Second Edition

Living Religions

A Brief Introduction

Mary Pat Fisher

CONSULTANTS:

LEE W. BAILEY *Ithaca College (retired)*

SAVINDER KAUR GILL *Mahidol University, Thailand*

KARMA LEKSHE TSOMO *University of San Diego*

RANDALL NADEAU *Trinity University*

ELLEN M. UMANSKY *Fairfield University*

SCOTT W. SUNQUIST *Pittsburgh Theological Seminary*

ZAYN KASSAM *Pomona College*

GURPREET SINGH *Gobind Sadan Institute, New Delhi*

CHRISTINE E. GUDORF *Florida International University*

PEARSON

Upper Saddle River, NJ 07458

Library of Congress Cataloging-in-Publication data is available upon request from the Library of Congress

Editor in Chief: Dickson Musslewhite
Senior Editor: David Repetto
Editorial Assistant: Patrick Walsh
Associate Marketing Manager: Lindsey Prudhomme
Senior Managing Editor: Mary Rottino
Senior Operations Specialist: Brian Mackey

Pearson Education Ltd.
Pearson Education Australia PTY, Limited
Pearson Education Singapore, Pte. Ltd
Pearson Education North Asia Ltd
Pearson Education, Canada, Ltd
Pearson Educación de Mexico, S.A. de C.V.
Pearson Education–Japan
Pearson Education Malaysia, Pte. Ltd

This book was designed and produced by
Laurence King Publishing Ltd, London
www.laurenceking.co.uk

Every effort has been made to contact the copyright holders, but should there be any errors or omissions, Laurence King Publishing Ltd would be pleased to insert the appropriate acknowledgment in any subsequent printing of this publication.

Commissioning Editor: Melanie White
Senior Editor: Susie May
Picture Researcher: Emma Brown
Designer: Andy Prince
Map: Advanced Illustration Ltd., Cheshire

Printed in Thailand

Front Cover: 20 October 2005, Chandigarh, India: Married Hindu women pray for the well-being of their husbands during the Hindu festival of Karva Chauth.
© AJAY VERMA/Reuters/Corbis

Prentice Hall
is an imprint of

www.pearsonhighered.com

10 9 8 7 6 5 4 3 2 1
ISBN-13: 978-0-20-563564-1
ISBN-10:   0-20-563564-4

CONTENTS

CHAPTER 4
BUDDHISM   70

CHAPTER 5
DAOISM AND CONFUCIANISM   98

PREFACE

Religion is not a museum piece. Religion is a vibrant force in the lives of many people around the world, and many religions are presently experiencing a renaissance.

Living Religions: A Brief Introduction is a sympathetic approach to what is living and significant in the world's major religious traditions and in various new movements that are arising. This book provides a clear and straightforward account of the development, doctrines, and practices of the major faiths followed today. The emphasis throughout is on the personal consciousness of believers and their own accounts of their religion and its relevance in contemporary life.

Special features of this edition

This second edition has been thoroughly revised and updated. In preparing the text I have worked with a team of specialist consultants who have provided detailed suggestions and resources for improving the text in light of recent scholarship.

As violence perpetrated in the name of religion is increasingly in the news, this edition includes extensive coverage of this disturbing aspect of many major religions and also new religious movements, such as the continual disruption of so many people's lives in West Asia along religious lines. There are also discussions of government attitudes toward religions, such as the Chinese government's evolving policies about religious practices. This edition includes the work of religious leaders who are actively opposing violence in the name of religion, such as the activities of the late Cambodian Buddhist Venerable Maha Ghosananda, who led peace walks through landmine-infested areas of Burma. Distinctions are made between the basic teachings of religions, none of which condones wanton violence, and the ways in which religions have been politicized. Every religion is struggling with its responses to modernity, including fundamentalist and exclusivist responses, and these struggles are discussed in each chapter. The roots of militancy in the name of religion are also carefully explored.

People of many faiths are looking at ways in which their religious practices and beliefs affect the environment. This edition, therefore, includes material on religious approaches to contemporary ecological concerns, such as the high dams that are threatening traditional cultures in India and strip-mining of sacred Navajo and Hopi lands. Included are contemporary responses of religious leaders of all stripes—from liberals to Christian evangelicals—to ominous signs of climate change. Many other social issues are now being taken up by religious leaders, with examples in this edition such as the efforts of African leaders to stem the scourge of AIDS.

Women's voices and women's contributions are woven into the discussions of each religion, and they include those of female theologians who are bringing vital new perspectives to religious scholarship. The increased participation of Jewish and Christian women as leaders in congregational worship as well as in theology is brought forth, and also new trends in Muslim feminist scholarship. This edition also includes extended coverage of popular religious practices, such as rituals and festivals.

This new edition preserves and improves upon the special features of the first edition.

Personal interviews with followers of each faith provide interesting and informative first-person accounts of each religion as perceived from within the tradition. I have presented these first-person quotations from many people, from a Siberian shamaness to a Holocaust survivor, in "Interview" feature boxes and also in excerpts woven throughout the text. The first-person interview boxes focus on how the practitioner of each faith experiences the beliefs and rituals of his or her tradition.

Religion in Public Life feature boxes portray the spiritual roots of people who are making significant contributions to modern society. For example, in the Judaism chapter, Rabbi David Saperstein speaks of his deep involvement in Reform Jewish social activism. In the final chapter, "Religion in a New Era," a special feature box on Jimmy Carter looks at how his being a committed Christian provides the moral underpinning of his peace work.

Quotations from primary sources are incorporated throughout the book to give a direct perception of the thinking and flavor of each tradition, such as Laotzi's Daoist principle of being like flowing water, which is "the softest thing on Earth. Yet its silken gentleness will easily wear away the hardest stone."

Pedagogical aids are present throughout the text. Key terms are defined and highlighted in boldface when they first appear and are included in an extensive glossary. Review questions and Discussion questions are given at the end of each chapter, designed to enhance further thought and understanding. Also included at the end of the book there are chapter-by-chapter lists of suggested reading and Internet resources, providing addresses for generally accurate and useful websites. Following this Preface, there is a world map indicating the global distribution of religions and also a timeline so that their historical developments can be understood side by side.

Organization of this book

Chapter 1: Religious Responses looks at religious phenomena as a whole, bringing out patterns that transcend differences between the various faiths. It explores theories as to why religions have been major social features from the distant past to the present, and examines varied ways that humans have tried to comprehend and worship invisible sacred realities. Attention is also given to atheists' assertions that religions are unscientific, built on human imagination. The chapter delves into the dialogue between science and religion, as well as the contemporary tension between fundamentalist and liberal perspectives, and between those who would increase or deny women's place in religious leadership.

Chapter 2: **Indigenous Sacred Ways** notes the continued existence of pockets of people still practicing their native lifeways to some extent, despite the subversive influences of global religions and global culture. Although the indigenous sacred ways are quite diverse, they tend to have in common certain features such as intimate relationship with spirits in the local environment. This intimacy is now being threatened by economic development, and traditional elders express concern for the future.

Chapter 3: Hinduism attempts to sort out the great array of rituals and beliefs collectively referred to as "Hinduism." It looks at ancient Vedic spiritual culture and its scriptures, and then the major philosophical and theistic paths that have evolved in the Indian sub-continent. Another avenue to understanding is also explored as the "Hindu way of life," with its rituals, castes, duties, life stages and goals, gurus, pilgrimages, and festivals. The chapter ends with a look at the contemporary Hindu identity movement and its involvement with Indian politics.

Chapter 4: Buddhism explores the life and legends of Gautama Buddha and elucidates his basic teachings about the Dharma. It looks at the major paths that evolved as Buddhism spread eastward throughout Asia. The chapter looks at current manifestations of Buddhist popularity in the West, and also streams of socially engaged Buddhism.

Chapter 5: Daoism and Confucianism begins with analysis of ancient Chinese traditions that have nurtured the later seemingly divergent paths of Daoism and Confucianism. The section on Daoism follows current scholarship in studying not only the literati tradition, with figures such as Laotzi and Zhuangzi, but also organized and folk Daoism and practices thought to lead to longevity and immortality. The Confucian section of the chapter traces the life of Kong fuzi, his teachings about essential virtues, and the teachings of his followers. Modern interaction of these ancient ways with atheist communism in China and with other contemporary cultures in East Asia is explored with reference to renewed interest in both Daoism and Confucianism.

Chapter 6: Shinto carefully explores the threads of traditional Japanese spirituality referred to as "Shinto," characterized by worship of natural beauty and the spirits of nature, purification, festivals, and shrine rituals. Mixed with Buddhist and Confucian influences, and also historically developed into State Shinto (which was denounced after Japan's defeat in World War II), and submerged in modernization, Shinto is difficult to define as a separate religious entity today, but its traces survive in tens of thousands of shrines in Japan. Zoroastrianism is shrinking in membership, but survives as an important religion in itself and an historical bridge between Eastern and Western religions. Several pages are therefore devoted to Zoroastrian tradition between the preceding chapters on Eastern religions and the following chapters on Western traditions.

Chapter 7: Judaism traces the threads of Jewish history in Biblical times, as Rabbinic Judaism has developed, and as they are evolving in today's world. It looks at the teachings and practices and holy days that define Jewish spirituality, at the significant contributions of Jewish feminist thought, and the manifestations of contemporary Jewish renewal.

Chapter 8: Christianity traces the life and teachings of the historical Jesus and his disciples, and the history of various branches of the Christian Church. Despite the many divisions in global Christianity, certain central beliefs and practices are found to characterize the movement as a whole. As the Church continues to evolve, contemporary trends discussed include evangelicalism, Pentecostalism, Liberation Theology, feminist scholarship and activism, ecumenism, and the "Great Reversal" in which the majority of Christians are now from non-Western countries.

Chapter 9: Islam follows the life of the Prophet Muhammad and his Companions, introduces the Qur'an, and then summarizes the central teachings and Five Pillars of the faith. It explores the division between Sunnis and Shi'as and also examines Sufi spirituality. The rapid spread of Islam and development of great Islamic cultures is followed, succeeded by centuries of decline and domination by Western civilizations. The resurgence of Islam in the modern world and its mixtures with politics are then examined.

Chapter 10: Sikhism begins with the appearance of non-sectarian saints in northern India and then follows the lives of the ten Sikh Gurus, from Guru Nanak to Guru Gobind Singh, who named the holy scripture as his successor. Central beliefs and practices of Sikhs are explored, followed by contemporary issues in Sikh communities in India as well as in their farflung diaspora.

Chapter 11: Religion in a New Era looks first at new religious movements which are continually arising, sometimes with apocalyptic expectations, sometimes centered around someone's supernatural powers or revelations, sometimes as offshoots or combinations of older religions. Other types of new religious movements discussed are nature spirituality (such as Neo-Paganism, goddess spirituality, and deep ecology), universalist religions such as Bahai, and New Age spirituality. In the contemporary world of religiously pluralistic cultures, boundaries are hardening in some places, terrorism is increasing, and religion and politics are often mixed. At the same time, there is a growing interfaith movement, and many religions are seeking to help people suffering from social problems such as the HIV/AIDS pandemic and poverty.

Acknowledgments

In order to try to understand each religion from the inside, I have traveled for many years to study and worship with devotees and teachers of all faiths, and to interview them about their experience of their tradition. People of all religions also come to the Gobind Sadan Institute for Advanced Studies in Comparative Religions, in New Delhi, where it is my good fortune to meet and speak with them about their spiritual experiences and beliefs.

In preparing this book, I have worked directly with consultants who are authorities in specific traditions and who have offered detailed suggestions and resources. For breadth of scholarship, I have engaged the help of a new group of consultants for each edition. For this edition, a number of very helpful and dedicated scholars have carefully reviewed the various chapters and made excellent suggestions for their improvement in the light of current scholarship. My hard-working associate Lee W. Bailey of Ithaca College (retired) has not only served as a consultant but has also prepared the Review questions and Discussion questions, and the lists of Internet resources. Savinder Kaur Gill of Malaysia, and now of Mahidol University, Thailand, conducted extensive original fieldwork to contribute information on the Orang Asli of Malaysia. The other consultants who have served as excellent advisers on particular chapters are Karma Lekshe Tsomo of University of San Diego, Randall Nadeau of Trinity University, Ellen M. Umansky of Fairfield University, Scott W. Sunquist of Pittsburgh Theological Seminary, Zayn R. Kassam of Pomona College, Gurpreet Singh of the Gobind Sadan Institute for Advanced Studies in Comparative Religion, and Christine E. Gudorf of Florida International University. I am extremely grateful for their generous and enthusiastic help, and for the assistance of the scholars who served as consultants to the previous edition and are specifically acknowledged therein.

Living Religions has been extensively reviewed throughout all its editions by professors teaching courses in world religions. Reviewers have included Robert Imperato, Saint Leo University; Sallie King, James Madison University; Jonathan Brumberg-Kraus, Wheaton College; George Mummert, Moberly Area Community College; Robert Badra, Kalamazoo Valley Community College; Hugh Urban, Ohio State University; John Gilman, San Diego State University; David Suter, St. Martin's College; Jeffrey Brodd, California State University, Sacramento; Mark MacWilliams, St Lawrence University; Mark Webb, Texas Technical University; Maurine Stein, Prairie State College; James Hicks, Forsyth Technical Community College; David Carlson, Franklin College; Ross Aden, Rock Valley College; Athena DeGangi, New Hampshire Community Technical College, Nashua.

For this edition, the reviewers were: Robert Badra, Kalamazoo Valley Community College; Kenneth Rose, Christopher Newport University; Gary Sligh, Lake-Sumter Community College; Laura E. Shulman, Northern Virginia Community College; Jean-Pierre Kamuabo, Wake Technical Community College; Michael Candelaria, University of New Mexico; Todd Lavin, Clarion University of Pennsylvania; Harold W. Bruen, Wake Technical Community College; Jeffrey Kaplan, University of Wisconsin, Oshkosh; Brett Hendrickson, Arizona State University; Dexter E. Callender, University of Miami; Charles Bunce, Mount St. Mary's College; Russ Butkus, University of Portland; James Ford, Rogers State University; and Michael T. Bradley, Jr., Georgia Perimeter College.

For this edition Alan Nykamp has also been very helpful in transcribing original interviews and Margaret Krebs has generously helped again in obtaining essential books. My husband Edward G. Fisher provided valuable editorial assistance. Among other people who have helped to review and amplify this edition with new materials are Riffat Hassan, Ali Mohammed Naqvi, Paulette Skiba, Sonam Wangmo, Galina Ermolina, I. H. Azad Faruqi, Bert Gunn, Swami Dharamananda, Sister Santacitta, Noordin Kassam, Gurbachan Singh, Ronki Ram, Rajinder Singh, and Somjit Dasgupta. May I express my deep gratitude toward them all.

As always, Laurence King Publishing has provided me with excellent editorial help. Lee Ripley has been supportive as ever. Susie May and Melanie White have guided this edition with brilliance, efficiency, and discernment. And at Prentice Hall, Dave Repetto has been very enthusiastic and helpful.

Finally, I cannot adequately express my gratitude to my own revered teacher, the late Baba Virsa Singh of Gobind Sadan. People of all faiths from all over the world came to him for his spiritual blessings and guidance. In the midst of sectarian conflicts, his place continues to be an oasis of peace and harmony. Now more than ever, we are learning to regard each other as members of one human family. May God bless us all to move in this direction.

Mary Pat Fisher

Gobind Sadan Institute for Advanced Studies
in Comparative Religion, New Delhi

TEACHING AND LEARNING RESOURCES FOR *LIVING RELIGIONS*

Whether you want to enhance your lectures, create tests, or assign outside material to reinforce content from the text, you and your students will find the most comprehensive set of instructional materials available with *Living Religions* to reinforce and enliven the study of world religions.

INSTRUCTOR RESOURCES

Instructor's Manual with Test Item File
This manual includes chapter outlines, key terms, and summaries. As in previous editions, there are class activities and discussion questions. New to this edition will be a list of relevant movies pertaining to each chapter. Test questions have been moved to the end of the manual in their own section. ISBN: 0-13-235686-4

Test Generator
This computerized test bank includes the test item file and allows flexibility in creating tests, editing questions, and adding instructor generated items. ISBN: 0-13-603003-3

Power Point Slides
New to this edition, these slides are illustrated with many of the photos from the text and also contain chapter outlines, provocative quotes, key terms and timelines from each religion. ISBN: 0-13-603228-1

The Sacred World: Encounters with the World's Religions CD-Rom
Included with each new copy of the book is the *Sacred World* CD-Rom, a multimedia exploration of the rituals and beliefs in nine of the world's major religions. Religions included are: Judaism, Christianity, Islam, Hinduism, Buddhism, Confucianism and Taoism (Daoism), Sikhism, Jainism, and Shinto. ISBN: 0-13-184090-8

Instructor's Resource CD-Rom
The Instructor's Resource CD-Rom contains the instructor manual, test items, power points and other resource material available with the text to allow maximum flexibility preparing lectures. ISBN: 0-13-603279-6

Course Management Resources
MyReligionLab in Black Board   ISBN: 0-13-603563-9
MyReligionLab in WebCT   ISBN: 0-13-603653-8

STUDENT RESOURCES

MyReligionLab
MyReligionLab provides an outstanding array of student and faculty resources for learning and teaching with Fisher's *Living Religions*. Students are given robust self-assessment opportunities, including quizzes with feedback, access to over 75 dynamic video clips of the world's religions with assessment questions, and a unique collection of primary and secondary sources reflecting the world's major scriptural traditions.
Access code   ISBN: 0-13-603225-7
Stand alone access code   ISBN: 0-13-603227-3

Companion Website
Visit **www.prenhall.com/fisher** for quick online study resources.

SafariX Textbooks Online is an exciting choice for students looking to save money. As an alternative to purchasing the print textbook, students can *subscribe* to the same content online and save on the suggested list price of the book. With a SafariX e-textbook, students can search the text, make notes online, print out reading assignments that incorporate lecture notes, and bookmark important passages for later review.
ISBN: 0-13-603004-1

TIME Special Edition: World Religions
In partnership with TIME magazine, Prentice Hall offers a special TIME edition containing recent articles on world religions.
ISBN 0-13-145781-0

The Prentice Hall Atlas of World Religions
Through the use of over 50 visually arresting maps, this atlas shows the origins, historical development, and present state of all the world's religions. ISBN 0-13-193885-1

Penguin Bundle Program Prentice Hall offers significant discounts on titles relevant to the study of world religion from the acclaimed Penguin Classics Series.

The predominant forms of religions in the world today

Legend:

- ⬚ (diagonal hatch) Indigenous ways
- ⬚ (diagonal hatch) Hinduism and Islam
- ⬚ (vertical lines) Buddhism
- ⬚ (dotted) China: Remnants of Confucianism, Buddhism, Daoism
- ⬚ (horizontal lines) Japan: Shinto, Buddhism, Sects
- ⬚ (plain) Christianity (Roman Catholicism, Protestantism, Eastern Orthodox)
- ⬚ (fine dots) Islam
- ⬚ (stippled) Indigenous ways and global religions

RUSSIAN FEDERATION

...LAND
ESTONIA
LATVIA
LITHUANIA
BELARUS
...KRAINE
MOLDOVA
GEORGIA
ARMENIA
TURKEY
...REECE
SYRIA
LEB.
ISRAEL
Judaism
...GYPT
JORDAN
KUWAIT
SAUDI
ARABIA
ERITREA
YEMEN
OMAN
...SUDAN
ETHIOPIA
SOMALIA
...NDA
KENYA
...M:
P.
...NGO
TANZANIA
...BIA
MALAWI
...ZAMBIA
MOZAMBIQUE
...BABWE
BOTSWANA
SWAZILAND
LESOTHO
...OUTH
...FRICA
MADAGASCAR

KAZAKHSTAN
UZBEKISTAN
KYRGYZSTAN
TAJIKISTAN
TURKMENISTAN
AZER.
IRAN
AFGHANISTAN
PAKISTAN
NEPAL
BANGLADESH
INDIA
Sikhism
Parsism
(Zoroastrianism)
SRI LANKA

MONGOLIA
CHINA
NORTH
KOREA
SOUTH
KOREA
JAPAN
TAIWAN
HONG KONG
MYANMAR
(BURMA)
THAILAND
LAOS
VIETNAM
CAMBODIA
MALAYSIA
PHILIPPINES
INDONESIA
PAPUA
NEW
GUINEA

NORTH PACIFIC
OCEAN

SOUTH PACIFIC
OCEAN

INDIAN OCEAN

AUSTRALIA

NEW ZEALAND

TIMELINE	2000 BCE	1500	1000	500	0 CE
INDIGENOUS	Neolithic reverence for nature, mother goddess, ancestors ←				
HINDUISM	Indus River cultures with goddess and indigenous religions c. 2500 BCE ←	*Vedas* first written c. 1500 BCE	Vyasa systematizes *Upanishads* c. 1000–500 BCE	*Ramayana* and *Mahabharata* in present form 400 BCE–200 CE Patanjali systematizes *Yoga Sutras* by 200 BCE	*The Laws of Manu* compiled by 100–300 CE
BUDDHISM			Gautama Buddha c. 563–483 BCE	King Ashoka spreads Buddhism c. 258 BCE Theravada Buddhism develops 200 BCE–200 CE	Mahayana Buddhism develops c. 100 CE Asvaghosha writes *Acts of the Buddha* 2nd C. CE
DAOISM AND CONFUCIANISM				Laozi c. 600–300 BCE Confucius c. 551–479 BCE Liezi c. 475–221 BCE	Mencius c. 390–305 BCE Zhuangzi c. 365–290 BCE Educational system based on Confucian Classics from 206 BCE
SHINTO	Shinto begins in pre-history as local nature- and ancestor-based traditions				
JUDAISM	Abraham c. 1900–1700 BCE?	Exodus from Egypt led by Moses c. 1250 BCE King David c. 1010–970 BCE King Solomon builds First Temple c. 950 BCE		First Temple destroyed; Jews exiled 586 BCE	Jerusalem falls to Romans; Jewish Diaspora begins 70 CE Canon of Tanakh agreed c. 90 Rabbinical tradition develops 1st–4th c. CE Mishnah c. 200 CE
CHRISTIANITY					Jesus c. 4 BCE – 30 CE Letters of Paul 48–68 CE Gospels written down c. 70–95 CE
ISLAM					
SIKHISM					
NEW RELIGIOUS MOVEMENTS					

300	600	900	1200	1500	1800	2000 CE
	Viking invasions carry Norse religion into northern Europe 800–1100			European colonialists invade indigenous cultures in Americas from 1492	Slave trade introduces African religions into Americas from 1550	Hopi Message to the U.N. General Assembly 1992
Puranas written down 500–1500	*Bhakti* movement 600–1800	Sankara organizes Vedanta school c. 788–820	Kabir c. 1440–1518	Mirabai c. 1500–50	Mahatma Gandhi 1869–1948; Paramahansa Yogananda 1893–1952; V.D. Savarkar "Hindutva" 1923	
	Buddhism declared national religion of Tibet 700s	Persecution of Chinese Buddhists begins 845	Chan Buddhism to Japan as Zen 13th c.		Buddhism spreads in the West 20th c.	
Ge Hong on alchemy 200–300 CE	Emperor declares Daoism official religion c. 400–448; Japan imports Confucianism c. 500–600	Song dynasty: Neo-Confucianism 960–1279; Zhou Dunyi 1017–73; Zhang Zai 1020–77; Zhang Boudan, *Awakening to Perfection* 1075–8			End of Confucianism as state ideology in China 1911; Cultural Revolution attacks religions 1966–76; Confucian and Daoist revival in East Asia from 1980s	
	Shinto name adopted 6th century CE				State Shinto established 1868	
	Jerusalem Talmud c. 500; Babylonian Talmud c. 600		Maimonides c. 1135–1204	Mass expulsion of Jews from Spain 1492	Baal–Shem Tov begins Hasidism c. 1700–60; Nazi Holocaust 1933–1945; Independent state of Israel 1948; Six–Day War 1967; Conflict between Hezbollah and Israel 2006	
Athanasius 296–373 CE; Council of Nicea: divinity of Jesus 325 CE; Augustine 354–430 CE; Official religion of Roman Empire 392 CE; Canon of Bible set c. 400	Consolidation of papal power 800–1300		Anselm of Canterbury 1033–1109; Western and Eastern churches split 1054	Monastic orders proliferate 14th c.; Spanish Inquisition established 1478; Protestantism begins with Martin Luther's "95 Theses" 1517; Council of Trent 1545–63	Methodism: John Wesley 1707–88; Mother Teresa 1910–97; Martin Luther King 1929–1968; Vatican II 1962; Pope Benedict XVI elected 2005	
	Muhammad 570–632; Spread of Islam begins 633; Canon of Qur'an set 650	Islam's cultural peak under Abbasids 750–1258; *Sahih Bukari* by 870; *Sahih Muslim* by 875; Ibn Sina 980–1037	Al-Ghazali 1058–1111; Ibn Rushid 1126–98; Ibn 'Arabi 1165–1240; Turks conquer Constantinople 1453	Akbar becomes Mughal emperor 1556	Muslim-majority Pakistan separates from Hindu-majority India 1947; Sufi Order of the West 1910	OPEC; Muslim resurgence 1970s; 9/11 Attacks in U.S. 2001; U.S. and allies invade Iraq 2003
				Guru Nanak 1469–1539; Guru Gobind Singh initiates Khalsa 1699; Guru Granth Sahib installed as Guru 1708	British massacre Sikhs in Amritsar 1919; Sikhs demand separate state 1984; Celebration of 300th anniversary of Khalsa 1999	
				Bahá'u'lláh 1817–92; Mormon Church founded 1822; Jehovah's Witnesses 1872; Theosophical Society 1875	Sun yung Moon founds Unification Church 1954; Parliament of the World's Religions 1993, 1999, 2004	

CHAPTER 1
RELIGIOUS RESPONSES

Before sunrise, members of a Muslim family rise in Malaysia, perform their purifying ablutions, spread their prayer rugs facing Mecca, and begin their prostrations and prayers to Allah. In a French cathedral, worshipers line up for their turn to have a priest place a wafer on their tongue, murmuring, "This is the body of Christ." In a South Indian village, a group of women reverently anoint a cylindrical stone with milk and fragrant sandalwood paste and place around it offerings of flowers. The monks of a Japanese Zen Buddhist monastery sit cross-legged and upright in utter silence, broken occasionally by the noise of the *kyosaku* bat falling on their shoulders. On a mountain in Mexico, men, women, and children who have been dancing without food or water for days greet an eagle flying overhead with a burst of whistling from the small wooden flutes they wear around their necks.

These and countless other moments in the lives of people around the world are threads of the tapestry we call "religion." The word is probably derived from the Latin, meaning "to tie back," "to tie again." All of religion shares the goal of tying people back to something behind the surface of life—a greater reality, which lies beyond, or invisibly infuses, the world that we can perceive with our five senses.

Attempts to connect with this greater reality have taken many forms. Many of them are organized institutions, such as Buddhism or Christianity. These institutions are complexes of such elements as leaders, beliefs, rituals, symbols, myths, scriptures, ethics, spiritual practices, cultural components, historical traditions, and management structures. Moreover, they are not fixed and distinct categories, as simple labels such as "Buddhism" and "Christianity" suggest. Each of these labels is an abstraction that is used in the attempt to bring some kind of order to the study of religious patterns that are in fact complex, diverse, ever-changing, and overlapping. In addition, not all religious behavior occurs within institutional confines. Some spiritual experience is that of individuals who belong to no institutionalized religion but nonetheless have an inner life of prayer, meditation, or direct experience of an inexplicable presence. Such personal, non-institutionalized patterns can be referred to as **spirituality**, as distinct from **religion**, a term that can be used to refer to more formalized responses to an invisible sacred reality, as shaped by a particular tradition.

Religion is such a complex and elusive topic that some contemporary scholars of religion are seriously questioning whether "religion" or "religions" can be studied at all. They have determined that no matter where and at what point they try to grab the thing, other parts will get away. Nonetheless, this difficult-to-grasp subject is central to many people's lives and has assumed great political significance in today's world so it is important to try sincerely to understand it. In this introductory chapter, we will try to develop some understanding of religion in a generic sense—why it exists, its various patterns and modes of interpretation, its encounters with modern science, its inclusion or exclusion of women, and its potentially negative aspects—before trying in the subsequent chapters to understand the major traditions known as "religions" practiced around the world today.

Why are there religions?

In many cultures and times, religion has been the basic foundation of life, permeating all aspects of human existence. But from the time of the European Enlightenment, religion has become in the West an object to be studied, rather than an unquestioned basic fact of life. Cultural anthropologists, sociologists, philosophers, psychologists, and even biologists have peered at religion through their own particular lenses, trying to explain what religion is and why it exists, to those who no longer take it for granted. In the following pages we will briefly examine some of the major theories that have evolved.

Materialistic perspective: humans invented religion

During the nineteenth and twentieth centuries, **scientific materialism** gained considerable prominence as a theory to explain the fact that religion can be found in some form in every culture around the world. The materialistic point of view is that the supernatural is imagined by humans; only the material world exists.

An influential example of this perspective can be found in the work of the nineteenth-century philosopher Ludwig Feuerbach (1804–1872). He reasoned that deities are simply projections, objectifications of human qualities such as power, wisdom, and love onto an imagined cosmic deity outside ourselves. Then we worship it as Supreme and do not recognize that those same qualities lie within ourselves; instead, we see ourselves as weak and sinful. Feuerbach developed this theory with particular reference to Christianity as he had seen it.

Following this theory of the divine as a projection of human qualities and emotions, psychoanalyst Sigmund Freud (1856–1938) described religion as a collective fantasy, a "universal obsessional neurosis"—a replaying of our loving and fearful relationships with our parents. Religious belief gives us a God powerful enough to protect us from the terrors of life, and will reward or punish us for obedience or nonobedience to social norms. From Freud's extremely sceptical point of view, religious belief is an illusion springing from people's infantile insecurity and neurotic guilt; as such it closely resembles mental illness.

Other scientific materialists believe that religions have been created or at least used to manipulate people. Historically, religions have often supported and served secular power. The nineteenth-century socialist philosopher Karl Marx (1818–1883), author of *The Communist Manifesto*, argued that a culture's religion—as well as all other aspects of its social structure—springs from its economic framework. In Marx's view, religion's origins lie in the longings of the oppressed. It may have developed from the desire to revolutionize society and combat exploitation, but in failing to do so, it became otherworldly, an expression of unfulfilled desires for a better, more satisfying life:

Man makes religion: religion does not make man. . . . The religious world is but the reflex of the real world. . . . Religion is the sigh of the oppressed creature, the sentiment of a heartless world, and the soul of soulless conditions. It is the opium of the people. . . . [1]

According to Marx, not only do religions pacify people falsely; they may themselves become tools of oppression. For instance, he charged Christian authorities of his times with supporting "vile acts of the oppressors" by explaining them as due punishment of sinners by God. Other critics have made similar complaints against Eastern religions that blame the sufferings of the poor on their own misdeeds in previous lives. Such interpretations and uses of religious teachings lessen the perceived need for society to help those who are oppressed and suffering. Marx's ideas thus led toward twentieth-century atheistic communism, for he had asserted, "The abolition of religion as the illusory happiness of the people is required for their real happiness."[2]

Functional perspective: religion is useful

Another line of reasoning has emerged in the search for a theory explaining the universal existence of religions: They are found everywhere because they are functional—useful both for society and for individuals.

One version of this theory is based on sociology. Pioneering work in this area was done by French sociologist Emile Durkheim (1858–1917). He proposed that humans cannot live without organized social structures, and that religions are a glue that holds a society together, for they teach social virtues such as love, compassion, altruism, justice, and discipline over our desires and emotions. The role of religion in the social process of identity formation at individual, family, community, and national levels is now being carefully examined, for people's identification with a particular religion can be manipulated to influence social change.

Biology also offers some functional reasons for the existence of religion. For instance, in *Is God a Virus?* John Bowker asserts that religions are organized systems that serve the essential biological purpose of bringing people together for their common survival. Religion is universal because it protects gene replication and the nurturing of children. He proposes that because of its survival value, the potential for religiosity may be genetically inherent in human brains. However, such mechanistic arguments are subject to criticism that they are not fully scientific, for they do not explain features of religions, such as celibacy or self-sacrifice, that do not enhance reproductive fitness.

Religious faith is also good for our health. Research by the Center for the Study of Religion/Spirituality and Health at Duke University found that those who attend religious services or read scriptures frequently are significantly longer lived, less likely to be depressed, less likely to have high blood pressure, and nearly ninety percent less likely to smoke. Many other studies have indicated that patients with strong faith recover faster from illness and operations.

Many medical studies have also been done on the potential of prayer to heal, but with mixed results. However, meditation has been proved to reduce mental stress and help develop positive emotions, even in the face of great difficulties. Citing laboratory tests of the mental calmness of Buddhists who practice "mindfulness" meditation, the 14th Dalai Lama points out:

Over the millenniums, many practitioners have carried out what we might call "experiments" in how to overcome tendencies toward destructive emotions. The world today needs citizens and leaders who can work toward ensuring stability and engage in dialogue with the "enemy"—no matter what kind of aggression or assault they may have endured. If humanity is to survive, happiness and inner balance are crucial. We would do well to remember that the war against hatred and terror can be waged on this internal front, too.[3]

From the point of view of individuals, there are many explanations for the usefulness of religion. Religions propose ideals that can radically transform people. Mahatma Gandhi (1869–1948) was a shy, fearful child. His transformation into one of the great political figures of the twentieth century occurred as he meditated on the great Hindu scripture, the **Bhagavad-Gita**, particularly the second chapter, which he says was "inscribed on the tablet of my heart."[4] It reads, in part:

He is forever free who has broken
Out of the ego-cage of I *and* mine
To be united with the Lord of Love.
This is the supreme state. Attain thou this
And pass from death to immortality.[5]

For many, the desire for material achievement offers a sense of purposefulness. But once achieved, material goals may seem hollow. A longing for something more lasting and meaningful may arise. The Buddha said:

Look!
The world is a royal chariot, glittering with paint.
No better.
    Fools are deceived, but the wise know better.[6]

According to some Eastern religions, the concept that we are distinct, autonomous individuals is an illusion; what we think of as "our" consciousnesses and "our" bodies are in perpetual flux. Freedom from problems lies in accepting temporal change and devaluing the "small self" in favor of the eternal self. The ancient sages of India called it "This eternal being that can never be proved, . . ."[7]

We may look to religions for understanding, for answers to our many questions about life. We have difficulty accepting the notion that this life is all there is. We are born, we struggle to support ourselves, we age, and we die. If we believe that there is nothing more, fear of death may inhibit enjoyment of life and make all human actions seem pointless.

It appears that throughout the world man [sic] has always been seeking something beyond his own death, beyond his own problems, something that will be enduring, true and timeless. He has called it God, he has given it many names; and most of us believe in something of that kind, without ever actually experiencing it.

Jiddu Krishnamurti[8]

For those who find security in specific answers, some religions offer **dogma**—systems of doctrines proclaimed as absolutely true and accepted as such. Absolute faith provides some people with a secure feeling of rootedness, meaning, and orderliness in the midst of rapid social change. Religions may also provide rules for living, governing everything from diet to personal relationships. Such prescriptions may be seen as earthly reflections of the order that prevails in the cosmos. Some religions, however, encourage people to explore the perennial questions by themselves, and to live in the uncertainties of not knowing intellectually, breaking through old concepts until nothing remains but truth itself.

A final need that draws some people to religion is the discomforting sense of being alone in the universe. This isolation can be painful, even terrifying. The divine may be sought as a loving father or mother, or as a friend. Alternatively, some paths offer the way of self-transcendence. Through them, the sense of isolation is lost in mystical merger with the One Being, with the Ultimate Reality.

Belief perspective: Ultimate Reality exists

From the point of view of religious belief, there truly is an underlying reality that cannot readily be perceived. Human responses to this Supreme Reality have been expressed and institutionalized as the structures of religions.

How have people of all times and places come to the conclusion that there is some Unseen Reality? Some simply accept what has been told to them or what is written in their holy books. Others have come to their own conclusions. In general, we have two basic ways of apprehending reality: rational thought and nonrational modes of knowing. Both modes have been highly developed in Indian religious traditions. The eminent twentieth-century philosopher and erstwhile President of India, S. Radhakrishnan (1888–1975) observed:

> *Every attempt at solving the problem of the ultimate basis of existence from a religious point of view has come to admit an Absolute or God. Rationalistic logic and mystic contemplation favour as a rule the former conception, while ethical theism is disposed to the latter. Hindu thought believes in the evolution of our knowledge of God. We have to vary continually our notions of God until we pass beyond all notions into the heart of the reality itself, which our ideas endeavour to report.*[9]

Another path to belief is through deep questioning. Martin Luther (1483–1546), father of the Protestant branches of Christianity, recounted how he searched for faith in God through storms of doubt, "raged with a fierce and agitated conscience."[10]

The human mind does not function in the rational mode alone; there are other modes of consciousness. In his classic study *The Varieties of Religious Experience*, the philosopher William James (1842–1910) concluded:

> *Our normal waking consciousness, rational consciousness as we call it, is but one special type of consciousness, whilst all about it, parted from it by the flimsiest of screens, there lie potential forms of consciousness entirely different. . . .*
>
> *No account of the universe in its totality can be final which leaves these other forms of consciousness quite disregarded.*[11]

To perceive truth directly, beyond the senses, beyond the limits of human reason, beyond blind belief, is often called **mysticism**. The Irish writer George William Russell (1867–1935) describes lying on a hillside:

> when, suddenly, I felt a fiery heart throb, and knew it was personal and intimate, and started with every sense dilated and intent, and turned inwards, and I heard first a music as of bells going away . . . the winds were sparkling and diamond clear, yet full of colour as an opal, as they glittered through the valley, and I knew the Golden Age was all about me, and it was we who had been blind to it . . .[12]

Encounters with Unseen Reality are given various names in spiritual traditions: **enlightenment**, **realization**, illumination, *kensho*, **awakening**, self-knowledge, **gnosis**, ecstatic communion, "coming home." Such a state may arise spontaneously, as in near-death experiences, or may be induced by meditation, fasting, prayer, chanting, drugs, or dancing.

Many religions have developed meditation techniques that encourage intuitive wisdom, perceived as a natural faculty within or an external voice, to come forth. The consciousness is initially turned away from the world, even from one's own feelings and thoughts. Often a concentration practice, such as staring at a candle flame, is used to collect the awareness into a single, unfragmented focus. Once the mind is quiet, distinctions between inside and outside drop away. The seer becomes one with the seen, in a fusion of subject and object through which the inner nature of things seems to reveal itself.

Kabir, a fifteenth-century Indian weaver who was inspired alike by Islam and Hinduism and whose words are included in Sikh scripture, described this state:

> The blue sky opens out farther and farther,
> the daily sense of failure goes away,
> the damage I have done to myself fades,
> a million suns come forward with light,
> when I sit firmly in that world.[13]

Our ordinary experience of the world is that our self is separate from the world of objects that we perceive. But this **dualistic** understanding may be transcended in a moment of enlightenment in which the Real and our awareness of it become one. The *Mundaka Upanishad* says, "Lose thyself in the Eternal, even as the arrow is lost in the target." For the Hindu, this is the prized attainment of liberation, in which one enters into awareness of the eternal reality. This reality is then known with the same direct apprehension with which one knows oneself. The Sufi Muslim mystic Abu Yazid in the ninth century CE said, "I sloughed off my self as a snake sloughs off its skin, and I looked into my essence and saw that 'I am He.'"[14]

This spontaneous experience of being grasped by Reality is the essential basis of religion, according to the influential German professor of theology Rudolf Otto (1869–1937). The experience is ineffable, "*sui generis* and irreducible to any other; and therefore, like every absolutely primary and elementary dictum, while it admits of being discussed, it cannot be strictly defined."[15] This experience of the Holy, asserts Otto, brings forth two general responses in a person: a feeling of great awe or even dread, and a feeling of great attraction.

Understandings of Sacred Reality

In the struggle to understand what the mind cannot readily grasp, individuals and cultures have come to rather different conclusions. Mircea Eliade (1907–1986) was a very influential scholar who helped to develop the field of **comparative religion**. This discipline attempts to understand and compare religious patterns found around the world. He used the terms "sacred" and "profane": the **profane** is the everyday world of seemingly random, ordinary, and unimportant occurrences. The **sacred** is the realm of extraordinary, apparently purposeful, but generally imperceptible forces. In the realm of the sacred lie the source of the universe and its values. However relevant this dichotomy may be in describing some religions, there are some cultures that do not make a clear distinction between the sacred and the profane. Many tribal cultures who have an intimate connection with their local landscape feel that spiritual power is everywhere; there is nothing that is not sacred. Trees, mountains, animals—everything is perceived as being alive with sacred presence.

Approached by different ways if knowing, by different people, from different times and cultures, the sacred has many faces. The ultimate reality may be conceived as **immanent** (present in the world) or **transcendent** (existing above and outside of the material universe). Many people perceive the sacred as a personal Being, as Father, Mother, Teacher, Friend, Beloved, or as a special deity. Religions based on one's relationship to the divine Being are called **theistic**. If the Being is worshiped as a singular form, the religion is **monotheistic**. If many attributes and forms of the divine are emphasized, the religion may be labeled **polytheistic**. Religions which hold that beneath the multiplicity of apparent forms there is one underlying substance are called **monistic**.

Some people believe that the sacred reality is usually invisible but occasionally appears visibly in human **incarnations**, such as Christ or Krishna, or in special manifestations, such as the flame Moses reportedly saw coming from the center of a bush but not consuming it. Or the deity that cannot be seen may be described in human terms. Christian theologian Sallie McFague thus writes of God as "lover" by imputing human feelings to God:

> God as lover is the one who loves the world not with the fingertips but totally and passionately, taking pleasure in its variety and richness, finding it attractive and valuable, delighting in its fulfilment. God as lover is the moving power of love in the universe, the desire for unity with all the beloved.[16]

There have always been **exclusivist** religious authorities who claim they worship the only true deity and label all others as "pagans" or "nonbelievers." When such rigid positions are taken, often to the point of violent conflicts or forced conversions, there is no room to consider the possibility that all may be talking about the same indescribable thing in different languages or referring to different aspects of the same unknowable Whole—which may be defined as **universalism**.

Atheism is the belief that there is no deity. Atheists may reject theistic beliefs because they seem to be incompatible with the existence of evil in the world, or because there is little or no concrete proof that God exists, or because theistic beliefs seem unscientific, or because they inhibit human independence.

A movement called "New Atheism" is attacking religious faith as being not only wrong, but actually evil because it can be used to support violence.

Agnosticism is not the denial of the divine but the feeling, "I don't know whether it exists or not," or the belief that if it exists it is impossible for humans to know it. Ultimate reality may also be conceived in **nontheistic** terms. It may be experienced as a "changeless Unity," as "Suchness," or simply as "the Way." There may be no sense of a personal Creator God in such as understandings.

These categories are not mutually exclusive, so attempts to apply the labels can sometimes confuse us rather than help us understand religions. Mystics may have personal encounters with the divine and yet find it so unspeakable that they say it is beyond human knowing. The Jewish scholar Maimonides (1135–1204) asserted that:

> the human mind cannot comprehend God. Only God can know Himself. The only form of comprehension of God we can have is to realize how futile it is to try to comprehend Him.[17]

Jaap Sahib, the great hymn of praises of God by the Tenth Sikh Guru, Guru Gobind Singh, consists largely of the negative attributes of God, such as these:

> Salutations to the One without colour or hue,
> Salutations to the One who hath no beginning.
> Salutations to the Impenetrable,
> Salutations to the Unfathomable . . .
> O Lord, Thou art Formless and Peerless
> Beyond birth and physical elements. . . .
> Salutations to the One beyond confines of religion. . . .
> Beyond description and Garbless
> Thou art Nameless and Desireless.
> Thou art beyond thought and ever Mysterious.[18]

Some people believe that the aspect of the divine that they perceive is the only one. Others feel that there is one being with many faces, that all religions come from one source.

Given the centrality in religions of religious experiences, in this book we will keep delving into them in order to try to understand the various religions that are practiced today. To use Mircea Eliade's term, we will be exploring the **phenomenology** of religion—its specifically sacred aspects—rather than explaining religions only in terms of disciplines such as history, politics, economics, sociology, or psychology. This involves an appreciative investigation of religious phenomena in order to comprehend their spiritual intention and meaning. We will also strive for "thick description," a term used by the cultural anthropologist Clifford Geertz, not only reporting outward behaviors but also attempting to explain their meaning for believers.

Worship, symbol, and myth

Many of the phenomena of religion are ways of worship, symbols, and myths. Worship consists in large part of attempts to express reverence and perhaps to enter into communion with that which is worshiped or to request help with problems such as ill health, disharmony, or poverty. Around the world, rituals, sacraments, prayers, and spiritual practices are used to create a sacred atmosphere or state of consciousness necessary to convey requests for help, to sanctify and explain the meaning of life stages such as birth, puberty, marriage, and death, or to provide spiritual instruction.

When such worshipful actions are predictable and repeated rather than spontaneous, they are known as **rituals**. Group rituals may be conducted by priests or other ritual specialists or by the people themselves. There may be recitation of prayers, scriptures or stories, sharing of food, purification by water, lighting of candles, and offerings to the divine. Professor Antony Fernando of Sri Lanka explains that when offerings are made to the deities:

> *Even the most illiterate person knows that in actual fact no god really picks up those offerings or is actually in need of them. What people offer is what they own. . . . Sacrifices and offerings are a dramatic way of proclaiming that they are not the ultimate possessors of their life and also of articulating their determination to live duty-oriented lives and not desire-oriented lives.*[19]

Believers build statues and buildings through which to worship the divine, but these are not the divine itself. Because people are addressing the invisible, it can be suggested only through metaphor. Deepest consciousness cannot speak the language of everyday life; what it knows can be suggested only in **symbols**—images from the material world that are similar to spiritual experiences.

Our religious ceremonies are but the shadows of that great universal worship celebrated in the heavens by the legions of heavenly beings on all planes, and our prayers drill a channel across this mist separating our earthbound plane from the celestial ones through which a communication may be established with the powers that be.

Pir Vilayat Inayat Khan[20]

Tracing symbols throughout the world, researchers find many similarities in their use in different cultures. Unseen Reality is often symbolized as a Father or Mother, because it is thought to be the source of life, sustenance, and protection. It is frequently associated with heights, with its invisible power perceived as coming from a "place" that is spiritually "higher" than the material world. The sky becomes heaven, the abode of the god or gods and perhaps also the pleasant realm to which good people go when they die. The area beneath the surface of the earth is often perceived as an "underworld," a dangerous place where life is different to life on the surface.

Some theorists assert that in some cases these common symbols are not just logical associations with the natural world. Most notably, the psychologist Carl Jung (1875–1961) proposed that humanity has a collective unconscious, a global psychic inheritance of archetypal symbols, such as the great mother and the trickster, from which geographically separate cultures have drawn.

Symbols are also woven together into **myths**—symbolic stories that communities use to explain the universe and their place within it. Joseph Campbell

(1904–1987), who analyzed myths around the world, found that they have four primary functions: mystical (to evoke awe, love, wonder, gratitude); cosmological (to explain the universe through the existence and actions of spiritual powers or beings); sociological (to create an orderly society, teach ethical codes); and psychological (to open doors to inner exploration, the development of one's full potential, and adjustment to life cycle changes). Understood in these senses, myths are not the work of primitive imagination; they can be deeply meaningful and transformational, forming a sacred belief structure that supports the laws and institutions of the religion and the ways of the community, as well as explaining the people's place within the cosmos.

Absolutist and liberal interpretations

Within each faith people often have different ways of interpreting their traditions. The **orthodox** stand by an historical form of their religion, strictly following its established practices, laws, and creeds. Those who resist contemporary influences and affirm what they perceive as the historical core of their religion could be called **absolutists**. In our times, many people feel that their identity as individuals or as members of an established group is threatened by the sweeping changes brought by modern industrial culture. The breakup of family relationships, loss of geographic rootedness, decay of clear behavioral codes, and loss of local control may be very unsettling. To find stable footing, some people may try to stand on selected religious doctrines or practices from the past. Religious leaders may encourage this trend toward rigidity by declaring themselves absolute authorities or by telling the people that their scriptures are literally and exclusively true. They may encourage antipathy or even violence against people of other religious traditions.

The term **fundamentalism** is often applied to this selective insistence on parts of a religious tradition and to violence against people of other religions. This use of the term is misleading, for no religion is based on hatred of other people and because those who are labeled may not be engaged in a return to the true basics of their religion. A Muslim "fundamentalist" who insists on the veiling of women, for instance, does not draw this doctrine from the foundation of Islam, the Holy Qur'an, but rather from historical cultural practice in some Muslim countries. A Sikh "fundamentalist" who concentrates on externals, such as wearing a turban, sword, and steel bracelet, overlooks the central insistence of the Sikh Gurus on the inner rather than outer practice of religion. A Hindu "fundamentalist" who objects to the presence of Christian missionaries working among the poor ignores one of the basic principles of ancient Indian religion, which is the tolerant assertion that there are many paths to the same universal truth. Rev. Valson Thampu, editor of the Indian journal *Traci*, writes that this selective type of religious extremism "absolutises what is spiritually or ethically superfluous in a religious tradition. True spiritual enthusiasm or zeal, on the other hand, stakes everything on being faithful to the spiritual essence."[21]

A further problem with the use of the term "fundamentalism" is that it has a specifically Protestant Christian connotation. The Christian fundamentalist movement originated in the late nineteenth century as a reaction to liberal trends, such as historical-critical study of the Bible, which will be explained below. Other labels may, therefore, be more cross-culturally appropriate, such as "absolutist," "extremist," or "reactionary," depending on the particular situation.

Those who are called religious **liberals** take a more flexible approach to religious tradition. They may see scriptures as products of a specific culture and time rather than the eternal voice of truth, and may interpret passages metaphorically rather than literally. If activists, they may advocate reforms in the ways their religion is officially understood and practiced. Those who are labeled **heretics** publicly assert controversial positions that are unacceptable to the orthodox establishment. **Mystics** are guided by their own spiritual experiences, which may coincide with any of the above positions.

Historical-critical study of scriptures

Non-faith-based research methods reveal that scriptures seem to be a mixture of polemics against opponents of the religion, myths, cultural influences, ethical instruction, later interpolations, mistakes by copyists, literary devices, actual history, and genuine spiritual inspiration.

To sort out these elements, the Bible—and more recently, scriptures of other religions—has, since the end of the eighteenth century, been analyzed objectively as a literary collection written within certain historical and cultural contexts, rather than as the absolute word of God. One area of research is to try to determine the original or most reliable form of a particular text. Another is to ferret out its historical aspects, with help from sources such as archaeological findings. Such research may conclude that material about a certain period may have been written later and include perspectives from that later period, or that a text attributed to one person may be a collection of writings by different people. Other areas of research are the intended audience, the language and meanings of the words, and whether a scripture or passage follows a particular literary form, such as poetry, for instance, narrative, or sayings. Another area is the **redaction**, editing and organizing, of the scripture and the development of an authorized canon that speaks not only to the local community but also to a wider audience. Yet another approach looks at the universal and contemporary relevance of the text, rather than its historicity.

The encounter between science and religion

Divisions among absolutist, liberal, and sceptical interpretations of religion are related to the development of modern science. Like religion, science is engaged in searching for universal principles that explain the facts of nature. The two approaches have influenced each other for thousands of years.

In ancient Greece "nature philosophers" tried to understand the world through their own perceptions of it. By contrast, Plato (c. 427–347 BCE) distrusted the testimony of the human senses. He distinguished between what is perceived by the senses and what is accessible through reason, between body and soul, appearance and reality, objects and ideas. He believed the soul was superior to the body, and the activity of reason preferable to the distraction of the senses, a value judgment that dominated Western thought through the Middle Ages.

In the seventeenth century, knowledge of nature became more **secularized** as scientists developed models of the universe as a giant machine, whose ways could be discovered by human reason. However, even though they studied its component parts and mathematically quantified its characteristics, many scientists regarded these as the work of a divine Creator or Ruler.

During the eighteenth-century Enlightenment, rational ways of knowing were increasingly respected. The sciences were viewed as progressive; some thinkers attacked institutionalized religions and dogma as superstitions. And the old unitary concepts of science and religion received another serious challenge in 1859, when the naturalist Charles Darwin (1809–1882) published *The Origin of Species*, which propounded the theory of evolution by natural selection. Darwin demonstrated that certain genetic mutations give an organism a competitive advantage over others of its species, and thus its lineage is naturally more likely to survive—a process that has directed the development of all forms of life. This contradicted a literal understanding of the biblical Book of Genesis, in which God is said to have created all life in only six days. By the end of the nineteenth century, all such beliefs of the Judeo-Christian tradition were being questioned.

However, during the twentieth and twenty-first centuries science has in some senses moved back toward a more nuanced understanding of religious belief. Science itself is now being questioned. Scientists have given up trying to find absolute certainties. Contemporary scientific research makes it clear that the cosmos is mind-boggling in its complexity and that what we perceive with our five senses is not ultimately real. For instance, the inertness and solidity of matter are only illusions. Each atom consists mostly of empty space with tiny particles whirling around in it. These subatomic particles—such as neutrons, protons, and electrons—cannot even be described as "things."

As science continues to question its own assumptions, new hypotheses are being suggested about the nature of the universe. "Superstring theory" proposes that it may not be made of particles, but rather of tiny vibrating strings and loops of strings. And that whereas we think we are living in four dimensions of space and time, there may be at least ten, with the unperceived dimensions "curled up" or "compactified" within the four dimensions we can perceive.

New branches of science are finding that the universe is not always predictable. Whereas scientific models of the universe were until recently based on the assumption of stability and equilibrium, physicist Ilya Prigogine observes that "today we see instability, fluctuations, irreversibility at every level."[22]

In the work of physicists such as David Bohm (1917–1994), physics approaches **metaphysics**—philosophy based on theories of subtle realities that transcend the physical world. Bohm described the dimensions we see and think of as "real" as the *explicate* order. Behind it lies the *implicate* order, in which separateness resolves into unbroken wholeness. Beyond may lie other subtle dimensions, all merging into an infinite ground that unfolds itself as light. This scientific theory is very similar to descriptions by mystics from all cultures about their intuitive experiences of the cosmos. They speak of realities beyond normal human perceptions of space and time.

One of the major conflicts between science and religion is that between

Creationism—religious concepts of intentional divine creation of all life forms—and **Darwinism**—the scientific concept of a universe evolving mechanistically by processes such as genetic mutations and random combinations of elements. Creationism has developed some scientific backing in the contemporary **intelligent design** movement, which holds that scientific discoveries of the complexities of life can be said to prove the existence of an Intelligent Designer, for they seem to be far beyond what could happen through evolutionary processes.

> *The most beautiful and profound emotion that we can experience is the sensation of the mystical. It is the sower of all true science. He to whom this emotion is a stranger, who can no longer wonder and stand rapt in awe, is as good as dead. To know that what is impenetrable to us really exists, manifesting itself as the highest wisdom and the most radiant beauty which our dull faculties can comprehend only in their most primitive forms—this knowledge, this feeling is at the center of true religiousness. . . . A human being is part of the whole. . . . He experiences himself, his thoughts and feelings as something separated from the rest—a kind of optical delusion of his consciousness. . . . Our task must be to free ourselves from this prison by widening our circle of compassion to embrace all living creatures, and the whole [of] nature in its beauty.*
>
> *Albert Einstein*[23]

Scientists are continually revealing a universe whose perfections suggest purposefulness. They have found, for instance, that stars could never have formed if the force of gravity were ever so slightly different. Biologists find that the natural world is an intricate harmony of beautifully elaborated, interrelated parts. Even to produce the miniature propeller that allows a tiny bacterium to swim, some forty different proteins are required.

The question then arises: Can the complex maps that produce life be the consequences of chance arrangements of atoms, or are they the result of deliberate design by some First Cause? Current research has demonstrated that the development of complex biochemical systems, such as the Krebs citric acid cycle, which unleashes the chemical energy stored in food to support life, can be explained by Darwinian mechanics. Evolutionary studies are revealing more and more evidence of what appear to be gradual changes in organisms. Even so, some scientists working in these areas maintain religious faith in a Creator.

In the dialogue between science and religion, four general positions have emerged. In the conflict model, which is most apparent in issues such as creation, some scientists have faith in scientific method and some religionists have faith in a Creator God whose existence cannot be scientifically proved. A second position is that science and religion are separate. Science deals with quantifiable physical reality, religion with the unquantifiable. A third position is dialogue, in which scientists and religious believers find common ground in interpreting religious propositions as metaphors and bases for the moral use of scientific research. A fourth is integration, in which science and religion overlap. An example is the intelligent design movement, which suggests that the odds against chance evolution of life's complexities and perfections may lead to belief in a Creator.

Scientists themselves have no answers that can be expressed in scientific terms.

The renowned theoretical physicist Stephen Hawking asks, "What is it that breathes fire into the equations and makes a universe for them to describe?"[24]

Women in religions

Another long-standing issue in the sphere of religion is the exclusion of women in male-dominated systems. Most institutionalized religions are **patriarchal**, meaning that men lead like father figures. Women are often relegated to the fringes of religious organizations, given only supporting roles, thus reflecting existing social distinctions between men and women. In some cases, women are even considered incapable of spiritual realization or dangerous to men's spiritual lives. Founders of religion have in many cases attempted to temper cultural restraints on women. Jesus, for example, apparently included women among his close disciples, and the Prophet Muhammad gave much more respect to women than the surrounding culture had. However, the institutions that developed after the prophets often reverted to exclusion and oppression of women, sometimes giving a religious stamp of approval to gender imbalances.

Although women are still barred from equal spiritual footing with men in many religions, this situation is now being widely challenged. The contemporary feminist movement includes strong efforts to make women's voices heard in the sphere of religion. Women are trying to discover their own identity, rather than having their identities defined by others. Scholars are bringing to light the histories of many women who have been religious leaders. Feminists are challenging patriarchal religious institutions that have excluded women from active participation. They are also challenging gender-exclusive language in holy texts and authoritarian masculine images of the divine. Their protests also go beyond gender issues to question the narrow and confining ways in which religious inspiration has been institutionalized. At prestigious Christian seminaries in the United States, women preparing for the ministry now outnumber men and are radically transforming views of religion and religious practice. Many women are deeply concerned about social ills of our times—violence, poverty, ecological disaster—and are insisting that religions be actively engaged in insuring human survival, and that they be life-affirming rather than punitive in approach.

Negative aspects of organized religions

Tragically, religions have often split rather than unified humanity, have oppressed rather than freed, have terrified rather than inspired. Institutionalization of religion is part of the problem. As institutionalized religions spread the teachings of their founders, there is the danger that more energy will go into preserving the outer form of the tradition than into maintaining its inner spirit. Max Weber (1864–1920), an influential early twentieth-century scholar of the sociology of religion, referred to this process as the "routinization of charisma." **Charisma** is the rare quality of personal magnetism often ascribed to founders of religion. When the founder dies, the center of the movement may shift to those who turn the original inspirations into routine rituals and dogma.

There is also the danger that power may devolve to those who have charisma but no genuine connection with divine wisdom. Since the human needs that religions answer are so strong, those who hold religious power are in a position to dominate and control their followers. In fact, in many religions leaders are given this authority to guide people's spiritual lives, for their wisdom and special access to the sacred are valued. Because religions involve the unseen, the mysterious, these leaders' teachings may not be verifiable by everyday physical experience. They must more often be accepted on faith and it is possible to surrender to leaders who are misguided or unethical. Religious leaders, like secular leaders, may not be honest with themselves and others about their inner motives. They may mistake their own thoughts and desires for divine guidance. Some people believe, however, that the most important thing for the disciple is to surrender the ego; even an unworthy leader can help in this goal simply by playing the role of one to whom one must surrender personal control.

Another potential problem is exaggeration of guilt. Religions try to help us make ethical choices in our lives, to develop a moral conscience. But in people who already have perfectionist or paranoid tendencies, the fear of sinning and being punished can be exaggerated to the point of neurosis or even psychosis by blaming, punishment-oriented religious teachings. If people try to leave their religion for the sake of their mental health, they may be haunted with guilt that they have done a terribly wrong thing. Religions thus have the potential for wreaking psychological havoc on their followers.

Another potentially negative use of religion is escapism. Because some religions, particularly those that developed in the East, offer a state of blissful contemplation as the reward for spiritual practice, the faithful may use religion to escape from their everyday problems. Psychologist John Welwood observes that Westerners sometimes embrace Eastern religions with the unconscious motive of avoiding their unsatisfactory lives. He calls this attempt "spiritual bypassing."

Because religions may have such a strong hold on their followers—by their fears, their desires, their deep beliefs—they are potential centers for political power. When church and state are one, the belief that the dominant national religion is the only true religion may be used to oppress those of other beliefs within the country. Religion may also be used as a rallying point for wars against other nations, casting the desire for control as a holy motive. Throughout history, huge numbers of people have been killed in the name of eradicating "false" religions and replacing them with the "true" religion. Rather than uniting us all in bonds of love, harmony, and mutual respect, this has often divided us with barriers of hatred and intolerance.

In our times, dangerous politicized polarizations between religions are increasing in some areas, albeit cooling off in others. Some of the most worrisome conflicts are pitting Christians and Jews against Muslims to such an extent that some have predicted a catastrophic "clash of civilizations." No religion has ever sanctioned violence against innocent people, but such political clashes have given a holy aura to doing just that, posing a grave threat to life and peace. Sadism, terrorism, wars over land and resources, political oppression, and environmental destruction can all be given a thin veneer of religious sanctification, thus obscuring their evil aspects.

His Highness the Aga Khan, spiritual leader of Ismaili Shia Muslims, maintains that the real problem today is a "clash of ignorance."[25] This is not the time to think of the world in terms of superficial, rigid distinctions between "us" and "them." It is the time when we must try to understand each other's beliefs and feelings clearly, carefully, and compassionately, and bring truly religious responses into play. To take such a journey does not mean forsaking our own religious beliefs or our scepticism. But the journey is likely to broaden our perspective and thus bring us closer to understanding other members of our human family. Perhaps it will bring us closer to Unseen Reality itself.

Review questions

1. Describe major positive and negative ways of understanding Unseen Reality. Consider sacred/profane, immanent/transcendent, theism/monotheism/polytheism/monism/nontheism, incarnations, atheism, agnosticism, and phenomenology.
2. Describe four major intellectual positions on the relationship between science and religion. Give examples for each.

Discussion questions

1. In view of materialistic arguments rejecting the reality of religion and spirituality, what kinds of experiences, language, and arguments can offer affirmations of sacred realities? Are they convincing or not? Why?
2. How are the changing social impacts of gender, education, and technologies affecting religion today? Do you think these trends are all good? Why?

CHAPTER 2

INDIGENOUS SACRED WAYS

"Everything is alive"

Here and there around the globe, pockets of people still follow local sacred ways handed down from their remote ancestors and adapted to contemporary circumstances. These are the traditional **indigenous** people—descendants of the original inhabitants of lands now controlled by larger political systems in which they may have little influence. Their distribution around the world, suggested in the map opposite, reveals a fascinating picture with many indigenous groups surviving in the midst of industrialized societies.

Indigenous people comprise at least four percent of the world population. Some who follow the ancient spiritual traditions still live close to the earth in non-industrial, small-scale cultures; many do not. But despite the disruption of their traditional lifestyles, many indigenous people maintain a sacred way of life that is distinctively different from all other religions. These enduring ways, which indigenous people may refer to as their "original instructions" on how to live, were almost lost under the onslaught of genocidal colonization, conversion pressures from global religions, mechanistic **materialism**, and the destruction of their natural environments by the global economy of limitless consumption.

Much of the ancient visionary wisdom has disappeared. To seek paying jobs and modern comforts such as electricity, many people have shifted from their natural environments into urban settings. There are few traditionally trained elders left and few young people willing to undergo the lengthy and rigorous training necessary for spiritual leadership in these sacred ways. Nevertheless, in our time there is a renewal of interest in these traditions, fanning hope that what they offer will not be lost.

To what extent can [indigenous groups] reinstate traditional religious values in a world gone mad with development, electronics, almost instantaneous transportation facilities, and intellectually grounded in a rejection of spiritual and mysterious events?

Vine Deloria, Jr.[1]

Understanding indigenous sacred ways

Outsiders have known or understood little of the indigenous sacred ways, many of which have long been practiced only in secret. The Buryats living near Lake Baikal in Russia were thought to have been converted to Buddhism and Christianity centuries ago; however, almost the entire population of the area gathered for indigenous ceremonies in 1992 and 1993.

In parts of aboriginal Australia, the indigenous teachings have been underground for 200 years since white colonialists and Christian missionaries appeared. As aborigine Lorraine Mafi Williams explains:

> We have stacked away our religious, spiritual, cultural beliefs. When the missionaries came, we were told by our old people to be respectful, listen and be obedient, go to church, go to Sunday school, but do not adopt the Christian doctrine because it takes away our cultural, spiritual beliefs.[2]

Not uncommonly, the newer global traditions have been blended with the older ways. For instance, Buddhism as it spread often adopted existing customs, such as the recognition of local deities. Now many indigenous people practice one of the global religions while still retaining many of their traditional ways.

Until recently, researchers into native sacred ways had little basis for understanding them. Many were anthropologists who approached them from the nonspiritual perspective of Western science or the Christian understanding of religion. Knowing that researchers from other cultures did not grasp the truth of their beliefs, native peoples have at times given them incorrect information in order to protect the sanctity of their practices.

Academic study of traditional ways is now becoming more sympathetic and self-critical, however, as is apparent in this statement by Gerhardus Cornelius Oosthuizen, a European researching African traditional religions:

> [The] Western worldview is closed, essentially complete and unchangeable, basically substantive and fundamentally non-mysterious; i.e. it is like a rigid programmed machine. . . . This closed worldview is foreign to Africa, which is still deeply religious. . . . This world is not closed, and not merely basically substantive, but it has great depth . . . and is truly mysterious; this world is restless, a living and growing organism.[3]

Indigenous spirituality is a **lifeway**, a particular approach to all of life. It is not a separate experience, like meditating or going to church. Rather, it ideally pervades all moments. As an elder of the Huichol in Mexico puts it:

> Everything we do in life is for the glory of God. We praise him in the well-swept floor, the well-weeded field, the polished machete, the brilliant colors of the picture and embroidery. In these ways we prepare for a long life and pray for a good one.[4]

In most native cultures, spiritual lifeways are shared orally and there are no written scriptures. This helps to keep the indigenous sacred ways dynamic and flexible, and the sacred experience fresh. These accounts are often rich in symbols, metaphors, and humor which are not easily understood by outsiders but are central to a people's understanding of how life works.

The lifeways of many small-scale cultures are meaningful only in the context of the land on which they live and their way of life. The people generally respect the rights of others and make no attempt to convert outsiders to theirs. Such worldviews are not inevitably linked to materially simple ways of life. The Dene Tha of northwestern Alberta, Canada, live in houses built by the government and ride snowmobiles, but still seek spiritual help from "animal helpers" and find meaning and guidance in their visionary experiences.

The doors to understanding indigenous forms of spirituality are now opening. Firstly, traditional elders are concerned about the potential for planetary disaster. Some are beginning to share their basic values in hopes of preventing industrial societies destroying the earth. Secondly, those of other faiths are beginning to recognize the value of indigenous ways. Thirdly, many people who have not grown up in native cultures are attempting to embrace indigenous spiritual ways, finding their own traditions lacking in qualities for which they long. However, they may disrupt or alter the indigenous practices. Osage theologian George Tinker describes what is often "the first Indian casualty" in North America:

> Well-meaning New Agers drive in from New York and Chicago or fly in from Austria and Denmark to participate in annual ceremonies originally intended to secure the well-being of the local, spatially configured community. These visitors see little or nothing of the reservation community . . . pay little attention to the poverty and suffering of the people there and finally leave having achieved only a personal, individual spiritual high.[5]

Indigenous traveling teachers are swamped with eager students. But many native peoples feel that their sacred ways are all they have left and worry that even these may be sold, stolen, and ruined.

Cultural diversity

This chapter considers the faith-ways of indigenous peoples as a whole. However, behind these generalizations lie many differences in social contexts, as well as in religious beliefs and practices. Some scholars today even question whether "indigenous" is a legitimate category in the study of religions, for they see it as a catchall "other" category consisting of sacred ways that do not fit within any of the other major global categories of organized religions.

To be sure, there are hundreds of different tribal traditions in North America alone, and at least fifty-three different ethnolinguistic groups in the Andean jungles. And Australian aboriginal lifeways, which are some of the world's oldest surviving cultures, traditionally included over 500 different clan groups, with differing beliefs, living patterns, and languages.

Indigenous traditions have evolved within materially as well as religiously diverse cultures. Some are descendants of civilizations with advanced urban technologies. When the Spanish conqueror Cortés took over Tenochtitlán (which now lies beneath Mexico City) in 1519, he found it a beautiful clean city with elaborate architecture, indoor plumbing, an accurate calendar, and advanced systems of mathematics and astronomy. Former African kingdoms were highly culturally advanced with elaborate arts, such as intricate bronze and copper casting, ivory carving, goldworking, and ceramics. Recently, some Native American tribes have become quite materially successful via economic enterprises, such as gambling complexes. And some indigenous groups use modern technologies such as the Internet to promote their concerns.

At the other extreme are those few cultures that still maintain a survival strategy of hunting and gathering. For example, some Australian aborigines continue to live as mobile foragers, though restricted to government-owned stations. A nomadic survival strategy necessitates simplicity in material goods; whatever can be gathered or built rather easily at the next camp need not be dragged along. But material simplicity is not a sign of spiritual poverty. The Australian aborigines have complex **cosmogonies**, or models of the origins of the universe and their purpose within it, as well as a working knowledge of their own bioregion.

Some traditional people live in their ancestral enclaves, somewhat sheltered from the pressures of modern industrial life, though not untouched by the outer world. Tribal peoples have lived deep in the forests and hills of India for thousands of years, utilizing the trees and plants for their food and medicines, although within the twentieth century their ancestral lands were taken over for "development" projects and encroached upon by more politically and economically powerful groups, rendering many of the seventy-five million Indian tribal people landless laborers. The Hopi people have continuously occupied a high plateau area of the southwestern United States for between 800 and 1,000 years; their sacred ritual calendar is tied to the yearly farming cycle.

Other indigenous people visit their sacred sites and ancestral shrines but live in more urban settings because of job opportunities. The people who participate in ceremonies in the Mexican countryside include subway personnel, journalists, and artists of native blood who live in Mexico City.

In addition to variations in lifestyles, indigenous traditions vary in their adaptations to dominant religions. Often native practices have become interwoven with those of global religions, such as Buddhism, Islam, and Christianity. In Southeast Asia, household Buddhist shrines are almost identical to the spirit houses in which the people still make offerings to honor the local spirits. The Dahomey tradition from West Africa was carried to Haiti by African slaves and called **Vodou**, from *vodu*, one of the names for the chief non-human spirits. Forced by the European colonialists to adopt Christianity, worshipers of Vodou secretly fused their old gods with their images of Catholic saints. In Cuba, Yoruba slaves did the same, resulting in the practices known as **Santeria** (see Chapter 11).

While interaction with larger state societies or colonial powers has been extremely detrimental to indigenous peoples around the world, adaptation of the dominant religions has at times allowed the traditional people to survive. Indigenous people sometimes earnestly try to practice the dominant religion, and in doing so they bring new life into it, as in the lively practice of Christianity in rural Africa. In other places, forced converts may practice the new religion only indifferently. A third outcome is the mixing of traditions to produce a new hybrid.

Despite their different histories and economic patterns, and their geographical separation, indigenous sacred ways do have some characteristics in common. Perhaps from ancient contact across land-bridges that no longer exist, there are similarities between the languages of the Tsalagi in the Americas, Tibetans, and the aboriginal Ainu of Japan. Similarities in the myths of geographically separate peoples can be accounted for by global diffusion by trade, travel, and other kinds of contact, and by parallel origin because of the similarities in human experience, such as birth and death, and wonder at the cosmos and our place in it.

Certain symbols and metaphors are repeated in the inspirational art and stories of many traditional cultures around the world, but the people's relationships to, and the concepts surrounding, these symbols are not inevitably the same. Nevertheless, the following sections look at some recurring themes in the spiritual ways of diverse small-scale cultures.

The circle of right relationships

For many indigenous peoples, everything in the cosmos is intimately interrelated. A symbol of unity among the parts of this sacred reality is a circle. This is not used by all indigenous people; the Navajo, for instance, regard a completed circle as stifling and restrictive. However, many other indigenous people hold the circle sacred because it is infinite—it has no beginning, no end. Time is circular for it keeps coming back to the same place. Life revolves around the generational cycles of birth, youth, maturity, and physical death, the return of the seasons, the cyclical movements of the moon, sun, stars, and planets.

This understanding of life as a complex of circles is thought to be the perfect framework for harmony. As Lame Deer, a Lakota Sioux holy man, explained:

> With us the circle stands for the togetherness of people who sit with one another around the campfire, . . . The camp in which every tipi had its place was also a ring. The tipi was a ring in which people sat in a circle and all the families in the village were in turn circles within a larger circle, part of the larger hoop which was the seven campfires of the Sioux, representing one nation. The nation was only a part of the universe, in itself circular and made of the earth, which is round, of the sun, which is round, of the stars, which are round. The moon, the horizon, the rainbow—circles within circles within circles, with no beginning and no end.[6]

To maintain the natural balance of the circles of existence, most indigenous peoples have traditionally been taught that they must develop right relationships with everything that is. Their relatives include the unseen world of spirits, the land and weather, the people and creatures, and the power within.

Relationships with spirit

Many indigenous traditions worship a Supreme Being who they believe created the cosmos. This being is known by the Lakota as "Wakan Tanka" or "Great Mysterious" or "Great Spirit." African names for this being are attributes, such as "All-powerful," "Creator," or "the one who began the forest." The Supreme Being is often referred to as male, but is female in some groups. Some tribes of the southwestern United States call her "Changing Woman"—sometimes young, sometimes old, the mother of the earth, associated with women's reproductive cycles and birth, the creatrix. Many traditional languages make no distinction between male and female pronouns, and some see the divine as androgynous, arising from the interaction of male and female aspects of the universe.

Awareness of one's relationship to the Great Power is thought to be essential, but the power itself remains unseen and mysterious. An Inuit spiritual adept described his people's experience of:

> *a power that we call Sila, which is not to be explained in simple words. A great spirit, supporting the world and the weather and all life on earth, a spirit so mighty that [what it says] to mankind is not through common words, but by storm and snow and rain and the fury of the sea; all the forces of nature that men fear. But Sila has also another way of [communicating]; by sunlight and calm of the sea, and little children innocently at play, themselves understanding nothing. . . . When all is well, Sila sends no message to mankind, but withdraws into endless nothingness, apart.[7]*

To traditional Buryats of Russia, the chief power in the world is the eternally blue sky, Tengry. African myths suggest that the High God was originally so close to humans that they became disrespectful. The All-powerful was like the sky, which was once so close that children wiped their hands on it, and women broke off pieces for soup and bumped it with their sticks when pounding grain.

It cannot be said that indigenous concepts of, and attitudes toward, a Supreme Being are necessarily the same as that which Western monotheistic religions refer to as God or Allah. In African traditional religions, much more emphasis tends to be placed on the transcendent dimensions of everyday life and doing what is spiritually necessary to keep life going normally. Many unseen powers are perceived to be at work in the material world. In various traditions, some of these are perceived without form, as mysterious and sacred presences, others as having more definite, albeit invisible, forms and personalities. These may include deities with human-like personalities, the nature spirits of venerable trees and mountains, animal spirit helpers, personified elemental forces, ancestors who still take an interest in their living relatives, or the *nagas*, known to the traditional people of Nepal as invisible serpentine spirits who control the circulation of water in the world and also within our bodies.

Continued communication with ancestors is extremely important to some traditional Africans, who understand that the person is not an individual, but a composite of many souls—the spirits of one's parents and ancestors. Rev. William Kingsley Opoku, International Coordinator of the African Council for Spiritual Churches, says:

> *Our ancestors are our saints. Christian missionaries who came here wanted us to pray to their saints, their dead people. But what about our saints? ... If you are grateful to your ancestors, then you have blessings from your grandmother, your grandfather, who brought you forth. . . . Non-Africans came in and said we should not obey our ancestors . . . This has been a mental bondage, a terrible thing.[8]*

Food and drink are set out for the "living dead" (ancestors who have died within living memory), acknowledging that they are still engaged with people's lives.

The Dagara of Burkina Faso in West Africa are familiar with the *kontombili*, who look like humans but are only about one foot tall, because of the humble way they express their spiritual power. Other West African groups recognize a great pantheon of deities, the **orisa** or *vodu*, each the object of special cult worship. The *orisa* embody the dynamic forces in life, such as Oya, goddess of death and change, experienced in tornadoes, lightning, winds, and fire; and Obatala, the source of creativity, warmth, and enlightenment.

The spirits are thought to be available to those who seek them as helpers, as intermediaries between the people and the power, and as teachers. A right relationship with these spirit beings can be a sacred partnership. As we will later see, those who are considered most able to call on the spirits for help are the shamans who have dedicated their lives to this service.

Kinship with all creation

In addition to the unseen powers, all aspects of the tangible world are believed to be imbued with spirit. Josiah Young III explains that in African traditional religion, both the visible and invisible realms are filled with spiritual forces:

> The visible is the natural and cultural environment, of which humans, always in the process of transformation, are at the center. The invisible connotes the numinous field of ancestors, spirits, divinities, and the Supreme Being, all of whom, in varying degrees, permeate the visible. Visible things, however, are not always what they seem. Pools, rocks, flora, and fauna may dissimulate invisible forces of which only the initiated are conscious.[9]

Within the spiritually charged visible world, all things may be understood as spiritually interconnected. Everything is therefore experienced as family. In African traditional lifeways, "we" may be more important than "I," and often refers to a large extended family and ancestral village, even for people who have moved to the cities. In indigenous cultures, the community is paramount, and it may extend beyond the living humans in the area. Many traditional peoples know the earth as their mother. The land one lives on is part of her body.

Some feature of the natural environment—such as a mountain or canyon—may be perceived as the center from which the world was created. This heightens the perceived sacredness of the land. Western Tibet's Mount Kailas, high in the Himalayas, is seen as the center of the earth, a sacred space where the earthly and supernatural meet. Spiritual specialists therefore climb the mountain seeking visions. The Western Apache remember vivid symbolic narratives about the exploits of people in specific places and contemplate them as aids to making their minds smooth, steady, and resilient.

Native people consider themselves caretakers of their mother, the earth. They are now raising their voices against the destruction of the environment, warning of the potential for global disaster. Nepali shamans report that the klevel of Lake Mansarovar at the base of Mount Kailas is low and the spirits are unhappy. Some indigenous visionaries say they hear the earth crying. Contemporary Australian aboriginal elder Bill Neidjie speaks of feeling the earth's pain:

> I feel it with my body,
> with my blood.
> Feeling all these trees,
> all this country . . .
> If you feel sore . . .
> headache, sore body
> that mean somebody killing tree or grass.

You feel because your body in that tree or earth. ...
You might feel it for two or three years.
You get weak . . .
little bit, little bit . . .
because tree going bit by bit . . .
dying.[10]

The earth abounds with living presences, in traditional worldviews. Rocks, bodies of water, and mountains—considered inanimate by other peoples—are personified as living beings. Visionaries can see the spirits of a body of water, and many traditional cultures have recognized certain groves of trees as places where spirits live. As a Pit River Indian explained, "Everything is alive. That's what we Indians believe."[11] Australian aboriginal people see their landscape in terms of the "everywhen" of the **Dreaming**, the time when the ancestors appeared from beneath the surface of the earth, investing the environment with their own presence and establishing the law.

All creatures may be perceived as kin, endowed with consciousness and the power of the Great Spirit. Many native peoples know that all things depend on each other, and that they have a reciprocal, rather than dominating, relationship with all beings. Hawaiian *kahuna* (shaman-priest) Kahu Kawai'i explains:

How you might feel toward a human being that you love is how you might feel toward a dry leaf on the ground and how you might feel toward the rain in the forest and the wind. There is such intimacy that goes on that everything speaks to you and everything responds to how you are in being—almost like a mirror reflecting your feelings.[12]

Even the dreams of indigenous peoples are often related to their particular environment and are understood as providing guidelines for proper ways to act. Trees, animals, insects, and plants are all to be approached with caution and consideration. If one must cut down a tree or kill an animal, one must first explain one's intentions and ask forgiveness. Those who harm nature may themselves be harmed in return. Tribal peoples of Madhya Pradesh in central India will avoid killing a snake, for they feel its partner would come after them to seek revenge. When a Buryat cuts a tree to build a house, he must first offer milk, butter, rice, and alcohol to the spirits of the forest and ask their forgiveness. The Yup'ik of southwestern Alaska know animals as thinking, feeling fellow beings, and believe that if humans treat animal populations carefully as guests, they will come back in plentiful numbers the following year and offer themselves to the hunters.

There are many stories of indigenous people's relationships with non-human creatures. Certain trees tell healing specialists which herbs to use. Australian aboriginal women are adept at forming hunting partnerships with dogs. Birds are thought to bring messages from the spirit world. A crow, a wild yak, and a pack of silver wolves revealed the sacred path to Mount Kailas in Tibet. A Hopi elder said he spent three days and nights praying with a rattlesnake. "Of course he was nervous at first, but when I sang to him he recognized the warmth of my body and calmed down. We made good prayer together."[13]

Relationships with power

Another common theme in indigenous lifeways is developing an appropriate relationship with spiritual energy.

> *All animals have power, because the Great Spirit dwells in all of them, even a tiny ant, a butterfly, a tree, a flower, a rock. The modern, white man's way keeps that power from us, dilutes it. To come to nature, feel its power, let it help you, one needs time and patience for that. . . . You have so little time for contemplation. ... It lessens a person's life, all that grind, that hurrying and scurrying about.*
>
> Lame Deer, Lakota nation[14]

In certain places and beings, the power of spirit is believed to be highly concentrated. It is referred to as *mana* by the people of the Pacific islands. This is the vital force that makes it possible to act with unusual strength, insight, and effectiveness.

Tlakaelel, a contemporary spiritual leader of the descendants of the Toltecs of Mexico, describes how a person might experience this power when looking into an obsidian mirror traditionally made to concentrate power:

> *When you reach the point that you can concentrate with all your will, inside there, you reach a point where you feel ecstasy. It's a very beautiful thing, and everything is light. Everything is vibrating with very small signals, like waves of music, very smooth. Everything shines with a blue light. And you feel a sweetness. Everything is covered with the sweetness, and there is peace. It's a sensation like an orgasm, but it can last a long time.[15]*

Sacred sites may be recognized by the power believers feel there. Some have been used again and again by successive religions, either to capitalize on the energy or to co-opt the preceding religion. Chartres Cathedral in France, for instance, was built on an ancient ritual site. In New Zealand, the traditional Maori people know of the revivifying power of running water, such as waterfalls (understood by scientists as places of negative ionization, which do indeed have an energizing effect). The Maori elders have told the public of the healing power of a certain waterfall on North Island; the area is now dedicated to anyone who needs healing.

Because power can be built up through sacred practices, the ritual objects of spiritually developed persons may have concentrated power. Special stones and animal artifacts may also carry power. A person might be strengthened by the spiritual energy of the bear or the wolf by wearing sacred clothing made from its fur. Power can also come to one through visions or by being given a sacred pipe or the privilege of collecting objects into a personal sacred bundle.

In some cultures women are thought to have a certain natural power; men have to work harder for it. Women's power is considered mysterious, dangerous, uncontrolled. It is said to be strongest during menstruation. Women are secluded during their menstrual periods in many cultures, not necessarily because they are considered polluting. Among the Yurok of northern California, houses have a separate back room for women who are menstruating so that they can concentrate on their inner selves, becoming inwardly stronger and purified by the flow of blood. In certain rituals in which both men and women participate, women's menstrual blood is often thought to diminish or weaken the ritual or the men's spiritual power. In most Native American nations that have sweat lodge ceremonies for ritual purification, menstruating women are not allowed to enter the lodge. A few cultures, such as the Ainu of Japan, have prized menstrual blood as a potent offering returned to the earth.

Gaining power is both desirable and dangerous. If misused for personal ends, it may turn against the person. To channel spiritual power properly, native people are taught that they must live within certain strict limits. Those who seek power or receive it unbidden are supposed to continually purify themselves of any selfish motives and dedicate their actions to the good of the whole.

Spiritual specialists

In a few remaining hunting and gathering tribes, religion is a relatively private matter. Each individual has direct access to the unseen. Although spirit is invisible, it is considered a part of the natural world. Anyone can interact with it spontaneously, without complex ceremony and without anyone else's aid.

More commonly, however, the world of spirit is thought to be dangerous. Although everyone is expected to observe certain personal ways of worship, such as offering prayers before taking plant or animal life, many ways of interacting with spirit are thought to be best left to those who are specially trained for the roles. These specialists are gradually initiated into the secret knowledge that allows them to act as intermediaries between the seen and the unseen. They sacrifice themselves through ritual purification, struggle, hardship, and protocol in order to remain in proper relationship with the spirits.

Storytellers and other sacred roles

Specialists' roles vary from one group to another, and the same person may play several roles. One common one is that of storyteller. Because the traditions are oral, these people must memorize long and complex stories and songs so that sacred traditions can be remembered and taught, generation after generation. The orally transmitted epics of the Ainu of Japan are up to 10,000 "lines" long. Chants of the Yoruba *orisa* comprise 256 "volumes" of 800 verses each.

The Yoruban chants include an explanation of the genesis of the earth. When time began, where the earth now exists there was only a vast watery area, with a dim and misty atmosphere. The *orisa* lived in an upper world of light until Obatala decided to see if solid land could be created on earth for the *orisa* to inhabit. He had a sacred gold chain made for his descent, and carried a shell of sand, a white hen, a palm nut, and a black cat. He climbed down to the watery world by means of the chain, but it was too short. Thus he poured the sand downward and then released the hen, who by scratching in the sand created the contours of the earth. Obatala settled on the land and planted his palm nut, which sent its seed far and wide, developing the plant life of the earth. At first he was alone, with only the black cat as his companion, but later many things happened, accounting for the features of the earth and its inhabitants as we know them today. The golden chain is a common mythological symbol of a World Axis connecting heaven and earth; the palm tree also commonly appears in myths of the World Tree, giver and protector of the first forms of life on earth.

Such stories are important clues to understanding the universe and one's place in it. What is held only in memory cannot be physically destroyed, but if a tribe is small and all its storytellers die, the knowledge is lost. This happened on a large scale during contacts with colonial powers, as native people were killed by war and imported diseases. Professor Wande Abimbola, who is trying to preserve the oral tradition of the Yoruba, has made thousands of tapes of the chants, but there are few people who can understand and interpret their meaning.

Bards carry the energy of ancient traditions into new forms. In Africa, poets are considered "technicians of the sacred," conversing with a dangerous world of spirits. Drumming creates a rhythmic environment in which the people can draw close to the unseen powers and players of the "talking drums" are highly valued as communicators with the spirits, ancestors, and Supreme Being. As the Akan of Ghana say:

The thumb, finger with mouth, wake up and speak!
The thumb armed with sticks for drumming
Is more loquacious and more eloquent
Than a human being sleeping;
Wake up and come![16]

"Tricksters" such as foxes often appear in the stories of indigenous traditions. They are paradoxical, transformative beings. Sacred clowns may endure the shame of behaving as fools during public rituals in order to teach people through humor. A sacred fool, called **heyoka** by the Lakota, must be both innocent and wise about human nature, and have a visionary relationship with spirit.

Life is holiness and everyday humdrum, sadness and laughter, the mind and the belly all mixed together. The Great Spirit doesn't want us to sort them out neatly.
                              Leonard Crow Dog, Lakota medicine man[17]

Another coveted role is to be a member of a secret society in which one can participate by initiation or invitation only, whether to enhance one's prestige or to draw closer to the spirit world. During ceremonies members often wear special costumes to hide their human identities and help them take on the personas of spirits they are representing. In African religions, they periodically appear as impersonators of animal spirits or of dead ancestors, demonstrating that the dead are still watching the living and protecting the village.

Women also have secret societies, whose activities are little known by outsiders. Among aboriginal peoples of Australia, members are initiated into separate but interrelated roles for males and females. For instance, when boys are separated from the tribe for circumcision by the men's secret society, the women's society has its own separation rituals and may stage ritual fights with the men's society. But the rituals for both sexes refer to **Dream Time**, in which there is no male/female differentiation.

Sacred dancers likewise make the unseen powers visible. Body movements are a language in themselves expressing the nature of the cosmos, a language that is understood through the stories and experiences of the community. Such actions keep the world of the ancestors alive for succeeding generations.

In some socially stratified societies there are priests and priestesses. Specially trained and dedicated, they carry out the rituals that ensure proper functioning of the natural world, and perhaps also communicate with particular spirits or deities. In West Africa, though priests or priestesses may have part-time earthly occupations, they are expected to stay in a state of ritual purity and spend much of their time communicating with the spirit being. Mediums associated with the temples enter a state of trance or allow themselves to be possessed by gods or spirits in order to bring messages to the people.

Mystical intermediaries

Another distinctive type of spiritual specialist is found among many indigenous peoples. They are called by many names, but the Siberian and Saami word **"shaman"** is a generic term for those who are mystical intermediaries between the physical and non-physical world for specific purposes, such as healing. Archaeological research has confirmed that shamanic methods are at least 20,000 to 30,000 years old. They are remarkably similar around the globe.

Mystical intermediaries may use their skills to benefit others. They are not to be confused with sorcerers, who practice black magic to harm others or promote their own ends, interfering with the cosmic order. Spiritual power is neutral; its use depends on the practitioner. What Native Americans call "**medicine** power" does not originate in the **medicine person**. Black Elk explained:

> Of course it was not I who cured. It was the power from the outer world, and the visions and ceremonies had only made me like a hole through which the power could come to the two-leggeds. If I thought that I was doing it myself, the hole would close up and no power could come through.[18]

There are many kinds of medicine. One heals physical, psychological, and spiritual problems. Techniques used include physical approaches to illness, such as herbs, massage, and cauterization. But the treatments are given to the whole person—body, mind, and spirit, with emphasis on healing relationships within the group—so there may also be divination, prayer, chanting, and ceremonies in which group power is built up and spirit helpers are called in. If an intrusion of harmful power, such as the angry energy of another person, seems to be causing the problem, the medicine person may attempt to suck it out with the aid of spirit helpers, then dry vomit the invisible intrusion into a receptacle.

These healing methods are now beginning to earn respect from the scientific medical establishment. Medicine people are permitted to attend indigenous patients in some hospitals, and in the United States, the National Institute of Mental Health has paid Navajo medicine men to teach young Indians the ceremonies that have often been more effective in curing the mental health problems of Navajos than has Western psychiatry.

In addition to healing, certain mystical intermediaries are thought to have gifts such as being able to talk with plants and animals, control the weather, and prophesy. A gift highly developed in Africa is that of divination, using techniques such as reading patterns revealed by a casting of cowrie shells.

Mystical intermediaries are contemplatives, Lame Deer explains:

> The wicasa wakan [holy man] wants to be by himself. . . . He likes to meditate, leaning against a tree or rock, feeling the earth move beneath him, feeling the weight of that big flaming sky upon him. That way he can figure things out. Closing his eyes, he sees many things clearly. What you see with your eyes shut is what counts. . . . He listens to the voices of the wama kaskan—all those who move upon the earth, the animals. He is as one with them. From all living beings something flows into him all the time, and something flows from him.[19]

The role of shaman may be hereditary or it may be recognized as a special gift. Either way, training is rigorous. To work in a mystical state of ecstasy, moving between ordinary and non-ordinary realities, shamans must experience physical death and rebirth. Some have near-death experiences. Uvavnuk, an Inuit shaman, was initiated when she was struck by a lightning ball. After she revived, she had great power, which she dedicated to serving her people. Other potential mystical intermediaries undergo rituals of purification, isolation, and bodily torment until they make contact with a helping spirit.

For many mystical intermediaries, their role is not a matter of choice. The spirit enters whom it will. Tsering, an aged Nepali *dhami* (shaman), relates:

> We never wanted to become dhamis. In fact, we tried hard to get the gods to leave us. We pleaded, performed worship ceremonies, even carried manure around with us to offend them, but nothing seemed to work. When calamities began to hit my family—when my brother died falling off the roof and our best horse drowned in the river—I realized I had no choice and had to make the initiatory journey to Kailas.[20]

Once there, the new *dhamis* had to plunge naked with unbound hair into freezing Lake Mansarovar in order to commune with the spirits. On returning to their village, their deities insisted they prove their spiritual connection by feats such as drinking boiling oil. Thereafter, those *dhamis* were respected as authorities.

Potential mystical intermediaries must undergo lengthy training in spiritual techniques, the names and roles of the spirits, and secrets and myths of the tribe. They are taught by older shamans and reportedly by the spirits. If the spirits do not accept and teach them, he or she is unable to carry the role.

The helping spirits—often spirit animals—that contact would-be shamans during the death-and-rebirth crisis become essential partners in their work, their guardian spirits who give them special powers. A shaman may take on its persona of the animal. Many tribes believe healing specialists need the powers of the bear; Lapp shamans became wolves, reindeer, bears, or fish.

Mystical intermediaries may be able to enter parallel, spiritual realities at will to bring back knowledge, power, or help for those in need. Techniques for entering the altered state of consciousness this requires are the same around the world: drumming, rattling, singing, dancing, and sometimes hallucinogenic drugs. These open what the Huichol shamans of Mexico call the *narieka*—the doorway of the heart, the channel for divine power, where human and spirit worlds meet. It is often experienced and represented as a pattern of concentric circles.

An Interview with Nadezhda Ananyevna Stepanova

One of the remaining traditional shamans of Buryatia, Nadezhda Ananyevna Stepanova comes from a family of powerful shamans. Her mother tried to prevent her becoming a shaman. Buddhist lamas had spread the impression that shamans were to be avoided, that they were ignorant, primitive servants of dark, lower spirits. But when a shaman receives a true spiritual call, to deny that pull is dangerous. Nadezhda explains:

"When I was twenty-six, I was told I would be a shaman, a great shaman. When I told Mother, she said, 'No, you won't.' She took a bottle, went to her native town, and then came back. 'Everything will be taken away; you won't become a shaman,' she said. I became seriously ill, and Mother was paralyzed. I understood then: We were both badly ill because she went against the gods.

"Nobody could heal me. Then one seer said, 'You must cure.' I replied, 'I don't know anything about curing.' But a voice inside me said, 'If you don't become a shaman, you will die. You will be overrun by a lorry with a blue number.' I began to collect materials about medicine, about old rites. Then I could do a lot, for all we need is seeing and feeling. I was initiated by the men shamans of all the families, each praying to his god in a definite direction, for every god has his direction. I sat in the middle. Every shaman asked his gods to help me, to protect me, to give me power. The ritual was in early March. It was very frosty and windy, and I was only lightly dressed, but I wasn't cold at all. The wind didn't touch me. I sat motionless for about four hours, but I was not cold.

"I began to cure. The main thing to me is to help a person if I can. I pray to my gods, ask them for mercy, I ask them to pay attention, to help. I feel the pain of those who come to me, and I want to relieve it. I have *yodo*— bark from a fir tree scratched by a bear; its smoke purifies. I perform rituals of bringing back the soul; often they work. My ancestors are very close to me; I see them as well as I see you.

"Last year in the island Olkhon in Lake Baikal, there was a great gathering of shamans from Tchita, Irkutsk, Ulan-Ude, Yakutiya, and Buryatia to pray to the great spirits of Baikal about the well-being and prosperity of the Buryat land. For a long time these spirits were not turned to. They were forgotten by the people, and they fell asleep. They could not take an active part in the life of people; they could not help them any more. *Teylagan*, the prayer of the shamans for the whole Buryatia, was to awaken the great spirits. We had always prayed to thirteen northern *nainkhats*, the great spirits of this area. But when the Buddhists came, persecution began, and people prayed secretly, only for their families. They could not pray for the whole Buryat nation, and they did not. They forgot. Shamans were killed. Then the atheistic Soviet regime tried to make us forget the faith, and we forgot. The most terrible thing about them was that they wanted to make people forget everything, to live by the moment and forget their roots. And what is man without roots? Nothing. It is a loss of everything. That is why now nobody has compassion for anybody. Now we are reaping the fruit: robbery, drinking, drugs. This is our disaster. That is why we must pray to our own gods."[21]

The "journey" then experienced by mystical intermediaries is typically into the Upperworld or the Lowerworld. To enter the latter, they descend mentally through a real hole in the ground, such as a spring, cave, animal burrow, or ceremonial hole regarded as a navel of the earth. These entrances lead into tunnels that open into bright landscapes. Reports of such journeys include what the journeyer saw and physical sensations, such as what the walls of the tunnel felt like.

The shaman encounters beings in the Lowerworld, and may bring something back if the client needs it—a lost guardian spirit or a lost soul, for instance, to revive a person in a coma. Often a river must be crossed as the boundary between the worlds of the living and the dead. An old man or woman may assist this passage through the Underworld. Where indigenous ways have been subdued, this process is retained only in myths, such as the Orpheus story.

Group observances

Indigenous ways are community-centered. Through group rituals, traditional people honor the sacred and affirm their bonds with each other and all creation. Humans can help to maintain the harmony of the universe by such observances.

In order to maintain the natural balance and to ensure success in the hunt or harvest, ceremonies must be performed with exactitude. For instance, there is a specific time for the telling of specific stories. Chona, a Tohono O'odham (Papago) medicine woman, told anthropologist Ruth Underhill:

> I should not have told you this [the origin of Coyote, who helped to put the world in order, with a few mistakes]. These things about the Beginning are holy. They should not be told in the hot time when the snakes are out. The snakes guard our secrets. If we tell what is forbidden, they bite.[22]

Rituals often take people out of everyday consciousness and into awareness of the presence of the sacred. In such states, individuals may experience a heightened group consciousness that binds them together as a community.

Each group has its own ways of ritual dedication to the spirits of life, but they tend to follow certain patterns everywhere. Some are rites of passage that honor major points in the life cycle, such as birth, naming, puberty, marriage, and death, and assist people in the transition from one state to another. When a Hopi baby is twenty days old, it is presented at dawn to Father Sun for the first time and officially given a name. Its face is cleansed with sacred cornmeal, a ceremony that will be repeated at death for the journey to the Underworld.

Girls commonly go through a ceremony to mark their first menstruation, which signals the end of childhood and preparation for becoming wives and mothers. For both boys and girls, the rituals of puberty typically involve separation from the community, a transition phase in which they are secluded with no clear identity and prepared for adulthood, and a third phase when they are reincorporated into the community with a new adult identity. Girls in traditional Lakota households spend the transition time practicing skills such as stitching and cooking.

There are also collective rituals to support the group's survival strategies. In farming communities these include ways of asking for rain, of insuring the growth of crops, and of giving thanks for the harvest. In the Great Drought of 1988, Sioux holy man Leonard Crow Dog was asked by three non-native Midwestern communities to perform rainmaking ceremonies for them.

Ritual dramas about the beginnings and sacred history of the people engage performers and spectators on an emotional level through the use of special costumes, body paint, music, masks, and perhaps sacred locations. These dramas provide a sense of orderly interface among humans, the land, and the spiritual world. They also dramatize mysticism, drawing people toward direct contact with the spirit world. Those who have visions and dreams are supposed to share them with others, which is often done through dramatization.

According to legend, the Plains Indians were given the sacred pipe by White Buffalo Calf Woman as a tool for communicating with the mysteries and understanding the ways of life. The bowl of the pipe represents the female aspect of the Great Spirit, the stem the male aspect. When they are ritually joined, the power of the spirit is thought to be present as the pipe is passed around the circle for collective communion with each other and with the divine.

Groups also gather for ritual purification and spiritual renewal of individuals. Indigenous peoples of the Americas "smudge" sites and possessions, cleansing them with smoke from special herbs, such as sage and sweetgrass. Many groups make an igloo-shaped "sweat lodge" into which hot stones are carried. People huddle together in the dark around the stone pit. When water is poured on the stones, intensely hot steam sears bodies and lungs. Everyone prays earnestly. Leonard Crow Dog says of the *inipi* (sweat lodge):

> The inipi *is probably our oldest ceremony because it is built around the simplest, basic, life-giving things: the fire that comes from the sun, warmth without which there can be no life;* inyan wakan, *or* tunka, *the rock that was there when the earth began, that will still be there at the end of time; the earth, the mother womb; the water that all creatures need; our green brother, the sage; and encircled by all these, man, basic man, naked as he was born, feeling the weight, the spirit of endless generations before him, feeling himself part of the earth, nature's child, not her master.*[23]

Pilgrimages to sacred sites are often communal. Buryats gather on top of Erde, the mountain where the spirit of the earth lives, and join hands to encircle it; a great energy is said to appear in the huge circle. The Huichol Indians of western Mexico make a yearly journey to a desert they call Wirikuta, the Sacred Land of the Sun, where they feel that creation began. They gather their supply of peyote cactus here. Peyote has the power to alter consciousness: it is their "little deer," a spirit who helps them to communicate with the spirit world.

When indigenous groups are broken up, they lose the cohesive power of group rituals. Africans taken to the New World as slaves lost not only their individual identities but also their membership in tight-knit groups. To re-establish shared spiritual traditions among African-Americans, Professor Maulana Ron Karenga created a celebration, Kwanzaa, based on indigenous African "first fruits" harvest festivals. Using symbolic objects to create a special atmosphere (such as fruit and vegetables, candles, and a "unity cup," all called by their Swahili names), families and groups of families meet from December 26 to January 1 to explore their growth over the past year. They look at their experiences of the "seven principles"—unity, self-determination, collective work, family-centeredness, purpose, creativity with limited resources, and confidence—and reward each other for progress by giving gifts.

Individual observances

It is considered important for each person to experience a personal connection with the spirits. The people acknowledge and work with them in many everyday ways. For instance, someone searching for herbs does not to take the first plant found; an offering is made to it, with the prayer that its relatives will understand the person's needs. Guardian spirits and visions may be sought by everyone, not just mystical specialists. The shaman may have more spirit helpers and more power, but visionary experiences and opportunities for worship are available to all. Thus, indigenous traditions have been called "democratized shamanism."

Temples to the spirits may exist, but one can also worship them anywhere. Wande Abimbola observes:

> Big temples aren't necessary to worship the orisa, even though there are temples for most orisa in Africa. If you are a devotee of Ifa, you can carry the objects of Ifa in your pocket. If you want to make an offering to Ogun, put any piece of iron on the floor and make an offering to it. It's just like a Christian would carry a Bible or maybe a cross.[24]

To open themselves for contact with the spirit world, individuals in many indigenous cultures undergo a **vision quest**. After ritual purification, they are sent alone to a sacred spot to cry to the spirits to help them in their journey.

Pre-puberty or the onset of puberty is commonly thought to be the best time for vision quests, for children are closest to the spirit world. Among the Dene Tha, children are informally encouraged to go out to the bush before the age of puberty and spend time alone, seeking a spirit helper.

Adults may also make vision quests before undertaking a sacred mission, such as the sun dance. Indigenous Mexican leader Tlakaelel describes the vision quest as he observes it:

> You stay on a mountain, desert, or in a cave, isolated, naked, with only your sacred things, the things that you have gained, in the years of preparation—your eagle feathers, your pipe, your copal [tree bark used as incense]. You are left alone four days and four nights without food and water. During this time when you are looking for your vision, many things happen. You see things move. You see animals that come close to you. Sometimes you might see someone that you care about a lot, and they're bringing water. You feel like you're dying of thirst, but there are limits around you, protection with hundreds of tobacco ties. You do not leave this circle, and this vision will disappear when they come to offer the water or sometimes they will just drop it on the ground. Or someone comes and helps you with their strength and gives you messages.[25]

One is not supposed to ask for a vision for selfish personal reasons. The point of this individual ordeal, which is designed to be physically and emotionally stressful, is to ask how one can help the people and the planet.

Contemporary issues

Traditional spiritual wisdom has been largely obliterated in many parts of the world by those who wanted to take the people's lands or save their souls with some other path to the divine. Under the slogan "Kill the Indian and save the man," the American founder of the boarding school system for native children took them from their families and transformed their cultural identity, presenting their ways as inferior and distancing them from participation in the traditional sacred life. They were exposed to the "modern" worldview, which does not believe in miracles, supernatural healings, or divine intervention—contradicting thousands of years of received wisdom in their own tradition.

Native Americans who converted to Christianity have sometimes been missionaries themselves. Sometimes Natives converted to try to appease the dominant non-Natives, but sometimes they embraced the "White Man's Faith," even though it was the religion of the oppressor, because of the personal example of these missionaries. A young nineteenth-century Choctaw Christian named Kanchi, for example, drowned while trying to save teenagers whose raft swamped as the Choctaw tribe crossed the Mississippi River under forcible removal from their ancestral lands. The tribe members read his Bible in his memory and eventually formed a new Christian community in what is now Oklahoma. Indigenous spirituality has become so mixed with Christianity that many Native American Christians are now trying to re-examine their religious lives and identities.

A similar policy of attempted acculturation was conducted between the 1880s and 1960s with Australian aboriginal children. In 1998, Australian citizens tried to apologize for this "attempted genocide," with some 300,000 signatures in Sorry Books and hundreds of emotional multiracial ceremonies in churches, schools, and cities across Australia.

In Mexico, decades of rebellion of indigenous people against central rule and cultural suppression seemed to be turning a corner in 2001, when rebel leaders from the south were welcomed by tens of thousands as they entered Mexico City to request political autonomy for the ten million indigenous people of Mexico. Chiapas rebel leader Subcommander Marcos declared, "It is the hour of the Indian people, of the people of the color of the earth. What they fear is that there is no more 'you' and 'us,' because we are all the color of the earth."[26] However, alterations to a bill which would have brought considerable autonomy for the indigenous people mean they may have fewer legal rights than before.

In Africa, traditional religion is still strong among some groups, such as the Yoruba, whose priest-diviners are still respected. However, in contemporary urban African areas, the traditional interest in the flow of the past into the present has been rapidly replaced by a Westernized view of time, with its perpetual anxiety about the future. This has led to severe psychological disorientation and social and political instability. Those whose spiritual cultures have been merged with world religions such as Islam, Buddhism, or Christianity are examining the relationship of their earlier tradition to the intercultural missionary traditions. African scholars have noted, for instance, that to put God in the forefront, as Christians do, damages the greater social importance of ancestor spirits in African traditional religions.

Indigenous peoples have also been victims of development. In Zimbabwe, thousands of Vaduma people were displaced when their lands were flooded to

create a lake for irrigating an area hundreds of kilometers away. Jameson
Kurasha of the University of Zimbabwe describes the effects this had:

> When the "idea" of development was imposed on them, families were separated by
> a massive stretch of water. Now the Murinye Mugabe families are alienated from
> each other. They are now peoples without a tangible past to guide and unite them
> because their past (i.e. ancestors) are either buried or washed away by the lake.
> They are basically a people without a home to point to. The separation has left a
> cultural damage that will never be restored.[27]

In Malaysia, the indigenous Orang Asli people and anthropologists, sociologists, and development workers feel that the government is intentionally but
discreetly forcing the people from their traditional homelands so that it can
appropriate the timber-rich land. So long as the Orang Asli live in the forests,
especially if they were even granted land rights to their ancestral lands, individual state governments cannot get access to the timber revenues. Critics think this
is why the government is making efforts to "integrate" the Orang Asli into Malay
culture in the name of "development," including relocation, education, and
Islamization, in order to detach them from their spiritual affinity to their land.

In the United States, reservations on which thousands of Navajos and Hopis
were living were found to be sitting on the largest coal deposit in the country—
the 4,000-square-mile "Black Mesa." In 1966, the Navajo and Hopi tribal
councils signed agreements allowing Black Mesa to be strip-mined by utility
companies to provide electricity for southwestern cities, and, presumably, economic development for the tribes. Since then, the sacred land has been devastat-
ed, ancient archaeological sites have been destroyed, thousands of Navajos have
been displaced, and aquifers are drying up as 1.3 billion gallons of pure water per
year have been used to pump the coal slurry to a power plant hundreds of miles
away. The Black Mesa Trust is pressing for legal action that would pose limits on
future damage to the area and curb pressure tactics being used against the
indigenous people.

Modern development schemes—as well as plunder of natural resources for
profit—are being called into question by traditional peoples around the world,
and attempts have begun to re-establish the validity of the ancient wisdom. In
India, officials in the Ministry of Environment and Forests acknowledge that the
remaining sacred groves of the indigenous people are treasure-houses of bio-
diversity and should not be destroyed. In such areas, it is often shamans who
teach the tribal people the importance of protecting trees and vegetation.

In northern Thailand, damage from rainy season floods and sedimentation was
so severe in 1995 that villagers whose houses and fields were destroyed revived
an ancient indigenous ritual to apologize to the Mae Chaem River. Respectful
relationships with the river had lapsed with the introduction of modern water
control technologies, such as dams and irrigation projects. At dawn, in the rain,
villagers made altars in the river, filling them with sweets, nuts, sugar cane, foods,
and cigarettes as offerings to the spirits of the forest, the earth deities, and the
guardian spirits of the river. In their prayers, they asked forgiveness of the river
for misuse of the water and requested that the water level be lowered.

Some indigenous people feel their traditional sacred ways are not only valid,
but actually essential for the future of the world. They see them as antidotes to

mechanistic, dehumanizing, environmentally destructive ways of life. Rather than regarding their ancient way as inferior, intact groups such as the Kogi of the high Colombian rainforest feel they are the elder brothers of all humanity, responsible for keeping the balance of the universe and re-educating their younger brothers who have become distracted by desire for material gain.

Differences of opinion and lifestyle between native people who live tradition-ally and those who have embraced industrial materialistic culture have led to rifts within the communities. There are people for and against selling mineral rights to community land for economic gain. Some indigenous people also question the ethics of developing gambling casinos as a base for economic self-sufficiency. But gameplaying has interesting precedents in many world religions and was trad-itionally part of sacred rites in many indigenous cultures. For instance, ceremonial throwing of dice has been symbolically associated with the cycles of death and rebirth, and the movement of the sun, moon, and stars.

In the 2000 United States census, over four million people said they were at least partly Native American, over twice as many as made that claim during the 1990 census. Possible reasons for this movement toward adopting a previously stigmatized indigenous identity include the potential for a share in gambling revenues, scholarships for minority students, and the new-found popularity of native spiritual traditions. There is thus considerable tension over the issue of native credentials, complicated by centuries of intermarriage.

While some elders long for exclusiveness, others are adopting modern technologies to bring international attention to and find support for their causes. Personal visions and ancient prophecies about the dangers of a lifestyle that ignores the earth and the spiritual dimensions of life are leading native elders around the world to raise their voices together. They assert spiritual insights about the state of the planet, political matters, and lifestyle issues; and seek converts not to their path but to a respect for all of life, which they feel is essential for the harmony of the planet.

A respected elder of the Hopi nation, the late Thomas Banyacya, made a stirring appeal to the United Nations in 1992, in which he explained Hopi prophecies about our times. According to these, the creator made a perfectly balanced world but when humans turned away from spiritual principles for selfish reasons it was destroyed by earthquakes. The few survivors developed the second world, but repeated their mistakes, and the world was destroyed by the Ice Age. The few people who survived spoke one language and developed high technologies but when they turned away from natural laws and spiritual principles, the third world was destroyed by a great flood which is remembered in the ancient stories of many peoples. Now we are living in the fourth world. According to Hopi time lines, we are in the final stages of decay.

Many people have said that indigenous peoples are myths of the past, ruins that have died. But the indigenous community is not a vestige of the past, nor is it a myth. It is full of vitality and has a course and a future. It has much wisdom and richness to contribute. They have not killed us and they will not kill us now. We are stepping forth to say, "No, we are here. We live."

Rigoberta Menchú of the K'iché Maya[28]

Winona LaDuke

As the narrator of Winona LaDuke's semi-fictional novel, *Last Standing Woman*, puts it, her clanspeople have a special destiny:

In times past, they were warriors, the ogichidaa, those who defended the people. Sometimes we still are. We are what we are intended to be when we have those three things that guide our direction—our name, our clan, and our religion.[29]

Winona herself is a prime example. She is continually in the news as a fighter on behalf of the future of the earth and its disadvantaged peoples. When in 1996 she ran as the Green Party candidate for Vice-President of the U.S., she campaigned for reforms oriented toward long-term survival:

I am interested in reframing the debate on the issues of this society, the distribution of power and wealth, abuse of power, the rights of the natural world, the environment, and the need to consider an amendment to the U.S. Constitution in which all decisions made today would be considered in light of the impact on the seventh generation from now.[30]

Winona now lives on her father's traditional tribal lands in northern Minnesota in the White Earth Reservation. She is trying to re-establish an economic base that will allow her Anishinaabe people to return to their land and to have the legal right to control its use. The land is of spiritual as well as economic importance to her people.

The project she initiated has already repurchased over 1,300 acres of former tribal lands, and is trying to add more through further purchases, bequests, and legislation. The lands include burial grounds with undisturbed birch and sugar maple forests, and a 715-acre area encompassing two lakes, nesting sites for waterfowl, wild rice, and many medicinal plants. The latter is earmarked to teach Anishinaabe children their traditional cultural practices, and demonstrate to the world their value for planetary survival.

Winona, a Harvard-educated journalist, lives in a lakeside log cabin on the reservation with her two children, trying to teach them traditional beliefs. She has no fear of fighting against large-scale vested interests. In 1994 she chained herself to a paper company's gates to protest their clearance of forests including thousand-year-old trees to make phone books. The publicity led other companies to cancel their contracts with that company.

An Anishinaabe tribal prophecy indicates that the people of the seventh fire—the current period—will look around and discover the things they had lost. With loss of the land had come loss of traditional spiritual principles. At the end of *Last Standing Woman*, the narrator speaks in the year 2018, describing her culture, which has rediscovered its spiritual traditions:

To understand our relationship to the whole and our role on the path of life. We also understand our responsibility. We only take what we need, and we leave the rest. We always give thanks for what we are given. What carries us through is the relationship we have to the Creation and the courage we are able to gather from the experience of our aanikoobijigan, our ancestors, and our oshkaabewisag, our helpers.[31]

Review questions

1. How do indigenous sacred ways have an ecological perspective?
2. What effects do indigenous sacred ways' rituals seem to have, such as storytelling, drumming, initiations, healing, self-sacrifice, and vision quests?
3. What are some important effects of the clashes between indigenous and industrial societies?

Discussion questions

1. Should and can indigenous sacred ways be reconciled with modern industrial/commercial pressures? If not, why? If so, what should be required on each side?
2. How should global religions relate to indigenous sacred ways?

CHAPTER 3

HINDUISM

"With mind absorbed and heart melted in love"

In the Indian subcontinent there has developed a complex variety of religious paths. Some of these are relatively unified religious systems, such as Buddhism, Jainism, and Sikhism. Most of the other Indian religious ways have been categorized together as if they were a single tradition named "Hinduism." This term is derived from a name applied by foreigners to the people living in the region of the Indus River, and was introduced in the nineteenth century under colonial British rule as a category for census-taking.

An alternative label preferred today is **Sanatana Dharma**. *Sanatana*, "eternal" or "ageless," reflects the belief that these ways have always existed. **Dharma**, often translated as "religion," encompasses duty, natural law, social welfare, ethics, health, and transcendental realization. *Dharma* is thus a holistic approach to social coherence and the good of all, a concept corresponding to order in the cosmos.

The spiritual expressions of Sanatana Dharma range from extreme asceticism to extreme sensuality, from the heights of personal devotion to a deity to the heights of abstract philosophy, from metaphysical proclamations of the oneness behind the material world to worship of images representing a multiplicity of deities. According to tradition, there are actually 330 million deities in India. The feeling is that the divine has countless faces.

The extreme variations within Sanatana Dharma are reflections of its great age. Few of the myriad religious paths that have arisen over the millennia have been lost. They continue to co-exist in present-day India. Some scholars of religion argue that these ways are so varied that there is no central tradition that can be called Hinduism proper.

In villages, where the majority of Indians live, worship of deities is quite diverse and does not necessarily follow the more reified and philosophical Brahmanic tradition that is typically referred to as "Hinduism." Since it is not possible here to trace all these diffuse, widely scattered strands in their complex historical development, we will instead explore the main facets of Sanatana Dharma thematically: its philosophical and metaphysical elements, then its devotional and ritual aspects, and, finally, its features as a way of life. These are not in fact totally separate categories, but we will separate them somewhat for clarity. Afterward, we will look at global and political aspects of the contemporary practice of Hinduism.

Philosophical and metaphysical origins

The Brahmanic tradition can be traced back to the Vedic age, thousands of years ago. The metaphysical beliefs in the Vedas were elaborated into various schools of thought by philosophers and sages. These beliefs were brought forth experientially by various methods of spiritual discipline.

> *Truth is one; sages call it by various names.*   *Rig Veda*

Vedic age

Many of the threads of Sanatana Dharma may have existed in the religions practiced by the aboriginal Dravidian peoples of India. There were also advanced urban centers in the Indus Valley from about 2500 BCE or even earlier until 1500 BCE. Major fortified cities with elaborate plumbing and irrigation systems and paved, right-angled streets have been found by archaeologists at Harappa, Mohenjo-Daro, and Dholavira; the culture they represent is labeled the Indus Valley civilization.

In the **Aryan Invasion Theory** of Western historians, first advanced by the influential German scholar Max Müller in 1848, the highly organized cultures of the Indus Valley and the villages in other parts of the subcontinent were overrun by lighter-skinned nomadic invaders from outside India. The theory argues that the **Vedas**, the religious texts often referred to as the foundations of Sanatana Dharma, were the product of the invaders, and not of indigenous Indians. These invaders were identified as **Aryans**, said to be among the Indo-European tribes thought to have migrated outward from the steppes of southern Russia during the second millennium BCE.

Today the Aryan Invasion Theory is contested by many scholars and by Hindu nationalists who refuse to believe their religion is foreign-born. The Vedas sing the praises of the Indian subcontinent, and do not refer to any other homeland. The term "Aryan" has been incorrectly used as a racial classification. It has no racial connotations, and is taken from the word *arya*, used in the Vedas to mean a noble person who speaks **Sanskrit** (the ancient language in which the Vedas were written) and practices the Vedic rituals. Contrary to the former theory of an invasion of the Indus Valley by outsiders with superior military hardware, current archaeological and linguistic research suggests that historical changes in the pre-Vedic Indus Valley habitations were the results of many small migrations rather than violent invasive conflict, and that evolution of religion in India was continuous rather than divided into distinctly different periods in which indigenous ways were replaced by imported ways.

If the Aryan Invasion Theory is not true, many ideas about the origins and evolution of Sanatana Dharma that have been prevalent among historians of religion for the last 150 years must be re-examined.

The Indus script still has not been deciphered, so the religious meaning of artifacts such as tiny animal figurines and narrative scenes on seals and pottery is yet unknown. Representations of trees with what appear to be deity figures suggest that worship may have taken place in natural settings under trees considered sacred—such as the peepul tree, which even in contemporary India is thought to be so sacred that it should not be cut down, even when its great trunk threatens walls and buildings. There are male figures apparently seated in meditation, some of them with horns, which have been interpreted as evidence of ancient practice of yogic postures or worship of the deity Siva (or Shiva). There are also many decorated female figurines, which may indicate worship of a goddess. Researchers find evidence of many levels of religious practice, from local cults to what may have been established state religions of the elite.

The relationship between ancient Indus Valley spirituality and the Vedas is also not yet clear. And the Vedas themselves are the foundation of upper-caste Brahmanic Hinduism, but not necessarily of all forms of Sanatana Dharma.

Although their origins and antiquity are still unknown, the Vedas themselves can be examined. They are a revered collection of ancient sacred hymns comprising four parts. The earliest are the *Samhitas*, hymns of praise in worship of deities. Then appeared the **Brahmanas**, directions about performances of the ritual sacrifices to the deities. The *Brahmanas* explain the symbolic correspondences between the microcosm of the ritual process and the "real world" in which rituals are performed. Some people went to the forests to meditate as recluses; their writings form the third part of the Vedas—the *Aranyakas*, or "forest treatises." Last came the **Upanishads**, consisting of teaching from highly realized spiritual masters. They explain the personal transformation that results from psychic participation in the ritual process.

These sacred teachings seem to have been written down by the middle of the first millennium BCE, though we know that they are much older than their earliest written forms. After being revealed to sages, they were transmitted orally from teacher to student and may then have been written down over a period of eight or nine hundred years. According to orthodox Hindus, the Vedas are not the work of any humans. They are the breath of the eternal, as "heard" by the ancient sages, or **rishis**, and later compiled by Vyasa. The name "Vyasa" means "Collector." He was traditionally considered to be one person, but scholars think it likely that many people were acting as compilers.

The Vedas are thought to transcend human time and are thus as relevant today as they were thousands of years ago. The **Gayatrimantra**, a verse in a Vedic hymn, is still chanted daily by the devout as the most sacred of prayers:

> *Aum [the primordial creative sound],*
> *Bhu Bhuvah Svah [the three worlds: earth, atmosphere, and heaven],*
> *Tat Savitur Varenyum,*
> *Bhargo Devasya Dheemahe [adoration of the glory, splendor, and grace that radiate*
>   *from the Divine Light that illuminates the three worlds],*
> *Dhiyo Yo Nah Prachodayat [a prayer for liberation through awakening of the light*
>   *of the universal intelligence].*[1]

The oldest of the known Vedic scriptures—and among the oldest of the world's existing scriptures—is the **Rig Veda**. This praises and implores the blessings of the **devas**—the controlling forces in the cosmos, deities who consecrate every part of life. The major *devas* included **Indra** (god of thunder and bringer of welcome rains), **Agni** (god of fire), **Soma** (associated with a sacred drink), and **Ushas** (goddess of dawn). The *devas* included both opaque earth gods and transparent deities of the sky and celestial realms. But behind all the myriad aspects of divinity, the sages perceived one unseen reality. This reality, beyond human understanding, ceaselessly creates and sustains everything that exists, encompassing all time, space, and causation.

The *Upanishads* are thought to have developed last, around 600 to 400 BCE. They represent the mystical insights of *rishis* who sought ultimate reality through their meditations in the forest. Many people consider these philosophical and metaphysical reflections on Vedic religion the cream of Indian thought, among the highest spiritual literature ever written. They were not taught to the masses but rather were reserved for advanced seekers of spiritual truth. The word *Upanishad* embraces the idea of the devoted disciple sitting down by the teacher to receive private spiritual instruction about the highest reality, loosening all doubts and destroying all ignorance. Emphasis is placed not on outward ritual performances, as in the earlier Vedic religion, but on inner experience as the path to realization and immortality.

The *rishis* explain that the bodily senses are made for looking outward; the eyes, ears, nose, tongue, and skin are enticed by sensory pleasures. But ultimately these are fleeting, impermanent. They pass away and then one dies, never having experienced what is of greater value because it is infinite, everlasting. What is real and lasting, they found, can be discovered only by turning away from transient worldly things. They taught their pupils to turn their attention inward and thus discover a transcendent reality from within. This unseen but all-pervading reality they called Brahman, the Unknowable: "Him the eye does not see, nor the tongue express, nor the mind grasp."[2]

From Brahman spring the multiplicity of forms, including humans. The joyous discovery of the *rishis* was that they could find Brahman as the subtle self or soul (**atman**) within themselves. One of the *rishis* explained this relationship thus:

> *In the beginning there was Existence alone—One only, without a second. He, the One, thought to himself: Let me be many, let me grow forth. Thus out of himself he projected the universe, and having projected out of himself the universe, he entered into every being. All that is has its self in him alone. Of all things he is the subtle essence. He is the truth. He is the Self. And that, . . . THAT ART THOU.*
>
> *Chandogya Upanishad*[3]

When one discovers the inner self, *atman*, and thus also its source, Brahman, the self merges into its transcendent source, and one experiences unspeakable peace and bliss.

The Upanishads express several doctrines central to all forms of Sanatana Dharma. One is **reincarnation**. In answer to the universal question, "What happens after we die?" the *rishis* taught that the soul leaves the dead body and enters a new one. One takes birth again and again in countless bodies—perhaps as an animal or some other life form—but the self remains the same. Birth as a human being is a precious and rare opportunity for the soul to advance toward its ultimate goal of liberation from rebirth and merging with the Absolute Reality.

An important related concept is that of **karma**. It means action, and also the consequences of action. Every act we make, and even every thought and every desire we have, shape our future experiences. Our life is what we have made it.

And we ourselves are shaped by what we have done: "As a man acts, so doe become. . . . A man becomes pure through pure deeds, impure through impure deeds."[4] Not only do we reap in this life the good or evil we have sown; they also follow us after physical death, affecting our next incarnation. Ethically, this is a strong teaching, for our every move has far-reaching consequences.

The ultimate goal, however, is not creation of good lives by good deeds, but a clean escape from the *karma*-run wheel of birth, death, and rebirth, or **samsara**. To escape from *samsara* is to achieve **moksha**, or liberation from the limitations of space, time, and matter through realization of the immortal Absolute. Many life-times of upward-striving incarnations are required to reach this transcendence of earthly miseries. This desire for liberation from earthly existence is one of the underpinnings of classical Hinduism, and of Buddhism as well.

Major philosophical systems

In addition to the Vedas, elaborate philosophical systems were developed long ago in India. They all have certain features in common:

1 All have deep roots in the Vedas and other scriptures but also in direct personal experiences of the truth through meditation;
2 All hold ethics to be central to orderly social life. They attribute suffering to the law of *karma*, thereby suggesting incentives to more ethical behavior;
3 All hold that the ultimate cause of suffering is people's ignorance of the Self, whch is omniscient, omnipotent, omnipresent, perfect, and eternal.

Two other major philosophical systems born in India—Jainism and Buddhism—do not acknowledge the authority of the Vedas but nevertheless draw on many of the same currents as Sanatana Dharma. Prominent among the philosophical systems that are related to the Vedas are **Samkhya**, **Advaita Vedanta**, and yoga.

Samkhya

The Samkhya system, though undatable, is thought to be the oldest in India. Its founder is said to be the semi-mythical sage Kapila. Its principles appear in Jainism and Buddhism from the sixth century BCE, so the system probably pre-ceded them and may be of pre-Vedic origin.

Samkhya philosophy holds that there are two states of reality. One is the **Purusha**, the Self, which is eternally wise, pure, and free, beyond change, beyond cause. The other is **Prakriti**, the cause of the material universe. All our suffering stems from our false confusion of Prakriti with Purusha, the eternal Self. A dualistic understanding of life is essential, according to this system, if we are to distinguish the ultimate transcendent reality of Purusha from the temporal appearances of Prakriti, which bring us happiness but also misery and delusion.

An illuminating story is told about Indra, who was once king of the gods. He was forced by the other *devas* to descend to earth in the body of a boar. Once there, he began to enjoy the life, wallowing in the mud, mating, and siring baby pigs. The *devas* were *aghast*; they came down to try to convince him to return, but

Indra had forgotten his kingly state and insisted on remaining as a boar. The *devas* tried killing his babies; he was distraught but simply mated to have more piglets. Then the *devas* killed his mate. Indra grieved his loss but stayed in the mud. They finally had to kill him as well to bring him back to his senses. His soul could then see the body of the boar it had been inhabiting and was glad to return to heaven. The moral is that we, too, are like gods who forget the heights from which we came, so intent are we on the joys and sorrows of earthly life.

Advaita Vedanta

Whereas Samkhya is a dualistic system, Advaita ("non-dualist") Vedanta is generally monistic, positing a single reality. It is based on the *Upanishads*: its founder is said to be Vyasa, systematizer of the *Upanishads*. The eminent philosopher Shankara (or Sankara) reorganized the teachings many centuries later, probably between the eighth and ninth centuries CE.

Whereas one view of the *Upanishads* is that the human self (*atman*) is an emanation of Brahman, Shankara insisted that the *atman* and Brahman are actually one. According to Shankara, our material life is an illusion. It is like a momentary wave arising from the ocean, which is the only reality. Ignorance consists in thinking that the waves are different from the ocean. The absolute spirit, Brahman, is the essence of everything, and it has no beginning and no end. It is the eternal ocean of bliss within which forms are born and die, giving the false appearance of being real.

That which makes us think the physical universe has its own reality is **maya**, the power by which the Absolute veils itself. *Maya* is the illusion that the world as we perceive it is real. Shankara uses the metaphor of a coil of rope that, at dusk, is mistaken for a snake. The physical world, like the rope, does actually exist but we superimpose our memories and subjective thoughts upon it. Moreover, he says, only that which never changes is truly real. Everything else is changing, impermanent. In ignorance we think that we exist as individuals, superimposing the notion of a separate ego-self on the underlying absolute reality of pure being, pure consciousness, pure bliss. It is a mistake to identify with the body or the mind, which exist but have no unchanging reality. When a person reaches transcendent consciousness, superimposition stops and the oneness of reality is experienced.

Yoga

From ancient times, people of the Indian subcontinent have practiced spiritual disciplines designed to clear the mind and support a state of serene, detached awareness. This desired state of balance, purity, wisdom, and peacefulness of mind is described as *sattvic*. It is distinctly different from two other general states of mind: active and restless, or lethargic and dull. The practices for increasing *sattvic* qualities are known collectively as **yoga**. It means "yoke" or "union"— referring to union with the true Self, the goal described in the *Upanishads*.

The sages distinguished four basic types of people and developed yogic practices that are particularly suitable for each type, in order that each can attain the desired union with the Self. For meditative people, there is raja yoga, the path of mental concentration. For rational people, there is jnana yoga, the path of rational inquiry. For naturally active people, there is karma yoga, the path of right action. For emotional people, there is bhakti yoga, the path of devotion.

Raja yoga   Some believe that the *sadhanas*, or practices of **raja yoga**, were known as long ago as the Neolithic Age and were practiced in the Indus Valley culture. By 200 BCE, a yogi named Patanjali (or perhaps a series of people taking the same name) had described a system for attaining the highest consciousness through raja yoga—the path of mental concentration. Patanjali's *Yoga Sutras* is a book of 196 terse sayings called **sutras**.

Yogis say that it is easier to calm a wild tiger than it is to quiet the mind, which is like a drunken monkey that has been bitten by a scorpion. The problem is that the mind is our vehicle for knowing the Self. If the mirror of the mind is disturbed, it reflects the disturbance rather than the pure light within. The goal of yogic practices is to make the mind absolutely calm and clear.

Patanjali distinguishes eight "limbs" of the yogic path: moral codes (*yama-niyama*), physical conditioning (*asana*), breath control (*pranayama*), sense control (*pratyahara*), concentration (*dharana*), meditation (*dhyana*), and the state of peaceful spiritual absorption (*samadhi*).

The moral and ethical principles that form the first limb of yogic practice are truth, non-violence, non-stealing, continence, and non-covetousness, plus cleanliness, contentment, burning zeal, self-study, and devotion to God. The *asanas* are physical postures used to cleanse the body and develop the mind's ability to concentrate. Regulated breathing exercises are also used to calm the nerves and increase the body's supply of *prana*, or invisible life energy. Breath is thought to be the key to controlling the flow of this energy within the subtle energy field surrounding and permeating the physical body. Its major pathway is through a series of **chakras**, or subtle energy centers, along the spine. To raise the energy from the lowest, least subtle chakra at the base of the spine to the highest, most subtle energy center at the crown of the head is the goal of *kundalini* yoga practices, with **kundalini** referring to the latent energy at the base of the spine. Ideally, the opening of the highest chakra leads to the bliss of union with the Sublime. In its fully open state, the crown chakra is depicted as a thousand-petaled lotus, effulgent with light.

In addition to these practices using the body and breath, Indian thought has long embraced the idea that repetition of certain sounds has sacred effects. It is said that some ancient yogic adepts could discern subtle sounds and that **mantras** (sacred formulas) express an aspect of the divine in the form of sound vibration. The sound of the mantras was believed to evoke the reality they named. The language used for these verbal formulas since ancient times was Sanskrit. It was considered a re-creation of the actual sound-forms of objects, actions, and qualities, as heard by ancient sages in deep meditation. The most cherished sound vibrations are the "unheard, unstruck" divine sounds inaudible to our outer ears.

Chanting sacred syllables is thought to still the mind and attune the devotee to the Divine Ground of Existence. Indians liken the mind to the trunk of an elephant, always straying restlessly here and there. If an elephant is given a small stick to hold in its trunk, it will hold it steadily, losing interest in other objects. In the same way, the mantra gives the restless mind something to hold, quieting it by focusing awareness in one place. If chanted with devoted concentration, the mantra may also invoke the presence and blessings of the deity.

Many forms of music have also been developed in India to elevate a person's attunement and may go on for hours if the musicians are spiritually absorbed.

Another way of steadying the mind is concentration on a visual form—a candle flame, the picture of a saint or guru, the **OM** symbol, or **yantras**. A *yantra* is a linear image with complex cosmic symbolism. Large *yantras* are also created as designs of colorful seeds for ritual invocations of specific deities.

One-pointed concentration ideally leads to a state of meditation. In meditation, all worldly thoughts have dissipated. Instead of ordinary thinking, the clear light of awareness allows insights to arise spontaneously as flashes of illumination. There may also be phenomena, such as colored lights, visions, waves of ecstasy, or visits from supernatural beings. The mind, heart, and body may gradually be transformed.

The ultimate goal of yogic meditation is **samadhi**: a super-conscious state of union with the Absolute. Swami Sivananda attempts to describe it:

> *Words and language are imperfect to describe this exalted state. . . . Mind, intellect and the senses cease functioning. . . . It is a state of eternal Bliss and eternal Wisdom. All dualities vanish in toto. . . . All visible merge in the invisible or the Unseen. The individual soul becomes that which he contemplates.*[5]

Jnana yoga The path of rational inquiry—*jnana yoga*—employs the rational mind rather than trying to transcend it by concentration practices. In this path, ignorance is considered the root of all problems. Our basic ignorance is our idea of our selves as being separate from the Absolute. One method is continually to ask, "Who am I?" The seeker discovers that the one who asks the question is not the body, not the senses, not the pranic body, not the mind, but something eternal beyond all these. The guru Ramana Maharshi explains:

> *After negating all of the above-mentioned as "not this," "not this," that Awareness which alone remains—that I am. . . . The thought "Who am I?" will destroy all other thoughts, and, like the stick used for stirring the burning pyre, it will itself in the end get destroyed. Then, there will arise Self-realization.*[6]

In the *jnana* path, the seeker must also develop spiritual virtues (calmness, restraint, renunciation, resignation, concentration, and faith) and have an intense longing for liberation. The ultimate wisdom is spiritual rather than intellectual knowledge of the self.

> *Spiritual knowledge is the only thing that can destroy our miseries for ever; any other knowledge removes wants only for a time.*
>
> *Swami Vivekananda*[7]

Karma yoga   In contrast to these ascetic and contemplative practices, another way is that of helpful action in the world. **Karma yoga** is service rendered without any interest in its fruits and without any personal sense of giving. The yogi knows that the Absolute performs all actions, and all actions are gifts to the Absolute.

This consciousness leads to liberation from the self in the very midst of work. Krishna, speaking as the Absolute, explains these principles in the *Bhagavad-Gita*:

> *The steadily devoted soul attains unadulterated peace because he offers the results of all activities to Me; whereas a person who is not in harmony with the divine, who is greedy for the fruits of his labor, becomes entangled.*[8]

Bhakti yoga   The final type of spiritual path is the one embraced by most Indian followers of Sanatana Dharma. It is the path of devotion to a personal deity, *bhakti yoga*. *Bhakti* means "to share," to share a relationship with the Supreme. For the *bhakta* (devotee), the relationship is that of intense love. Bhakta Nam Dev described this deep love in sweet metaphors:

> *Thy Name is beautiful, Thy form is beautiful, and very beautiful is Thy love, Oh*
>   *my Omnipresent Lord.*
> *As rain is dear to the earth, as the fragrance of flowers is dear to the black bee, and*
>   *as the mango is dear to the cuckoo, so is the Lord to my soul.*
> *As the sun is dear to the sheldrake, and the lake of Man Sarowar to the swan, and*
>   *as the husband is dear to the wife, so is God to my soul.*
> *As milk is dear to the baby and as the torrent of rain to the mouth of the sparrow-*
>   *hawk who drinks nothing but raindrops, and as water is dear to the fish, so is*
>   *the Lord to my soul.*[9]

Bhaktas' devotion is thought to be more dear to the Supreme than ritualistic piety. The story is told that a pious **brahmin** came daily to offer ritual worship to a stone statue of the deity Siva. One day he was horrified to see wild flowers and partly eaten pork decorating the shrine. These had been left by a hunter who stopped to worship Siva in his own fashion. Hoping to teach the *brahmin* a lesson, Siva appeared to him in a dream commanding that he watch from hiding while the hunter expressed his devotion. When the hunter then came to worship, he saw blood oozing from the eye of the statue. Without hesitation, he plucked out his own eye to place it on that of the idol. The bleeding stopped, but the statue's other eye started bleeding. The hunter prepared to pull out his other eye when Siva manifested himself, healed the hunter, and took him as one of his chosen devotees, called "the beloved of the eye."

A vision of a deity like that in the story is what the *bhakta* hopes for. Bhakta Ravi Das, a shoemaker who became a highly regarded spiritual teacher because of his intense devotion, implored his beloved: "I am a sacrifice unto You, my Omnipresent Lord. Why are you silent? For many births I have been separated from you. This life I dedicate to You. I live only with the hope of you. It is so long since I have seen You."[10]

Mirabai, a fifteenth-century Rajput princess, was married to a ruler at a young age, but from her childhood she had been utterly devoted to the deity Krishna. When she continued to spend all her time in devotions to Krishna, an infuriated in-law tried to poison her. It is said that Mirabai drank the poison while laughingly dancing in ecstasy before Krishna; in Krishna's presence the poison seemed like nectar to her and did her no harm. The Beloved One is said to respond and to be a real presence in the fully devoted *bhakta's* life.

In the *bhakti* path, even though the devotee may not transcend the ego in *samadhi*, the devotee's whole being is surrendered to the deity in love. Ramakrishna explains why the *bhakti* way is more appropriate for most people:

> As long as the I-sense lasts, so long are true knowledge and Liberation impossible. . . . [But] how very few can obtain this Union [Samadhi] and free themselves from this "I"? It is very rarely possible. Talk as much as you want, isolate yourself continuously, still this "I" will always return to you. Cut down the poplar tree today, and you will find tomorrow it forms new shoots. When you ultimately find that this "I" cannot be destroyed, let it remain as "I" the servant.[11]

Religious foundations and theistic paths

In ancient Vedic times, elaborate fire sacrifice rituals were created, controlled by *brahmins* (priests). Specified verbal formulas, sacred chants, and sacred actions were to be used by the priests to invoke the breath behind all of existence. This universal breath was later called **Brahman**, the Absolute, the Supreme Reality.

After a period when Brahmanic ritual and philosophy dominated Sanatana Dharma, the *bhakti* approach became prominent around 600 CE. It opened spiritual expression to *shudras* (a caste of manual laborers and artisans) and women, and has since been the primary path of the masses. It may also have been the initial way of the people, as it is difficult to pray to the impersonal Absolute of the *Upanishads*. More personal worship of a Divine Being can be inferred from the goddess and Siva-like low reliefs found in the archaeological sites of ancient India. Worship of major deities probably persisted during the Vedic period and was later given written expression. Eventually **bhakti**—intense devotion to a personal manifestation of Brahman—became the heart of Hinduism as the majority of people now experience it.

Of all the deities worshiped by Hindus, there are three major groupings: **Saktas** who worship a Mother Goddess, **Saivites** who worship the god Siva, and **Vaishnavites** who worship the god Vishnu. Each devotee has his or her own "chosen deity," but will honor others as well.

Ultimately, many Hindus rest their faith in one genderless deity with three basic aspects: creating, preserving, and destroying. The latter activity is seen as a merciful act that allows the continuation of the cosmic cycles.

Saktas

An estimated fifty million Hindus worship some form of the goddess. Some of these Saktas follow a Vedic path; some are more independent. As we have seen, worship of the feminine aspect of the divine probably dates back to the pre-Vedic period. Her power is called *sakti* and is often linked with *kundalini*. Erotic, sensual imagery is often used to symbolize her abundant creativity.

The feminine principle is worshiped in many forms. At village level, especially in southern India, local deities are typically worshiped as goddesses. Rather than taking human-like forms, their presence may be represented by round stones, trees, *yantras*, or small shrines without images. They are intimately concerned with village affairs, unlike the great goddesses of the upper class, access to whose temples was forbidden to those of low caste.

The great goddesses have been worshiped both in the plural and in the singular, in which case one goddess represents the totality of deity—eternal creator, preserver, and destroyer. **Durga** is often represented as a beautiful woman with a gentle face but ten arms holding weapons with which she vanquishes the demons who threaten the *dharma*; she rides a lion. She is the blazing splendor of God incarnate, in benevolent female form.

Kali is the divine in its fierce form. In her aspect as the destroyer of evil she may be portrayed dripping with blood, carrying a sword and a severed head, and wearing a girdle of severed hands and a necklace of skulls. What appears as destruction is a means of transformation. With her sword she cuts away all personal impediments to realization of truth, for those who sincerely desire to serve the Supreme. At the same time, she opens her arms to those who love her. Some worship her with blood offerings from animal sacrifices, but some *sakti* temples are doing away with this, at the behest of animal lovers.

Fearsome to evil-doers, but loving and compassionate to devotees, Kali wears a mask of ugliness. The divine reality is a wholeness encompassing both creation and destruction. In Hindu thought, death and birth are linked, each giving way to the other in eternal cycles. All beings, all phenomena, are inter-related parts of the same divine essence. Sanskrit scholar Leela Arjunwadkar observes that there is a deeply sensed unity among all beings in classical Indian literature:

> That is why we find all types of characters in Sanskrit literature—human beings, gods and goddesses, rivers, demons, trees, serpents, celestial nymphs, etc., and their share in the same emotional life is the umbilical cord that binds all to Mother Nature.[12]

From ancient times, worship of the divine female has been associated with worship of nature, particularly great trees and rivers. The Ganges is an especially sacred female presence, and her waters are thought to be extraordinarily purifying. Pilgrims bathe in them at sunrise, and corpses or the ashes of the dead are placed in them so that their sins will be washed away.

Sacred texts called **Tantras** instruct worshipers how to honor the feminine divine. Ways of worship include concentration on *yantras*, meditation with the hands in *mudras* (positions that reflect and invoke a particular spiritual reality), *kundalini* practices, and use of mantras. One such text gives a thousand different "names" or attributes of the Divine Mother as mantras for recitation, such as "*Sri mata* (She who is the auspicious Mother) and *Sri maha rajni* (She who is the Empress of the Universe)."[13]

Sakti worship has also been incorporated into worship of the gods. Each is thought to have a female consort, often portrayed in close physical embrace signifying the eternal unity of male and female principles in the oneness of the divine. Here the female is often conceived as the life-animating force; the transcendent male aspect is inactive until joined with the productive female energy.

The female is highly venerated in Hinduism. Women are thought to make major contributions to the earthly life, which includes *dharma* (order in society), marital wealth (bearing sons in a patriarchal society), and the aesthetics of sensual pleasure. They are mythologically associated with wealth, beauty, splendor, and grace. As sexual partners, they help to activate the spiritualizing life-force. No sacrifice is complete unless the wife participates as well as the husband.

In the ideal marriage, husband and wife are spiritual partners. Marriage is a vehicle for spiritual discipline, service, and advancement toward a spiritual goal. Men and women are thought to complement each other, although the ideal of liberation has traditionally been intended largely for the male.

Women were not traditionally encouraged to seek liberation through their own spiritual practices. A wife's role is usually linked to that of her husband, who is seen as her god and teacher. For centuries, it was hoped that a widow would choose to be cremated with her dead husband in order to remain united with him. In early Vedic times, women were relatively free and honored members of society, participating equally in important spiritual rituals. But by the nineteenth century wives were like servants of the husband's family. With expectations that, on marriage, the girl will take a large dowry to the boy's family, girls are such an economic burden that many are aborted, or killed at birth. There are cases today of women being beaten or killed by the husband's family after their dowry has been handed over. Nevertheless many women in contemporary India have been well educated, and many have attained high political positions.

Saivites

Siva or Shiva is a personal, many-faceted manifestation of the attributeless supreme deity. In older systems he is one of the three major aspects of deity: Brahma (Creator), Vishnu (Preserver), and Siva (Destroyer). Saivites nevertheless worship him as the totality, with many aspects. As Swami Sivasiva Palani, Saivite editor of *Hinduism Today*, explains: "Siva is the unmanifest; he is creator, preserver, destroyer, personal Lord, friend, primal Soul"; and he is the "all-pervasive underlying energy, the more or less impersonal love and light that flows through all things."[14] Siva is sometimes depicted dancing above the body of the demon he has killed, reconciling darkness and light, good and evil, creation and destruction, rest and activity in the eternal dance of life.

Siva is also the god of yogis, for he symbolizes asceticism. He is often shown in austere meditation on Mount Kailas, clad only in a tiger skin, with a snake around his neck. The latter signifies his conquest of the ego.

Siva has various saktis or feminine consorts, including Durga. He is often shown with his devoted spouse **Parvati**. Through their union, cosmic energy flows freely, seeding and liberating the universe. Nevertheless, they are seen mystically as eternally chaste. Siva and his sakti are also expressed as two aspects of a single being. Some sculptors portray Siva as androgynous, with both masculine and feminine physical traits. Tantric belief incorporates an ideal of balance of male and female qualities within a person. This unity is often expressed abstractly, as a **lingam** within a **yoni**, a symbol of the female vulva.

The lingams used in worship of Siva are naturally occurring or sculpted cylindrical forms honored since antiquity. Those shaped by nature, such as stones polished by rivers, are most highly valued. Tens of thousands of devotees each year undergo dangerous pilgrimages to high mountain caves to venerate large lingams naturally formed of ice. While the lingam may resemble an erect phallus, most Siva-worshipers focus on its symbolic meaning, which is abstract and asexual. They see it as a nearly amorphous, "formless" symbol for the unmanifest, trascendent nature of Siva—beyond time, space, cause and form—whereas the yoni represents the manifest aspect of Sivaness.

Saivism encompasses traditions that have developed outside Vedic-based Brahmanism. These include sects such as the Lingayats, whose ways of Siva worship underwent a strong reform movement in the twelfth century, refusing caste divisions, brahminical authority, and the belief that menstruating women are polluted. They practice strict vegetarianism and regard men and women as equals.

Another branch is represented by the sixty-three great Saivite saints of Tamil Nadu in southern India, who from the seventh century onward expressed great love for Siva. They experienced him as the Luminous One, present everywhere in subtle form but apparent only to those who love him. For this realization, knowledge of the scriptures and ascetic practices are useless. Only direct personal devotion will do.

Siva's son Ganesh, a deity with the head of an elephant, guards the threshold of space and time and is, therefore, invoked for his blessings at the beginning of any new venture. Ganesh was the subject of an extraordinary event that happened in temples in many parts of India, as well as in Hindu temples in other parts of the world. On September 21, 1995, statues devoted to Ganesh began drinking milk from spoons, cups, and even buckets offered by devotees. Scientists suggested explanations such as mass hysteria or capillary action in the stone, but the phenomenon lasted only one day.

Vaishnavites

In contrast to Sakti and Siva, **Vishnu** is beloved as the tender, merciful deity. In one myth, a sage was sent to determine who was the greatest of the gods by trying their tempers. The first two, Brahma and Siva, he insulted and was soundly abused in return. When he found Vishnu, the god was sleeping. Knowing of Vishnu's good-naturedness, the sage increased the insult by kicking him awake. Instead of reacting angrily, Vishnu tenderly massaged the sage's foot, concerned that he might have hurt it. The sage exclaimed, "This god is the mightiest, since he overpowers all by goodness and generosity!"

Vishnu has been worshiped since Vedic times and came to be regarded as the Supreme as a person. According to ideas appearing by the fourth century CE, he has appeared in many earthly incarnations, some of them animal forms. Many deities have been drawn into this complex, in which they are interpreted as incarnations of Vishnu. Most beloved of these have been Rama, subject of the *Ramayana* (see page 53), and Krishna (see page 54). However, many people still revere Krishna without reference to Vishnu.

Popular devotion to Krishna takes many forms. If Krishna is regarded as the transcendent Supreme Lord, the worshiper humbly lowers himself or herself. If Krishna is seen as master, the devotee is his servant. If Krishna is loved as a child, the devotee takes the role of loving parent. If Krishna is the divine friend, the devotee is his friend. And if Krishna is the beloved, the devotee is his lover. The latter relationship was popularized by the ecstatic sixteenth-century Bengali saint and sage Sri Caitanya, who adored Krishna as the flute-playing lover. Following Sri Caitanya, the devotee makes himself (if a male) like a loving female, to experience the bliss of Lord Krishna's presence. This form of devotion was carried to America in 1965, organized as the International Society for Krishna Consciousness, and spread to other countries. Its followers are Hare Krishnas.

Vishnu is often associated with his consort, **Lakshmi**, who is also an ancient goddess worshiped in her own right. Associated with prosperity and regal power, Lakshmi is often depicted as a radiant woman sitting on a water-borne lotus flower. The lotus floats pristine on the water but has its roots in the mud, thus representing the refined spiritual energy that rises above worldly contamination. The lotus also symbolizes the fertile growth of organic life, as the world is continually reborn on a lotus growing out of Vishnu's navel.

The epics and Puranas

Personal love for a deity flowered in the spiritual literature that followed the Vedas. Two major classes of scriptures that arose after 500 BCE (according to Western scholarship) were the **epics** and the **Puranas**. These long heroic narratives and poems popularized spiritual knowledge and devotion through national myths and legends. They were particularly useful in spreading Hindu teachings to the masses at times when Buddhism and Jainism—movements born in India but not recognizing the authority of the Vedas—were winning converts.

In contrast to the rather abstract depictions of the Divine Principle in the *Upanishads*, the epics and Puranas represent the Supreme as a person, or rather as various human-like deities. As T. M. P. Mahadevan explains:

> The Hindu mind is averse to assigning an unalterable or rigidly fixed form or name to the deity. Hence it is that in Hinduism we have innumerable god-forms and countless divine names. And, it is a truth that is recognized by all Hindus that obeisance offered to any of these forms and names reaches the one supreme God.[15]

Two great epics, the **Ramayana** and the **Mahabharata**, present the Supreme usually as Vishnu, who intervenes on earth during critical periods in the cosmic cycles. Each world cycle lasts 4,320,000 years. Two thousand of these world cycles are the equivalent of one day and night in the life of Brahma, the Creator god. Each world cycle is divided into four ages, or *yugas*.

Dharma—moral order in the world—is natural in the first age. In the second age people must be taught their proper roles in society. During the darker third age, revealed values are no longer recognized, people lose their altruism and willingness for self-denial, and there are no more saints. In the final age, **Kali Yuga**, the world is at its worst, with egotism, ignorance, recklessness, and war rampant. According to Hindu time reckoning, we are now living in a Kali Yuga period that began in 3102 BCE. Such an age is described thus:

> When society reaches a stage where property confers rank, wealth becomes the only source of virtue, passion the sole bond of union between husband and wife, falsehood the source of success in life, sex the only means of enjoyment, and when outer trappings are confused with inner religion . . .[16]

Each of these lengthy cycles witnesses the same events. The balance shifts from the true *dharma* to dissolution and then back to the *dharma* as the gods are victorious over the anti-gods. The Puranas list the many ways that Vishnu has incarnated in the world when *dharma* is decaying. For instance, he is said to have incarnated great **avatars** such as Krishna and Rama to help uplift humanity. It is considered inevitable that Vishnu will continually return in answer to the pleas of suffering humans. It is equally inevitable that he will meet resistance from "demonic forces," which are also part of the cosmic cycles.

Ramayana The epics deal with the eternal play of good and evil, symbolized by battles involving the human incarnations of Vishnu. Along the way, they teach examples of the virtuous life—responsibilities to others as defined by one's social roles. One is first a daughter, son, sister, brother, wife, husband, mother, father, or friend in relationship to others, and only secondarily an individual.

The *Ramayana*, a long poetic narrative in the Sanskrit language thought to have been compiled between approximately 400 BCE and 200 CE, is attributed to the bard Valmiki. Probably based on old ballads, it is much beloved and is acted out with great pageantry throughout India every year. It depicts the duties of relationships, portraying ideal characters, such as the ideal servant, the ideal brother, the ideal wife, the ideal king. In the story, Vishnu incarnates as the virtuous prince Rama in order to kill Ravana, the ten-headed demon king of Sri Lanka. Rama is heir to his father's throne, but the mother of his step-brother compels the king to banish Rama into the forest for fourteen years. Rama, a model of morality, goes willingly, observing that a son's duty is always to obey his parents implicitly, even when their commands seem wrong. He is accompanied into the ascetic life by his wife Sita, the model of wifely devotion in a patriarchal society, who refuses his offer to remain behind in comfort.

Eventually Sita is kidnapped by Ravana, who woos her unsuccessfully in his island kingdom and guards her with all manner of terrible demons. Although Rama is powerful, he and his half-brother Lakshman need the help of the monkeys and bears in the battle to get Sita back. Hanuman the monkey becomes the hero of the story. He symbolizes the power of faith and devotion to overcome our human frailties. In his love for the Lord he can do anything. The bloody battle ends in single-handed combat between Ravana and Rama. Rama blesses a sacred arrow with Vedic mantras and sends it straight into Ravana's heart. In what may be a later addition to the poem, when Rama and Sita are reunited, he accuses her of infidelity, so, to prove her innocence, she undergoes an ordeal by fire in which Agni protects her.

Another version of the *Ramayana*, perhaps as elaborated by later ballad-singers, has Rama ordering Sita into the forest because his subjects are suspicious of what may have happened while she was in Ravana's captivity. She is abandoned near the ashram of Valmiki. There she takes shelter and gives birth to twin boys. Years later, Valmiki and the sons attend a great ritual conducted by King Rama, and the boys sing the *Ramayana*. There is an emotional reunion of the children with their father. Thereupon, Sita, a daughter of the earth, begs the earth to receive her if she has been faithful to Rama. With these words, she becomes a field of radiance and disappears into the ground:

> *O Lord of my being, I realize you in me and me in you. Our relationship is eternal. Through this body assumed by me, my service to you and your progeny is complete now. I dissolve this body to its original state.*
>
> *Mother Earth, you gave form to me. I have made use of it as I ought to. In recognition of its purity may you kindly absorb it into your womb.*[17]

Mahabharata   The other famous Hindu epic is the *Mahabharata*, a Sanskrit poem of more than 100,000 verses. Perhaps partly historical, it may have been composed between 400 BCE and 400 CE. The plot concerns the struggle between the sons of a royal family for control of a kingdom near what is now Delhi. The story teaches the importance of sons, the duties of kingship, the benefits of ascetic practice and righteous action, and the qualities of the gods. In contrast to the idealized characters in the *Ramayana*, the *Mahabharata* shows all sides of human nature, including greed, lust, intrigue, and the desire for power. It is thought to be relevant for all times and all peoples. A serial dramatization of the *Mahabharata* has drawn huge television audiences in contemporary India. It teaches one primary ethic: that the happiness of others is essential to one's own happiness. This consideration of others before oneself is a central dharmic virtue.

The eighteenth book of the *Mahabharata*, which may have originally been an independent mystical poem, is the *Bhagavad-Gita* ("Song of the Supreme Exalted One"). Krishna, revered as a manifestation of the Supreme, appears as the charioteer of Arjuna, who is preparing to fight on the virtuous side of a battle that will pit brothers against brothers, thus occasioning a treatise about the conflict that may arise between our earthly duties and our spiritual aspirations.

Before they plunge into battle, Krishna instructs Arjuna in the arts of self-transcendence and realization of the eternal. The eternal instructions are still central to Hindu spiritual practice. Arjuna is enjoined to withdraw his attention from the impetuous demands of the senses, ignoring all feelings of attraction or aversion. This will give him a steady, peaceful mind. He is instructed to offer devotional service and to perform the prescribed Vedic sacrifices, but for the sake of discipline, duty, and example alone rather than reward—to "abandon all attachment to success or failure . . . renouncing the fruits of action in the material world."[18]

Actually, Lord Krishna says those who do everything for love of the Supreme transcend the notion of duty. Everything they do is offered to the Supreme, "without desire for gain and free from egoism and lethargy."[19] Thus they feel peace, freedom from earthly entanglements, and unassailable happiness.

This yogic science of transcending the "lower self" by the "higher self" is so ancient that Krishna says it was originally given to the sun god and, through his agents, to humans. But in time it was lost, and Krishna is now renewing his instructions pertaining to "that very ancient science of the relationship with the Supreme."[20] He has taken human form again and again to teach the true religion:

> *Whenever and wherever there is a decline in religious practice . . . and a predominant rise of irreligion—at that time I descend Myself.*
>
> *To deliver the pious and to annihilate the miscreants, as well as to re-establish the principles of religion, I advent Myself millennium after millennium.*[21]

Krishna says that everything springs from his Being:

> *There is no truth superior to Me. Everything rests upon Me, as pearls are strung on a thread. . . .*
>
> *I am the taste of water, the light of the sun and the moon, the syllable* om *in Vedic mantras; I am the sound in ether and ability in man. . . .*

> All states of being—goodness, passion or ignorance—are manifested by My
> energy. I am, in one sense, everything—but I am independent. I am not under the
> modes of this material nature.[22]

This supreme Godhead is not apparent to most mortals. The deity can be
known only by those who love him, and for them it is easy, for they remember
him at all times: "Whatever you do, whatever you eat, whatever you offer or give
away, and whatever austerities you perform—do that . . . as an offering to Me."
Any small act of devotion offered in love becomes a way to him: "If one offers Me
with love and devotion a leaf, a flower, fruit, or water, I will accept it."[23]

The Puranas The Puranas, poetic Sanskrit texts that narrate the myths of
ancient times, were probably compiled between 500 and 1500 CE. There are a
total of eighteen Puranas—six about Vishnu, six about Brahma, and six about
Siva. They popularize the more abstract teachings in the Vedas and *Upanishads* by
giving them concrete form. The most well known and loved is the *Bhagavata
Purana*, which includes the life story of Krishna. Most Western Indologists think
it was written about the ninth or tenth century CE, but in Indian tradition it was
written down at the beginning of Kali Yuga by Vyasa.

In the *Bhagavata Purana*, the supreme personality of Godhead is portrayed first
in its vast dimensions—the Being whose body animates the material universe. We
know this universe is only one of millions of material universes. Each is like a bub-
ble in the eternal spiritual sky, arising from the pores of the body of Vishnu, and
these bubbles are created and destroyed as Vishnu breathes out and in, a cosmic
conception so vast that it is impossible to grasp it. It is much easier to comprehend
Vishnu in his incarnation as Krishna. A wise teacher in the *Bhagavad-Gita*, in the
Bhagavata Purana Krishna is a much-loved child, raised by cowherds.

The boy Krishna mischievously steals balls of butter from the neighbors and
wanders garlanded with flowers through the forest, happily playing his flute and
he playfully steals the hearts of the *gopis*, the cowherd girls. His favorite is the
lovely Radha, but through his magical ways, he multiplies himself so that each
thinks that he dances with her alone. Each is so much in love with Krishna that
she feels she is one with him and desires only to serve him.

Eventually Krishna is called away on a heroic mission, never returning to the
gopis. Their grief at his leaving and their intense longing for him serve as models
for the *bhakti* path—the way of extreme devotion. In Hindu thought, the emotional longing of the lover for the beloved is one of the most powerful vehicles
for concentration on the Supreme Lord.

The Hindu way of life

Although there is no single founder, devotional tradition, or philosophy which
can be said to define Sanatana Dharma, everyday life is so imbued with spiritually meaningful aspects that spirituality is never far from one's mind. Those we will
examine here include rituals, castes and social duties, life stages, home *puja*, homage to the guru, fasting, prayer, auspicious designs, reverence paid to trees and
rivers, pilgrimages, and religious festivals.

Rituals

From the cradle to the cremation ground, the Hindu's life is wrapped up in rituals. There are sixteen rites prescribed in the ancient scriptures to purify and sanctify the person in his or her journey through life, including rites at the time of conception, birth, name-giving, starting education, first leaving the family house, starting studies of Vedas, marriage, and death. The goal is to continually elevate the person above his or her basically animal nature.

Public worship—*puja*—is usually performed by *pujaris*, or *brahmin* priests, who are trained in Vedic practices and the recitation of Sanskrit texts. They conduct ceremonies in which the sacred presence is made tangible through employing all the senses. Siva-lingams may be anointed with precious substances, such as ghee (clarified butter), honey, or sandalwood paste, with offerings of rosewater and flowers. In a temple, devotees may receive **darsan** (visual contact with the divine) through the eyes of the images. Mantras and ringing bells are heard. Incense and flowers fill the area with uplifting fragrances. **Prasad**, food sanctified by being offered to the deities and/or one's guru, is eaten by devotees, who experience it as sacred and spiritually charged.

In temples, the deity image is treated like a living king or queen. Fine-haired whisks may be waved before it, purifying the area for its presence. Aesthetically pleasing meals are presented on its own dishes. During visiting hours, the deity holds court. In the morning, the image is ritually bathed and dressed in sumptuous clothes; at night, it may be put to rest in bedclothes. If it is hot, arrangements are made for the deity to take an afternoon in privacy. For festivals, the deity is paraded through the streets. The great Jagganath festival, held once every twelve years in Puri, was attended by some one and a half million devotees in 1996, all clambering up for *darsan* of the deity, pulled in a massive sixteen-wheeled chariot (misspelled as "juggernaut" in English). Loving service to the divine makes it real and present.

Ritual fire ceremonies around a **havan**, or sacred fire place, are conducted by *brahmin* pandits, following ancient Vedic traditions. Fruits, fragrances, herbs and grains, and ghee are placed in the fire as offerings to the deities, as invoked and praised by chants, and are conveyed by Agni, god of fire. The fire reminds devotees of the brightness of the divine and the power of truth which illuminates the darkness. Havans may be conducted to celebrate a particular deity, or at the behest of a patron for the sake of his health or good fortune.

Death ceremonies are also carried out by fire. Soon after death, washed, rubbed with sandalwood paste, and dressed in fresh clothes, the body is wrapped in white sheets and carried to a burning ground. Flowers are placed on the shrouded body and logs are stacked around it to make a fierce fire. Pandits may chant Vedic verses that cleanse the body and assist the soul's passage to the spiritual realm. The senior mourner—usually the eldest surviving son—carries a clay pot of water around the body three times, gradually pouring out the water, then dashes the pot to the floor to signify the end of this earthly body. He then lights the pyre. Alternatively, the shrouded body may be placed in an electric crematorium. After the burning the remaining bits of bone and ash are ritually immersed in the waters of a holy river. The mourners are now visually assured that the soul has been set free and the body is no more. Cremation is satisfying in the context of Sanatana Dharma, in which the body is regarded as a disposable vehicle for the immortal soul.

Castes, duties, and life goals

The **caste** system which still shapes lives in modern India to a considerable extent goes back to the Vedic age. Because the Vedic sacrifices were a reciprocal communion with the gods, priests who performed the public sacrifices had to be carefully trained and maintain high standards of ritual purity. Those so trained—the *brahmins*—comprised a special occupational group. The orderly working of society included a clear division of labor among four major occupational groups, which later became entrenched as castes. The *brahmins* were the priests and philosophers, specialists in the life of the spirit. The next group, later called **kshatriyas**, were the nobility of feudal India: kings, warriors, and vassals. Their general function was to guard and preserve the society; they were expected to be courageous and majestic. **Vaishyas** were the economic specialists: farmers and merchants. The **shudra** caste were the manual laborers and artisans. Even lower than these original four castes were those "outcastes" who came to be considered **untouchables**. They carried on work such as removing human waste and corpses, sweeping streets, and working with leather from the skins of dead cows—occupations that made their bodies and clothing abhorrent to others.

Over time, Vedic religion was increasingly controlled by the *brahmins*, and contact between castes was limited. Caste membership became hereditary. The caste system became as important as the Vedas in defining Hinduism until its social injustices were attacked in the nineteenth century. One of its opponents was Mahatma Gandhi, who renamed the lowest caste *harijans*, "the children of God." In 1948 the stigma of "untouchability" was legally abolished, though many caste distinctions still linger in modern India. Marriage across caste lines, for instance, is often disapproved of. If a boy and girl—one of whom is from the lowest caste—fall in love, sometimes the families from both sides will kill them rather than allow their marriage, to prevent disgrace or retribution.

Despite its abuses, the division of labor represented by the caste system is part of Sanatana Dharma's strong emphasis on social duties and sacrifice of individual desires for the sake of social order. Its purpose is to uplift people from worldly concerns and to encourage them to behave according to higher laws. The Vedas, other scriptures, and historical customs have all conditioned the Indian people to accept their social roles. These were set out in a major document known as the Code of Manu, compiled by 100 CE. In it are laws governing all aspects of life, including the proper conduct of rulers, dietary restrictions, marriage laws, daily rituals, purification rites, social laws, and ethical guidance. It prescribes hospitality to guests, for everyone is the deity incarnate, and the cultivation of such virtues as contemplation, truthfulness, compassion, non-attachment, generosity, pleasant dealings with people, and self-control. It condemns untouchables to living outside villages, eating only from broken dishes, and wearing only clothes removed from corpses. On the other hand, the code proposed charitable giving as the sacred duty of the upper castes, and thus provided a safety net for those at the bottom of this hierarchical system: "A householder must give as he is able and to those who do not cook for themselves, and to all beings one must distribute without detriment."[24]

Sanatana Dharma also holds up four major goals that define the good life. One is *dharma*, carrying out one's responsibilities and duties for the sake of social and cosmic order. *Artha* is success in worldly activities including the pursuit of wealth and advantage. *Kama* refers to love and sensual pleasures, and to aesthetic expression. Many religious paths regard eroticism as an impediment to spiritual progress, but the *Mahabharata* proposes that *dharma* and *artha* both arise from *kama*, because without desire and creativity there is no striving. The ultimate goal is *moksha*, liberation from the cycle of death and rebirth. Its attainment marks the end of all the other goals.

Life stages

The process of attaining spiritual realization or liberation is thought to take at least a lifetime, and probably many lifetimes. Birth as a human being is prized as a chance to advance toward spiritual perfection. In the past, spiritual training was usually available to upper-caste males only; women and *shudras* were excluded. It was preceded by an initiation ceremony in which the boy received the **sacred thread**, a cord of three threads to be worn across the chest from the left shoulder.

A Brahmin male's lifespan was divided into four periods of approximately twenty-five years each. For the first period he is a chaste student at the feet of a teacher. Next comes the householder stage, when he is expected to marry, raise a family, and contribute to society. He then starts to detach himself from worldly pursuits and turn to meditation and scriptural study. By seventy-five, he is able to withdraw totally from society and become a **sannyasin**.

The *sannyasin* is a contemplative who cuts himself off from wife and family, declaring, "No one belongs to me and I belong to no one." Some *sannyasins* live in comfortable temples; others wander alone—sometimes wearing no clothes—with only a water jar, a walking staff, and a begging bowl as possessions. Some In silence, the *sannyasin* is supposed to concentrate on practices that will finally release him from *samsara* into cosmic consciousness.

Most contemporary Hindu males do not follow this path to its *sannyasin* conclusion in old age, but many Hindus still become *sannyasins*. Some of them renounce the world at a younger age and join a monastic order, living in an **ashram**, a retreat community that has developed around a teacher.

Home puja

Both women and men carry on *puja* (worship) in their homes. Nearly every home in India has a shrine with pictures or small statues of deities, and many have a prayer room set aside for worship. For *puja*, ritual purity is emphasized; the time for prayer and offerings to the deities is after bathing in the morning or washing in the evening. *Puja* is an everyday observance, although among orthodox families, menstruating women are considered unclean and are not allowed to approach the shrines. Typically, a small oil lamp and a smoldering stick of incense are waved before the deities' images. If the devotee or family has a guru, a picture of him or her is usually part of the shrine.

An Interview with Somjit Dasgupta

In Sanatana Dharma, many forms of dance, song, and instrumental music have evolved as means of spiritual expression. Somjit Dasgupta is an accomplished Indian musician whose *ragas* softly played on the stringed *sarod* touch a deep place in the soul. He explains,

"My Guru was Radhikamohan Maitreya, whose main instrument was the *sarod*. For music, there has been no distinction between Hindu or Muslim tradition. When the Muslim rulers came here, they preached from the ashrams. Some of the old Hindu musicians were converted and joined the Muslim courts.

"In our old Sanskrit texts, it is written, 'There is no education, no learning beyond music.' In the Indian tradition, it is *sangeet*—collective worship and singing.

"Meditation was there in other parts of the world also, but it was very special in this part of the world. Meditation means to sit and see within yourself. Once my Guru told me, 'What do you mean by sound? Sound is some cluster of frequencies that you are hearing. In that way, I am Radhikamohan Maitreya: I am a cluster of frequencies. And you are Somjit Dasgupta. Some other set of frequencies created you. That's why your self and my self are joined in different ways, giving us different personalities. But our aim is to go back to the primordial frequency, through this *sadhana*, this spiritual practice. Everybody in every *sadhana* has to go through music. With our finger touch, by Guru's grace, our aim is to reach that primordial frequency. And there, there is no myself. No self is there. That is eternity. This thing

my Guru gave me. I cannot say it is an achievement. It is as though you are going back to your father's place.' I asked, 'What is there?' He said, 'Some day I will tell you.'

"Then he told me about one song, which says, 'The same single *Omkar* [the Ultimate Reality as primordial vibration] is spread throughout the world. It has no form, no dimensions. In the primordial frequency there is nothing, nobody, only *Omkar*. When I see That personally, I enjoy That personally, I feel That personally, then only can I think about the Almighty.'

"He also told me about another song from the *drupad* musical tradition, which contains the seed, the essence. It says '*Chaitanya*—the primordial sensations, presence, and sensitivity within me—is eternal. *Bindu* is where you touch to experience that Chaitanya. When you are touching your instrument, that is your touching point. Beyond all these things is that same existence, that same primordial frequency.'

"He taught me fourteen songs about the Guru, containing the inner essence of dharma. One says, 'There is no knowledge beyond the Guru. There is no spiritual practice, no meditation beyond the Guru. All kinds of inner enlightened knowledge finish in eternity: There my Guru stays, with all the blessings.'

"Our work is not to perform on the stage or anything like that. It is that whatever you get from your Guru, your entire existence is to pass that on, so that this teaching can give that essence for the future. So the main thing is to keep this teaching alive. The rest is up to the Guru, and the Almighty."[25]

The guru

Most practicing Hindus seek to place themselves at the feet of a spiritual teacher, or **guru,** the title applied to venerable spiritual guides. Gurus do not declare themselves as teachers; people are drawn to them because of their spiritual status. Gurus are often regarded as enlightened or "fully realized" individuals. They do not provide academic instruction. Rather, they give advice, example, and encouragement to those seeking enlightenment or realization.

> *Anyone and everyone cannot be a guru. A huge timber floats on the water and can carry animals as well. But a piece of worthless wood sinks, if a man sits on it, and drowns him.*
>
> *Ramakrishna*[26]

The Siddha tradition of southern India specializes in "teaching" by **shaktipat**—the power of a glance, word, touch, or thought. A disciple of the late Swami Muktananda describes the effect, referring to him as "Baba" (Father):

When a seeker receives shaktipat, *he experiences an overflowing of bliss within and becomes ecstatic. In Baba's presence, all doubts and misgivings vanish, and one experiences inner contentment and a sense of fulfillment.*[27]

Disciples love and honor their guru as their spiritual parent. The guru does not always behave as a loving parent; often disciples are treated harshly, to test their faith and devotion or strip away the ego. But true devotees are grateful to serve their guru, out of love. They often bend to touch the feet or hem of the robe of the guru, partly out of humility and partly because great power is thought to emanate from the feet. Humbling oneself before the guru is considered necessary in order to receive the teaching. A common metaphor is that of a cup and a pitcher of water. If the cup (the disciple, or *chela*) is full, no water (spiritual wisdom) can be poured into it from the pitcher (the guru). And if the cup is on the same level as the pitcher, there can be no pouring. The cup must be empty and below the pitcher; then the water can be freely poured into it.

Fasts, prayers, and auspicious designs

Orthodox *brahmins* observe many days of fasting and prayer, corresponding to auspicious points in the lunar and solar cycles or times of danger, such as the four months of the monsoon season. The ancient practice of astrology is so highly regarded that many couples are now choosing birth by Caesarean section for the purpose of selecting the most auspicious moment for their child's birth.

Many expressions of Indian spirituality, particularly in rural areas, are not encapsulated within Brahmanic traditions but have an existence of their own. Such, for instance, are the home-made designs daily laid out before homes at dawn. Women create them to protect their households by inviting in a deity such as Lakshmi. Typically made of edible substances, such as rice flour, the designs are soon dismantled by insects and birds, but they help to fulfill the dharmic requirement to feed a thousand souls every day.

Reverence of trees and rivers

Practices such as worship under large trees stretches back into pre-history and continues at countless small shrines today. There is a strong taboo against cutting certain sacred trees, such as the peepul, which sprouts wherever it can gain the slightest foothold. In some parts of India, whole tracts of virgin forest are kept intact by villagers, who protect both animal and plant life with the understanding that the area is the home of a deity. These sacred groves are now viewed by environmentalists as important islands of biological diversity.

Not only forests but also hilltops, mountains, and river sources are often viewed as sacred and their natural environment thus protected to a certain extent. The Narmada River, one of India's most sacred, is regarded by millions of people as a goddess (as are most Indian rivers). Its banks are lined with thousands of temples devoted to Mother Narmada and Lord Shiva. Pilgrims reverently circumambulate its entire 815-mile (1,312-km) length. However, the river and its huge watershed are the subjects of the world's largest water development scheme. When the reservoir created by the highest of the dams is filled, some 245 villages will be submerged, temples and all. The inhabitants of the watershed that will be inundated are closely linked to their local sacred landscape, and one of them explains, "Our gods cannot move from this place. How can we move without them?"[28] Fierce conflicts have been raging since 1990 between environmentalists and social activists who claim the high dams will adversely affect at least one million people in the watershed, and modernists who regard such dams, as Nehru said, as "the secular temples of modern India."[29]

High dams are not the only threat to sacred rivers. Religious practices themselves may lead to high levels of water pollution. Mass bathing on auspicious occasions is accompanied by wastes, such as butter oil, flowers, and human excreta (contrary to scriptural injunctions about proper behavior in sacred rivers). The remains of dead bodies reverently immersed in the sacred rivers may be incompletely cremated. Immersion of idols of Ganesh or Durga on holy days as a symbol of purification (as explained in the next section) has become a major source of water pollution. In one year alone, ritual immersion of idols in Calcutta added to the Hoogli River an estimated 17 tons of varnish and 32 tons of paints, including manganese, lead, mercury, and chromium.[30]

Pilgrimages

Pilgrimages to holy places and sacred rivers are thought to be special opportunities for personal purification and spiritual elevation. Millions of pilgrims yearly undertake strenuous climbs to remote mountain sites that are thought to be blessed by the divine. One of the major pilgrimage sites is Amarnath cave. At an altitude of 11,090 feet (3,380 m) in the Himalayas of Kashmir, ice has formed a giant stalagmite, which is highly revered as a Siva lingam. Pilgrims may have been trekking to this holy place in the high Himalayas for up to three thousand years. The 14,800-feet (45-km) footpath over a glacier is so dangerous that 250 people were killed by freak storms and landslides in 1996, but tens of thousands of devotees have continued to undertake the pilgrimage. Similarly, Saktas trek up to Saktipithas, fifty-one pilgrimage spots in the Indian subcontinent that are thought to mark abodes of the goddess or places where parts of Her body now rest.

The places where great saints and teachers have lived also automatically become places of pilgrimage during their lives and after they pass on. Their powerful vibrations are felt to still permeate and bless these sites. One such place is the holy mountain of Arunachala in southern India. The great saint Ramana Maharshi (1879–1951) lived there so absorbed in Ultimate Consciousness that he neither talked nor ate and had to be force-fed by another holy man. But the needs of those who gathered around him drew out his compassion and wisdom, and he spontaneously counseled them in their spiritual needs.

Festivals

Sanatana Dharma honors the divine in so many forms that almost every day a religious celebration is being held in some part of India. Sixteen religious holidays are honored by the central government so that everyone can leave work to join in the throngs of worshipers. These are calculated partially on a lunar calendar, so dates vary from year to year. Most Hindu festivals express spirituality in its happiest aspects. Group energy attracts the gods to overcome evils, and humorous abandon helps merry-makers transform their fears.

On a midwinter night in northern India, people celebrate Lohari by building a bonfire and throwing popcorn, peanuts, and sesame candies into it. The feeling is that one is symbolically throwing away one's evils, and invoking blessings for the year to come. Families who have given birth to a male child during the past year perform this ceremony for his auspicious future. Holi is the joyful celebration of the death of winter and return of spring.

In July or August a special day, Naga Panchami, is devoted to the *nagas*, or snakes, considered powerful gods by the indigenous peoples. In southern Indian villages, where they are especially honored, thousands of live snakes are caught and exhibited. Worshipers sprinkle vermilion and rice on the hoods of cobras, considered especially sacred. On Naga Panchami, farmers abstain from ploughing to avoid disrupting any snake-holes.

In August or September, Vaishnavites celebrate Krishna's birthday (Janmashtami). Devotees fast and keep a vigil until midnight, retelling stories of Krishna's life or reading his enlightened wisdom from the *Bhagavad-Gita*. In some places his image is placed in a cradle and lovingly rocked by devotees. Elsewhere, pots of milk, curds, and butter are strung high above the ground to be seized by young men who form human pyramids to get to them. They romp about with the pots like Krishna, playful stealer of the milk products he loved.

At the end of the summer, it is Ganesh who is honored, especially in western and southern India, during Ganesh Chaturti. Special potters make clay images of the elephant-headed remover of obstacles, son of Parvati who formed him from her body's dirt and sweat, and set him to stand guard while she bathed. As she wouldn't let Siva in, her angry spouse smashed the boy's head into a thousand pieces. Parvati demanded that the boy be restored to life with a new head, but the first one found was that of a baby elephant. To soothe Parvati's distress at the transplant, Siva granted Ganesh the power of removing obstacles. The elephant-headed god is now the first to be invoked in all rituals. After days of being sung to and offered sweets, his images are carried to a body of water and bidden farewell with prayers for an easy year until the next Ganesh Chaturti.

In different parts of India, the first nine or ten days of Asvina, the lunar month corresponding to September or October, are dedicated either to the Durga Puja (in which elaborate images of the many-armed goddess celebrate her powers to vanquish the demonic forces) or to Dussehra (which marks Rama's nine nights of worshiping Durga before killing Ravana on the tenth day). The theme of both Durga Puja and Dussehra is the triumph of good over evil.

Twenty days later, on the night of the new moon, is Divali, the happy four-day festival of lights. Variously explained as the return of Rama after his exile, the *puja* of Lakshmi (goddess of wealth, who visits only clean homes), and the New Year of those following one of the Indian calendars, it is a time for tidying business establishments and financial records, cleaning and illuminating houses with oil lamps, wearing new clothes, gambling, feasting, honoring clay images of Lakshmi and Ganesh, and setting off fireworks.

Initially more solemn is Mahashivaratri, a day of fasting and a night of keeping vigil to earn merit with Siva. During the ascetic part of the observance, many pilgrims go to sacred rivers or special tanks of water for ritual bathing. Siva lingams and statues are venerated, and the faithful stay awake throughout the night, chanting and telling stories of their Lord. In one of the stories, a discussion among Brahma, Vishnu, and Siva leads to Siva's manifesting as a pillar of fire and challenging the others to touch the ends, which they will not. A reformist group, Arya Samaj, decries what it considers superstition and idolatry and honors the day as the end of a week-long celebration of their reform. They carry out Vedic fire sacrifices and hold spiritual talks, throwing personal offerings into the fire on the last day.

Every few years, millions of Hindus of all persuasions gather for the immense Kumbha Mela. It is held alternately at four sacred spots where drops of the holy nectar of immortality are said to have fallen. On one day in 2001, in what has been recorded as the largest ever gathering of human beings for a single purpose, over twenty-five million people amassed at the point near Allahabad where the Jumna River meets the sacred Ganges and the invisible Saraswati. There they took a purifying bath in the frigid waters on the most auspicious date, as determined by astrologers. Among the Kumbha Mela are huge processions of ascetic **sadhus** from various orders, many of whom leave their retreats only for this festival. They gather to discuss religious matters and also social problems, sometimes leading to revisions of Hindu codes of conduct. Many of the lay pilgrims are poor people who undergo great hardships to reach the site.

Hinduism in the modern world

Hinduism did not develop in India in isolation. Christianity may have put down roots in India as long ago as 70 CE. Muslims began taking over certain areas beginning in the eighth century CE; during the sixteenth and seventeenth centuries a large area was ruled by the Muslim Mogul emperors. Islam and Hinduism generally co-existed, despite periods of intolerance, along with Buddhism and Jainism, which had also grown up within India. Indian traders carried some aspects of Sanatana Dharma to Java and Bali, where Hinduism survives today with a unique Balinese flavor.

When the Mogul Empire collapsed, European colonialists moved in. Ultimately the British dominated, and in 1857 India was placed under direct British rule. Christian missionaries set about correcting abuses they perceived in certain Hindu practices, such as widow-burning and the caste system. But they also taught those who were being educated in their schools that Hinduism was "intellectually incoherent and ethically unsound."[31] Some Indians believed them and drifted away from their ancient tradition.

Modern movements

To counteract Western influences, Mahatma ("Great Soul") Gandhi (1869–1948) encouraged grassroots nationalism, emphasizing that the people's strength lay in awareness of spiritual truth and in non-violent resistance to military or industrial oppression. He claimed that these qualities were the essence of all religions, including Hinduism, which he considered the universal religion.

In addition to being made a focus for political unity, Hinduism itself was revitalized by a number of spiritual leaders. One of these was Ramakrishna (1836–1886), who was a devotee of the Divine Mother in the form of Kali. Eschewing ritual, he communicated with her through intense love. He practiced Tantric disciplines and the *bhavanas* (types of loving relationships). These brought him spiritual powers, spiritual insight, and reportedly a visible brilliance, but he longed only to be a vehicle for pure devotion:

> I seek not, good Mother, the pleasures of the senses! I seek not fame! Nor do I long
> for those powers which enable one to do miracles! What I pray for, O good Mother,
> is pure love for Thee—love for Thee untainted by desires, love without alloy, love
> that seeketh not the things of the world, love for Thee that welleth up unbidden out
> of the depths of the immortal soul![32]

Ramakrishna worshiped the divine through many Hindu paths, as well as Islam and Christianity, and found the same One in them all. Intoxicated with the One, he had continual visions of the Divine Mother and ecstatically worshiped her in unorthodox, uninhibited ways. For instance, once he fed a cat some food that was supposed to be a temple offering for the Divine Mother, for she revealed herself to him in everything, including the cat. He also placed his spiritual bride, Sarada Devi, in the chair reserved for the deity, honoring her as the Great Goddess.

The pure devotion and universal spiritual wisdom Ramakrishna embodied inspired what is now known as the Ramakrishna Movement, or the Vedanta Society. A famous disciple, named Vivekananda (1863–1902), carried the eternal message of Sanatana Dharma to the world beyond India and excited so much interest in the West that Hinduism became a global religion. He also reintroduced Indians to the profundities of their great traditions.

Within India Hinduism has also been influenced by reform movements such as Brahmo Samaj and Arya Samaj. The former defended Hindu mysticism and *bhakti* devotion to an immanent deity. The latter advocated a return to what it saw as the purity of the Vedas, rejecting image worship, devotion to a multiplicity of deities, priestly privileges, and popular rituals. Contemporary Arya Samaj leader and social activist Swami Agnivesh is sharply critical of what has become of religions in general in India, and advocates reawakening of social conscience as a spiritual imperative.

> *Do not care for doctrines, do not care for dogmas, or sects, or churches, or temples;*
> *they count for little compared with the essence of existence in each [person], which is*
> *spirituality. . . . Earn that first, acquire that, and criticize no one, for all doctrines*
> *and creeds have some good in them.*
>
> *Ramakrishna*[33]

Global Hinduism

Hinduism is also experiencing vibrant growth beyond the Indian subcontinent, partly among expatriates and partly among converts from other faiths. For the past hundred years, many self-proclaimed gurus have left India to develop followings in other countries. Some were fraudulent, with scandalous private behavior or motives of wealth and power. Despite increased Western wariness of gurus, some of these movements have continued to grow.

Many non-Indians discovered Sanatana Dharma by reading *Autobiography of a Yogi*, by Paramahansa Yogananda (1893–1952). The book describes his intriguing spiritual experiences with Indian gurus and also explains principles of Sanatana Dharma in loving fashion. Yogananda traveled to the United States and began a movement, the California-based Self-Realization Fellowship, which has survived his death and is still growing under the supervision of Western disciples, with centers, temples, and living communities in forty-six countries.

Another still-flourishing example is the Netherlands-based Transcendental Meditation (TM) movement, which was begun by Maharishi Mahesh Yogi in the 1960s. For a fee, he and his disciples teach people secret mantras and assert that repeating the mantra for twenty minutes twice each day will bring great personal benefits. These range from enhanced athletic prowess to increased satisfaction with life. By paying more money, advanced practitioners can also learn how to "fly." That is, they take short hops into the air while sitting cross-legged. The organization claims a success rate of sixty-five percent in ending drug and alcohol addiction. TM has now entered politics as well. It is a vast global organization,complete with luxurious health spas in Europe, a Vedic "theme park" near Niagara Falls in Canada, Vedic-based development projects in Africa, colleges, universities, and Maharishi Schools of Management in many countries, and an ashram for 10,000 people in India.

Another rather unlikely success story is found in ISKCON, the International Society for Krishna Consciousness. In 1965, the Indian guru A. C. Bhaktivedanta Swami Prabhupada arrived in the United States, carrying the asceticism and *bhakti* devotion of Sri Caitanya's tradition of Krishna worship from India to the heart of Western materialistic culture. Adopting the dress and diet of Hindu monks and nuns, his initiates lived in temple communities. Their days began at 4 a.m. with meditation, worship, chanting of the names of Krishna and Ram, and scriptural study, with the aim of turning from a material life of sense gratification to one of transcendent spiritual happiness. During the day, they chanted and danced in the streets to introduce others to the bliss of Krishna, distributed literature (especially Swami Prabhupada's illustrated and esteemed translation of the *Bhagavad-Gita*), attracted new devotees, and raised funds. Despite schisms and scandals, the movement has continued since Swami Prabhupada's death in 1977, and is growing in strength in various countries, particularly in India and eastern Europe. In England, a great mansion has been turned into an ISKCON temple, which also serves Indian immigrants as a place to celebrate major festivals.

An American devotee who is a descendant of the Ford automobile family is building a large village industries park, tourism hospitality complex, and Vedic planetarium near the global headquarters of ISKCON in India. The planetarium is designed to research and showcase the scientific accuracy of ancient Vedic descriptions of the cosmos.

Some contemporary gurus are also enjoying great global popularity. One of the most famous at present is Mata Amritanandamayi, a seemingly tireless, motherly saint from South India who takes people from all walks of life into her arms. In large-scale gatherings around the world, the "hugging saint" may embrace up to 70,000 people at a stretch, through the night and into the next day. She encourages her "children" to find personal solace and compassion for others through worship of the divine in any form. Many of her followers regard "Amma" herself as the personification of the Divine Mother.

Hindu identity

At the same time that Hinduism is reaching around the world, some Hindu groups within India are giving Hinduism a strongly nationalistic thrust. In particular, the RSS—Rashtriya Svayamsevak Sangh—arose early in the twentieth century, espousing Hindu cultural renewal in order to combat the ills of modernity and return to an idealized past referred to as "Ram Rajya," the legendary kingdom of Lord Ram, when Hindu virtues were maintained by a perfect ruler. This movement gave organized expression to the ideals of V. D. Savarkar, who wrote of an ancient Hindu nation and *Hindutva* ("Hindu-ness"), excluding Muslims and Christians as aliens in India, in contrast to the historical evidence that Sanatana Dharma is a noncentralized, evolving composite of variegated ways of worship,

The RSS continues to be a powerful force shaping politics in India today. Its activities run counter to the secularism established by India's constitution, which recognizes the multi-cultural, multi-religious fabric of the country and does not confer favored political status on any religion. But in the eyes of what could be called Hindu "fundamentalists," secularism is a cover the political elite have used to hide their corruption. Under its guise, they feel, people are being robbed of their religious values and identity, which the RSS, the religious organization Vishva Hindu Parishad (VHP), and political parties such as the Bharatiya Janata Party (BJP) say they are trying to restore, claiming the moral high ground even while engaging in illegal activities.

A major focus of these activities has been the small town of Ayodhya, which according to Hindu mythology is the birthplace of Lord Ram. According to Hindutva belief, Babur, the Muslim Mughal ruler, had the main temple commemorating Ram's birthplace torn down and the Babri Mosque built on its ruins. In 1992, some 200,000 Hindu extremists managed to enter Ayodhya and tear down the Babri Mosque. This was followed by Hindu-Muslim violence throughout India.

The RSS has tens of thousands of branches in Indian villages and cities where Hindu men and boys meet for games, martial arts training, songs, lectures, and prayers to the Hindu nation, conceived as the Divine Mother. Its leader has urged throwing Christian missionaries out of India and has asserted that all Indians are Hindus. There are an estimated 12,000 RSS schools in India in which children are, according to the National Steering Committee for Textbook Evaluation, being taught from texts "designed to promote bigotry and religious fanaticism in the name of inculcating knowledge of culture in the young generation."[34]

Political affiliates of the RSS with a "Hindu agenda"—particularly the BJP (Bharatiya Janata Party)—have become powerful in Indian politics. It was the leading party in the central government in power in 2002 when one coach of a train carrying volunteers who were seeking to illegally construct the new temple in Ayodhya caught fire in the state of Gujarat and was surrounded by a presumably Muslim mob. Fifty-nine Hindus burned to death, and terrible inter-religious violence followed. Perhaps two thousand people, most of them Muslims, were killed by mobs while officials did little to stop them.

Extremist Hindu groups are trying to woo Christian converts back to Hinduism and actively oppose Christianity in India. In recent years, Christian nuns were raped, priests killed, Bibles burned, and churches and Christian schools destroyed, apparently by the extremists. Some "untouchable" Hindus have converted to Christianity, Buddhism, or Islam because those religions do not make caste distinctions. Christians in particular have offered social services for the poor such as schools and hospitals. An estimated fifty percent of all Christians in India were formerly of low-caste origin. Indian Christian scholars point to interfaith tolerance as one of the essential qualities of Hinduism. But to ardent Hindu fundamentalists, this tolerance does not extend to choosing what it regards as "foreign" religions such as Christianity.

Tensions continue to run high between Hindus and Muslims in Kashmir, where efforts to become independent of India often pit Hindus and Muslims against each other. Serious political concerns are often obscured by divisions along religious lines, and peace continues to be elusive.

Such conflicts are not in keeping with Sanatana Dharma's ideal of tolerance for many ways to the divine. Although tensions between religions exist in many regions of India, what predominates is the spirit of accommodation with which the various communities have lived side by side for hundreds of years.

The Indian Supreme Court has formally defined Hindu beliefs in a way that affirms universality rather than exclusiveness. According to the Court's definition, to be a Hindu means:

1 Acceptance and reverence for the Vedas as the foundation of Hindu philosophy;
2 A spirit of tolerance, and willingness to understand and appreciate others' points of view, recognizing that truth has many sides;
3 Acceptance of the belief that vast cosmic periods of creation, maintenance, and dissolution continuously recur;
4 Acceptance of belief in reincarnation;
5 Recognition that paths to truth and salvation are many;
6 Recognition that there may be numerous gods and goddesses to worship, without necessarily believing in worship through idols;
7 Unlike other religions, absence of belief in a specific set of philosophic concepts.[35]

Dr. Karan Singh

Globally active in an extraordinary number of public posts and projects, Dr. Karan Singh is also one of the world's most respected spokesmen for Hinduism. He was born wealthy, as heir to the Maharaja of Jammu and Kashmir, but has never retired from a life of intense public service. In fact, he turned over his entire princely inheritance to the service of the people of India and converted his palace into a museum and library.

A brilliant orator, Dr. Karan Singh quotes extensively and effectively from the Vedas in his talks and says he has been deeply influenced by them—in particular, the *Upanishads*. He states:

The Upanishads *are the high-water mark of Hindu philosophy. They are texts of tremendous wisdom and power. They represent some of the deepest truths with regard to the all-pervasiveness of the divine. One is the concept that every individual encapsulates a spark of the divine, the* atman. *There is also the concept of the human race as an extended family. Then there is the concept that "The truth is one; the wise call it by many names." That is the ultimate unity of all religions. We also have the concept of the welfare of the many, the happiness of the many.*

Busy though he is, Dr. Karan Singh always takes time daily to perform his private *puja* (worship ceremonies). He is a worshiper of Lord Siva. Before Lord Siva, he also worships the goddess.

As part of my daily routine, I have my own puja. *I do it in the morning, again at night before going to bed, and in the course of the day. Ours is not a religion where you go once a week to a church and that's it. Hinduism is supposed to be*

something which permeates your entire consciousness. Therefore these puja *sessions are supposed to be ways of reminding yourself of the divinity.*

Despite his personal devotion to Lord Siva, Dr. Karan Singh emphasizes that Hinduism supports acceptance of all manifestations of the divine, and therefore all religions.

The exclusivism or monopolistic tendencies in religions who claim that they have the sole agency in the sphere of the divine is not acceptable in this day and age. We have got to accept the fact that there are multiple paths to the divine. We have to not only accept them—we have to respect whoever is traveling on his or her path. That has come to me particularly from the Vedanta tradition.

Although Dr. Karan Singh has often been deeply involved in government, he is free from the taint of corruption and scandal that mars so many political careers. He attributes his clear reputation partly to the fact that the was born into "favorable financial circumstances," and also to his religious upbringing:

Not being corrupt is part of the basic religious teachings around the world. We are brought up on the stories of Raja Harish Chandra, who gave up everything for the sake of truth, and Sri Rama, who gave up everything for the sake of his father's word, and so on. Those sort of mythological stories based on truth and the quest for truth are very strong in wisdom. And if you are pursuing the path of truth, then I presume that automatically rules out your being corrupt.[36]

Finally, Hindu scholar and statesman Karan Singh observes that the vast understandings of the ancient Vedas will always make them relevant to the human condition:

We, who are children of the past and the future, of earth and heaven, of light and darkness, of the human and the divine, at once evanescent and eternal, of the world and beyond it, within time and in eternity, yet have the capacity to comprehend our condition, to rise above our terrestrial limitations, and, finally, to transcend the throbbing abyss of space and time itself. This, in essence, is the message of Hinduism.[37]

Review questions

1. Describe major philosophical themes of Hinduism: Brahman, *atman*, reincarnation, *karma, samsara, moksha*, Samkhya, Advaita Vedanta, and Yoga.
2. Describe major Hindu ritual practices: Brahmins, Vishnu, Siva, the Mother Goddess, Tantras, women's roles, lingams, Rama, Krishna, *puja, darsan, prasad*.

Discussion questions

1. How can Hinduism embrace such a wide continuum of contradictory social beliefs and practices—universalism and simultaneously its divisive caste system, treatment of women, and exclusivist nationalism?
2. How can Hinduism embrace such a wide continuum of contradictory views of the relation of spirit and body—severe *sadhu* asceticism and elaborate, sensuous images of gods and goddesses?
3. Can and should Hinduism's beliefs and practices be reconciled with modern industrial society? Discuss reincarnation, *karma, Vedanta, chakras*, polytheism, asceticism, *darsan*, gurus, reverence for trees and rivers, caste, universalism.

CHAPTER 4

BUDDHISM

"He will deliver by the boat of knowledge the distressed world"

The man who came to be known as the Buddha preached an alternative to the ritual-bound Brahmanism of sixth-century BCE India. The Buddha taught about earthly suffering and its cure. Many religions offer comforting supernatural solutions to the difficulties of earthly life. Early Buddhism was quite different: it held that liberation from suffering depends on our own efforts. The Buddha taught that by understanding how we create suffering for ourselves we can become free.

The effort involved in taking responsibility for our own happiness and our own liberation may seem unappealing and unlikely to attract many followers. On the contrary, the Buddha's teachings spread far and wide from his native India throughout Asia, becoming the dominant religion in many countries. The new path took on devotional and mystical qualities from earlier local traditions, with various Buddhas and bodhisattvas to whom one could appeal for help. Now, more than two and a half thousand years after the Buddha's death, the path he taught is attracting considerable interest in the West.

The life and legend of the Buddha

Although the Buddha was apparently an historical figure, what we know about him is not documented, but is derived from stories passed down through generations of followers. His prolific teachings were probably not collected in written form until several hundred years after his death. In the meantime, they were apparently transmitted orally, chanted by monks, groups of whom were responsible for remembering specific parts of the teachings.

Only a few factual details of the Buddha's life have been retained. While stories about his life are abundant in authorized Buddhist texts, these were never organized into a unified canonical biography. Extant complete biographies date from four centuries after his passing. These venerate the Buddha as a legendary hero, and were written by story-teller poets rather than historians. An example of such a sacred biography is Asvaghosa's epic, the *Buddhacarita* (Acts of the Buddha), composed in the first century CE.

The one who became the Buddha (a generic term meaning "Awakened One") was reportedly born near what is today the border between India and Nepal. He was named Siddhartha Gautama, meaning "wish-fulfiller" or "he who has reached his goal." It is said that he lived for over eighty years during the fifth century BCE, though his life may have extended either into the late sixth or early fourth century. His father was apparently a wealthy landowner serving as one of the chiefs of a *kshatriya* clan, the Shakyas who lived in the foothills of the Himalayas. The family name, Gautama, honored an ancient Hindu sage whom the family claimed as ancestor or spiritual guide. His mother Maya is said to have given birth to him in the garden of Lumbini near Kapilavastu. The epics embellish his birth story as a conception without human intercourse, in which a white elephant carrying a lotus flower entered his mother's womb during a dream. He is portrayed as the reincarnation of a great being who had been born many times before and took birth on earth once again out of compassion for all suffering beings.

According to legend, the child was raised in the lap of luxury, with fine clothes, white umbrellas for shade, perfumes, cosmetics, a mansion for each season, the female musicians, and a harem of dancing girls. He was also trained in martial arts and married to at least one wife, who bore a son. Despite this life of ease, Siddhartha was reportedly unconvinced of its value, and the gods arranged for him to see "four sights" his father had tried to hide from him: a bent old man, a sick person, a dead person, and a mendicant seeking lasting happiness rather than temporal pleasure. Seeing the first three sights, he was dismayed by the impermanence of life and the existence of suffering, old age, and death. The monk piqued his interest in a life of renunciation. At the age of twenty-nine Siddhartha renounced his wealth, left his wife and newborn son (whom he had named "Rahul," or "fetter"), shaved his head, and donned the coarse robe of a wandering ascetic. He embarked on a life in pursuit of a very difficult goal: finding the way to total liberation from suffering.

Many Indian *sannyasins* were already leading the homeless life of poverty and simplicity considered appropriate for seekers of spiritual truth. Although the future Buddha later developed a new spiritual path that departed significantly from Brahmanic tradition, he first tried traditional methods. He headed southeast to study with a *brahmin* teacher who had many followers, then with another who helped him reach an even higher mental state.

Unsatisfied, still searching, Siddhartha reportedly underwent six years of extreme self-denial techniques: nakedness, exposure to great heat and cold, breath retention, a bed of brambles, severe fasting. Finally he acknowledged that this extreme ascetic path had not led to enlightenment.

Siddhartha then shifted his practice to a Middle Way that rejected both self-indulgence and self-denial. He revived his failing health by accepting food once more and began a period of reflection. On the night of the full moon in the sixth lunar month, it is said that he sat in deep meditation beneath a tree in a village now called Bodh Gaya, and finally experienced supreme awakening. After passing through four states of serene contemplation, he recalled all his previous lives. Then he had a realization of the wheel of repeated death and rebirth, in which past good or bad deeds are reflected in future lives. Finally, he realized the cause of suffering and the means for ending it. After this awakening or enlightenment, it is said that he was radiant with light.

According to legend, Siddhartha was tempted by Mara, the personification of evil, to keep his insights to himself, for they were too complex and profound for ordinary people to understand. But the Buddha compassionately determined to set the wheel of the Dharma in motion and began by teaching in Sarnath, the

Deer Park. He then spent decades walking and teaching ever-increasing groups of followers all over northern India. The Enlightened One's teachings and personality were apparently so compelling that many people were transformed simply by meeting him. Gradually he became known as "Shakyamuni Buddha," the "sage of the Shakya clan." Out of the abundant and varied scriptures later attributed to Shakyamuni Buddha, historians agree on the validity and centrality of a core of teachings that became known as the **Dharma** (in the Pali dialect: *Dhamma*)* that he taught: the Four Noble Truths, the Noble Eightfold Path, the Three Marks of Existence, and other guidelines for achieving liberation from suffering.

The newly awakened Buddha walked across northern India for forty-five years as a mendicant with an alms bowl, giving teachings and advice to people of all sects and classes. Many young men decided to become monks (**bhikshus**; Pali: *bhikkhus*), emulating his life of poverty and spiritual dedication. Many others adopted his teachings but continued to live as householders.

The **Sangha**—the monastic order that developed from the Buddha's early disciples—accepted people from all castes and levels of society. The Buddha's stepmother Mahaprajapati, who had raised him after the death of his mother, and his wife, Yashodara, became **bhikshunis** (Pali: *bhikkhunis*), members of the order of nuns that the Buddha founded. After the death of his father King Shuddhodana, the Buddha's stepmother asked permission to enter the Sangha. When the Buddha hesitated to admit her, she and five hundred women from the court shaved their heads, put on yellow robes, and walked a great distance to Vaishali, where he was, making the same request. At last he agreed, reportedly on the condition that Mahaprajapati observe eight special rules, a story that has been used to subordinate nuns to the order of monks, regardless of seniority. The Buddha's alleged reluctance to admit women to the Sangha is today a matter of much speculation. Some think that later monks may have added the rules or that the eight special rules were laid down with the monks' weaknesses in mind. Be this as it may, in the context of patriarchal Indian society, for women to leave their homes and become itinerant mendicants would probably have been perceived as socially disruptive, as well as difficult for women of the court. According to Hindu social codes, a woman could not lead the renunciate life and could achieve spiritual salvation only through personal devotion, especially devotion to her husband. By contrast, the Buddha asserted that women were as capable as men of achieving enlightenment.

Traditional accounts of the Buddha's death at the age of eighty are evidence of his selfless desire to spare humankind from suffering. His last meal, served by a blacksmith, inadvertently included some poisonous mushrooms or perhaps spoiled pork. Severely ill and recognizing his impending death, the Buddha pushed on to his next teaching stop at Kushinara, teaching a young man along the way. He sent word to the blacksmith not to blame himself, for his offering of food accrued great merit. When the Buddha reached his destination, he lay down

---

* Buddhist terms have come to us both in **Pali**, an Indian dialect first used for preserving the Buddha's teachings (the Buddha himself probably spoke a different ancient dialect), and in Sanskrit, the language of Indian sacred literature. For instance, the Pali *sutta* (aphorism) is equivalent to the Sanskrit *sutra*. In this chapter Sanskrit will be used, as it is more familiar to Westerners, except in the section on Theravada, which uses Pali.

on a stone couch. As his monks came to pay their last respects, he urged them to tend to their own spiritual development:

You must be your own lamps, be your own refuges. . . . A monk becomes his own lamp and refuge by continually looking on his body, feelings, perceptions, moods, and ideas in such a manner that he conquers the cravings and depressions of ordinary men and is always strenuous, self-possessed, and collected in mind.[1]

He designated no successor and appointed no one to lead the order. But the Buddhist teachings and the monastic order survived and spread widely. His closest helper, Ananda, explained that before passing away the Buddha made it clear that his followers should take the Dharma and ethical discipline as their support. Followers should study the Dharma, put it into practice, and be able to defend the Dharma in the face of criticism.

One way the Buddhist tradition spread was through the dissemination of bone relics remaining after the Buddhist cremation. It is said that relics were given to messengers from seven clans who built dome-shaped reliquaries called **stupas** to commemorate the Buddha's final liberation (*parinirvana*). The Buddha's physical passing is memorialized by images in which he is serenely lying on his side. These stupas and images became the focus of great devotion to the Buddha. Inscriptions dating back to the third century BCE or even earlier show that priests as well as laypeople made pilgrimages to these sacred sites. Standing before them, followers sense the Buddha's presence.

The Dharma

Buddhism is often described as a nontheistic religion. There is no personal God who creates the world or to whom prayers can be directed. Buddhists at the 1993 Parliament of the World's Religions in Chicago found it necessary to explain to people of other religions that they do not worship the Buddha:

Shakyamuni Buddha, the founder of Buddhism, was not God or a god. He was a human being who attained full Enlightenment through meditation and showed us the path of spiritual awakening and freedom. Therefore, Buddhism is not a religion of God. Buddhism is a religion of wisdom, enlightenment and compassion. Like the worshippers of God who believe that salvation is available to all through confession of sin and a life of prayer, we Buddhists believe that salvation and enlightenment are available to all through removal of defilements and delusion and a life of meditation. However, unlike those who believe in God who is separate from us, Buddhists believe that Buddha which means "one who is awake and enlightened" is inherent in us all as Buddhanature or Buddhamind.[2]

Unlike other Indian sages, the Buddha did not focus on descriptions of an unseen reality, the nature of the soul, life after death, or the origin of the universe. He said that curiosity about such matters was like a man who, having been wounded by a poisoned arrow, refused to get it pulled out until he was told the caste and origin of his assailant, his name, his height, the color of his skin, and all details about the bow and arrow. In the meantime, he died.

Being religious and following dhamma *has nothing to do with the dogma that the world is eternal; and it has nothing to do with the other dogma that the world is not eternal. For whether the world is eternal or otherwise, birth, old age, death, sorrow, pain, misery, grief, and despair exist. I am concerned with the extinction of these.*[3]

The Buddha spoke of his teachings as a raft to take us to the farther shore, rather than a description of the shore or something to be carried around once we get there. The farther shore is **nirvana** (Pali: *nibbana*) or liberation, the goal of spiritual effort; the planks of the raft are insights into the truths of existence and teachings about the path to liberation.

In his very first sermon at Sarnath, the Buddha set forth the Four Noble Truths, the foundation for all his later teachings:

1 Life inevitably involves suffering, is imperfect and unsatisfactory.
2 Suffering originates in our desires.
3 Suffering will cease if all desires cease.
4 There is a way to realize this state: the Noble Eightfold Path.

The Buddha was neither pessimistic nor optimistic about our human condition. Sri Lankan monk and scholar Walpola Rahula speaks of the Buddha as "the wise and scientific doctor for the ills of the world."[4] To look at the diagnosis and treatment of our human condition one step at a time, the First Noble Truth is the existence of *dukkha*: suffering and frustration. We all experience grief, sickness, old age, physical pain, mental anguish, and eventually death. We may be happy for a while, but our happiness is not permanent. Even our identity is impermanent. There is no continual "I." What we regard as a "self" is simply an ever-changing bundle of fleeting feelings, sense impressions, ideas, and evanescent physical matter. One moment's identity leads to the next like one candle being lit from another, but no two moments are the same.

The Second Noble Truth is that the origin of *dukkha* is desire—for sensory pleasures, for fame and fortune, for things to stay as they are or become different—and in attachment to things and ideas. The reason that desire leads us to suffering, the Buddha taught, is that we do not understand the true, impermanent nature of the things we desire, which are changing all the time. We seek to grasp things and hold onto life as we want it to be, but we cannot since everything is in a constant state of flux.

In Buddhism, unhappiness is the inevitable companion of happiness. Sunshine gives way to rain, flowers wilt, friends die, and our bodies age and decay. As the contemporary monk Ajahn Sumedho points out, "trying to arrange, control and manipulate conditions so as to always get what we want, always hear what we want to hear, always see what we want to see, so that we never have to experience unhappiness or despair, is a hopeless task."[5]

To remedy this situation, the Buddha taught awareness of *dukkha*, **anitya** (Pali: *anicca*, impermanence), and **anatman** (Pali: *anatta*). According to this revolutionary and unique doctrine, there is no separate, permanent, or immortal self; instead, a human being is an impermanent composite of interdependent physical, emotional, and cognitive components. Insight into *anatman* is spiritually valuable because it reduces attachment to one's mind, body, and selfish desires. Even suffering is useful, because it helps us to see things as they really are. When we realize that everything changes and passes away, moment by moment, we become aware that nothing in this world is permanent and independent. There are only momentary configurations within a continual process of change. Once we have grasped these basic facts of life, we can be free in this life, and free from another rebirth.

The Third Noble Truth is that *dukkha* can cease if desires cease. In this way, illusion ends, insight into the true nature of things dawns, and nirvana is achieved. One lives happily and fully in the present moment, free from self-centeredness and full of compassion for others. One can serve them purely, without thought of oneself. The Fourth Noble Truth is that only by following a path of morality, concentration, and wisdom—the Noble Eightfold Path—can desire and suffering be extinguished.

The Noble Eightfold Path to liberation

The Buddha set forth a systematic approach so that human beings could extricate themselves from suffering and achieve the final goal of liberation. The Noble Eightfold Path offers ways to avoid non-virtuous actions and create merit for a happy life and a favorable rebirth. Perfecting this path means final escape from the cycle of death and rebirth, and obtaining the peace of nirvana.

The first aspect of the Noble Eightfold Path is right understanding—comprehending reality correctly through deep realization of the Four Noble Truths. Initially, this means seeing through illusions, such as a little more wealth bringing happiness. Gradually one learns to question old assumptions in the light of the Four Noble Truths. Everything we do and say is governed by the mind. The Buddha said if our mind is defiled and untrained, suffering will follow us just as a chariot follows a horse. If our mind is purified and well trained, then our actions will be meritorious and we will naturally experience happiness.

The second aspect is right thought or motives. The Buddha encourages us to uncover any "unwholesome" emotional roots behind our thinking, such as a desire to hide our imperfections or avoid contact with others. As we discover and weed out such emotional blocks, our thought becomes free from the limitations of self-centeredness—relaxed, clear, and open.

The third aspect is right speech. The Buddha taught his followers to relinquish the propensity to lie, gossip, speak harshly, or engage in divisive speech, and instead to use communication in the service of truth and harmony. He also advised us to speak to ourselves and others in a positive way: "May you be well and happy today."

The fourth aspect is right action, which begins with observing the five basic precepts for moral conduct: to avoid destroying life, stealing, sexual misconduct, lying, and intoxicants. Beyond these, all actions should be based on clear understanding. "Evil deeds," said the Buddha, are those "done from motives of partiality, enmity, stupidity, and fear."[6]

The fifth is right livelihood—being sure that one's way of making a living does not violate the five precepts. One's trade should not harm others or disrupt social harmony.

Right effort, the sixth aspect, means striving continually to cut off unwholesome states in the past, present, and future. This is not a way for the lazy.

The seventh aspect, right mindfulness, is particularly characteristic of Buddhism, for the way to liberation is said to be through disciplining the mind. The idea is to be aware in every moment. The **Dhammapada** (Sayings of the Dharma), a very early text, includes this pithy injunction:

> *Check your mind.*
> *Be on your guard.*
> *Pull yourself out*
> *as an elephant from mud.*[7]

The eighth aspect, right meditation, applies mental discipline to the quieting of the mind itself. The Buddha explained that the mind is "subtle, invisible, treacherous."[8] Skillful means are therefore needed to understand and control its restless nature. When the mind is completely stilled, it becomes a quiet pool in which the true nature of things is clearly reflected. The various schools of Buddhism that developed over the centuries have taught different techniques of meditation, but this basic principle remains the same.

Try to be mindful, and let things take their natural course. Then your mind will become still in any surroundings, like a clear forest pool. All kinds of wonderful, rare animals will come to drink at the pool, and you will clearly see the nature of all things. You will see many strange and wonderful things come and go, but you will be still. This is the happiness of the Buddha.
*   Achaan Chah, meditation master, Wat Pa Pong, Thailand*[9]

The wheel of birth and death

Buddhist teachings about rebirth are slightly different from those of Hindu orthodoxy, for there is no eternal soul to be reborn. In Buddhism, one phenomenon or event acts as the cause that sets another into motion. The central cause in this process is *karma* (Pali: *kamma*)—our actions of body, speech, and mind. The impressions of our virtuous and non-virtuous actions shape our experience moment-by-moment. When we die, this process continues, passing on the flame to a new life in a realm of existence that reflects our past *karma*.

This wheel of birth and death operates primarily because of the three root afflictions: greed, hate, and delusion. The opposites of these afflictions—nongreed (such as generosity, renunciation for others' sake), non-hate (such as friendliness, compassion, and patience), and non-delusion (such as mental clarity and insight)—act as causes to ultimately leave the circle of birth and death.

In Buddhist thought, not only do sentient beings take birth many times, but they also take on many different forms, creating an interconnected web of life. This has important implications for one's relationships with all life.

In all, there are thirty-one planes of existence. Whether interpreted as psychological metaphors or metaphysical realities, these include hell beings, hungry ghosts (beings tormented with unsatisfied desires), animals, humans, and gods. All these states of rebirth are imperfect and impermanent. Sentient beings circle round and round, life after life, caught in this cycle of *samsara*, repeatedly experiencing aging, decay, suffering, death, and painful states of rebirth, until finally they achieve nirvana, which is beyond cause and effect.

Nirvana

The Buddha said little about nirvana, the goal of Buddhist practice, but described it as a desirable state of mind. The only way to end the cycle of suffering is to end all craving and lead a life free of attachment that has no karmic consequences. One enters a state that the Buddha called "quietude of heart,"[10] "a state beyond grasping, beyond aging and dying,"[11] "the unborn, . . . undying, . . . unsorrowing, . . . stainless, the uttermost security from bonds."[12] For the **arhant** (Pali: *arhat, arahat*), a worthy one, who has found nirvana in this life:

> *No suffering for him*
> *who is free from sorrow*
> *free from the fetters of life*
> *free in everything he does.*
> *He has reached the end of his road. . . .*
>
> *Like a bird invisibly flying in the sky,*
> *he lives without possessions,*
> *knowledge his food, freedom his world,*
> *while others wonder. . . .*
>
> *He has found freedom—*
> *peaceful his thinking, peaceful his speech,*
> *peaceful his deed, tranquil his mind.*[13]

When an *arhant* dies, individuality disappears and the being enters the ultimate state of nirvana. The Buddha remained silent when he was asked what happens to an *arhant* after death. Why? At one point he picked up a handful of leaves from the forest floor and asked his disciples which were more numerous, the leaves in his hand or those in the forest. When they replied, "Very few in your hand, lord; many more in the grove," he said:

> *Exactly. So you see, friends, the things that I know and have not revealed are more*
> *than the truths I know and have revealed. And why have I not revealed them?*
> *Because, friends, there is no profit in them; because they are not helpful to holiness;*
> *because they do not lead from disgust to cessation and peace, because they do not*
> *lead from knowledge to wisdom and nirvana.*[14]

Buddhism spreads abroad

After the Buddha attracted a group of disciples, he began to send them out in all directions to help teach the Dharma. Two hundred years after the Buddha died, a powerful Indian king named Ashoka led a huge military campaign to extend his empire. After he saw the tremendous loss of life on both sides, he reportedly felt great remorse, became a Buddhist, and began to espouse non-violence. He had inscriptions written on rocks and pillars throughout his empire teaching the Dharma, with an emphasis on developing an attitude of social responsibility. Under Ashoka's leadership, Buddhism was disseminated throughout the kingdom and outward to other countries, beginning its development as a global religion. After Ashoka's death, *brahmins* reasserted their political influence and Buddhists were persecuted in some parts of India. By the time of the twelfth-century Muslim invasions of India, Buddhism was in decline and never became the dominant religion in the Buddha's homeland.

As the Buddha's teachings expanded and adapted to local cultures, various schools of interpretation developed. Of the earliest Buddhist schools, only the one today known as **Theravada** ("Way of the Elders") survives. This school is prevalent in Southeast Asian countries such as Sri Lanka, Myanmar (formerly Burma), Thailand, Cambodia, and Laos. The schools that developed somewhat later are collectively known as **Mahayana** ("Great Vehicle"). This school gradually became dominant in Nepal, Tibet, China, Korea, Mongolia, Vietnam, and Japan. Followers of all these traditions are in general agreement about the Four Noble Truths, the Noble Eightfold Path, and the teachings about *karma*, *samsara*, and nirvana.

Theravada: the path of mindfulness

Theravadin Buddhists study the early scriptures in Pali, honor the life of renunciation, and follow mindfulness meditation teachings. These characteristics are more obvious among intellectuals and monastics; ordinary lay people tend to be devotional in their practices.

The Pali Canon   Buddhists who follow the Theravada tradition study a large collection of ancient scriptures preserved in the Pali language of ancient India. This ancient **canon**, or authoritative collection of writings, is called the Pali Canon. This collection is also referred to as the **Tipitaka** (Sanskrit: *Tripitaka*, "Three Baskets," because of the old practice of storing palm-leaf manuscripts in wicker baskets). The "Three Baskets" are three collections of sacred writings: rules of monastic discipline, Dharma teachings, and scholastic treatises. After the Buddha's death, leading members of the community of monks started compiling an authoritative canon of teachings and monastic discipline. According to Buddhist lore, this was done by a council of five hundred elders who had studied directly with the Buddha. Venerable Ananda reportedly recited the Buddha's discourses from memory and another close disciple rehearsed the discipline of the monastic order. Then the elders agreed on a definitive body of the Buddha's teachings, which were recited orally until the first century BCE, when the *sutras* (Pali: *suttas*) were written down. In addition to the Tipitaka, Theravadins accept certain non-canonical Pali works, such as later commentaries.

The Triple Gem   Like Buddhists of all schools, those who follow the Theravada go for refuge in the **Triple Gem**: the Buddha (the Enlightened One), the Dharma (the teachings he gave), and the Sangha (community). To become a Buddhist, a person goes for refuge in these three jewels by reciting the Pali formula: *Buddham* *saranam gacchami* ("I go to the Buddha for refuge"), *dhammam saranam gacchami* ("I go to the Dharma for refuge"), *sangham saranam gacchami* ("I go to the Sangha for refuge"). One takes refuge in the Buddha not by praying to him for help, but by honoring him as a supreme teacher and inspiring model. In a sense, taking refuge in the Buddha is honoring the Buddha-wisdom within each of us.

The Dharma is like a medicine that can cure our suffering, but it will not work unless we take it. In the Pali Canon, it is described as immediate, timeless, leading to calmness, known only through direct experience and personal effort.

The Sangha is ultimately the community of realized beings; on the conventional level, the Sangha is the order of *bhikshus* and *bhikshunis* who have renounced worldly life in order to follow, preserve, and share the Dharma.

The Buddha established one of the world's first monastic orders, and the Sangha remains very strong in Theravada countries. There are presently about half a million Theravadin monks in Southeast Asia. To simplify their worldly lives and devote themselves to studying and teaching the Dharma, monks and nuns shave their heads, dress in simple robes, own only a few basic material items, eat no solid foods after noon, practice celibacy, and depend on the laity for food, clothing, and medical supplies. Early every morning the monks set forth with an alms bowl, and laypeople regard offering food to them as merit-making. The monks reciprocate by offering spiritual guidance, chanted blessings, and performing social services, such as offering advice and education.

Buddhist monasteries are at the center of village life. They are left open, and people come and go throughout the day. The monks hold a revered social position as models of self-control, kindness, and intelligence. In Thailand, it is common for young men to take temporary vows as monks—often for the duration of the rainy season when there is little farmwork. They wear saffron robes, set forth with shaven heads and alms bowls, and receive religious instruction while practicing a life of simplicity.

In contrast to the monks, there has traditionally been little social support for Buddhist nuns in Southeast Asia. Provisions were made during the time of the Buddha for women monastics to live in their own monasteries, practicing the same lifestyle as monks, but the order of fully ordained nuns (*bhikshunis*) disappeared in Theravadin countries about a thousand years ago. Many early Buddhist scriptures are egalitarian toward women's capacity for wisdom and attainment of nirvana, but spiritual power has remained in the hands of monks and there has been little opportunity for nuns to teaching and lead.

Over time, some of the monks and the texts they edited apparently became somewhat sexist. Because the monks are celibate, they are not allowed to come into direct contact with women, and many believe women hinder their spiritual development. Feminist scholars object to this interpretation.

There are now attempts to revive full ordination for nuns in Theravadin countries. A landmark event occurred in 1998, when 135 nuns from many countries received full ordination in Bodh Gaya. According to the code of discipline, ordination of nuns is possible only if a quorum of both ordained monks and nuns is present. The lack of ordained nuns had been used by conservative monks to block women's ordination. But in China, Taiwan, Japan, and Korea, orders of fully ordained nuns have continued, and in Bodh Gaya the requisite number of ten *bhikshus* and ten *bhikshunis was assembled*, and presided over the full ordination of *bhikshunis* from Sri Lanka. The order of nuns had become extinct there almost a thousand years ago.

Meditation   The Theravada tradition tries to preserve what are thought to be the Buddha's original teachings, including a wide variety of meditation techniques. The two major branches of meditation practice are *samatha* (calm) and **vipassana** (insight). One begins the practice by increasing one's attentiveness to a specific object, as a way of calming (*samatha*) and focusing the mind. One then proceeds to the practice of *vipassana* by developing insight into *dukkha, anicca,* and *anatta*.

As taught by the Burmese meditation master Mahasi Sayadaw, the way to begin *vipassana* practice is simply to watch oneself breathing in and out, with attention focused on the rise and fall of the abdomen. To keep the mind concentrated on this movement, rather than being distracted this way and that by unconscious, conditioned responses, one continually makes concise mental notes of what is happening: "rising" and "falling." Inevitably other thoughts and feelings will arise in the restless mind. As they do, one simply notes what they are—"imagining," "wandering," "remembering"—and then returns the attention to the rising and falling of the breath. Bodily sensations will appear, too, and one handles them the same way, noting "itching," "tight," "tired," and so on. Periods of sitting meditation are alternated with periods of walking meditation, in which one notes the exact movements of the body in great detail: "lifting," "moving," and "placing." If ecstatic states or visions arise in the process of meditation, one is told simply to note them and let them pass away without attachment. In the same way, emotions that arise are simply observed, accepted, and allowed to pass away, rather than labeled "good" or "bad." By contrast, says Dharma teacher Joko Beck, we usually get stuck in our emotions:

> *Everyone's fascinated by their emotions because we think that's who we are. We're afraid that if we let our attachment to them go, we'll be nobody. Which of course we are! When you wander into your ideas, your hopes, your dreams, turn back— not just once but ten thousand times if need be, a million times if need be.*[15]

The truths of existence as set forth by the Buddha—*dukkha* (suffering), *anicca* (impermanence), and *anatta* (no eternal self)—will become apparent during this process. As one continues the practice, the mind becomes calm, clear, attentive, and flexible, free from likes and dislikes. This same type of mindfulness can be carried over into every activity of the day.

Devotional practices   In addition to the contemplative and philosophical traditions described above, many lay Buddhists and also many monastic practitioners of Theravada Buddhism in Southeast Asia are likely to turn to the Buddha in devotion, taking refuge in his protective presence and power. Temples, halls, and roadside shrines have been built with images of the Buddha before which people bow, light candles, burn incense, offer flowers, press bits of gold leaf onto Buddha images, and make aspirations and prayers. Some monastics and intellectuals— including Protestant Christians who became interested in Buddhist studies in the late nineteenth century—have labeled such practices antithetical to the spirit of

Buddhism, which they understand as rationalistic, philosophical, non-ritualistic, non-iconic, and nontheistic. Despite the increasing commercialization of Buddhist imagery, some commentators are now trying to trace the history of image-oriented worship. Popular devotional practices are so widespread and so influential in popular Buddhist practice that scholars have begun to examine them as perhaps being part of the mainstream of Buddhism.

A key text in this regard is the *Mahaparinibbana Sutta*, a Pali scripture that describes the Buddha's cremation and the dispersal of his relics. The text also deals with the issue of devotionalism, recounting that, before his death, the Buddha recommended the commemoration of his relics alongside dedicated practice of the Dharma: "Whoever lays wreaths or puts sweet perfumes and colors . . . with a devout heart, will reap benefit and happiness for a long time."[16] Simultaneously, the text advocates devotion to the Dharma as a way of respecting, revering, and paying homage to the Buddha. When lay Buddhists recite the refuge formula, taking refuge in the Buddha, the Dharma, and the Sangha, they may experience this refuge not merely as a philosophical idea, but as a way of connecting with the timeless presence of the Buddha.

In one popular ritual in northern Thailand, a network of threads attached to a large statue of the Buddha is used in special ceremonies to conduct his spiritual power to the Sangha, holy water, amulets, or new images to be consecrated. The 108 squares formed overhead by the strings are believed to form a magical cosmos whose sacred energy touches the earth through cords hanging downward.

Followers may consider the Buddha's power to be present in relics from his cremated body. Images of the Buddha may also be placed in stupas, reliquary mounds reaching toward the sky—a practice perhaps derived from earlier indigenous spiritual traditions. For instance, a tiny bone chip believed to be a relic of the Buddha is enshrined at Doi Suthep Temple in Chiang Mai in Thailand. Flocks of pilgrims climb the 290 steps to the temple and request blessings by acts such as pressing squares of gold leaf onto an image of the Buddha, and lighting three sticks of incense to honor the Triple Gem. So great are the powers associated with relics that huge processions carrying what is thought to be the Buddha's tooth have been used by the governments in Sri Lanka and Myanmar to legitimize their claims to temporal power.

Cherished images of the Buddha proliferate in temples and in roadside shrines that are almost identical to the indigenous spirit shrines. These physical images are a reminder of the Buddha's teachings and give a sense of his protective, guiding presence. In Southeast Asia, aspects of Theravada Buddhism are often adopted by shamans for greater efficacy in healing rituals. In Sri Lanka, the *yakeduras* invoke the power of the Buddha and the Dharma to ward off evil spirits and help cure spiritually afflicted people. In the cosmic hierarchy, the Buddha and Dharma are considered powerful and therefore useful in subduing lesser forces. Even monks are seen as magical protectors of sorts, and followers often request chanted blessings for protection.

As in all Buddhist cultures, Buddhist temples are important centers for community identity and integration. There the monks not only teach the Dharma, but also preside over festivals to improve the harvest, ceremonies to assist the dead to achieve a better rebirth, and ceremonies to invoke the blessings of the deities. All these events generate a festive atmosphere and communal joy.

Mahayana: the path of compassion and wisdom

Additional Buddhist practices and teachings began to appear in a wide range of scriptures from the early centuries CE. These developments beyond the Pali scriptures gradually evolved into what is called Mahayana, the Great Vehicle. The Mahayana scriptures emphasize the practice of compassion and wisdom by both monastics and laypeople, toward the goal of liberating all sentient beings from suffering. Its traditions honor all the teachings set forth in the Pali Canon and, in addition, accept the extensive Mahayana literature originally found in Sanskrit and later translated into Chinese, Tibetan, and other languages. This praises the deeds and qualities of innumerable Buddhas and bodhisattvas, and inspires practitioners to develop the compassion and wisdom needed to become bodhisattvas and eventually Buddhas themselves.

The Mahayana scriptures emphasize the importance of religious experience. The Dharma is not embodied only in scriptures; for the Mahayanist it is the source of a transformative experience that awakens the quest for enlightenment as the greatest value in life and seeks to embody the Dharma in every aspect of life. Each school—and there are many branches within Mahayana—offers a special set of methods, or "skillful means," for awakening. These methods are quite varied, in contrast to the uniformity of Theravada, but the Mahayana traditions also share many common characteristics.

Bodhisattvas   An early Mahayana scripture, the *Lotus Sutra*, defended its innovative ideas by claiming that earlier teachings were skillful means for those with lower capacities. The idea is that the Buddha geared his teaching to his audience, and that his teachings were presented in different ways and at different levels of completeness in accordance with the readiness of his audience to understand them. Some researchers explain this as a way to give credit to the earlier teachings while going beyond them. Like other Mahayana texts, the *Lotus Sutra* claimed there was a higher goal than the *arhant*'s achievement of liberation, namely, to aspire to become a **bodhisattva** (a being who is dedicated to liberating others from suffering) and work to achieve the perfect enlightenment of a Buddha. The *Lotus Sutra* says that all beings have the capacity for Buddhahood and are destined to attain it eventually. Both monastics and laity are urged to take the bodhisattva vow and work to become fully enlightened. Today Mahayana Buddhists in East Asia express this commitment in the Four Great Bodhisattva Vows compiled in China in the sixth century CE by Tiantai Zhiyi, founder of the Tiantai School:

> Beings are infinite in number, I vow to save them all;
> The obstructive passions are endless in number, I vow to end them all;
> The teachings for saving others are countless, I vow to learn them all;
> Buddhahood is the supreme achievement, I vow to attain it.

His Holiness the Fourteenth Dalai Lama, representing the Tibetan tradition, says:

> The motivation to achieve Buddhahood in order to save all sentient beings is really
> a marvelous determination. That person becomes very courageous, warm-hearted,
> and useful in society.[17]

> *You are not just here for yourself alone, but for the sake of all sentient beings. Keep your mind pure, and warm.*
>
> Soen Nakagawa-roshi[18]

The concept of the selfless bodhisattva is not just an ideal for earthly conduct; numerous bodhisattvas are believed to be present and available to hear the followers' petitions. On the path to Buddhahood, bodhisattvas practice the ten perfections (*paramitas*): generosity, ethical conduct, patience, diligence, concentration, wisdom, and so on. As emanations of wisdom and compassion, they are sources of inspiration and blessing.

The most popular bodhisattva in East Asia is Guanyin (Japanese: Kannon), who symbolizes compassion and extends blessings to all. Although this being is depicted as male (Avalokiteshvara) in Indian images, the *Lotus Sutra* says that Guanyin will take any form that is needed to help others, and lists thirty-two examples. In East Asia, Guanyin is typically represented as female, often as the giver or protector of young children. An image of Guanyin holding a baby has become especially popular in East Asia as a source of inspiration and blessing for women and children.

The Three Bodies of Buddha   In Theravada, Buddha is an historical figure who died like any other human being, but who left the Dharma as a guide to liberation from suffering. By contrast, in Mahayana the Buddha came to be regarded as a universal principle. Metaphysically, Buddha is said to be an immanent presence in the universe with three aspects, or "bodies." The first aspect is the enlightened wisdom of a Buddha, which is formless; the second is the body of bliss, or celestial aspect of a Buddha that communicates the Dharma to bodhisattvas; and the third is the body of transformation, by which a Buddha manifests in various forms to help liberate suffering beings. It was in this third body that the Buddha appeared for a time on the earth as the historical figure Shakyamuni Buddha.

In Mahayana, the Buddhas are seen to embody perfect purity, boundless compassion, omniscient wisdom, and many other enlightened qualities. Although some may interpret the Buddhas and bodhisattvas as metaphors for aspects of enlightened awareness, others regard them as living presences that are able to impart blessings and guidance. Both Theravada and Mahayana are nontheistic, in that the existence or non-existence of gods is not a primary concern, yet ordinary people are inclined to seek help in times of need.

Mahayana scriptures portray Buddhas and bodhisattvas moving swiftly through intergalactic space and time, appearing in multiple forms at different world systems simultaneously. In the Tibetan tradition, for example, the Fourteenth Dalai Lama is regarded as a human emanation of Avalokiteshvara, the bodhisattva of compassion. Many Tibetan monks, nuns, and laypeople followed him into exile after the communist takeover of Tibet and have set up a community in the mountains of northern India, in Dharamsala, to be near him. Practitioners are not to be attached to these appearances, but receive teachings and draw great inspiration from them.

Emptiness As in Theravada, the Mahayana schools affirm that there is an ultimate reality, which is the true nature of things. This "suchness" is simply the lack of any essence or permanent, independent reality, however. In accordance with the universal law of cause and effect, all conditioned phenomena arise and perish continuously, and lack true existence. In the Udana scripture from the Pali Canon, the Buddha stated, "O monks, there is an unborn, undying, unchanging, uncreated. If it were not so, there would be no point to life, or to training." But even nirvana, a non-regressive state of liberation from mental afflictions, suffering, and rebirth, is empty in that it lacks true or independent existence.

Sunyata, voidness or emptiness, is one of the most complex and paradoxical of the Mahayana teachings. The concept was elaborated by the Indian philosopher Nagarjuna around the second and third century CE, based on the earlier Perfection of Wisdom scriptures. All compounded things arise and pass away, as a process of events dependent on other events, and have no independent origin and no eternal reality. Thus, the world of phenomena—*samsara*—is empty of inherent existence. Nirvana is also empty in that it is a thought construct, even though it is not dependent on conditions.

In the Perfection of Wisdom scriptures, a student who has received lengthy teachings on *sunyata* is asked whether he understands them. He declares, "In truth, nothing has been taught." Everything being empty, there is nothing to cling to, so one who realizes emptiness is free to experience reality directly and be compassionate without attachment. The concepts of selflessness and emptiness help practitioners understand things "as they are" and help them overcome attachment to things, including attachment to concepts.

The Perfection of Wisdom scriptures that celebrate the liberating experience of emptiness are foundational for most Mahayana schools. What is distinctive and startling about Mahayana is the application of the idea of emptiness to all things, including the teachings of the Buddha. In the *Heart Sutra* that is used liturgically throughout East Asia, the core doctrines of traditional Buddhism are systematically shattered: the bodhisattva Guanyin sees that the five aggregates of a person (form, sensation, perception, karmic formations, and consciousness) are each empty of absolute self-nature; they exist only relative to other aggregates. With this realization, the bodhisattva becomes free of delusion. Next, birth and death, purity and defilement, increase and decrease are seen as empty; the six sense objects, the six sense organs, and the six sense awarenesses are seen as empty; life and death are seen as empty; the Four Noble Truths and Eightfold Path are seen as empty. Even knowledge and attainment are empty. With this "perfection of wisdom," there are no obstacles and no fear. Having seen through the illusion of true existence, even the ultimate existence of the core Buddhist teachings, one attains nirvana. In the *Heart Sutra*, this is epitomized in the mantra: *Gate, Gate, paragate, parasamgate, bodhi, svaha!* ("Gone, gone, gone beyond, gone completely beyond, awakened, so be it!").

Zen: the great way of enlightenment

Buddhism was transmitted from India to China beginning around the first century CE and thence to Korea, Japan, and Vietnam, absorbing elements of Daoism along the way. Around the fifth century, according to tradition, a south Indian monk named Bodhidharma traveled to a monastery in northern China, where he spent nine years in silent meditation, "facing the wall." On this experiential foundation, he became recognized as the first patriarch of the radical path that came to be called Ch'an Buddhism, from the Sanskrit word *dhyana*, meaning meditation. Although this account of its origins and founder is not accepted by scholars as completely factual, it is known that the Ch'an school was transmitted to Japan, where it is known as **Zen**.

Zen claims to preserve the essence of the Buddha's teachings through direct experience, triggered by mind-to-mind transmission of the Dharma. Instead of focusing on scriptures, Buddhas, and bodhisattvas, Zen emphasizes direct insight into the true nature of one's own mind, known as **Buddha-nature**. A central way of direct insight is *zazen* (sitting meditation). "To sit," said the Sixth Zen Patriarch, "means to obtain absolute freedom and not to allow any thought to be caused by external objects. To meditate means to realize the imperturbability of one's original nature."[19]

The Great Way is not difficult
for those who have no preferences.
When love and hate are both absent
everything becomes clear and undisguised.
Make the smallest distinction, however,
and heaven and earth are set infinitely apart.   *Sengtsan*[20]

Instructions in the manner of sitting are quite rigorous: one must maintain an upright posture and not move during the meditation period, to avoid distracting the mind. Skillful means are then applied to make the mind one-pointed and clear. One beginning practice is simply to watch and count each inhalation and exhalation from one to ten, starting over from one if anything other than aware-ness of the breath enters the mind. Although this practice sounds simple, the mind is so restless that many people must work for months before finally getting to ten without having to start over. Getting to ten is not really the goal; the goal is the process itself, the process of recognizing what comes up in the mind and gently letting it go without attachment or preferences.

As one practices *zazen*, undisturbed by phenomena, one becomes inwardly calm and the natural mind is revealed in its original purity. This "original mind" is spacious and free, like an open sky. Thoughts and sensations may float through it like clouds, but they arise and then disappear, leaving no trace. What remains is insight into "thusness," the true nature of things. In some Zen schools, this perception of thusness comes in a sudden burst of insight, or *kensho*.

When the mind is calmed, action becomes spontaneous and natural. Zen prac-titioners are taught to rest in the natural simplicity of their own Buddha-nature. It is said that two Zen monks, on gaining a glimpse of enlightenment, ran naked through the woods scribbling on rocks. On the other hand, the Zen tradition links spontaneity with intense, disciplined concentration. In the art of calligraphy, the perfectly spontaneous brushstroke is executed with the whole body in a single breath, yet this is the outcome of years of attentive practice. Giving ourselves fully to the moment—when pouring tea, being aware only of pouring tea—is a simplicity that most have yet to realize. Then we are fully present in the moment, whether we are painting, serving tea, sweeping, or simply breathing. In such a moment, the "thusness" of life, its unconditioned reality, is revealed.

Another tool, used in the Rinzai Zen tradition, is the **koan**. Attention is focused ardently on a question that boggles the mind, such as "What was your original face before your parents were born?" As Roshi Philip Kapleau observes, "*Koans* deliberately throw sand into the eyes of the intellect to force us to open our Mind's eye and see the world and everything in it undistorted by our concepts and judgments." To concentrate on a *koan*, one must look closely at it without thinking about it, experiencing it directly. Beyond abstractions, Roshi Kapleau explains, "The import of every *koan* is the same: that the world is one interdependent Whole and that each separate one of us is that Whole."[21]

The aim of Zen practice is enlightenment, often experienced as a flash of insight known as *satori*. One directly experiences the interrelatedness of all existence, often in a sudden recognition that nothing is separate from oneself. As one Zen master put it:

> The moon's the same old moon,
> The flowers exactly as they were,
> Yet I've become the thingness
> Of all the things I see![22]

All aspects of life become, at the same time, utterly precious and utterly empty, "nothing special." This paradox cannot be grasped intellectually; it can only be realized through direct intuitive awareness.

Pure Land: devotion to Amitabha Buddha

Zen is a practice of inner awareness with great attention given to every action and this requires years of disciplined meditation. Other forms of Buddhist practice that developed in India and East Asia had greater popular appeal. The most widespread Buddhist school in East Asia is known as **Pure Land** Buddhism. At times of great social upheaval (for instance, when the government became corrupt and society was falling apart), it was widely thought that people had become so degenerate that it was nearly impossible for them to attain enlightenment through their own efforts.

Instead, many became devoted to Amitabha Buddha, the Buddha of Boundless Light. Amitabha (who became known as **Amida** in Japan) was believed to have been an ancient prince who vowed to attain enlightenment. After he did, he used his pure virtue to prepare a special Pure Land of Bliss for all who called his name. In Japan, the original abstract Indian Buddhist concept of a Pure Land far to the west to which devotees return after death was transformed into concrete images. The Japanese had an ancient tradition of worshiping mountains as the realm to which the dead ascend and from which deities descend to earth. They began to depict Amida Buddha riding on clouds billowing over the mountains, coming to welcome his dying devotees.

Many people contributed to the growth of Pure Land Buddhism into a mass movement. In Japan, the thirteenth-century religious leader Shinran broke with monastic tradition by marrying and emphasized the principle that salvation comes through repeating the name of Amida Buddha with sincere trust, not by separating oneself from society. The Jodo Shinshu school developed by Shinran's followers became a major Buddhist movement throughout the world. The monk Genshin described the ineffable pleasures of being reborn into the Pure Land upon death:

> *Rings, bracelets, a crown of jewels, and other ornaments in countless profusion adorn his body. And when he looks upon the light radiating from the Buddha, he obtains pure vision, and because of his experiences in former lives, he hears the sounds of all things. And no matter what color he may see or what sound he may hear, it is a thing of marvel.*[23]

Many believers interpret these passages literally, anticipating that if they have sufficient faith in the saving power of Amitabha, they will enjoy a beautiful life after death. But some understand the Pure Land as a state that can be achieved in this life—a metaphor for the experience of enlightenment in everyday life, in which one's former identity "dies" and one is reborn into an expanded state of consciousness. Some modern thinkers have emphasized creating a Pure Land in the human realm, making their goal transformation of this world by purifying it of social evils such as oppression, pollution, and sexism.

Nichiren: salvation through the Lotus Sutra

While some Pure Land Buddhists despair of purifying themselves by their own efforts and therefore humbly beseech the grace of Amida Buddha, other Buddhists stress the importance of striving to reform not only ourselves but also society. One example was a thirteenth-century Japanese fisherman's son who named himself Nichiren. For Nichiren, the highest truths of Buddhism were embodied in the *Lotus Sutra*, a large compilation of parables, verses, and descriptions of innumerable beings who support the teachings of the Buddha. Nichiren gave particular attention to two of these beings: the Bodhisattva of Superb Action, who staunchly devotes himself to spreading the Perfect Truth, and the Bodhisattva Ever-Abused, who is persecuted because of his insistence on revering everyone with unshaken conviction that each person is potentially a Buddha. Nichiren himself was repeatedly abused by the authorities, but persisted in his efforts to reform Buddhism in Japan and spread what he considered its purified essence, the bodhisattva ideal, to the world. The phrase chanted by Nichiren and his followers, *"Namu myoho rengekyo,"* pays homage to the *Lotus Sutra*. Today it is chanted by Nichiren monks, nuns, and laypeople by the hour. The chant is thought to slowly reveal the profound meaning of the *Lotus Sutra* as it works inwardly, beyond thought. In our time, some Nichiren followers undertake long peace walks. In one peace effort sponsored by Nipponzan Myohoji in 1995, people walked from Auschwitz in Poland to Hiroshima and Nagasaki in Japan, to commemorate the fiftieth anniversary of the end of World War II, making a plea for non-violence and respect for all of life. They beat hand drums while chanting *"Namu myoho rengekyo,"* and bowed to the Buddha in each person they met, whether or not they were friendly, as a contribution to world peace. The founder of Nipponzan Myohoji, the Most Venerable Nichidatsu Fujii, strongly influenced Gandhi's doctrine of non-violence. Before he passed away in 1985 at the age of a hundred, he explained:

We do not believe that people are good because we see that they are good, but by believing that people are good we eliminate our own fear and thus we can intimately associate with them. To believe in the compassionate power of the Supreme Being which we cannot see is a discipline in order to believe in the invisible good in others.[24]

Civilization has nothing to do with having electric lights, airplanes, or manufacturing atomic bombs. It has nothing to do with killing human beings, destroying things or waging war. Civilization is to hold one another in mutual affection and respect.[25]

The chanting of *"Namu myoho rengekyo"* has led to more than seventy Peace Pagodas, in many countries, built with donated materials and labor, by people of all faiths who pray for world peace and the elimination of all weapons.

Soka Gakkai International is another important offshoot of Nichiren's movement, which is based in Japan but has millions of members around the world. Its founders call for a peaceful world revolution through transformation of individual consciousness. They combine the central practice of chanting *"Nam myoho rengekyo"* with modern social activism in areas such as humanitarian relief, environmental awareness, human rights, literacy, and cultural and interfaith exchanges. Members are encouraged to develop their "unlimited potential" for hope, courage, and altruism.

Another new branch of Buddhism inspired by the *Lotus Sutra* is Rissho Kosei-kai, founded in the 1930s by Rev. Nikkyo Niwano and Myoko Naganuma to bring the message of the *Lotus Sutra* to the world in practical ways in order to encourage happiness and peace. Members meet to discuss ways of applying the Buddha's teachings to specific problems in their own lives. The organization, which is active in international inter-religious activities, asserts that "The Eternal Buddha, invisible but present everywhere, is the great life-force of the universe, which sustains each of us."[26]

The Bodhisattva loves all living beings as if each were his only child.

Vimalakirtinirdesha Sutra

Vajrayana: the indestructible path

Of the many branches of Mahayana Buddhism, perhaps the most elaborate is **Vajrayana**. It developed in India, was transmitted to Tibet, and has been practiced in Nepal, Bhutan, Sikkim, and Mongolia. Currently it is practiced throughout the Tibetan diaspora and increasingly in North America and Europe.

Prior to the introduction of Buddhism from India, the mountainous Tibetan region was home to a shamanic religion called Bön. In the seventh century CE a Tibetan king named Songtsan became interested in Buddhism and sent a group of students to India to study it. The journey from Tibet to India was difficult and many students died in the searing heat of the Indian plains. Only one member of a second group survived the arduous trip across the Himalayas, returning with many Sanskrit texts. After some of these works were translated into Tibetan,

Songtsan declared Buddhism the national religion and encouraged Buddhist virtues in his subjects. Bön proponents are said to have sabotaged the new religion, until finally a tantric adept, Padmasambhava, was invited to Tibet in the eighth century CE. Eventually, it is said, he subdued and converted the local Bön deities and, along with his consort Yeshe Tsogyal, established the tantric Buddhist teachings in Tibet. Although the Tibetans' understanding of Buddhism was no doubt influenced by earlier beliefs, and elements such as the use of prayer flags and an emphasis on practices for the dying may reflect Bön concerns, the Tibetans spent many centuries attempting to understand the Indian Buddhist teachings as purely as possible.

After a decline in the tenth century, when some misinterpreted the tantric teachings, a teacher named Atisha was invited from the center of Buddhist learning at Nalanda, India, to set things right. Under Atisha, Tibetan Buddhism became a complex path with three stages, said to have been prescribed by the Buddha. The first is quieting the mind and relinquishing attachments through meditation practice, as emphasized in the early Buddhist teachings. The second is intensive training in compassion and wisdom, as emphasized in the Mahayana teachings. The third is the advanced esoteric path called Vajrayana ("the diamond vehicle") or Tantrayana, a rigorous path to nurture enlightenment within a single lifetime that developed in India.

Vajrayana aspirants are guided through a series of tantric practices by qualified teachers, or **lamas**. Some of these teachers are recognized as incarnate bodhisattvas and carefully trained from a young age to help others advance toward enlightenment.

> The masses have their heads on backwards. If you want to get things right, first look at how they think and behave, and consider going the opposite way.
> Lama Drom Tonpa, 11th century[27]

Vajrayana initiates practice **deity yoga**: meditating on themselves in the form of a Buddha or bodhisattva in order to embody the enlightened qualities that the practitioner wishes to manifest. These radiant forms are themselves imagined and therefore lacking true existence, but meditating on them is considered a way to understand one's own true nature. Some of these meditational deities are shown in wrathful form, such as Mahakala, defender of Dharma, while others, such as Amitabha, are shown in peaceful form.

The highest Vajrayana practices use the subtle vital energies of the body to transform the mind. A subtle and profound state of consciousness is produced after lengthy practice; when the "gross mind" is neutralized, the "subtle mind" manifests powerfully as "the clear light of bliss." This innermost subtle mind of clear light is the true empty quality of one's own mind. Once it is realized, one is said to be capable of attaining Buddhahood in a single lifetime.

The practices used to transform the mind may also enable supernormal powers such as levitation, clairvoyance, and warming the body from within while sitting naked in the snow. Milarepa, the famous Tibetan poet-saint, whose enlightenment was won through great austerities, once sang this song:

> Blissful within, I don't entertain
> The notion "I'm suffering,"
> When incessant rain is pouring outside.
>
> Even on peaks of white snow mountains
> Amidst swirling snow and sleet
> Driven by new year's wintry winds
> This cotton robe burns like fire.[28]

The communist Chinese overran Tibet between 1950 and 1959, destroying countless ancient monasteries and scriptures and killing an estimated one-sixth of the population over decades of occupation. The beloved Fourteenth Dalai Lama, spiritual and political leader of Tibet, escaped to India in 1959. The town of Dharamsala in the mountains of northern India where he established his head-quarters has become a magnet for spiritual seekers. Despite persecution, religious practice and meaning still pervade every aspect of Tibetan life, from house-raising to ardent pilgrimages. Monks and laypeople alike meditate on **thangkas** and **mandalas**, visual aids to concentration and illumination, which portray Buddhas and bodhisattvas in a diagram representing an ideal universe. A favorite practice is the chanting of mantras, especially the mantra of the bodhisattva of compassion, Avalokiteshvara: *Om mani padme hum*. These syllables evoke an awareness of the treasure of compassion for all living beings that lies within the heart of each of us. To help manifest this compassion, mantras are repeatedly recited, written out thousands of times, spun in prayer wheels, and printed on prayer flags so that the repetition of the mantra continues as they blow in the wind.

Festivals

Since Buddhism has evolved into different forms in different countries, most of its festivals are not uniformly celebrated. The typical ways that laypeople observe them are to go in the morning to their temple or monastery, make offerings of food to the monks, renew their commitment to the Five Precepts, and listen to a talk about the Dharma. They may then offer food to the poor. In a gesture of respect for the Triple Gem—the Buddha, Dharma, and Sangha—they may circum-ambulate a stupa three times. In the evening, there may be chanted recitations of the Buddha's teachings and meditation practice.

The most important Buddhist festival is *Vesak*, which according to Theravadins marks the Buddha's birth, enlightenment, and death, all of which were said to have miraculously occurred on the same day. For Mahayana Buddhists, *Vesak* marks the day of the Buddha's enlightenment. Vajrayana Buddhists celebrate four distinct days commemorating the Buddha's conception, birth, enlighten-ment, and death. The Buddha is said to have been born on the full moon of the month *Vaisakha*, which falls in April and May. In general, devout Buddhists gather at temples or monasteries before dawn to hear stories about the Buddha's life, to wash images of him, to make offerings of flowers, candles, and incense, and carefully to observe the Five Precepts, including refraining from any kind of killing.

On the full moon day of the third lunar month, *Magha* (approximately March), some Buddhists celebrate Magha Puja Day, also known as "Sangha Day."

His Holiness the Dalai Lama

Surely one of the best-known and most-loved spiritual leaders in the world, His Holiness the Fourteenth Dalai Lama is a striking example of Buddhist peace and compassion. Wherever he goes, he greets everyone with evident delight. His example is all the more powerful because he is the leader in exile of Tibet, a small nation which knew extreme oppression and suffering during the twentieth century.

The simplicity of His Holiness's words and bearing belie his intellectual power. His Holiness was a peasant child just two years old in 1937 when he was located and carefully identified as the reincarnation of the Thirteenth Dalai Lama. He was formally installed as the Fourteenth Dalai Lama when he was only four and a half years old, thus becoming the spiritual and temporal ruler of Tibet. He was raised and rigorously educated in the Potala in Lhasa. One of the world's largest buildings, it then contained huge ceremonial halls, thirty-five chapels, meditation cells, government storehouses, national treasures, all records of Tibetan history and culture in seven thousand volumes, plus thousands of illuminated volumes of the Buddhist scriptures.

A rigorous grounding in religion, maintains the Dalai Lama, brings steadiness of mind in the face of any misfortunes. He says:

> Humanitarianism and true love for all beings can only stem from an awareness of the content of religion. By whatever name religion may be known, its understanding and practice are the essence of a peaceful mind and therefore of a peaceful world.[29]

The Dalai Lama's equanimity of mind was seriously challenged by the Chinese invasion and oppression of his small country. In 1959, when he escaped from Tibet to lessen the potential for bloodshed during a widespread popular revolt against the Chinese, Tibet was home to more than six thousand monasteries. Only twelve of them were still intact by 1980. It is said that at least one million Tibetans died as a direct result of the Chinese occupation, and the violence against the religion, culture, and people of Tibet continues today as Chinese settlers fill the country.

In the face of the overwhelming military power of the Chinese, and armed with Buddhist precepts, the Dalai Lama has tried to steer his people away from violent response to violence. He explains:

> The best way to solve problems is through human understanding, mutual respect. On one side make some concessions; on the other side take serious consideration about the problem. There may not be complete satisfaction, but something happens. At least future danger is avoided. Non-violence is very safe.[30]

While slowly, patiently trying to influence world opinion so that the voice of Tibet will not be extinguished by Chinese might, the Dalai Lama has established an entire government in exile in Dharamsala, India, in the Himalayas. In his effort to keep the voice of Tibet alive. In the process, he has emerged as a great moral leader in the world. His quintessentially Buddhist message to people of all religions is that only through kindness and compassion toward each other and the cultivation of inner peace shall we all survive.

It commemorates a major event early in the Buddha's teachings when, after giving the sermon to his first disciples at the Deer Park in Sarnath, he went to Rajagaha city to address 1,250 *arhants* who came to pay their respects and listen to his teachings. They were all ordained by the Buddha.

Many other days are celebrated on local and national levels, such as the Festival of the Tooth in Sri Lanka honoring the Buddha's tooth relic, which is normally hidden within a series of caskets in a special temple but is on this day paraded through the streets on the back of a richly decorated elephant. In Thailand, there is a special Festival of Floating Bowls on the full moon night of the twelfth lunar month. Bowls made of leaves and flowers with candles and incense sticks are floated upon the water of rivers and canals. As people let them go, they feel that their bad luck is also floating away.

Buddhism in the West

Images of the Buddha are now enshrined around the world, for the path that began in India has gradually spread to the West as well as throughout Asia. An important phase of this transmission was in the twentieth century, when North American and European countries became vibrant centers of Buddhism. Scholars are studying Buddhist traditions and many people are learning Buddhist meditation practices. The exodus of over 100,000 people from Tibet since 1959, including many high lamas, has led to the establishment of Tibetan Buddhist centers in many Western countries as well as in Southeast Asia and India, the Dalai Lama's home in exile. Several hundred thousand Westerners have some spiritual involvement with Tibetan Buddhism.

Over four hundred Zen meditation centers are flourishing in North America alone and there are many Zen monasteries that give training in *zazen* and offer a monastic lifestyle as a permanent or temporary alternative to the stress and confusion of modern life.

Intensive *vipassana* meditation retreats lasting up to three months are held in Theravadin centers such as the Insight Meditation Society in rural Barre, Massachusetts. Theravadin teachers from Southeast Asia and Europe make frequent visits to conduct retreats, and American teachers who have undertaken rigorous training in Southeast Asia under traditional meditation masters are also emerging as respected teachers. An American monk named Venerable Sumedho, trained in traditional Theravada Buddhism in Thailand, has established monastic forest communities and meditation centers in England, Switzerland, Italy, and the United States. In contrast to the low profile of Buddhist women in Asia, many Buddhist centers in the West are led by women, who are explaining traditional Buddhist teachings to Westerners in fresh, contemporary ways. Some are exemplars of dedicated spiritual practice, such as Tenzin Palmo, a British woman who became a Tibetan Buddhist nun and lived alone for twelve years in a cave located 13,200 feet (4,000 m.) high in the Himalayas.

The Vietnamese monk Venerable Master Thich Nhat Hanh now lives in exile in southern France, conducting retreats for both women and men in a community called Plum Village. When he travels internationally, large audiences gather and derive inspiration from his teachings. He speaks simply, using familiar examples, and emphasizes bringing the awareness fostered by meditation into everyday life, rather than making spirituality a separate compartment of one's life. He says:

> *When we walk in the meditation hall, we make careful steps, very slowly. But when we go to the airport, we are quite another person. We walk very differently, less mindfully. How can we practice at the airport and in the market.*[31]

Buddhism is often embraced by people in the West because of their longing for peace of mind in the midst of a chaotic materialistic life.

Many psychotherapists are studying Buddhism for its insights into the mind and human suffering. For instance, Richard Clarke, who is both a Zen teacher and a psychotherapist, feels that a discipline such as Zen should be part of the training of counselors and therapists.

Are Westerners able to achieve enlightenment by taking Buddhist workshops here and there? Particularly in the case of Tibetan Buddhist practices, Westerners often want to be initiated into the most highly advanced teachings without taking time for years of patient practice and being inwardly transformed by the step-by-step foundational teachings. Can teachings developed within a specific cultural context be directly transplanted into the soil of an entirely different culture? Most Westerners who are adopting Buddhist practices are living in highly materialistic cultures with different priorities and values, rather than in traditional Buddhist cultures or monastic settings. In their impatience to get results, many shop around from one teacher to the next and experiment with one practice after the next, rather than persisting over a long time in one path.

Another crucial issue is how to train teachers for the West. Two large Tibetan Buddhist organizations from the Gelukpa order have opened nearly six hundred centers for study and meditation around the world but do not have enough fully trained lamas to staff all these centers. Traditional training takes up to twenty-five years of rigorous study and debate of the finer points of Buddhist philosophy, logic, meditation, cosmology, psychology, and monastic life. Close guidance by an advanced teacher has traditionally been considered essential, but this is not possible for all the Western aspirants, given the shortage of qualified teachers and the language problems entailed.

Given the differences in culture, background, and motivation, are Western students and their teachers creating new forms of Buddhism adapted to Western ways? How authentic are these new forms? Some observers feel Western Buddhism is closer to what they construe as the core of early Buddhism than are later developments in the East, with an emphasis on inner practice rather than outer forms. Western Buddhists tend to be oriented to achieving enlightenment by their own efforts, which is reportedly what the Buddha prescribed, and are searching for ways to achieve this. Whether or not Western Buddhism conforms to early patterns, it seems to be evolving in new directions, with some Westerners remaking it in their own image. For instance, in *Buddhism Without Beliefs* the American Buddhist Stephen Bachelor emphasizes a secularized version of Buddhism, stripped of belief in rebirth and karma. An important difference between Western Buddhism and historical developments in Asia is the Western tendency to support equal participation of women, as renunciates, teachers, and lay practitioners. In recent years, Buddhists in Asia, confronted by modernization, consumerism, globalization, and new social attitudes, are taking directions similar to those of Western Buddhists.

Since 1987, Buddhist women from Asia and the West have joined hands and begun holding international gatherings to enhance the role of women in Buddhism. The international Association of Buddhist Women, Sakyadhita or "Daughters of the Buddha," is working to improve conditions for women's Buddhist practice and education, full ordination of women, and training of women as teachers of Buddhism.

Socially engaged Buddhism

An emerging focus in contemporary Buddhist practice is the relevance of Buddhism to social problems. Contrary to popular assumptions, the Buddha did not advise people to permanently leave society to seek their own enlightenment. Sri Lankan Buddhist monk Walpola Rahula explains:

> It may perhaps be useful in some cases for a person to live in retirement for a time in order to improve his or her mind and character, as preliminary moral, spiritual, and intellectual training, to be strong enough to come out later and help others. But if someone lives an entire life in solitude, thinking only of their own happiness and salvation, without caring for their fellow beings, this surely is not in keeping with the Buddha's teaching which is based on love, compassion, and service to others.[32]

Buddhism has always been engaged with the wider society and political life. In Thailand, for instance, the king is the bearer of the Buddhist heritage, and thus has sacred legitimization. But Thailand also has a tradition of socially-conscious lay practice of Buddhism. The renowned Thai monk Buddhadasa Bhikkhu (1906–1993) was a great critic of capitalism, teaching that it increases egoism and selfishness, causing distress both to the individual and to society.

In Vietnam, Thich Nhat Hanh and other socially active Buddhists refused to take sides with either North Vietnam or South Vietnam during the Vietnam War, for they felt both were oppressing the common people and exploiting American soldiers. They worked hard to bring a negotiated end to the war, and helped the suffering people as best they could by evacuating villagers, helping to rebuild damaged buildings, taking care of orphans, and providing medical care to people from all sides. They believed that all life is precious and interdependent—violence and suffering affect everyone—and meditated to generate selfless compassion, according to the teachings of the Buddha, who said:

> Hatred is never appeased by hatred. It is appeased by love. This is an eternal law. Just as a mother would protect her only child, even at the risk of her own life, even so let one cultivate a boundless heart towards all beings. Let one's thoughts of boundless love pervade the whole world.[33]

However, Buddhism's link with politics has not always been entirely altruistic. In Sri Lanka, a selective interpretation of Theravada Buddhist tradition has been used to bolster nationalistic sentiments among the Sinhalese Buddhist majority against the Tamil (mostly Hindu and Muslim) minority. As in many contemporary fundamentalist movements elsewhere, a chauvinistic, rigid version of religious identity developed in response to rapid colonization, modernization, and Westernization. The reaffirmation of Buddhist identity became a tool of ethnic oppression of the minority, leading to a violent separatist movement among the Tamils and decades of civil strife.

In general, however, the Buddha's emphasis on compassion has prevailed, and even as social activists, Buddhists have tended to be guided by Buddhist principles of non-violence, compassion, and social justice. In this posture, some contemporary Buddhists have tried to correct injustice, oppression, famine, cruelty to animals, nuclear testing, warfare, and environmental devastation. E. F. Schumacher preached what he called "Buddhist economics," to affirm human beings' willingness to live simply, generously, and humanely with each other. Ajahn Pongsak, a Thai Buddhist monk, was so troubled by the devastation of the northern Thai forests that he rallied 5,000 villagers to reforest an area by building a tree nursery. He taught them the importance of a respectful relationship with the forest as their own home, their own parent. He says:

> A mind that feels no gratitude to the forest is a coarse mind indeed—without this basic siladhamma [dharma], how can a mind attain enlightenment? . . . The times are dark and siladhamma is asleep, so it is now the duty of monks to reawaken and bring back siladhamma. Only in this way can society be saved.

Cambodians are recovering from decades during which the Khmer Rouge murdered over one million people. Buddhists have played major roles in peacemaking and rebuilding the country. The monks of Buddhism for Development, for instance, have gone to the villages and cities to carry out community development projects. The most instrumental figure has been Venerable Maha Ghosananda (1929–2007), whose entire family was killed during the Pol Pot regime. In addition to political initiatives, he led many peace marches of monks, nuns, and laypeople through areas infested with land mines, and counseled people facing issues such as domestic violence, HIV/AIDS, deforestation, and dire poverty.

Another notable example of using Buddhist teachings as an antidote to violence is Daw Aung San Suu Kyi, leader of the National League for Democracy in Burma (Myanmar). Living by Buddhist principles to counteract fear and cope with government oppression, she has been an outspoken advocate of democratic social change.

Buddhism was returned to its native India after some one thousand years' absence by the bold action of a converted Buddhist activist, Dr. B. R. Ambedkar (1891–1956). Born an untouchable Hindu, he was the chief architect of India's new democratic constitution, and built into it many provisions to end the oppression of the traditional Hindu caste system. When he publicly converted to Buddhism shortly before his death, he inspired almost half a million untouchables to do likewise. Despite this, he openly questioned and changed certain Buddhist teachings. Among them was the emphasis on renunciation and meditation rather than social engagement.

In the midst of the civil strife between the Sinhalese Buddhist majority and the Hindu and Muslim Tamil minority in Sri Lanka, the Buddhist monks of the Sarvodaya Shramadana Sangamaya movement have tried to promote harmony and rural development. The founder, a Buddhist schoolteacher named Dr. A. T. Ariyaratne, asserts that renunciation is not the best path for most people. They can

An Interview with Karma Lekshe Tsomo

Karma Lekshe Tsomo is an American from Hawai'i who has become a very active Tibetan Buddhist nun. Her story illustrates the unusual pathways by which many Westerners come to adopt Buddhism. Lekshe explains, "I was very much attracted to the teachings of Jesus as a child, but there were a lot of unanswered questions for me, especially about the meaning of life and what happens to us after we die.

"When I was about twelve, I read some books on Buddhism. At once I thought, 'Wow, home free!' When I was nineteen, I went to Japan, Thailand, India, and Nepal. On the way I had a really clear and beautiful dream that I was a nun.

"It wasn't until I arrived at the Tibetan Library in Dharamsala that I got a real systematic education. As I burst into the classroom for the first time, there on a cushion was a little lama with a yellow pointed hat, and he was explaining, 'At the second stage after death you will see a faint smoke.' I thought, 'Bingo! This is it!' So I sat at his feet for six years.

"The more I studied Buddhism and the more I practiced, the more I wanted to dedicate my whole life to it. In 1977 I met Gyalwa Karmapa and six months later I told him I wanted to be ordained.

"Life in India was tremendously difficult. The Himalayas were icy cold in the winter. No indoor plumbing. I was living in a mud hut at seven to eight thousand feet. Plus I was so poor. I had no support as a nun. The Tibetans were refugees and were already having enough trouble taking care of their own community. Things got really difficult. I would go to the *pujas* [devotional ceremonies], get the *prasad* [offerings], and live on that.

The fourth year, an American woman invited me to take lunch with her family for two rupees a day, so I got some sort of a balanced meal once a day. Otherwise, it was very tough.

"Despite so many challenges, I knew without question that the best place to study Buddhism was right there. Not only were the teachers some of the greatest scholars the Tibetan tradition has ever produced, but also because study was combined with practice—meditation practices. The tenor of the teachings was to transform the mind. I thought, 'I may not know the inner workings of Buddhist philosophy, but I think I am becoming a better person.'

"We began to notice that conditions for Buddhist women to practice were not the same as for men. Conditions and facilities for education for nuns were lagging way behind. Fortunately, since Buddhism is a rather logical and sensible path, once you question people about whether women have equal capacity for enlightenment and liberation, they have to admit that they do, because the Buddha himself said so. Sometimes, however, social reality doesn't match theory. I work with Sakyadhita International Association of Buddhist Women trying to gain equal opportunities for women to study, equal facilities for meditation practice, and also opportunities for women to become ordained if they so wish. It seems that once women get an opportunity for education, they express a deep concern for the needs of others in their communities. There are 300 million Buddhist women out there. They are a tremendous resource for peace, goodwill, and energy to work for the benefit of humanity."

best realize their spiritual potential in the midst of society, working for its better-ment. He and the monks of the Sarvodaya movement have engaged people of all religions in thousands of villages in work camps where they come together to eliminate social decadence and poverty by developing schools, nutrition programs, roads, and irrigation canals and to learn to live by the Four Noble Truths and the Eightfold Path.

Sulak Sivaraksa, founder of the International Network of Engaged Buddhists, explains that socially engaged Buddhism does not mean promoting Buddhism per se:

> The presence of Buddhism in society does not mean having a lot of schools, hospitals, cultural institutions, or political parties run by Buddhists. It means that the schools, hospitals, cultural institutions, and political parties are permeated with and administered with humanism, love, tolerance, and enlightenment, characteristics which Buddhism attributes to an opening up, development, and formation of human nature. This is the true spirit of nonviolence.[34]

Even when one intends to be non-violent in one's approach to life, difficult ethical questions may arise. For example, scholars of Buddhist medical ethics are trying to determine how best to apply Buddhist principles to issues such as abor-tion, reproductive technologies, genetic engineering, organ transplants, suicide, coma patients, and euthanasia. Although the issues seem modern, some were addressed during the time of the Buddha, according to the scriptures. Euthanasia, for instance, is the subject of a number of stories. The general principle seems to be to avoid taking human life, even when the person requests help in dying. However, careful reading of the texts seems to allow a dying person to refuse life-extending technology, for death is one of the realities of life that must be faced.

Buddhism is thus as relevant today, and its insights as necessary, as in the sixth century, when the one who became Shakyamuni Buddha renounced a life of ease to save all sentient beings from suffering.

Review questions

1. Tell the story of the Buddha's enlightenment. Examine the Four Noble Truths, the Eightfold Path, the Middle Way, and freedom from delusions.
2. Describe the main similarities and the important differences of the Theravada, Mahayana, and Vajrayana traditions. Describe their geographical development and name and quote a main text in each tradition.
3. Explain the trends in Buddhism today. Explore meditation, women, and social engagement.

Discussion questions

1. What are the major similarities and differences between Hinduism and Buddhism? Why do you think these developed?
2. What reality do Buddhists refer to as most important? What is it named? How is it different from theism? Is this difference important?
3. Do you think there is a proper role for Buddhism in Western society?

CHAPTER 5

DAOISM AND CONFUCIANISM

The unity of opposites

While India was giving birth to Hinduism, Jainism, and Buddhism, three other major religions were developing in East Asia. Daoism and Confucianism grew largely in China, from similar roots but with different emphases, and spread to Japan and Korea; Shinto (see Chapter 6) is considered distinctively Japanese. All three are associated primarily with their homelands. Buddhism spread to East Asia, and its practice has often been mixed with the native traditions.

In East Asia, religions are subtly blended and practiced, and although Daoism and Confucianism may seem quite opposite to each other, they co-exist as complementary value systems in East Asian societies.

In this chapter Chinese words are transliterated according to the Pinyin system, which has replaced the Wade-Giles system. Thus "Daoism" is the Pinyin transliteration; "Taoism" was the Wade-Giles transcription of the same word. When terms are first used, the Wade-Giles equivalent is given in parenthesis.

Ancient traditions

Chinese civilization is old and continuous. By 2000 BCE, people were living in settled agrarian villages in the Yellow River Valley, with a written language, musical instruments, and skillful work in bronze, silk, ceramics, and ivory. Their spiritual ways permeate all religious developments in China, Korea, and Japan. A major feature is the veneration of ancestors, whose spirits remain closely bonded to their living descendants for some time. Respect must be paid to them—especially the family's founding ancestor and those recently deceased—through funerals, mourning rites, and sacrifices. The rituals, *li,* are essential; ancestors will help their descendants, if treated with proper respect, or cause trouble if ignored.

Kings, even those of the earliest Chinese dynasty, sought their ancestors' help through the medium of oracle bones—shells or bones onto which the diviner scratched the questions the king wanted the ancestors to answer. When touched with a hot poker the bones cracked, forming patterns, which the diviner interpreted as answers from the ancestors. Later, demons and ghosts who had been ignored or ill-treated during their lifetime were seen as causing so much mischief that efforts were made to thwart them, including gongs and firecrackers, appeals through mediums, spirit-walls to keep them from entering doorways, exorcisms, prayers, incense, and fasts. These activities continue today.

To the early Chinese and in continuing popular belief, the world is full of invisible spirits. In addition to ancestors, there are deified humans who have died but are still available to help the people.

The world is also full of nature spirits. Plants, animals, rivers, stones, mountains and stars are vitalized by cosmic energy and often personified and honored as deities. From early times, Chinese people made offerings to these beings and sought their aid with personal problems, sometimes through a shaman who can communicate with the spirit world.

According to a belief that can be traced back at least to the earliest historical dynasty, the Shang (c. 1751–1123 BCE), there is also a great being referred to as *Shangdi* (**Shang Ti**), the Lord-on-High, ruler of the universe, the supreme ancestor of the Chinese. Deities governing aspects of the cosmos and the local environment are subordinate to him. This deity is conceived of as being masculine and closely involved in human affairs, though not as a Creator God.

During the Zhou (Chou) dynasty (c. 1122–221 BCE), the focus shifted to Heaven (*Tian*) as an impersonal power controlling the universe. The emperors of the ruling dynasty developed the idea of the of Heaven" to justify their rule. The Mandate is the self-existing moral law of virtue, the supreme reality. Rulers have a moral duty to maintain the welfare of the people and a spiritual duty to conduct ceremonies for the highest heavenly beings.

There has long existed in China a belief that the cosmos is a manifestation of an impersonal self-generating energy called *qi* (*ch'i*). This has two aspects whose interplay causes the ever-changing phenomena of the universe. **Yin** is dark, receptive, and "female"; **yang** is bright, assertive, and "male". Wisdom lies in recognizing and moving with their ever-shifting, but regular and balanced, patterns. This creative rhythm of the universe is the **Dao** (**Tao**), or "way." As traditionally diagramed, yin and yang interpenetrate each other (represented by the small circles). As soon as one aspect reaches its fullest point, it begins to diminish, while at its polar opposite increases. Nothing is outside this process.

Many forms of divination were devised to harmonize with the cosmic process. One system developed during the Zhou dynasty was eventually written down as the *Yijing* (*I Ching*), or *Book of Changes, and* is regarded as a classic text in both Daoism and Confucianism. From the Han dynasty (206 BCE–220 CE), the *Yijing* was highly elaborated with commentaries by scholars. To use it, one purifies the divining objects—such as yarrow stalks or coins, symbolizing yin and yang—asks a question, casts the objects six times, then consults the *Yijing* for symbolic interpretation of the yin–yang combinations.

The pattern of throws is diagramed in the *Yijing* as a hexagram, with yin represented as a broken line and yang by a straight line. For example, hexagram number 46, called Sheng or "Pushing Upward," has been likened to a tree emerging from the earth, growing slowly and invisibly:

Thus the superior person of devoted character
Heaps up small things
In order to achieve something high and great.[1]

Another set of commentaries is based on the two trigrams within the hexagram. In the case of hexagram 46, the upper pattern of three yin lines can be interpreted as devotion and yielding, and the lower pattern of two yang lines above one yin line suggests gentleness. According to the commentaries, these non-aggressive qualities will ultimately lead to supreme success.

By studying and systematizing the ways of humans and nature, the ancient Chinese tried to order their actions in order to steer a coherent course within the changing cosmos. They recognized that any extreme action will produce its opposite as a balancing reaction and strived for a middle way of discretion and moderation. From these roots gradually developed two contrasting ways of harmonizing with the cosmos—the more mystically religious ways, which are collectively called Daoism, and the more political and moral ways, which are known as Confucianism. Like yin and yang, they interpenetrate and complement each other, and are themselves evolving dynamically.

Daoism—the way of nature and immortality

Daoism is as full of paradoxes as the Buddhist tradition it influenced: Chan or Zen Buddhism. It has been adored by Westerners who seek a carefree, natural way of life as an escape from the industrial rat race. Yet beneath its precepts of the simple life in harmony with nature is a tradition of great mental and physical discipline. As it has developed over time, Daoism includes efforts to align oneself with the unnamable original force (the Dao), ceremonial worship of deities from the Jade Emperor to the Kitchen God, and cultivation of physical and spiritual strength. Some Daoist scriptures counsel indifference about birth and death; others teach ways of attaining physical immortality. These variations developed within an ancient tradition that had no name until it had to distinguish itself from Confucianism. "Daoism" is actually a label invented by scholars and awkwardly stretched to cover a philosophical or "literati" tradition, a multitude of self-cultivation and longevity techniques, and an assortment of religious sects which probably developed at least in part from the early philosophical texts and practices. Religious Daoism itself is often an amalgam, with the Daoist way of natural life and meditation as its base, plus Confucian virtues, health disciplines, rituals and theology inspired by Buddhism, and immortality as its final goal.

Teachings of Daoist sages

The specific origin of Daoist philosophy and practices is unclear. In China, tradition attributes the publicizing of these ways to the Yellow Emperor, who supposedly ruled from 2697 to 2597 BCE. He was said to have studied with an ancient sage and to have developed meditation, health, and military practices based on what he learned. After ruling for one hundred years, he ascended to heaven on a dragon's back and became one of the Immortals.

The philosophical or **literati** form of Daoism has been pursued by intellectuals and artists over the millennia, who explore the concepts about the Dao expressed in ancient texts and perhaps also try to apply them to their social and political environment in the effort to create a condition of harmony known as the Great Peace. The two most salient texts of the Daoist literati tradition are the *Dao de jing* and the *Zhuangzi*. The *Dao de jing* (*Taote Ching*, "The Classic of the Way and its Power") is second only to the Bible in the number of Western translations, for its ideas are not only fascinating but also elusive for translators. According to tradition, the book was written by Laozi (Lao-tzu), a curator of the royal library of the Zhou dynasty, for a border guard as he left society for the mountains at the reported age of 160. The guard recognized Laozi as a sage and begged him to leave behind a record of his wisdom. Laozi reportedly complied by inscribing the 5,000 words now known as the *Dao de jing*. This is traditionally said to have happened during the sixth century BCE, with Laozi purportedly fifty-three years older than Confucius. But archaeological finds date the earliest existent version of the *Dao de jing* to 350 BCE and suggest it was an alternative to Confucianism. Some think the *Dao de jing* was an oral tradition, derived from the teachings of several sages, and question whether Laozi ever existed.

The book's central philosophy is a practical concern with improving harmony in life. It says that one can best harmonize with the natural flow of life by being receptive and quiet. These teachings were elaborated more emphatically and humorously by a sage named Zhuangzi (Chuang-tzu) (c. 365–290 BCE). He, too, was a minor government official for a while but left political involvement for a hermit's life of freedom and solitude. Unlike Laozi, whose philosophy was addressed to those in leadership positions, Zhuangzi asserted that the best way to live in a chaotic, absurd civilization is to become detached from it.

At the heart of Daoist teachings is the idea of Dao, the "unnamable," the "eternally real."[2] Contemporary Master Da Liu asserts that Dao is so ingrained in Chinese understanding that it is a basic concept that cannot be defined, like "goodness." Moreover, Dao is a mystical reality that cannot be grasped by the mind. The *Dao de jing* says:

> *The Dao that can be told of*
> *   Is not the Absolute Dao,*
> *The Names that can be given*
> *   Are not Absolute Names.*
> *The Nameless is the origin of Heaven and Earth;*
> *The Named is the Mother of All Things . . .*
> *These two (the Secret and its manifestations)*
> *   Are (in their nature) the same; . . .*
> *They may both be called the Cosmic Mystery:*
> *Reaching from the Mystery into the Deeper Mystery*
> *Is the Gate to the Secret of All Life.*[3]

Chapter 25 of the *Dao de jing* is more explicit about the mysterious Unnamable:

> *There is a thing confusedly formed,*
> *Born before heaven and earth.*
> *Silent and void*
> *It stands alone and does not change,*
> *Goes round and does not weary.*

It is capable of being the mother of the world.
I know not its name
So I style it "the way."
I give it the makeshift name of "the great."[4]

Although we cannot describe the Dao, we can live in harmony with it. Ideally, says Laozi:

Humans model themselves on earth,
Earth on heaven,
Heaven on the way,
And the way on that which is naturally so.[5]

There are several basic principles for the life in harmony with Dao. One is to experience the transcendent unity of all things, rather than separation. This realization can only be attained when one ceases to feel any personal preferences. Daoism is concerned with direct experience of the universe, accepting and cooperating with things as they are, not with setting standards of morality, not with labeling things as "good" or "bad." Zhuangzi asserts that herein lies true spirituality:

Such a man can ride the clouds and mist, mount the sun and moon, and wander beyond the four seas. Life and death do not affect him. How much less will he be concerned with good and evil![6]

The Daoist sage takes a low profile in the world. He or she is like a valley, allowing everything needed to flow into his or her life, or like a stream. Flowing water is a Daoist model for being. It bypasses and gently wears away obstacles rather than fruitlessly attacking them, effortlessly nourishes the "ten thousand things" of material life, works without struggling, leaves all accomplishments behind without possessing them. Laozi observes:

Water is the softest thing on earth,
Yet its silken gentleness
Will easily wear away the hardest stone.

Everyone knows this;
Few use it in their daily lives.
Those of Tao yield and overcome.[7]

This is the uniquely Daoist paradox of **wu wei**—"actionless action," or taking no intentional or invasive action contrary to the natural flow of things. *Wu wei* is spontaneous, creative activity proceeding from the Dao, action without ego-assertion, letting the Dao take its course. Zhuangzi uses the analogy of a butcher whose knife stays sharp because he lets his hand be guided by the carcass, finding the spaces between the bones where the blade will glide through. Even when difficulties arise, the sage does not take unnecessary action.

> Sweet music and highly seasoned food
> Entertain for a while,
> But the clear, tasteless water from the well
> Gives life and energy without exhaustion.
>
> *Laozi[8]*

The result of *wu wei* is non-interference. Much of Laozi's teaching is directed at rulers, that they might guide society without interfering with its natural course. Nothing is evil, but things may be out of balance. The world is naturally in harmony; Dao is our original nature. But according to tradition, the Golden Age of Dao declined as humans departed from the "Way." "Civilization," with its intellectual attempts to improve on things and rigid views of morality leads to world chaos. How much better, Laozi advises, to accept not-knowing, moving freely in the moment with the changing universe.

Then again, Daoism places great value on withdrawal to a contemplative life and love of nature. The latter is greatly aided by **feng shui** (geomancy). By observing the contours of the land and the flows of wind and water, specialists in *feng shui* can reportedly determine the best places for the harmonious placement of a temple, dwelling place, or grave.

The literati Daoist seeks to find the still center, save energy for those times when action is needed, and take a humble, quiet approach to life.

The ethical effects of such a philosophy are designed to harmonize humanity with the cosmos. Heaven, earth, and humanity arise from the same source, the Dao, first cause of the cosmos. For this reason, all things on earth are to be loved and allowed to exist and develop according to their nature. As the sage Ge Hong (283–343 CE) writes in the *Inner Chapters of the Master who Embraces Simplicity*, "Universal Dao acts on non-interference [*wu wei*], that is, lets everything be natural, no matter what relationship among them and how different they are." The Daoist feels "I am one with all things."

Only Dao is to be pursued, rather than material gain or fame. Laozi says, "The five colors blind the eye. The five tones deafen the ear. The five flavors dull the taste. Racing and hunting madden the mind. Precious things lead one astray."[9] By contrast, he says, "I have three treasures which I hold and keep. The first is mercy; the second is economy; the third is daring not to be ahead of others."[10]

Furthermore, there should not be a great gap between the rich and the poor. Just as Heaven makes adjustments between surpluses and deficiencies, the rich should desire to share with the poor. But as Laozi observes:

> The human way is just not so.
> It reduces those who are deficient,
> To offer those who have surpluses.
> Who can offer his surpluses to the world?
> Only a person of Dao.[11]

Organized and folk Daoism

Since the second century CE, Daoist-organized groups or sects have employed practices such as alchemy, faith-healing, sorcery, and the use of talismans, and have converted these into institutionalized and distinctive social movements with detailed rituals, clergy, and revealed texts. Since antiquity people have burnt incense and made offerings in order to communicate with the invisible spirits involved in their destinies. In temple worship, these practices are institutionalized, with detailed ritual instructions and a priesthood. However, folk practices may transcend the restrictions, including making offerings of non-vegetarian foods. Liu Zhongyu, of a branch of the Dragon Gate sect of the Complete Perfection lineage in Hong Kong, pragmatically explains, "In fact, it is forbidden in Daoism to give things such as pig's heads as offerings. But as the people have long been doing so, Daoism has to let things take their own course."[12]

One of the most familiar spirits, the Kitchen God, is usually worshiped at family level, although he was at one time listed in official Daoist spirit pedigrees as the Great Emperor and Controller of Destinies of the Eastern Kitchen. According to folk belief, he sits in the kitchen watching the family so that he can report their virtues and failings to the Jade Emperor each year. Sometimes, humorous ruses are used to insure that he does not give a bad report. One is to make an offering before he sets off for Heaven that is so intoxicating that he forgets about the family's flaws. Another is to offer him sweet maltose that is so sticky that he cannot open his mouth to speak when he meets the Jade Emperor.

People vow to do a good deed if a prayer request is granted. Accordingly, they may offer incense, candles, or food to the spirits to redeem the vow once they feel the spirits have blessed them with success. Sometimes the vow-redeeming promises are more elaborate, such as releasing a captive animal, or sculpting a statue of a deity. Many people vow to do a performance to please the deities, often including singing, dancing, music, or beating drums.

As in ancient times, Chinese villages make collective offerings to local spirits or organize processions inviting them to visit their region, bless them, and protect them from harm. Talismans are made for protection, with the written characters presumed to have magical power to control the spirits.

The ancient practice of worshiping certain people as divine, appointed to heavenly office after they died, is encompassed by organized Daoism. For example, a virtuous daughter of the Lin family saved members of her own family and others in distress during the Song dynasty, and now she is worshiped as Tian ho (Tien-hou), the Holy Mother in Heaven, especially in coastal regions.

The institutionalization of ancient practices, with community priests serving as ritual specialists, developed as the Han dynasty (206 BCE–220 CE) was declining amidst famine and war; its eventual fall was presaged in 184 CE, when followers of a leader known as a faith healer and advocate of egalitarian ideas rebelled in eight of China's twelve provinces. Simultaneously, in western China, Zhang Daoling (Chang Tao-ling) had a vision in which he was appointed representative of the Dao on earth and given the title Celestial Master. He advocated similar practices of healing by faith and developed a quasi-military organization of religious officials, attracting numerous followers. The older Han religion had involved demons and exorcism, belief in an afterlife, and a god of destinies. These roles were now ascribed to a pantheon of celestial deities, who were controlled by the new Celestial Master priesthood led by Zhang's family. This hereditary clergy performed imperial investitures as well as village festivals. After the sack of the northern capitals early in the fourth century, the Celestial Masters and other aristocrats fled south and established themselves in southeast China. Today the Celestial Masters tradition is thriving in Taiwan and Hong Kong, but is also being revived in mainland China.

In approximately 365 CE another aristocratic family in exile in southern China began receiving revelations from a deceased member, Lady Wei. These revelations of the names and powers of newly discovered deities, meditation methods, alchemy, and rituals were recorded in exquisite calligraphy and transmitted to a few advanced disciples. This elite group of celibates called their practices "Highest Purity Daoism." They looked down on the Celestial Master tradition as crude, and avoided village rituals and commoners. Instead, they focused on meditations for purifying the body with divine energies so as "to rise up to heaven in broad daylight." Although the Highest Purity Daoism did not reach the mass of the people, its texts and influence continue to be revered today as the elite tradition of Daoism.

In the late fourth century, another group arose in the wake of Highest Purity. The Numinous Treasure school assimilated many elements of Buddhism, creating a medley of new meditation practices, divine beings, rituals, scriptures, heavens, rebirth, and hells. This was succeeded in the twelfth century by Complete Perfection, which has been the dominant monastic school ever since. It unites Daoist inner alchemy with Chan Buddhist meditation and Confucian social morality. Actively monastic, it focuses on meditation and non-attachment to the world. Its major center is the White Cloud Monastery in Beijing, headquarters of the government-approved Chinese Daoism Association. It is also the foundation for most Hong Kong Daoist temples and martial arts groups.

The many revealed scriptures of Daoist movements were occasionally compiled and canonized by the court. The present Daoist canon was compiled in 1445 CE. Containing about 1,500 scriptures, it has only recently begun to be studied by non-Daoist scholars. It includes a wealth of firsthand accounts by mystical practitioners—poems of visionary shamanistic journeys, advanced meditation practices, descriptions of the perfected human being, methods for ascending to heavenly realms and achieving immortality, and descriptions of the Immortals and the heavenly bureaucracies.

At death Daoist or Buddhist priests may be hired by families to perform rituals to help the deceased appear before the Ten Hell Judges, and join in the rituals of grave-cleaning in April and the liberation and feeding of hungry ghosts in August. Every temple has a shrine to Tudi gong (T'u-ti Kung), Lord of the Earth, who can transport offerings to deceased loved ones.

Longevity and immortality

A third way of practicing Daoism revolves around individual spiritual practices for the sake of self-cultivation, longevity, and perhaps immortality. Daoist texts refer to powerful ascetic practices traditionally passed down secretly from teacher to pupil. These teachers lived in the mountains; great Daoist teachers are said to be still hidden in the remote mountains of China and Korea.

The aim of the longevity practices is to use the body's energy to become strong and healthy, and to intuitively perceive the order of the universe. Within our body is the spiritual micro-universe of the "three treasures" needed for the preservation of life: generative force (*jing*), vital lifeforce (*qi*), and spirit (*shen*). These are said to be activated by breathing techniques, vocalizations, vegetarian diets, gymnastics, absorbing solar and lunar energies, sexual techniques, visualizations, and meditations.

The process of "inner alchemy" begins with the practitioner building a reservoir of *jing* energy in the "cauldron" several inches below the navel, whence it rises up the spine as a vapor, transmuted into *qi* energy. *Qi* is in turn transmuted into *shen* in an upper cauldron in the head, drops down to illuminate the heart center, and then descends to an inner area of the lower cauldron. There it forms what is called the Immortal Fetus, which adepts can reportedly raise through the Heavenly Gate at the top of the head and thus leave their physical body for various purposes, including preparation for life after death. In addition, the adept learns to draw the *qi* of heaven and earth into the micro-universe of the body, unifying and harmonizing inner and outer.

> *The secret of the magic of life consists in using action in order to attain non-action.*
> *The Secret of the Golden Flower*[13]

In contrast to physical practices to lengthen life and lead to immortality, Zhuangzi had counseled indifference to birth and death: "The Master came because it was time. He left because he followed the natural flow. Be content with the moment, and be willing to follow the flow."[14] Laozi referred enigmatically to immortality or long life realized through spiritual death of the individual self, the body and mind transmuted into selfless vehicles for the eternal. As Professor Huai-Chin Han notes, people who are interested in Daoist practices:

> *usually forget the highest principles, or the basis of philosophical theory behind the cultivation of Tao [Dao] and the opening of the ch'i [qi] routes for longevity. . . . Longevity consists of maintaining one's health, slowing down the ageing process, living without illness and pain, and dying peacefully without bothering other people. Immortality does not mean indefinite physical longevity; it indicates the eternal spiritual life.*[15]

A quiet contemplative life in natural surroundings, with peaceful mind, health-maintaining herbs, healthy diet, practices to strengthen the inner organs and open the meridians (subtle energy pathways known to Chinese doctors), and meditations to transmute vital into spiritual energy, brings a marked tendency to longevity. Chinese literature and folk knowledge contain many references to sages thought to be centuries old. They live hidden in the mountains, and are said to be somewhat translucent. The most famous of the legendary long-lived are the Eight Immortals, humans who were said to have gained immortality, each with his or her own special magical power.

One of the most revered celestial beings has always been the Queen Mother of the West. She guards the elixir of life and is the most wondrous incarnation of yin energy. The Daoist canon also includes the writings of female Daoist sages who undertook the rigors of Daoist meditation practices and reportedly mastered its processes of inner transformation. In her mystical poetry, the twelfth-century female sage Sun Bu-er describes the ultimate realization:

All things finished.
You sit still in a little niche.
The light body rides on violet energy,
The tranquil nature washes in a pure pond.
Original energy is unified, yin and yang are one;
The spirit is the same as the universe.[16]

Daoism today

Historically, whenever the central Chinese government has been strong, it has tended to demand total allegiance to itself as a divine authority and to challenge or suppress competing religious groups. The emperors of ancient China either claimed divine origin or referred to themselves as the Sons of Heaven appointed from on high. Confucian scholars were suppressed and their books burned by the Qin (Ch'in) dynasty (221–206 BCE), shamans were forbidden during the Han dynasty, Buddhists were persecuted during the Tang dynasty, the Taiping rebellion of the nineteenth century attempted to purge China of Daoism and Buddhism, and during the Cultural Revolution of 1966 to 1976, zealous Red Guards destroyed Daoist, Buddhist, and Confucian temples and books. However, during the economic liberalization of the late twentieth century in mainland China, in spite of an atheistic communist ideology, temples were maintained as historic sites, pilgrimages to temples in natural sites and religious tourism were encouraged, and an explosion of temple building occurred.

All forms of Daoist practice are still actively undertaken today, in communist mainland China, Taiwan, Hong Kong, and Chinese communities overseas. Chinese temples combine Confucian, Buddhist, and Daoist elements, but the liturgies tend to be Daoist.

Both Daoist and Buddhist groups continue to be recipients of new revelations and scriptures. These texts, known as "precious scrolls," emanate from deities such as the Golden Mother of the Celestial Pool. It is believed that in the past the Divine Mother sent Buddha and Laozi as her messengers but that now the crisis of the present world requires her direct intervention.

Starting in the 1980s, a few ancient Daoist practitioners in China tried to teach student groups so that the disciplines could be transmitted. They met with many bureaucratic obstacles within communist China but received support from Chinese communities and scholars abroad. The Communist Party is still officially anti-religious, but there is a great resurgence of religious practice, in the country-side and in the cities. After the violent attempts of the Cultural Revolution to stamp out religion, shrines and halls for worshiping clan ancestors are sprouting and new Daoist and Buddhist temples, Muslim mosques, and Christian churches are being built. Party policy seems to be turning toward the pragmatic view that religious and cultural traditions can perhaps play a "positive role" in building social stability in the midst of rapid social and economic change. Religious organizations must register with the government and operate under its control. There are also hundreds of local Daoist associations in the provinces of China.

Hong Kong, which has inherited Chinese traditions, has long been home to many Daoist temples and activities. The Peng Ying Xian Guan (Fung Ying Seen Koon) branch of Complete Perfection Daoism began early in the twentieth century as an attempt by two Dragon Gate priests to develop a secluded holy place for self-cultivation, as a cure for decaying social morality. Many pilgrims came to their Quiet Chamber for Cultivating the Dao, and then to more and more buildings encouraging a variety of Daoist practices. Now the organization sponsors a free clinic, a school, lectures for teaching the Dao, training classes for priests and study of rites and scriptures, and rituals to pray for blessings and redeem lost souls.

To unite Daoists and promote social welfare, the Hong Kong Taoist Association is developing schools to combine education with Daoist enlightenment and character-building, giving lectures encouraging morality, building and repairing Daoist temples, and organizing festivals observed by all Daoist temples. Similar associations exist in Taiwan, Malaysia, and Singapore.

Academic study of Daoism is intensifying with the help of Daoist religious organizations, university scholars, social science research institutes, and cultural and artistic institutions. The activities of the Chinese government's Center for Religious Studies include a major project to republish the entire Daoist canon with extensive explanatory material from current research.

Interest in Daoist practices and philosophy has boomed in the West from the middle of the twentieth century. The many masters and centers in the United States include organized religious institutions, societies for self-cultivation, and practitioners of techniques for spiritual development, health, and longevity. Many people outside China are benefiting from acupuncture therapy, which uses traditional spiritual knowledge of the subtle energy meridians that run through the organs and spine for medicinal purposes. Traditional Chinese herbal medicine is also of increasing interest, as are energy training practices. Of these, **Taiji quan** (T'ai chi ch'uan) was developed in the eighteenth century as a training for martial arts, and is practiced today by many Chinese at dawn and dusk for their health. It looks like slow swimming in the air, with continual circular movement through a series of dance-like postures. They are considered manifestations of the unobstructed flow of *qi* through the body. According to the *Taiji Quan Classics*, "In any action the entire body should be light and agile and all of its parts connected like pearls on a thread."[17] Taiji quan is often physically beneficial in controlling blood pressure, muscular coordination, and balance.

In the early twentieth century, a weakly tuberculosis patient cured himself by practicing the energy training disciplines from an old Daoist inner alchemical text describing traditional meditation and longevity techniques. He learned to detect the inner movements of *qi* within himself and wrote about them in contemporary biomedical terms. Others also became interested in the traditional health exercises. The self-cultivation systems are now generally known as **Qigong** (Ch'i-kung) and are widely used not only in China but also in the West to cure diseases, increase physical vitality, and improve concentration. Some people today claim that the combination of meditation methods, breath control, martial arts, and diet are even helpful in thwarting the ravages of AIDS.

The most famous of these claims have been made by Li Hongzhi, who in 1992 developed a form of Qigong that mixed Buddhism with Daoist energy practices, producing a hybrid known as **Falun Gong** or **Falun Dafa**. He proposed that he would spiritually install a "falun" or Dharma Wheel in followers' abdomens so that they could perform advanced energy practices. His system also differs from other forms of Qigong in that it emphasizes ethics—the development of three cardinal virtues: truthfulness, benevolence, and forbearance. Li, who moved to the United States, claims that practitioners of Falun Dafa can attain excellent health, supernatural power, and cosmic enlightenment if they develop the cardinal virtues as well as carrying on the daily exercises. These are taught for free by volunteers at thousands of locations around the world. Falun Dafa now claims millions of followers. But in China, the movement has been severely repressed since 1999 because the government fears that it may gain political power. Practitioners of Falun Dafa have been imprisoned and tortured to discourage others from joining the movement, which the government portrays as an evil cult using the pretence of religion to practice political and criminal activities. The government has even cracked down on other forms of Qigong which it once supported, and legislation has been passed that may be used to suppress any mystical Chinese group and any other religious group that has not been sanctioned by the Chinese Communist Party.

Nonetheless, there is general government support for resurgent Daoism and interest in Daoism is running high in many other countries, replete with numerous websites, international Daoist organizations, and international scholarly conferences. In the Western popularization of Daoism, classic Daoist texts are even being used by businesses to teach management practices.

Confucianism—the practice of virtue

To trace a different strand of Eastern religion, we return to the sixth century BCE, a period of great spiritual and intellectual flourishing in many cultures. It roughly coincided with the life of the Buddha, the Persian Empire, the Golden Age of Athens, the great Hebrew prophets, and in China with the life of another outstanding figure. Westerners call him Confucius and his teaching Confucianism. His family name was Kong; the Chinese honored him as Kong fuzi (Master Kong) and called his teaching **Jujiao** (the teaching of the scholars). It did not begin with Confucius. Rather, it is based on the ancient Chinese beliefs in the Lord on High, the Mandate of Heaven, ancestor worship, spirits, and the efficacy of rituals. Confucius developed from these roots a school of thought that emphasizes the cultivation of moral virtues and the interaction between human rulers and Heaven, with political involvement as the way to transforming the world. This philosophy became highly influential in China and still permeates the society, despite great political changes. It exists not only as a school of thought but also as the practice of religious ethics, as a political ideology, and as the link between the state and the Mandate of Heaven.

For two thousand years, Daoism, Buddhism, and Confucianism have co-existed in China, contributing mutually to the culture. Both Daoism and Buddhism emphasize the ever-changing nature of things in the cosmos, whereas Confucianism focuses on ways of developing a just and orderly society.

Individuals often harmonize the apparently opposite characteristics of Daoism and Confucianism in their own lives. Professor Yu Yingshi explains that Daoism and Confucianism can co-exist because in Chinese tradition there are no major divisions between mind and matter, utopian ideals and everyday life:

For Chinese, the transcendental world, the world of the spirit, interpenetrates with the everyday world though it is not considered identical to it. If we use the tao to represent the transcendental world and the Confucian ideal of human relationships to represent the human world, we can see how they interface. The tao creates the character of these human relations. For these relations to exist as such, they must follow the tao, they cannot depart from the tao for a moment. These two worlds operate on the cusp of interpenetration, neither dependent on nor independent of the other. So mundane human relationships are, from the very beginning, endowed with a transcendental character.[18]

Master Kong's life

Confucius was born in approximately 551 BCE, during the Zhou dynasty, into a family whose ancestors had been prominent in the previous dynasty. They had lost their position through political struggles, and his father, a soldier, died when the boy was only three years old. Although the young boy was determined to be a scholar, the family's financial straits necessitated his taking such humble work as overseeing granaries and livestock. He married at the age of nineteen and had at least two children. His mother died when he was twenty-three, and during three years of mourning he lived ascetically and studied ancient ceremonial rites (*li*) and imperial institutions. When he returned to social interaction, he gained some renown as a teacher of *li* and of the arts of governing.

It was a period of political chaos, with the stability of the early Zhou dynasty giving way to disorder. As central power weakened, feudal lords held more power than kings of the central court, ministers assassinated their rulers, and sons killed their fathers. Confucius felt that a return to classical rites and standards of virtue was the only way out of the chaos, and he unsuccessfully sought rulers who would adopt his ideas. He then turned to a different approach: training young men to be wise and altruistic public servants. He proposed that the rulers should perform classical rites and music properly so that they would remain of visibly high moral character and thus inspire the common people to be virtuous. He thus instructed his students in the "Six Classics" of China's cultural heritage: the *Yijing*, poetry, history, rituals, music and dance, and the Spring and Autumn Annals of events in his state, Lu. According to tradition, it was Confucius who edited older documents pertaining to these six areas and put them into the form now known as the Confucian Classics. There are now only five; the treatises on music were either destroyed or never existed. Of his role, Confucius claimed only: "I am a transmitter and not a creator. I believe in and have a passion for the ancients."[19]

Confucius's work and teachings were considered relatively insignificant during his lifetime. After his death in 479 BCE, interstate warfare increased, ancient family loyalties were replaced by large and impersonal armies, and personal virtues were replaced by laws and state control. After the brutal reunification of China by the Qin and Han dynasties, however, rulership required more cultured bureaucrats who could embody the virtues advocated by Confucius. In the second century BCE the Confucian Classics thus became the basis of the civil service examinations for the scholar-officials who were to serve in the government. The life of the gentleman-scholar devoted to proper government became the highest professed ideal. Eventually temples were devoted to the worship of Confucius as the model for unselfish public service, human kindness, and scholarship. However, the official state use of the Confucian Classics can be seen as a political device to give the government a veneer of civility.

The Confucian virtues

Foremost among the virtues that Confucius felt could save society was **ren** (**jen**). Translations of this central term include innate goodness, love, benevolence, perfect virtue, humaneness, and human-heartedness. In Chapter IV of *The Analects*, Confucius describes the rare person who is utterly devoted to *ren* as one who is not motivated by personal profit but by what is moral, is concerned with self-improvement rather than public recognition, is ever mindful of parents, speaks cautiously but acts quickly, and regards human nature as basically good.

The prime exemplar of *ren* should be the ruler. Rulers were required to rule not by physical force but by the example of personal virtue:

> *Confucius said: If a ruler himself is upright, all will go well without orders. But if he himself is not upright, even though he gives orders they will not be obeyed. . . . One who governs by virtue is comparable to the polar star, which remains in its place while all the stars turn towards it.* "[20]

Asked to define the essentials of strong government, Confucius listed adequate troops, adequate food, and the people's trust. But of these, the only true necessity is that the people have faith in their rulers. To earn this faith, the ruling class should "cultivate themselves," leading lives of virtue and decorum. They should continually adhere to *ren*, always reaching upward, cherishing what is right, rather than reaching downward for material gain.

The modern Chinese character for *ren* is a combination of "two" and "person," conveying the idea of relationship. Those relationships emphasized by Confucians are the interactions between parent and child, older and younger siblings, husband and wife, older and younger friend, ruler and subject. In these relationships, the first is considered superior to the second. Each relationship is nonetheless based on distinct but mutual obligations and responsibilities. This web of human relationships supports the individual like a series of concentric circles.

At the top, the ruler models himself on Heaven, serving as a parent to the people and linking them to the larger cosmic order through ritual ceremonies. Confucius says that this was the source of the greatness of Yao—a sage king of c. 2357 BCE: "It is Heaven that is great and Yao who modeled himself upon it."[21]

In Confucius's ideal world, there is a reciprocal hierarchy in which each knows his place and respects those above him. As the *Great Learning* states it, peace begins with the moral cultivation of the individual and order in the family. This peace extends outward to society, government, and the universe itself like circular ripples in a pond.

The heart of moral rectification is filial piety to parents. In Confucian doctrine, there are three grades of filial piety: the lowest is to support one's parents, the second is not to bring humiliation to one's parents and ancestors, and the highest is to glorify them. In the ancient *Book of Rites*, as revived by Confucius, deference to one's parents is scrupulously defined. For instance, a husband and wife should go to visit their parents and parents-in-law, whereupon:

On getting to where they are, with bated breath and gentle voice, they should ask if their clothes are (too) warm or (too) cold, whether they are ill or pained, or uncomfortable in any part; and if they be so, they should proceed reverently to stroke and scratch the place. They should in the same way, going before or following after, help and support their parents in quitting or entering (the apartment). In bringing in the basin for them to wash, the younger will carry the stand and the elder the water; they will beg to be allowed to pour out the water, and when the washing is concluded, they will hand the towel. They will ask whether they want anything, and then respectfully bring it. All this they will do with an appearance of pleasure to make their parents feel at ease.[22]

Confucius supported the ancient Chinese custom of ancestor veneration, as an extension of filial piety—indeed, as the highest achievement of filial piety.

Confucius said relatively little about the supernatural, preferring to focus on the here-and-now: "While you are not able to serve men, how can you serve the ghosts and spirits?"[23] He made a virtue of *li* (the rites honoring ancestors and deities), suggesting that one make the sacrifices with the feeling that the spirits were present. According to some interpreters, he encouraged the rites as a way of establishing earthly harmony through reverent, ethical behavior. The rites should not be empty gestures; he recommended that they be outwardly simple and inwardly grounded in *ren*.

Although Confucius did not speak much about an unseen Reality, he asserted that *li* are the earthly expressions of the natural cosmic order. *Li* involves right conduct in terms of the five basic relationships essential for a stable society: kindness in the parent and filial piety in the child; gentility in the older brother and respect in the younger; affectionate behavior in the husband and sincerity in the wife; humane consideration in the older friend and deference in the younger friend; and benevolence in rulers and loyalty in subjects.

Everything should be done with a sense of propriety. Continually eulogizing the typical gentleman of China's ancient high civilization as the model, Confucius used examples such as the way of passing someone in mourning. Even if the mourner were a close friend, the gentleman would assume a solemn expression and "lean forward with his hands on the crossbar of his carriage to show respect; he would act in a similar manner towards a person carrying official documents."[24] Even in humble surroundings, the proprieties should be observed: "Even when a meal consisted only of coarse rice and vegetable broth, [the gentleman] invariably made an offering from them and invariably did so solemnly."[25]

Divergent followers of Confucius

The Confucian tradition has been added to by many later commentators. Two of the most significant were Mengzi (Mencius) and Xunzi (Hsun Tzu).

A little over a hundred years after Confucius died, the "Second Sage" Mengzi (commonly latinized as Mencius) was born. During his lifetime (c. 390–305 BCE) Chinese society became even more chaotic. Like his predecessor, the Second Sage tried to share his wisdom with embattled rulers, but to no avail. He, too, took up teaching, based on stabilizing aspects of the earlier feudal system.

Mengzi's major additions to the Confucian tradition were his belief in the goodness of human nature and his focus on the virtue of *yi*, or righteous conduct. Mengzi emphasized the moral duty of rulers to govern by the principle of humanity and the good of the people. If rulers are guided by profit motives, this self-centered motivation will be reflected in all subordinates and social chaos will ensue. On the other hand, "When a commiserating government is conducted from a commiserating heart, one can rule the whole empire as if one were turning it in one's palm."[26] This is a natural way, says Mengzi, for people are naturally good: "The tendency of human nature to do good is like that of water to flow downward."[27] Heaven could be counted on to empower the righteous.

Another follower quite disagreed with this assessment. This was Xunzi, who seems to have been born when Mengzi was an old man. Xunzi argued that human nature is naturally self-centered and that Heaven is impersonal, operating according to natural laws rather than intervening on the side of good government or responding to human wishes ("Heaven does not suspend the winter because men dislike cold"[28]). Humans must hold up their own end. Their natural tendency, however, is to envy, to compete, and to desire personal gain and sensual pleasure. The only way to constrain these tendencies is to teach and legally enforce the rules of *li* and *yi*. Though naturally flawed, humans can gradually attain sagehood by persistent study, patience, and good works and thereby form a cooperative triad with Heaven and earth.

Xunzi's careful reasoning provided a basis for the new legalistic structure of government. The idealism of Mengzi was revived much later as a Chinese response to Buddhism and became required for civil service examinations from the thirteenth to the twentieth centuries. However, their points of agreement are basic to Confucianism: the appropriate practice of virtue is of great value; humans can attain this through self-cultivation; and study and emulation of the ancient sages are the path to harmony in the individual, family, state, and world.

The state cult

Since ancient times, as we have seen, rulers have been regarded as the link between earth and Heaven. This understanding persisted in Chinese society, but Confucius and his followers had elaborated the idea that the ruler must be virtuous for this relationship to work. During the Han dynasty, Confucius's teachings were at last honored by the state. The Han scholar Dong Zhongshu (Tung Chungshu, c. 179–c. 104 BCE) set up an educational system based on the Confucian Classics that lasted until the twentieth century. He used Confucian ideals to unite the people behind the ruler, who himself had to be subject to Heaven.

During this period, civil service examinations based on the Confucian Classics were established as a means of attaining government positions. The Confucian Classics were established as the Five Classics and the Four Books as the standard textbooks during the Song dynasty by the **Neo-Confucian** scholar Zhu Xi (Chu Hsi, 1130–1200 CE). *His Reflections on Things at Hand* gave a metaphysical basis for Confucianism: the individual is intimately linked with all the cosmos, "forming one body with all things." According to Zhang Zai's (Chang Tsai) *Western Inscription*:

> *Heaven is my father and earth is my mother and even such a small creature as I*
> *finds an intimate place in their midst. Therefore, that which extends throughout the*

universe I regard as my body and that which directs the universe I regard as my nature. All people are my brothers and sisters and all things are my companions. The great ruler [the emperor] is the eldest son of my parents [Heaven and Earth], and the great ministers are his stewards. . . . To rejoice in Heaven and to have no anxiety—this is filial piety at its purest.[29]

By becoming more humane one can help to transform not only oneself but also society and even the cosmos. The Neo-Confucianists thus stressed the importance of meditation and dedication to becoming a "noble person."

Women were encouraged to offer themselves in total sacrifice to others. Confucian women had previously been expected to take a subordinate role in the family and in society, but at the same time to be strong, disciplined, wise, and capable in their relationships with their husbands and sons. In Neo-Confucianism, such virtues were subsumed under an extreme ideal of self-sacrifice.

Although Confucius had counseled restrained use of *li*, Neo-Confucianism included an increased emphasis on offerings, as practiced since ancient times and set forth in the traditional *Book of Rites* and *Etiquette and Ritual*, which had been reconstructed during the Han dynasty. These rites were thought to preserve harmony between humans, Heaven, and earth. At the family level, offerings were made to propitiate the family ancestors. Government officials were responsible for ritual sacrifices to beings such as the gods of fire, literature, cities, mountains, waters, the polar star, sun, moon, and former rulers. The most important ceremonies were performed by the emperor, to give thanks and ask blessings from Heaven, earth, gods of the land and agriculture, and the dynastic ancestors. Traditionally these were performed at the tops of five holy mountains in the four cardinal directions and the center of the kingdom, each associated with a particular season and symbolic meaning, such as rites for spring and new growth that were held in the east. Of these, the highest ritual was the elaborate annual sacrifice to Shangdi at the white marble Altar of Heaven by the emperor. He was considered Son of Heaven, the "high priest of the world." Both he and his large retinue prepared themselves by three days of fasting and keeping vigil. In a highly reverent atmosphere, he then sacrificed a bull, offered precious jade, and sang prayers of gratitude to the Supreme.

Confucianism under communism

The performance of rituals was a time-consuming and major part of government jobs, carried out on behalf of the people. But as China gradually opened to the West in recent centuries, a reaction set in against these older ways, and the last of the imperial dynasties was overthrown in 1911. In the 1920s Republic, science and social progress were glorified by radical intellectuals of the New Culture movement who were opposed to all the old systems. Under the communist regime established in 1949, communism took the place of religion, attempting to transform the society by secular means. Party Chairman Mao Zedong was venerated almost as a god, with the "Little Red Book" of quotations from Chairman Mao replacing the Confucian Classics.

During the Cultural Revolution (1966–76), Confucianism was attacked as one of the "Four Olds"—old ideas, culture, customs, and habits. The revolution attempted to destroy the hierarchical structure Confucianism had idealized and to prevent the intellectual elite ruling the masses. Contrary to the Confucian virtue of filial piety, young people denounced their parents at public trials, and scholars were objects of derision. An estimated one million people were attacked. Some were killed, some committed suicide, and millions suffered.

Mao said he had hated Confucianism from his childhood. What he disliked was the intellectual emphasis on studying the Classics, the "superstitious" rituals, and the oppression of the lowest members of Chinese society—women and peasants. He urged peasants to overthrow all authoritarian traditions.

Nevertheless, in some respects, Confucian morality continued to form the basis of Chinese ethics. Mao particularly emphasized the (Confucian) virtues of selfless service to the people and of self-improvement for the public good:

> *All our cadres, whatever their rank, are servants of the people, and whatever we do is to serve the people. How then can we be reluctant to discard any of our bad traits?*[30]

For decades, communist China prided itself on being the most law-abiding country in the world. The streets were safe, and tourists found that if they could not understand the currency, they could trust taxi drivers to take the exact amount, and no more, from their open wallets. But recently there has been a rise in crime and official corruption. The society has changed abruptly since China opened its doors to the West in 1978, undermining what remained of traditional Confucian virtues. The government blames the influx of materialistic values, resulting from the indiscriminating embrace of the underside of Western culture and the rapid shift toward a free market economy. In 1989, Zhao Ziyang (Chao Tzu-yang), then Communist Party leader, urged officials to maintain Confucian discipline (without naming it that) in the midst of the changes: "The Party can by no means allow its members to barter away their principles for money and power."[31] But when the people picked up this cry, aging leaders chose to brutally suppress popular calls for greater democracy and an end to official corruption; they did so in the name of another Confucian value: order in society.

For their part, the intellectuals of the democracy movement had tried to do things in the proper way but were caught on the horns of the poignant Chinese dilemma. Under Confucian ethics, it has been the continuing responsibility of scholars to play the role of upright censors. On the other hand, scholars had to remain loyal to the ruler, for they were subjects and observing one's subservient position as a subject preserved the security of the state. The leaders of the democracy movement tried to deal with this potential conflict by ritualized, respectful action: in 1989 they formally walked up the steps of the Great Hall of the People in Tiananmen Square to present their written requests to those in power. But they were ignored and brutally suppressed.

Again, in 1995, forty-five of China's most distinguished scholars and scientists delivered a petition to the government urging freedom of thought and accountability of the government to the public, in order to end socially corrosive corruption. Now, in twenty-first-century China, as noted earlier, popular and intellectual interest in various religions is increasing. Evangelical Christianity has grown so vigorous that China is now home to the second largest evangelical Christian community in the world, and there are more Catholics in China than in Ireland. Buddhists account for the majority of religious adherents, with 320,000 nuns and monks in 16,000 Chinese temples and monasteries. Islam is strong in northwest China, home of most of China's eighteen million Muslims. The officially atheistic Communist Party is showing signs of regarding religions as having a certain social usefulness, but it also attempts to control religious activities and beliefs through its Religious Affairs Bureau and police, conducting "patriotic education" classes for religious officials that include Marxist-Leninist principles. While Confucianism is not recognized as a "religion"—the five religions officially permitted in China being Buddhism, Islam, Daoism, Protestantism, and Catholicism—its philosophy and ethics are attracting new attention, and the government has sponsored dozens of "Confucian Institutes" in other countries for the study of Chinese culture and language.

Among intellectuals, conferences have been held on the mainland in China and also in Taiwan and Singapore to discuss Confucianism. Today it is being analyzed not as an historical artifact but as a tradition that is relevant to modern life, with the potential to contribute to cultural identity, economic progress, social harmony, and a personal sense of the meaning of human life.

Confucianism may inform capitalistic behavior as well as Marxist communism. There is now talk of "Capitalist Confucianism"—business conducted according to Confucian ethics such as humanity, trustworthiness, sincerity, and altruism.

Confucian values are also being reappraised as a significant addition to holistic education. In them is imbedded the motivation to improve and become a responsible and ethical member of one's family and society. Self-perception, according to Confucian ideals, is a lifelong process. Thus the Neo-Confucians developed multi-stage learning programs that extend beyond formal schooling. Confucianism has always promoted education as the only means to social reform, and encourages a sense of voluntary service to the community. In the moral and spiritual vacuum left after the demise of fervent Maoism, Confucianism may also help restore a sense of holy purpose to people's lives. The traditional feeling was that the Mandate of Heaven gives transcendent meaning to human life.

Chinese authorities have recently reintroduced the teaching of Confucius in elementary schools as a vehicle for encouraging social morality. After a gap of more than half a century, the Confucian-based civil service examinations are being partially reintroduced in the selection of public servants. Earlier castigated as "feudal institutions," Confucian academies are being described as fine centers for learning. Chinese authorities are also reviving aspects of the religious cult, such as observance of the birthday of Confucius, perhaps mostly for the sake of tourism. In 1995, the Confucian Temple in Qufu, the home of Confucius, was declared a UNESCO World Heritage site, and in 2004 over three million tourists visited the Temple for gala celebrations of Master Kong's birthday.

Confucianism in East Asia

Countries near China, which have historically been influenced by China politically and culturally, also show signs of having been influenced by Confucian values. Singapore has since 1978 sponsored an annual courtesy campaign to inspire virtuous behavior in the midst of fast-paced modern life. In one recent year, the campaign's focus was courteous use of mobile phones.

An Interview with Ann-ping Chin

Ann-ping Chin grew up in Taiwan, the daughter of parents from the northern part of mainland China. She teaches Confucianism and Daoism at Wesleyan University and has visited China five times to do research on the continuing changes in that society.

"Lots of things are changing in China. First of all, the economic boom is changing women's perceptions of themselves and of their family. For instance, if a woman is determined to have a profession of her own, in this huge marketplace of China this implies that she would become involved in a private enterprise or begin one herself. If she does that, this means that she would have to consider child-rearing as secondary.

"Divorce is very common. Family units are breaking up and children have less security—there are all the problems that we associate with divorce in the West. The woman simply says, 'Look—I'm going to leave or you leave.'

"Making money is now the most important thing for the Chinese. It's finally a free market. From an initial impression, perhaps you can say that the fundamental Confucian values are disappearing. Through more than two thousand years of Chinese history, both in traditional Confucian teachings and in Daoist teachings as well, you find a tremendous deprecation of the idea of making money—of taking advantage or making a profit, be it in money or in human relationships. Now, unless you have the determination to make money, you are not considered a true man in Chinese society.

"On the other hand, I would say that the very basic relationships of parents and children, and of friends to friends are still very strong. The Chinese have given up their relationship with the ruler; that's really a joke. The relationship between husband and wife is much more complicated. Men love the idea of having a very devoted wife. They know that is perhaps impossible, but they still yearn for it. And they still value the traditional qualities that you find in the biographies of virtuous women.

"Other values have been abandoned. I'm very disturbed and saddened, pained, by what is happening to the Chinese scholars. They cannot go out and do private enterprise, for they are scholars. They get paid a very pathetic amount of money each month, not enough to make ends meet. Scholars have always been really respected even though people didn't understand them. But now there isn't even that respect since the society is placing so much emphasis on making money.

"My parents both came from very scholarly backgrounds. They passed down to us the traditions without the formalities or rigidities, so we were extremely fortunate. I think my father passed down to us his love of students, his love of teaching, and of the very special relationship between teachers and disciples. It's not obedience— rather, it's a concern that the disciple expresses toward the teacher.

"My father's character had a profound effect on me. He always tried to do the right thing. And to do the right thing sometimes can be so difficult. This was the only way that he could live—to always try to do the right thing, whether it was for a friend, or for us, for my mom, for his own parents, or for strangers. He would never compromise that."

In Korea, where few people consider themselves adherents of Confucianism as a religion, lectures and special events are sponsored by hundreds of local Confucian institutes to promote Confucian teachings. In some cases, Confucianism is associated with particular clans in East Asia, and thus with political favoritism. Some Korean institutes are politically conservative, opposing women's efforts to revise family laws. The Korean Overseas Information Service advocates a flexible, liberal version of the tradition, open to other cultures and all religions but still providing a firm foundation for social order.

> *Confucianism can present contemporary Koreans with a set of practical standards of conduct in the form of rituals and etiquette. Extensive introduction of Western modes of behavior led to the confusion and adulteration of Korea's native behavior pattern. Civility and propriety in speech and deportment enhance the dignity of man. Rites and conduct befitting to a civilized people should be refined and adjusted to the conditions of the time. . . . Korea should, through its Confucian heritage, sustain the tradition of propriety and modesty and defend the intrinsically moral nature of man from submergence in economic and materialistic considerations.*[32]

Confucian organizations in Hong Kong, Taiwan, and other parts of East Asia are attempting to restore religious versions of Confucianism, such as the worship of Confucius himself or study of the Confucian Classics.

Confucian thought has also played a significant role in Japan. It entered Japan during the seventh century when Chinese political thought and religious ideas first began to have significant influence there. It left its mark on the first constitution of Japan, on the arrangement of government bureaucracy, and in the educational system. From the twelfth to the sixteenth century, Confucianism was studied in Zen Buddhist monasteries. Then from the seventeenth to the nineteenth century, Confucianism began to spread more widely among the people of Japan because of its adoption as an educational philosophy in public and private schools. Confucian moral teachings became the basis for establishing proper human relationships in the family and in Japanese society.

Both Confucianism and Shinto were used by the Japanese military during the pre-war period to inculcate a nationalist expansionist ideology. More in keeping with the original motives of Confucianism, some scholars have observed that Japan's effective modernization in the last one hundred years is partly due to values derived from Confucianism. These include a high regard for diligence, consensus, moral self-cultivation, frugality, and loyalty.

Dr. Mary Evelyn Tucker, noted scholar of East Asian Studies and the relationships between religions and the environment, concludes that Confucianism is not outdated. Rather, it can be seen as quite relevant now and for the future as well, for "It aims to promote flourishing social relations, effective educational systems, sustainable agricultural patterns, and humane political governance within the context of the dynamic, life-giving processes of the universe."[33]

Review questions

1. What are the reasons for and against Daoism's reluctance to portray gods, exemplified by the saying "The Dao that can be told of is not the Absolute Dao"?
2. In what ways is Confucianism "religious" and in what ways not "religious"?
3. What were the motives of the communists who overthrew Confucian Chinese society? Why was Confucianism revived later?

Discussion questions

1. Do you think that ethics require a transcendent source such as gods/goddesses or the Mandate from Heaven to give them a motivating force?
2. Are there themes in Daoism and Confucianism that would help resolve industrial society's ecology crisis?
3. Does Confucianism's emphasis on moderation and harmony stifle progressive corrections of social injustices such as patriarchy's treatment of women?

CHAPTER 6

SHINTO

The way of the kami

Japan has embraced and adapted many religions that originated in other countries, but also has its own local traditions closely tied to nature and the unseen world. These have been referred to collectively as a religion in themselves, under the label of "Shinto." However, according to current scholarship, Shinto is not a single self-conscious religious tradition but rather an overarching label applied to ways of honoring the spirits in nature. These ways have at times been combined with imperial myths supporting the worldly rulers.

Many modern Japanese combine practices from several religions, for each offers something different. Confucianism informs organizations and ethics, Buddhism and Christianity offer ways of understanding suffering and the after-life, traditional veneration of ancestors links the living to their family history, and the ways called "Shinto" harmonize people with the natural world and have led to many forms of popular religious culture, such as festivals and visits to shrines.

The roots of "Shinto"

Shinto has no founder, no orthodox canon of sacred literature, and no explicit code of ethical requirements. The meanings of many of its elaborate rituals are unknown by many who practice them. Historically, individual clans apparently worshiped a particular deity as their own ancestor, along with other unseen beings and natural forces, but such worship was localized until the eighth century CE, when the term "Shinto" came into use to distinguish indigenous Japanese ways from Buddhism and other imported religions. The label "Shinto" was formed from the words *shin* (divine being) and *do* (way). The major chronicles of "Shintoism" were written down—the *Kojiki* and *Nihongi*—but contemporary scholars do not regard them as uniquely Japanese, for they seem to be greatly influenced by Buddhist, Confucian, Korean, and Chinese thought.

During the Tokugawa "Enlightenment" period in Japan (1600–1868), thinkers made another effort to define the "native" Japanese religion, as opposed to foreign incursions, by collating various texts, popular practices, and myths.

Then, in 1868, the Meiji Restoration brought the Emperor Meiji and an imperial state apparatus into power. To confront subjugation by Western colonial powers, the Meiji regime at first tried to copy the West and then turned to conservatism and nationalism, with emphasis on worship of the emperor. The extreme nationalism fostered by this trend, supported by religious veneration of the emperor, came to an end with World War II, with the victors forcing Japan to separate church and state.

Now the priests who run the many shrines in Japan are again promoting Shinto as a religion unto itself, native to Japan. In this chapter we will examine the characteristics of Japanese culture that the priests attribute to Shinto.

Kinship with nature

Despite industrial pollution and urbanization, Japan is a country of exquisite natural beauty. The islands marry mountains to sea, and the interiors are laced with streams, waterfalls, and lush forests. Even the agriculture is beautiful, with flowering fruit trees and terraced fields. The people reportedly lived so harmoniously with this environment that they had no separate word for "nature" until they began importing modern Western ideas late in the nineteenth century. Living close to nature, they organized their lives around the seasons, honoring the roles of the sun, moon, and lightning in their rice farming. Mount Fuji, greatest of the islands' volcanic peaks, was honored as the sacred embodiment of the divine creativity that had thrust the land up from the sea. The sparkling ocean and rising sun were loved as earthly expressions of the sacred purity, brightness, and awesome power at the heart of life.

> To be fully alive is to have an aesthetic perception of life because a major part of the world's goodness lies in its often unspeakable beauty.
>
> Rev. Yukitaka Yamamoto, Shinto priest[1]

Although industrialization and urbanization have blighted some of the natural landscape, the sensitivity to natural beauty survives in small-scale arts. In rock gardening, flower arranging, the tea ceremony, and poetry, Japanese artists honor the simple and natural. If a rock is placed "just right" in a garden, it seems alive, radiating its natural essence. In a tea ceremony, great attention is paid to each natural sensual delight, from the purity of water poured from a wooden ladle to the genuineness of the clay vessels. These arts are often linked with Zen Buddhism, but the sensitivities seem to derive from the ancient Japanese ways, and have thus been attached to the idea of Shinto as a religion.

Honoring the kami

Surrounded by nature's beauty and power, the Japanese people found the divine all around them. According to Japanese mythology:

> In primeval ages, before the earth was formed, amorphous matter floated freely about like oil upon water. In time there arose in its midst a thing like a sprouting reedshoot, and from this a deity came forth of its own.[2]

This deity gave birth to many **kami**, or spirits, two of which—the Amatsu ("heavenly") Kami—were told to organize the material world. Standing on the Floating Bridge of Heaven, they stirred the ocean with a jeweled spear. When they pulled it out of the water, it dripped brine back into the ocean, where it coagulated into eight islands (interpreted either as Japan or the whole world). To rule this earthly kingdom they created the Kami Amaterasu, literally "the one who illuminates the sky," or Goddess of the Sun. The Amatsu Kami also gave birth to the ancestors of the Japanese. All of the natural world—land, trees, mountains, waters, animals, people—is thus joined in kinship as the spiritual creation of the *kami*.

Although the word *kami* (a way of pronouncing the character *shin*) is usually translated as "god" or "spirit," these translations are not exact. *Kami* can be either singular or plural, for the word refers to a single essence manifesting in many places. Rather than evoking an image, like the Hindu or Mahayana Buddhist deities, *kami* refers to a quality. It means, literally, "that which is above," and also refers to that which evokes wonder and awe. The *kami* harmonize heaven and earth and guide the solar system and the cosmos. It/they tend to reside in beautiful or powerful places, such as mountains, certain trees, unusual rocks, waterfalls, whirlpools, and animals. In addition, it/they manifest as wind, rain, thunder, or lightning. *Kami* also appear in abstract forms, such as the creativity of growth and reproduction. Since the seventh century CE, using the imported Chinese idea of the Mandate of Heaven, the emperor himself came to be revered as a *kami*—a living god, the divinely descended ruler upon whom the well-being of the country depends. In general, explains Sakamiki Shunzo, *kami* include:

> *all things whatsoever which deserve to be dreaded and revered for the extraordinary and preeminent powers which they possess. . . . [Kami] need not be eminent for surpassing nobleness, goodness, or serviceableness alone. Malignant and uncanny beings are also called* kami, *if only they are the objects of general dread.*[3]

To follow the *kami* is to bring our life into harmony with nature, Shinto adherents feel.

Shrines

Recognizing the presence of *kami*, humans have built shrines to honor it/them. There are even now more than 100,000 Shinto shrines in Japan. Shrines may be as small as beehives or elaborate temple complexes covering thousands of acres. Some honor *kami* protecting the local area; some honor *kami* with special responsibilities, such as healing or protecting crops from insects. The shrines are situated on sites thought to have been chosen by the *kami* for their sacred atmosphere. At one time, every community had its own guardian *kami*.

The greatest number of these shrines are dedicated to Inari, the god of rice. His messengers are foxes, so the shrines have statues of foxes, rather than the statues of dogs or lions that are often placed to guard shrine entrances. Other shrines include imperial shrines previously funded and administered by the government, shrines dedicated to Hachiman, the *kami* of war, Sengen shrines dedicated to the princess who is considered the guardian deity of Mount Fuji, and shrines dedicated to clan founders. Perhaps the most important shrine is the Ise Shrine, a complex of over one hundred shrines. Historians think they were first constructed in their current form in 690 CE. The main shrine is the place of worship of the *kami* Ameraterasu, and is thought to hold the Sacred Mirror, believed to have been given to the first emperor by the gods. It is considered so sacred that the general public is kept at a distance by fences.

It is thought that the earliest places of worship were sacred trees or groves, perhaps with some enclosure to demarcate the sacred area. Shrine complexes that developed later also have some way of indicating where sacred space begins: tall gate-frames, known as *torii*, walls, or streams with bridges, which must be crossed to enter the holy precinct of the *kami*. Water is a purifying influence, and basins of water are provided for washing one's mouth and hands before passing through the *torii*. Statues of guardian lions may further protect the *kami* from evil intrusions, as do ropes with pendants hanging down.

In temple compounds, one first comes to a public hall of worship, behind which is an offering hall where priests conduct rites. Beyond that is the sacred sanctuary, which is entered only by the high priest. Here the spirit of the *kami* is invited to dwell within a special natural object or perhaps a mirror, which reflects the revered light of brightness and purity, considered the natural order of the universe. If there is a spiritually powerful site already present—a waterfall, a crevice in a rock, a hot spring, a sacred tree—the spirit of the *kami* may dwell there. Some shrines are completely empty at the center. In any case, the worshipers do not see the holy of holies; their worship is imageless. As Kishimoto Hideo explains:

> *A faithful believer would come to the simple hall of a Shinto sanctuary, which is located in a grove with a quiet and holy atmosphere. He may stand quite a while in front of the sanctuary, clap his hands, bow deeply, and try to feel the deity in his heart. . . . Shinto being a polytheistic religion, each sanctuary has its own particular deity. But seldom do the believers know the individual name of the deity whom they are worshiping. They do not care about that. . . . The more important point for them is whether or not they feel the existence of the deity directly in their hearts.[4]*

The *kami* of a place may be experienced as energies rather than pictured as forms. At times Shinto has been strongly **iconoclastic** (opposed to images of the divine). In the eighteenth century, for instance, a famous Shinto scholar wrote:

> *Never make an image in order to represent the Deity. To worship a deity is directly to establish a felt relation of our heart to the living Divinity through sincerity or truthfulness on our part. If we, however, try to establish a relation between Deity and man indirectly by means of an image, the image will itself stand in the way and prevent us from realizing our religious purpose to accomplish direct communion with the Deity. So an image made by mortal hands is of no use in Shinto worship.[5]*

Ceremonies and festivals

To properly encourage the spirit of the *kami* to dwell in the holy sanctuary, long and complex ceremonies are needed. In some temples, it takes ten years for the priests to learn them. The priesthood was traditionally hereditary. One temple has drawn its priests from the same four families for over a hundred generations. Not uncommonly, the clergy may be priestesses. The priests may be assisted by *miko*, young unmarried women dressed in white kimonos. Neither priests nor priestesses live as ascetics; it is common for them to be married, and they are not traditionally expected to meditate. Rather, they are considered specialists in the arts of maintaining the connection between the *kami* and the people.

Everything has symbolic importance, so rites are conducted with great care. The correct materials in temple furnishings, the nine articles held by priests during ceremonies (such as branch, gourd, sword, and bow), the bowing, the sharp clapping of hands, beating of drums, the waving of a stick with paper strips—everything is established by tradition and performed with precision. Traditionally, there are no personal prayers to the *kami* for specific kinds of help, but rather a reverent recognition of the close relationship between the *kami*, the ancestors, the people, and nature. When people have made a pilgrimage to a special shrine, they often take back spiritual mementos of their communion with the *kami*, such as a paper symbol of the temple encased within a brocade bag.

Followers of the way of the *kami* may also make daily offerings to the *kami* in their home. Their place of worship usually consists of a high shelf on which rests a miniature shrine, with only a mirror inside. The daily home ritual may begin with greeting the sun in the east with clapping and a prayer for protection for the household. Then offerings are placed before the shrine: rice for health, water for cleansing and preservation of life, and salt for the harmonious seasoning of life. When a new house is to be built, the blessings of the *kami* are ceremonially requested.

Another feature of Japanese popular culture that is associated with shrine worship is festivals, which are held throughout the year and throughout a person's life. They begin four months before the birth of a baby, when the soul is thought to enter the fetus. Thirty-two or thirty-three days after the infant's birth, its parents take it to the family's temple for initiation by the deity. In a traditional family, many milestones—such as coming of age at thirteen, or first arranging one's hair as a woman at sixteen, marriage, turning sixty-one, seventy-seven, or eighty-eight—are celebrated with spiritual awareness and ritualism.

Seasonal festivals remind people that they are descendants of the *kami*, and are exuberant affairs in which the people and *kami* join in celebrating life. Many are held to ensure good crops and give thanks for them.

All local shrines celebrate their own *kami* with a festival that usually includes a great parade in which the local *kami* is thought to be taken out of the shrine where it lives and carried through the streets in a portable shrine in order to show it the world outside. The *kami* may be accompanied by elaborate floats and music-makers. During the festivals, offerings of rice, fish, and vegetables may be presented to the *kami*, as well as offerings of music, dance, and praises. Everyone present is blessed by the priests with water flung from *sakaki* tree branches dipped into sanctified water.

One of the biggest annual festivals is New Year's. It begins in December with ceremonial housecleaning, the placing of bamboo and pine "trees" at doorways of everything from homes to offices and bars to welcome the *kami*, and dressing in traditional kimonos. On December 31, there is a national day of purification. On New Year's day, people watch the first sunrise of the year and try to visit a shrine as well as friends and relatives.

Many ceremonies honor those reaching a certain age. For instance, on January 15, those who are twenty years old are recognized as fully-fledged adults, and on November 15, children who are three, five, or seven years old (considered delicate ages) are taken to a shrine to ask for the protection of the *kami*. On February 3, the end of winter, people throw beans to toss out bad fortune and invite good, and at shrines the priests shoot arrows to break the power of misfortune. A month-long spring festival is held from March to April, with purification rites and prayers for a successful planting season. The month of June is devoted to rites to protect crops from insects, blights, and bad weather. Fall brings thanksgiving rites for the harvest, with the first fruits offered to the *kami* and then great celebrating in the streets.

Purification

In the traditions collectively referred to as Shinto or **kannagara** *(harmony with the kami)*, the world is beautiful and full of helpful spirits. Sexuality *per se* is not evil; the world was created by mating deities, and people have traditionally bathed together communally in Japan. However, ritual impurity is a serious problem that obscures our originally pristine nature; it may offend the *kami* and bring about calamities, such as drought, famine, or war.

The quality of impurity or misfortune is called **tsumi**. It can arise through defilement by corpses or menstruation, hostility toward others or the environment, or natural catastrophes. In contrast to repentance required by religions that emphasize human sinfulness, *tsumi* requires purification. One way of removing it is paying attention to problems as they arise:

> To live free of obstructing mists, problems of the morning should be solved in the morning and those of the evening should be solved by evening. Wisdom and knowledge should be applied like the sharpness of an axe to the blinding effect of the mists of obstruction. Then may the kami purify the world and free it of tsumi.[6]

The *kami* of the high mountain rapids will carry the *tsumi* to the sea, where the whirlpool *kami* will swallow it and the wind *kami* will blow it to the netherworld, where *kami* of that place absorb and remove it.

> After this has been completed, the heavenly kami, the earthly kami and the myriad of kami can recognise man as purified and everything can return to its original brightness, beauty and purity as before since all tsumi has wholly vanished from the world.[7]

People may also be purified in a kind of spontaneous movement that washes over them, often in nature, bringing them into awareness of unity with the universe. Hitoshi Iwasaki, a Shinto priest, says that he likes to look at the stars at night in the mountains where the air is clear:

> When I am watching the thoroughly clear light of the stars, I get a pure feeling, like my mind being washed. I rejoice to think this is a spiritual **misogi** [purification ritual]. . . . Master Mirihei Ueshiba, the founder of Aikido, is said to have looked upon the stars one night, suddenly realized he was united with the universe, and burst into tears, covering his face with his hands. We human beings, not only human beings but everything existing in this world, are one of the cells which form this great universe.[8]

In addition to personal ways of cleansing, there are ritual forms of purification. One is **oharai**, a ceremony commonly performed by Shinto priests, which includes the waving of a branch from a sacred *sakaki* tree, to which are attached white streamers (the Japanese version of the shaman's medicine fan of feathers or the Hindu yak-tail whisk, used to sweep through the air and purify an area). *Oharai* is today performed on cars and new buildings.

Before people enter a Shinto shrine, they splash water on their hands and face and rinse their mouth to purify themselves in order to approach the *kami*. Water is also used for purification in powerful ascetic practices, such as *misogi*, which involves standing under a waterfall. Sprinkling salt on the ground or on ritual participants is also regarded as purifying.

Such ritual practices all have inner meaningfulness. At Tsubaki Grand Shrine in Japan, priests purify hundreds of new cars every weekend, and the same practice has been adopted at Tsubaki Shrine in California. There, Tetsuji Ochiai explains to new car owners whose cars are being ritually purified that they themselves must also practice mental purification for the sake of traffic safety.

Buddhist and Confucian influences

Over time, the ways of the *kami* that have been labeled "Shinto" have blended with other religions imported into Japan, particularly Buddhism, first introduced into Japan in the sixth century CE, and Confucianism, which has been part of Japanese culture since its earliest contact with China.

Buddhism is still practiced side-by-side with the ways called Shinto. The fact that their theologies differ so significantly has been accepted by the people as covering different kinds of situations. The Japanese often go to Shinto shrines for life-affirming events, such as conception, birth, and marriage, and to Buddhist temples for death rites. Buddhist monks of medieval times tried to convince the Japanese that the Shinto *kami* were actually Buddhist deities. The two religions were therefore closely interwoven in many ways throughout Japanese history, until the Meiji Government promoted its version of Shinto as part of its program of nationalistic revival in the nineteenth century, distinguishing it from Buddhism, which was denounced for its foreign origins. Parallel worship of the two paths continues.

Reverence toward the *kami* is mixed with Buddhist practices in traditions such as ritual ascent of sacred mountains in search of enlightenment. Mountain caves are considered to have special powers in Japan because of the spiritual power of the mountains plus that of the *kami* who are thought to spend the winters there. To reach the cave of Omine-san, a sacred mountain in Nara Prefecture, pilgrims and ascetics climb up a steep trail to the cave mouth while chanting the Buddhist Heart Sutra. Small shrines dedicated to various *kami* and also Buddhist figures are encountered on the mountainside. Crawling into the cave and then up a narrow shaft into an elevated upper chamber, pilgrims find themselves in a dark, wet, womb-like world with secretions dripping from the rocks. This sacred natural space in the deep recesses of the mountain is considered an excellent place for progressing toward full realization of the truth by Buddhist practices such as chanting of the Heart Sutra.

As for Confucianism, seventeenth-century Japanese Confucian scholars attempted to free themselves from Buddhism and to tie the Chinese beliefs they were importing to the ancient Japanese ways. One, for instance, likened *li* to the way of the *kami* as a means of social cohesion. Another stressed reverence as the common ground of the two paths and was himself revered as a living *kami*. The

Neo-Confucianists' alliance with the ways of the *kami* to throw off the yoke of Buddhism made the somewhat formless Japanese traditions more self-conscious. Scholars began to study and interpret them. The combination of Confucian emphasis on hierarchy and devotion to the *kami* helped pave the way for the establishment in 1868 of the powerful Meiji monarchy.

State Shinto

The Meiji regime took steps to promote Shinto as the spiritual basis for the government. The state cult, amplifying the Japanese traditions of ancestor veneration, had taught since the seventh century that the emperor was the offspring of Amaterasu, the Sun Goddess. *Naobi no Mitma* ("Divine Spirit of Rectification"), written in the eighteenth century, expressed this ideal:

> *This great imperial land, Japan, is the august country where the divine ancestral goddess Amaterasu Omikami was born, a superb country. . . . Amaterasu deigned to entrust the country with the words, "So long as time endures, for ten thousand autumns, this land shall be ruled by my descendants."*
>
> *According to her divine pleasure, this land was decreed to be the country of the imperial descendants . . . so that even now, without deviation from the divine age, the land might continue in tranquility and in accord with the will of the* kami, *a country ruled in peace.*[9]

It had been customary for the imperial family to visit the great shrine to the Sun Goddess at Ise to consult the supreme *kami* on matters of importance. But Emperor Meiji carried this tradition much farther. He decreed that the way of the *kami* should govern the nation. This way was labeled State Shinto and was administered by government officials rather than Shinto priests, whose objections were silenced, and many of the old rituals were suppressed. State Shinto became the tool of militaristic nationalists as a way to enlist popular support for the throne and the expanding empire.

An illustration of the profound changes in Shinto ushered in by the Meiji "Restoration" occurs in pre- and post-Meiji versions of the Oracles of the Three Shrines. These are scrolls with sayings attributed to the *kami* of three major shrines. The versions popular before the Meiji Restoration emphasize virtues such as honesty, compassion, and purity. A version prepared in the Meiji period taken from the eighth-century imperial cult asserts a direct link between the *kami* and the emperor.

After Japan's defeat in World War II, Emperor Hirohito, Meiji's grandson, also known as the Showa Emperor, became little more than a ceremonial figurehead. He had previously been held up as a god, not to be seen or touched by ordinary people. At the end of the war he officially declared himself human.

"Sect Shinto"

During the social changes of the nineteenth and twentieth centuries, many new religious sects appeared that had their roots in practices of communicating with the *kami*. In rural areas, certain women had long been acting as shamans by falling into trances, from which the *kami* would speak through them. Some of these shamanistic women developed a following of their own, leading to movements that were labeled "Sect Shinto" by the Meiji regime. Some of these movements are still popular today. For example, the Tenrikyo movement was founded by Miki Nakayama in 1838. She was acting as a trance medium for the healing of her son when she was reportedly possessed by ten *kami*, including the chief God the Parent. They proclaimed through her, "Miki's mind and body will be accepted by us as a divine shrine, and we desire to save this three-thousand-world through this divine body."[10] It is said that she later spontaneously composed 1711 poems under divine inspiration, and that these became the sacred scriptures of a new religion. One of these begins with this revelation:

> *Looking all over the world and through all ages, I find no one who has understood My heart. No wonder that you know nothing, for so far I have taught nothing to you. This time I, God, revealing Myself to the fore, teach you all the truth in detail.*[11]

Tenrikyo has continued to be popular since Miki's death, and she is revered as the still-living representative of the divine will.

Another new movement, called Oomoto, developed from revelations given to Madame Nao Deguchi when she was reportedly possessed by the previously little-known *kami* Ushitora no Konjin in 1892. The revelations criticized the "beastly" state of humanity, with:

> *the stronger preying on the weaker. . . . If allowed to go on in this way, society will soon lose the last vestiges of harmony and order. Therefore, by a manifestation of Divine Power, the Greater World shall undergo reconstruction, and change into an entirely new creation. . . . The Greater World shall burst into bloom as plum blossoms at winter's end.*[12]

As developed by Madame Deguchi's relatives and successors, the Oomoto movement survived persecution by the Meiji regime. It has denied that it is a Shinto sect and now has a universalist approach, recognizing founders of other religions as *kami*. Its leaders travel around the world encouraging self-examination, environmental restoration, and global religious cooperation.

Shinto today

In general, the ways attributed to Shinto are indigenous to Japan. Elsewhere, it is common only in Hawaii and Brazil, where many Japanese settled. Most Japanese who visit shrines and pray to the *kami* do not think of themselves as Shinto adherents. This label is applied mostly by the priestly establishment.

In Japan, reaction to the horrors of World War II, the elimination of the imperial mythology of State Shinto, and a desire for modernization threatened institutionalized Shinto. The Japanese Teachers Association taught rejection of the imperial family, Japanese history, and the beliefs and practices associated with Shinto. The Japanese flag—a red circle on a white background—became a symbol of the past, although its symbolism transcends history. The red circle signifies the rising sun and the white background purity, righteousness, and national loyalty.

An Interview with Hitoshi Iwasaki

Hitoshi Iwasaki is a young Shinto priest struggling to educate himself in the suppressed ancient ways of his people. He has officiated at the Shinto shrine in Stockton, California, and at its parent shrine in Japan, Tsubaki Grand Shrine in the Mie Prefecture, where a fine waterfall is used for *misogi*.

"We Japanese are very fortunate. We are grateful for every natural phenomenon and we worship the mountain, we worship the river, we worship the sea, we worship the big rocks, waterholes, winds.

"Unfortunately, after World War II, we were prohibited from teaching the Shinto religion in schools. We never learned about Shinto at school. Many young Japanese know the story of Jesus Christ, but nothing about Shinto. The government is not against Shinto. [The silence comes from] newspapers, the media, and the teachers' union, because they were established just after World War II. They have a very left-wing attitude [and associate Shinto with State Shinto]. Ordinary Japanese people don't link Shinto with politics nowadays, but the teachers' union and newspapers never give credence to religion, Shinto, or Japanese old customs.

"Against this kind of atmosphere, we learned in the school that everything in Japan was bad. Shinto and Japanese customs were bad. Many young people are losing Japanese customs. But I went to Ise Shrine University, where I learned that Shinto is not just State Shinto. Some young people like me study Japanese things and they become super-patriots. That's the problem. There is no middle, just super-left or super-right.

"I learned Shinto partly by learning aikido. The founder was a very spiritual person who studied in one of the Shinto churches. In Shinto we don't have services, we don't preach, we don't do anything for people who want to be saved. But I want to introduce the idea of Shinto to the people of the United States and young Japanese and I can do it through aikido. I think I learned the way of nature through aikido practice. We are born as a child of *kami*, which means we are part of the universe, like a tree. People practice aikido not to fight but to be a friend, to unite.

"In Japan some people are going to Shinto. They were all doing Zen before, but Zen is very difficult. In waterfall purification there is no choice, just standing under the waterfall.

"My friend, a Shinto priest, went to the Middle East, a complete desert. He says it was difficult to explain Shinto there. For them, nature is the enemy. They have to fight nature.

"In Japan we have water everywhere. Now the big rivers and streams are polluted. But people come to the shrines. People gather because this is a sacred place from ancient times where people have come to pray. And other people want to go where people are gathered, so some of the shrines become vacation places, surrounded by souvenir shops. Many come to Shinto shrines and pray Buddhist prayers. Why not? Buddha is one of the *kami*. Everything has *kami*."

But the shrines remain and are visited by more than eighty million Japanese at New Year. People often visit more as tourists than believers, but many say they experience a sense of spiritual renewal. Long-established households have their *kami* shelf, often next to the Buddhist family altar.

Despite the fact that Japan is now one of the most technologically advanced countries in the world, with business its primary focus, there still seems to be a place for ritual—and in some cases, heartfelt—communion with the intangible *kami* that, in traditional belief, permeate all of life. Modern life has ultimately encouraged renewed interest in *kannagara*. Rapid and extreme urbanization, industrial pollution, and despoliation of the natural environment have brought backlashes from concerned citizens who are urging a return to appreciation of the natural beauty of their homeland, traditionally the abode of the *kami*.

Some Shinto adherents explain it as a universal natural religion, rather than an exclusively Japanese phenomenon, and try to explain the way of harmony with the *kami* to interested non-Japanese, without striving for conversions. A Shinto shrine in California offers ritual ways of experiencing one's connection with nature and learning to see the divine in the midst of life.

Within Japan, there are new attempts to teach children the thousands-of-years-old rice cultivation ceremony, and with it, values such as co-existence and "co-prosperity" with the natural environment and with each other.

Review questions

1. Explain the Shinto involvement in nature and environmental concerns. Refer to *kami*, mountains, waterfalls, sexuality, and *kannagara*.
2. Describe the purposes of some Shinto rituals, such as those for life cycles and seasons. Consider aesthetic beauty, priests/priestesses, shrines, *torii*, mirrors, *oharai*, cars, and iconoclasm.
3. Explain the purpose of purification in Shinto, both personal and collective. Take into account *misogi*, *tsumi*, and Mt. Fuji.

Discussion questions

1. What elements of Confucianism and Buddhism can be found in Shinto? Discuss meditation, death, social cohesion, and social hierarchy.
2. Why do you think Shinto is so closely tied to Japanese nationalism? Discuss patriotism, emperor deification, war, and post-World War II changes.

ZOROASTRIANISM

A bridge between East and West

Zoroastrianism, a religion from ancient Iran, has perhaps only 130,000 practitioners, but for more than a thousand years it may have been the official religion of the vast Iranian Empire which extended from Iraq or Turkey to India. In some ways it bridges Eastern and Western religions. Its origins are synchronous with, and similar to, Hinduism, it is thought to have influenced Buddhism, and it introduced beliefs that are similar to those later found in Jewish, Christian, and Muslim religions. Supplanting polytheism, it brought an early form of monotheism, which was subsequently central to those "Western" faiths, as well as to Sikhism, which was born on Indian soil.

In the early faith, people worshiped gods representing the elements, aspects of nature, and abstract principles, such as justice and obedience. These often corresponded with those of the Vedic Indians and were similarly named *daevas*, like the Indian *devas*, meaning "Shining Ones," with the highest gods called *Ahuras* ("Lords"). The ritual worship was designed, as in India, to maintain the natural order, truth, and righteousness of the universe by re-enacting the sacrifice that led to its creation.

Zarathushtra's mission

Whereas the faith is known in Iran as Mazdayasna—"the worship of the Wise Lord, Ahura Mazda"—Western scholars refer to it by the name of one of its great reformers, the prophet Zarathushtra (Greek: Zoroaster) who may have lived between 1100 and 550 BCE. German philosopher Karl Jaspers has referred him as one of the great figures of the **"Axial Age,"** which he dated as approximately the sixth century BCE. During that period great religious leaders and thinkers appeared in many parts of the ancient world, including the sages who wrote the *Upanishads*, the Buddha, Mahavira, Confucius, Laozi, and Socrates.

It is thought Zarathushtra trained as a priest in the Indo-Iranian tradition, and was a mystical seeker who spent many years in spiritual retreat. At the age of thirty, he is said to have had a vision of a great shining being, Vohu Manah, the embodiment of the loving mind, who led him into the presence of Ahura Mazda, the creator God. Ahura Mazda was surrounded by angelic presences manifesting six attributes of the divine. Scholars suggest these represent earlier Indo-Iranian deities, transformed by Zarathushtra to suit his monotheistic belief but still retaining their association with forces of nature—the earth, the arch of the sky, water, plants, cattle, and fire.

Zarathushtra said he experienced communion with Ahura Mazda and his attributes on many occasions, and as a result he reportedly determined that in contrast to the multiplicity of gods worshiped by the Indo-Iranians, Ahura Mazda was the Supreme Lord. Zarathushtra denounced all cruelty, selfishness, distortion, and hypocrisy in the name of religion. He insisted that Ahura Mazda creates only goodness and should be worshiped by good thoughts, words, and deeds. There is a cosmic battle between sustaining and destroying forces, and to assure the victory of good over evil, humans must dedicate themselves as spiritual warriors for goodness.

Zarathushtra poured forth his adoration for the Supreme in metric verses called **Gathas**. "Speak to me as friend to friend," he implores Ahura Mazda. "Grant us the support which friend would give to friend."[1] The only words of the prophet that have been retained, the Gathas are the major source of information about Zarathushtra's life and theology, but are written in an ancient language whose meanings are now obscure.

Zarathushtra was long unable to convince anyone else to follow him in honoring Ahura Mazda above all other gods. At last he journeyed to another kingdom and convinced its king, Vishtapa, of the truth of his understanding. Vishtapa adopted Zarathushtra's creed and proclaimed it the state religion. Zarathushtra is said to have preached for almost fifty years until his assassination at the age of seventy-seven.

Spread of Zoroastrian beliefs

It is difficult to trace the later spread of Zarathushtra's teachings. The Magi—a tribe of priestly specialists in western Iran whose practices included magic and astrology—seem to have become involved with transmitting Zoroastrianism some time after Zarathushtra died, but they may have altered it significantly.

Ahura Mazda was apparently revered by the Achaemenid kings of the great Persian Empire, set up in the mid-sixth century BCE by King Cyrus, who seems to have been a follower of Ahura Mazda. However, he and the succeeding Achaemenid kings left no written mention of Zarathushtra. Cyrus's reign was noted for its religious tolerance as well as its power and wealth. The Jews within the empire were allowed to practice their own religion but may have adopted Zoroastrian beliefs such as the belief that there is an evil aspect in life, an immortal soul, and reward or punishment in an afterlife—for these were absent from earlier Judaic religion. From Judaism, they may have passed into Christianity and Islam.

The tradition of devotion to Ahura Mazda was threatened by the 331 BCE invasion of Alexander, known as "The Great" in the West but "The Accursed" in Iran. According to Zoroastrian belief, he ransacked the capital of Persepolis, destroying fire temples, burning the library containing the holy scriptures of Zarathushtra, and killing so many Zoroastrian priests that oral transmission of many scriptures was lost. It is thought that the Gathas survived because many people knew them by heart.

Two centuries later, Zoroastrianism was re-established in a shrunken Iranian empire by the Parthians, who ruled for almost five hundred years to 224 CE. Its surviving teachings were reassembled as the **Avesta**, or "holy texts." Under the Sassanids of the third to mid-seventh centuries CE, it became the state religion, serving the aristocracy of Iran, and was one of the major religions of the ancient world.

A major threat to Zoroastrianism came from the spread of Islam after the death of Muhammad in 632 CE. A number of Persian Zoroastrians avoided conversion to Islam by migrating to western India, whose spiritual origins were similar to their own, where they were called **Parsis** ("Persians"). They consecrated a sacred fire, which is said to have burned continuously ever since. Some Parsis migrated to what is now Pakistan.

The numbers of Zoroastrians in Iran dwindled over the centuries under Muslim dominance, but detailed instructions about the faith's rituals and customs were preserved in the **Pahlavi** texts, written or translated in Middle Persian from about the ninth century CE. A small community of believers still survives in Iran. Today, India—particularly the Mumbai area—is the major center of Zoroastrian population.

Zoroastrian teachings

There is uncertainty about exactly what Zarathustra taught, but enough is known for his theology and its later transformations to be sketched.

The primacy of Ahura Mazda

Zarathushtra is considered the first of the monotheists of the Western traditions, in the sense that he elevated one god above all others worshiped by the earlier Iranians. He refers to this God, Ahura Mazda, by the masculine gender. In the *Gathas he* makes impassioned pleas to Ahura Mazda to make him a more fit spiritual vehicle, so that he can "dedicate to Mazda the life-breath of his whole being."[2] He asks for guidance in the mission of protecting "the poor in spirit, the meek and lowly of heart, who are Thine." He emphasizes the need for clear thought in this mission:

> *O Lord of Life, we long for Thy mighty Fire of Thought which is an enduring, blazing Flame bringing clear guidance and joy to the true believer, but as for the destruction-loving, this quickening Flame overcomes his evil in a flash.[3]*

Although Zarathushtra perceived Ahura Mazda as the one Eternal Being, he also described six divine powers that radiate from the godhead: The Good Mind, Righteousness, Absolute Power, Devotion, Perfection, and Immortality. After his death, these were personified and worshiped as beings, and uttering their names was thought to bring great power. These Bountiful Immortals, the **Ameshta Spenta**, are chief among the angels, who include deities worshiped by the earlier Iranians. One of these is Mithra, guardian of the light, protector of the truth, and bestower of wealth.

The choice between good and evil

Zarathushtra wrestled with the problem of the existence of evil. Many Western scholars describe Zarathushtra's theology as cosmic dualism, with Ahura Mazda opposed by a dark force of equal power. Others feel that this was a later development and that the original teaching was that although there were two opposing forces Ahura Mazda was the stronger.

Zarathushtra did speak of two opposing powers: *Spenta Mainyu*, the good spirit, and *Angra Mainyu*, the evil spirit. The two principles will always actively oppose each other in humans and in creation as a whole until the good spirit is at last victorious. Evil, Zarathushtra asserts, is not all-powerful or eternal, but to assure the victory of good over evil, humans must dedicate themselves as spiritual warriors on the side of Spenta Mainyu.

Heaven, hell, and resurrection

At death, Zoroastrians believe, each of us is judged according to the total goodness or evilness of our thoughts, words, and deeds. The greater the goodness, the wider the bridge to heaven, the Kingdom of Light. The greater the evil, the narrower the bridge, until it is so narrow that souls cannot cross. They fall into hell, House of the Lie, a murky, woeful place.

By natural law, good deeds bring their own reward and evil deeds their just punishment, and Zoroastrians feel that the effects of actions will be felt both in the present and in an afterlife. Tehmurasp Rustamji Sethna explains:

> *When a man's actions are good he has self-confidence and usually people say he has nothing to worry about, his road is clear. On the other hand, if a man's actions are bad, it is usually said he is following a precarious path and any moment he will fall.[4]*

There is no eternal hell in Zoroastrianism, for good is ultimately victorious. With the help of all individuals who choose goodness over evil, the world will reach a state of perfection in which all souls, living or dead, are liberated forever from evil. This time is the *Frashokereti,* the "refreshment" of the world in which all of creation is resurrected into perfected immortality. This refreshment requires the contributions of many people. Zoroastrianism therefore places great emphasis on the moral responsibility of each person, for the good of the whole.

Religious practices

An important ritual is the act of tying the sacred cord (*kusti*) around one's mid-section, while reciting a prayer to keep evil at bay, traditionally performed at least five times a day. Symbolically, the faithful are girding themselves as soldiers for Ahura Mazda, strengthening their resolve to follow the spiritual path. The *kusti* is worn by both males and females.

Zoroastrian rituals also emphasize purification. Water is venerated as a means or symbol of purification. The devout dip their fingers into water, apply it to their eyes and forehead, and raise their hands in prayer to Ahura Mazda. It is a sin to pollute water or place anything dead in it. The other element emphasized in Zoroastrian rituals is fire, long used in Indo-Iranian tradition for its purifying, transformative power.

When the physical body dies, Zoroastrians carry it to a Tower of Silence, a circular building open at the top so that vultures can alight on the corpse to pick the bones clean. This is done to avoid polluting the earth with decaying flesh. The survivors continue to pray for the departed and continue to observe death anniversaries at which the *fravashi,* or eternal principle and guide, of the deceased person is invoked, to help the living in their good works.

Zoroastrianism today

The number of Zoroastrians is falling toward possible extinction. Conversion to the faith is not emphasized, partly because of a desire not to dilute the teachings or the identity as a distinct faith community. In contemporary Iran, there is little incentive to convert, for Zoroastrians, like Jews and Christians, are tolerated but limited in their privileges under Muslim rule. Historically, however, many Muslims converted to Zoroastrianism during the last years of the Pahlavi dynasty.

When the Parsis were influenced by Westernization and Protestant missionary activity, they became somewhat embarrassed about the mystical aspects of their faith. Some began reciting their prayers in English rather than the ancient Avestan language, and interpreting what they were doing as talking to God rather than uttering powerful sacred mantras. They tended to de-emphasize rituals and beliefs in an evil spirit and the end of the temporal world in favor of the more abstract philosophy and ethical standards of the Gathas.

The pendulum now seems to be swinging in the other direction. Training is still available in Iran and India for the hereditary lineage of Zoroastrian priests, and there is considerable interest in preserving and understanding the tradition. Religious historians, metaphysicians, and linguists have attempted to translate the ancient language, uncover the deep significance behind the rituals, and sift out the origins of the tradition from the thousands of years of later accretions. Such efforts have brought a renewed sense of pride and appreciation within Zoroastrianism.

CHAPTER 7

JUDAISM

A covenant with God

Judaism is the diverse tradition associated with the Jewish people, who may be defined either as a religious group or as an ethnic group.

In religious terms, Jews are those who experience their history as a dialogue with God. In a religious sense, "Israel" refers to those who answer the call of God and acknowledge and strive to obey the one God, through the Torah. As a nation, "Israel" is an originally nomadic people that throughout its history has been dispersed and oppressed. After the horrors of the Holocaust in the twentieth century, some Jews founded a homeland in Israel, the center of their ancestors' faith. Others live in communities around the world. Many who consider themselves Jews have been born into a Jewish ethnic identity but do not feel or practice a strong connection to Jewish religious traditions.

A history of the Jewish people

The Jewish sense of history begins with the stories recounted in the Hebrew Bible or **Tanakh** (a different version of which Christians call "the Old Testament"). They begin with the creation of the world by a supreme deity, or God, and progress through the patriarchs, matriarchs, and Moses who spoke with God and led the people according to God's commandments, and the prophets who heard God's warnings to those who strayed from them. But Jewish history does not end where the stories of the Tanakh end, about the second century BCE. After the holy center of Judaism, the Temple of Jerusalem, was captured and destroyed by the Romans in 70 CE, Jewish history is that of a dispersed people, finding unity in their evolving teachings and traditional practices, which were eventually codified in the great compendium of Jewish law and lore, the **Talmud**.

Biblical stories

Although knowledge of the early history of the Children of Israel is based largely on the narratives of the Tanakh, scholars are uncertain of the historical accuracy of the accounts. Some of the people, events, and genealogies set forth cannot be verified by other evidence, such as archaeological findings or references to the Israelites in the writings of neighboring peoples. It may be that the Israelites were too small and loosely organized a group to be noted by historians of other cultures. No mention of Israel appears in other sources until about 1230 BCE, but biblical narratives and genealogies place Abraham, said to be the first patriarch of the Israelites, at about 1700 to 1900 BCE.

Jews hold the **Pentateuch**, the "five books of Moses" at the beginning of the Tanakh, as the most sacred part of the scriptures. Traditionalists believe these were divinely revealed to Moses and written down by him as a single document. Some contemporary biblical researchers disagree. On the basis of clues, such as the use of variant names for God, they speculate that these books were oral traditions reworked and set down later by several different sources with the intent of interpreting the formation of Israel from a religious point of view, as the results of God's actions in human history. The Pentateuch seems to have assumed its final form in the days of Ezra the Scribe (fifth century BCE).

Some of the stories in the Pentateuch, such as the Creation, the Garden of Eden, the Great Flood, and the Tower of Babel, are similar to earlier Mesopotamian legends. In the narratives of the continuing history of the Israelites, only the last four books (I and II Samuel and I and II Kings) are thought to be edited directly from contemporary sources. Although the accuracy of many of the stories has not yet been independently documented, they are of great spiritual significance in Christianity and Islam as well as in Judaism. They are also politically important, for along with the Talmud they later gave a scattered people a special sense of group identity and of God's active role in Jewish history.

From creation to the God of Abraham   The Hebrew scriptures begin with a sweeping poetic account of the creation of heaven and earth by God in six days, from the time of "the earth being unformed and void, with darkness over the surface of the deep and a wind from (or: the spirit of) God sweeping over the water."[1] After creating the material universe, God created man and woman in the divine "image" or "likeness," placing them as masters of the earth, rulers of "the fish of the sea, the birds of the sky, and all the living things that creep on the earth."[2] God is portrayed as a transcendent Creator, without origins, gender, or form, a being utterly different from what has been created. Since Hebrew has no gender-neutral pronouns, God is generally—though not always—described in male singular terms. This creation story (in Genesis 1 and 2:1–4) is attributed by scholars to the "priestly source," thought to be editors writing immediately before or after the exile of the Jews to Babylon in 586 BCE.

A second, probably earlier, version of the creation story follows, beginning in Genesis 2:4. It is thought to be a contribution to the scriptures from the "Yahwist source," which used the word transliterated as "Yahweh" for the supreme male deity. Instead of presenting woman as the equal of man, it portrays her as an offshoot of Adam, the first man, formed to keep him company. This version has commonly been interpreted as blaming woman for the troubles of humanity, although this reading is not supported in the Hebrew manuscripts. According to the legend of Adam and Eve, originally God placed the first two humans in a garden paradise. The woman Eve ("mother of all the living") was promised wisdom by a serpent (later often interpreted as a symbol of Satan) to tempt her to taste the fruit of the tree of knowledge of good and evil, against God's command. She gave some to Adam as well. According to the legend, this ended their innocence. God cursed the serpent and the land, and banished Adam and Eve from their garden; their lives were no longer paradisical nor were they immortal, for they no longer had access to the "tree of life."

The theme of exile reappears continually in the Hebrew Bible, and in later

Jewish history the people are rendered homeless again and again. The biblical narratives emphasize that the people risk God's displeasure every time they stray from God's commands. They are repeatedly exiled from their spiritual home and continually seek to return to it.

A more optimistic interpretation developed later. This was the feeling that the Jewish people were spread throughout the world by God's will, for a sacred purpose: to be good citizens of whatever land they reside in, and to help raise the imperfect world back up to the condition of perfection in which God had created it. Israel would find its way home only when all of creation was lifted up. The rabbinic tradition, which began in the first century CE and has shaped Jewish theology into the modern period, emphasized that the way out of exile was through study and righteous living. Commandments have their origin in God and, if followed, will lead humanity back to a life in harmony with God.

Covenant   A unique belief introduced into Jewish theology was the idea of a covenantal relationship between the Jewish people and God. On the people's side, obedience to God is expected. On the divine side, God grants special favors and is bound by his own ethical agreements to the people. The paradigm for this relationship is the covenant between God and Abraham on behalf of the Jewish people. A more universal covenant with humanity as a whole is portrayed in the story of Noah, said to be the sole righteous man of his time.

According to the biblical narrator, God despairs of the general wickedness of humans, regrets having created them, and sends a great flood "to destroy all flesh under the sky."[3] Non-biblical evidence from archaeology, geology, and legends of other peoples supports the belief that a great flood occurred in Mesopotamia, grounding at least part of the narrative in historical fact. In the biblical story, God establishes a covenant with Noah and gives directions for the building of an ark, which saves Noah's family and two of each of God's creatures. God promises never again to destroy the created world or to interfere with the established natural order, with the rainbow as a sign of this covenant.

God does, however, continue to intervene in history, according to the narrators. Ten generations after the legend of Noah, the narrative focuses on Abraham, Isaac, and Jacob (the "patriarchs"), and their wives, Sarah, Rebecca, Leah, and Rachel (the "matriarchs"). According to the biblical narratives, Abraham was born in Ur (now in Iraq), migrated to Haran (now in Turkey), and then was called by God to journey to Canaan. With his wife Sarah and his household, he left the land of his father and also the religion of his father, a worshiper of the old gods.

Abraham is held up as an example of obedience to God's commands. Without hesitation, he is said to undergo circumcision (cutting away of the foreskin of the penis) as an initiatory rite, a sign of the covenant in which God agrees to be the divine protector of Abraham and his descendants, with all males to be likewise circumcised on the eighth day after birth.

According to the biblical narrative, God tested Abraham by demanding he sacrifice his most precious possession, his beloved son Isaac. When Abraham prepares to sacrifice Isaac, the Lord stops him, satisfied that "now I know that you fear God."[4] The Hebrew word *yirah*, usually translated as "fear" of God, also implies "awe of God's greatness," or what Rabbi Lawrence Kushner calls "trembling in the presence of ultimate holiness."[5]

Early monotheism   Scholars disagree on whether pure monotheism—the worship of a single God of the universe, exclusive of any other divine beings—was practiced by the early patriarchs. It is known that the polytheistic religion of the Canaanites, who paid homage to a high male god called El, and a Great Mother Goddess named Asherah, had some influence on that of the Israelites, who apparently incorporated or adapted elements of the older faiths of the area into their own. The hymns recorded in the biblical book of Psalms, for example, may have roots in Canaanite traditions. However, the ultimate thrust of Judaism was the rejection of the gods of surrounding peoples. The Israelites came to see themselves as having been chosen by a single divine patron. In their patriarchal culture, this God was perceived as a ruler in a close relationship to the people, like a parent to children, or a sovereign to vassals.

Israel's birth in struggle   It is unclear who the people of the biblical narratives were. Some scholars think "Hebrew" is derived from the generic term *habiru*, used for low-class, landless people who lived as outlaws and were often hired as mercenaries. Another derivation may relate to the Hebrew word *ivrim*, meaning nomads or wanderers. Others point to *'ibri* as the biblical word for Hebrew, meaning "children of Eber," an ethnic term. But because of frequent moving and intermarrying, the Israelites were of mixed ethnic stock, including Hebrew, Aramaean, and Canaanite. **Semite** is a modern term applied to Jews, Arabs, and others of eastern Mediterranean origin whose languages are classified as Semitic; it is often inaccurately used as an ethnic designation.

According to the genealogies in the Pentateuch, the people who became known as Israelites were the offspring of Israel (first called Jacob), grandson of Abraham. Jacob received the new name after wrestling all night with an angel of God. "Israel" means "the one who struggled with God." This story in which a human being struggles and finally is reborn at a higher level of spirituality has been taken as a metaphor for the spiritual evolution of the people of Israel. As a result of the struggle, Israel the patriarch receives both a new name and the promise that many nations will be born from him. The nation Israel—"the smallest of peoples"[6]—is perceived as the spiritual center for the world to grow toward God. This is its destiny, though Jews do not feel it has yet been fulfilled.

Egypt: bondage and exodus   Jacob/Israel is said to have had one daughter and twelve sons by his two wives and their two maidservants. The sons became the progenitors of the twelve tribes of Israel. The whole group left Canaan for Goshen in Egypt during a famine. Exodus, the second book of the Tanakh, opens about four centuries later with a statement that the descendants of Israel had become numerous. To keep them from becoming too powerful, the reigning pharaoh ordered that they be turned into slaves for construction projects. He also ordered midwives to kill all boy babies born to the Israelite women.

One who escaped this fate was Moses, an Israelite of the tribe of Levi, who was raised in the palace by the pharaoh's own daughter. He is said to have fled the country after killing an Egyptian overseer who was beating an Israelite worker. While he lived in exile in Midian, the oppression of the Israelites in Egypt grew worse and worse.

According to the scriptural Book of Exodus, Moses was chosen by God to defy the pharaoh and lead the people out of bondage, out of Egypt. On a mountain, an angel of God appeared to him from within a bush blazing with fire but not consumed by it. God called to him out of the bush and yet cautioned, "Do not come closer. Remove your sandals from your feet, for the place on which you stand is holy ground."[7] When God told Moses to go rescue "My people, the Israelites, from Egypt,"[8] Moses demurred, but God insisted:

> *I will be with you . . . Thus you shall say to the Israelites, "Ehyeh [I Am] sent me to you. . . . The LORD, the God of your fathers, the God of Abraham, the God of Isaac, and the God of Jacob, has sent me to you."[9]*

The word given in this biblical translation as "LORD" is considered too sacred to be pronounced. In the Hebrew scriptures it is rendered only in consonants as YHWH or YHVH; the pronunciation of the vowels is not known.

With his brother Aaron to act as spokesperson, Moses returned to Egypt. Many chapters of Exodus recount miracles used to convince the pharaoh to let the people go into the wilderness to worship their God. These included a rod that turned into a serpent, plagues of locusts and frogs, lasting darkness, and finally the Lord killing all firstborn children and creatures. The Israelites were spared this fate, marking their doors with the blood of a lamb so that the Lord would pass over them. (Passover commemorates this story.) The pharaoh at last let the Israelites go. The redemption from bondage by the protection of the Lord has served ever since as a central theme in Judaism.

According to the scriptural account, the Lord's presence led the Israelites, manifesting as a pillar of cloud by day and of fire by night. The armies of the pharaoh pursued them until Moses stretched his staff toward the sea and God caused an east wind to blow all night, dividing the waters so that the Israelites could pass through safely on a dry seabed. As the Egyptians tried to follow, God told Moses again to hold out his arm over the sea, and the walls of water crashed down on them, drowning every one.

From the wilderness to Canaan   According to the Pentateuch, God told Moses that he would lead the people back to Canaan. First, however, it was necessary to travel to the holy Mount Sinai to re-establish the covenant between God and the people. The Lord is said to have descended to its summit in a terrifying show of lightning, thunder, fire, smoke, and trumpeting. God is said to have then given the people through Moses a set of rules for righteous living, later called the Torah. Among them were the utterances that Christians call "The Ten Commandments", on stone tablets. God also gave a set of social norms, prescribed religious feasts, and detailed instructions for the construction of a portable tabernacle with a holy ark, the **Ark of the Covenant**, in which to keep the stone tablets on which God inscribed the commandments.

During the forty days that Moses was on the mountain receiving these instructions, the people who had just agreed to a holy covenant with God became disturbed and impatient. The biblical account says that under Aaron's reluctant supervision, they melted down their gold jewelry and cast it into the form of a golden calf, practicing what the authors of the biblical narratives considered idol-worship, which had been explicitly forbidden by God. Moses is said to have been so outraged by their idolatry that he smashed the stone tablets and destroyed the idol. He ordered the only people still siding with YHWH, the Levites, to slay 3,000 of those who had strayed.

After another forty-day meeting with God on the summit of Mount Sinai, Moses returned with stone tablets on which God had inscribed the commandments. Moses' face was said to be so radiant from his encounter with God that he had to veil it. Aaron and his sons were invested as priests, the tabernacle was constructed as directed, and the people set off for the land of Canaan, with the Presence of the Lord filling the tabernacle.

Acceptance of the laws given to Moses at Mount Sinai brought a new dimension to the covenant between God and Israel. God had freed the Jews from slavery and extinction at the hands of the Egyptians, and now the Jews freely agreed to accept the Torah.

Carrying the Ark representing this covenant, the Israelites had to wander for forty years through the desert before they could re-enter the promised land, fertile Canaan, which at that time belonged to other peoples. But the Israelites' God did not forsake them. Every day they found their daily bread scattered on the ground, in the form of an unknown food, which they named manna.

A stone inscription, the Merneptah Stele, written for the Egyptian Pharaoh Merneptah, places the Hebrews as being in Canaan about 1207 BCE. Through what was described as the miraculous help of God, they fought many battles against the kings and tribes of Canaan. Archaeological evidence indicates that every Canaanite town was destroyed from one to four times between the thirteenth and eleventh centuries BCE, though the identity of the conquerors is not known. At Sinai, God had vowed to oust the inhabitants of the lands into which the Israelites advanced, warning them against adopting the local spiritual practices: "No, you must tear down their altars, smash their pillars, and cut down their sacred posts."[10] The editors of the scriptures clearly considered the Canaanite religion spiritually invalid and morally inferior to their own. But the Israelites' attention to their God was not absolute. According to the scriptures, whenever they turned away from YHWH, forgetting or worshiping other gods, surrounding peoples found them easy prey.

The first Temple of Jerusalem   David, the second king of Israel, is remembered as Israel's greatest king. An obscure shepherd, David was chosen by the prophet Samuel to be anointed on the head with oil, for thus were future kings found and divinely acknowledged in those times. Composer and singer of psalms, David was summoned to the court of the first Israelite king, Saul, to play soothing music whenever an evil spirit seized the king. When Saul and his son were killed in battle, David was made king. By defeating or making allegiances with surrounding nations, David created the beginnings of a secure, prosperous Israelite empire. He made the captured city of Jerusalem its capital and brought the Ark of the Covenant there.

Under the reign of King Solomon (son of David), a great Temple was built in Jerusalem. It was to be a permanent home for the Ark, which was housed in the innermost sanctum, and a place for making the burned offerings of animals, grain, and oil to the divine. There already existed an ancient practice among pre-Israelite peoples of using high places for altars where sacrifices were made to the gods. After centuries of wandering worship, the Israelites now had a central, stationary place where God would be most present to them. God is said to have appeared to Solomon after the fourteen-day Temple dedication ceremony and pledged: "I consecrate this House which you have built and I set My name there forever. My eyes and My heart shall ever be there."[11]

The Temple became the central place for sacrifice. But Solomon accumulated great personal wealth, at the expense of the people, and built altars to the gods of his wives, who came from other nations. This so angered the Lord, according to the scriptures, that he divided the kingdom after Solomon's death. An internal revolt of the ten northern tribes established a new kingdom of Israel, independent of Jerusalem and the dynasty of David. The southern kingdom, continuing in its allegiance to the house of David and retaining Jerusalem as its capital, renamed itself Judah, after David's tribe.

Prophets such as Elijah warned the people against worshiping gods other than the Lord, and exhorted them to end their evil ways. Over the centuries, these prophets were men and women who had undergone transformational ordeals that made them instruments for the word of God. The "early prophets," such as Elijah, focused on the sin of idolatry; the "later prophets" warned that social injustice and moral corruption would be the ruin of the Jewish state.

By the reign of King Hoshea of Israel, the kingdom was so corrupt and idolatrous that, in the scriptural interpretation, God permitted the kingdom of Assyria to overtake what was left of it. Assyria carried off most of the Israelites to exile among the **Gentiles** (non-Jewish people). Most of the Israelites became dispersed within Assyria; these people who thenceforth lost a distinct ethnic identity are known as the "Ten Lost Tribes of Israel." This destruction of the northern kingdom took place in 722 BCE and is attested in Assyrian annals.

Judah maintained its independence, declining and continually warned of impending doom by its prophets, until King Nebuchadnezzar of Babylonia (which by 605 BCE had taken over the Assyrian Empire) captured Jerusalem. In 586 BCE the walls of Jerusalem were battered down and its buildings put to the torch by the Babylonians. The great Temple was emptied of its sacred treasures, the altar dismantled, and the building destroyed. Many Judaeans were taken to exile in Babylonia, where they were thenceforth known as "Jews," since they were from Judah.

The prophets interpreted these events as reasonable punishment by God for Judah's idolatry and misbehaviors. Nevertheless, Isaiah and a later anonymous prophet prophesied that God would soon usher in a new era of peace and justice among all peoples, from his holy Temple in Jerusalem.

> *I never could forget you.*
> *See, I have engraved you*
> *On the palms of My hands . . .*
>
> *Isaiah 49:15–16*

Return to Jerusalem

After fifty years of exile in Babylon, a small group of devoted Jews, probably fewer than 50,000, returned to their holy city and land, now called Judaea. They were allowed to return by the Persian king, Cyrus. But most of the Jews did not return to Jerusalem from Babylon, which was now their home. They were thenceforth said to be living in the **diaspora**, from the Greek word for "disperse." They always remembered Zion as a central part of their faith, but also learned to establish their creative lives in the diaspora.

King Cyrus authorized the rebuilding of the Temple in Jerusalem, which was completed in 515 BCE. The second Temple became the central symbol to a scattered Jewish nation. A new emphasis on Temple rites developed, with an hereditary priesthood tracing its ancestry to Aaron.

The priestly class, under the leadership of Ezra, a priest and a scribe, also undertook to revise, or redact, the stories of the people, editing the Pentateuch to reveal the hand of God. Some scholars think that it was these priestly editors who wrote the creation account in Genesis 1.

The Torah was now established as the spiritual and secular foundation of the dispersed nation. In approximately 430 BCE, Ezra the scribe set the precedent of reading for hours from the Torah scrolls in a public square. These "five books of Moses" were accepted as a sacred covenant.

As the Jews lived under foreign rule—Persian, Greek, Parthian, and then Roman—Judaism became open to cross-cultural religious borrowings. Some scholars think concepts of Satan, the hierarchy of angels, reward or punishment in an afterlife, and the final resurrection of the body on the Day of Judgment made their way into Jewish belief from the Zoroastrianism of the Persians, for they were absent from earlier Judaic religion. However, they were not uniformly accepted. Greek lifestyle and thought were introduced into the Middle East by Alexander the Great in the fourth century BCE. The rationalistic, humanistic influences of Hellenism led many Jews, including the priests in Jerusalem, to adopt a Hellenistic attitude of scepticism rather than unquestioning belief.

Tension between traditionalists and those embracing Greek ways came to a head during the reign of Antiochus IV Epiphanes, a Hellenistic ruler of Syria (175–164 BCE), which held political sovereignty over the land of Israel. Antiochus seems to have tried to achieve political unity by forcing a single Hellenistic culture on all his subjects, abolishing the Torah as the Jewish constitution, burning copies of the Torah, killing families who circumcised their sons, building an altar to Zeus in the Temple in Jerusalem, and sacrificing a hog on it (in defiance of the Mosaic law against eating or touching dead pigs as unclean). The Maccabean rebellion, led by the Hasmon family of priests, called in Hebrew the Maccabees ("Hammers"), won a degree of independence for Judaea in 164 BCE. It established a new and independent kingdom, once again called Israel and centered around Jerusalem, and ruled by the Hasmonean family. This lasted until its conquest by the Roman general Pompey in 63 BCE, and was the last independent Jewish nation until the twentieth century.

Under the Hasmonean kings, three sects of Jews formed in Judaea. The **Sadducees** were priests and wealthy businesspeople, conservatives intent on preserving the letter of the law. The **Pharisees** were more liberal citizens from all classes who sought to study the applications of the Torah to everyday life. A third general movement was uncompromising in their piety and their disgust with what they considered a corrupted priesthood. The Jewish historian Josephus describes one of its groups: the **Essenes**. Its initiated members were males who dressed in white, shared their property, avoided luxury, and emphasized ritual purity. What may have been a similar or related group retreated to the desert soon after the Hasmonean takeover of the high priesthood in 152 BCE, and developed a fortified compound at Qumran, near the Dead Sea. Their leader was the "Teacher of Righteousness," a priest, reformer, and mystic whose name was not uttered. The community's extensive library, of this community, now known as the Dead Sea Scrolls, was discovered near Qumran in 1947.

Scholars are studying these scrolls for clues to the period between biblical and rabbinic Judaism (to be discussed in the next section). It is possible that members of the sect that collected and wrote them were scattered throughout Palestine, with Qumran their center for study and initiation into states of higher ritual purity and thus closer contact with God. They apparently maintained intense loyalty to Jerusalem as the Holy City and were preparing themselves for a cosmic battle in which the "Sons of Light" would defeat the "Sons of Darkness" and establish a reign of utmost purity centered in Jerusalem.

Eventually the conflicts among the Hasmoneans erupted into civil war. The Roman general Pompey was called in from Syria in 63 BCE to choose between contenders to the Hasmonean throne, but he took over the country instead. There followed four centuries of oppressive Roman rule of Judaea.

Under Roman rule, belief grew among Jews—including the sects living in the desert—about a messianic age in which the people would at last be rescued from their sufferings and Jews would return to their homeland. This belief had been voiced by earlier prophets. For instance, the prophet Ezekiel received a vision in which God showed him a valley of scattered dry human bones, which God reunited and brought back to life.

As well as anticipating the national redemption of Israel, with the Jewish people returning to the land of Israel, the prophets had foreseen a universal destiny for Israel. Combining the particular and universal orientations of Judaism, they had prophesied an "End of Days" in which disaster would be followed by universal redemption, in which all nations would recognize the one God.

Under oppressive Seleucid Greek rule of Palestine, **apocalyptic** literature became very popular. Such literature sees the world in terms of good and evil, predicts God's victory over evil, asserts that God will then reward good people and punish evil people, and urges people to live righteous lives in preparation for that time. Among some Jews, the belief grew that a person, a **Messiah,** would come to bring evil times to an end and establish the reign of peace. In the biblical book of Daniel, probably written while Jews were being persecuted by the Seleucid emperor Antiochus IV (175–164 BCE), Daniel describes a vision of "one like a human being" who would come on heavenly clouds, and on him the white-haired, fiery-throned "Ancient of Days" would confer "everlasting dominion" over all people, a kingship "that shall not be destroyed."[12] By the first century CE, expectations had developed that through the Messiah, God would gather the chosen people and not only free them from oppression but also reinstate Jewish political sovereignty in the land of Israel. Then all nations would recognize that Israel's God is the God of all the world. The messianic end of the age, or end of the world, would be heralded by great oppression and wickedness. Many felt this time was at hand. There were some who felt that Jesus was the Messiah.

Spurred by anti-Roman militias called **Zealots**, some Jews rose up in armed rebellion against Rome in 66 CE. The rebellion was suppressed, and after heroic resistance, the Jewish defenders were slaughtered in the holy walled city of Jerusalem in 70 CE. The Roman legions destroyed the Jewish Temple in Jerusalem, leaving only a course of foundation stones standing. This Temple has never been rebuilt; the foundation stones, called the Western Wall, have been a place of Jewish pilgrimage and prayer for twenty centuries. The Essene movement was apparently annihilated in this uprising.

A second followed in 132–135 CE. Ultimately, Jerusalem was reduced to ruins, along with all Judaean towns. Those Jews who had not been executed were forbidden to read the Torah, observe the Sabbath, or circumcise their sons. None was allowed to enter Jerusalem when it was rebuilt as the Roman city Aelia Capitolina, except on the anniversary of the destruction of the Temple, when they could pay to lean against all that remained of it—the Western Wall—and lament the loss of their sacred home. Judaea was renamed Palestine after the ancient Philistines. Judaism no longer had a physical heart or geographic center.

Rabbinic Judaism

Judaism could have died then, as its people scattered throughout western Asia and the Mediterranean countries. One group who survived the destruction of Judaea were the **rabbis**, inheritors of the Pharisee tradition and the founders of rabbinic Judaism, which has defined the major forms of Jewish practice over the last two thousand years. Another was the movement that had formed around Jesus of Nazareth, later known as Christianity. Between them they kept the teachings of the Tanakh vibrantly alive. Both used the Hebrew Bible as a foundation document, but from it they have developed in their own ways.

The rabbis were teachers, religious decision-makers, and creators of liturgical prayer. No longer were there priests or Temple for offering sacrifices. The substitute for animal sacrifice was liturgical prayer and ethical behavior. Without the Jerusalem Temple, the community gained new importance. The people met in **synagogues**, which simply means "meeting places," to read the Torah and worship communally, praying simply and directly to God. A *minyan*—a quorum of ten adult males—had to be present for community worship.

Everyone was taught the basics of the Torah as a matter of course, but, from the age of five or six, many men also occupied themselves with deep study of the scriptures. Women were excluded or exempted from formal Torah study. Women's family responsibilities at home were considered primary for them. They were responsible for keeping the strict dietary laws, preparing for the Sabbath and other home-centered aspects of Jewish religious life, lighting the Sabbath candles, caring for young children, teaching their daughters the commandments that they would be expected to fulfill as women, and regulating sexual expression in the marriage according to rabbinic laws in order to maintain ritual purity in their homes. Although they were under sacred obligation to pray, women did not receive much religious education. By contrast, literacy was highly valued for men, and this characteristic persisted through the centuries even in the midst of largely illiterate societies. It is said that in the afterlife one can see the Jewish sages still bent over their books studying. This is Paradise.

The revealed scriptures were closed; what remained was to interpret them as indications of God's word and will in history. This process continues to the present, giving Judaism a continually evolving quality in tandem with unalterable roots in the ancient books of Moses. Centering the religion in books and teachings rather than in a geographical location or a politically vulnerable priesthood has enabled the dispersed community to retain a sense of unity across time and space, as well as a common heritage of law, language, and practice.

The rabbis set themselves the task of thoroughly interpreting the Hebrew scriptures. Their process of study, called **Midrash**, yielded two types of interpretation: legal decisions, called *halakhah* ("proper conduct"), and non-legal teachings, called *haggadah* (folklore, sociological and historical knowledge, theological arguments, ritual traditions, sermons, and mystical teachings).

In addition to delving into the meanings of the written Torah, the rabbis undertook to apply the biblical teachings to their contemporary lives, in very different cultural circumstances from those of the ancients, and to interpret scripture in ways acceptable to contemporary values. The model for this delicate task of living interpretation had been set by Hillel the Elder, who taught from about 30 BCE to 10 CE, probably overlapping with the life of Jesus. He was known as a humble and pious scholar, who stressed loving relationships, good deeds, and charity toward the less-advantaged. He also established a valuable set of rules for flexible interpretation of the Torah.

What is hateful to you, do not do to your neighbor:
that is the entire Torah;
the rest is commentary;
go and learn it.

Hillel the Elder[13]

The process of Midrash yielded a vast body of legal and spiritual literature, known in Jewish tradition as the oral Torah. According to rabbinical tradition, God gave Moses two versions of the Torah at Sinai: the written Torah, which appears in the five books of Moses, and the oral Torah, a larger set of teachings, which was memorized and passed down through the generations to the early rabbis. After the fixing of the Jewish canon—the scriptures admitted to the Tanakh in about 90 CE—the rabbinical schools set out to systematize all the commentaries and the oral tradition, which was continually evolving on the basis of expanded and updated understandings of the original oral Torah. In about 200 CE, Judah the Prince completed a terse edition of legal teachings of the oral Torah, which was thenceforth known as the **Mishnah**.

The Mishnah's legal principles for social order are based on logical analysis of how, and why, things are. It sets up hierarchical classifications, such as levels of women's status and domestic responsibilities according to the number of slave girls they bring when married. If, for instance, she brings one slave girl, the wife does not have to grind flour, bake bread, or do laundry, but she must prepare the meals, feed her child, make the bed, and work in wool. This detailing of the woman's obligations to the household economy makes clear her status within the family: She enjoys rights and protection from her husband and benefits from the expectations that she be creative and a moral beacon.

Despite this subordination of women to men, there are also directives about men's responsibility to women—such as a husband's obligation to give sexual pleasure to his wife—and the responsibility of rulers and privileged members of society to insure legal justice for all people and to provide for the material well-being of the lower classes, widows, orphans, and resident aliens. Accordingly, Jews have often been prominent in movements for social justice. The ultimate point in the hierarchy is God.

The Mishnah became the basic study text for rabbinic academies in Judaea and Babylonia, and after several centuries the Mishnah and the rabbis' commentaries on it were organized into the Talmud. This is a vast compendium of law, Midrash, and argument. It does not have a beginning, middle, and end in any traditional sense. It records disagreements among rabbis and sometimes leaves them standing. Drawing on "prooftexts" from the Torah, the rabbis came to different and often inventive conclusions.

There are two authorized Talmuds. Both have the same Mishnah; what differs is the additional commentaries, or **Gamara**. The Jerusalem Talmud is the earlier one, written down about 400 CE. It emphasizes continual study of the Torah as a spiritual practice, a primary way of coming to know the will and ways of God. Studying the Torah is said to increase one's holiness and spiritual power.

The Babylonian Talmud grew out of the other major center of rabbinical study: Babylonia. Completed about 500 CE, it is more developed as an encyclopedia of the Torah, for Jewish life in Babylonia was less precarious. The Babylonian Talmud was better preserved than the Jerusalem Talmud, and it has become the dominant version in Jewish theology and law. It, too, describes study of the Torah as essential to Israel's destiny as a nation upholding God's laws.

Midrash is still open-ended, for significant commentaries and commentaries on commentaries have arisen over the centuries. Rabbis have often disagreed in their interpretations of the Torah, and these disagreements, sometimes between rabbis from different centuries, are presented together. This continual interweaving of historical commentaries, as if all Jewry were present at a single marathon Torah-study event, has been a significant unifying factor for the far-flung, often persecuted Jewish population of the world.

In the process of **exegesis**, rabbis have introduced new ideas into Judaism, while claiming they were merely revealing what already existed in the scriptures. Notions of the soul are not found in the Tanakh, but appear in the Talmud and Midrash. The ways in which God is referred to and perceived also change. In the early biblical narratives, the Lord appears to the patriarchs and Moses in dramatic forms, such as the burning bush. Later, the prophets are visited by angelic messengers, and sometimes hear a divine inner voice speaking to them. In the rabbinical mystical literature, God is even more transcendent and less anthropomorphic. God's presence in the world, in relationship to the people, is called the **Shekhinah**, a feminine noun that often represents the nurturing aspect of God, sometimes depicted as a radiant, winged presence.

The rabbis also developed prayers that over time replaced sacrifices in the Temple. These are still used in contemporary Jewish liturgy. For instance, the *Kaddish*, exaltation of God's name recited repeatedly in Jewish prayer services, is preserved in Aramaic, the language of Babylonia, the great center of early rabbinical Judaism.

> *May His great name be praised to all eternity.*
> *Hallowed and honored, extolled and exalted, adored and acclaimed be the name of*
> *the Holy One, though He is above all the praises, hymns, and songs of adoration*
> *which men can utter.*
>
> *Excerpt from the Kaddish*[14]

At the same time that rabbinical Judaism was further developing beliefs and liturgy for public worship, Christianity was developing as an institution. Scholars think that Jesus was influenced by the Essenes and may have lived with them for a while, but that he was more closely related to the Pharisees and the school of Hillel. He emphasized holiness in worldly life and, like the Jewish prophets, observance of the spirit and the full ethical implications of the law, not merely fulfillment of the letter of the Law. His early apostles emphasized rabbinic traditions holding that, with the arrival of the Messiah and the age of messianic redemption, observance of the ritual laws would be abrogated. The apostle Paul, the major missionary of the Christian sect, preached to both Jews and Gentiles in the diaspora that with the advent of Jesus, God would accept them without their practicing circumcision and Mosaic laws governing many aspects of daily life and hygiene. Belief or disbelief in Jesus and the launching of the messianic age had very practical implications as to whether they observed Jewish law in their daily lives. Both monotheistic and from common stock, Judaism and Christianity grew farther and farther apart.

Judaism in the Middle Ages

In the early centuries of the Common Era, the Jewish population of the land of Israel declined. Some Jews settled in other regions of the Roman Empire, and larger numbers established themselves beyond the boundaries of Rome among the Zoroastrian Persians in Mesopotamia. The city of Babylon, which already had a sizable Jewish population dating back to the biblical exile, became the major center of Jewish intellectual activity, a position it would hold well into the tenth century. The authoritative Babylonian Talmud received its final editing in the middle of the sixth century CE.

Even when the Talmud was complete, the rabbinic enterprise continued. The two great Babylonian rabbinic academies were appealed to with questions from far-flung Jewish communities. Their answers, which were binding on all Jews, and the questions themselves, became a new and enduring form of legal writing, *Responsa* literature, which continues to the present.

When Baghdad became the capital city of the great Abbasid Empire in the eighth century, Jewish life concentrated around that city. Jews were treated relatively well under Islamic rule. Like Christians, they were recognized as a "People of the Book," and allowed to maintain their religious traditions and run their communities autonomously as long as they paid a substantial head tax in acknowledgment of their subordinate status. In Baghdad, as throughout the Islamic Middle East, many Jews were prosperous merchants, professionals, and craftsmen. In the early Middle Ages, in fact, Jews tended to dominate trade between Muslim and Christian realms because of their facility with languages and ability to find supportive co-religionists in virtually any community.

Life under Islamic rule was intellectually exciting for the Jewish community, which had rapidly adopted Arabic as its spoken language. During its early centuries, Islam was far advanced beyond Christian Europe in its explorations of science, medicine, philosophy, poetry, and the fine arts. Jews living in Muslim countries benefited from an atmosphere of cultural creativity and tolerance, and developed Jewish religious philosophy and Hebrew secular poetry. Many Jews were well-known physicians. Muslim Spain, in particular, where some Jews rose to high political position in its courts, is renowned for its outstanding Hebrew poets and major philosophical and scientific Jewish writers.

From time to time, however, Jews were threatened by intolerant Muslim rulers and were forced to flee to other territories. The great scholar and physician Maimonides (1135–1204) was forced to leave his ancestral home of Córdoba, Spain, in the mid-twelfth century; he and his family eventually settled in Egypt. Considered one of the greatest of all Jewish intellectuals, Maimonides is particularly famous for his synthesis between reason and faith. In writings such as *The Guide of the Perplexed* he spoke on behalf of the rationality that had characterized Judaism since the dawning of the rabbinic age:

> *What is man's singular function here on earth? It is, simply, to contemplate abstract intellectual matters and to discover truth. . . . And the highest intellectual contemplation that man can develop is the knowledge of God and his unity.*[15]

Jews who lived in Christian countries were less exposed to the vibrant intellectual energy of the Islamic world between the seventh and twelfth centuries. Christian Europe was primarily a feudal agricultural society in which literacy mainly belonged to the Church. Jews, who were primarily merchants, were among the few town dwellers, and generally lived under charters of protection from the ruler of the area. In France and Germany, Jewish intellectual life flourished, but Christians assumed the financial functions. Jews became expendable, and throughout the later Middle Ages there was a pattern of expulsions of Jews from countries in which they had long lived.

Anti-semitism, or prejudice against Jews, had long been simmering among Christians. While Jews and Christians, like all humans, suffered from hatred and unwarranted attacks, Jews were hated all the more because Jesus was a Jew but many of his own people never accepted Christian claims that he was the Messiah. Jews were blamed for his murder and for preventing his messianic successes by not believing in him.

Beginning in 1095, Jews became victims of Christian crusaders traveling through Europe to defend the Holy Land. They had been provoked by rumors that Christians were being harmed there by Muslims, with Jews as their accomplices. Believing in the holiness of their mission, crusaders and orders of knights also attacked Jews as non-conformists who did not agree with the doctrines of the Christian Church. They massacred so many Jews that many formerly prosperous Jewish communities in Germany were wiped out.

In the twelfth century, rumors were spread in England that Jews were engaged in ritual murders of Christians, and many were subsequently slaughtered. Then, in thirteenth-century Germany, Jews were accused of stealing the consecrated bread used by Christians for communion with Jesus, and then torturing it. Such strange rumors were never verified, but they spread rapidly, and with them, killings of Jews. In the fourteenth century, Jews were blamed for the Plague and were either killed or forced out of many countries. In 1492, tens of thousands of Jews were forced to leave Spain, where they had lived for over a thousand years. Some fled to safety in Portugal or Italy, or the Muslim realms of North Africa and the Ottoman Empire of Turkey. Others chose to convert to Christianity rather than to leave their homeland even though staying in Spain as *conversos* (converted Jews) would expose them to the dreaded Inquisition, which had been established in Spain in 1483. The Inquisition represented the Roman Catholic Church, and its mission was to discover perceived heretics within the Christian community. It had no power over Jews, but it did have jurisdiction over the large numbers of Jews who had converted to Christianity, and who might be practicing their former religion in secret. The Inquisition, which had the power to torture the accused and to execute the convicted, continued to function in Spain and in Spanish territories well into the eighteenth century.

There was further deterioration of Jewish life in western Europe in the sixteenth and seventeenth centuries. After 1555, those Jews who remained in some cities of Italy and Germany were forced to live in **ghettos**, special Jewish-only quarters, which were often walled in and locked at night and during Christian holy days, to limit mixing between Christians and Jews.

During the later Middle Ages, Poland had become a haven for the expelled Jews of western Europe. They rapidly grew in numbers, finding in their new home an enclave of peace and prosperity. By the sixteenth and early seventeenth centuries eastern Europe had become the major European center of Jewish life and scholarship. Jews lived an intensely religious life in villages and towns that were almost completely Jewish, speaking Yiddish, a distinctive Jewish language based on the medieval German they had spoken in western Europe.

In 1648, the flourishing of the Ashkenazi Jewish communities of central and eastern Europe suffered a great setback when the Cossack peasants of the Ukraine revolted against Polish rule. Associating Jewry with their Roman Catholic Polish oppressors and being violently anti-semitic as well, Greek Orthodox people led terrible massacres against the Jews, which were followed by even more killing as Poland collapsed.

In this time of despair in both eastern and western Europe, Jews were heavily taxed and ill-treated. Their longing for deliverance from danger, poverty, and oppression fueled the old messianic dream. Among the "pseudo-Messiahs" who rose to the occasion, the most famous was Shabbatai Tzevi (1626–1676) of Smyrna, a Turkish port. A rather unstable personality, he became convinced that it was his calling to be the Messiah. A young man named Nathan, who became his enthusiastic prophet, sent letters to Jews throughout Europe, Asia, and Africa announcing that the Messiah had at last appeared in his master. Many believed him and prepared for their return to the Holy Land. However, when Tzevi entered the Ottoman Empire, he was arrested and put in jail. Given the choice of converting to Islam or being executed, he chose conversion and was given a government position. The shock to his supporters was terrible.

Kabbalah and Hasidism

Mystical yearning has always been a part of Jewish tradition. The fervent experience of and love for God is an undercurrent in several writings of the biblical prophets, and is incorporated into the Talmud as well. Some mystical writings are found outside the biblical canon, in the extra-biblical collections of texts known as the Apocrypha and the Pseudepigrapha. The apocryphal Book of Enoch describes the ascent to God as a journey through seven heavenly spheres to an audience with the King of the celestial court. The core mystical encounter with indescribable sanctity is based on the vision of the prophet Isaiah (Isaiah 6), and includes the chant of the heavenly court, *"Kadosh, Kadosh, Kadosh"* ("Holy, Holy, Holy"), which is included in all Jewish communal prayer.

In the Middle Ages, Jewish mystical traditions, known as **Kabbalah**, began to be written down. The most important of these books is the Zohar ("Way of Splendor"). The Zohar is a massive and complex offering of stories, explanations of the esoteric levels of the Torah, and descriptions of visionary practice and experiences. It depicts the world we perceive with our senses as but a lower reflection of a splendid higher world. During the sixteenth century Kabbalah's most influential leader was Isaac Luria (1534–1572). He explained creation as the beaming of the divine light into ten special vessels, some of which were shattered by the impact because they contained lower forces that could not bear the intensity of the light. The breaking of the vessels spewed forth particles of evil as well as fragments of light into the world. Humans have a great responsibility to help end chaos and evil in the world by regathering the "sparks of holiness" in the unclean realms to repair the holy vessels. This concept of *tikkun olam* (repairing the world) has continued to be very important in Jewish thought, emphasizing the relationship between God and humans as a covenantal one with reciprocal responsibilities in which both are working together to uplift the world, and where every human act, both good and bad, has ultimate significance. To this end, Luria asked his followers to follow strict ascetic purification practices, prayer, and observance of the commandments of the Torah, and to chant sacred formulas.

Lurianic Kabbalism resurfaced in a very different form in the eighteenth century as **Hasidism**, the path of ecstatic piety. It developed in Ukraine and Poland, where Jews had become subject to legal limitations, poverty-stricken, and fearful for their lives from riots and murders. The rabbis had little to offer them, retreating into academic debates about legal aspects of the Torah.

Into this grim setting came the Baal Shem Tov (1700–1760), a beloved healer and Hasidic teacher, who offered a joyful version of Jewish holiness. He believed that Torah study and obedience to the letter of the law were not superior to deep-felt, pure-hearted prayer; everyone is capable of the highest enlightenment. He asserted that the divine could be found everywhere, in the present, thereby de-emphasizing the perennial waiting for a future Messiah. "Leave sorrow and sadness," he cried; "man must live in joy and contentment, always rejoicing in his lot."[16] Followers of the Baal Shem Tov worshiped through joyous songs and ecstatic, swaying prayer, and found God in the midst of the ghetto.

God can be found everywhere, emphasized the Baal Shem Tov, but can be seen only by those who are not taken in by surface appearances and who really want to find him. God is here in the midst of even the most mundane everyday activities; if carried out in remembrance of God, even eating, drinking, and working become holy acts. It is through the ups and downs of everyday life that the soul advances toward God. The highest goal is *devekut*, "cleaving" to God, free of the egotism and vanity that separate humans from the Holy One.

> *As the hand held before the eye conceals the greatest mountain, so the little earthly life hides from the glance the enormous lights and mysteries of which the world is full, and he who can draw it away from before his eyes, as one draws away a hand, beholds the great shining of the inner worlds.*
>
> *Attributed to Reb Nachman of Bratislava*

Soon an estimated half of all eastern European Jews were followers of the Hasidic path. Spread of the teachings is credited to Dov Ber, who emphasized the importance of the **tzaddik**, or enlightened saint and teacher, called *rebbe* (or Reb) when ordained as a Hasidic spiritual guide. Dov Ber urged Hasidim to take spiritual shelter with a *tzaddik*, whose prayers and wisdom would be more powerful than their own because of the *tzaddik*'s personal relationship with God. This idea stirred enormous opposition from non-Hasidic leaders, who believed that each Jew should be his or her own *tzaddik*. While the position of *tzaddik* became hereditary and was sometimes subject to exploitation by less-than-holy lineage carriers, such charismatic leadership remains a central element and perhaps one of the enduring attractions of modern Hasidism. The religious fervor associated with Hasidism clearly continues as an influence within Judaism, and many of the Hasidic movements themselves still thrive, despite the devastation of the Holocaust and the challenges of modernity.

Judaism and modernity

In the late eighteenth and nineteenth centuries, the great majority of Jews lived in eastern European countries such as Poland and Russia, which were little affected by the eighteenth-century European movement called the Enlightenment. The Enlightenment, however, provided new opportunities and better conditions for the Jews in western Europe. It played down tradition and authority in favor of tolerance, reason, and material progress. In such a rational atmosphere, restrictions on Jews began to decrease. The French Revolution (1789–1792) brought equality for the masses, including Jews living in France, and in the course of the nineteenth century this trend slowly spread to other European nations. Ghettos were torn down, and some Jews even ascended to positions of prominence in western European society. The Rothschild family, for instance, became international financiers, benefactors, and patrons of the arts.

Inspired by Enlightenment views and liberated from the social restrictions that had kept them isolated as a religious community, some "Enlightenment Jews" of Europe embarked on a path of secularization and acculturation that has brought a sea-change in Judaism in the modern world. Baruch Spinoza (1632–1677) questioned the divine source of the Torah, the authority of rabbis, and the sacredness of ritual. Moses Mendelssohn (1729–1786), adopting the Enlightenment ideal of the universalism of humanity, urged Jews to learn German and dress and comport themselves as non-Jews. He also urged governments to separate Church and State, and tolerate their citizens' different beliefs.

Opponents of these trends warned that in the name of Enlightenment Judaism could lose its distinctive position at the center of Jewish life, and that in adapting to the surrounding culture Jews would cease to observe their traditional rituals. Reformers, for their part, insisted that those very halakhic observances were standing in the way of Jews' integration into modern life. In the face of this threat to the integrity of their received religious traditions, some scholars and rabbis asserted the validity of the Oral Law as the word of God, the proper framework for all life, and encouraged Jews not only to live by *halakhah* but also to segregate themselves from non-Jewish secular culture. This position led to what came to be called **Orthodox Judaism**. One of its staunchest advocates was Moses Sofer (1762–1839), the leader of Central European traditional Judaism.

Meanwhile, the reform movement—which became known as **Reform Judaism**—was moving farther and farther away from its traditional moorings. In the second decade of the nineteenth century, the New Israelite Temple Association in Hamburg, Germany, adopted changes that were beginning to appear elsewhere: hymns and sermons in the vernacular instead of Hebrew, a shorter version of the liturgy, emphasis on the Saturday service rather than the traditional prayers three times every weekday, and choirs and organ music as in Christian churches. The reformers also prepared a prayerbook that omitted references to Jews' longing for a personal Messiah and return to Zion.

As these developments were occurring in Europe in response to modernity, in favor of adaptation to or segregation from the surrounding culture, Judaism was also evolving in the Americas. In 1654 a small group of Sephardic Jews who had eventually emigrated to Brazil after their ancestors were expelled from Spain and Portugal by Christian Inquisitors sought to enter the colony of New Amsterdam as refugees. Despite resistance from the local authorities, the Dutch West India Company decreed that they should be admitted to the colony and allowed to live and trade there, because many wealthy Jews in Amsterdam were shareholders in the company. During their twenty-four years in Brazil as the first organized Jewish community in the "New World," the emigrants had enjoyed a period of legal equality and economic freedom. In the New Amsterdam colony as well, they were protected by a 1663 directive from the Dutch West India Company that the colony should allow people to pursue their own religions, so long as they did not cause any trouble.

With the independence of the United States and the framing of its Constitution, Jews as well as other minorities were automatically granted equal rights, under the ideals of equality of all humans and separation of Church and State. The new country became a haven for persecuted minorities, and by 1880 there were 250,000 Jews in the United States, mostly of German origin, and middle-class in occupations and attitudes. Between 1881 and the early 1920s, immigration to the United States totaled two million, mainly Jews from eastern Europe, prompted by virulent anti-semitism in Czarist Russia and endemic Jewish poverty in both Russia and eastern provinces of Austria–Hungary. Today, the United States, with approximately six million Jews, has the largest Jewish population in the world. It continues to be a highly diverse population, consisting of both Jews who are religiously affiliated and those who are not. We will return later to the modern development of various branches of Judaism, but first will look at another major influence on the shape of modern Judaism: the Holocaust, the overwhelmingly tragic event of Jewish history.

The Holocaust

For many Jews the defining event of the twentieth century was the **Holocaust**, the murder of almost six million European Jews by the Nazi leadership of Germany during World War II. These Jews constituted over a third of the Jewish people in the world and half of all Jews in Europe.

Anti-semitism had been part of Greco–Roman culture, and had been present in Europe since the Roman Empire first adopted Christianity as its state religion in the fourth century CE. New and virulent strains of this disease appeared in western Europe at the end of the nineteenth century. Racist theories spread that those of "pure" Nordic blood were genetically ideal, while Jews were a dangerous "mongrel" race.

Reactionary anti-Jewish feelings also resurfaced late in the nineteenth century in Russia and in eastern Europe, where Jews formed a sizable minority of the population and where they were accumulating wealth and establishing a presence in higher educational circles. Jews were increasingly associated with left-wing movements pushing for social change, even though many Jewish socialists such as Leon Trotsky were non-observant Jews. Trotsky's leadership in the violent Bolshevik Revolution and the Red Army brought terrible reprisals, called **pogroms**, against Jewish communities by the White Russians in the civil war. In a thousand separate incidents, up to 70,000 Jews were killed by unrestrained rioting mobs.

In the aftermath of Germany's defeat in World War I and the desperate economic conditions that followed, Adolf Hitler's Nazi Party bolstered its popular support by blaming the Jews for all of Germany's problems. Germany, the Nazis claimed, could not regain its health until all Jews were stripped of their positions in German life or driven out of the country. Demands to eliminate the Jews for the sake of "racial hygiene" were openly circulated. Seeing the writing on the wall, many Jews, including eminent professionals, managed to emigrate, leaving their homes, their livelihoods, and most of their possessions behind. Others stayed, hoping that the terrifying signs would prove to be short-lived.

With Hitler's rise to power, acts of violence against Jews in Germany were instigated by his Nazi thugs and laws were passed that separated Jews from the rest of the population and deprived them of their legal and economic rights. When Hitler annexed Austria in 1938 and then invaded Poland, Denmark, Norway, Belgium, Holland, and France, several million more Jews fell under Nazi control.

Immediately after World War II began with the German invasion of Poland in 1939, systematic oppression started, with orders to all Polish Jews to move into the towns, where walled ghettos were created to confine them. Jews were made to wear a yellow or white badge with the Star of David on it to reveal their stigmatized status, and since all other jobs were taken away from them, they could do only menial labor.

Along the Russian front, special "Action Groups" were assigned to slaughter Jews, gypsies, and commissars (heads of government departments) as the German troops advanced, and to incite the local militia to do the same. One cannot comprehend the numbers of men, women, and children killed in these mass murders—34,000 at Babi Yar, 26,000 at Odessa, 32,000 at Vilna—probably totaling hundreds of thousands.

By 1942, large-scale death camps had been set up by the Nazis to facilitate the "Final Solution"—the total extermination of all Jews in Europe. From the ghettos Jews were transported by cattle cars (in which many suffocated to death) from all over Europe to concentration camps. There they were starved, worked to death as slaves, tortured, "experimented" on, and/or shipped to extermination camps. Industrial-scale gas chambers were found to be the most efficient means of killing.

The governments of some countries, to a greater or lesser extent, tried to protect their Jews; also some individuals, at great personal risk, in every part of Europe, hid Jews or tried to help them escape. For example, Chiune Sugihara, a Japanese diplomat stationed in Lithuania, and then Berlin and Prague, managed to issue Japanese transit visas to some 10,000 Jews, ignoring all risks to himself in order to help them quickly escape from danger. But there was little outcry against Hitler's genocidal actions from the outside world. In hindsight, many historians have concluded that Hitler's hideous policy could have been slowed by determined resistance from free Allied countries.

No modern Jewish thinker can ignore the challenge that the Holocaust poses to traditional Jewish beliefs of an omnipotent and caring God. Elie Wiesel (b. 1928), who as a boy survived a Nazi death camp in Poland, but lost all his other family members and was witness to and sufferer of great atrocities, was so embittered against God that he could not bring himself to utter the traditional prayers:

> Why should I bless Him? In every fiber I rebelled. Because He had had thousands of children burned in His pits? Because He kept six crematoria working night and day, on Sundays and feast days? Because in His great might He had created Auschwitz, Birkenau, Buna, and so many factories of death? How could I say to Him: "Blessed art Thou, Eternal, Master of the Universe, Who chose us from among the races to be tortured day and night, to see our fathers, our mothers, our brothers, end in the crematory?"[17]

Wiesel says that we cannot turn away from the questions about how it could happen, for genocidal actions are being undertaken against other minority groups in our times as well.

Zionism and contemporary Israel

Zionism is the Jewish movement dedicated to the establishment of a politically viable, internationally recognized Jewish state in the biblical land of Israel. While political Zionism was a reaction to increasing anti-semitism in Europe in the late nineteenth century, it is a movement with deep roots in Judaism and Jewish culture. The desire to end the centuries-long exile from **Zion** (the site of the Jerusalem Temples) was a central theme in all Jewish prayer and in many religious customs. Jewish messianism is focused around a descendant of King David who will return his united people to the land of Israel, where Jewish sovereignty will be eternally re-established in an atmosphere of universal peace.

Zionism became an organized international political movement under the leadership of the journalist Theodor Herzl (1860–1904), who believed that the

Jews could never defend themselves against anti-semitism until they had their own nation. Herzl worked to provide political guarantees for the Jewish settlement that existed in Palestine through the nearly two thousand years of exile and to offer institutional support to encourage Jews from around the world to immigrate to Palestine through the formation of various Zionist organizations. Simultaneously, pioneers, mainly secular Jews from eastern Europe, began increasing the Jewish presence on the land. The 1917 Balfour Declaration stated Britain's support for limited Jewish settlement in Palestine following World War I. While most Jews worldwide also applauded this Zionist victory, not all supported the movement. Most Reform Jews believed the destiny of Jews was to be lived out among the Gentiles, where the Enlightenment had fueled hopes of a freer future and where Jews hoped they could be recognized as legitimate citizens of the countries in which they lived. Some support for Zionism came from traditional Orthodox Jews, but not all of them embraced the idea. Many felt it was God who had punished the people for their unfaithfulness by sending them away from the promised land and that only God would end the exile.

Nonetheless, by a United Nations decision in 1947, Palestine was partitioned into two areas, one to be governed by Jews and the other by Arabs, with Jerusalem an international zone. The Jews accepted the plan, and in 1948 declared Israel an independent Jewish State with full rights for minorities. However, the Arabs did not accept the partition and as soon as British troops moved out, Israel was attacked by its Arab neighbors—Jordan, Iraq, Syria, Lebanon, and Egypt. Outnumbered, Israel nonetheless managed to control a larger area than was allotted to it in the partition plan, bringing many Arabs under its rule. Arabs who fled to avoid violence were not allowed into the surrounding countries; they were kept in refugee camps, in which for generations people have continued to live in distress and growing hatred for Israel. Egypt and Jordan kept sending guerrilla troops, known as *fedayeen*, to attack the Israelis, whose sovereignty they refused to recognize.

When an attack by Arab neighbors and Palestinians seemed imminent in 1967, Israel launched a stunningly successful pre-emptive strike—the "Six-Day War." Nevertheless, the Arab countries still refused to recognize Israel's nationhood and Palestinian resistance grew. In 1973, Egypt and Syria launched a surprise attack which the smaller but militarily superior Jewish forces managed to thwart. Despair over attaining any lasting peace with the surrounding Arabs brought hardliners to the fore in Israeli politics. They saw in expanded settlements a fulfilment of biblical prophecy and a defense against Palestinian terrorism.

From time to time, peace has seemed almost possible, but it has not yet happened. Informal frameworks for Palestinian–Israeli settlement such as the Geneva Accords of 2003 offered some hope of decreasing hostilities by creating two independent states of Palestine and Israel, but they have not satisfactorily dealt with major sticking points. One of these is the "Right of Return" sought by Palestinian refugees from the 1948–1949 war and their descendants. Countering this, some Jews point out that over 600,000 Jews had to flee their homes in Arab countries where they were persecuted after the creation of Israel. There is also Palestinian concern that the new state of Palestine would consist only of isolated, dependent enclaves under Israeli control. Yet another problem is control of and access to sites which are holy to both Muslims and Jews such as the Temple

Mount in Jerusalem, known to Muslims as the place where the Prophet Muhammad began his Night Journey to the seven heavens.

One attempt by Jews to protect themselves from Palestinians has been the building of massive security fences and walls up to twenty-five feet high that impede the two communities mixing. Critics claim that while these are supposedly built to stop Palestinian suicide bombers, they are actually ways of appropriating more land and water resources. Palestinian communities are turned into isolated cages in which farmers are cut off from their fertile land and water, and in some cases, from the other side of their now-divided villages. However, hopes of more peaceful co-existence between Israel and Palestine have grown with the withdrawal of Jewish settlers from the West Bank and Gaza Strip. And many Israelis and Jews in other countries are actively seeking peace and reconciliation with Palestinians. Efforts persist to keep person-to-person contacts open between Israeli Jews and those who have historically been pitted their opponents. Women's encounters have been particularly fruitful in developing interfaith friendships that transcend political violence and separation.

Tensions also exist within the Jewish community in Israel. Jewish settlers have come to Israel from many backgrounds. Those of eastern European origin—the Ashkenazi who founded the state—tend to regard themselves as superior to settlers from other areas. Ultra-Orthodox religious authorities insist on strict observance of religious rituals, assert considerable control over education and politics, and claim that converts consecrated by Reform and Conservative rabbis in the United States are not really Jews. The Orthodox rabbis generally favor hardline political policies in Israel, and yet Orthodox Jews are exempted from military service. There is also internal dissension over relationships with the Palestinians. Some sympathize with the their situation, while Religious Zionists believe the land has been promised to them by God for the redemption of the Jewish people and eventually the entire world. The ancient Zionist vision remains unfulfilled. Aviezer Ravitzky comments, "As the rabbis said, the End of Days continues to 'tarry.'"[18]

Although the dream of a sovereign Torah-based nation is still elusive, Israel is nonetheless a unique home or place of pilgrimage for Jews, and many immigrants are still arriving from countries such as India, Yemen, Morocco, Ethiopia, and the former Soviet Union. According to the Law of Return passed in 1950, any Jew is granted automatic citizenship in Israel. Even though only an estimated fifteen percent of Israelis claim to live completely by religious laws, and most Israeli Jews describe themselves as "non-religious," Israel is a country in which businesses close and buses stop running on the Jewish Sabbath, Jewish holidays are national holidays, and most people celebrate Passover, marry other Jews, and light the Chanukah menorah if not the Sabbath candles. Jewish identity in Israel thus retains something of its religious roots even among the secular-minded.

Torah

It is difficult to outline the tenets of the Jewish faith. As we have seen, Jewish spiritual understanding has changed repeatedly through history. Rationalists and mystics have often differed. Since the nineteenth century, there has been disagreement between liberal and traditional Jews, to be discussed later.

Nevertheless, there are certain major themes that can be extricated from the vast history and literature of Judaism. Jewish teachings are known as the **Torah.** In its narrowest sense, the Torah refers to the Five Books of Moses. On the next level, it means the entire Hebrew Bible and the Talmud, the written and the oral law. For some, "Torah" can refer to all sacred Jewish literature and observance. At the highest level, Torah is God's will, God's wisdom.

The one God

The central Jewish belief is monotheism. It has been stated in different ways in response to different cultural settings (emphasizing the divine unity when Christians developed the concept of the Holy Trinity, for instance, and emphasizing that God is formless and ultimate holiness in opposition to the earthly local gods). But the central theme is that there is one Creator God, the "cause of all existent things."[19]

God is everywhere, even in the darkness, as David sings in Psalms:

Where can I escape from Your spirit?
Where can I flee from Your presence?
If I ascend to Heaven, You are there:
if I descend to Sheol [the underworld],
You are there too.

If I take wing with the dawn
to come to rest on the western horizon,
even there Your hand will be guiding me,
Your right hand will be holding me fast.

Psalm 139:7–14

This metaphysical understanding of God's oneness is difficult to explain in linear language, which refers to the individual objects perceived by the senses. As the eleventh-century Spanish poet and mystical philosopher Ibn Gabirol put it, "None can penetrate . . . the mystery of Thy unfathomable unity."[20]

One of the most elegant attempts to "explain" God's oneness has been offered by the great twentieth-century thinker Abraham Joshua Heschel (1907–1972). He linked the idea of unity to eternity, explaining that in eternity, "past and future are not apart; here is everywhere, and now goes on forever." Time as we know it is only a fragment, "eternity broken in space." According to Heschel:

The craving for unity and coherence is the predominant feature of a mature mind. All science, all philosophy, all art are a search after it. But unity is a task, not a condition. The world lies in strife, in discord, in divergence. Unity is beyond, not within, reality. . . . The world is not one with God, and this is why his power does not surge unhampered throughout all stages of being. Creature is detached from the Creator, and the universe is in a state of spiritual disorder. Yet God has not withdrawn entirely from this world. The spirit of this unity hovers over the face of all plurality, and the major trend of all our thinking and striving is its mighty intimation. The goal of all efforts is to bring about the restitution of the unity of God and world.[21]

> *Plurality is incompatible with the sense of the ineffable. You cannot ask in regard to*
> *the divine: Which one? There is only one synonym for God: One.*
>
> > *Abraham Joshua Heschel[22]*

In traditional Judaism, God is often perceived as a loving Father who is none-theless infinitely majestic, sometimes revealing divine power when the children need chastising.

Love for God

The essential commandment to humans is to love God. The central prayer in any Jewish religious service and the inscription on the *mezuza* at the doorpost of every traditional Jewish home is the *Shema Israel*:

> *Hear, O Israel! The Lord is our God, the Lord alone. You shall love the Lord your*
> *God with all your heart and with all your soul and with all your might. Take to*
> *heart these instructions with which I charge you this day. Impress them upon your*
> *children. Recite them when you stay at home and when you are away, when you lie*
> *down and when you get up. Bind them as a sign on your hand and let them serve*
> *as a symbol on your forehead; inscribe them on the doorposts of your house and on*
> *your gates.*
>
> > *Deuteronomy 6:4–9*

Even Maimonides, the great proponent of reason and study, asserted the pri-macy of love for God. He emphasized that one should not love God from selfish or fearful motivations, such as receiving earthly blessings or avoiding problems in the life after death. One should study the Torah and fulfill the commandments out of sheer love of God.

The sacredness of human life

Humans are the pinnacle of creation, created in the "image" of God, according to the account of Creation in Genesis 1. Jews do not take this passage to mean that God literally looks like a human. It is often interpreted in an ethical sense: that humans are so wonderfully endowed that they can mirror God's qualities, such as justice, wisdom, righteousness, and love.

All people are potentially equal; they are said to be common descendants of the first man and woman. But they are also potentially perfectible, and in raising themselves they uplift the world. God limited the divine power by giving humans free will, involving them in the responsibility for the world's condition, and their own. If we are suffering, according to the Talmud, we should examine our own deeds.

The German scholar Martin Buber (1878–1965) described the relationship between God and humans as reciprocal:

> *You know always in your heart that you need God more than everything; but do*
> *you not know too that God needs you—in the fulness of His eternity needs you?*
> *How would man exist, how would you exist, if God did not need him, did not need*

you? You need God, in order to be—and God needs you, for the very meaning of your life. . . . There is divine meaning in the life of the world . . . of human persons, of you and of me. . . . We take part in creation, meet the Creator, reach out to him, helpers and companions.[23]

Human life is sacred, rather than lowly and loathsome; Judaism celebrates the body. Sexuality within marriage is holy, and the body is honored as the instrument through which the soul is manifested on earth. Indeed, according to some thinkers, body and soul are an inseparable totality.

> *I praise You, for I am awesomely, wondrously made.*   *Psalm 139:14*

Law

Because of the great responsibility of humankind, traditional Jews give thanks that God has revealed in the written and oral Torah the laws by which they can be faithful to the divine will and fulfill the purposes of Creation by establishing a Kingdom of God here on earth, in which all creatures can live in peace and fellowship. In the words of the biblical prophet Isaiah, speaking for God,

The wolf and the lamb shall graze together,
And the lion shall eat straw like the ox,
And the serpent's food shall be earth.
In all my sacred mount
Nothing evil or vile shall be done.[24]

To the extent that traditional Jews act according to the Torah, they feel they are upholding their part of the ancient covenant with God.

The Torah, as indicated through rabbinic literature, is said to contain 613 commandments, or **mitzvot** (singular: **mitzvah**). Jewish law does not differentiate between sacred and secular life, so these include general ethical guidelines such as the Ten Commandments and the famous saying in Leviticus 19:18—"Love your fellow as yourself"—plus detailed laws concerning all aspects of life, such as land ownership, civil and criminal procedure, family law, sacred observances, diet, and ritual slaughter. The biblical Book of Genesis sets forth the Noahide Code of seven universal principles for a moral and spiritual life: idolatry, blasphemy against God, murder, theft, sexual behaviors outside marriage, and cruelty to animals are all prohibited, and the rule of law and justice in society is affirmed as a positive value.

From the time of its final editing in Babylonia in the mid-sixth century CE, the Talmud, together with its later commentaries, has served as a blueprint for Jewish social, communal, and religious life. Through the rabbinic tradition, law became the main category of Orthodox Jewish thought and practice, and learned study of God's commandments one of the central expressions of faith.

From a contemporary viewpoint, Ismar Schorsch notes that many ancient commandments are ecologically useful, for they restrain how humanity uses the natural environment. They are addressed to humans not as wise masters of the earth, as in the first account of Creation in Genesis, but as the disobedient Adam and Eve of the second Creation story, who must be saved from themselves lest they destroy the planet, "for as the Bible so often avers: the land ultimately belongs to its Creator and we mortals are but His tenants."[25]

Suffering and faith

Jewish tradition depicts the universe as being governed by an all-powerful, personal God who intervenes in history to reward the righteous and punish the unjust. Within this context, Jews have had considerable difficulty in answering the eternal question: Why must the innocent suffer? This question has been particularly poignant since the Holocaust.

The Hebrew Bible brings up the issue with the parable of Job, a God-fearing and wealthy man. In a conversation with God, Satan predicts that Job will drop his faith and blaspheme the Lord if he is stripped of his possessions. With God's assent, Satan tests Job by destroying all he has, including his children and his health. On hearing the news of his children's deaths

> Job arose, tore his robe, cut off his hair, and threw himself on the ground and worshiped. He said, "Naked came I out of my mother's womb, and naked shall I return there; the Lord has given, and the Lord has taken away, blessed be the name of the Lord."[26]

With an itchy inflammation covering him from head to foot, Job begins to curse his life and to question God's justice. In the end, he acknowledges not only God's power to control the world but also his inscrutable wisdom, which is beyond human understanding. God rewards him with long life and even greater riches than he had before the test.

Debate over the meanings of this story has continued over the centuries. One rabbinical interpretation is that Satan was cooperating with God in helping Job grow from fear of God to love of God. Another is that faith in God will finally be rewarded in this life, no matter how severe the temporary trials. Another is that those who truly desire to grow toward God will be asked to suffer more, that their sins will be expiated in this life so that they can enjoy the divine bliss in the life to come. Such interpretations assume a personal, all-powerful, loving God doing what is best for the people, even when they cannot understand God's ways. In such belief, God is seen as always available, like a shepherd caring for his sheep, no matter how dark the outer circumstances.

> Though I walk through a valley of deepest darkness,
> I fear no harm, for You are with me;
> Your rod and Your staff—they comfort me.
>
> *Psalm 23:4*

On the other hand, oppression and then the Holocaust have led some Jews to complain to God in anguish. They, too, feel close to God, but in a way that allows them to scream at God, as it were. In questioning the justice of history, they hold God responsible for what is inexplicably monstrous. But even in the Holocaust, there were those who held fast to hope for better times. As they walked to their death in Nazi gas chambers, some were reciting the hymn *Ani maamin*: "I believe with complete faith in the coming of the Messiah, and even though he may delay, nevertheless I anticipate every day that he will come."[27]

Sacred practices

Since the rabbinic period began, a major Jewish spiritual practice has been daily scriptural study. Boys were traditionally taught how to read and write ancient Hebrew and how to interpret scripture through the process of exegesis, by means of the oral Torah. This required extensive knowledge of the scriptures and concentrated intellectual effort. This classical pattern continues today even in the diaspora, where some children continue to be trained in special schools to carry on the study of the Torah, thus encouraging them not only to learn and obey the commandments but also through rational analysis to delve into deeper understanding of truth.

In addition to study, a Jew is urged to remember God in all aspects of life, through prayer and observance of the commandments. These commandments are not otherworldly. Many are rooted in the body, and spiritual practices often engage all the senses in awareness of God.

Boys are ritually circumcised when they are eight days old, to honor the seal of God's commandment to Abraham. Orthodox Jews consider women ritually impure during their menstrual periods and for seven blood-free days afterwards, during which time they and their husbands are prohibited from having sexual intercourse with each other. At the end of this forbidden period Orthodox Jewish women undertake complete immersion in a **mikva**, a special deep bath structure, symbolizing their altered state. Marital sex is sacred, with the Sabbath night the holiest time for making love. By contrast, adultery is strictly forbidden as one of the worst sins against God, for Jewish tradition is extremely concerned with maintaining pure lines of descent.

What one eats is also of cosmic significance, for according to the Torah some foods are definitely unclean. For example, the only ritually acceptable, or **kosher**, meats, are those from warmblooded animals with cloven hoofs which chew their cuds, such as cows, goats, and sheep. Poultry is kosher, except for birds of prey, but shellfish is not. Meat is also kosher only if it has been butchered in the traditional way with an extremely sharp, smooth knife by an authorized Jewish slaughterer. Great pains are taken to avoid eating blood; meat must be soaked in water and then drained on a salted board before cooking. Meat and milk cannot be eaten together, and separate dishes are maintained for their preparation and serving.

These dietary instructions are laid out in the biblical Book of Leviticus, which quotes God as saying to Moses and Aaron, "For I the Lord am He who brought you up from the land of Egypt to be your God: you shall be holy, for I am holy."[28] The rules of diet, if strictly followed, give Jews a feeling of special sacred identity and link them to the eternal authority of the Torah.

Some contemporary Jews feel that consciousness about what they eat should be extended to environmental considerations. To them, the styrofoam box in which a cheeseburger is sold at fast-food places is as much a problem as the mixing of meat and milk. Nuclear power-generated electricity used for cooking might itself be non-kosher, as long as there is no safe provision for disposing of nuclear waste.

For traditional observant Jews, the morning begins with a prayer before they open their eyes to thank God for restoring the soul. The hands must then be washed before reciting blessings and, for all traditional male Jews, putting a special fringed rectangle of cloth around the neck. It is usually worn under the clothes as a reminder of the privilege of being given divine commandments. For weekday morning prayers men also put *t'fillin*, or phylacteries, small leather boxes containing biblical verses about the covenant with God, on the forehead and the upper arm, held against the heart, in fulfillment of the Shema command-ment, as literally understood: "Bind them [the Shema's words about the primacy of love for God] as a sign on your hand and let them serve as a symbol on your forehead." Traditional Jewish men also wear a fringed prayer shawl, or *talit*, whose fringes act as reminders of God's commandments, and keep their heads covered at all times, if possible.

Traditionally, prayers are recited on waking and at bedtime. In addition, three prayer services are chanted daily in a synagogue by men if there is a *minyan* (quorum of ten). Women can say them also, but they are excused from rigid schedules partly because of their household responsibilities, and partly because of the belief that women have a more intuitive sense of spirituality.

Jews are also expected to give thanks continually. One should recite a hundred benedictions to God every day. To this end, there is a blessing to be said every time one takes a drink of water. There is even a blessing to be recited after using the toilet:

> *Blessed art thou, our God, Ruler of the universe, who hast formed (human) beings in wisdom, and created in them a system of ducts and tubes. It is well known before thy glorious throne that if but one of these be opened, or if one of those be closed, it would be impossible to exist in thy presence. Blessed art thou, O God, who healest all creatures and doest wonders.[29]*

The Jewish **Sabbath** is observed as an eternal sign of the covenant between the Jews and God. The Sabbath runs from sunset Friday night to sunset Saturday night, because the Jewish "day" begins with nightfall. The Friday night service welcomes the Sabbath as a bride and is often considered an opportunity to drop away the cares of the previous week so as to be in a peaceful state for the day of rest. Just as God is said to have created the world in six days and then rested on the seventh, all work is to cease when the Sabbath begins.

The Saturday morning service incorporates public and private prayers, singing, and the reading of passages from the Pentateuch and Prophets sections of the Hebrew Bible. Torah scrolls are kept in a curtained ark on the wall facing Jerusalem. They are hand-lettered in Hebrew and are treated with great rever-ence. It is a great honor to be "called up" to read from the Torah.

More liberal congregations may place emphasis on an in-depth discussion of the passage read. Often it is examined not only from an abstract philosophical perspective but also from the point of view of its relevance to political events and everyday attempts to live a just and humane life. Torah study, and study of all Jewish literature, is highly valued as a form of prayer in itself, and synagogues

An Interview with Herman Taube

Herman Taube is a poet, Professor Emeritus of Jewish Studies and Yiddish Literature, and volunteer chaplain to nursing home patients. He emigrated to the United States in 1947 from Poland with his wife, who had earlier been sent to a concentration camp where her younger sister and mother died. During World War II, Herman was a medic working side by side with Russian Orthodox and Muslim doctors in Uzbekhistan to aid people in a refugee camp. He says:

"If you do charitable work—if you help in clinics, if you help unfortunate children, if you go into the jails to help inmates—this is God's work. It is not the responsibility of the rich only to help the poor. Even the poorest man has to give charity. This is the law in Jewish religion.

"Maimonides says, and Jews are saying every morning in their prayers, that a human being has to believe every day in the coming of the Messiah. Messiah does not come with a long beard and a donkey. Messiah can be you. Messiah can be a man on the street who helps a fellow human being. In the Hebrew Bible, in the Talmud, there are quotations indicating that the Messiah will come in a generation which is full of innocence or full of guilt—one of the two. And he will spiritually lead the people away from evil. I think this will become a messianic era.

"Look at the fall of communism, the fall of fascism in our generation. Something is changing. You don't have to go far—look at Washington. You see good people living in the streets, with no roof over their head. They cannot make a meal. On the other side, you see those big parties where people spend millions. There is a need for a messianic age, a need for a better world.

"A reporter asked me, 'Can you believe in God after the Holocaust?' Belief is not something static. My wife and I sometimes ask, 'Where was God?' A million and a half Jewish children were killed. Little boys and girls who were just learning how to say, 'Mama,' and the grandmother said, 'How big is the baby?' and tried to pick up their hands. And this child was taken and thrown into a lamppost. So yes, there are questions. We have no answers.

"Why did Polish people, nuns, and plain peasants risk their lives to save Jewish people, when they knew that for saving a Jew's life their house would be burned down? And their children were taken into forced labor. Why did the people of Assisi save sixty Jewish people under the noses of the Nazis? The Vatican wasn't too helpful, didn't speak up, but they, the simple people, risked their lives. So there is goodness in the world, too. There is goodness and Godness in the hearts of those people.

"The Talmud says God said, 'You don't believe in me? So you don't believe in me. But keep my commandments. Care for the poor and for the widows.' This is exactly what a lot of those Messiahs are doing.

"My wife doesn't like to be interviewed. It's like pulling off a bandage from an open wound. Even after forty-five years, it comes to the holidays and she's missing her mother and her sister. That unbelievable guilt feeling: Why did we survive and they die?

"I believe in God. There is a Power above us that rules our life. We do not see it, we cannot comprehend it. But there is something. I do not deny Him—or Her; maybe it's a Her. And I don't deny my roots."

usually have libraries for this purpose, sometimes in the same space that is used for worship.

In Hasidic congregations, the emphasis falls on the intensity of praying, or *davening*, even in saying fixed prayers from the prayer book. Some sway their bodies to induce the self-forgetful state of ecstatic communion with the Loved One. Others quietly shift their attention from earthly concerns to "cleave to God." The rabbinical tradition states the ideal in prayer: "A person should always see himself as if the Shekhinah is confronting him."[30]

In addition to, or instead of, going to a service welcoming the Sabbath, observant families usually begin the Sabbath eve with a special Friday night dinner. The mother lights candles to bring in the Sabbath light; the father recites a blessing over the wine. Special braided bread, *challah*, is shared as a symbol of the double portions of manna in the desert. The rituals help to set a different tone for the day of rest, as do commandments against working, handling money, traveling except by foot, lighting a fire, cooking, and the like. The Sabbath day is set aside for public prayer, study, thought, friendship, and family closeness, with the hope that this renewed life of the spirit will then carry through the week to come.

It is customary to recognize coming of age, at thirteen, in Jewish boys by the **Bar Mitzvah** ("son of the commandment") ceremony. The boy has presumably undertaken some religious instruction, including learning to pronounce Hebrew, if not always to understand it. He is called up to read a portion from the Torah scroll and recite a passage from one of the books of the Prophets, in Hebrew, and then perhaps to give a short teaching about a topic from the reading. Afterwards there may be a simple *kiddush*, a celebration with blessing of wine and sweet bread or cake, but a big party is more likely. This custom of welcoming the boy to adult responsibilities has been extended to girls in non-Orthodox congregations in the **Bat Mitzvah** ("daughter of the commandment").

Holy days

Judaism follows an ancient lunar calendar of annual holidays and memorials linked to special events in history. The spiritual year begins with the High Holy Days of Rosh Hashanah and Yom Kippur. Rosh Hashanah (New Year's Day), a time of spiritual renewal in remembrance of the original creation of the world, is celebrated on the first two days of the seventh month (around the fall equinox). For thirty days prior to Rosh Hashanah, each morning synagogue service brings the blowing of the *shofar* (a ram's horn that produces an eery, unearthly blast) to remind the people that they stand before God. At the service on the eve of Rosh Hashanah, a prayer is recited asking that all humanity will remember what God has done, that there will be honor and joy for God's people, and that righteousness will triumph while "all wickedness vanishes like smoke."[31]

The ten Days of Awe follow Rosh Hashanah. People are encouraged to change inwardly, by looking at their mistakes of the past year. It is said that during this period, God makes it easier for a person to be repentant and is also more likely to accept repentance. A biblical passage from the prophet Isaiah is cited: "Seek ye the Lord while He may be found, Call ye upon Him while He is near."[32]

Yom Kippur completes the High Holy Days, renewing the sacred covenant with

God in a spirit of atonement and cleansing. Historically, this was the only time when the high priest entered the Holy of Holies in the Temple of Jerusalem, and the only time that he would pronounce the sacred name of the Lord, YHWH, in order to ask for forgiveness of the people's sins. Today, there is an attempt at personal inner cleansing, and individuals must ask pardon from everyone they may have wronged during the past year. If necessary, restitution for damages should be made. Congregations also confess their sins communally, ask that their negligence be forgiven, and pray for their reconciliation to God in a new year of divine pardon and grace.

Sukkot is a fall harvest festival. A simple outdoor booth (a *sukkah*) is built and decorated as a dwelling place of sorts for seven days. Usually this is done as a ritual act, but seeking a deeper experience of the meaning of Sukkot, some contemporary Jews are actually attempting to live in the *sukkah* they construct. Michael Lerner relates:

> *The idea of moving out of my apartment or house to live in a* sukkah *always seemed impractical to me until I tried it. Living in a temporary shelter— particularly one with a water-permeable roof made of twigs, reeds, vines, tree branches, and other forms of vegetation arranged in such a way that one can see through them to the stars—has a special effect of reconnecting urban and suburban dwellers to the natural order, and to the transitory nature of our carefully constructed forms of material security.*[33]

The fragile home reminds the faithful that their real home is in God, who sheltered their ancestors on the way from Egypt to the promised land of Canaan. Some contemporary groups also pray for peace amid our vulnerability to nuclear war. Participants hold the *lulav* (a bundle made of a palm branch, myrtle twigs, and willow twigs) in one hand and the *etrog* (a citrus fruit) in the other and wave them together toward the four compass directions and to earth and sky, praising God and acknowledging him as the unmoving center of creation. Traditionally there was an offering of water, precious in the desert lands of the patriarchs, and great merrymaking. During the Second Temple days, the ecstatic celebration even included burning of the priests' old underclothes. The day after the seven-day Sukkot festival is Simhat Torah ("Joy in Torah"), ending the yearly cycle of Torah readings, from Creation to the death of Moses, and beginning again.

Near the winter solstice, the darkest time of the year, comes Hanukkah, the Feast of Dedication. Each night for eight nights, another candle is lit on a special candle holder. The amount of light gradually increases like the lengthening of sunlight. Historically, Hanukkah was a celebration of the victory of the Maccabean Rebellion against the attempt by Antiochus to force non-Jewish practices on the Jewish people. According to legend, when the Jews regained access to the Temple, they found only one jar of oil left undefiled, still sealed by the high priest. It was enough to stay alight for only one day, but by a miracle, the oil stayed burning for eight days. Many Jewish families also observe the time by nightly gift-giving. The children have their own special Hanukkah pastimes, such as spinning the *dreidel*, a top with four letters on its sides as an abbreviation of the sentence "A great miracle happened there."

As the winter rainy season begins to diminish in Israel, some Jews celebrate the reawakening of nature on Tu B'shvat. Observances lavish appreciation on a variety of fruits and plants. In Israel, the time is now marked by the planting of trees to help restore life to the desert.

On the full moon of the month before spring comes Purim. It commemorates the legend of Esther, queen of Persia, and Mordecai, who saved their fellow Jews from destruction by the evil viceroy Haman. It has been linked to Mesopotamian mythology about the goddess Ishtar, whose spring return brings joy and fertility. Purim is a bawdy time of dressing in costumes and mocking life's seriousness, and the jokes frequently poke fun at sacred Jewish practices. As the story of Esther is read from an ornate scroll, the congregation responds with noisy stomping, rattles, horns, and whistles whenever Haman's name is read. Purim is also celebrated with gifts of money to the poor and gifts of food to friends and family.

The next major festival is Pesach, or Passover, which celebrates the liberation from bondage in Egypt and the spring-time advent of new life. It was the tenth plague, death to all first-born sons of the Egyptians, that finally brought the pharaoh to relent. The Israelites were warned to slaughter a lamb for each family and mark their doors with its blood so that the angel of death would pass over them. They were to roast the lamb and eat it with unleavened bread and bitter herbs. So quickly did they depart that they didn't even have time to bake the bread, which is said to have baked in the sun as they carried it on their heads. The beginning of Pesach is still marked by a **Seder** dinner, with the eating of unleavened bread (*matzah*) to remember the urgency of the departure, and bitter herbs as a reminder of slavery, so that they would never impose it on other peoples. Also on the table are *charoset* (a sweet fruit and nut mixture, a reminder of the mortar that the enslaved Israelites molded into bricks) and salt water (a reminder of the tears of the slaves) into which parsley or some other plant (a reminder of spring life) is dipped and eaten. Children ask ritual questions about why these things are done, as basic religious instruction. A movement for contemporary **liturgical** renewal has yielded many new scripts for the Seder—such as special liturgies for feminists, for secular Zionists, and for co-celebration of Pesach with Muslims.

A new holy day may be celebrated in April or May: Holocaust Memorial Day. Observances often include the singing in Yiddish of a song from the Jewish Resistance Movement. In part:

> *Never say that you are*
> *going your last way,*
> *though leaden skies*
> *blot out the blue of day.*
> *The hour for which we*
> *long will certainly appear.*[34]

In Israel, Holocaust Remembrance Day is observed with a country-wide minute of silence, in which all traffic, speaking, and movement stop entirely. This is a powerful secular ritual that enables secular and religious Jews to remember the Holocaust together.

Early summer brings Shavuot, traditionally identified with the giving of the Torah to Moses at Mount Sinai and the people's hearing of the voice of God. It is likely that Shavuot was initially a summer harvest festival that later was linked with the revelation of the Torah. In Israeli kibbutzim, the old practice of bringing the first fruits to God has been revived. Elsewhere, the focus is on reading the Ten Commandments and on presenting the Torah as a marriage contract between God and Israel. In some congregations, Shavuot is a time to celebrate children's graduation from religious school.

Then come three weeks of mourning for the Temples, both of which were destroyed on the ninth day of the month of Av (July or August), Tisha Be-av. This is traditionally a time of fasting and avoidance of joyous activities. Some feel that there is no longer cause for mourning because even though the Temple has not been rebuilt, the old city of Jerusalem has been recaptured. Others feel that we are all still in exile from the state of perfection.

Contemporary Judaism

Within the family of Judaism, there are many groups, many different focuses, and many areas of disagreement. Current disputes include the degree of adherence to the Torah and Talmud, requirements for conversion to Judaism, the extent of the use of Hebrew in prayer, and the full participation of women.

Major branches today

To a certain extent, contemporary Jews may be divided along historic ethnic lines. The majority—at least 65 percent—are descendants of the **Ashkenazim**, who originally migrated to Italy from West Asia during the first and second centuries CE, and then spread through central and eastern Europe, and thence to the Americas. The second largest grouping is the **Sephardim**, descendants of those who migrated to Spain from West Asia in the eighth and ninth centuries, and thence to North Africa, the Americas, and back to West Asia. These ethnic distinctions account for certain cultural, linguistic, and dietary differences.

As we saw earlier, other distinctions among Jews who are religiously observant have developed as Judaism has encountered the modern world. Judaism, like all modern religions, has struggled to meet the challenge of secularization: the idealization of science, rationalism, industrialization, and materialism. The response of the Orthodox has been to stand by the Torah as the revealed word of God and the Talmud as the legitimate oral law. Orthodox Jews feel that they are bound by the traditional rabbinical *halakhah*, as a way of achieving closeness to God. But within this framework there are great individual differences, with no central authority figure or governing body. Orthodoxy includes mystics and rationalists, Zionists and anti-Zionists. The Orthodox also differ greatly in their tolerance for other Jewish groups and in their degree of accommodation of the surrounding secular environment. **Modern Orthodoxy** values secular knowledge and integration with non-Jewish society so that its members can be enriched by interaction with the modern world and also help to uplift it; at the same time, Modern Orthodoxy, which first developed in nineteenth-century western Europe, is dedicated to the national and religious significance of Israel and to Jewish law as divinely given. **Religious Zionism**, which is based on the teachings of Rabbi Abraham Isaac Kook (1864–1935), places central emphasis on resettlement of the Jewish people in Israel as the working out of a divine plan for the salvation not only of Jews but also for the whole world. Involvement with secular society is permissible only when such involvement is beneficial for the state of Israel. **Haredi (Ultra-Orthodox)** Judaism—which may overlap with Religious Zionism, especially in Israel—is generally in favor of a degree of detachment from non-Jewish culture, so that the community can focus on study of the Torah. Some Haredi groups practice complete withdrawal from the secular world and the rest of the Jewish community, while others, such as the **Lubavich Hasidim** (originally from Lithuania, with strong communities in many countries), are devoted to extending their message to as many Jews as possible, using all the tools of modern technology for their sacred purpose. The Lubavich, who offer highly structured and nurturing communities in which male–female roles are strictly defined and an all-embracing piety and devotion to a charismatic leader are universally shared, have had considerable success in attracting young Jews to their way of life.

The Reform (or **Liberal**) movement, at the other end of the spectrum, began in nineteenth-century Germany as an attempt to help modern Jews appreciate their religion rather than regarding it as antiquated, meaningless, or even repugnant. In imitation of Christian churches, synagogues were redefined as places for spiritual elevation, with choirs added for effect, and the Sabbath service was shortened and translated into the vernacular. The liturgy was also changed to eliminate references to the hope of return to Zion and animal sacrifices in the Temple. Women and men were allowed to sit together in the synagogue, in contrast to their traditional separation. Halakhic observances were re-evaluated for their relevance to modern needs, and Judaism was understood as an evolving, open-ended religion rather than one fixed forever by the Torah. Reform congregations are numerous in North America, where they are continually engaged in a "creative confrontation with modernity." Rather than exclusivism, Reform rabbis cultivate a sense of the universalism of Jewish values.

It is not surprising that Reform Judaism, particularly in North America, has been at the forefront in the establishment of interfaith dialogue and faith-based social activism, in cooperation with non-Jewish groups. Rabbi Maria Feldman of the Religious Action Center of Reform Judaism affirms:

> To be a Reform Jew is to hear the voice of the prophets in our head; to be engaged in the ongoing work of tikkun olam; to strive to improve the world in which we live. The passion for social justice is reflected in the ancient words of our prophets and sages and in the declarations of our Movement's leaders throughout its history. The ancient command "Tzedek, Tzedek Tirdof! Justice, justice shall you seek!" constantly reverberates in our ears.[35]

Reform Judaism is not fully accepted in Israel, where the Israeli Rabbinate, which has considerable civil and political power, does not recognize the authority of non-Orthodox rabbis.

The liberalization process has also given birth to other intermediate groups. With roots in mid-nineteenth-century responses to the liberal Reform movement in Germany, **Conservative Judaism** sought to maintain ("conserve") traditional laws and practices while using modern means of historical scholarship, sponsoring critical studies of Jewish texts from all periods. In the United States, it received a boost in 1902 when the famous scholar Solomon Schechter became president of the Jewish Theological Seminary, which thenceforth became a major center of

Rabbi David Saperstein

Judaism has produced many notable philanthropists and social activists. In twenty-first century United States political arenas, the voice of Rabbi David Saperstein is heard again and again, advocating social change and social justice.

Rabbi Saperstein comes from a family of rabbis. His two great-grandfathers were Orthodox rabbis, his great-uncles, father, and uncle were highly regarded Reform rabbis, and his brother Marc is a leading Jewish scholar. His wife, Ellen Weiss, is involved in social issues as Vice President for News at National Public Radio. His father Harold Saperstein was the rabbi of Temple Emanuel in Lynbrook, Long Island, and his mother Marcia taught current events to generations of high school students in the synagogue.

Dedicated, energetic, and hard-working, Rabbi Saperstein is perhaps best known as the Director of the Religious Action Center of Reform Judaism, a powerful center for social justice advocacy on Capitol Hill in Washington, D.C. He is also active in helping to build interfaith coalitions for various causes and is the Co-Chairman of the Coalition to Preserve Religious Liberty.

Rabbi Saperstein is also an attorney who teaches seminars at Georgetown University Law School in Jewish Law and First Amendment Church-State Law. An effective writer and speaker, he bases his arguments about controversial subjects in biblical teachings. He has something significant to say about a range of contemporary issues, from torture of political prisoners to globale warming. For instance, in lobbying the United States Senate with reference to proposed legislation on hate crimes, he said:

> We cannot stand idly by while hate crimes destroy the sense of community that we and so many others have worked so hard to build. This is an issue that hits especially close to home for the Jewish people. . . . More than that, though, we are ever mindful that Jews are far from the only victims of senseless hatred. It is a painful bond we share with all too many others. . . . Hate crimes are more than mere acts of violence. . . . They are a betrayal of the promise of America.[36]

Social action is at the heart of lived Jewish faith, according to Rabbi Saperstein:

> Is it not self-evident that we cannot fulfill our destiny to be a light to the nations, that we cannot respond to God's central call to us to be a holy people, if we retreat from struggles for justice, peace, and equality in our nation and in our world? . . . we Jews do not continue for continuity's sake alone, do not exist for existence's sake alone—but are called for a holy purpose and a holy mission: to be God's partners in shaping a better and more hopeful world.
>
> This vision resonates through the entire prophetic tradition, the rabbinic creation of the world's first social welfare system, the immense charitable undertakings of organized Jewish communities in the diaspora for over 1,000 years—and in Judaism's magnificent contributions to the evolution of contemporary democracy and human rights.[37]

Jewish scholarship. Conservative Jews believe Jews have always searched and added to their laws, liturgy, Midrash, and beliefs to keep them relevant and meaningful in changing times. Conservative women have long served as cantors and have been ordained as rabbis since 1985. To avoid confusion with political conservatism, Conservative Judaism is now in many places called "Masorti" Judaism, from the Hebrew word meaning "traditional."

Rabbi Mordecai Kaplan, an influential American thinker who died in 1983, branched off from Conservatism and founded a movement called **Reconstructionism**. He held that the Enlightenment had changed everything and that strong measures were needed to preserve Judaism in the face of rationalism. Kaplan asserted that "as long as Jews adhered to the traditional conception of the Torah as supernaturally revealed, they would not be amenable to any constructive adjustment of Judaism that was needed to render it viable in a non-Jewish environment."[38] He defined Judaism as an "evolving religious civilization," both cultural and spiritual, and asserted that the Jewish people are the heart of Judaism. The traditions exist for the people, and not vice versa, he said. Kaplan denied that the Jewish people were specially chosen by God, an exclusivist idea. Rather, they had chosen to try to become a people of God. Kaplan created a new prayer book, deleting traditional portions he and others found offensive, such as derogatory references to women and Gentiles, references to physical resurrection of the body, and passages describing God as rewarding or punishing Israel by manipulating natural phenomena.

In the United States, home of the world's largest Jewish community, there has been a great shift in leadership within Orthodoxy, Conservatism, and Reform organizations. For example, the seminaries of all three have "baby boomers" as their presidents, and in 2007 neither the President of Yeshiva University—where mostly Orthodox males study the Torah, Mishnah, and Talmud—nor the Chancellor of the Jewish Theological Seminary were rabbis.

In addition to those who affiliate with a religious movement, there are many Jews who identify themselves as secular Jews, affirming their Jewish origins and maintaining various Jewish cultural traditions while eschewing religious practice. There are also significant numbers of people of Jewish birth, particularly in North America and western Europe, whose Jewish identity is vestigial at best, and unlikely to survive in future generations. The possibilities for total assimilation into Western culture are evident in statistics indicating that over fifty percent of Western Jews marry non-Jews. In most cases, neither spouse in such a marriage converts, and research indicates that it is highly unlikely that their children will identify as Jews. Thus, one of the great ironies of the liberty offered to the Jewish people by democratic secular societies is the freedom to leave Judaism as well as to affirm it.

Jewish feminism

In contrast to the option of leaving Judaism, some feminists are coming back to religious observance, but not in the traditional mold, which they regard as patriarchal and sexist. Since the mid-twentieth century, women have taken an active role in claiming their rights to full religious participation—for instance, to be counted as part of a *minyan*, to be called up to read from the Torah, and to be ordained as rabbis. They are also redefining Judaism from a feminist perspective. Part of this effort involves trying to reconstruct the history of significant biblical women, for the Torah was written down by men who devoted far more space to the doings of men than of women. There are hints, for instance, that there were powerful prophetesses, such as Miriam and Huldah, but very little information is given about them. There have also been post-biblical women scholars, writers, and teachers, women who supported synagogues and Jewish publications from their earnings as businesswomen, and women who were active in social reform, and their stories and names are being uncovered.

In the past fifty years, Jewish feminists have tackled liturgical issues, changing language to gender-neutral and gender-inclusive terms for worshipers and for God. The Hebrew scriptures describe God as both female and male, validating translations from the Hebrew that use gender-neutral language. Nevertheless, there was resistance and even shock over these attempts to replace references to God as "He." In 1981, feminist Rita Gross wrote that this shock

> mirrors and legitimizes the profoundly androcentric [male-oriented] character of Jewish society, especially "spiritual Judaism" or the religious dimensions of being Jewish. It expresses a profound and long-standing alienation between women or femaleness and the central values of Jewish religious tradition—an alienation that I believe stretches to the origins of our tradition. That usage and the alienation it reflects is also the most basic explanation for the traditional exclusion of women from almost all the most meaningful and most normative dimensions of Judaism— its covenanted, "religious" and "spiritual" aspects.[39]

Since then, as a result of feminist efforts, gender-neutral liturgy and women's participation in synagogue worship have become quite common in contemporary Judaism. In Reform, Conservative, and Reconstructionist synagogues, women may be counted in the *minyan* and called up to recite blessings and read from the Torah. Many have been ordained as rabbis, invested as cantors who lead the prayer service, and installed as presidents of synagogues as well as heads of philanthropical organizations. Many liberal congregations use prayer books with gender-neutral language. Even in Orthodox congregations, the Jewish Orthodox Feminist Alliance serves as a resource "for a community constantly balancing tradition and modernity, . . . guided by the principle that *halakhic* Judaism offers many opportunities for observant Jewish women to enhance their ritual observance and to increase their participation in communal leadership."[40]

There is also a feminist critique of women's position in the state of Israel. Women among the early Zionist settlers envisioned a society in which men and women would work side by side and each apply their full capabilities to the creation of a new society. Even though laws were created that supported gender equality, traditional sexual divisions of labor were perpetuated, especially once the Orthodox parties took a major role in the formation and governance of the state. Judith Plaskow links the discrimination against women in Israel to the disempowerment of other minorities, including Palestinians and non-Ashkenazi Jews. She argues passionately:

> The recognition of diverse constituencies as parts of larger communities involves an obligation to redefine communal life as the sum of all pieces. When one part has been accustomed to speaking for the whole—male Ashkenazi Jewish Israelis for

Israelis, elite male Jews for Jews, middle-class white feminists for women—this definition may mean dislodging long-fixed patterns of dominance with difficult and dramatic results.[41]

Jewish renewal

Both men and women from varied backgrounds are being attracted to newly revitalized expressions of Jewish spirituality. After the Holocaust, many Jews had retreated from religious observance to avoid being conspicuous. Now, not only are some Jews becoming comfortable with being openly religious, but also conversions to Judaism seem to be increasing.

Although anti-semitism continues to flare up here and there, many non-Jews are developing sensitivity against negative stereotyping of Jews. The Evangelical Lutheran Church in America has issued an apology for the anti-Jewish writings of Martin Luther, father of Protestant Christianity. In part, they declared:

> *As did many of Luther's own companions in the sixteenth century, we reject this violent invective, and yet more do we express our deep and abiding sorrow over its tragic effects on subsequent generations. In concert with the Lutheran World Federation, we particularly deplore the appropriation of Luther's words by modern anti-Semites for the teaching of hatred toward Judaism or toward the Jewish people in our day. . . . We recognize in anti-Semitism a contradiction and an affront to the Gospel, a violation of our hope and calling, and we pledge this church to oppose the deadly working of such bigotry.[42]*

In post-Soviet Russia, where under Stalin Jews had been so persecuted that only a few rabbis remained in all of Russia, there are now Jewish seminaries and universities, schools, and kindergartens. Rabbi Dovid Karpov, whose congregation serves one hundred and fifty free hot meals a day in Moscow, says that Judaism has begun to flourish again after years of secrecy and danger:

> *Now we can celebrate holidays such as Hanukkah openly. It is not yet a mass movement, but there are more people than you can count on your fingers. We feel that soon we will see the fruit of our work. Judaism survives despite all the persecutions. The new world is coming very soon and it will have a very different form. The Messiah is coming. The time will soon come when we will have the peace that everyone is waiting for. It will happen sooner than anyone can imagine.[43]*

Contemporary Jewish renewal is not just an absence of fear. It is an active search for personal meaning in the ancient rituals and scriptures, and the creation of new rituals for our times. There are now numerous small *havurot*, or communities of Jews, who are not affiliated with any formal group but get together on a regular basis to worship and celebrate the traditions. They favor a democratic organization and personal experience, and are often engaged in trying to determine what parts of the traditions to use and how. Some incorporate study groups, continuing the ancient intellectual tradition of grappling with the ethical, philosophical, and spiritual meanings of the texts. Some are bringing fresh ideas to traditional celebrations, so that they are actively transformational rather than simply matters of empty habit.

From highly conservative to highly liberal quarters, there are now attempts to renew the ancient messianic ideal of Judaism, that by its practice the world might be healed.

Review questions

1. Which major areas of Jewish history are recounted in the Tanakh? Outline their main themes and give some characters.
2. What is a Jewish covenant? Describe three major covenants.

Discussion questions

1. How does the ongoing interpretation of sacred Jewish texts interact with the ancient texts? Discuss the two creation accounts: the first in Genesis Chapter 1 to 2:4, and the second from 2:4 through Chapter 3. What do the different sequences of plant and animal creation imply about how to interpret biblical texts?
2. What are the important differences among the major branches of contemporary Judaism? If you had a choice, which branch would you join and why?
3. Describe the evolving role of women in Judaism. Discuss Eve, Sarah, Mishnah, Shekhinah, *minyan*, and Rita Gross. Why has it changed?

CHAPTER 8

CHRISTIANITY

"Jesus Christ is Lord"

Christianity is a faith based on the life, teachings, death, and resurrection of Jesus. He was born as a Jew about two thousand years ago in Roman-occupied Palestine. He taught for fewer than three years and was executed by the Roman government on charges of sedition. Nothing was written about him at the time, although, some years after his death, attempts were made to record what he had said and done. Yet his birth is now celebrated around the world and since the sixth century has been used as the major point from which public time is measured, even by non-Christians. The religion centered around him has more followers than any other.

In studying Christianity we will first examine what can be said about the life and teachings of Jesus, based on accounts in the Bible and on historians' knowledge of the period. We will then follow the evolution of the religion as it spread to all continents and became theologically and liturgically more complex. This process continues in the present, in which there are not one but many different versions of Christianity.

The Christian Bible

The Bibles used by various Christian churches consist of the Hebrew Bible (called the "Old Testament"), and in some cases non-canonical Jewish texts called the Apocrypha, and what Orthodox Christians call the Deuterocanonical books, plus the twenty-seven books of the "New Testament" written after Jesus's earthly mission.

Traditionally, the holy scriptures have been reverently regarded as the divinely inspired Word of God. Furthermore, in Eastern Orthodox Christianity, "the Gospel is not just Holy Scripture but also a symbol of Divine Wisdom and an image of Christ Himself."[1] Given the textual complexity of the Bible, some Christians have attempted to clarify what Jesus taught and how he lived, so that people might truly follow him.

The field of theological study that attempts to interpret scripture is called **hermeneutics**. In Jewish tradition, rabbis developed rules for interpretation. In the late second and early third centuries CE, Christian thinkers developed two highly different approaches to biblical hermeneutics. One of these stressed the literal meanings of the texts; the other looked for allegorical rather than literal meanings.

During medieval times, allowance was made for interpreting scriptural passages in at least four ways: literal, allegorical, moral (teaching ethical principles), and heavenly (divinely inspired and mystical, perhaps unintelligible to ordinary think-ing). This fourfold approach was later followed by considerable debate on whether the Bible should be understood on the basis of its own internal evidence or whether it should be seen through the lens of Church tradition. During the eight-eenth century, critical study of the Bible from a strictly historical point of view began in western Europe. This approach, now accepted by many Roman Catholics, Protestants, and some Orthodox, is based on the literary method of interpreting ancient writings in their historical context, with their intended audience and desired effect taken into account. In the nineteenth and twentieth centuries, emphasis shifted to questions about the process of hermeneutics, such as how to understand ancient texts that came from other cultures, how individual passages relate to the whole text, how the biblical message is conveyed through the medium of language, and how it is grasped by people in modern contexts.

There is very little historical proof of the life of Jesus outside of the Bible, but extensive scholarly research has turned up some shreds of evidence. The Jewish historian Josephus (born in approximately 37 CE), who was captured by the Romans and then defected to their side, wrote extensively about other details of Jewish history that have been confirmed by archaeological discoveries. He made two brief references to Jesus that may have been given a positive slant by Christian copyists, but are nonetheless now regarded as proof that Jesus did exist. In the *Baraitha* and *Tosefta*, supplements to the Jewish Mishnah, there are a few references to "Yeshu the Nazarene" who was said to practice "sorcery" (healings) and was "hanged."

What Christians believe about Jesus's life and teachings is based largely on biblical texts, particularly the first four books of the New Testament, which are called the **gospels** (good news). On the whole, they seem to have been originally written about forty to sixty years after Jesus's death. They are based on the oral transmission of the stories and discourses, which may have been influenced by the growing split between Christians and Jews. The documents, thought to be pseudo-nymous, are given the names of Jesus's followers Matthew and John, and of the apostle Paul's companions Mark and Luke. The gospels were first written down in Greek and perhaps Aramaic, the everyday language that Jesus spoke, and then copied and translated in many different ways over the centuries. They offer a composite picture of Jesus as seen through the eyes of the Christian community.

Three of the gospels, Matthew, Mark, and Luke, are so similar that they are called the **synoptic** gospels, referring to the fact that they can be "seen together" as presenting rather similar views of Jesus's career, though they are organized somewhat differently. Most historians think that Matthew and Luke are largely based on Mark and another source called "Q." This hypothesized source would probably be a compilation of oral and written traditions. It is now thought that the author of Mark put together many fragments of oral tradition in order to develop a connected narrative about Jesus's life and ministry, for the sake of propagating the faith.

The other two synoptic gospels often parallel Mark quite closely but include additional material. The gospel according to Matthew (named after one of Jesus's original disciples, a tax collector) is sometimes called a Jewish Christian gospel. It represents Jesus as a second Moses as well as the Messiah ushering in the Kingdom of Heaven, with frequent references to the Old Testament. Matthew's stories emphasize that the Gentiles (non-Jews) accept Jesus, whereas the Jews reject him as savior.

Luke, to whom the third gospel is attributed, is traditionally thought to have been a physician who sometimes accompanied Paul the apostle. The gospel seems to have been written with a Gentile Christian audience in mind. Luke presents Jesus's mission in universal rather than exclusively Jewish terms and accentuates the importance of his ministry to the underprivileged and lower classes.

The Gospel of John, traditionally attributed to "the disciple Jesus loved," is of a very different nature from the other three. It concerns itself less with following the life of Jesus than with seeing Jesus as the eternal Son of God, the word of God made flesh. It is seen by many scholars as being later in origin than the synoptic gospels, perhaps having been written around the end of the first century CE. By this time, there was apparently a more critical conflict between Jews who believed in Jesus as the Messiah, and the majority of Jews, who did not recognize him as the Messiah they were awaiting. The Gospel of John seems to concentrate on confirming Jesus's Messiahship, and also to reflect Greek influences, such as a dualistic distinction between light and darkness. It is also more mystical and devotional in nature than the synoptic gospels.

> *The light shines on in the dark, and the darkness has never mastered it.*
> *The Gospel of John, 1:5*

Other gospels circulating in the early Christian Church were not included in the canon of the New Testament. They include magical stories of Jesus's infancy, such as an account of his making clay birds and then bringing them to life. The Gospel of Thomas, one of the long-hidden manuscripts discovered in 1945 by a peasant in a cave near Nag Hammadi, Egypt, is of particular interest. Some scholars feel that its core may have been written even earlier than the canonical gospels. It contains many sayings in common with the other gospels but places the accent on mystical concepts of Jesus:

> *Jesus said: I am the Light that is above*
> *them all. I am the All,*
> *the All came forth from me and the All*
> *attained to me. Cleave a (piece of) wood,*
> *I am there; lift up the stone and you will*
> *find Me there.*[2]

The life and teachings of Jesus

It is not possible to reconstruct from the gospels a single chronology of Jesus's life nor to account for much of what happened before he began his ministry. Nevertheless, the stories of the New Testament are important to Christians as the foundation of their faith. And after extensive analysis most scholars have concluded on grounds of linguistics and regional history that many of the sayings attributed to Jesus by the gospels may be authentic.

Birth

According to the Christian doctrine of the incarnation, Jesus is the divine Son of God who "became flesh" by being conceived and born as a human being. The biblical book of Colossians states, "In him the whole fullness of deity dwells bodily" (Colossians 2:9).

Most historians think Jesus was probably born a few years before the first year of what is now called the **Common Era**. When sixth-century Christian monks began figuring time in relationship to the life of Jesus, they may have miscalculated slightly. Traditionally, Christians have believed that Jesus was born in Bethlehem. This detail fulfills the rabbinic interpretation of the Old Testament prophecies that the Messiah would be born in Bethlehem, the home of David the great king, and in the lineage of David. Both Matthew and Luke offer genealogies tracing Jesus to David. Some scholars suggest that Jesus was actually born in or near Nazareth, his own home town in Galilee. This region, whose name meant "Ring of the Gentiles" (non-Jews), was not fully Jewish; it was also scorned as somewhat countrified by the rabbinic orthodoxy of Judaea. Both Judaea and Galilee were ruled by Rome at the time.

According to the gospels, Jesus's mother was Mary, who was a virgin when she conceived him by the Holy Spirit; her husband was Joseph, a carpenter from Bethlehem. Luke states they had to go to Bethlehem to satisfy a Roman ruling that everyone must travel to their ancestral cities for a census. When they had made the journey, there was no room for them in the inn, so the baby was born in a stable among the animals. He was named Jesus, which means "God saves." This well-loved birth legend exemplifies the humility that Jesus taught. According to Luke, those who came to pay their respects were poor shepherds to whom angels had appeared with the glad tidings that a Savior had been born to the people. Matthew tells instead of Magi, sages from "the east," who may have been Zoroastrians and who brought the Christ child symbolic gifts of gold and frankincense and myrrh, confirming his divine kingship and his adoration by Gentiles.

Preparation

No other stories are told about Jesus's childhood in Nazareth until he was twelve years old, when, according to the Gospel of Luke, he accompanied his parents on their yearly trip to Jerusalem for Passover. Left behind by mistake, he was said to have been discovered by his parents in the Temple discussing the Torah with the rabbis; "all who heard him were amazed at his understanding and his answers." When scolded, he reportedly replied, "Did you not know that I must be in my Father's house?"[3] This story is used to demonstrate his sense of mission even as a boy, his knowledge of Jewish tradition, and the close personal connection between Jesus and God. In later accounts of his prayers, he spoke to God as "Abba," a very familiar Aramaic and Hebrew word for father.

The New Testament is also silent about the years of Jesus's young manhood. What is described, is the ministry of John the Baptist, a prophet citing Isaiah's prophecies of the coming Kingdom of God. He was conducting baptism in the Jordan River in preparation for this. Apocalyptic expectations were running high, with Israel chafing under Roman taxation and rule.

According to all four gospels, at the age of about thirty Jesus came to John to be baptized. John was calling people to repent of their sins and be spiritually purified and sanctified by immersion in the river. He felt it improper to perform this ceremony for Jesus, whom Christians consider sinless, but Jesus insisted. One explanation for his insistence is that this became a ceremony of his consecration to God as the Messiah. The gospel writer reports:

> When he came up out of the water, immediately he saw the heavens opened and the Spirit descending upon him like a dove; and a voice came from heaven. "Thou art my beloved Son; with thee I am well pleased."[4]

Another interpretation is that Jesus's baptism was the occasion for John's publicly announcing that the Messiah had arrived, beginning his ministry. A third interpretation is that by requesting baptism, Jesus identified himself with sinful humanity. Even though he had no need for repentance and purification, he accepted baptism on behalf of all humans.

After being baptized, Jesus reportedly undertook a forty-day retreat in the desert wilderness, fasting. During his retreat, the gospel writers say he was tempted by Satan to use his spiritual power for secular ends, but he refused.

Ministry

In John's gospel, Jesus's baptism and wilderness sojourn were followed by his gathering of the first disciples, the fisherman Simon (called Peter), Andrew (Peter's brother), James, and John (brother of James), who recognized him as the Messiah. Jesus warned his disciples they would have to leave their possessions and human attachments to follow him—to pay more attention to the life of the spirit than to physical comfort and wealth. Jesus said it was extremely difficult for the wealthy to enter the kingdom of heaven. God, the Protector, takes care of physical needs, which are relatively unimportant:

> Is not life more than food, and the body more than clothing? Look at the birds of the air; they neither sow nor reap nor gather into barns, and yet your heavenly Father feeds them. Are you not of more value than they? And which of you by being anxious can add one cubit to his span of life?[5]

Jesus taught that his followers should concentrate on laying up spiritual treasures in heaven, rather than material treasures on earth, which are short-lived. Because God is like a generous parent, those who love God and want to follow the path of righteousness should pray for help, in private: "Ask, and it will be given you; seek, and you will find; knock, and it will be opened to you."[6]

As Jesus traveled, speaking, he is said to have performed many miracles, such as turning water into wine, healing the sick, restoring the dead to life, walking on water, casting devils out of the possessed, and turning a few loaves and fish into enough food to feed a crowd of thousands, with copious leftovers. Jesus reportedly performed these miracles quietly and compassionately; the gospels interpreted them as signs of the coming Kingdom of God.

The stories of the miracles performed by Jesus have symbolic meanings taken from the entire Jewish and early Christian traditions. In the sharing of the loaves and fishes, for instance, it may have been more than physical bread that Luke was talking about when he said, "and all ate and were satisfied."[7] The people came to

Jesus out of spiritual hunger, and he fed them all, profligate with his love. Bread often signified life-giving sustenance. Jesus was later to offer himself as "the bread of life."[8] On another level of interpretation, the story may prefigure the Last Supper of Jesus with his disciples, with both stories alluding to the Jewish tradition of the Great Banquet, the heavenly feast of God, as a symbol of the messianic age. The fish were a symbol of Christ to the early Christians; what he fed them was the indiscriminate gift of himself.

Theological interpretations of the biblical stories are based on the evidence of the Bible itself, but people also bring their own experiences to them. To William, a twentieth-century Nicaraguan peasant, the miracle was not the multiplication of the loaves but the sharing: "The miracle was to persuade the owners of the bread to share it, that it was absurd for them to keep it all while the people were going hungry."[9]

Jesus preached and lived by truly radical ethics. In contrast to the prevailing patriarchal society and extensive proscriptions against impurity, he touched lepers and a bleeding woman to heal them; in his "table fellowship," he ate with people of all classes. In a culture in which the woman's role was strictly circumscribed, he welcomed women as his disciples. Mary Magdalene, Mary the mother of James the younger and Joses, Salome the mother of the disciples James and John, Mary of Bethany, Martha, Susanna, and Joanna are among those mentioned in the gospels. Some of them traveled with Jesus and even helped to support him and his disciples financially, a great departure from orthodox Jewish tradition. In addition, wives of some of Jesus's first male disciples who were married apparently accompanied them as they traveled with Jesus (1 Corinthians 9:5). His was a radically egalitarian vision.

He also extended the application of Jewish laws: "You have heard that it was said to the men of old," Jesus began, "You shall not kill; and whoever kills shall be liable to judgment. But I say to you that every one who is angry with his brother shall be liable to judgment."[10] Not only should a man not commit adultery; it is wrong even to look at a woman lustfully. Rather than taking revenge with an eye for an eye, a tooth for a tooth, respond with love. If a person strikes you on one cheek, turn the other cheek to be struck also. If anyone tries to rob you of your coat, give him your cloak as well. And not only should you love your neighbor, Jesus says:

> Love your enemies and pray for those who persecute you, so that you may be sons of your Father who is in heaven; for he makes his sun rise on the evil and on the good, and sends rain on the just and on the unjust.[11]

The extremely high ethical standards of the Sermon on the Mount (Matthew 5–7) may seem impossibly challenging. Who can fully follow them? And Jesus said these things to people who had been brought up with the understanding that to fulfill incompletely even one divine commandment is a violation of the Law. But when people recognize their helplessness to fulfill such commandments, they are ready to turn to the divine for help. Jesus pointed out, "With man this is impossible, but not with God; all things are possible with God."[12]

The main thing Jesus taught was love. He stated that to love God and to "love your neighbor as yourself"[13] were the two great commandments in Judaism, upon which everything else rested. To love God means placing God first in one's life, rather than concentrating on the things of the earth. To love one's neighbor means selfless service to everyone, even to those despised by the rest of society. Jesus often horrified the religious authorities by talking to prostitutes, tax-collectors, and the poorest and lowliest of people. He set an example of loving service by washing his disciples' feet. This kind of love, he said, should be the mark of his followers, and at the Last Judgment, when the Son of Man judges the people of all time, he will grant eternal life in the kingdom to the humble "sheep" who loved and served him (Matthew 25:37–40).

Jesus preached that God is forgiving to those who repent. He told a story likening God to the father who welcomed with gifts and celebration his "prodigal son" who had squandered his inheritance and then humbly returned home. He told story after story suggesting that those who considered themselves superior were more at odds with God than those who were aware of their sins. Those who sincerely repent—even if they are the hated toll-collectors, prostitutes, or ignorant common people—are more likely to receive God's forgiveness than are the learned and self-righteous. Indeed, Jesus said, it was only in childlikeness that people could enter the kingdom of heaven. In a famous series of statements about supreme happiness called the **Beatitudes**, Jesus is quoted as promising blessings for the "poor in spirit,"[14] the mourners, the meek, the seekers of righteousness, the pure in heart, the merciful, the peacemakers, and those who are persecuted for the sake of righteousness and of spreading the gospel.

Jesus's stories were typically presented as **parables**, in which familiar earthly situations were used to make a spiritual point. He spoke of parents and children, of masters and servants, of sowing seeds, of fishing (Matthew 13:47–50).

As we have seen, messianic expectations were running very high among Jews of that time, oppressed as they were by Roman rule. They looked to a time when the people of Israel would be freed and the authority of Israel's God would be recognized throughout the world. Jesus reportedly spoke to them again and again about the fulfillment of these expectations: "The time is fulfilled, and the kingdom of God is at hand; repent, and believe in the gospel"[15]; "I must preach the good news of the kingdom of God . . . for I was sent for this purpose."[16] He taught them to pray for the advent of this kingdom: "Thy kingdom come, Thy will be done on earth as it is in heaven."[17] However, in contrast to expectations of secular deliverance from the Romans, Jesus seems to refer to the kingdom as manifestation of God's full glory, the consummation of the world.

Every one who drinks of this water will thirst again, but whoever drinks of the water that I shall give him will never thirst; the water that I shall give him will become in him a spring of water welling up to eternal life.

Jesus, as quoted in the Gospel of John, 4:13–14

Jesus's references to the kingdom, as reported in the gospels, indicate two seemingly different emphases: one that the kingdom is expected in the future, and the other that the kingdom is already here. In his future references, as in the apocalyptic Jewish writings of the time, Jesus said that things would get much worse right before the end. He seemed to foretell the destruction of Jerusalem by the Romans that began in 70 CE. But:

An Interview with David Vandiver

Born into a devout small-town Southern Baptist family, David Vandiver describes the evolution of his understanding and practice of Christianity.

"The primary values as I grew up were ones of honesty, fairness, and caring for others. It was not until much later in my life that the vast scope of values held by Christians in differing places in the world came to my attention. I was not aware, for example, that there were Christians who believed God wanted them to influence politics for justice, work for equal rights for all people, protect the natural environment, or make peace with other nations and peoples of differing faiths. Our form of faith did a good job of supporting what was valuable in society, but did little to tear down what was destructive. We had no cause to practice tolerance because we were all so similar, except for the African Americans in our town—about twenty percent of the population— who were already Christian and from whom we, as Anglo-Americans, wished to stay separated. I grew up with racism all around me.

"Nonetheless, as a high school youth in the early 1970s, I joined my friends in dragging my church into the foray of the U.S. Civil Rights Movement because I couldn't see Jesus as one who would keep any group of people powerless and poor. Christianity was a voice for the downtrodden and oppressed of the world, and if I was to follow Jesus, I would have to take up their cause for justice in some way.

"The most accessible way for me to take up this cause was a vocation as a Christian minister. It guided me to a Masters of Divinity in Pastoral Counseling at a Baptist seminary. It was here that I began to consider the teachings of Jesus the Christ more deeply. What did it mean to 'love my neighbor as myself'? In practical terms, it came to mean that I could not simply spend the rest of my life pursuing a comfortable living while ignoring the fact that millions are living in poverty and oppression.

"Early in my seminary days, I was married to a wonderful woman, who lost her life in an automobile accident four months after our wedding. I found myself doubting the existence of a caring God. I was plunged into a dark night of the soul and feared I would never escape it. Slowly it began to dawn on me that my plight was not mine alone; that millions had suffered and were suffering similar losses. It became clear to me that anything good and loving in life was a gift, sent as a precious favor.

"I saw that following Jesus would take me out of the mainstream of the world in order to love it fully. On the other hand, I was painfully aware of the impossibility of loving others unconditionally. What as a child was an inherent identity became a life-long journey that I would never fully complete.

"Vocationally and geographically, I have found a home as the manager of a wilderness camp for inner-city children from Washington. I am reminded of how I grew up, unaware of the larger world around me. I work to help them find the tools that will assist them in loving those they find difficult to love: their enemies, abusers, oppressors, and those who ignore them. Those who have given me those tools have held up the imperatives of Jesus to love the world, even those whom I find difficult to love."

then will appear the sign of the Son of man in heaven, and then all the tribes of the earth will mourn, and they will see the Son of man coming on the clouds of heaven with power and great glory; and he will send out his angels with a loud trumpet call, and they will gather his elect from the four winds, from one end of heaven to the other.[18]

It was his mission, he said, to gather together everyone who could be saved.

Challenges to the authorities

As Jesus traveled through Galilee, many people gathered around him to be healed. Herod Antipas, a Jew who had been appointed by the Romans as ruler of Galilee, had already executed John the Baptist and may have been concerned that Jesus might be a trouble-maker, perhaps one of the Zealots of Galilee who were stirring up support for a political uprising against the Romans. Jesus therefore moved outside Herod's jurisdiction for a while, to carry on his work in Tyre and Sidon (now in Lebanon).

According to the gospels, Jesus was also regarded with suspicion by prominent Jewish groups of his time—the emerging Pharisees (the shapers of rabbinic Judaism), Sadducees (the temple priests and upper class), and the scribes (specially trained laymen who copied the written law and formulated the oral law of Judaism). Jesus seems not to have challenged Mosaic law, but rather, its interpretations in the evolving rabbinic traditions and the hypocrisy of some of those who claimed to be living by the law. It is written in the Gospel of Matthew that the Pharisees and scribes challenged Jesus's disciples for not washing their hands before eating. Jesus responded:

"What goes into the mouth does not make a man unclean; it is what comes out of the mouth that makes him unclean. . . ."[19]

"Alas for you, scribes and Pharisees, you hypocrites! You who are like whitewashed tombs that look handsome on the outside, but inside are full of dead men's bones and every kind of corruption. In the same way you appear to people from the outside like good honest men, but inside you are full of hypocrisy and lawlessness."[20]

Many seemingly anti-Jewish statements in the New Testament are suspected by some modern scholars as additions or interpretations dating from the period after Jesus's death, when rabbinic Judaism and early Christianity were competing for followers. Nevertheless, more universal teachings are apparent in such stories attributed to Jesus. For instance, in all times and all religions there have been those who do not practice what they preach when claiming to speak with spiritual authority.

Jesus is said to have also confronted those who were making a living by charging a profit when exchanging money for Temple currency and selling animals for sacrificial offerings (Mark 11:15–18).

According to the gospel accounts, Jesus appropriated to himself the messianic prophecies of Second Isaiah. It is written that he privately asked his disciples, "Who do you say that I am?" Peter answered, "You are the Christ."[21] "Christ" is Greek for "anointed one," a translation of the Aramaic word *M'shekha* or

Messiah, which also means "perfected" or "enlightened one." His disciples later spoke of him as the Messiah after he died and was resurrected. And his follower Martha, sister of Lazarus whom Jesus reportedly raised from the dead, is quoted as having said to Jesus, "I now believe that you are the Messiah, the Son of God who was to come into the world."[22] Some contemporary biblical scholars have concluded, however, that Jesus rejected the title of Messiah, for it might have been misunderstood.

According to the gospel tradition, a transcendental phenomenon, the "**Transfiguration**," was witnessed by three disciples. Jesus had climbed a mountain to pray, and as he did:

> *He was transfigured before them, and his face shone like the sun, and his garments became white as light. And behold, there appeared to them Moses and Elijah, talking with him. . . . When lo, a bright cloud overshadowed them, and a voice from the cloud said, "This is my beloved Son, with whom I am well pleased; listen to him."[23]*

The presence of Moses and Elijah placed Jewish law and prophecy behind the claim that Jesus is the Christ. They were representatives of the old covenant with God; Jesus brought a new dispensation of grace.

Jesus claimed that John the Baptist was Elijah come again. The authorities had killed John the Baptist, and, Jesus prophesied, they would attack him, too, not recognizing who he was. John quotes Jesus as saying things like "My teaching is not mine, but his who sent me"; "I am the light of the world"; "You are from below, I am from above; you are of this world, I am not of this world"; and "Before Abraham was, I am."[24] Jesus characterized himself as a good shepherd who is willing to lay down his life for his sheep. Foreshadowing the **Crucifixion**, he said he would offer his own flesh and blood as a sacrifice for the sake of humanity. His coming death would mark a "new covenant" in which his blood would be "poured out for many for the forgiveness of sins."[25]

It is possible that such passages were later interpolations by the early Christians as they tried to explain the meaning of their Master's life and death when the New Testament was in the process of formation.

Crucifixion

The anti-institutional tenor of Jesus's teachings did not endear him to those in power. Jesus knew that to return to Jerusalem would be politically dangerous. But eventually he did so, at Passover. He reportedly entered the town on a donkey, accompanied by multitudes who cried:

> *"Hosanna! Blessed be he who comes in the name of the Lord! Blessed be the kingdom of our father David that is coming! Hosanna in the highest!"[26]*

However, Jesus warned his disciples that his end was near. At the Last Supper, a meal during the Passover season, he is said to have given them instructions for a ceremony with bread and wine to be performed thenceforth to maintain an ongoing communion with him. However, one of the disciples would betray him, he said. This one, Judas, had already done so, selling information leading to Jesus's arrest for thirty pieces of silver.

Jesus took three of his followers to a garden called Gethsemane, on the Mount of Olives, where he is said to have prayed intensely that the cup of suffering would pass away from him, if it be God's will, "yet not what I will, but what thou wilt."[27] The gospels often speak of Jesus's spending long periods in spontaneous prayer. It is possible to interpret Jesus's prayer at Gethsemane as a confirmation of his great faith in God's mercy and power. In the words of New Testament theologian Joachim Jeremias:

> Jesus takes into account the possibility that God may rescind his own holy will . . .
> The Father of Jesus is not the immovable, unchangeable God who in the end can
> only be described in negations. He is not a God to whom it is pointless to pray. He is
> a gracious God, who hears prayers and intercessions, and is capable in his mercy of
> rescinding his own holy will.[28]

Nevertheless, after praying Jesus said, according to Mark's gospel, "It is all over. The hour has come."[29] A crowd including Judas approached with swords and clubs; they led Jesus away to be questioned by the chief priest, elders, and scribes.

All four gospels include "**passion narratives**" describing Jesus's sufferings during his betrayal, trial, and execution by crucifixion. Matthew and Mark report a hearing before the high priest, Joseph Caiaphas. The high priest asked Jesus, "Are you the Christ?" Jesus reportedly answered:

> You have said so. But I tell you, hereafter you will see the Son of man seated at the
> right hand of Power, and coming on the clouds of heaven.[30]

Caiaphas pronounced this to be blasphemy, punishable by death according to Jewish law. However, under the Romans the Sanhedrin (supreme Jewish court made up of chief priests, elders, and law teachers) was forbidden to pass the death sentence. Jesus was taken to Pontius Pilate, the Roman governor, for sentencing. To Pilate's question, "Are you King of the Jews?" Jesus is said to have replied, "You have said so."[31] According to the biblical accounts, Pilate seems to prefer to let Jesus off with a flogging. But the crowd demands that he be killed as he is a challenger to the earthly king, Caesar. The Gospel of John reports that Pilate asks Jesus, "What have you done?" and Jesus replies:

> My kingdom does not belong to this world. My kingly authority comes from
> elsewhere." "You are a king then?" said Pilate. Jesus answered, "King is your
> word. My task is to bear witness to the truth. For this was I born; for this I came
> into the world, and all who are not deaf to truth listen to my voice." Pilate said,
> "What is truth?" and with those words went out again to the Jews.[32]

At last, unable to pacify Jesus's critics, Pilate turned him over to his military guard for execution by crucifixion. The victim was typically tortured or beaten brutally with whips, then hung or nailed onto a wooden cross to die. The guards put a crown of thorns on Jesus's head and paraded him and his cross to the hill called Golgotha ("Place of the Skull"). The accusation—"This is Jesus, King of the Jews"—was set over his head, and two robbers were crucified alongside him. The authorities, the people, and even the robbers (one of them, at least, according to Luke) mocked him for saying he could save others when he could not even save himself.

Jesus hung there for hours until, according to the gospels, he cried out, "My

God, my God, why hast thou forsaken me?"[33] This is the first line of Psalm 22, which is actually a great proclamation of the faith in God of one who is persecuted. Then Jesus died. This event is thought to have happened on a Friday some time between 27 and 33 CE. A wealthy Jewish disciple named Joseph of Arimathea asked Pilate for Jesus's body, which Joseph wrapped in a linen shroud and placed in his own tomb, with a large stone against the door. A guard was placed at the tomb to make sure that no followers would steal the body and claim that Jesus had risen from the dead.

Resurrection and Ascension

That seemed to be the end of it. Jesus's disciples were terrified, so some of them hid, mourning and disheartened. The whole religious movement could have died out, as did other messianic cults. However, what is reported next in varying gospel accounts seemed to change everything. Some of the women who had been close to Jesus and had traveled with him from Galilee—Mary Magdalene, plus, according to different gospels, Mary mother of James, Joanna, Salome, and perhaps others—visited the tomb on Sunday to prepare the body for a proper burial, a rite that had been postponed because of the Sabbath. Instead, they found the tomb empty, with the stone rolled away. Angels then appeared and told them Jesus had risen from death. The women ran and brought two of the male disciples, who witnessed the empty tomb with the shroud folded.

Then followed numerous reports of appearances of the risen Christ to various disciples. He dispelled their doubts about his **Resurrection**, having them touch his wounds and even eating a fish with them. He said to them, as recounted in the Gospel of Matthew:

> *All authority in heaven and on earth has been given to me. Go therefore and make disciples of all nations, baptizing them in the name of the Father and of the Son and of the Holy Spirit, teaching them to observe all that I have commanded you; and lo, I am with you always, to the close of the age.*[34]

The details of the appearances of the resurrected Jesus differ considerably from gospel to gospel. However, some scholars think that to have women as the first witnesses to the empty tomb suggests there must be some historical truth in the claims of Jesus's Resurrection, for no one trying to build a case would have rested it on the testimony of women, who had little status in a patriarchal society. Feminist scholar Elisabeth Schüssler Fiorenza finds deep meaning in the presence of women disciples at the time of Jesus's death and resurrection. The gospels mention a woman who anoints Jesus, a sign that she recognizes him as the Messiah. The reports that it is women who faithfully visit the tomb suggest that, as Schüssler Fiorenza puts it,

> *Whereas according to Mark the leading male disciples do not understand this suffering messiahship of Jesus, reject it, and finally abandon him, the women disciples who have followed Jesus from Galilee to Jerusalem suddenly emerge as the true disciples in the passion narrative. They are Jesus' true followers who have understood that his ministry was not rule and kingly glory but* diakonia, *"service" (Mark 15:41). Thus the women emerge as the true Christian ministers and*

witnesses. The unnamed woman who names Jesus with a prophetic sign-action in Mark's Gospel is the paradigm for the true disciple. While Peter had confessed, without truly understanding it, "you are the anointed one," the woman anointing Jesus recognizes clearly that Jesus' messiahship means suffering and death.[35]

It was the Resurrection that turned defeat into victory for Jesus, and discouragement into powerful action for his followers. As the impact of all they had seen set in, the followers came to believe that Jesus had been God present in a human life, walking among them.

According to two gospel accounts, after the resurrected Jesus appeared to his disciples, encouraging them to carry the gospel to the whole world, he ascended into heaven. The end of the gospel of Mark, which is thought to be a later addition to the chapter, adds, "and sat down at the right hand of God" (Mark 16:19). Some Christians believe that Jesus miraculously ascended bodily into the highest heaven, an invisible realm in the sky where God is sitting with Jesus beside him, as an advocate for his faithful followers. Whether understood metaphorically or literally, the **Ascension** is an article of Christian faith. It is further extended in the Acts of the Apostles into belief that Jesus will return bodily to the earth in the future (Acts 1:10–11).

The early Church

Persecution became the lot of Jesus's followers. But by 380 CE, despite strong opposition, Christianity became the official religion of the vast Roman Empire. As it became the establishment, rather than a tiny, scattered band of dissidents within Judaism, Christianity continued to define and organize itself.

From persecution to empire

The earliest years of what became the mainstream of Christianity are described in the New Testament books that follow the gospel accounts of the life of Jesus. "The Acts of the Apostles" was presumably written by the same person who wrote the Gospel of Luke, for the style is the same, both books are addressed to the same person named Theophilus, and Acts refers back to the Gospel of Luke as an earlier part of a single history of the rise of Christianity. Acts is followed by letters to early groups of Christians, most of them apparently written by Paul, a major organizer and **apostle** (missionary), in about 50 to 60 CE.

Like the gospel accounts, the stories in these biblical books are examined by many contemporary scholars as possibly romanticized, idealized documents, used to convert, to increase faith, to teach principles, and to establish Christian theology, rather than to accurately record historical facts.

According to Acts, an event called **Pentecost** galvanized the early Christians into action. At a meeting of the disciples, something that sounded like a great wind came down from the sky, and what looked like tongues of fire swirled around to touch each one's head. The narrative states that they all began speaking in different languages, so that all who listened could understand in their own language. Some mocked them, saying they were drunk, but Peter declared that they had been filled with the Spirit of God, as the Old Testament prophet Joel had prophesied would happen in the last days before the onset of the kingdom of God. He testified that the Jesus whom the people had crucified had been raised up by God, who had made him "both Lord and Christ."[36] Reportedly, 3,000 people were so convinced that they were baptized that day.

One of the persecutors of Christians was Saul. He was a Pharisee tentmaker who lived during the time of Jesus but never met him. Instead, after Jesus died, he helped to throw many of his followers into prison and sentence them to death. Acts relates that on the way to Damascus in search of more heretics, he saw a light brighter than the sun and heard the voice of Jesus asking why Saul was persecuting him. This resistance was useless, said the vision of Jesus, who then appointed him to do the opposite—to go to both Jews and Gentiles:

> to open their eyes, that they may turn from darkness to light and from the power of Satan to God, that they may receive forgiveness of sins and a place among those who are sanctified by faith in me.[37]

This meeting with the risen Christ, and through him, God, was an utterly transformational experience for Saul. He wrote about his previous life:

> I count everything sheer loss, because all is so far outweighed by the gain of knowing Christ Jesus my Lord, for whose sake I did in fact lose everything. I count it so much garbage, for the sake of gaining Christ and finding myself incorporate in him, with no righteousness of my own, no legal rectitude, but the righteousness which comes from faith in Christ, given by God in response to faith. All I care for is to know Christ.[38]

Saul was baptized and immediately began promoting the Christian message under his new name, Paul. His indefatigable work in traveling around the Mediterranean was of great importance in shaping and expanding the early Christian Church. He was shipwrecked, stoned, imprisoned, and beaten, and probably died as a martyr in Rome, but nothing short of death deterred him from his new mission.

Paul tried to convince Jews that Jesus's birth, death, and Resurrection had been predicted by the Old Testament prophets. This was the Messiah they had been waiting for, and now, risen from death, he presided as the cosmic Christ, offering God's forgiveness and grace to those who repented and trusted in God rather than in themselves. Some Jews were converted to this belief, and the Jewish authorities repeatedly accused Paul of leading people away from Jewish law and tradition. There was not only one Jewish tradition, however. The Pharisees, for instance, did not see God as belonging only to Israel, but rather as the parent watching over and taking care of every individual. They addressed God by new names, such as *Abinu she-Bashamayim* ("Our Father Who art in Heaven"), the same form of address by which Jesus reportedly taught his followers to pray to God (Matthew 6:9). However, a major difference remained between Jews and Christians over the central importance given to Jesus. It is possible that Jesus himself may not have claimed that he was the Messiah, and that it was Paul who developed this claim. To this day, Jews tend to feel that to put heavy emphasis on the person of Jesus takes attention away from Jesus's message and from God.

In Paul's time, those Jews who emphasized that Jews had been especially chosen by God were offended by interpretations of Jesus's life and teachings that saw Christianity as a universal mission of salvation for all peoples. These interpretations made the new sect, Christianity, seem irreconcilable with exclusive versions of Judaism, and the gap between the two became deep and bitter. The New Testament writings reflect the criticisms of the early Christians against the large Jewish majority who did not accept Jesus as their Messiah. These polemics have been echoed through the centuries as anti-semitism. Only in Jerusalem did Jewish leaders have the authority to persecute Christians as dissidents. Opposition in Israel led to their spreading out to carry the gospel elsewhere, thus helping to expand their mission, but Christian animosity toward Jews lingered, to resurface in virulent forms from time to time.

Paul also tried to sway Gentiles: worshipers of the old gods whose religion was in decline, supporters of the emperor as deity, ecstatic initiates of mystery cults, and followers of dualistic Greco-Roman philosophers who regarded matter as evil and tried to emancipate the soul from its corrupting influence. He taught them that God did not reside in any idol but yet was not far from them, "For in him we live and move and have our being."[39] Hellenistic Jewish philosophers such as Philo (c. 20 BCE–c. 50 CE) had tried to bridge Jewish religion and Greek thought in intellectual circles; Christian missionaries took this approach to the masses. For Gentiles embracing Christianity, Paul and others argued that the Jewish tradition of circumcision should not be required of them (as for example in Romans 2:29). As Paul interpreted the gospel, salvation came by repentant faith in the grace of Christ, rather than by observance of a traditional law. In Paul's letter to the Church in Rome, he argues that even Abraham was **justified**, or accepted by God in spite of sin, because of his great faith in God rather than by his circumcision. Greco-Romans had idealized the male human body, with great athletic spectacles performed by nude men, so the necessity of altering the human form would have been a barrier to their acceptance of Paul's teachings. Shifting away from circumcision as a traditional requirement was a significant example of the enculturation of Christianity as it evolved in various contexts and began to distinguish itself from Judaism.

Christianity spread rapidly and soon became largely non-Jewish in membership. By 200 CE, it had spread throughout the Roman Empire and into Mesopotamia, despite fierce opposition. Many Christians were subjected to imprisonment, torture, and confiscation of property, because they rejected polytheistic beliefs, idols, and emperor worship in the Roman Empire. They were suspected of being revolutionaries, with their talk of a Messiah, and of strange cultic behaviors, such as their secret rituals of symbolically drinking Jesus's blood and eating his flesh. Persecution did not deter the most ardent of Christians; it united them intimately to the passion and death of Christ. In addition to martyrdom, many early Christians embraced a life of ascetic self-denial by fasting, wearing coarse clothes, renouncing sexuality, spending hours in prayer and contemplation, and serving others. They sought to be living sacrifices, giving up the pleasures of the material world for the sake of loving and serving God.

With the rise of Constantine to imperial rule early in the fourth century CE, opposition turned to the official embracing of Christianity. Constantine said that God showed him a vision of a cross to be used as a standard in battle. After he used it and won in 330 CE, he instituted tolerance of Christianity alongside the state cult, of which he was the chief priest. Just before his death, Constantine was baptized as a Christian.

By the end of the fourth century CE, people of other religions were stripped of all rights, and ordered into Christian churches to be baptized. Some paid outward service to Christianity but remained inwardly faithful to their old traditions. As Christianity became the favored religion, many converted for secular reasons.

By the end of the fifth century CE, Christianity was the faith claimed by the majority of people in the vast former Roman Empire. It also spread beyond the empire, from Ireland in the west to India and Ceylon (Sri Lanka) in the east.

Evolving organization and theology

During its phenomenal growth from persecuted sect to state religion throughout much of the ancient world, Christianity was developing organizationally and theologically. By the end of the first century CE, it had a bureaucracy that carried on the rites of the Church and attempted to define mainstream Christianity.

One form that was judged to be outside the mainstream was Gnostic Christianity, which appeared as a movement in the second century CE. **Gnosticism** means mystical perception of knowledge. The Nag Hammadi library found in Egypt presents Jesus as a great Gnostic teacher. His words are interpreted as the secret teachings given only to initiates. "He who is near to me is near to the fire," he says in the Gospel of Thomas.[40] The Gnostics held that only spiritually mature individuals could apprehend Jesus's real teaching: that the Kingdom of Heaven is a present reality experienced through personal realization of the Light.

When the New Testament canon of twenty-seven officially sanctioned texts was set and translated into Latin in the fourth century, the Gnostic gospels were not included. Instead, the Church treated possession of Gnostic texts as a crime against Church law because the Christian faith community felt that Jesus had not taught an elitist view of salvation and had not discriminated against the material aspect of creation.

What became mainstream Christianity is based not only on the life and teachings of Jesus, as set forth in the gospels selected for the New Testament, but also on the ways that they have been interpreted over the centuries. One of the first and most important interpreters was Paul. His central contribution—which was as influential as the four gospels in shaping Christianity—was his interpretation of Jesus's death and Resurrection.

Paul spoke of *agape*—altruistic, self-giving love—as the center of Christian concern. He placed it above spiritual wisdom, asceticism, faith, and supernatural "gifts of the Spirit," such as the ability to heal, prophesy, or spontaneously speak in unknown tongues. Love was applied not only to one's neighbors but also to one's relationship with the divine. It was love plus gnosis—knowledge of God, permeated with love—that became the basis of contemplative Christianity, as it was shaped by the "Fathers" of the first centuries.

Let all that you do be done in love.   *1 Corinthians 16:14*

The cross, with or without an image of Jesus crucified on it, became a central symbol of Christianity. It marked the path of suffering service, rather than political domination, as the way of conquering evil and experiencing union with a compassionate God. To participate in Jesus's sacrifice, people could repent of their sins, be baptized, and be reborn to new life in Christ. In the early fifth century CE the bishop Augustine, one of the most influential theologians in the history of western Christianity, described this spiritual rebirth thus:

> *Where I was angry within myself in my chamber, where I was inwardly pricked, where I had sacrificed, slaying my old man and commencing the purpose of a new life, putting my trust in Thee—there hadst Thou begun to grow sweet unto me and "hadst put gladness in my heart."*[41]

Rowan Williams, the twenty-first-century theologian and Archbishop of Canterbury, leader of the Anglican Church, explains this repentance and spiritual resurrection as:

> *the refusal to accept that lostness is the final human truth. Like a growing thing beneath the earth, we protest at the darkness and push blindly up in search of light, truth, home—the place, the relation where we are not lost, where we can live from deep roots in assurance. "Because I live, you will live also."*[42]

The expectation of the coming of God's kingdom and final judgment of who would go to heaven and who to hell, so fervent in the earliest Christianity, began to wane as time went by and the anticipated events did not happen. The notion of the Kingdom of God began to shift to the indefinite future, with emphasis placed on a preliminary judgment at one's death. There was nevertheless the continuing expectation that Christ would return in glory to judge the living and the dead and bring to fulfillment the creation." This belief in the "Second Coming" of Christ is still an article of faith today for some Christians; others regard it as symbolic of a pointing to the certainty of God's coming rule of love and peace.

Reflecting on the life of Jesus and their experience of the risen Christ, Christians believed that the transcendent and invisible God had become immanent and visible in Jesus. This led to the early development of the doctrine of the **Holy Trinity**, which speaks of three equal "persons" within one divine being: Father, Son, and Holy Spirit. The Father is the one who sends the Son to become incarnate in Jesus with the mission to reveal God's love to the world. The Son or Word manifests God in the world in many ways, but the incarnation in Jesus is a culmination of that revelation. The Holy Spirit, or Holy Ghost, who Jesus promises will be sent after his death, is the power and presence of God, actively guiding and sustaining the faithful.

Although Jesus had spoken in parables with several levels of meaning, the evolving Church found it necessary to articulate some of its beliefs more openly and systematically. A number of **creeds**, or professions of faith, were composed for use in religious instruction and baptism, to define who Jesus was and his relationship to God, and to provide clear stands in the face of various controversies. The Emperor Constantine was particularly concerned to bring doctrinal unity among the Christian churches which he had legalized and whose beliefs he was promoting throughout his widespread empire. One major controversy concerned the teachings of Arius, a leader of the congregation in Alexandria. The issue was the relationship between God and Jesus. The Christians worshiped Jesus, but at the same time came from monotheistic Jewish tradition, in which God alone is worshiped. Was Jesus therefore somehow the same as God? To Arius, the "Son of God" is a metaphor; it does not mean that Jesus has the same status as God, for Jesus was a human being. Opponents of this belief argued that Jesus is properly worshiped as the incarnation of God.

Constantine convened a general council of the elders of all area churches in Nicaea in 325 CE to settle this critical issue. After decades of controversy, Arius's beliefs were ultimately rejected in the framing of the **Nicene Creed**, tradition-ally dated to another council held in Constantinople in 381 CE (and thus some-times referred to as the Niceno-Constantinopolitan Creed). It is still the basic profession of faith for many Christian denominations in both East and West, including all Orthodox churches, and has been proposed as a basis for unifying all Christians:

> *We believe in one God, the Father, the almighty, maker of heaven and earth, of all that is, seen and unseen. We believe in one Lord, Jesus Christ, the only Son of God, eternally begotten of the Father, God from God, Light from Light, true God from true God, begotten not made, of one Being with the Father. Through him all things were made. For us men and for our salvation he came down from heaven; by the power of the Holy Spirit he became incarnate of the Virgin Mary, and was made man. For our sake he was crucified under Pontius Pilate; he suffered death and was buried. On the third day he rose again in accordance with the Scriptures; he ascended into heaven and is seated at the right hand of the Father. He will come again in glory to judge the living and the dead, and his kingdom will have no end. We believe in the Holy Spirit, the Lord, the giver of life, who proceeds from the Father (and from the Son). With the Father and the Son he is worshiped and glorified. He has spoken through the Prophets. We believe in one holy, **catholic**, and apostolic Church. We acknowledge one baptism for the forgiveness of sins. We look for the resurrection of the dead, and the life of the world to come. Amen.*

As we will see later, the small phrase "and from the Son" was added to the creed by the Western part of the Church in the early Middle Ages and became a major point of disagreement between the Western Church and the Eastern Christian churches, which did not add it.

Christology—the attempt to define the nature of Jesus and his relationship to God—received further official clarification during the Council of Chalcedon in 451, which issued a statement that allows considerable leeway in Christological interpretations by declaring Jesus is of "two natures"—perfectly divine and also perfectly human. The Council of Chalcedon defined Jesus as:

> *perfect in divinity and humanity, truly God and truly human, consisting of a rational soul and a body, being of one substance with the Father in relation to his divinity, and being of one substance with us in relation to his humanity, and is like us in all things apart from sin (Hebrews 4:15). He was begotten of the Father before time in relation to his divinity, and in these recent days was born from the Virgin Mary, the Theotokos [Mother of God], for us and for our salvation.*

Early monasticism

Alongside the development of doctrine and the consolidation of church structure, another trend was developing. Some Christians were turning away from the world to live in solitary communion with God, as ascetics. There had been a certain amount of asceticism in Paul's writings. He himself was celibate, as he believed that avoiding family entanglements helped one to concentrate on the Lord.

By the fourth century CE, Christian monks—and apparently also some remarkable ascetic women referred to as *ammas* (mothers)—were living simply in caves in the Egyptian desert with little regard for the things of the world. They had no central organization but tended to learn from the examples of other ascetics. Avoiding emphasis on the supernatural powers that often accompany the ascetic life, they told stories demonstrating the virtues they valued, such as humility, submission, and the sharing of food. For example, an earnest young man was said to have visited one of the desert fathers and asked how he was faring. The old man sighed and said, "Very badly, my child." Asked why, he said, "I have been here forty years doing nothing other than cursing my own self each day, inasmuch as in the prayers I offer, I say to God, 'Accursed are those who deviate from Your commandments.'"[43] The young seeker was moved by such humility and made it his model.

The desert fathers and mothers were left to their own devices at first. In Christian humility, they avoided judging or trying to teach each other and attempted to be, at best, harmless. But by the fifth century CE, the monastic life shifted from solitary, unguided practice, to formal spiritual supervision. Group monasteries and structures for encouraging obedience to God through an abbot or abbess were set up, and rules devised to help monks persevere in their calling. The Rule of St. Benedict became a model for all later monastic orders in the West, with its emphasis on poverty, chastity, and obedience to the abbot, and its insistence that each monastery be economically self-sufficient through the labor of the monastics. The Benedictines have been famous over the centuries for their practice of hospitality to pilgrims and travelers, and are today active participants in interreligious monastic dialogue.

The carefree man, who has tested the sweetness of having no personal possessions, feels that even the cassock which he wears and the jug of water in his cell are a useless burden, because these things, too, sometimes distract his mind.

A Desert Father[44]

The Eastern Orthodox Church

Christianity's history has been marked by internal feuds and divisions. One of the deepest schisms occurred in 1054, when the Roman Catholic Church, whose followers were largely in the West, and the Eastern Orthodox Church split apart.

The history of the Orthodox Church

Late in the third century CE, the Roman Empire was divided into two: an eastern and a western section. In the fourth century CE, Constantine established a second seat in the east, in Constantinople (now Istanbul, Turkey). It was considered a "second Rome," especially after the sack of Rome by the Goths in 410. The two halves of the Christian world grew apart, divided by language (Latin in the west, Greek in the east), culture, and religious differences.

In the western half, religious power was becoming more and more centralized in the Roman **pope** and other high officials. The Byzantine east was organized into a number of **sees**. The five major sees were those of Rome, Constantinople, Alexandria, Antioch, and Jerusalem. But this distinction was for organizational purposes; spiritually, all bishops, regardless of the status of the cities with which they are associated, are to today thought to be equal as successors to the original apostles, equally empowered to perform the sacraments and teach the faith. Rome was accorded a "primacy of honor" but not supreme jurisdiction.

The east did not recognize the Roman pope's claim to universal authority. By the early Middle Ages, there were also doctrinal disagreements. In its version of the Niceno-Constantinopolitan Creed, for example, the Western Church added the *filioque*, a formula professing that the Holy Spirit came from the Father "*and from the Son*"; the Eastern Church retained what is considered the more original text, professing that the Holy Spirit proceeds only from the Father.

In 1054, leaders of the eastern and western factions excommunicated each other over the disagreement about the Holy Spirit, and over the papal claim, celibacy for priests (the Eastern Church requires celibacy for bishops only), and whether the eucharistic bread should be leavened or unleavened. To the Eastern Church, the last straw was its treatment by crusaders.

From 1095 to about 1290, waves of Christians poured out of Europe in what were presented as **"Holy crusades"** to recapture the holy land of Palestine from Muslims, defend the Byzantine Empire against Muslim Turks, and in general wipe out the enemies of Christianity. It was a tragic and bloody time. One of the many casualties was the tenuous relationship between the Eastern and Western Churches. When crusaders entered Constantinople in 1204, they tried to intervene in local politics. Rebuffed, they ravaged the city. They destroyed the altar and sacred icons in Hagia Sophia, the Church of the Holy Wisdom (later a Muslim mosque), and placed prostitutes on the throne reserved for the patriarch of the region. Horrified, the Orthodox Church ended its dialogue with Rome and proceeded on its own path, claiming to be the true descendant of the apostolic Church. Despite periodic attempts at reconciliation the Eastern and Western Churches are still separate.

The Russian Orthodox Church

When the Muslim Ottoman Turks took Constantinople in the fifteenth century, Russia became more prominent in the Orthodox Church, calling itself the "third Rome." The Orthodox Church had spread throughout the Slavic and eastern Mediterranean countries.

Russian Orthodox Christianity was closely associated with Russian national history since its adoption by Vladimir I in 988. But it was severely repressed by the Soviet government during the twentieth century. Lenin saw institutionalized religion as a divisive, backward force in society, an apology for oppression. Following the 1917 Revolution, anti-Church propaganda was broadcast, and many intellectuals who wanted the good of society left the Church. Lenin proclaimed that all Church property belonged to the State. Thousands of monasteries and churches were taken over during the Revolution, and in the early 1920s thousands of priests, nuns, and lay Christians were killed. During the 1930s more monasteries and churches were closed, and great numbers of clergy were imprisoned. Bishops who refused to accept Soviet control issued what is called the Solovky Memorandum.

The bishops were imprisoned in the Solovky labor camp; many were killed there. It is estimated that some 40,000 priests were killed from 1918 to 1940. Out of almost 80,000 churches and chapels in the Russian Empire in 1914, only a few hundred or a thousand remained by the beginning of World War II. Under Khrushchev, a new campaign against religion was unleashed, and perhaps two-thirds of the remaining Orthodox churches were closed.

Nevertheless, the Orthodox Church did not die, for it was deeply rooted in the minds and hearts of the people. In the mid-1980s, the Russian Orthodox Church had an estimated 50 million members. Most of those who dared to worship publicly were the *babushkas*—old women who were apparently not regarded as politically dangerous.

After decades of oppression, the Russian Orthodox Church witnessed a great change in government policy in 1988, the celebration of its first millennium in Russia and Ukraine. Mikhail Gorbachev's government approached its leaders, asking their help with *perestroika* and returning some church buildings, which had been turned into museums or warehouses. Some 1,700 churches were reopened in 1988 and 1989, and each was immediately filled with worshipers. Seminaries for new clergy report a great increase in enrolment. Late in 1989, Gorbachev ended seven decades of suppression of religion, pronouncing the right of the Soviet faithful to "satisfy their spiritual needs."[45]

Nevertheless, many people are disillusioned with the contemporary Russian Orthodox Church because of its politics. Its staff included many KGB agents, and some Church leaders felt they had to make compromises in order to survive at all as a religion under Soviet rule. Now the Russian Orthodox Church has very powerful influence in government policy and is strongly supported by political leaders from all parties, including communists.

Since the early days of the Soviet Union, there have also been Orthodox Christians who refused to collaborate or compromise with the government. At the risk of their jobs and lives, some Christian laypeople and priests began to worship secretly in what became known as catacomb churches, just as the early Christians had worshiped in catacombs to evade persecution.

Even today, some Orthodox Christians continue to worship in secret rather than subject their congregations to the registration requirements of the state and disapproval of the official Church. Bishop Feodor, bishop of underground Christians in Moscow, Riga, and the Far East, objects to the assertive power of the Russian Orthodox Church:

If the Church has pride, it has no holy power. We are all brothers in Adam and in Christ. We are all baptized by God. This is true for each Christian. If you cannot love your brother who is next to you, how can you love one you cannot see, such as Christ, who has not been with us for two thousand years?[46]

The Orthodox world today

There are fifteen self-governing Orthodox Churches worldwide, each having its own leader, known as patriarch, metropolitan, or archbishop. Most Orthodox Christians live in Russia, the Balkan states, and eastern Europe, in formerly communist countries where the teaching and propagation of Christianity was severely restricted. Autocephalous (independent) churches there include the large Church of Russia, which is dominated by the Patriarchate of Moscow, plus the Churches of Serbia, Bulgaria, Romania, Albania, Poland, and the Czech Republic. The original and still central Patriarchate of Constantinople is based within Turkey, as a small minority within a Muslim country, which has no Orthodox seminaries. This Patriarchate includes islands in the Aegean and the Mount Athos peninsula. The latter was historically a great center of Orthodox monasticism, but its population of monks declined considerably in the twentieth century when emigration of monks was prohibited by communist regimes. Now women have agitated to be allowed to enter Mount Athos, where even female animals are banned. Traditionalists maintain that Mount Athos is the only truly monastic community left in the world and should continue its antique ways unchanged and undistracted; women counter that the ban on women is degrading, a "sexist, anti-democratic decision taken by men, not by God."[47]

The Patriarchate of Alexandria is based in Egypt and includes all of Africa, where Orthodoxy arose independently in Uganda and has been embraced with considerable enthusiasm. The Patriarchate of Antioch consists mostly of Orthodox Christian Arabs in Syria and Lebanon. The Patriarchate of Jerusalem is charged with guarding the Holy Places of Christianity.

The Greek Orthodox Church dominates religious life in Greece and is assisting in reviving interest in the classical books and arts of Orthodox spirituality. In the Church of Cyprus, the archbishop is also traditionally the political leader of the people. The Church of Sinai consists of only one monastery.

Extensive emigration, particularly from Russia during the first few years of communist rule, created large Orthodox populations in Western countries. Some retain direct ties to their home patriarchate, such as the New York-based Archdiocese of the Greek Orthodox Church in North and South America. Alongside that, the Orthodox Church in America was granted its independence in 1970, and now claims over four million members in a country where Protestantism and Roman Catholicism are the predominant forms of Christianity. Missionary activity by the Russian Orthodox Church also established Orthodoxy in China, Korea, Japan, and among the indigenous peoples in Alaska.

Distinctive features of Orthodox spirituality

Over the centuries, the individual Orthodox Churches have probably changed less than have the many descendants of the early Western Church. There is a strong conservative tradition, attempting to preserve the pattern of early Christianity. Even though the religious leaders can make local adaptations suited to their region and people, they are united in doctrine and sacramental observances. Any change that will affect all churches is decided by a **synod**—a council of officials trying to reach common agreements, as did the early Church. Although women are important in local Church affairs, they cannot be ordained as priests or serve in hierarchical capacities.

In addition to the Bible, Orthodox Christians honor the writings of the saints of the Church. A collection called the *Philokalia* consists of texts written by Orthodox masters between the fourth and fifteenth centuries. "Philokalia" means love of the exalted, excellent, and beautiful—the transcendent divine source of life and truth. The *Philokalia* is essentially a Christian guide to the contemplative life for monks, but is also for laypeople. A central practice is "unceasing prayer": the continual remembrance of Jesus or God, often by repeating a verbal formula. The most common is the "Jesus prayer": "Lord Jesus Christ, Son of God, have mercy on me, a sinner." The repetition of the name of Jesus brings purification of heart and singularity of desire. To call upon Jesus is to experience his presence in oneself and in all things.

The Orthodox Church has affirmed that humans can approach God directly. Some may even see the light of God and be utterly transformed by it:

> *He who participates in the divine energy, himself becomes, to some extent, light: he is united to the light, and by that light he sees in full awareness all that remains hidden to those who have not this grace; . . . for the pure in heart see God . . . who, being Light, dwells in them and reveals Himself to those who love Him, to His beloved.*[48]

Another distinctive feature of Orthodox Christianity is its veneration of **icons,** stylized paintings of Jesus, his mother Mary, and the saints. They are created by artists who prepare for their work by prayer and ascetical training. There is no attempt at earthly realism, for they represent the reality of the divine world. They are beloved as windows to the eternal. Some icons are said to have spiritual powers, heal illnesses, and transmit the holy presence. Believers kiss the icon reverently and pray before it.

Some major icons in an Orthodox church are placed on an iconostasis, a screen that separates the congregation from the Holy of Holies, which can be entered only by the clergy. On either side of the opening to the altar are icons of Jesus and the Virgin Mary.

Orthodox choirs sing the divine liturgy in many-part harmony, producing an ethereal and uplifting effect. Everything strives toward that beauty to which the *Philokalia* refers. Archimandrite Nathaniel of the Russian Othodox Pskova-Pechorsky Monastery, which has been a place of uninterrupted prayer for almost six hundred years despite eight hundred attacks on its walls and numerous sieges, speaks of the ideal of beauty in Orthodox Christianity:

> *The understanding of God is the understanding of beauty. Beauty is at the heart of our monastic life. The life of prayer is a constant well of beauty. We have the beauty of music in the Holy Liturgy. The great beauty of monastic life is communal life in Christ. Living together in love, living without enmity, as peaceful with each other as one dead body is peaceful with another dead body, we are dead to enmity.*[49]

Medieval Roman Catholicism

In the West, from the sixth to tenth centuries CE, the old Roman Empire gradually fell to non-Christian invaders. Islam also made spectacular advances in areas previously converted to Christianity. However, the Angle and Saxon invaders of England were slowly converted to Christianity. By the fourteenth century, most of central and western Europe was claimed for Christianity, and missionaries spread the faith to isolated areas of Asia.

The Holy Roman Empire was politically decentralized into feudal kingdoms, with the Christian Church the major force uniting Europe. The chief factors sustaining Christianity were its centralized organization under the Western pope and Eastern Orthodox Byzantine leaders and the periodic refreshing of its spiritual wellsprings through monasticism and mysticism.

Papal power

During the late first and early second centuries CE, some men and women followed a charismatic Christian life, leaving home to preach, baptize, prophesy, and perhaps die as martyrs; others moved toward an institutionalized patriarchal Church. By the beginning of the second century, a consolidation of spiritual power had begun with clergy and bishops (superintendents) administering Church affairs in each city or region. While some women ministered to women, as deacons, the clergy and bishops had to be male, with wife and children. The bishops of the chief cities of the Roman Empire had the greatest responsibilities and authority, with the greatest prestige held by the Bishop of Rome, eventually known as the pope. By the fifth century, Pope Leo I argued that all popes were apostolic successors to Peter, the "rock" on which Jesus in Matthew's gospel said he would found his Church. The Roman emperor passed an edict that all Christians were to recognize the authority of the Bishop of Rome.

The strongest of Church administrators during these early centuries was Gregory I ("the Great"), who died in 604 CE. Wealthy by birth but ascetic by choice, he devoted his personal fortune to founding monasteries and feeding the poor. Longing for the quiet life of a monk, he was convinced to be pope at a time of pestilence, floods, and military invasions. Even in this setting, he provided for the physical needs of the poor, promoted the discipline of the clergy (including the Western ideal that priests should be celibate in order to concentrate on piety and ministry without family obligations and to avoid having to share Church property with wives and children), revamped the liturgy (Gregorian chanting is named after him), and re-established the Church as a decent, just institution carrying high spiritual values.

Pope Gregory also sent missionaries to convert England to Christianity. They were ultimately successful, partly because of the royal protection the missionaries and converts won and partly because rather than destroying the old religious shrines, Gregory instructed the missionaries to replace the idols of indigenous deities with relics of martyrs and saints—bits of bone, cloth, even dirt from their graves—which they carried to England.

The papacy began to wield tremendous secular power. Beginning in the eighth century, its approval conferred divine sanction on feudal kings. In the ninth century the Church produced documents old and new believed to legitimate the hierarchical authority of the papacy over the Church, and the Church over society, as the proper means of transmitting inspiration from the divine to humanity. Those who disagreed could be threatened with **excommunication**. This exclusion from participation in the sacraments cut a person off from the redemption of the Church (blocking one's entrance to heaven in the afterlife), as well as from the benefits of the Church's secular power. Crusades were launched under the auspices of the Church, with war used ostensibly in defense of the faith, with no restraints on the treatment of the "**infidel**."

This centralization of power became a major unifying element in the Europe of the Middle Ages. Kingdoms broke up between 800 and 1100 as Vikings invaded from the north and Magyars from the east. For the sake of military protection, peasants gave up their freedom to feudal lords. The feudal lords in turn began to war among themselves. In the midst of the ensuing chaos, people looked to the pope as an orderly wielder of power.

Church and states were at times locked in a struggle for dominance, with popes alternately supporting, dominating, and being deposed by secular rulers. The power of the papacy was also somewhat limited by the requirement that the pope be elected by a council of cardinals. The position could not become hereditary. But it was open to intrigue, scandal, and power-mongering.

The thirteenth century saw the power of the papacy placed behind the **Inquisition**, an ecclesiastical court set up in 1229 to investigate and suppress heresy. This instrument of terror was based on Augustine's concept that heretics should be controlled for the sake of their own eternal salvation, out of love for their souls. But whereas Augustine saw fines and imprisonment as reasonable coercion to help people change their minds, in some cases the medieval Inquisitors had them tortured and burned to deter others from dangerous views.

Though strong, the papacy was often embroiled in its own political strife. During the fourteenth century, the popes left their traditional seat in turbulent Rome for the more peaceful climate of Avignon, France. There they built up an elaborate administrative structure, increasingly involved in worldly affairs. After the papacy was persuaded to return to Rome, a would-be reformer, Pope Urban IV, turned to terror tactics to get his way. At one point he had five cardinals tortured and killed. Many people refused to follow him; for a while they followed an "anti-pope" they established in Avignon.

Intellectual revival and monasticism

Although the papacy was subject to abuses, mirrored on a lesser scale by the clergy, Christian spirituality was vigorously revived in other quarters of medieval society. During the twelfth and thirteenth centuries great universities developed in Europe, often from cathedral schools. Theology was considered the greatest of the sciences, with Church ideals permeating the study of all areas of life. Soaring Gothic cathedrals were built to uplift the soul to heavenly heights, for God was perceived as being enthroned in the heavens, far above the workaday world.

The yearning for spiritual purity was particularly pronounced in monasticism. It was largely through monks and nuns that Christian spirituality survived and spread. Monasteries also became bulwarks of Western civilization. In Ireland, particularly, they were the centers of larger communities of laypeople and places of learning within illiterate warring societies.

During the twelfth century many new monastic orders appeared in the midst of a massive popular re-invigoration of spiritual activity. A major influence was a community in Cluny, France. Its monks specialized in liturgical elaborations and prayer, leaving agricultural work to serfs. An alternative direction was taken by the Cistercians, Gregorians, and Carthusians. They returned to St. Benedict's Rule of combining manual work and prayer; "to labor is to pray," said the monks. The Carthusians lived cloistered lives as hermits, meeting each other only for worship and business matters. Despite such austere practices, people of all classes flocked to monastic life as a pious refuge from decadent society.

> *It is not only prayer that gives God glory but work. . . . He is so great that all things give Him glory if you mean they should.*
>
> *Gerard Manley Hopkins*[50]

In contrast to monks and nuns living cloistered lives, mendicant friars, or brothers, worked among the people. In 1215, the Dominican Order was instituted primarily to teach the faith and refute heresies. A famous Dominican scholar, Thomas Aquinas, created a monumental work, *Summa Theologiae*, in which rational sciences and spiritual revelations were joined in an immense, consistent theological system. Aquinas was much influenced by the recovery of the classical writings of Aristotle that had been preserved by Muslims and returned to Europe through Spain.

Franciscans, following the lead of the beloved St. Francis of Assisi (see below), wandered about without personal property or established buildings, telling people about God's love and accepting charity for their meager needs. The mendicant Dominicans and Franciscans, still noted as missionaries today, became one of the major features of medieval Christianity.

In addition to organized orders of nuns, there was a grassroots movement among thirteenth-century German and Flemish women to take private vows of chastity and simplicity. These women, who were called "beguines," lived frugally by their own work. Because they were not organized into a religious order, they chose their own lifestyles, intending simply to live "religiously." At times persecuted because it did not fit into any traditionally sanctioned pattern, the movement persisted, drawing tens of thousands of women. Eventually they built small convents for themselves; by the end of the fourteenth century, there were 169 beguine convents in Cologne, the heart of the movement.

Medieval mysticism

Mysticism also flowered during the Middle Ages, renewing the spiritual heart of the Church. Especially in cloistered settings, monks and nuns contemplated the meanings of the scriptures for the soul. Biblical stories of battles between heroes and their enemies were, for instance, interpreted as the struggle between the soul and baser desires. Beyond this rational thought, some engaged in non-conceptual prayer, simply resting receptively in the presence of God.

One remarkable mystic was the German abbess Hildegard of Bingen (1098–1179). Founder of two monasteries on the Rhine, from a young age she experienced frequent visions, which she recorded in several books of revelations. She wrote treatises on medical and scientific matters as well as much fine spiritual poetry, and achieved considerable fame as a composer. Corresponding with popes, emperors, and kings, she remained privately devoted to mystic thought and to prophecy.

In thirteenth-century Italy, there was the endearing figure of St. Francis of Assisi (1182–1226). The carefree son of a merchant, he underwent a spiritual transformation after a vision in which Jesus spoke to him from the cross, saying: "Repair my Church." He traded his fine clothes for simple garb and "left the world"[51] for a life of poverty, caring for lepers and rebuilding dilapidated churches. Eventually he understood that his mission was to rebuild the Church by re-emphasizing the gospel and its commands of love and poverty. A band of brothers, and then of sisters led by the saintly Clare, gathered around him. The friars preached, worked, begged, tended lepers, and lived a life of penance and prayer while wandering from town to town. St Francis was known for his rapport with animals and is often pictured with birds on his shoulders. Two years before his death, he received the "stigmata," replicas on his body of the crucifixion wounds of Jesus. This was interpreted as a sign of his union with Christ by suffering, prayer, holiness, and love.

The flowering of English mysticism during the fourteenth century was exemplified by Julian of Norwich (1342–c. 1416). As a girl, she had prayed that when she reached the age of thirty (the age at which Jesus began his public mission) she would have an illness that would bring her an understanding of his Passion (the sufferings of his final days). As requested, she did indeed become so ill when she was thirty that she almost died. During this crisis, she had visions and conversations with Christ, which revealed the boundless love with which he continually offers himself for humanity. Her writings delve into the perennial problem of reconciling the existence of evil with the experience of a loving God, whom she sometimes referred to as "God our Mother."

An anonymous fourteenth-century English writer contributed a work called *The Cloud of Unknowing*. Christianity then and now largely follows what is called the affirmative way, with art, liturgy, scriptures, and imagery to aid devotion. But the author of *The Cloud* spoke to those prepared to undertake the negative way of abiding in sheer love for God, with no thoughts. God cannot be known through ideas or physical images; "a naked intent toward God, a desire for him alone, is enough."[52] In the silence of wordless prayer, his light may pierce the cloud of human unknowing that obscures the divine from the seeker.

Fourteenth-century Italy witnessed unprecedented degradation among the clergy, while the papacy occupied itself with organizational matters in Avignon. In this spiritual vacuum, laypeople gathered around saintly individuals to imbibe the atmosphere of their genuine devotion. One of the most celebrated of these was Catherine of Siena, "mother of thousands of souls." In her efforts to restore spiritual purity and religious discipline to the Church, she gained the ear of Pope Gregory XI, helping to convince him to return to Rome.

The Protestant Reformation

Despite the genuine piety of individuals within the Catholic Church, some who clashed with its authority claimed that those in power seemed often to have lost touch with their own spiritual tradition. With the rise of literacy and printing in the late fifteenth century, many Christians were rediscovering early Christianity and comparing it unfavorably with what the Roman Catholic Church had made of it. Roman Catholic fund-raising or church-building financial activities were particularly criticized. These included **indulgences** (remission of the punishment for sin by the clergy in return for services or payments), the sale of relics, purchases of masses for the dead, spiritual pilgrimages, and the earning of spiritual "merit" by donating to the Church.

Salient among the reformists was Martin Luther (1483–1546). Luther was a monk, priest, and Professor of Biblical Studies at the University of Wittenberg. He struggled personally with the question of how one's sins could ever be totally atoned for by one's own actions. The Roman Catholic Church's position was that to be forgiven of post-baptismal sins, people should repent and then confess their sins to a priest and be pardoned. In addition, the punishment after death due to sins could be remitted either for the performance of prescribed penances or through the granting of an indulgence. Indulgences could even be purchased to make sure that the souls of those who had died repentant were freed from **Purgatory** (the intermediate place of purifying suffering for those who died in a state of repentance and grace but who were not yet sufficiently stainless to enter heaven). The Castle Church at Wittenberg housed an immense collection of relics, including what were believed to be hairs from the Virgin Mary and a thorn from the "crown" of thorns placed on Jesus's head before he was crucified. This relic collection was deemed so powerful that those who viewed them on the proper day and contributed sufficiently to the Church could receive indulgences from the pope freeing themselves or their loved ones from almost two million years in Purgatory.

By intense study of the Bible, Luther began to emphasize a different approach. Both Paul and Augustine could be interpreted as saying that God, through Jesus, offered salvation to sinners in spite of their sins. This salvation was offered by God's grace alone and received solely by repentant faith. The good works and created graces prescribed by Catholics to earn merit in heaven were not part of original Christianity, Luther argued. Salvation from sin comes from faith in God, which itself comes from God, by grace. This gift of faith brings justification (being found righteous in God's sight) and then flowers as unselfish good works, which characterize the true Christian:

> From faith flows love and joy in the Lord, and from love a joyful, willing and free mind that serves one's neighbor willingly and takes no account of gratitude or ingratitude, of praise or blame, of gain or loss. . . . As our heavenly father has in Christ freely come to our help, we also ought freely to help our neighbor through our body and its works, and each should become as it were a Christ to the other.[53]

In 1517 Luther invited the university community to debate this issue with him, by the established custom of nailing his theses to the door of the church. He apparently had no intention of splitting with the Church. But a papal bull (decree) of June 15, 1520 excommunicated him.

Cut off from Rome, Luther sought support from the secular princes of Germany. For reasons sometimes more political than spiritual, many came over to his side and helped to enforce his ideas. Although there were some attempts at compromise by followers of both Luther and Rome, conciliatory efforts collapsed.

Luther's evolving theology took him farther and farther from the institutions of the Roman Catholic Church. He did not think the Bible supported its tradition that pope, bishops, priests, and monks should have spiritual authority over laypeople; instead, he asserted that there is "a priesthood of all believers." He also felt that the sacred rites, or **sacraments**, of the Church were ways of nourishing faith instituted by Jesus and that they included only **baptism** and the **Eucharist** (also known as the Lord's Supper, Holy Communion, or **mass**).

Another major reformer who eventually broke with Rome was the Swiss priest Ulrich Zwingli (1484–1531). He rejected practices not mentioned in the Bible, such as abstaining from meat during Lent, veneration of relics and saints, religious pilgrimages, and celibacy for monks and priests. Zwingli asserted that the Lord's Supper should be celebrated only as a memorial of Jesus's sacrifice; he did not believe in the myserious presence of Jesus's blood and body in the consecrated wine and bread. He even questioned the spiritual efficacy of rituals such as masses for the dead and confession of one's sins to a priest:

> It is God alone who remits sins and puts the heart at rest, so to Him alone ought we to ascribe the healing of our wounds, to Him alone display them to be healed.[54]

The ideals of these reformists were adopted by many Christians. The freedom of scriptural interpretation opened numerous options. Protestantism, as the new branch of Christianity came to be called, was never as monolithic as the Roman Catholic Church had been. Reform movements branched out in many directions, leading over time to a great proliferation of Protestant **denominations** (organized groups of congregations).

A major seat of Protestantism developed in Geneva, under John Calvin (1509–1564). He shared the reform principles of salvation by faith alone, the exclusive authority of the Bible, and "the priesthood of all believers." But Calvin carried the doctrine of salvation by faith to a new conclusion. To him, the appropriate response to God is a zealous piety and awe-struck reverence in which one "dreads to offend him more than to die."[55] Human actions are of no eternal significance because God has already decided the destiny of each person. By grace, some are to be saved; for God's own reasons, others are predestined to be damned eternally. Although there was therefore nothing that people could do about it, their behavior would reveal which fate awaited them.

Although only God knew who was saved, there are three signs which humans could recognize: profession of faith, an upright life, and participation in the sacraments. Calvin felt the Church has the right to chastise and, in some extreme situations, excommunicate those who seemed to violate its sanctity. Calvin envisioned a holy commonwealth in which the Church, government, and citizens cooperate to create a society dedicated to the glory and mission of God.

Calvin's version of Christianity made its followers feel that they should fear no one except God. Convinced that they were predestined to do God's will, they were impervious to worldly obstacles to the spread of their faith. **Calvinism** became the state religion of Scotland and also had a following in England.

Concurrently, the Church of England separated from the Church of Rome when Henry VIII declared the English Church's independence from the Church of Rome. His daughter Elizabeth I finalized the breach with Rome in the Elizabethan Settlement of 1559. Now called **Anglicanism**, this form of Christianity is in communion with Old Catholics and also shares some similarities with the Protestant churches. The Anglican Church retains many of the Roman Catholic rituals but rejects the authority of the Roman Catholic pope (referring instead to its Archbishop of Canterbury as its spiritual leader) and allows priests to marry. One of its thirty-seven autonomous Churches is the Protestant Episcopal Church in the United States, a name referring to its being a Church with bishops. Another offshoot is Methodism. It originated with the evangelist John Wesley (1703–1791), who emphasized personal holiness and methodical devotions. He traveled an average of 8,000 miles (12,874 km) a year by horseback to promote "vital practical religion and by the grace of the life of God to beget, preserve, and increase the life of God in the souls of men."[56]

Martin Luther's reformation of the German Church led directly to present-day **Lutheranism**. This maintains a strong emphasis on liturgy and sacraments and is currently practiced mostly in Germany, Scandinavia, the Baltics, and the northeastern United States. As the Protestant Reformation progressed, political entities in Europe chose specific forms of Christianity as their official religions. Spain, France, and Italy remained largely Roman Catholic. Northern Germany was largely Lutheran. Ireland split between Catholicism and Protestantism, leading to wars that continue today. The two major Reformed Churches that sprang from Calvinism were the Scottish movement called **Presbyterianism** (in which the congregation is governed by **presbyters**, who rank second below bishops, ministers, and elders) and **Congregationalism** (which emphasizes the independence of each local church and the "priesthood" of all members). Some Polish and Hungarian communities adopted a form of **Unitarianism**, which rejected original sin, the Trinity, and Jesus's divinity in favor of a simple theism and imitation of Jesus.

Some Protestant groups that were outlawed by the Church of England emigrated to new colonies in North America. These are sometimes referred to as "Free churches," being independent of government endorsement. One of the largest groups is the **Baptists**, a denomination in which people are baptized as conscious adult believers rather than as infants. **Quakers** (formally known as the Religious Society of Friends) date from the seventeenth-century followers of George Fox. They traditionally worshiped without any liturgy or minister, in the hope that as they sat in worshipful silence, God would speak through any one of their members.

During the nineteenth and twentieth centuries, yet more Protestant churches sprang up in the United States, including evangelical churches—those emphasizing salvation by personal faith in Jesus, personal conversion, the importance of the Bible, and preaching instead of ritual. **Seventh Day Adventists** believe that the Second Coming of Christ will soon occur, and they regard the Bible as an absolute guide to faith and spiritual practice in anticipation of his return. **Jehovah's Witnesses** criticize other Christian churches as having developed false doctrines from the second century onward, and they urge people to leave these "false religions" and prepare for a coming time when all who do not hold true belief will be destroyed.

Protestant missionary societies and evangelists were also active in carrying the gospel to Asia and Africa, where many independent denominations have evolved, and to South America, where Protestant groups are gaining strongholds in areas that had formerly been largely Roman Catholic since the Spanish conquests of these countries. This multi-culturalism and contemporary **evangelism** will be examined in detail at the end of this chapter.

Despite the great diversity among Protestant denominations, most share several characteristics that distinguish them somewhat from Orthodoxy and Roman Catholicism, though the Catholic Church's positions are now much closer to those of Protestants as a result of the profound changes introduced in 1962 by the Second Vatican Council. Both take the Bible as their foundation, but differ on how it is to be interpreted. Protestants tend to follow Martin Luther in believing that the individual's conscience and reason are the ultimate guides to understanding the scripture. This is in contrast to Roman Catholics who assert the authority of Church tradition and the infallibility of the Vatican's pronouncements about essentials of the faith, and Orthodox, who regard the Bible as a "verbal icon" of Christ and thus tend to focus more on venerating it than on interpreting it. A second point that has divided Protestants and Roman Catholics is the Protestant belief that we can achieve salvation only by God's grace, through repentance and faith; Roman Catholics support the doctrine of salvation by both faith and good works. A third divisive issue is that of spiritual authority. Protestantism asserts the "priesthood of all believers" and the individual's direct relationship to God and Jesus, in contrast to Roman Catholicism, which stands on mediation of God's grace through the officials of the Church. The officials differ in many respects, such as the provision that Protestant ministers can be married, unlike Catholic priests, who are expected to remain celibate in the belief that restraint of physical desires enhances spirituality. Fourth, Protestants have radically redefined the Roman Catholic and Orthodox concept of sacraments; Luther and Zwingli insisted that the only holy sacraments are those instituted by Jesus and regarded even those as instructive or commemorative rather than as mystical vehicles for God's grace. The sacraments and their meanings for Protestants, Roman Catholics, and Orthodox believers will be examined in depth later in this chapter.

The Roman Catholic Reformation

As the Protestant reformers were defining their positions, so was the Roman Catholic Church. Because reform pressures were underway in Catholicism before Luther, Catholics refer to the movement as the Catholic Reformation, rather than the "Counter-Reformation," as Protestants call it. However, the Protestant phenomena provoked the Roman Catholic Church to clarify its position through councils of bishops, especially the Council of Trent (1545–1563). It attempted to legislate moral reform among the clergy, to tighten the Church administration, and to recognize officially the absolute authority of the pope as the earthly vicar of God and Jesus Christ. It also took historic stands on a number of issues, emphasizing that these were dogmas, or authoritative truths. For example, one of the fundamental doctrines of the Roman Catholic Church is the dogma of **original sin**. All humans are said to be morally defective, or "fallen," having inherited a sinful nature from the first human ancestors. They can be saved from this condition only by the grace of God, as mediated through the death and Resurrection of Jesus, and the cleansing sacrament of baptism.

The Council of Trent reiterated that salvation requires "good works" as well as faith. These include acts of mercy, veneration of the saints, relics, and sacred images, and participation in the sacraments. In the sacrament of the Eucharist, the Council reiterated the doctrine of **transubstantiation**: what appear to be bread and wine are transformed into the body and blood of Christ.

In addition to the actions of the Council of Trent, the Roman Catholic Church gradually chose more virtuous popes than some in the past, and several new monastic orders grew out of the desires for reform. The Jesuits offered themselves as an army for God at the service of the pope. The Society of Jesus, as the order was formally called, was begun by Ignatius Loyola (1491–1556) in the sixteenth century. His *Spiritual Exercises* is still regarded as an excellent guide to meditation and spiritual discernment. However, it was as activists and educators in the everyday world that Jesuits were highly influential in the Reformation, and they were among the first to carry Roman Catholicism to Asia.

Roman Catholicism was carried to the western hemisphere and the Philippines by Spanish *conquistadores*. At home, Spain was host to a number of outstanding mystics during the sixteenth and seventeenth centuries. St. Teresa of Avila (1515–1582), a Carmelite nun, became at mid-life a dynamo of spiritual activity, in an order of ascetic Reformed (or Discalced, which means "barefooted") Carmelite nuns and monks. Discalced Carmelites usually pray much, and eat and sleep little. Despite her organizational activity, St. Teresa was able to maintain a calm sense of deep inner communion with God. In her masterpiece entitled *The Interior Castle*, she described the state of "spiritual marriage":

> *Here it is like rain falling from the heavens into a river or a spring; there is nothing but water there and it is impossible to divide or separate the water belonging to the river from that which fell from the heavens.*[57]

St. Teresa's great influence fell onto a young friend, now known as St. John of the Cross. He became a member of one of the Carmelite houses for men; when imprisoned by Carmelites who opposed the reforms, he experienced visions and wrote profound spiritual poetry. For John, the most important step for the soul longing to be filled with God is to surrender all vestiges of the self. This state he called the "dark night of the soul," a relinquishing of human reasoning into a state of not-knowing into which the pure light of God may enter without resistance. He is considered one of the great masters of the spiritual life.

The impact of the Enlightenment

Major potential threats to Christianity arose during the eighteenth-century Enlightenment in Europe. Intellectual circles exalted human reason and on this basis rejected faith in biblical miracles and revelations. Some people felt that nineteenth-century scientific advances undermined the biblical story of the creation of the world. However, many nineteenth-century scientists were devout

Christians who viewed the truth of science as supporting the truth of faith. There emerged two opposing trends: a liberal one, trying to join faith with modern knowledge, and a conservative one, emphasizing the conflict between faith and science. Both views spread rapidly, dividing between them much of Christendom, especially Protestantism.

Although fundamentalism began as a reaction to a broadening and secularizing of mainline Protestant Christianity, which was accepting much of modern biological and social sciences, the movement developed into a powerful political and social force that now rejects much of what it considers secular: public education, big government, and social programs run by the government. An attitude of withdrawing from the negative influence of the modern world dominates this movement.

In 1911, "fundamentalists" in the United States published as their uncompromising tenets the total inerrancy of the Bible, and Christ's literal virgin birth, substitutionary atonement, bodily resurrection, and anticipated second coming. Meanwhile, "modernist" theologians were interpreting such concepts in symbolic terms, with an aversion to dogmatism. Individuals were encouraged to judge religious beliefs by their own experience.

Undaunted, and in some cases invigorated, by these challenges to traditional faith, Protestantism developed a strong missionary spirit, joining Roman Catholic efforts to spread Christianity to every country, along with colonialism. As John Wesley, the founder of Methodism, had explained:

> I looked upon all the world as my parish; . . . that in whatever part of it I am, I judge it meet, right, and my bounden duty to declare unto all that are willing to hear, the glad tidings of salvation.[58]

The "social gospel" movement brought Protestant churches to the forefront of efforts at social and moral reform. Women, long excluded from important positions in the Church, played major roles in Church-related missionary and reform efforts, such as the abolition of slavery; they cited certain biblical passages as supporting equality of the sexes. When Sarah Grimke (1792–1873) and other women were criticized by their Congregational church for speaking publicly against slavery, Grimke asserted, "All I ask of my brethren is that they will take their feet from off our necks and permit us to stand upright on that ground which God has designed us to occupy."[59]

Liberal trends in Protestant theology led to efforts to analyze the Bible as literature. What, for instance, were the earliest texts? Who wrote them? How did they relate to each other? Who was the historical Jesus? Such questions were unthinkable in earlier generations. However, now in New Testament scholarship there is an interest in studying the texts as they are, receiving them as a whole, rather than analyzing and pulling them apart, in Enlightenment fashion, as if dissecting a frog.

The Second Vatican Council

In the meantime, the Roman Catholic and Eastern Orthodox Churches continued to defend tradition against the changes of modern life. A general council of the

Roman Catholic hierarchs was held in 1869–1870. It found itself embroiled chiefly in the question of papal infallibility, a doctrine it ultimately upheld. The pope, proclaimed the bishops of the council, can never err when he speaks from the seat of his authority (*ex cathedra*), on matters of faith and morals.

In 1962, Pope John XXIII, known for his holiness and friendliness, convened the Second Vatican Council for the express purposes of updating and energizing the Church and making it serve the people better as a living force in the modern world rather than being an old, embattled citadel. When questioned about his intentions, he demonstrated by opening a window to let in fresh air. With progressives and traditionalists often at odds, the majority nevertheless voted for major shifts in the Church's mission.

Many of the changes involved the liturgy of the mass, or the Eucharist. Rather than celebrate it in Latin, which most people did not understand, the liturgy was to be translated into the local languages. Rites were to be simplified. Greater use of sacred music was encouraged, and not just formal, traditional organ and choir offerings.

For the first time the laity were to be invited to participate actively. After Vatican II thus unleashed creativity and simplicity in public worship, entirely new forms appeared, such as informal folk masses—with spiritual folk songs sung to guitar accompaniment.

Another major change was the new emphasis on **ecumenism**, in the sense of rapprochement among all branches of Christianity. The Roman Catholic Church acknowledged that the Holy Spirit is active in all Christian churches, including Protestant denominations and the Eastern Orthodox churches. It pressed for a restoration of unity among all Christians, proclaiming that each could preserve its traditions intact. It also extended the concept of revelation, increasing the hope of dialogue with Jews, with whom Christians share "spiritual patrimony,"[60] and with Muslims, upon whom the Church "looks with esteem," for they "adore one God" and honor Jesus as a prophet. Appreciative mention was also made of other world religions as ways of approaching the same One whom Christians call God. Specifically described were Hinduism ("through which men contemplate the divine mystery") and Buddhism ("which acknowledges the radical insufficiency of this shifting world").[61]

Vatican II clearly marked major new directions in Catholicism. Its relatively liberal, pacifist characteristics are still meeting with some opposition within the Church decades later. In the late twentieth century, conservative elements in the Vatican began to reverse the direction taken by Vatican II to some extent, to the dismay of liberal Catholics. In the final section of this chapter, concerning current trends in Christianity, we will note several ways in which the renewed conservatism in the Vatican is being expressed.

Central beliefs in contemporary Christianity

The history of Christianity is characterized more by divisions than by uniformity among Christian groups. The Church is vast and culturally diverse, and Christian theologies are complex and intricate. Nevertheless, there are a few basic motifs on which the majority of faithful Christians would probably agree today.

A central belief is the divine Sonship of Jesus—the assertion that Jesus is the incarnation of God. According to the Gospel of John, before Jesus's death he told his disciples that he would be going to "my Father's house . . . to prepare a place for you." When they asked how they would find the way to that place, Jesus reportedly said:

I am the way, I am the truth and I am life. No one comes to the Father except by me. . . . Anyone who has seen me has seen the Father. . . . It is the Father who dwells in me doing his own work.[62]

Throughout most of Christian history, there has been the belief that Jesus was the only incarnation of God. Interestingly, Thomas Aquinas argued that although God could become incarnate in multiple incarnations (as in Hindu belief), he chose to do so only once, in Christ. Contemporary theologian Paul Knitter calls for a less exclusive approach that still honors Jesus's unique contribution:

What Christians do know, on the basis of their praxis of following Jesus, is that his message is a sure means for bringing about liberation from injustice and oppression, that it is an effective, hope-filled, universally meaningful way of realizing Soteria *[human welfare and liberation of the poor and oppressed] and promoting God's kingdom. . . . Not those who proclaim "only Lord, only Lord," but those who* do *the will of the Father will enter the kingdom (Matthew 7:21–23).*[63]

For Christians, Jesus is the Savior of the world, the one whom God sent to redeem people from their sins and reconcile them with God. Matthew reports that Jesus said he "did not come to be served, but to serve, and to give up his life as a ransom for many."[64] His own suffering and death are regarded as a substitute sacrifice on behalf of all those who follow and place their faith in him. According to the Gospel of John,

God loved the world so much that he gave his only Son, that everyone who has faith in him may not die but have eternal life. It was not to judge the world that God sent his Son into the world, but that through him the world might be saved.[65]

According to one strand of Christian belief, humanity has a sinful character, illustrated in the Old Testament by the fall of Adam and Eve. We have lost our original purity. Given free will by God, we have chosen disobedience rather than surrender to his will. We cannot save ourselves from our fallen condition; we can only be forgiven by the compassion of a loving God. Christians such as Methodists and Quakers are more optimistic about human nature.

Through fully surrendered faith in Jesus, Christians hope to be washed of their egotistical sinfulness, regenerated, made righteous, adopted by God, sanctified, and glorified in the life to come. These are the blessings of salvation, which Christians feel Jesus won for them by his sacrifice.

Although Christians worship Jesus as Savior, as the incarnation of a merciful God, they also see him as a human being showing fellow humans the way to God. His life is seen as the model for human behavior. Archbishop Desmond Tutu of South Africa emphasizes his identification with the human condition:

God does not occupy an Olympian fastness, remote from us. He has this deep, deep solidarity with us. God became a human being, a baby. God was hungry. God was tired, God suffered and died. God is there with us.[66]

This is the central mystery of Christianity: that God became human in order to lead people back to God.

The human virtue most often associated with Jesus is love. Many Christians say they experience Jesus's love even though he is no longer walking the earth in human form. And in turn, they have deep love for Jesus. Those who are experiencing problems are comforted to feel that Jesus is a living presence in their lives, supporting them spiritually, loving them even in the darkest of times.

> *The basic thrust of Jesus's message is to invite us into divine union, which is the sole remedy for the human predicament.*
>
> Father Thomas Keating[67]

In addition to being the paragon of love, Jesus also provides a model of sinlessness. To become like God, humans must constantly be purified of their lower tendencies. This belief has led some Christians to extremes of penance, such as the monks who flogged themselves and wore hairshirts so that their conscience might always be pricked. In a milder form, confession of one's sinfulness is a significant part of Christian tradition. There is an emphasis on self-discipline to guard against temptations, on examination of one's own faults, and on rituals, such as baptism, that help to remove the contamination that is innate in humanity. Although one must make these efforts at purification, most Christians believe that it is only through the grace of God—as mediated by the saving sacrifice of Jesus—that one can be delivered from sin and rise above ordinary human nature toward a divine state of sinlessness.

Sacred practices

Imitation of the model set by Jesus in his own life is the primary practice of Christians. In the widely read fourteenth-century book, *The Imitation of Christ*, people are encouraged to aspire to Jesus's own example as well as his teachings:

> *O how powerful is the pure love of Jesus, which is mixed with no self-interest, nor self-love! . . . Where shall one be found who is willing to serve God for naught?*[68]

In addition to the inner attempt to become more like Jesus, Christians have a variety of spiritual practices. Although forms and understandings of these vary among the branches of Christendom, they may include public worship services with sermons and offering of the sacraments, celebrations of the liturgical year, private contemplation and prayer, and devotions to Mary and the saints.

Worship services and sacraments

Christian worship typically takes place in a church building, which may be revered as a sacred space. The late-nineteenth-century Russian Orthodox saint Ioann Kronshtadtsky (d. 1908) explained:

> *Entering the church you enter some special realm which is not like the visible one. In the world you hear and see everything earthly, transient, fragile, liable to decay, sinful. In the church you see and hear the heavenly, the non-transient, the eternal,*

the holy. A temple is the threshold of heaven. It is like the heaven itself, because here is God's throne, the service of angels, the frequent descent of the Holy Spirit. . . . Here everything from icons to censer and the priests' robes fills you with veneration and prayer; everything tells you that you are in God's shrine, face to face with God himself.[69]

The word sacrament can be translated as "mystery." In Roman Catholicism and Orthodoxy, the sacraments are the sacred rites that are thought capable of transmitting the mystery of Christ to worshipers. Roman Catholic and Eastern Orthodox churches observe seven sacraments: baptism (initiation and symbolic purification from sin by water), confirmation (of membership in the Church), Eucharist (the ritual meal described below), penance (confession and absolution of sins), extreme unction (anointing of the sick with oil, especially before death), holy orders (consecration as a deacon, priest, or bishop), and matrimony. In general, Protestant churches recognize only baptism and the Eucharist as sacraments and have a less mystical understanding of their significance.

The ritual of public worship, or liturgy, usually follows a set pattern, though in some churches the actions of the Holy Spirit are thought to inspire spontaneous expressions of faith.

In most forms of Christianity, the central sacrament is the Holy Eucharist (also called Holy Communion, mass, or Lord's Supper). It is a mystery through which the invisible Christ is thought to grant communion with himself. Believers are given bread, which is received as the body of Christ, and a sip of wine or grape juice, understood as his blood. The priest or minister may ritually consecrate the bread and wine and share them among the people. In Roman Catholic or Orthodox masses, the wine and the bread are thought to be transformed by the Holy Spirit into the blood and body of Christ. They are treated with profound reverence. In sharing the communion "meal", the people are united with each other as well as with Christ. The traditional ideal was to take communion every day and certainly every Sunday (the Sabbath).

In the Bible Jesus is pictured setting the pattern for this sacrament at what is called the Last Supper, the meal he shared with his inner circle before his capture. The body and blood of Christ are seen as the spiritual nourishment of the faithful, which gives them eternal life in the midst of earthly life.

The partaking of sacred bread and wine is the climax of a longer liturgy of Holy Communion. The communion service, often called a mass in Catholicism, begins with liturgical prayers, praise, and confession of sinfulness. A group confession chanted by some Protestant congregations enumerates these flaws:

Most merciful God, we have sinned against you in thought, word, and deed, by what we have done and by what we have left undone. We have not loved you with our whole heart; we have not loved our neighbors as ourselves.[70]

Catholics were traditionally encouraged to confess their sins privately to a priest before taking communion, in the sacrament of **penance**, or "reparation for guilt" (also called "reconciliation"). After hearing the confession, the priest pronounces forgiveness and blessing over the penitent, or perhaps prescribes a penance. Orthodox Christians were also traditionally expected to spend several days in contrition and fasting before receiving communion. The reason for the emphasis on purification is that during the service the church itself is perceived as the Kingdom of God, in which everything is holy. In Orthodox services, the clergy walk around the church, swinging an incense censer to set apart the area as a sacred space and to lift the prayers of the congregants to God.

In all Christian churches, passages from the Old and New Testaments may be read and the people may sing hymns, songs of praise or thanksgiving to God. They may be asked to recite a credal statement of Christian beliefs, and to make money offerings. There may be an address by the priest or minister (a sermon or a homily) on the readings for the day. These parts of the liturgy constitute the Liturgy of the Word, in which Christ is thought to be present as the living Word, addressing the people through scripture and preaching. In Protestant churches, the Liturgy of the Word is often offered without the communion service.

In both Protestantism and Roman Catholicism, there are now attempts at updating the liturgy to make it more meaningful and personally relevant for contemporary Christians. One innovation that seems to have taken hold everywhere is the "sharing of the peace." Partway through the worship service, congregants turn to everyone around them to hug or shake hands and say, "The Peace of Christ be with you"—"and also with you."

As well as regular liturgies and the sacrament of the mass or communion, there are special events treated in sacred ways. The first to be administered is the sacrament of baptism. It involves immersing the person in water or, more often, pouring sanctified water (representing purification) on the candidate's head, while invoking the Holy Trinity. In a recent ecumenical document, the World Council of Churches defined the general meaning of the practice:

> By baptism, Christians are immersed in the liberating death of Christ where their sins are buried, where the "old Adam" is crucified with Christ, and where the power of sin is broken. . . . They are raised here and now to a new life in the power of the resurrection of Jesus Christ.[71]

Aside from adult converts to Christianity, the rite is usually performed on infants, with parents taking vows on their behalf. There are arguments that infant baptism has little basis in the Bible and that a baby cannot make the conscious repentance of sin and "conversion of heart" implied in the ceremony. Baptists and several other Protestant groups therefore reserve baptism for adults.

A second ceremony—**confirmation**—is often offered in early adolescence in Roman Catholicism and Protestantism. After religious instruction, a group of young people make a conscious and personal commitment to the Christian life.

Some Christians observe special days of fasting. Russian Orthodox Old Believer priest Father Appolinari explains fasting as a way of *soprichiastna*, of becoming part of something very large, the spiritual aura of the Lord.

The liturgical year

Christian churches celebrate a yearly cycle of festivals, leading the worshiper through the life of Jesus and the gift of the Spirit. As the faithful repeat this cycle year after year, they hope to enter more deeply into the mystery of God in Christ, and the whole body of believers in Christ theoretically grows toward the kingdom of God.

Christmas and Epiphany   There are three major events in the Church calendar, each associated with a series of preparatory celebrations. The first is the season of light: **Christmas** and **Epiphany**. Christmas is the celebration of Jesus's birth on earth as the incarnation of God. Epiphany means "manifestation" or "showing forth." It celebrates the recognition of Jesus's spiritual kingship by the three Magi (in the Western Church), his acknowledgement as the Messiah and the beloved Son of God when he is baptized by John the Baptist, and his first recognized miracle, the turning of water into wine at the wedding in Cana.

In early Christianity, Epiphany was more important than the celebration of Jesus's birth. The actual birth date is unknown, but the setting of the date near the winter solstice allowed Christianity to take over the older "pagan" rites celebrating the return of longer periods of daylight at the darkest time of year. In the Gospel of John, Jesus is "the true light that enlightens every man,"[72] the light of the divine appearing amid the darkness of human ignorance.

Advent, the month preceding Christmas, is supposed to be a time of joyous anticipation. But in industrialized countries, it is more likely a time of frenzied marketing and buying of gifts, symbolizing God's gift of Jesus to the world.

In some countries churches stage pageants re-enacting the birth story, with people taking the parts of Mary, Joseph, the innkeeper who has no room, the shepherds, and the three Magi. Since the nineteenth century, it has been traditional to cut or buy an evergreen tree (a symbol of eternal life, perhaps borrowed from indigenous ceremonies) and erect it in one's house, decorated with lights and ornaments. On Christmas Eve some Christians gather for a candlelit "watchnight" service, welcoming the turn from midnight to a new day in which Christ has come into the world. On Christmas Day, Catholic and Protestant children are sometimes told that presents have been magically brought by St. Nicholas, a fourth-century bishop noted for his great generosity. The exchange of gifts may be followed by a great feast.

Easter   The most religiously significant event of the Christian liturgical year is **Easter**. It commemorates Jesus's death (on "Good Friday") and Resurrection (on Easter Sunday, which falls in the spring but is celebrated at different times by the Eastern and Western Churches). Like Christmas, Easter is a continuation of earlier rites associated with the spring equinox, celebrating the regeneration of plant life and the return of warm weather. It is also related to Pesach, the Hebrew Passover, the Jewish spring feast of deliverance.

Liturgically, Easter is preceded by a forty-day period of repentance and fasting, called **Lent**. Many Christians perform acts of asceticism, prayer, and charity, to join in Jesus's greater sacrifice. In the Orthodox Church, the last Sunday before Lent is dedicated to asking forgiveness. People request forgiveness from each other, bowing deeply. In the West, Lent begins with Ash Wednesday, when many Christians have ash smudges placed on their foreheads by a priest who says, "Remember, man, thou art dust and unto dust thou shalt return." On the Sunday before Easter, Jesus's triumphal entry into Jerusalem is honored by the waving of palm or willow branches in churches and the proclaiming of Hosannas. His death is mourned on "Good Friday." The mourning is jubilantly ended on Easter Sunday, with shouts of "Christ is risen!"

In Russia, the Great Vigil welcoming Easter morning lasts from midnight until dawn, with the people standing the entire time.

Ascension   Ascension may be celebrated as one of the major holy days in the Christian liturgical calendar, honoring the bodily Ascension of Jesus to heaven. It is celebrated on the Thursday that occurs forty days after Easter, or on the following Sunday. Apparently this event has been celebrated since the early centuries of Christianity. Solemn liturgical observances focus on readings from biblical accounts and credal statements regarding the religious significance of the Ascension. In medieval England, the Ascension was celebrated by a triumphal torchlight procession with a banner portraying a lion above a dragon, symbolizing the ascended Christ's triumph over Satan.

Pentecost   Fifty days after the Jewish Passover (which Jesus is thought to have been celebrating at the Last Supper with his disciples) comes the Jewish Shavuot (which celebrates the giving of the Torah to Moses, as well as the first fruits of the harvest). Jews nicknamed it Pentecost, which is Greek for "fiftieth." Christians took over the holiday but gave it an entirely different meaning.

In Christianity, Pentecost commemorates the occasion described in Acts when the Holy Spirit descended upon the disciples after Jesus's death, Resurrection, and Ascension, filling them with the Spirit's life and power and enabling them to speak in foreign tongues. In early Christianity, Pentecost was an occasion to baptize those who had been preparing for admission to the Church.

The Transfiguration and Assumption   Some Christian Churches also emphasize two other feast days. On August 6, people honor the Transfiguration of Jesus on the mountain, revealing his supernatural radiance. On August 15, they celebrate the Assumption of Mary, known as "The Falling Asleep of the Mother of God." These feasts are prominent in the Eastern Church, which generally places more emphasis on the ability of humanity to break out of its earthly bonds and rise into the light, than on the heaviness and darkness of sin.

Contemplative prayer

The contemplative tradition within Christianity is beginning to re-emerge. The hectic pace and rapid change of modern life make periods of quietness essential. Many Christians, not aware of a contemplative way within their Church, have turned to Eastern religions for instruction in meditation.

One of the most influential twentieth-century Christian contemplatives was the late Thomas Merton (1915–1968). He was a Trappist monk who received a special dispensation to live as a hermit in the woods near his abbey in Kentucky. Merton lived simply in nature, finding joy in the commonplace, experienced attentively in silence. He studied and tried to practice the great contemplative traditions of earlier Christianity and reintroduced them to a contemporary audience through his writings. In meditative "prayer of the heart," or "contemplative prayer," he wrote:

> We seek first of all the deepest ground of our identity in God. We do not reason
> about dogmas of faith, or "the mysteries." We seek rather to gain a direct existential

*grasp, a personal experience of the deepest truths of life and faith, finding ourselves
in God's truths. . . . Prayer then means yearning for the simple presence of God, for
a personal understanding of his word, for knowledge of his will and for capacity to
hear and obey him.*[73]

Before he became a Christian monk, Merton had studied Eastern mysticism,
assuming that Christianity had no mystical tradition. He became friends with a
Hindu monk who advised him to read St. Augustine's *Confessions* and *The Imitation
of Christ*. These led Merton toward an appreciation of the potential of the
Christian inner life, aligned with a continuing openness to learn from Eastern
monasticism. He died while in Asia visiting Buddhist and Hindu monastics.

Spiritual renewal through inner silence has become an important part of some
Christians' practice of their faith. Syrian Orthodox Bishop Paulos Mar Gregorios
of India, past-President of the World Council of Churches, concluded from the
Bible evidence that Jesus himself was a contemplative.

A form of Christian meditation instituted by the Franciscans and still practiced
in many Catholic and Anglican churches is the Stations of the Cross. These are
fourteen plaques or paintings placed on the walls of the church depicting scenes
from the death of Jesus. As one sees him taking up the cross, falling three times
under its weight, being stripped of his clothes and being nailed to the cross, one
becomes painfully and humbly aware of the suffering that God's Son experienced
in manifesting as a human redeemer.

Contemplation of the humanness of Jesus is used to help believers identify
with him and thence to aspire to his divine model.

In Orthodoxy, the central contemplative practice is repetition of the Jesus
Prayer: "Lord Jesus Christ, have mercy on me" (and some add, "a sinner").
Eventually its meaning imbeds itself in the heart and one lives in a state of
unceasing prayer. An unknown nineteenth-century Russian peasant who lived
with continual repetition of the Jesus Prayer described its results:

*The sweetness of the heart, warmth and light, unspeakable rapture, joy, ease,
profound peace, blessedness, and love of life are all the result of prayer of the heart.*[74]

Devotion to Mary

Mary, the mother of Jesus, has not been in the forefront of historical theological
disputes. Veneration of Mary has come as much from the grassroots as from the
top. Drawings of her were found in the catacombs in which the early Christians
met; explicit devotion to her was well developed by the third or fourth century.
Despite the absence of detailed historical information, she serves as a potent and
much-loved spiritual symbol. She is particularly venerated by Roman Catholics,
Eastern Orthodoxy, and Anglicans.

Some researchers feel devotion to Mary is derived from earlier worship of the
Mother Goddess. They see her as representing the feminine aspect of the
Godhead. She is associated with the crescent moon, representing the receptive
willingness to be filled with the Spirit. In the story of the **Annunciation**—the
appearance of an angel who told her she would have a child conceived by the
Holy Spirit—her response was "Behold, I am the handmaid of the Lord; let it be
to me according to your word."[75] This receptivity is not seen as powerlessness.

Mary, like Christ, embodies the basic Christian paradox: that power is found in "weakness."

Whether or not devotion to Mary is linked to Mother Goddess worship, oral Christian traditions have given her new symbolic roles. One links her with Israel, which is referred to as the daughter of Zion or of Jerusalem in the Old Testament. God comes to her as the Holy Spirit, and from this love between YHWH and Israel, Jesus is born to save the people of Israel.

In the Orthodox and Catholic traditions, she is the Mother of God. In Russia, she is also revered as the protectress of all humanity, and especially the Russian people. Before he died on the cross, Jesus is said to have told John, the beloved disciple, that thenceforth Mary was to be his Mother. The story is interpreted as meaning that thenceforth all humanity was adopted by Mary.

Another role is that of the immaculate virgin. According to the gospels of Matthew and Luke, she conceived Jesus by heavenly intervention rather than human biology. Roman Catholicism asserts that at the Immaculate Conception, she herself was conceived without "original sin." Even in giving birth to Jesus, she remained a virgin. Orthodoxy does not insist on these doctrines, nor on the Catholic dogma that Mary ascended bodily to heaven after her physical death. The emphasis on virginity is a spiritual sign of being dedicated to God alone, rather than to any temporal attachments.

According to the faithful, Mary is not just a symbol but a living presence, like Christ. She is appealed to in prayer and is honored in countless paintings, statues, shrines, and churches dedicated to her name. Catholics are enjoined to repeat the "Hail Mary" prayer:

> *Hail, Mary, full of grace, the Lord is with thee. Blessed art thou among women, and blessed is the fruit of thy womb, Jesus. Holy Mary, Mother of God, pray for us sinners, now and at the hour of our death.*

Theologians point out that veneration of Mary is really directed toward God; Mary is not worshiped in herself but as the mother of Christ, reflecting his glory. If this were not so, Christians could be accused of idolatry.

Be this as it may, Mary has been said to appear to believers in many places around the world. At Lourdes, in France, it is claimed that she appeared repeatedly to a young peasant girl named Bernadette in the nineteenth century. A spring found where she indicated has been the source of hundreds of medically authenticated healings from seemingly incurable diseases. In 1531, in Guadalupe (within what is now Mexico City), Mary appeared to a converted Aztec, Juan Diego. She asked him to have the bishop build a church on the spot. To convince the sceptical bishop, Juan filled his cloak with the out-of-season roses to which she directed him. When he opened the cloak before the bishop, the petals fell away to reveal a large and vivid image of Mary, with Indian features.

Sightings of Mary continue around the world. What are perceived as her ethereal images have drawn crowds to worship before a large office window in Florida, before a closed church in eastern Europe, and at a site where she reportedly appeared two decades ago in Vietnam. In Mexico, her image is said to be seen frequently, manifesting in everything from dented car fenders and stovetops to garlic and fruits. Such is the perennial appeal of the holy mother.

Veneration of saints and angels

Roman Catholics and Orthodox Christians honor their spiritual heroes as saints. These are men and women who are recognized as so holy that the divine life of Christ is particularly evident in them. After their death, they are carefully judged by the Church for proofs of exalted Christian virtue, such as tolerance under extreme provocation, and of miraculous power. Those who are canonized by this process are subject to great veneration.

> *Each saint is a unique event, a victory over the force of evil. So many blessings can pour from God into the world through one life.*
>
> *Father Germann, Vladimir, Russia*[76]

Orthodox Christians are given the name of a saint when they are baptized. Each keeps an icon of this patron saint in his or her room and prays to the saint daily. Icons of many saints fill an Orthodox church, helping to make them familiar presences rather than names in history books. Saints are often known as having special areas of concern and power. For instance, St. Anthony of Padua is invoked for help in finding lost things. **Relics**, usually parts of the body or clothes of saints, are felt to radiate the holiness of the saints' communion with God. They are treasured and displayed for veneration in Catholic and Orthodox churches. It is said that saints' physical bodies were so transformed by divine light that they do not decay after death, and continue to emit a sweet fragrance.

Roman Catholics and Orthodox Christians also pray to the **angels** for protection. Angels are understood as spiritual beings who serve as messengers from and adoring servants of God. They are usually pictured as humans with wings. In popular piety, each person is thought to have a guardian angel for individual protection and spiritual help.

Contemporary trends

At the start of the third millennium since the birth of Jesus, Christianity is gaining membership and participation in some quarters and losing ground in others. The fall of communism in the former Soviet Union and its satellites has brought reopening and renovation of many churches and a renewed interest in spirituality throughout that large area. Orthodox Christianity has also received a boost from the activist approach of Ecumenical Patriarch Bartholomew, Archbishop of Constantinople, whose position makes him the leading voice in Orthodoxy. He is known as the "Green Patriarch" for his environmental activism, and has taken an active role in improving Orthodox relations with Roman Catholics and Protestants, and in conflict resolution where people of different religions are at war with each other. In Egypt, Orthodox Coptic Christians, heirs to the ancient tradition of the Desert Fathers, have long been submerged under Muslim rule, but the monasteries have begun to flourish again. The 16 million Coptic Christians have their own pope.

Roman Catholicism is experiencing divisions between conservatives and liberals.

After the liberal tendencies of Vatican II, Pope John Paul II reaffirmed certain traditional stands and strengthened the position of the right wing of the Church. In a 1995 encyclical, he insisted upon what he called the fundamental right to human life as opposed to the "culture of death," condemning abortion and euthanasia as "crimes which no human law can claim to legitimize" and condemning the death penalty.[77] In 2000, Cardinal Joseph Ratzinger, then head of the Vatican's highly conservative Congregation for the Doctrine of the Faith (the successor to the Inquisition), delivered *Dominus Jesu*," which proclaimed, "There exists a single Church of Christ, which subsists in the Catholic Church." Other Christian communities "are not churches in the proper sense" and non-Christians are in a "gravely deficient situation" regarding salvation.[78]

Despite his conservative stances, on a special "Day of Forgiveness" held during the Lenten season in the millennial year of 2000, Pope John Paul II delivered a statement asking forgiveness for the past sins of the Roman Catholic Church, including its treatment of Jews, other Christians, other religions, women, ethnic groups, indigenous peoples, and heretics. He also took a strong public stance opposing the American-led attack on Iraq in 2003 and expressing solidarity with the people of Iraq.

Nevertheless, the conservative trend in the Vatican was continued with the election of Cardinal Ratzinger in 2005 as the new pope, Benedict XVI. He is known for his defense of traditional Catholic doctrines and values, and has asserted concern about what he considers the danger of secularism in Christian social activism and charitable work.

In spite of the public attention paid to the pope as a person, the priesthood is dwindling in most Western countries, partly because Catholic priests are required to be celibate. Recent revelations of sexual abuse by some priests of their parishioners—often innocent children—have rocked people's confidence in the priesthood. In the United States, thousands of people have come forward with complaints of sexual abuse by their priests. American bishops have tried to repair the damage by apologizing, declaring "zero tolerance" for such behaviors, and paying large amounts of money to those who claim to have been abused, but they have refused to deny the Catholic tradition of celibate priests.

There is increased interest in participation by women (who are not allowed by the Vatican to be priests), and widespread disregard of papal prohibitions on effective birth control, abortion, test-tube conception, surrogate motherhood, genetic experimentation, divorce, and homosexuality.

The Vatican has responded to these trends by insisting on the value of tradition and authority. But many American Catholic leaders are concerned that, in the words of Father Frank McNulty of Newark, New Jersey, "people often do not perceive the church as proclaiming integral truth and divine mercy, but rather as sounding harsh, demanding."[79] Acting as a group, Roman Catholic bishops in the United States have issued statements deploring sexism as a "sin" (recommending that spiritual positions of responsibility and authority be opened to women and that non-sexist language be used in liturgy), supporting peace efforts, and insisting on the morality of economic social justice.

In Protestantism, traditional denominations in Europe and the United States are declining in membership. According to a Gallup poll, only a minority of the "unchurched" disagree with their denomination's teachings. They are more likely to drop away because of apathy, a lack of services, or a lack of welcome on the part of the minister. In the Anglican Church, the Archbishop of Canterbury, Rowan Williams, is waking people out of apathy by controversial actions, such as his support for the appointment of a homosexual bishop in New Hampshire. Opposition to this move has been so strong in Africa and other non-Western parts of the Anglican Church that some fear it may divide the global Anglican Communion, which encompasses 79 million people.

Although many traditional Christian churches are losing members, other groups and trends are taking vigorous root. These include evangelical and charismatic groups, non-Western Christian churches, liberation theology, feminist theology, creation-centered Christianity, and the ecumenical movement.

Evangelicalism

To evangelize is to preach the Christian gospel and convert people to Christianity. Evangelical theology, with its emphasis on experiencing the grace of God, has been important throughout the history of American Protestantism. The current evangelical movement has its roots in the fundamentalist–modernist controversy of the early twentieth century.

As discussed earlier, the fundamentalists were reacting against the liberal or modern movement in Christianity that sought to reconcile science and religion and use historical and archaeological data to understand the Bible. This movement had an optimistic view of human nature and stressed reason, free will, and self-determination. In response, a group of Christians called for a return to what they considered the "fundamentals" of Christian faith. The controversy received its most famous public expression in the Scopes trial in 1925 when John Thomas Scopes, a high school teacher in Tennessee, challenged a state law forbidding the teaching of Darwin's theory of evolution in schools.

Beginning in the 1930s and with waves of enthusiasm in the 1950s and late twentieth and early twenty-first centuries, heirs of the fundamentalist movement, who can broadly be called "**evangelicals**," have become a vigorous movement in many Protestant denominations. They study the Bible together and value being "born again" in Christ. They look back to great evangelists of the eighteenth and nineteenth centuries, such as the itinerant Methodist preacher John Wesley (1703–1791) and Charles Grandison Finney (1792–1875), whose preaching reportedly led hundreds of thousands of people to conversion experiences. In general, according to the definition by David Bebbington accepted by most scholars, contemporary Evangelicalism has four defining characteristics: conversionism (conviction that lives need to be changed), activism (the expression of the gospel in effort), biblicism (a particular and constant regard for the Bible), and crucicentrism (a stress on the sacrifice of Jesus on the cross). Evangelicals vary from conservative to liberal on other theological and ethical issues (such as the literal interpretation of the Bible and involvement in social issues such as peace movements and the alleviation of poverty).

Many evangelicals and other conservative Protestants anticipate the **rapture**—when Christians will be transported up to heaven to live with Jesus in immortal bodies. Popular Christian media in the United States have fanned the belief that the end times are imminent and one should be ready, a belief that has serious ramifications in political decision-making. Like all Protestants, Evangelicals practice the two sacraments of baptism and the Lord's Supper, but are much more concerned that the sacrament be personal and meaningful than that it be correctly done according to a book of worship. Their messages enjoy widespread visibility through international electronic media.

On the ground, evangelicalism is also making great strides in South America, in areas that were largely Roman Catholic as a result of colonization by Spain. In the early 1990s, an average of five evangelical churches were being established each week in Rio de Janeiro, most of them in the slum areas, offering to the very poor food, job training, day care, and perhaps conversion.

Spirit-oriented movements

There is a rising emphasis on charismatic experience—that is, divinely inspired powers—among Christians of all classes and nations. While fundamentalists stress the historical Jesus, charismatics feel they have also been touched by the "third person" of the Trinity, the Holy Spirit. They include members of Protestant Pentecostal churches but also Roman Catholics, members of mainline Protestant denominations, and Orthodox churches who are caught up in a contemporary spiritual renewal that harks back to the biblical descent of the Holy Spirit upon the disciples of Jesus, firing them with spiritual powers and faith.

Mainstream Christian churches, which have often rejected emotional spiritual experience in favor of a more orderly piety, are gradually becoming more tolerant of it. Among Roman Catholics the movement is often called "Charismatic Renewal," for it claims to bring true life in the Spirit back to Christianity. By broad definition, up to one-fourth of all Christians today could be considered members of this Spirit-oriented movement.[80]

This movement encompasses all those who look for the spiritual gifts mentioned numerous times in the letters attributed to Paul, suggesting that these were common manifestations in the early Church. In I Corinthians, Paul writes:

> To each is given the manifestation of the Spirit for the common good. To one is given through the Spirit the utterance of wisdom, and to another the utterance of knowledge according to the same Spirit, to another faith by the same Spirit, to another gifts of healing by the one Spirit, to another the working of miracles, to another prophecy, to another the discernment of spirits, to another various kinds of tongues, to another the interpretation of tongues. All these are activated by one and the same Spirit, who allots to each one individually just as the Spirit chooses.[81]

Pentecostals, adherents of a rapidly-growing world-wide version of the Spirit-oriented movement, generally look for a second experience of the Holy Spirit after the initial experience of salvation by belief in Jesus as Savior for the forgiveness of their sins; they require speaking in tongues as a sign of this "second grace" of baptism by the Holy Spirit. The **African Instituted Churches** (AICs) are richly varied, but usually are oriented toward healing and protection from evil, the most prominent aspects of African indigenous religions. Older African Instituted Churches have their roots in Western missionary efforts but generally left them behind as they adapted to African culture.

Under the alleged influence of the Spirit, Pentecostalist-charismatics stand and gesture as they lovingly sing praises of Jesus and God, speak in tongues, pray and utter praises, spontaneously heal by the laying on of hands and prayer, and bear witness to spiritual miracles. Spontaneous spiritual gestures are especially prevalent at large renewal sites.

Speaking of the descent of the Holy Spirit, Roman Bilas, Moscow head of the Union of Pentecostal Christians of Evangelical Faith, says passionately:

> *This moment when you really feel God's power in yourself brings so much peace and joy within you. It transforms you and society. There comes a sense of total forgiveness for your sins, and the ability in you to forgive others. At that moment, you start to speak in different languages, . . .*
>
> *We may also receive the gift of prophecy. . . . We check to see if the message is consistent with the Bible. If it is, then we will listen. Otherwise, the person is told not to speak publicly because he would create confusion in the Church.*
>
> *The main thing is that the person should be filled with God's Power. A nice-looking car will not move unless it is fueled. God's Power will only fill those who are pure.*[82]

The Great Reversal

Although contemporary Christianity was largely shaped in Europe and its North American colonies, the largest percentage of the Christian Church now lies outside these areas. It has great numerical strength in Africa, Latin America and parts of Asia. In 1970, Christianity was about 43 percent non-Western, whereas today it is about 65 percent non-Western. In this short span of time, many independent, indigenous churches have arisen in the world. Tens of millions of Chinese Christians are worshiping in their homes and in non-church buildings; hundreds of millions of Africans are members of African Instituted Churches. As soon as the Western colonial supports were taken away, Christianity exploded in Africa as an indigenous religion. To wit: Africa was 25 percent Christian in 1950, whereas it is 48 percent Christian today. Some of the most active areas in terms of outreach are now Brazil, Korea, China, India, southern Africa, and the United States.

Some signs of the times: instead of the old pattern in which the West sent missionaries to spread Christianity to Asia, Africa, and South America, congregations in those areas are being asked to send volunteers to the West to help spread the gospel in new missionary efforts there. Catholic prayer requests are being "outsourced" through the Vatican to India from the United States, Canada, and Europe, where there are not enough clergy to handle the requests. Churches in Europe are becoming empty of worshipers as the people become more and more secular in their approach to life.

The vigor of Christianity in the United States can be explained partly by the growth of evangelical and charismatic churches and linking fundamentalist Christianity with right-wing claims to patriotism and a defense of traditional American values. An equally important contribution is immigration. The majority of those who migrate to the United States are Christians, and migrants tend to build vital churches. Contemporary Christian migrants include Roman Catholic or Pentecostal Latin Americans, Presbyterian or Methodist Koreans, plus Christians from Africa, China, India, and West Asia. By contrast, most contemporary immigrants to Europe are Muslims.

Some of the most active remnants of Christianity in Europe are involved in peace and reconciliation movements and, like many Christian denominations in the United States, tried to oppose the US-led attack on Iraq. Around the globe, many fundamentalists feel they are fighting a cultural war against liberalism, secularism, and materialism—within as well as beyond Christianity. Spiritually diverse, Christianity is also politically and culturally diverse.

When Western missionaries spread Christianity to other regions, they often assumed that European ways were culturally superior to the indigenous ways and peoples. But some of these newer Christians have come to different conclusions. Theologians of the African Instituted Churches, for instance, reject the historical missionary efforts to divorce them from their traditions of honoring their ancestors. This effort tore apart their social structure, they feel, with no scriptural justification:

> As we became more acquainted with the Bible, we began to realise that there was nothing at all in the Bible about the European customs and Western traditions that we had been taught. What, then was so holy and sacred about this culture and this so-called civilization that had been imposed upon us and was now destroying us? Why could we not maintain our African customs and be perfectly good Christians at the same time? . . .
>
> We have learnt to make a very clear distinction between culture and religion. . . . [For instance], the natural customs of any particular nation or race must never be confused with the grace of Jesus Christ our Saviour, Redeemer and Liberator.[83]

Contemporary perceptions of Jesus have been deeply enriched by those from the inhabitants of poor Third World countries who have brought personal understanding of Jesus's ministry to the outcasts and downtrodden. In Asia, where Christians are usually in the minority, there is an emphasis on a Christ who is present in the whole cosmos and who calls all people to sit at a common table to partake of his generous love. In Latin America, Jesus is viewed as the liberator of the people from political and social oppression, from dehumanization, and from sin. In Africa, the African Instituted Churches have brought indigenous traditions of drumming, dancing, and singing into community worship of a Jesus who is seen as the greatest of ancestors—a mediator carrying prayers and offerings between humans and the divine, and watchful caretaker of the people.

Liberation theology

Although many Christians make a distinction between the sacred and the secular, some have involved themselves deeply with social issues as an expression of their Christian faith. For instance, the Baptist preacher, Martin Luther King, Jr. (1929–1968), became a great civil rights leader, declaring: "It was Jesus of Nazareth that stirred the Negroes to protest with the creative weapon of love."[84] This trend is now called **liberation theology**, a faith that stresses the need for concrete political action to help the poor. Beginning in the 1960s with Vatican II and the conference of Latin American bishops in Colombia in 1968, Roman Catholic priests and nuns in Latin America began to make conscious, voluntary

Archbishop Desmond M. Tutu

During the years of struggle against apartheid in South Africa, one voice that refused to be silenced was that of the Anglican Archbishop of Cape Town, Desmond Mpilo Tutu (b. 1931). Afterward, he served his country as Chairperson of the Truth and Reconciliation Commission, "looking a beast in the eye" to investigate abuses from all sides that were perpetrated during the apartheid era. In this capacity, he still refused to mute his criticisms of those wielding power, no matter what their race and stature. In 1995 he proclaimed,

> The so-called ordinary people, God's favourites, are sick and tired of corruption, repression, injustice, poverty, disease and the violation of their human rights. They are crying out "enough is enough!" It is exhilarating when you are able to say to dictators everywhere: "You have had it! You have had it! This is God's world and you will bite the dust!" They think it will not happen but it does, and they bite the dust comprehensively and ignominiously.
>
> We will want to continue to be the voice of the voiceless. It is the role of the church to be the conscience of society.[85]

The "Arch's" fearless stance on behalf of truth and justice for the oppressed earned him the Nobel Peace Prize in 1984. He confronted not only those in power but also those who sought change through violence and those in the Church who witnessed the horrors of apartheid but kept silent. He explains, "Our task is to be agents of the Kingdom of God, and this sometimes requires us to say unpopular things."[86]

The former archbishop feels that

> Faith is a highly political thing. At the centre of all that we believe as Christians is the incarnation—the participation of God in the affairs of this world. As followers of that God we too must be politically engaged. We need inner resources, however, in order to face the political demands of our time.[87]

How has Archbishop Tutu developed his inner resources? Through meditation, prayer, and fasting. He observes the traditional daily devotions of the Anglican Church, always starts meetings with prayer, and annually takes a long spiritual retreat. He regularly prays for others, and many are also praying for him; he asserts that intercessory prayer has practical effects. His spiritual confessor, Francis Cull, describes Archbishop Tutu's inner life as rooted in the Benedictine monastic discipline that underlies Anglican spirituality. He explains:

> As I ponder on the prayer life of Desmond Tutu I see the three fundamental Benedictine demands that there shall be: rest, prayer, and work and in that order. It is a remarkable fact, and it is one reason at least why he has been able to sustain the burdens he has carried, that he has within him a stillness and a need for quiet solitude. . . . The "rest" of which St. Benedict speaks is not a mere switching off; it is a positive attempt to fulfill the age-old command to rest in God. . . . [88]

efforts to understand and side with the poor in their struggles for social justice. A biblical basis for this approach is found in the Acts of the Apostles:

> *The group of believers was one in mind and heart. No one said that any of his belongings was his own, but they all shared with one another everything they had. . . . There was no one in the group who was in need. Those who owned fields or houses would sell them, bring the money received from the sale and turn it over to the apostles; and the money was distributed to each one according to his need.*[89]

The Peruvian theologian Gustavo Gutierrez (b. 1928), who coined the expression "theology of liberation," explains the choice of voluntary poverty as:

> *a commitment of solidarity with the poor, with those who suffer misery and injustice. . . . It is not a question of idealizing poverty, but rather of taking it on as it is—an evil—to protest against it and to struggle to abolish it.*[90]

For their sympathetic siding with those who are oppressed, Catholic clergy have been murdered by political authorities in countries such as Guatemala. They have also been strongly criticized within the Vatican. The movement has nevertheless spread to all areas where there is social injustice. Bakole Wa Ilunga, Archbishop of Kananga, the Democratic Republic of Congo (formerly Zaire), reminds Christians that Jesus warned the rich and powerful that it would be very difficult for them to enter the kingdom of heaven. By contrast:

> *Jesus liberates the poor from the feeling that they are somehow less than fully human; he makes them aware of their dignity and gives them motives for struggling against their lot and for taking control of their own lives.*[91]

Taking control is not easy for those who are oppressed minorities. In the United States, the Church offers the large African-American community of Christians a way of developing an alternative reality in the midst of poverty, urban violence, and discrimination.

The practical activities of the Black Church range from building shelters and arranging jobs to treatment for addiction, campaigns against police brutality, voter registration drives, and leadership training. Even without social empowerment, people often feel inwardly empowered and cherished by the presence of Jesus in their lives.

Despite the vibrancy of liberation theology, racism has not been eradicated in Christianity. Pioneering Black theologian James H. Cone proclaims it is time to end the silence over this issue. He claims, "The challenge for Black theology in the twenty-first century is to develop an enduring race critique that is so comprehensively woven into Christian understanding that no one will be able to forget the horrible crimes of white supremacy in the modern world."[92]

Feminist theology

The issue of taking control of one's life and defining one's identity has also been taken up by feminists within the Christian Church. The Church institution has historically been dominated by men, although there is strong evidence that Jesus had active women disciples and that there were women leaders in the early churches. Reconstructing their history in the early Christian movement and the effects of patriarchical domination is a task being addressed by considerable in-depth scholarship at present. The effect of the apostle Paul in shaping attitudes toward women as he guided the developing Christian communities is one area of particular concern. Some of the statements attributed to him in the biblical Epistles seem oppressive to women; some seem egalitarian. He argues, for example, that men should pray or prophesy with their head uncovered but that women should wear a veil:

> *For a man ought not to have his head veiled, since he is the image and reflection of God; but woman is the reflection of man. Indeed, man was not made from woman, but woman from man. Neither was man created for the sake of woman, but woman for the sake of man.*[93]

Many contemporary scholars are trying to sort out the cultural and historical as well as the theological contexts of such statements. Elisabeth Schüssler Fiorenza, for example, explains:

> *I argue that women were not marginal in the earliest beginnings of Christianity; rather, biblical texts and historical sources produce the marginality of women. Hence texts must be interrogated not only as to* what they say *about women but also how they* construct what they say *or do not say.*[94]

Another area of feminist theological scholarship is the role models for women offered by the Bible. A central female figure in the New Testament is Mary, mother of Jesus. Ivone Gebara and Maria Clara Bingemer of Brazil look at Mary from the perspective of "the great masses of Latin America, the overwhelming majority of whom are poor, enjoy no adequate quality of life, and lack respect, bread, love, and justice."[95] While acknowledging that the dogmas developed by the Catholic Church about Mary may be inflated, they nonetheless reveal a well-spring of hope for women and other oppressed humans.

A third major area of Christian feminist theology is the concept of God. The Divine is commonly referred to as "He" or "Father," but scholarship reveals that this patriarchal usage is not absolute; there also existed other models of God as Mother, as Divine Wisdom, as Justice, as Friend, as Lover. Sally McFague points out that to envision God as Mother, for instance, totally changes our understanding of our relationship to the Divine:

> *What the father-God gives us is redemption from sins; what the mother-God gives is life itself, . . . not primarily judging individuals but calling us back, wanting to be more fully united with us. . . . All of us, female and male, have the womb as our first home, all of us are born from the bodies of our mothers, all of us are fed by our mothers. What better imagery could there be for expressing the most basic reality of existence: that we live and move and have our being in God?*[96]

Creation-centered Christianity

Another current trend in Christianity is an attempt to develop and deepen its respect for nature. In the Judeo-Christian tradition, humans are thought to have been given dominion over all the things of the earth. Sometimes this "dominion" was interpreted as the right to exploit, rather than the duty to care for, the earth. This view contrasts with indigenous beliefs that the divine resides everywhere, that everything is sacred, and that humans are only part of the great circle of life. Some Christians now feel that the notion of having a God-given right to control has allowed humans to nearly destroy the planet. In some cases, they are turning to indigenous spiritual leaders for help in extricating the planet from ecological destruction. Historian and passionate earth-advocate Father Thomas Berry feels that "we need to put the Bible on the shelf for twenty years until we learn to read the scripture of life."[97]

A Christianity that would accord greater honor to the created world would also tend to emphasize the miracle that is creation, thus helping to unite science and religion. Creation-centered Christians—such as the late Jesuit priest and paleontologist Teilhard de Chardin—see the mind of God in the perfect, intricate balances of chemistry, biology, and physics that allow life as we know it to exist.

Creation-centered Christianity is being passionately espoused by Matthew Fox, whose views as a Dominican theologian were not accepted by the Vatican. He now heads the University of Creation Spirituality in California. He opposes what he regards as the Roman Catholic tendency to focus on the sufferings of Jesus and thus encourage a perpetual sense of guilt, rather than Jesus's love of all life and his compassion for the sufferings of the weak, exploited, and oppressed.

Environmental concern is being expressed not only by liberal Christians. In the United States, evangelical leaders have become alarmed by signs of global warming and have joined efforts to get the government to pass laws designed to limit it. A 2006 statement signed by presidents of evangelical colleges, pastors of popular "megachurches," and leaders of social aid groups such as the Salvation Army urged passing of such legislation as appropriate according to Christian ethics, for "millions of people could die in this century because of climate change, most of them our poorest global neighbors."[98]

Ecumenical movement

The restoration of religious freedom to multitudes of Christians in formerly communist countries and the explosion of charismatic and African Instituted movements have increased the great diversity of Christian ways of worshiping. Another contemporary trend is the attempt to unify all Christians around some point of agreement or at least fellowship with each other.

Vatican II asserted that the Roman Catholic Church is the one Church of Christ, but opened the way to dialogue with other branches of Christianity by declaring that the Holy Spirit was active in them as well. The Orthodox Church likewise believes that it is the "one, holy, Catholic, and Apostolic Church." Although it desires reunion of all Christians and denies any greed for organizational power, it insists on uniformity in matters of faith. Orthodox and Roman Catholic Churches therefore do not share Holy Communion with those outside their respective disciplines. Some Protestant denominations have branches that also refuse to acknowledge each other's validity.

In the attempt to restore some bonds among all Christian churches, there are dozens of official ecumenical dialogues going on. The World Council of Churches, centered in Geneva, was founded in 1948 as an organizational body allowing Christian churches to cooperate on service projects even in the midst of their theological disagreements. Its Faith and Order Commission links three hundred culturally, linguistically, and politically, not to mention theologically, different Christian churches in working out the problems of Christian unity. However, the Orthodox Church representatives are always in the minority within the Council and therefore typically lose when decisions call for a majority vote. The consensus model for decision-making has been proposed as being closer to the original spirit of Christianity. As Father Denis G. Pereira explains:

> *This model may be more difficult and involve more time. But it is inspired by a spirit of love, respect and generosity rather than suspicion and competition. The method supposes that the Church must be always open to the Spirit of God, and that the Spirit often speaks through the least and the last, at times even through a minority of one.*[99]

As Christians around the world struggled to find an appropriate Christian response to the September 11, 2001 terrorist attacks on the United States, the World Council of Churches announced a "Decade to Overcome Violence." They proposed that the members would be using this decade as:

- *an opportunity to discover afresh the meaning of sharing a common humanity, to confirm our commitment to the unity of all God's people and to the ministry of reconciliation*

- *a call to repent for our own complicity in violence, and explore, from within our faith traditions, ways to overcome the spirit, logic and practice of violence*

- *a forum in which to work together for a world of peace with local communities, secular movements, and people of other faiths*

- *a time to analyze and expose different forms of violence and their interconnection, and to act in solidarity with those who struggle for justice and the integrity of creation.*[100]

Review questions

1. What are the major themes of Jesus's teachings? Quote from biblical texts.
2. What was the importance for the early Church of the following: Paul, Constantine, Gnosticism, the Trinity, the Nicene Creed, Christology, monasticism?
3. Outline the history and main principles of the three major branches of Christianity: Eastern Orthodoxy, Roman Catholicism, and Protestantism.
4. What are the major contemporary conflicts in the Christian Church?

Discussion questions

1. Why were Jesus's teachings radical?
2. What were some of the major historical reasons for the way Christianity developed? Discuss Judaism, persecution, empire, monasticism, the Orthodox–Catholic schism, mysticism, the Protestant Reformation, the Western Enlightenment.
3. What do you see as major reasons for the contemporary shifts in Christianity today? Discuss globalization, the papacy, liberation theology, evangelicals, charismatics, women, racial conflicts, ecology. What positions would you take on some of the conflicts? Why?

CHAPTER 9

ISLAM

"There is no god but God"

In about 570 CE, a new prophet was born. This man, Muhammad, is considered by Muslims to be the last of a continuing chain of prophets who have come to restore the true religion. They regard the way revealed to him, Islam, not as a new religion but as the original path of monotheism, which also developed into Judaism and Christianity.

After carrying the torch of civilization in the West while Europe was in its Dark Ages, in the twentieth century Islam began a great resurgence. It is now the religion of nearly one-fifth of the world's people. Its monotheistic creed is simple: "There is no god but God, and Muhammad is his Messenger." Its requirements of the faithful are straightforward, if demanding. But beneath them lie profundities and subtleties of which non-Muslims are largely unaware. In fact, ignorance about Islam and perceived targeting of Muslims in general by the U.S.-led "war on terrorism" have exacerbated a dangerous and growing divide between Muslims and non-Muslims in the contemporary world. Therefore it is extremely important to carefully study the origins, teachings, and modern history of this major world religion.

The Prophet Muhammad

Islam, like Christianity and Judaism, traces its ancestry to the patriarch Abraham. Isma'il (Ishmael) was said to be the son of Abraham and an Egyptian slave, Hagar. When Abraham's wife, Sarah, also bore him a son (Isaac), Abraham took Isma'il and Hagar to the desert valley of Becca (Mecca) in Arabia to spare them Sarah's jealousy.

The sacred book of Islam, the Holy Qur'an, received as a series of revelations to Muhammad, relates that Abraham and Isma'il together built the holiest sanctuary in Islam, the Ka'bah. It was thought to be the site of Adam's original place of worship; part of the cubic stone building is a venerated black meteorite. According to the Qur'an, God told Abraham that the Ka'bah should be a place of pilgrimage. It was regarded as a holy place by the Arabian tribes.

According to Islamic tradition, the region sank into historical oblivion as it turned away from Abraham's monotheism. For many centuries, the events of the rest of the world passed it by, aside from contact through trading caravans. Then into a poor clan of the most powerful of the tribes in the area was born a child named Muhammad ("the praised one"). His father died before he was born, and after the death of his mother and then his grandfather, Muhammad became the ward of his uncle, who put him to work as a shepherd.

God is *the* focus in Islam, the sole authority, not Muhammad. But Muhammad's life story is important to Muslims, for his character is considered a model of the teachings in the Qur'an. The stories of Muhammad's life and his sayings are preserved in literature called the **Hadith**, which report on the Prophet's **Sunnah** (sayings and actions). When he was a teenager, on a trip to Syria with his uncle, Muhammad was noticed by a Christian monk who identified marks on his body indicating his status as a prophet. As a young man, Muhammad managed caravans for a beautiful, intelligent, and wealthy woman named Khadijah. When she was forty and Muhammad was twenty-five, she offered to marry him. Khadijah became Muhammad's strongest supporter during the difficult and discouraging years of his early mission.

With Khadijah's understanding of his spiritual propensities, Muhammad began to spend periods of time in solitary retreat. These retreats were not uncommon in his lineage. They provided opportunities for contemplation, away from the world.

When Muhammad was forty years old, he made a spiritual retreat during the month called Ramadan. An angel in human-like form, Gabriel, reportedly came to him and insisted that he recite. Three times Muhammad demurred that he could not, for he was unlettered, and three times the angel forcefully commanded him. In desperation, Muhammad at last cried out, "What shall I recite?" and the angel began dictating the first words of what became the Qur'an:

Proclaim! (or Recite!)
In the name
Of thy Lord and Cherisher,
Who created—
Created man, out of
A (mere) clot
Of congealed blood:
Proclaim! And thy Lord
Is Most Bountiful,—
He Who taught
(The use of) the Pen,—
Taught man that
Which he knew not.[1]

Muhammad returned home, deeply shaken. Khadijah comforted him and encouraged him to overcome his fear of the responsibilities and ridicule of prophethood. The revelations continued intermittently, asserting the theme that it was the One God who spoke and who called people to **Islam** (which means complete, trusting surrender to God). According to tradition, Muhammad described the form of these revelations thus:

Revelation sometimes comes like the sound of a bell; that is the most painful way. When it ceases I have remembered what was said. Sometimes it is an angel who talks to me like a human, and I remember what he says.[2]

The Prophet shared these revelations with the few people who believed him: his wife, Khadijah; his young cousin, 'Ali; his friend, the trader Abu Bakr; and the freed slave, Zayd.

After three years, Muhammad was instructed by the revelations to preach publicly. He was ridiculed and defamed by the Qurayshites, the aristocrats of his tribe who operated the Ka'bah as a pilgrimage center and organized profitable trading caravans through Mecca. While Muhammad was somewhat protected by the influence of his uncle, his followers were subject to persecution. A dark-skinned Abyssinian slave named Bilal, who was among the first converts, was imprisoned and brought out daily under the hot sun, pinned to the ground with a heavy stone on his chest, and ordered to deny the Prophet and worship the old gods. He staunchly refused, saying, "One, one." Once bought by the Prophet's friend Abu Bakr, Bilal became the first **muezzin** (one who calls the people to prayer from a high place), illustrating the Prophet's discarding of racial and social class distinctions. Finally, according to some accounts, Muhammad and his followers were banished for three years to a desolate place where they struggled to survive by eating wild foods such as tree leaves.

The band of Muslims was asked to return to Mecca, but the persecution by the Qurayshites continued. Muhammad's fiftieth year, the "Year of Sorrows," was the worst of all: he lost his beloved wife Khadijah and his protective uncle. With his strongest backers gone, persecution of the Prophet increased.

According to tradition, at the height of his trials, Muhammad experienced the Night of Ascension. He is said to have ascended through the seven heavens to the far limits of the cosmos, and thence into the Divine Proximity. There he met former prophets and teachers from Adam to Jesus, saw paradise and hell, and received the great blessings of the Divine Presence.

Pilgrims to Mecca from Yathrib, an oasis to the north, recognized Muhammad as a prophet. They invited him to come to their city to help solve its social and political problems. Still despised in Mecca as a potential threat by the Qurayshites, Muhammad and his followers left Mecca secretly. Their move to Yathrib, later called al-Medina ("The City [of the Prophet]"), was not easy. The Prophet left last, accompanied (according to some traditions) by Abu Bakr. To hide from the pursuing Meccans, it is said they took refuge in a cave, where the Prophet taught his friend the secret practice of the silent remembrance of God.

This *hijrah* (migration) of Muslims from Mecca to Medina took place in 622 CE. The Muslim era is calculated from the beginning of the year in which this event took place, for it marked the change from persecution to appreciation of the Prophet's message.

In Medina, Muhammad drew up a constitution for the city of Yathrib/Medina that later served as a model for Islamic social administration. The departure of Muslims from Mecca was viewed with hostility and suspicion by the leaders of Mecca. Their assumption was that Medina had become a rallying point for enemies of the Meccans who, under Muhammad's leadership, would eventually attack and destroy Mecca. To forestall this, Mecca declared war on Medina, and a period of open conflict between the two cities followed.

Muhammad himself directed the first raid against a Meccan caravan on its return journey. The battle between Muslim emigrants and Meccans took place at Badr near Medina; the small group of Muslims was victorious.

According to the Qur'anic revelations, God had sent thousands of angels to help Muhammad. Furthermore, Muhammad threw a handful of pebbles at the Meccans and this turned the tide, for it was God who threw, and "He will surely weaken the designs of the unbelievers."[3] Enraged by the Islamic victory, Mecca made a surprise attack against Medina and routed the Muslims, injuring

Muhammad and scattering the Islamic forces. Within two years, Mecca had mounted a much larger force, including cavalry and numerous archers, for a siege intended to subdue Medina permanently. Warned by spies, the Muslims defended Medina with a large trench encircling the city. Unable to press their attack, the Meccans were forced to retreat. Rather than continue hostilities, Muhammad negotiated a truce between the two warring cities.

The Qur'anic revelations to Muhammad emphasize the basic religious unity of Jews, Christians, and Muslims, members of the same monotheistic tradition of Abraham. But most of the Jews of Medina refused to accept Islam, because it recognized Jesus and claimed to complete the Torah. In addition, they were politically allied to those who opposed the Prophet. Eventually, their farms were bought or appropriated by increasing numbers of Muslim converts, and some Jews were killed as political opponents. The Qur'an taught that the Jews and Christians had distorted the pure monotheism of Abraham; Muhammad had been sent to restore and supplement the teachings of the apostles and prophets. He was instructed to have the people face Mecca rather than Jerusalem during their prayers.

In 630 CE the Prophet returned triumphant to Mecca with such a large band of followers that the Meccans did not resist. Reportedly, only thirty people were killed in the historic conquest of Mecca. The Ka'bah was purged of its idols, and from that time it has been the center of Muslim piety. Acquiescing to Muhammad's political power and the Qur'anic warnings about the dire fate of those who tried to thwart God's prophets, many Meccans converted to Islam. Muhammad declared a general amnesty. Contrary to tribal customs of revenge, the Prophet showed his unusual gentleness by forgiving those who had been his opponents.

The Prophet then returned to Medina, which he kept as the spiritual and political center of Islam. From there, a number of campaigns were undertaken. In addition to northern Africa, the Persian states of Yemen, Oman, and Bahrain came into the fold. As the multi-cultural, multi-racial embrace of Islam evolved, the Prophet declared that the community of the faithful was more important than the older tribal identities that had divided people. The new ideal was a global family, under God. In his "Farewell Sermon," Muhammad stated, "You must know that a Muslim is the brother of a Muslim and the Muslims are one brotherhood."[4]

In the eleventh year of the Muslim era, Muhammad made a final pilgrimage to the Ka'bah in Mecca to demonstrate to the faithful the rites that were to be followed thenceforth. After his return to Medina, he became very ill. As he recognized that the end was near, he gave final instructions to his followers, promising to meet them at "the Fountain" in Paradise. Muhammad died in 632 CE. In the circumstances that followed Muhammad's death, his steadfast friend Abu Bakr was elected the first **caliph** (successor to the Prophet). Another possible successor was the trustworthy and courageous 'Ali, the Prophet's cousin and husband of his favorite daughter, Fatima. One tradition has it that the Prophet Muhammad actually transferred his spiritual light to Fatima before his death, but that in the midst of funeral arrangements, neither she nor 'Ali participated in the selection of the first caliph. The Shi'ite faction would later claim 'Ali as the legitimate heir.

Muhammad's own life has continued to be very precious to Muslims, and it is his qualities that a good Muslim tries to emulate. He always denied having any superhuman powers, and the Qur'an called him "a human being like you," just "a servant to whom revelation has come," and "a warner."[5] The only miracle he ever claimed was that, though unlettered, he had received the Qur'anic revelations in extraordinarily eloquent and pure Arabic. He did not even claim to be a teacher— "God guides those whom He will,"[6] he was instructed to say—although Muslims consider the Prophet the greatest of teachers.

Nevertheless, all who saw the Prophet remarked on his touching physical beauty, his nobility of character, the fragrance of his presence, his humility, and his kindness. Many stories are told of his affectionate compassion toward animals, children, women, widows, and orphans, contrary to prevailing customs. When asked the short cut to heaven, he reportedly said that Paradise lies under the feet of the mother. In his devotion to God, he quietly endured poverty so extreme that he tied a stone over his stomach to suppress the pangs of hunger. He explained, "I eat as a slave eats, and sit as a slave sits, for I am a slave (of God)." Although the Qur'an says that the Prophet is the perfect model for humanity, the purest vehicle for God's message, he himself perpetually prayed for God's forgiveness. When he was asked how best to practice Islam, he said, "The best Islam is that you feed the hungry and spread peace among people you know and those you do not know."[7]

Muhammad's mystical experiences of the divine had not led him to forsake the world as a contemplative. Rather, according to the Qur'an, the mission of Islam is to reform society, to actively combat oppression and corruption, "inviting to all that is good, enjoining what is right, and forbidding all that is wrong."[8] The Prophet's task—which Muslims feel was also undertaken by such earlier prophets as Moses and Abraham—is not only to call people back to faith but also to create a just moral order in the world as the embodiment of God's commandments.

The Qur'an

The heart of Islam is not the Prophet but the revelations he received. Collectively they are called the Qur'an ("reading" or "reciting"). He received the messages over a period of twenty-three years, with some later messages replacing earlier ones. At first they were striking affirmations of the unity of God and the woe of those who did not heed God's message. Later messages also addressed the organizational needs and social lives of the Muslim community.

After the *hijrah*, Muhammad heard the revelations and dictated them to a scribe; many of his companions memorized them. They are said to have been safeguarded against changes and omissions. Recited, the passages have a lyrical beauty and power that Muslims believe is unsurpassed; these qualities cannot be translated. The recitation is to be rendered in what is sometimes described as a sad, subdued tone, because the messages concern God's sadness at the people's waywardness. Muhammad said, "Weep, therefore, when you recite it."[9]

Recitation of the Qur'an is thought to have a healing, soothing effect, but can also bring protection, guidance, and knowledge. It is critical to recite it only in a purified state, for the words are so powerful that the one who recites it takes on a great responsibility. Ideally, one learns the Qur'an as a child, when memorization is easiest and when the power of the words will help to shape one's life.

During the life of the Prophet, his followers attempted to preserve the oral tradition in writing as an additional way of safeguarding it from loss. The early caliphs continued this effort until a council was convened by the third caliph around 650 CE to establish a single authoritative written text. This is the one still used. It is divided into 114 *suras* (chapters). The first is the **Fatiha**, the opening sura, which reveals the essence of the Qur'an:

> *In the name of God, Most Gracious, Most Merciful.*
> *Praise be to God,*
> *The Lord of the Worlds;*
> *Most Gracious, Most Merciful;*
> *Master of the Day of Judgment.*
> *Thee do we worship,*
> *And Thine aid we seek.*
> *Show us the straight way,*
> *The way of those on whom*
> *Thou has bestowed Thy Grace*
> *Those whose portion*
> *Is not wrath,*
> *And, who go not astray.*

The verses of the Qur'an are terse, but are thought to have multiple levels of meaning. Translator and commentator Abdullah Yusuf Ali notes that in the mystical early passages there are often three layers: (1) a reference to a particular person or situation; (2) a spiritual lesson; and (3) a deeper mystical significance.

The Qur'an often mentions figures and stories from Jewish and Christian sacred history, which is considered part of the fabric of Islam by Muslims. Islam is the original religion, according to the Qur'an. Submission has existed as long as there have been humans willing to submit. Adam was the first prophet. Abraham was not exclusively a Jew nor a Christian; he was a monotheistic, upright person who had surrendered to God. Jesus was a very great prophet.

Muslims believe the Jewish prophets and Jesus all brought the same messages from God. However, the Qur'an teaches that God's original messages have been added to and distorted by humans. For instance, Muslims do not accept the idea developed historically in Christianity that Jesus has the authority to pardon or atone for our sins. The belief that this power lies with anyone except God is considered a blasphemous human interpolation into what Muslims understand as the basic and true teachings of all prophets of the Judeo-Christian-Islamic tradition: belief in one God and in our personal moral accountability before God on the Day of Judgment. In the Muslim view, the Qur'an was sent as a final corrective in the continuing monotheistic tradition. Muslims, citing John 14:16, 26 from the Christian New Testament, believe that Jesus prophesied the coming of Muhammad when he promised that the **Paraclete** (advocate) would come to assist humanity after him.

The Qur'an revealed to Muhammad is understood as a final and complete reminder of the prophets' teachings, which all refer to the same one God, known in Arabic as **Allah** ("The God"). For example, in Sura 42, Muhammad is told:

> *Say: "I believe in whatever Book Allah has sent down; and I am commanded to judge justly between you. Allah is our Lord and your Lord! For us is the*

responsibility for our deeds, and for you for your deeds. There is no contention between us and you. Allah will bring us together, and to Him is our final goal.[10]

The central teachings

On the surface, Islam is a straightforward religion. Its teachings can be summed up simply, as in this statement by the Islamic Society of North America:

Islam is an Arabic word which means peace, purity, acceptance and commitment. As a religion, Islam calls for complete acceptance of the teachings and guidance of God.

A Muslim is one who freely and willingly accepts the supreme power of God and strives to organize his life in total accord with the teachings of God. He also works for building social institutions which reflect the guidance of God.[11]

This brief statement can be broken down into a number of articles of faith.

The Oneness of God and of humanity

The first sentence chanted in the ear of a traditional Muslim infant is the **Shahadah**—"*La ilaha illa Allah Muhammad-un Rasul Allah*" ("There is no god but God, and Muhammad is the Messenger of God"). Exoterically, the Shahadah supports absolute monotheism. As the Qur'an reveals in Sura 2:163:

Your God is One God:
There is no god but He,
Most Gracious, Most Merciful.

Esoterically, the Shahadah means that ultimately there is only one Absolute Reality; the underlying essence of life is eternal unity rather than the apparent separateness of things in the physical world. Muslims think that the Oneness of God is the primordial religion taught by all prophets of all faiths. Muhammad merely reminded people of it.

It has been estimated that over ninety percent of Muslim theology deals with the implications of Unity. God, while One, is referred to by ninety-nine names. These are each considered attributes of the One Being, such as *al-Ali* ("The Most High") and *ar-Raqib* ("The Watchful"). Allah is the name of God that encompasses all the attributes. Each of the names refers to the totality, the One Being.

Unity applies not only to the conceptualization of God, but also to every aspect of life. In the life of the individual, every thought and action should spring from a heart and mind intimately integrated with the divine. Islam theoretically rejects any divisions within itself; all Muslims around the globe are supposed to embrace as one family. All humans are a global family; there is no one "chosen people," for all are invited into a direct relationship with God. Science, art, and politics are not separate from religion. Individuals should never forget Allah; the Oneness should permeate their thoughts and actions. Abu Hashim Madani, an Indian Sufi sage, is said to have taught: "There is only one thing to be gained in life, and that is to remember God with each breath; and there is only one loss in life, and that is the breath drawn without the remembrance of God."[12]

> *"The 'remembrance of God' is like breathing deeply in the solitude of high mountains: here the morning air, filled with purity of the eternal snows, dilates the breast; it becomes space and heaven enters our heart."*
>
> *Frithjof Schuon[13]*

Prophethood and the compass of Islam

Devout Muslims feel that Islam encompasses all religions. Islam honors all prophets as messengers from the one God:

Say ye: We believe
In God, and the revelation
Given to us, and to Abraham,
Isma'il, Isaac, Jacob,
And the Tribes, and that given
To Moses and Jesus, and that given
To (all) Prophets from their Lord:
We make no difference
Between one and another of them:
And we bow to God in surrender.[14]

Muslims believe that the original religion was monotheism, but that God sent prophets from time to time as religions decayed into polytheism. Each prophet came to renew the message, in a way specifically designed for his culture and time. The Qur'anic revelations declared Muhammad to be the "Seal of the Prophets," the last and ultimate authority in the continuing prophetic tradition. The prophets are mere humans, although holy and powerful; none of them is divine, for there is only one Divinity.

Islam is thought to be the universal religion in its pure form. All scriptures of all traditions are also honored, but only the Qur'an is considered fully authentic, because it is the direct, unchanged, untranslated word of God. Whatever exists in other religions that agrees with the Qur'an is divine truth.

Human relationship to the divine

> *We are nearer to [a person] than his jugular vein.*
>
> *The Holy Qur'an, Sutra 50:16*

In Muslim belief, God is all-knowing and has intelligently created everything for a divine purpose, governed by fixed laws that assure the harmonious and wondrous working of all creation. Humans will find peace only if they know these laws and live by them. They have been revealed by the prophets, but the people often have not believed. To believe is to surrender totally to God. As the Qur'an states:

Farid Esack

Farid Esack, one of the world's most brilliant young Muslim scholars, grew up as a victim of apartheid in South Africa. His family was so poor that they had to beg for food and search through gutters for food. Farid says:

When you live in poverty and isolation, one of the things you hold on to is religion for your sanity, to keep you going. When you hear people crying in suffering and pain, instead of asking, "Where is God?", this is God crying out to you, "Why are you allowing this?"[15]

Thus it was not only poverty that drove Farid to risk his life again and again to build resistance to apartheid policies. It was also his deep commitment to Islam.

I was strangely and deeply religious as a child, with a deep concern for the suffering which I experienced and witnessed all around me. I dealt with these two impulses by holding on to an indomitable belief that for God to be God, God had to be just and on the side of the marginalized. More curious was a logic, based on a text in the Qur'an, "If you assist Allah then He will assist you and make your feet firm" (47:7). For me this meant that I had to participate in a struggle for freedom and justice and, if I wanted God's help in this, then I had to assist Him.[16]

In 1984 Farid and three friends founded the Call of Islam, which was very active in organizing resistance to apartheid, gender inequality, environmental destruction, and tensions between religions. After years fraught with danger, Farid found himself in a queue of the rural poor, to cast his vote for a freely elected government. He mused:

I thought of the pain our country had endured in its long march to freedom, the loneliness of exile, of detention without trial, the political murders, the dispossession, the sighs of the tired and the exploited factory and farm workers, the months of living on the run like a fugitive, the attacks by police dogs, the clandestine pamphleteering . . . all for a single mark with a cheap little lead pencil![17]

Can you imagine that we are the generation responsible for the death of apartheid? . . . Difficult as it was to sustain this belief at times, we did it.[18]

Farid is trying to show through intense Muslim scholarship that if a person of another religion is righteous, just, and God-fearing, he or she should be accepted by Muslims as a *mu'min* (believer), not a *kafir* non-believer.

Having served as a member of South Africa's Gender Equality Commission, Farid concludes:

In the Last Judgment, I will not be asked whether I succeeded or not. It is not our task to solve the problems of the world. We will only be asked what we did with the gifts He gave us. In Islam and in the Christian Gospels, it is said that God will ask you on the Day of Judgment, "When I was hungry, why did you not feed Me?"[19]

None believes in Our revelations save those who, when reminded of them, prostrate themselves in adoration and give glory to their Lord in all humility; who forsake their beds to pray to their Lord in fear and hope; who give in charity of that which We have bestowed on them. No mortal knows what bliss is in store for these as a reward for their labors.[20]

The Qur'an indicates that human history provides many "signs" of the hand of God at work bestowing mercy and protection on believers. Signs such as the great flood, which was thought to have occurred at the time of Noah, illustrate that non-believers and evil-doers ultimately experience great misfortune in this life or the afterlife. None is punished without first being warned by a messenger of God to mend his or her ways. Creation itself is a sign of God's compassion, as well as of God's omnipotent will.

According to Islam, the two major human sins involve one's relationship to God. One is **shirk** (associating anything else with divinity except the one God). The Qur'an instructs,

Say: "Oh People of the book!
Come to common terms as between us and you:
That we worship none but Allah;
That we associate no partners with Him;
That we erect not from among ourselves
Lords and patrons other than Allah."[21]

In other words, in Islam's pure monotheism one is enjoined not to worship anything but God—not natural forces, or mountains, or stones, or incarnations of God, or lesser deities, or human rulers. Idol-worship is vigorously denounced, as is worship of natural phenomena: "Adore not the sun nor the moon, but adore Allah Who created them."[22]

The other major sin is **kufr** (ungratefulness to God, unbelief, atheism). Furthermore, a major human problem is forgetfulness of God. God has mercifully sent us revelations as reminders. The veils that separate us from God come from us, not from God; Muslims feel that it is ours to remove the veils by seeking God and acknowledging the omnipresence, omniscience, and omnipotence of the Divine. For the orthodox, the appropriate stance is a combination of love and fear of God. Aware that God knows everything and is all-powerful, one wants to do everything one can to please God, out of both love and fear. This paradox was given dramatic expression by the Caliph 'Umar ibn al-Khattab:

If God declared on the Day of Judgment that all people would go to paradise except one unfortunate person, out of His fear I would think that I am that person. And if God declared that all people would go to hell except one fortunate person, out of my hope in His Mercy I would think that I am that fortunate person.[23]

The unseen life

Muslims believe that our senses do not reveal all of reality. In particular, they believe in the angels of God. These are non-physical beings of light who serve and praise God day and night. They are numerous, and each has a specific responsibility. For instance, certain angels are always with each of us, recording our good and bad deeds. The Qur'an also mentions archangels, including Gabriel, highest of the angelic beings, whose main responsibility is to bring revelations to the prophets from God. But neither he nor any other angel is to be worshiped, according to strict monotheistic interpretation of Islam, for the angels are simply utterly submissive servants of God. By contrast, according to Islamic belief, there is a non-submissive being called Satan. He was originally one of the *jinn*—immaterial beings of fire, whose nature is between that of humans and angels. He proudly refused to bow before Adam and was therefore cursed to live by tempting Adam's descendants—all of humanity, in other words—to follow him rather than God. According to the Qur'an, those who fall prey to Satan's devices will ultimately go to hell.

Popular Muslim piety also developed a cult of saints. The tombs of mystics known to have had special spiritual powers have become places of pilgrimage. Many people visit them out of devotion and desire for the blessings of the spirit, which is thought to remain in the area. This practice is frowned upon by some reformers, who assert that Muslim tradition clearly forbids worship of any being other than God.

The Last Judgment

In the polytheistic religion practiced by Arabs before Muhammad, the afterlife was only a shadow, without rewards or punishments. People had little religious incentive to be morally accountable. By contrast, the Qur'an emphasizes that after a period of repose in the grave, all humans will be bodily resurrected and assembled for a final accounting of their deeds. At that unknown time of the Final Judgment, the world will end cataclysmically: "The earth will shake and the mountains crumble into heaps of shifting sand" (Sura 73:14). Then comes the terrible confrontation with one's own life:

> The works of each person We have bound about his neck. On the Day of
> Resurrection, We shall confront him with a book spread wide open, saying,
> "Read your book."[24]

Hell is the grievous destiny of unrepentant non-believers—those who have rejected faith in and obedience to God and His Messenger, who are unjust and who do not forbid evil. Hell also awaits the hypocrites who even after making a covenant with God have turned away from their promise to give in charity and to pray regularly:

> It is a flaming Fire. It drags them down by their scalps; and it shall call him who
> turned his back and amassed riches and covetously hoarded them.[25]

Muslim piety is ever informed by this belief in God's impartial judgment of one's actions, and the responsibility to remind others of the fate that may await them.

Basically, Islam says that what we experience in the afterlife is a revealing of our tendencies in this life. Our thoughts, actions, and moral qualities are turned into our outer reality. We awaken to our true nature, for it is displayed before us. For the just and merciful, the state after death is a Garden of Bliss. Those who say, "Our Lord is God . . . shall have all that your souls shall desire. . . . A hospitable gift from One Oft-Forgiving, Most Merciful!" (Sura 41:30–32). The desire of the purified souls will be for closeness to God, and their spirits will live in different levels of this closeness. For them, there will be castles, couches, fruits, sweet-meats, honey, houris (beautiful virgin women), and immortal youths serving from goblets and golden platters. Such delights promised by the Qur'an are interpreted metaphorically to mean that human nature will be transformed in the next life to such an extent that the disturbing factors of this physical existence will no longer have any effect.

> *People are asleep, but when they die, they wake up.*
> *Hadith of the Prophet Muhammad*

By contrast, sinners and non-believers will experience the torments of hell, fire fueled by humans, boiling water, pus, chains, searing winds, food that chokes, and so forth. It is they who condemn themselves; their very bodies turn against them "on the Day when their tongues, their hands, and their feet will bear witness against them as to their actions" (Sura 24:24). The great medieval mystic al-Ghazali speaks of spiritual torments of the soul as well: the agony of being separated from worldly desires, burning shame at seeing one's life projected, and terrible regret at being barred from the vision of God. Muslims do not believe that hell can last forever for any believer, though. Only the non-believers will be left there; the others will eventually be lifted to paradise, for God is far more merci-ful than wrathful.

The Five Pillars

The basic spiritual practices incumbent on all Muslims are known as the Five Pillars of Islam. A Muslim must do his or her best to fulfill the Five Pillars because they are considered God's commandments.

Belief and witness

The first pillar of Islam (the Shahadah) is believing and professing the unity of God and the messengership of Muhammad: "There is no god but God, and Muhammad is the Messenger of God," to which Shi'ites add "and 'Ali is the Master of the believers." The Qur'an requires the faithful to tell others of Islam, so that they will have the information they need to make an intelligent choice. However, it rules out the use of coercion in spreading the message:

> *Let there be [or: There is] no compulsion*
> *In religion: Truth stands out*
> *Clear from Error: whoever*
> *Rejects Evil and believes*
> *In God hath grasped*
> *The most trustworthy*
> *Hand-hold, that never breaks.*[26]

The Qur'an insists on respect for all prophets and all revealed scriptures.

Daily prayers

The second pillar is the performance of a continual round of prayers (*salaat*). Five times a day, the faithful are to perform ritual ablutions with water (or sand or dirt if necessary), face Mecca, and recite a series of prayers and passages from the Qur'an, bowing and kneeling. Around the world, this joint facing of Mecca for prayer unites all Muslims into a single world family. When the prayers are recited by a congregation, all stand and bow shoulder to shoulder, with no social distinctions. In a mosque, women and men usually pray separately, with the women in rows behind the men, to avoid sexually distracting the men. There may be an imam, or prayer-leader, but no priest stands between the worshiper and God. On Friday noon, there is usually a special prayer service in the mosque. Remembrance of God is an everyday obligation; such remembrance continually polishes the rust from the heart.

Prayer is thought to strengthen belief in God's existence and goodness and carry this belief into the depths of the heart and every aspect of external life. Praying is also expected to purify the heart, develop the mind and conscience, comfort the soul, encourage the good and suppress the evil in the person, and awaken the innate sense of higher morality and higher aspirations. The words of praise and the bowing express continual gratefulness and surrender to the One. At the end of the prayers, one turns to the two guardian angels on one's shoulders to say the traditional greeting—"*Assalamu Alaykum*" ("Peace be on you")—and another phrase adding the blessing, "and mercy of God."

While mouthing the words and performing the outer actions, one should be concentrating on the inner prayer of the heart. The Prophet reportedly said, "Prayer without the Presence of the Lord in the heart is not prayer at all."[27]

To be aware of God's presence, one should not just be going through the motions, as an obligation five times a day. Ideally, in Muslim spirituality, one should be constantly remembering God inwardly, and one's whole life should become a means of worship. In the Qur'an, Muhammad was instructed: "Say: Truly, my prayer and my service of sacrifice, my life and my death, are for Allah, the Cherisher of the Worlds."[28]

Zakat

The Qur'an links prayer with **zakat**, charity or almsgiving, the third pillar. One's prayer is accepted only if one shares with others. At the end of the year, all Muslims must donate at least two and a half percent of their accumulated wealth to needy Muslims. This is designed to decrease inequalities in wealth and prevent personal greed. Its literal meaning is "purity," for it purifies the distribution of money, helping to keep it in healthy circulation.

Saudi Arabia devotes fifteen percent of its GDP to development and relief projects throughout the world. The Islamic Relief Organization it funds helps people of all religions, without discrimination, where there is need following disasters. Many stories from the life of the Prophet Muhammad teach that one should help others whether or not they are Muslims. For example, the Prophet's neighbor was Jewish. The Prophet reportedly gave him a gift every day, even though the neighbor daily left garbage at his door. Once the neighbor was sick, and the Prophet visited him. The neighbor asked, "Who are you to help me?" The Prophet replied, "You are my brother. I must help you."

Fasting

The fourth pillar is fasting. Frequent fasts are recommended to Muslims, but the only one that is obligatory is the fast during Ramadan, commemorating the first revelations of the Qur'an to Muhammad. For all who are beyond puberty, but not infirm or sick or menstruating or nursing children, a dawn-to-sunset abstention from food, drink, sexual intercourse, and smoking is required for the whole month of Ramadan.

Because Muslims use a lunar calendar of 354 days, the month of Ramadan gradually moves through all the seasons. When it falls in the summer, the period of fasting is much longer than in the shortest days of winter. The hardship of abstaining even from drinking water during these long and hot days is an unselfish surrender to God's commandment and an assertion of control over the lower desires. The knowledge that Muslims all over the world are making these sacrifices at the same time builds a special bond between haves and have-nots, helping the haves to experience what it is to be hungry, to share in the condition of the poor. Those who have are encouraged to be especially generous in their almsgiving during Ramadan.

Fasting is expected to allow the body to burn up impurities and provide one with "a Transparent Soul to transcend, a Clear Mind to think and a Light Body to move and act."[29] Many people feel that they are spiritually more sensitive and physically more healthy during Ramadan fasting, and they look forward eagerly to this period each year. Fasting liberates a person's body from the heaviness of food and it is also a lesson for the soul, teaching it not to allow anything into the mind and heart that would distract one from God. It is believed that control of the body's desires also builds the mastery needed to control the lower emotions, such as anger and jealousy.

Hajj

The fifth pillar is **hajj**, the pilgrimage to Mecca. All Muslims who are physically and financially able to do so are expected to make the pilgrimage at least once in their lifetime. It involves a series of symbolic rituals designed to bring the faithful as close as possible to God. Male pilgrims wrap themselves in a special garment of unsewn cloths, rendering them all alike, with no class distinctions. The garment is like a burial shroud, for by dying to their earthly life they can devote all their attention to God. It is a time for *dhikr*, the constant repetition of the Shahadah, the remembrance that there is no god but God.

Pilgrims walk around the ancient Ka'bah seven times, like the continual rotation around the One by the angels and all of creation, to the seventh heaven. Their hearts should be filled only with remembrance of God.

Another sacred site on the pilgrimage is the field of Arafat. It is said to be the place where Adam and Eve were taught that humans are created solely for the worship of God. Here pilgrims pray from noon to sunset to be forgiven of anything that has separated them from the Beloved. In addition, pilgrims carry out other symbolic gestures, such as sacrificing an animal and throwing stones at the devil,

An Interview with Dr. Syed M. Hussain

Dr. Syed M. Hussain is a specialist in kidney disorders, dialysis, and kidney transplants at a New Delhi hospital. He may be called for emergencies at any time, night or day, but observes the rules of fasting, particularly during Ramadan. He explains:

"Ramadan is a very holy month in the Muslim calendar. It is a ritual for Muslims to fast during this month so that you become a little more spiritual and healthier. At the same time, you also have the pinch of hunger. Many people in their lifetime who are very wealthy will never experience what is hunger and what is thirst. Fasting will make you understand what a hungry person is going through. Altogether, such sacrifices make you closer to life. You see that God has given you such beautiful things.

"During this holy month of Ramadan, Muslims usually take something in the morning between 4 and 4.30 a.m., and after that, they say their morning prayer at 5 to 5.30 a.m. Then they will fast until sunset, and then they will have their meal. The logic is that if one hundred thousand people are missing one or two meals, then one hundred thousand people are receiving their meals [when that money is given in charity]. This is also a philosophy of equality.

"As a doctor I see that if you are fasting, your system gets toned up. Your physical fitness increases and you become healthier. Your mental alertness rises. When I fast during Ramadan, my mind becomes very, very clear. I am relieved of bad thoughts, and when I see patients, I feel closer to them. When you see someone who suffers you recognize what he is going through. Then you

cannot be cruel. If you are cruel, you are not doing religious practice from the bottom of your heart—you are doing it just for show. There is no place for such things in any religion.

"If you fast for some time, your digestive tract gets a rest. When you give a rest to your digestive system, you also give rest to your brain and heart. If you are fasting, you are giving a rest to your entire system. Your metabolism will be low and you will not have anger; you will not fight or be cruel.

"In the hospital some of my colleagues will say, 'You are fasting, so let me hide and take my food.' I say, 'Don't worry—if I get upset when I see food, then my motive is defeated. Instead, you should get all the best food which I like, and I'll be happier, because that will give me more strength to control my *nafs* (inner passions).' That makes me a better person. All religions are religions of sacrifice. The more you sacrifice, the more you become a better person.

"I don't think any religion has any place for fighting and killing. No religion has a place for terrorist actions. Many people think that Islam is a fundamentalist religion, but no. Look at the basics in the Book. If ten people are practicing the wrong things, that doesn't make the system wrong. Some people may have deviated, but if you practice from the heart, then you are compassionate, you are soft, you are helping, and you are generous to all the people around you. If you at least help one person seriously in your life, then you have learned something in your life. You can show your face to God, that you have helped one of his creatures who was suffering. Otherwise what is life? It won't make any sense."[30]

represented by pillars. The animal sacrifice reminds the *hajjis* of Abraham's will-ingness to surrender to God that which was most dear to him, his own son, even though in God's mercy a ram was substituted for the sacrifice. Most of the meat is distributed to the needy, a service for which Saudi Arabia has had to develop huge preservation and distribution facilities. *Hajjis* also perform symbolic acts at the holy well of Zum-Zum, the spring that God is said to have provided for Hagar when she and Isma'il were left alone in the desert.

Hajj draws together Muslims from all corners of the earth for this intense spiritual experience. During the month of the pilgrimage, approximately three million pilgrims converge upon Mecca. To help handle them, the Saudi govern-ment built the immense King Abdul Aziz International Airport near Jedda. The journey was once so hazardous that many people and camels died trying to cross the desert in fulfillment of their sacred obligation.

Now there are new dangers from the presence of such masses of pilgrims. The Saudi government has tried to organize the sites to avoid tragedies, but in recent years hundreds of *hajjis* have died in stampedes and fires. To lessen the danger of cooking fires, the government has made arrangements for thousands of fireproof air-conditioned tents and trucks selling sealed fast-food meals.

Though considerably modernized now, *hajj* is still the vibrant core of the global Muslim community. To be a *hajji* is as much as ever a badge of pride. Throughout Muslim history, *hajj* has brought widely diverse people together, consolidating the center of Islam, spreading information and ideas across cultures, and sending pilgrims back into their communities with fresh inspiration.

Sunnis and Shi'as

The preceding pages describe beliefs and practices of all Muslims, although vary-ing interpretations of the beliefs have always existed. Groups within Islam differ on other issues. After Muhammad's death, resentments over his succession began to divide the unity of the Muslim community into factions. The two main opposing groups have come to be known as the **Sunni**, who now comprise about eighty percent of all Muslims worldwide, and the **Shi'a** (adj. Shi'ite).

As discussed earlier, a caliph was elected to lead the Muslim community after Muhammad's death. The office became a lifetime appointment. The first three caliphs, Abu Bakr, Umar, and Uthman, were elected from among the Prophet's closest companions. The fourth was 'Ali, the Prophet's cousin and son-in-law. He was reportedly known for his holy and chivalrous qualities, but the dynasty of Umayyads never accepted him as their leader, and he was assassinated by a fanatic, a former member of his own party. 'Ali's son Husayn, grandson of the Prophet, challenged the legitimacy of the fifth caliph, the Umayyad Mu'awiyya. When Mu'awiyya designated his son Yazid as his successor, Husayn rebelled and was massacred in 680 by Yazid's troops in the desert of Karbala along with many of his relatives, who were also members of the Prophet's family. This martyrdom unified Shi'ite opposition to the elected successors and they broke away, claiming their legitimate line of succession through the direct descendants of the Prophet, beginning with 'Ali. The two groups are still separate.

Sunni Muslims form most of the population in Saudi Arabia, Egypt, Turkey, northern African countries, Pakistan, Afghanistan, Central Asian countries of the former Soviet Union, and Indonesia. Syria and Iraq have more mixed populations of Sunnis and Shi'as. The major Shi'a majority country is Iran.

Sunnis

Those who follow the elected caliphs are "the people of the Sunnah" (the sayings and practices of the Prophet, as collected under the Sunni caliphs). They consider themselves traditionalists, and they emphasize the authority of the Qur'an and the Hadith and Sunnah. They believe Muhammad died without appointing a successor and left the matter of successors to the **ummah**, the Muslim community. They look to the time of the first four "rightly guided caliphs" (Abu Bakr, Umar, Uthman, and 'Ali) as the golden age of Islam. They regard the caliph as the leader of worship and the administrator of the **Shari'ah**, the sacred law of Islam. Sunnis regard not only the life of the Prophet but also the lives of the rightly guided caliphs—who had heard the revelations of the Prophet firsthand and been inspired by his personal example—and a few other close companions of the Prophet as the models for the ideal Muslim.

The Shari'ah is based chiefly on the Qur'an and Sunnah of Muhammad, who was the first to apply the generalizations of the Qur'an to specific life situations. Religion is not a thing apart; all of life is to be integrated into the spiritual unity that is the central principle of Islam. The Shari'ah specifies patterns for worship (the Five Pillars of Islam) as well as detailed prescriptions for social conduct, to bring remembrance of God into every aspect of daily life and practical ethics into the fabric of society. These prescriptions include injunctions against drinking intoxicating beverages, eating certain meats, gambling and vain sports, sexual relations outside of marriage, and sexually provocative dress, talk, or actions. They also include positive measures, commanding justice, kindness, and charity. Women are given many legal rights, including the right to own property, to divorce (according to certain schools of law), to inherit, and to make a will. These rights, divinely decreed during the time of the Prophet, fourteen hundred years ago, were not available to women in the West until the nineteenth century. Polygyny is allowed for men who have the means to support several wives, to bring all women under the protection of a husband. Women are allowed to inherit only half as much as men because men have the obligation to support women financially. The faithful are enjoined to exercise justice and honesty in their relationships and business interactions, to manage their wealth carefully, and to avoid arrogance.

The Shari'ah is said to have had a transformative effect on Muhammad's community. Before Muhammad, the people's highest loyalty was to their tribe. Tribes made war on each other with few restraints. Women had no rights. Children were often killed at birth either because of poverty or because they were females in a male-dominated culture. People differed widely in wealth. Drunkenness and gambling were commonplace. Within a short time, Islam made great inroads into these trad-itions, shaping tribes into a spiritual and political unity with a high sense of ethics.

In the second century of Islam, the Abbasid dynasty replaced the Umayyads, who had placed more emphasis on empire-building and administration than on spirituality. At this point, there was a great concern for purifying and regulating social and political life in accord with Islamic spiritual tradition. Mechanisms for establishing the Shari'ah were developed. Since then, Sunnis have felt that as life circumstances change, laws in the Qur'an, Hadith, and Sunnah should be continually interpreted by a consensus of opinion and the wisdom of learned men and jurists. For example, a contemporary Muslim faces new ethical questions not specifically addressed in the Qur'an and Hadith, such as whether or not test-tube fertilization is acceptable. Divorce has always been addressed by the Shari'ah, but the conditions under which a wife may petition for divorce have been closely examined in recent years.

Careful study of the Qur'an and Sunnah as the basis for legal opinions is undertaken by the **ulama**, scholars who devote their lifetimes to developing this knowledge. The most renowned school for the training of the *ulama* is al-Azhar in Cairo. Founded in the tenth century, it is the world's oldest university. A **fatwa**, or legal opinion, from the scholars of al-Azhar is considered authoritative by Sunni Muslims around the world.

Shi'a

The Shi'a feel that 'Ali was the rightful original successor to the Prophet Muhammad. Several weeks before his death, the Prophet reportedly took 'Ali's hand and said, "Whoever I protect, 'Ali is also his protector. O God, be a friend to whoever is his friend and an enemy to whoever is his enemy." This is construed by the Shi'a as a veiled way of designating 'Ali as his successor. They feel that spiritual power was passed on to 'Ali, and that the caliphate is based on this spiritual as well as temporal authority. They are ardently devoted to the memory of Muhammad's close relatives: 'Ali, Fatima (the Prophet's beloved daughter), and their sons Hasan and Husayn. The martyrdom of Husayn at Karbala in his protest against the alleged tyranny, oppression, and injustice of the Umayyad caliphs is held up as a symbol of the struggle against human oppression. It is commemorated yearly as 'Ashura, on the tenth day of the month of Muharram. Participants in mourning processions cry and beat their chests or, in some areas, offer cooling drinks to the populace in memory of the martyred Husayn. Shi'ite piety places great emphasis on the stories told of 'Ali and Husayn's dedication to truth and integrity, even if it leads to personal suffering, in contrast to the selfish power politics ascribed to their opponents.

Rather than recognize the Sunni caliphs, the Shi'a pay allegiance to a succession of seven or twelve **Imams** (leaders, guides). The first three were 'Ali, Hasan, and Husayn. According to a saying of the Prophet acknowledged by both Sunni and Shi'a:

> I leave two great and precious things among you: the Book of Allah and my
> Household. If you keep hold of both of them, you will never go astray after me.[31]

"Twelver" Shi'a believe there were a total of twelve Imams, legitimate hereditary successors to Muhammad. The twelfth Imam, they believe, was commanded by God to go into an occult hidden state to continue to guide the people and return publicly at the Day of Resurrection as the Mahdi. A minority of the Shi'a, the Nizari Isma'ilis, recognize a different person as the seventh Imam. This line of Imams has continued to the present forty-ninth Imam, HRH Prince Karim Aga Khan IV.

Unlike the Sunni caliph, the Imam combines political leadership (if possible) with continuing the transmission of Divine Guidance. This esoteric religious knowledge was given by God to Muhammad, from him to 'Ali, and thence from each Imam to the successor he designated from 'Ali's lineage. It includes both the outer and inner meanings of the Qur'an. The Shari'ah is therefore interpreted for each generation by the Imam, for he is closest to the divine knowledge.

Sufism

As well as the two orthodox traditions within Islam—Sunni and Shi'a—there is an esoteric tradition, said to date back to the time of the Prophet. He himself was at once a political leader and a contemplative with a deep prayer life. He reportedly said every verse of the Qur'an has both an inner and an outer meaning. Around him was a group of about seventy people, who lived in his Medina mosque in voluntary poverty, detached from worldly concerns, praying night and day. After the first four caliphs, Muslims of deep faith and piety, both Sunni and Shi'a, were distressed by the increasingly secular, dynastic, wealth-oriented characteristics of Muhammad's Umayyad successors. **Sufism** (Arabic: *tasawwuf*), the mystical inner tradition of Islam, also involved resistance to the legalistic, intellectual trends within Islam in its early development.

Sufis have typically understood their way as a corrective supplement to orthodoxy. For their part, some orthodox Sunnis do not consider Sufis to be Muslims. Sufis consider their way a path to God that is motivated by longing for the One. In addition to studying the Qur'an, Sufis feel that the world is a book filled with "signs"—divine symbols and elements of beauty that speak to those who understand. The intense personal journeys of Sufis and the insights that have resulted from their truth-seeking have periodically refreshed Islam from within. Much of the allegorical interpretation of the Qur'an and devotional literature of Islam is derived from Sufism.

The early Sufis turned to asceticism as a way of deepening their piety. The Prophet had said: "If ye had trust in God as ye ought He would feed you even as He feeds the birds."[32] Muhammad himself had lived in poverty, reportedly gladly so. Complete trust in and surrender to God became an essential step in the journey. **Dervishes** (poor mendicant mystics) with no possessions, no attachments in the world, were considered holy people like Hindu *sannyasins*. But Sufi asceticism is based more on inner detachment than on withdrawal from the world; the ideal is to live with feet on the ground, head in the heavens.

To this early asceticism was added fervent, selfless love. Its greatest exponent was Rabi'a (c. 713–801). A mystic of Iraq, she scorned a rich man's offer of marriage, saying she did not want to be distracted for a moment from God. All her attention was placed on her Beloved. Rabi'a emphasized disinterested love, with no selfish motives of hope for paradise or fear of hell. When no veils of self exist, the mystic dissolves into the One she loves.

The Beloved is all, the lover just a veil
The Beloved is living, the lover a dead thing.

Jalal al-Din Rumi[33]

In absolute devotion, the lover desires *fana*, total annihilation in the Beloved. This Sufi ideal was articulated in the ninth century CE by the Persian Abu Yazid al-Bistami. He is said to have fainted while saying the Muslim call to prayer. When he awoke, he observed that it is a wonder that some people do not die when saying it, overwhelmed by pronouncing the name Allah with the awe that is due to the One. In his desire to be annihilated in God, al-Bistami so lost himself that he is said to have uttered pronouncements such as "Under my garment there is nothing but God,"[34] and "Glory be to Me! How great is My Majesty!"

The authorities were understandably disturbed by such potentially blasphemous statements. Sufis themselves knew the dangers of egotistical delusions inherent in the mystical path. There was strict insistence on testing and training by a sufficiently trained, tested, and illumined **murshid** (teacher) or **shaykh** (spiritual master). Advanced practices were taught only to higher initiates. It was through the *shaykh* that the **barakah** (blessing, sacred power) was passed down, from the *shaykh* of the *shaykh*, and so on, in a chain reaching back to Muhammad, who is said to have transmitted the *barakah* to 'Ali.

A number of **tariqas** (esoteric orders) evolved, one of which traced its spiritual lineage back to Junayd of Baghdad (d. 910 CE). He taught the need for constant purification, a continual serious examination of one's motives and actions. He also knew it was dangerous to speak openly of one's mystical understandings; the exoteric-minded might find them blasphemous, and those who had not had such experiences would only interpret them literally and thus mistakenly. He counseled veiled speech, and much Sufi literature after his time is couched in metaphors accessible only to mystics.

Despite such warnings, the God-intoxicated cared little for physical safety and exposed themselves and Sufism to opposition. The most famous case is that of Mansur al-Hallaj (c. 858–922). After undergoing severe ascetic practices, he is said to have visited Junayd. When the master asked, "Who is there?", his disciple answered, *"ana'l-Haqq"* ("I am the Absolute Truth," i.e., "I am God"). After Junayd denounced him, al-Hallaj traveled to India and through the Middle East, trying to open hearts to God. He wrote of the greatness of the Prophet Muhammad, and introduced into the poetry of divine love the simile of the moth that flies ecstatic into the flame and, as it burns up, realizes Reality.

Political maneuverings made a possible spiritual revival a threat to authorities back home, and they imprisoned and killed al-Hallaj for his *"ana'l-Haqq."* However, al-Hallaj is considered by many to be one of the greatest Muslim saints, for it is understood that he was not speaking in his limited person. Like the Prophet, who had reportedly said, "Die before ye die,"[35] al-Hallaj had already died to himself so that nothing remained but the One.

> *What's in your head—toss it away! What's in your hand—give it up! Whatever happens—don't turn away from it. . . . Sufism is the heart standing with God, with nothing in between.*
>
> *Abu Sa'id Abu al-Khayr*[36]

A more moderate Sufism began to make its way into Sunni orthodoxy through Abu Hamid al-Ghazali (1058–1111). He had been a prominent theologian but left his prestigious position for a life of spiritual devotion. Turning within, he discovered mystical truths, which saved him from his growing scepticism about the validity of religion. Like all mystics, he urged awareness of the certainty of death as an antidote to entanglements in worldly concerns.

Al-Ghazali's persuasive writings combined accepted Muslim theology with the assertion that Sufism is needed to keep the mystical heart alive within the tradition. By the fourteenth century, three sciences of religion were generally accepted by the orthodoxy: jurisprudence, theology, and mysticism.

Over the centuries, other elements have been added to Sufism. Some Sufis have embraced teachings from various religions, emphasizing that the Qur'an clearly states that the same Voice has spoken through all prophets. Shihabuddin Suhrawardi (1153–1191), for instance, combined many currents of Islam with spiritual ideas from the Zoroastrians of ancient Iran and the Hermetic tradition from ancient Egypt. His writings are full of references to the divine light and hierarchies of angels.

Although Sufi teachings and practices have been somewhat systematized over time, they resist doctrinal, linear specification. They come from the heart of mystical experiences which defy ordinary logic. Paradox, metaphor, the world of creative imagination, of an expanded sense of reality—these characteristics of Sufi thought are better expressed through poetry and stories.

Poetry has been used by Sufis as a vehicle for expressing the profundities and perplexities of relationship with the divine. The Turkish dervish Jalal al-Din Rumi (c. 1207–1273), by whose inspiration was founded the Mevlevi Dervish Order in Turkey (famous for its "Whirling Dervishes" whose dances lead to transcendent rapture), was a master of mystical poetry. He tells the story of a devotee whose cries of "O Allah!" were finally answered by God:

> *Was it not I that summoned thee to service?*
> *Did not I make thee busy with My name?*
> *Thy calling "Allah!" was My "Here am I,"*
> *Thy yearning pain My messenger to thee.*
> *Of all those tears and cries and supplications*
> *I was the magnet, and I gave them wings.*[37]

The aim of Sufism is to become so purified of self that one is a perfect mirror for the divine attributes. The central practice is called *dhikr*, or "remembrance." It consists of stirring the heart and piercing the solar plexus, seat of the ego, by movements of the head, while continually repeating *"la ilaha illa Allah,"* which Sufis understand in its esoteric sense: "There is nothing except God." Nothing in this ephemeral world is real except the Creator; nothing else will last. As the seventy thousand veils of self—illusion, expectation, attachment, resentment, egocentrism, discontent, arrogance—drop away over the years, this becomes one's truth, and only God is left to experience it.

The spread of Islam

In the time of Muhammad, Islam combined spiritual and secular power under one ruler. This tradition, which helped to unify the warring tribes of the area, was continued under his successors. Islam expanded phenomenally during the centuries after the Prophet's death, contributing to the rise of many great civilizations. The *ummah* became a community that spread from Africa to Indonesia. Non-Muslims have the impression that it was spread by the sword, but this was not typically the case. The Qur'an forbids coercion in religion, recommending instead that Muslims invite others to the Way by their wisdom, beautiful teaching, and personal example. Islam spread mostly by personal contacts: trade, attraction to charismatic Sufi saints, appeals to Muslims from those feeling oppressed by Byzantine and Persian rule, unforced conversions. There were some military battles conducted by Muslims over the centuries, but they were not necessarily for the purpose of spreading Islam, and many Muslims feel that wars of aggression violate Muslim principles.

Muhammad's non-violent takeover of Mecca occurred only two years before he died. It was under his successors that Islam spread through West Asia and far beyond. Only a year after Muhammad died, a newly converted Qurayshite, Khalid ibn al-Walid (d. 642), commanded a series of campaigns that within seven years had claimed the entire Arabian peninsula and Syria for Islam. Newly Islamic Arab armies quickly swept through the Sassanian Persian Empire, which had stood for twelve centuries. Defeated in battle in 637 CE, the Persian emperor fled, leaving the capital in Arab hands. Within ten years of the Prophet's death, a mere 4,000 horsemen commanded by Amr ibn al-As took the major cities of Egypt, centers of the Byzantine Empire. Another wave of conquest soon penetrated into Turkey and Central Asia, North Africa, and north through Spain, to be stopped in 732 CE in France at the battle of Tours. At this point, only a hundred years after Muhammad died, the Muslim *ummah* under the Umayyad caliphs was larger than the Roman Empire had ever been.

Muslims cite the power of the divine will to establish a peaceful, God-conscious society as the reason why this happened. By contrast with their strong convictions, the populations they approached were often demoralized by border fighting among themselves and by grievances against their rulers. Many welcomed them without a fight. For example, the Christians of Damascus expected Muslim rule to be more bearable than Byzantine rule, so they opened the city gates to the Muslim armies. Jerusalem and Egypt accepted the Muslims in similar fashion. Syrian Christians at Shayzar under Byzantine rule reportedly went out to meet the Muslim commander and accompanied him to their city, singing and playing tambourines. In Spain, Visigoth rule and taxation had been oppressive; the persecuted Jews were especially glad to help Islam take over. Both Christians and Jews often converted to Islam.

Some historians cite economic factors as an underlying motive for Arabs' expansion beyond their original territory. Although Islamic civilization did become quite opulent, the central leadership did not always support the far-reaching adventures. The conquered peoples were generally dealt with in the humane ways specified in the Qur'an and modeled by Muhammad in his negotiations with tribes newly subjected to Muslim authority.

Monotheistic followers of revealed traditions, Christians and Jews, who like Muslims were "people of the book," were treated as **dhimmis**, or protected people. They were allowed to maintain their own faith, but not to try to convert others to it. The Dome of the Rock was built on the site of the old Temple of the Jews in Jerusalem, honoring Abraham as well as Muhammad in the city that is still sacred to three faiths: Judaism, Christianity, and Islam.

The Umayyad caliphs had their hands full administering this huge *ummah* from Damascus, which they had made its capital. They tended to focus more on organizational matters than on the spiritual life. Some were also quite worldly; Walid II, for example, is said to have enjoyed a pool filled with wine so that he could swim and drink at the same time.

Islamic culture

Under the Abbasids, who took over the caliphate in 750 CE, Muslim rule became more Persian and cosmopolitan and Islamic civilization reached its peak. The capital was moved to the new city of Baghdad. No more territories were brought under centralized rule, and merchants, scholars, and artists became cultural heroes. A House of Wisdom was built, with an observatory, library, and an educational institution where Greek and Syriac manuscripts on subjects such as medicine, astronomy, mathematics, and philosophy were translated into Arabic. In Cairo, Muslims built in 972 CE the great university and mosque, Al-Azhar, which is still important in Muslim scholarship.

In its great cities, Islam went through a period of intense intellectual and artistic activity, absorbing, transmitting, and expanding upon the traditions of other cultures. For instance, from Persia, which was to become a Shi'ite stronghold, it adopted a thousand-year-old tradition of exquisite art and poetry. To these cultural borrowings Islam added its own innovations. The new system of nine Arabic numerals and the zero derived from Indian numbers revolutionized mathematics by liberating it from the clumsiness of Roman numerals. A love of geometry and a spiritual understanding of numbers, from the One to infinite divisions, provided the basis for beautifully elaborated art and architectural forms. Muslim scholars' research into geography, history, astronomy, literature, and medicine lifted these disciplines to unprecedented heights.

The pivotal institution of Islamic society was the *ulama*, whose primacy and influence were unchallenged. The *ulama* were not only guardians of the faith but also the pervasive force holding together Islamic society. They were *qadis* (judges), *muftis* (jurisconsults), guides and pastors of the artisans' guilds, spiritual leaders, mosque imams, state scribes, the sole teachers of the civil and military schools, and market inspectors. The major sources of their economic power and their independence from the state were religious and private endowments, run and controlled by the *ulama*.

Although Baghdad was the capital of the Abbasids, independent caliphates were declared in Spain and Egypt. Muslim Spain was led by successors to the Umayyads and became a great cultural center. Córdoba, the capital, had seven hundred mosques, seventy libraries, three hundred public baths, and paved streets. Europe, by contrast, was in its Dark Ages; Paris and London were only mazes of muddy alleys. Spanish Muslim scientists developed a prototype of a flying machine, mechanical clocks, and highly accurate astronomical clocks, many centuries before such inventions were introduced into Europe through translations of Arabic manuscripts.

Tunisia and Egypt comprised a third center of Islamic power: the Shi'ite Fatimid caliphate (so named because they claimed to be descendants of Muhammad's daughter Fatima). While otherwise known for their brilliant cultural and scientific accomplishments, under the troubled Fatimid caliph, al-Hakim (985–c. 1021), the Fatimids broke with Islamic tradition and persecuted *dhimmis*; they also destroyed the Church of the Holy Sepulcher in Jerusalem, provoking European Christian crusades to try to recapture the Holy Lands.

Crusading Christians fought their way to Jerusalem, which they placed under siege in 1099. When the small Fatimid garrison surrendered, the crusaders slaughtered the inhabitants of the holy city. Eyewitnesses recount the beheading of 70,000 captives at the al-Aqsa mosque, near the altar site of the ancient Jewish temple. Severed hands and feet were piled everywhere. Anti-crusading Muslims led by the famous Salah-al-Din (known in the West as Saladin) retook Jerusalem in 1187 and treated its Christians with the leniency of Islam's highest ideals for the conduct of war. But widespread destruction remained in the wake of the crusaders, and a reservoir of ill-will against Christians lingered, to be exacerbated centuries later by European colonialism in Muslim lands.

The Islamic period in Spain was known for its tolerance of Judaism. But during the thirteenth century, Christians took Spain and later instituted the dread Inquisition against those not practicing Christianity. By the beginning of the six-teenth century, an estimated three million Spanish Muslims had either been killed or had left the country.

Eastward expansion

Its westward advance stopped at Europe, Islam carried its vitality to the north, east, and south. Although Mongol invasions from Central Asia threatened, the Mongols were converted to Islam; so were the Turks. While Uzbek Khan, Mongol leader from 1313 to 1340, desired to spread Islam throughout Russia, he maintained tolerance toward the Christians in the conquered lands. He granted a charter to the Orthodox Metropolitan concerning their treatment: "Their laws, their Churches; their monasteries and chapels shall be respected; whoever condemns or blames this religion, shall not be allowed to excuse himself under any pretext but shall be punished with death."[38]

Similar tolerance toward other religions was practiced by the Muslim Turks, but in 1453 the Turks conquered Constantinople, the heart of the old Byzantine Empire, and renamed it Istanbul; Hagia Sophia was turned into a mosque even though it did not face Mecca. At its height, the Turkish Ottoman Empire domin-ated the eastern Mediterranean as well as the area around the Black Sea.

Farther east, Islam was carried into northern India, where Muslims destroyed some Hindu idols and temples but allowed the Hindu majority a protected *dhimmi* status. The Chishti Sufi saints drew people to Islam by their great love for God. "The heart of a mystic is a blazing furnace of love which burns and destroys every-thing that comes into it because no fire is stronger than the fire of love," declared Khwaja Muinuddin Chishti.[39]

Under the Muslim Moguls, the arts and learning flourished in India. In the ecumenical spiritual curiosity of the Emperor Akbar, who rose to the Mogul throne in 1556, representatives from many traditions—Hindu, Zoroastrian, Jain, Christian—were invited to the world's first interfaith dialogues. Eventually Akbar devised a new religion that was a synthesis of Islam and all these other religions, with himself as its supposedly enlightened head, but it died with him, and

Muslim orthodoxy gained ascendancy with his grandson, Aurangzeb.

Under British colonization of India, tensions between Hindus and Muslims were inflamed, partly to help Britain divide and rule. India gained its independence under the influence of Mahatma Gandhi, who was unable to devise a political solution to the concerns of Muslims fearing domination by a Hindu-majority government. In 1947, West and East Pakistan (the East section now the independent nation of Bangladesh) were partitioned off to be Muslim-ruled and predominantly populated by Muslims, while India was to be run by Hindus. The creation of Pakistan was one of the major contemporary attempts to create a model nation based on the principles of Islam. Mohammed Ali Jinnah, the London-educated lawyer who is regarded as its founder, conceived of Pakistan as a modern, democratic state in which women, minorities, and human rights would be respected, according to Islam's tenets of tolerance, compassion, and justice. Millions lost their lives trying to cross the borders between the two countries, and the strife between the two faiths continues. In December 1992, militant Hindus set off communal violence by destroying a mosque in Ayodhya, India, in the belief it had been built by the Moguls on the site of an ancient temple to Lord Rama. Another wave of Hindu violence against Muslims occurred in the state of Gujarat in 2002, in retaliation for the burning of a train illegally carrying Hindu volunteers to build a new Ram temple on the site.

The greatest concentration of Muslims developed even farther east, in Indonesia, where Muslim traders and missionaries may have first landed as early as the tenth century CE. Nearly ninety percent of the people are now Sunni Muslims, but despite recent violence between Muslims, Hindus, and Christians, the government has attempted to preserve a secular, pluralistic society rather than establish Islam as the state religion. In 1989, then-President Suharto stated: "We want each and all religions existing and developing in our country to achieve progress in an atmosphere of unity and mutual respect."[40]

China and the former Soviet Union encompass tens of millions of Muslims. To the south, Islam spread into Africa along lines of trade. In competition with Christianity, Islam sought the hearts of Africans and eventually won in many areas. Many converted to Islam; many others maintained some of their indigenous ways in combination with Islam. The prosperous Mali Empire was headed by a Muslim, who made an awe-inspiring pilgrimage to Mecca with a gold-laden retinue of 8,000 in 1324. As the spread of Islam encompassed an increasing diversity of cultures, *hajj* became important not only for individuals but also for the religion as a whole, holding its center in Mecca in the midst of worldwide variations.

Relationships with the West

Although Islam honors the prophets of all traditions, its own religion and prophet were denounced by medieval Christian Europe. Some people fear that the medieval "clash of civilizations" may be replayed in our times if ignorance, distrust, and fear lead to exclusivist, simplistic, and violent responses to the rapid changes in the modern globalized world. Christianity had considered itself the ultimate religion and had launched its efforts to bring the whole world under its wings. Islam felt the same way about its own mission. In the struggle for souls, the Church depicted Muhammad as an idol-worshiper, an anti-Christ, the Prince of Darkness. Islam was falsely portrayed as a religion of many deities, in which Muhammad himself was worshiped as a god (thus the inaccurate label "Muhammadanism"). Europeans watched in horror as the Holy Lands became Muslim and the "infidel" advanced into Spain and elsewhere in Europe. Even though Muslim scholars and artists preserved, shared, and advanced the classic civilizations while Europe was benighted, the wealth of Arabic culture was interpreted in a negative light.

By the nineteenth century, Western scholars began to study the Arabic classics, but the fear and loathing of Muhammad and Muslims remained. The ignorance about, and negative stereotyping of, Muslims continues today.

> Borrow the Beloved's eyes. Look through them and you'll see the Beloved's face
>   everywhere. . . .
> Let that happen, and things you have hated will become helpers.
>
> Jalal al-Din Rumi[41]

Although it had enjoyed great heights of culture and political power, the Muslim world fell into decline. It seems that the Mongol invasions were at least partly responsible, for they eradicated irrigation systems and libraries and killed scholars and scientists, erasing much of the civilization that had been built up over five hundred years. Some Muslims today feel spiritual laxness was the primary reason that some previously glorious civilizations became impoverished Third World countries. Another theory is that Muslims were simply overtaken by stronger, better-equipped military and economic powers, such as the Mongols in the thirteenth century, and subsequently the Europeans.

During the late eighteenth and early nineteenth centuries, many Muslim populations fell under European domination. From the mid-twentieth century onward, most gained their independence as states that had adopted certain Western ideals and practices. In many cases, they had let go of some aspects of their Muslim heritage, considering it a relic that prevented success in the modern world. Arabic was treated as an unimportant language; Western codes of law replaced the Shari'ah in social organization. But Muslims were not totally Westernized, and resumed local rule with little training for self-government and participation in a world economy dominated by industrial nations.

Societies that had been structured along traditional lines fragmented from the mid-nineteenth century onward, as wide-ranging programs of reforms and modernization were unleashed throughout the Muslim world. The local autonomy of the traditional Islamic society was swept away and replaced by centralized regulations of Western origin. Traditional schools, markets, guilds, and courts lost much of their reason for being.

Before the colonial forces moved out, foreign powers led by Britain helped to introduce a Jewish state in West Asia. After long and terrible persecution in many countries, Jewish Zionists sought resettlement in Palestine, which they considered their ancient homeland. But some historians allege that the chief motive of the countries supporting this claim was to protect European interests. Lord Palmerston of Britain suggested that a wealthy Jewish population transplanted to

Palestine, and highly motivated to protect itself, would prop up the decaying Ottoman Empire so that it could serve as a bulwark against Russian imperialism; the new Jewish presence in Palestine would also serve as a check against the attempts of Egypt to create a pan-Islamic state encompassing Egypt, Syria, and the Arabian peninsula.

Islam in the United States

Even as Muslims were feeling humiliated by foreign domination elsewhere, they were growing in numbers and self-pride within the United States. Islam is the fastest growing religion in the United States, and may now be the second largest religion in the country. Two-thirds of American Muslims are immigrants; one-third are converts, most of them African Americans.

Conversion to Islam by African Americans was encouraged early in the twentieth century as a form of separatism from white oppression. The Christianity espoused by the dominant white population was interpreted as part of the pattern of oppression, and awareness grew that many of the slaves who had been brought from West Africa had been of Muslim faith. A number of movements developed to bring the former slaves back to their suppressed ancestral faith. For instance, in 1913 Noble Drew Ali (1886–1929) began a movement, eventually called the Moorish Science Temple of America, that was designed to begin teaching the elements of the faith to African Americans and thus give them a strong sense of their own identity. Members were encouraged to adopt Noble Drew Ali's understanding of Muslim lifestyles, with modest dress, gender separation, traditional family structure, and community solidarity.

Other movements had a strong nation-building character. In particular, under the leadership of Elijah Muhammad, who proclaimed himself a messenger of God, tens of thousands of African Americans became "Black Muslims," calling themselves the Nation of Islam. However, faith in Elijah Muhammad himself was shaken by allegations about his sexual relationships with his secretaries. Some followers—especially the influential leader Malcolm X and Warith Deen Muhammad, son of Elijah Muhammad—developed contacts with mainstream Muslims in other countries and came to the conclusion that Elijah Muhammad's version of Islam was far removed from Muslim orthodoxy. They steered converts toward what they perceived as the true traditions of Islam and alliance with the world Muslim community.

Others of African American heritage, especially Minister Louis Farrakhan, current leader of the Nation of Islam, maintain Elijah Muhammad's more political focus on unifying against white oppression, despite Islam's strong tradition of non-racism. However, politicization of Islamic identity is probably not the main aspect of the growth of Islam. Many American Muslims embrace their religion as a bulwark of discipline and faith against the degradations of materialism. The Nation of Islam has played a strong role in combating violence and drug abuse in some inner cities, and members are encouraged to observe a disciplined "December Fast" in contrast to the commercial frenzy of the Christmas season.

The homes of African American Muslims become places of refuge from the surrounding culture, with Qur'anic inscriptions, prayer spaces, cleanliness and lack of clutter, and windows covered as privacy screens. Soon after birth, children are placed with their mothers on their prayer rugs and gradually learn to recite portions of the Qur'an. They are carefully trained in politeness to elders, modest dress, and proper behavior. The environment these children encounter in public schools is a great contrast to this traditional upbringing. Young Muslim girls are taunted about their headscarves, and sex education classes, which begin at an early age, are offensive to Muslim parents who do not accept dating and extra-marital sexuality for their children. Some African American Muslim parents thus attempt to home-school their children.

Muslim resurgence

The Muslim world had lost its traditional structure and was generally helpless against manipulations by foreign nations until it found its power in oil. In the 1970s, the predominantly Muslim oil-rich nations found that by banding together they could control the price and availability of oil. OPEC (the Organization of Petroleum Exporting Countries) brought greatly increased revenues into pre-viously impoverished countries and strengthened their self-image as well as their importance in the global balance of power.

As the wealth suddenly poured in, it further disrupted established living pat-terns. Analysts feel that some people may have turned back to a more conservative version of Islam in an effort to restore a personal sense of familiarity and stability amid the chaos of changing modern life; the increase in literacy, urbanization, and communications helped to spread revived interest in Islam. There was also the hope that Islam would provide the blueprint for enlightened rule, bringing spiritual values into community and politics as Muhammad had done in Medina. It is thought that the Prophet had intentionally tried to create a united community in which each Muslim is responsible for his fellow human beings, in which no one should be hungry or unfairly treated, and in which the leader of the community is a just and religious person.

Traditionally, Muslims have seen the world as divided into *dar al-Islam*, "the abode of Islam" (those places where Muslims are a majority and Shari'ah governs worldly life), *dar al-sulh*, "the abode of peace" (where Muslims are a minority but can live in peace and freely practice Islam), and *dar al-harb*, "the abode of conflict" (where Muslims are in the minority, struggling to practice Islam).

As overt colonialism wanes, the world has become divided into autonomous nation-states with strong central governments. In this process, forty-three primarily Islamic nation-states have been created. They differ greatly in culture and in the degree to which each society is ruled by Islamic ethics. But all are now being reconsidered as possible frameworks for *dar al-Islam*, within which the Muslim dream of religion-based social transformation might be accomplished. Those who seek to establish Islamic states in which the sovereignty of God is supreme are often now referred to as **Islamists**.

Tradition and modern life

The resurgence of Islam takes several forms. One is a call for a return to Shari'ah rather than secular law derived from European codes. The orthodox feel the world must conform to the divine law, rather than diluting the law to accommodate it to the material world. In Iran, for instance, an attempt has been made to shape every aspect of life according to Shari'ah. Fasting during Ramadan is strictly enforced in Saudi Arabia and Iran, and restaurants in many Muslim countries close during the fasting hours. In Muslim-dominated northern Nigeria, a 1999 Shari'ah ruling barred men and women from traveling in the same public vehicles, in an effort to combat immorality and crime.

Private behaviors are also becoming more traditional. In particular, to honor the Qur'anic encouragement of physical modesty to protect women from being molested, many Muslim women have adopted *hijab* (veiling), covering their bodies except for hands, face, and feet, as they had not done for decades. In Saudi Arabia, some wear not only head-to-toe black cloaks but also full veils over their faces without even slits for their eyes. Some Muslim women assert they like dressing more modestly so that men will not stare at them. Others feel men are simply treating women as slaves.

In some Muslim-majority countries, women are allowed to join the workforce only if they are veiled. In Iran, replacing more Westernized customs with Muslim moral codes, including veiling of women, has allowed women from conservative backgrounds to leave their homes and enter public life without antagonizing their families. Now that a great number of Iranian Muslim women have been educated and entered the workforce and politics, they are a formidable part of reformist efforts to challenge the control of the male clerical elite over social life. They have also become active participants in contemporary Iranian attempts to reconcile Islam with human rights and democracy.

Women's rights to divorce and to choose their own marriage partners are among the hotly debated issues in contemporary attempts to define Shari'ah. Shari'ah has been locally adapted to various societies over the centuries; to attempt to restore its original form is to deny the usefulness of its flexibility. Some customs thought to be Muslim are actually cultural practices not specified in the basic sources; they are the result of Islamic civilization's assimilation of many cultures in many places. Muhammad worked side-by-side with women, and the Qur'an encourages equal participation of women in religion and in society. Veiling and seclusion were absorbed from conquered Persian and Byzantine cultures, particularly their upper classes; peasant women could not carry out their physical work under veils or in seclusion from public view.

Muslim women scholars are now re-examining the Qur'an and Hadith to determine the historical realities and principles of women's issues that have long been hidden behind an exclusively male interpretation of the traditions.

A problem with applying Shari'ah as civil law is that some ethical issues that arise today did not exist in their present form when the legal codes were created or were not specifically addressed by the Qur'an or Hadith. Artificial birth control methods, for example, were not available. However, infanticide was mentioned by the Qur'an: "Do not kill your children for fear of poverty. We will provide for them and for you." Does this mean all forms of population control are forbidden, or should the overpopulation of the earth be a major consideration today? According to Islamic legal reasoning, the method for determining such ambiguous issues is to weigh all the likely benefits and disadvantages of a course of action and discourage it if the disadvantages outweigh the advantages. For Muslim intellectuals who want to retain their faith within the context of modern life, the process of *ijtihad* (reasoned interpretation, independent judgment by a qualified scholar) is critical.

The global family of Islam is not a political unit; its unity under Arab rule broke up long ago. There is as yet no consensus among Muslim-majority states about how to establish a peaceful, just, modern society based on basic Muslim principles. But there is widespread recognition that there are problems associated with modern Western civilization that should be avoided, such as crime, drug abuse, corruption of values, and unstable family life.

> *Today everyone cries for peace but peace is never achieved, precisely because it is metaphysically absurd to expect a civilization that has forgotten God to possess peace.*
>
> Seyyed Hossein Nasr[42]

Outreach and education

Another sign of Muslim resurgence is the increase in outreach, as Muslims become more confident of the value of their faith. Islam is the fastest growing of all world religions, with over 1400 million followers. New mosques are going up everywhere. Some Muslims who constitute a minority in their countries are trying to assert their rights to practice their religion by praying five times a day, leaving work to attend Friday congregational prayer at noon, and wearing traditional head-coverings. Special Islamic satellite channels offer alternatives to Western-oriented programming that Muslims find offensive, and also act as a force for international Muslim unity.

A third sign of Muslim resurgence is the increasing attention being given to developing educational systems modeled on Islamic thought. Islam is not anti-scientific or anti-intellectual; on the contrary, it has historically bridged reason and faith and placed a high value on developing both in order to tap into the full-ness of human potential. Western education has omitted the spiritual aspects of life, so Muslims consider it incomplete and imbalanced.

While there are many excellent Muslim educational institutions, the numerous *madrasas*, traditional religious schools, typically teach a narrow version of Islam, ignoring its sophisticated cultural and scientific heritage and nuanced philosophy. Because some of these schools have proved to be breeding grounds for militants, fanning hatred of the West, particularly among the poor rural students, they are coming under closer scrutiny. The Sustainable Development Policy Institute in Islamabad released a report in 2003 which identified a number of troubling features of textbooks and curricula in Pakistan, including distorted interpreations of history, insensitivity to the country's diverse religions, glorifying violence, encouraging prejudices toward women, religious minorities and other countries, and outdated teaching practices.[43]

Pakistan is revising its textbooks to correct such points. Similarly, Saudi Arabia has been criticized for giving distorted religious messages through its schools, and is revising its curricula and textbooks to promote peace and harmony. Efforts are being made in some countries to increase the accuracy and sensitivity of portrayals of Islam in the education of non-Muslims.

Philanthropic projects funded by Muslims are also on the increase. Most notably, the Ismaili Shia Muslim community, under the direction of its current imam, His Highness the Aga Khan, has organized many award-winning public service projects under the aegis of the Aga Khan Development Network, one of the world's largest development networks.

Islam in politics

The facet of Islam that is of greatest concern around the world to both Muslims and non-Muslims is its association with politics. There are more frequent references to Islam and Qur'anic statements by political leaders. Some use this approach to support the status quo and glorify Islam's past heights. In Arabic countries, others have used Muslim idealism to rally opposition to ruling elites who are perceived as being corrupt or tied to the West. Some charismatic leaders have used their own interpretations of Islam to ignite violent expressions of frustration and hatred against Western global domination. These include suicidal terrorist attacks against civilian targets by those who have been assured their self-sacrifice will earn them entry to Paradise, contrary to Quranic passages refusing suicide and upholding the value and sanctity of each human life.

A major issue is the understanding of **jihad**. All Muslims are enjoined by the Qur'an to carry on jihad. Commonly mistranslated as "holy war," it means "striving." The Prophet Muhammad is said to have distinguished between two types of jihad. Of these, he said, the Greater Jihad is the struggle against one's lower self. It is the internal struggle between wrong and right, error and truth, selfishness and selflessness, hardness of heart and all-embracing love. This is reflected in outer attempts to keep society in a state of harmonious order, as the earthly manifestation of Divine Justice. The Lesser Jihad is an external effort to protect the Way of God against the forces of evil. This jihad is the safeguarding of one's life, faith, livelihood, honor, and the integrity of the Muslim community. The Prophet Muhammad reportedly said that "the preferred jihad is a truth spoken in the presence of a tyrant."[44]

Jihad is not to be undertaken for personal gain. The Qur'anic revelations that apparently date from the Medina period when the faithful were being attacked by Meccans make it clear that

> *To those against whom* *(They are) those who have*
> *War is made, permission* *Been expelled from their homes*
> *Is given (to fight), because* *In defiance of right,*
> *They are wronged;—and verily,* *(For no cause) except*
> *God is Most Powerful* *That they say, "Our Lord*
> *For their aid;* *Is God."[45]*

The Qur'an gives permission to fight back under such circumstances, and Islamic Shari'ah law gives detailed limitations on the conduct of war and the treatment of captives, to prevent atrocities.

Muhammad is considered the prototype of the true ***mujahid***, or fighter in the Path of God, one who values the Path of God more than life, wealth, or family.

By fasting and prayer, he continually exerted himself toward the One, in the Greater Jihad. In defending the Medina community of the faithful against the attacking Meccans, he was acting from the purest of motives. It is believed that a true *mujahid* who dies in defense of the faith goes straight to Paradise, for he has already fought the Greater Jihad, killing his ego.

The absolute conviction that characterizes jihad derives from the recognition of the vast disparity between evil and the spiritual ideal, both in oneself and in society. Continual exertion is thought necessary in order to maintain a peaceful equilibrium in the midst of changing circumstances. Traditionalists and radicals have differed in how this exertion should be exercised in society.

In terms of the Lesser Jihad, support can be found in the Qur'an both for a pacifist approach and for active opposition to unbelievers. The Qur'an asserts that believers have the responsibility to defend their own faith as well as to remind unbelievers of the truth of God and of the necessity of moral behavior. In some passages, Muslims are enjoined simply to stand firm against aggression. In other passages, Qur'an suggests active opposition to people who do not believe in the supremacy of the one God:

> *Tumult and oppression are worse than slaughter.*
> *Nor will they cease fighting you*
> *Until they turn you back from your faith*
> *If they can. . . .*
> *Fight them on*
> *Until there is no more tumult or oppression*
> *And there prevail justice and faith in God.*[46]

In addition to varying interpretations of Quranic passages regarding jihad, contemporary use of violence in the name of Islam involves a complex of varying historical, cultural, and political circumstances in different countries. There is as yet no political unity among Muslim states, but growing antagonism toward the West is tending to create a political unity in opposition to pre-emptive use of American military power against Muslim countries in the "war against terror."

One of the leading radical voices that emerged in the twentieth century was that of the Egyptian scholar and activist Sayyib Qutb (1906–1966). After World War II, he saw most Muslim countries being controlled either by corrupt monarchies or by cruel military dictatorships. He had also visited the United States, but was disgusted by its culture. Devoutly religious, he saw the sex, violence, and selfish greed in Western culture as the headwaters of evil that was spreading around the world. His writings during years of imprisonment by the Egyptian government before they eventually executed him have been pivotal in the thinking of all later Islamists.

Similar thinking later came to the fore in Iran, one of the first Muslim-majority countries in which violence was used in recent times to advance the cause of Islam. In predominantly Shi'ite Iran, the Pahlavi Shahs had tried to rapidly modernize their country, turning it into a major military and industrial power. In the process, they eroded the authority of the *ulama*. A revolutionary leader emerged from this disempowered group, the Ayatollah Khomeini (c. 1900–1989), and swept the Shah from power in 1979. Khomeini insisted that social transformation should be linked with spiritual reformation, but made some drastic changes in interpretation of

Islam in order to justify violent revolutionary behavior. He also attempted to export his revolution to other Muslim countries with Shi'ite populations that could carry on the work. He labeled Iraq "atheist" in response to the war initiated by Iraq against Iran over contested oilfields, denounced predominantly Sunni Saudi Arabia for its ties to the West, and inspired some Lebanese Shi'a to see their political struggle against Christians and Jews as part of a great world battle between Islam and the forces of Western imperialism and Zionism. He issued a *fatwa* (legal opinion) that Indian-born British author Salman Rushdie could be sentenced to death under Islamic law, because his novel, *The Satanic Verses*, seemed to defame the Prophet and his wives. Many people died in riots over the still-controversial book.

Khomeini's call for governmental change was not heeded, so radicals resorted to sabotage and terrorism as their most powerful weapons. Their surprise attacks on civilians tended to turn world opinion against Islam, rather than promoting its ideals. More moderate leadership is now in power in Iran.

Iraq has also seen Islam used as a rallying point for political power. When Saddam Hussein of Iraq tried to re-annex Kuwait, from which Iraq and Saudi Arabia had been separated in 1922 by a "divide and rule" decision of the occupying British forces, Islam was cast as a political football by both sides in the Gulf War. Hussein, an Arab nationalist, resorted to Islam as a means of mass mobilization against what he saw as Western intrusion in the Gulf. After the Gulf War, years of economic sanctions by the United Nations against Iraq over continuing suspicion of its military intentions created such hardships for the populace that Iraqis referred to the sanctions as a means of genocide.

Then the United States launched massive bombings of Iraq in 2003 in a campaign it said would "shock and awe" the Iraqi regime and liberate the people from the tyrannical rule of Saddam Hussein, as well as saving the world from what it claimed were Iraq's massive stockpiles of weapons of mass destruction. By contrast, many Muslims around the world perceived the American-led attacks and occupation of the country as an unprovoked attack on innocent Muslim civilians as well as an attempt to control its oil resources. No such weapons of mass destruction were found. Terrorist activity has now increased in Iraq and elsewhere in protest at the American-led invasion, and tens of thousands of Iraqi civilians have been killed in the chaotic aftermath of U.S. bombing. When Saddam Hussein was hanged at the end of 2006, many Muslims regarded him as a martyr for his resistance to American power.

In Afghanistan during the 1980s, the United States supported armed Muslim militants—including Osama bin Laden, the Saudi leader who ran terrorist-training camps in rural Afghanistan—to help them drive out the Soviet Union. When the Russian troops left, Afghanistan collapsed into factional fighting and chaos, from which emerged oppressive control by the Taliban from 1996 to 2001. Theirs was an extreme and exclusivist view of the ideal Muslim state. They discarded all secular laws and replaced them with their interpretation of Shari'ah. To deter crime, they organized public spectacles in which the hands of thieves were amputated and adulterers were whipped. While they succeeded in bringing a certain orderliness to the country, their methods outraged the outside world and contradicted the Prophet's insistence on compassion and tolerance. They kept women out of the workplace, denied them education, and insisted that they wear head-to-toe *burqas*. The tenacious Revolutionary Association of the Women of Afghanistan resisted the anti-women regimes of both the Taliban and other ruling factions in Afghanistan, documenting the raping, killing, and kidnapping of women by militia members as an instrument of social repression.

Under heavy military attack by the United States, the Taliban's political power in Afghanistan was broken. Hundreds of women in the capital city of Kabul shed their *burqas* publicly, demanding the right to work, education for their daughters, and a voice in politics. While a coalition backed by the United States tries to maintain order, based on a constitution that attempts to combine the teachings of the Qur'an with democracy, the country is still torn and poverty-stricken.

Since 1932, Saudi Arabia has been under the absolute monarchical control of the huge al-Sa'ud family. Friendly to the West and using its oil wealth lavishly, the regime is often criticized for exposing the populace to the corrupting influence of Western culture by allowing Western troops on its soil. Despite the plush modern lifestyles and technologies of the elite, the country is religiously conservative, harkening to the ideas of the eighteenth-century legal scholar and reformer Muhammad ibn 'Abd al-Wahhab, who urged discarding all practices not specifically approved by the Qur'an and Sunnah. Whereas **Wahhabism** has been recently blamed as a source of everything from fundamentalist interpretations of the Qur'an to violent terrorist movements, study of Ibn 'Abd al-Wahhab's voluminous writings shows that he did not use the Qur'an as justification for holy war. Wahhabism has also been blamed for severe oppression of women, including Saudi Arabia's insistence that women be covered by a full *burqa* from head to toe and ban on women's driving cars or leaving home unless accompanied by a close male relative. But current scholarship suggests such restrictions stem from local customs and laws rather than Ibn 'Abd al-Wahhab's life and writings, which reflect Muhammad's concern for women's rights.

The most well-known self-styled jihadi in the world is Osama bin Laden, an exiled member of the Saudi aristocracy. In his extremist mixture of religion with politics, martyrdom is an heroic cult, the world is strictly divided into good and evil sides, destruction of property and lives is justified, and the faithful are urged to undertake jihad on a global scale. Bin Laden's militant organization, Al Qaeda, is thought to be responsible for many acts of terrorism around the globe, including the devastating September 11, 2001 attacks on the World Trade Center and Pentagon in the United States which set in motion a sea-change in relationships between Muslims and non-Muslims everywhere. Al Qaeda's agenda is to strike back at the United States for its support for Israel and its intrusive presence in the Arabian peninsula, which bin Laden and others interpret as non-Muslim control over Muslim lands.

Contrary to United States government predictions, elimination of particular Al Qaeda leaders has not ended the movement, and its highly motivated operatives in many countries seem to be willing to risk their lives to continue the struggle against Western cultural and political domination.

Similarly, the 2004 Israeli assassination of Sheikh Ahmed Yassin, leader of the anti-Israeli grassroots Palestinian welfare organization Hamas, led to his replacement by a greater hardliner. When he, too, was assassinated less than a month later, the leadership went underground but violence further increased nonetheless, with Palestinian militants pledging "100 retaliations" for his death.[47] Before his assassination, Yassin had said, "The Palestinian people do not have Apache helicopters or F-16s (fighter-bombers) or tanks or missiles. The only thing they can have is themselves to die as martyrs."[48]

At present, despite attempts at encouraging dialogue, the major trend is an increase in tensions between Muslims and non-Muslims. Terrorist activities that have killed civilians have brought a backlash of anti-Muslim sentiments, with growing perception of Islam as a religion encouraging violence and fanaticism. The United States's "war on terrorism" has brought an increase in acts of terrorism and made it more difficult for moderate Muslim leaders to hold their ground against critics within their countries. As Islamophobia grows among non-Muslims, many leading Muslims are trying to explain to them that Islam does not equal violence.

The Qur'an permits the jihad of violence only under specific conditions. To fight, people must have been deprived of their right to live and support themselves. The action must be undertaken not by individuals but by the collective wisdom of the Muslim community. *Jihadis* are never allowed to harm women, children, or unarmed civilians. They cannot wilfully destroy property. The tactics of terrorists are therefore not permitted by the Qur'an. In general, relations with people of other religions are to be as tolerant as possible:

> *Do not argue with the followers of the earlier revelations otherwise than in a most kindly manner—unless it be such of them as are bent on evil-doing—and say: We believe in that which has been bestowed from on high upon us, as well as that which has been bestowed upon you; for our God and your God is one and the same, and it is unto Him that we all surrender ourselves. (Holy Qur'an 29:46)*

Nevertheless, after a long history of foreign domination which is now being repeated by the spread of Western culture and military might, many Muslims are so distressed they are willing to offer their lives as suicide bombers in the hopes that the world will pay attention to their grievances.

Particularly after September 11, 2001, and terrorist bombings in Madrid in 2004 and London in 2005, there have been hate crimes against Muslims as a result of a renewed idea among non-Muslims that Islam breeds violence and fanaticism. Suspicion of Muslims has grown to the extent that imams have been removed from airline flights for performing their prayers, France has outlawed Muslim headscarves in public schools in fear of Muslims' different communal identity, and the British government has proposed forbidding Muslim students to wear full-face veils in class, on the grounds that seeing a woman with veiled face makes non-Muslims "feel uncomfortable" and even fear that an intruder might be hiding behind the veil.[49]

Alongside such reactions, there are also attempts on the part of both Muslim and non-Muslim scholars at deeper understanding of the complex mixtures of religion with politics.

Islam for the future

Challenged to explain Islam to its critics, Muslim scholars and intellectuals are meeting at global conferences to formulate unified responses to current issues. There is a tendency toward rapprochement between Sunnis and Shi'as at some levels, with the understanding that their differences are not so much matters of religious doctrine as of historical conflicts over leadership. Religious modernists, Islamists, and secularists are all trying to understand the roots of extremism and to seek new ways of relating to and even shaping the rapidly-changing world. They feel that extremism is undermining Islam by contradicting its principles and spreading hatred for the religion.

While media attention is centered on sensational manifestations of Islamism in present-day societies, these deeper currents of thought are forward-looking, exploring how Islam can help to shape a new social order in the world.

Mahmoon-al-Rasheed, Founder of the Comprehensive Rural Educational, Social, Cultural and Economic Center in Bangladesh, maintains there is violence within and between nations because people have not developed a sense of duty toward each other and have not recognized how inseparably all people are related to each other. He proposes that Islamic values are not aimed at creating a political state but rather a harmoniously integrated world society, for:

> We cannot begin to realize our full potential until we have achieved a community which knows no limit but that of human society and renders all obedience to a Law common to all.[50]

> If one knows the true meaning of Islam, there will be no wars. All that will be heard are the sounds of prayer and the greetings of peace. Only the resonance of God will be heard. That is the ocean of Islam. That is unity. That is our wealth and our true weapon. Not the sword in your hand.[51]

Review questions

1. Outline Muhammad's life story, including dates, places, religious experiences, wars, his character, and his education.
2. Explain the Five Pillars of Islam, the ways they are practiced, and the purpose of each.
3. What are the most important religious themes and people that are common to Islam, Judaism, and Christianity?

Discussion questions

1. Why do you think, of all possibilities, "submission" (as distinct from "enlightenment" or "salvation," for example) is the major theme of Islam? What various forms does it take?
2. Do you think Islam promotes violence more or less than any other religion?
3. Are there good reasons for thinking that Islam and the West are engaged in a "clash of civilizations" or not?

CHAPTER 10
SIKHISM

"By the Guru's grace shalt thou worship Him"

Another great teacher made his appearance in northern India in the fifteenth century CE: Guru Nanak. His followers were called **Sikhs**, meaning "disciples, students, seekers of truth." In time, he was succeeded by a further nine enlightened Gurus, ending with Guru Gobind Singh (1666–1708). Despite the power of these Gurus, the spiritual essence of Sikhism is little known outside India and its diaspora (dispersed communities), even though Sikhism is the fifth largest of all world religions. Many Sikhs understand their path not as another sectarian religion but as a statement of the universal truth within, and transcending, all religions. Their beliefs and practices have been interpreted as an offshoot of Hinduism or a synthesis of the Hindu and Muslim traditions of northern India, but Sikhism has its own unique quality, independent revelation, and history. As awareness of Sikh spirituality spreads, Sikhism is becoming a global religion, although it does not actively seek converts. Instead, it emphasizes the universality of spirituality and the relevance of spirituality in everyday life.

The *sant* tradition

Before Guru Nanak, Hinduism and Islam had already begun to draw closer to each other in northern India. One of the foremost philosophers in this trend was the Hindu saint Ramananda, who held theological discussions with teachers from both religions. But a deeper marriage occurred in the hearts of *sants*, or "holy people," particularly Sufi mystics, such as Shaikh Farid, and Hindu *bhaktas*, such as Sri Caitanya. They shared a common cause in emphasizing devotion to the Beloved above all else. Many of them were from lower castes, but their spiritual realization was of great heights. They were basically non-sectarian monotheists who did not accept ritualism or casteism.

The most famous of the bridges between Hindu and Muslim is the fifteenth-century weaver Kabir (1440–1518). He was the son of Muslim parents and the disciple of Ramananda. Rather than taking the ascetic path, he remained at work at his loom, composing songs about union with the Divine that are at once earthly and sublime. He could easily transcend theological differences between religions, for he was opposed to outward forms, preferring ecstatic personal intimacy with God. Speaking for the One, he wrote:

O human, where dost thou seek Me?
Lo! I am beside thee.
I am neither in temple nor in mosque:

> *I am neither in Kaaba nor in Kailash:*
> *Neither am I in rites and ceremonies; nor in yoga and renunciation.*
> *If thou art a true seeker, thou shalt at once see Me: thou shalt meet Me in a moment*
> *   of time.*
> *Kabir says, "O Sadhu! God is the breath of all breath."[1]*

Guru Nanak

When Guru Nanak (1469–c. 1539) was born, the area of northern India called the Punjab was half-Muslim, half-Hindu, and ruled by a weak Afghan dynasty. For centuries, it had been the lane through which outer powers fought their way into India. In 1398, the Mongolian leader Tamerlane slaughtered and sacked Punjabis on his way to and from Delhi. Toward the end of Nanak's life, it was the Mughal emperor Babur who invaded and claimed the Punjab. This casting of the Punjab as a perpetual battleground became a crucial aspect of Sikhism.

What Sikhs believe about the life of Guru Nanak is based not so much on historic records as on ***janam-sakhis***—traditional stories about his life. The earliest collection of these was probably written down in the seventeenth century; others were written from the eighteenth to twentieth centuries. From historians' point of view, they reflect the biases and concerns of their times, such as early seventeenth-century opposition to the ritualism of Brahmanic Hinduism, and they recount many miraculous happenings that cannot be historically verified. The picture of Guru Nanak that has been handed down is thus a record of how he has been remembered by the faithful.

According to the *janam-sakhis*, Nanak was little concerned with worldly things. As a child he was of a contemplative nature, resisting the formalities of his Hindu religion. Even after he was married, it is said that he roamed about in nature and gave away any money he had to the poor. At length he took a job as an accountant, but his heart was not in material gain.

When Nanak was thirty, his life was transformed after immersion in a river, from which it is said he did not emerge for three days. Some people now think he was meditating on the opposite side, but in any case he could not be found until he suddenly appeared in town, radiant. According to one account, he had been taken into the presence of God, who gave him a bowl of milk to drink, saying that it was actually nectar (*amrit*) which would give him "power of prayer, love of worship, truth and contentment."[2] The Almighty sent him back into the world to redeem it from Kali Yuga (the darkest of ages). Later Nanak sang:

> *Me, the worthless bard, the Lord has blest with Service.*
> *Be it night or day, many a time He gives His call,*
> *And calls me verily into His presence.*
> *And there I praise Him and receive the robe,*
> *And the Nectar-Name [of God] becomes my everlasting food.[3]*

According to the *janam-sakhis*, after Nanak's disappearance in the river in 1499, he began traveling through India, the Himalayas, Afghanistan, Sri Lanka, and Arabia, teaching in his own surprising way. When people asked him whether he would follow the Hindu or Muslim path, he replied, "There is neither Hindu nor Mussulman [Muslim], so whose path shall I follow? I shall follow God's path. God is neither Hindu nor Mussulman."[4] Nanak mocked the Hindu tradition of throwing sacred river water east toward the rising sun in worship of their ancestors—he threw water to the west. If Hindus could throw water far enough to reach their ancestors thousands of miles away in heaven, he explained, he could certainly water his parched land several hundred miles distant in Lahore by throwing water in its direction. Another tradition has it that he set his feet toward the Ka'bah when sleeping as a pilgrim in Mecca. Questioned about this rude conduct, he is said to have remarked, "Then kindly turn my feet toward some direction where God is not."

Guru Nanak emphasized three central teachings as the straight path to God: working hard in society to earn one's own honest living (rather than withdrawing into asceticism and begging); sharing from one's earnings with those who are needy; and remembering God at all times as the only Doer, the only Giver. Encouraging people to stay in the world and to help others rather than live a life of detachment in search of spiritual fulfillment, at the end of his travels Guru Nanak settled with his family as a farmer. The multitudes of *sikhs* who came to him contributed foods or labor to a free community kitchen in which there were no caste distinctions. The Guru encouraged them to live a disciplined life of rising early in the morning to praise God and working hard to support themselves and share with those in need. To a society that stressed distinctions of caste, class, gender, and religions, Guru Nanak introduced the idea of a social order based on equality, justice, and service to all, in devotion to the One God whom he perceived as formless, pervading everywhere.

Nanak's commitment to practical faith, as opposed to external adherence to religious formalities, won him followers from both Hinduism and Islam. Before he died, they argued over who would dispose of his body. According to the *janam-sakhis*, he told Muslims to place flowers on one side of his body, Hindus on the other; the side whose flowers remained fresh the next day could bury or cremate him. The next day they raised the sheet that had covered his body and found nothing beneath it; all the flowers were still fresh, leaving only the fragrance of his being.

Oh my mind, love God as a fish loves water:
The more the water, the happier is the fish,
*   the more peaceful his mind and body.*
He cannot live without water even for a moment.
God knows the inner pain of that being without water.

Guru Nanak[5]

The succession of Gurus

There were eventually a total of ten Sikh Gurus, all of whom were thought to be transmitting the spiritual light of Nanak. Before he passed on, Guru Nanak passed his spiritual authority to Lehna, previously a devotee of the goddess Durga. Lehna had become so dedicated to Guru Nanak's mission that the Guru gave him the name Angad—a part of his body (*ang*). Although the spiritual transmission from Guru Nanak reportedly made him so powerful that he became famous for healing incurable diseases such as leprosy, Guru Angad (1504–1552) was a model of humility and service to the poor and needy. He continued the tradition of *langar* and served the people with his own hands. One of the many stories told of his humility concerns an ascetic who was jealous of the Guru's popularity. The monsoon rains which were essential for the crops had not come, so the ascetic used the opportunity to turn the farmers against Guru Angad. He taunted them that if the Guru was so powerful, he should call for rain. The desperate villagers begged Guru Angad to do so, but he replied that one should not interfere with God's ways; rain would come only when God so willed. The ascetic persisted in turning the people against him, telling them that he himself would magically bring the rains if they would get rid of the Guru. Thus the people drove Guru Angad away. Agreeably, he left the village. Refused shelter anywhere nearby, he settled in a forest. Thereafter the ascetic fasted and tried all his mantras, but the rains did not come. At last, Amar Das, who later became the third of the Sikh Gurus, learned of the situation and reproached the villagers for forsaking the sun for the light of a small lamp. Recognizing their mistake, the villagers begged Guru Angad to forgive them and return to the village. He did so, amid great rejoicing, and the rains came.

The Third and Fourth Gurus, Amar Das and Ram Das, developed organizational structures for the growing Sikh **Panth** (community) while setting personal examples of humility. Ram Das founded the holy city of Amritsar, within which the Fifth Guru, Guru Arjun Dev (1536–1606), built the religion's most sacred shrine, the Golden Temple. The Fifth Guru also compiled the sacred scriptures of the Sikhs, the **Adi Granth** (original holy book, now known as the **Guru Granth Sahib**), from devotional hymns composed by Guru Nanak, the other Gurus, and Hindu and Muslim saints, including spiritual figures from low castes. Among the latter are holy people such as Bhagat Ravi Das, a low-caste Hindu shoemaker who achieved the heights of spiritual realization. His powerful poetry incorporated into the Guru Granth Sahib includes this song:

> *When I was, You were not.*
> *When You are, I am not.*
> *As huge waves are raised in the wind in the vast ocean,*
> *But are only water in water,*
> *O Lord of Wealth, what should I say about this delusion?*
> *What we deem a thing to be,*
> *It is not, in reality.*
> *It is like a king falling asleep on his throne*
> *And dreaming that he is a beggar.*
> *His kingdom is intact,*
> *But separating from it, he suffers. . . .*
> *Says Ravi Das, the Lord is nearer to us than our hands and feet.*[6]

Emperor Akbar visited the Third and Fourth Gurus and was very pleased with the universalism of the Guru Granth Sahib. But his son and successor, Jehangir, was jealous of Guru Arjun Dev's popularity among Muslims, and thus had him tortured and executed in 1606 on a false charge. It is said that Guru Arjun Dev remained calmly meditating on God as he was tortured by heat, with his love and faith undismayed. His devotional hymns include words such as these:

Merciful, merciful is the Lord.
Merciful is my master.
He blesses all beings with His bounties.
Why waverest thou, Oh mortal? The Creator Himself shall protect you.
He who has created you takes care of you. . . .
Oh mortal, meditate on the Lord as long as there is breath in your body.[7]

To protect Sikhism and defend the weak of all religions against tyranny, the Sixth Guru, Hargobind (1595–1644), established a Sikh army, carried two swords (one symbolizing temporal power, the other, spiritual power), and taught the people to defend their religion. The tender-hearted Seventh Guru, Har Rai (1630–1661), was a pacifist who never used his troops against the Mughals. He taught his Sikhs not only to feed anyone who came to their door, but also to:

do service in such a way that the poor guest may not feel he is partaking of some charity but as if he had come to the Guru's house which belonged to all in equal measure. He who has more should consider it as God's trust and share it in the same spirit. Man is only an instrument of service: the giver of goods is God, the Guru of us all.[8]

The Eighth Guru, Har Krishan (1656–1664), succeeded to Guru Nanak's seat when he was five years old and died at the age of eight. When taunted by Hindu *pandits* (learned men) the "Child Guru" reportedly touched a lowly deaf and dumb Sikh watercarrier with his cane, whereupon the watercarrier expounded on the subtleties of the Hindu scripture, *Bhagavad-Gita*.

The ninth master, Guru Teg Bahadur (c. 1621–1675), was martyred. According to Sikh tradition, he was approached by Hindu *pandits* who were facing forced conversion to Islam by the Mughal emperor, Aurangzeb. The emperor viewed Hinduism as a totally corrupt, idolatrous religion, which did not lead people to God; he had ordered the destruction of Hindu temples and mass conversion of all Hindus, beginning in the north with Kashmir. Reportedly, one of the Kashmiri *pandits* dreamed that only the Ninth Guru, the savior in Kali Yuga, could save the Hindus. With the firm approval of his young son, Guru Teg Bahadur told the *pandits* to tell their oppressors they would convert to Islam if the Sikh Guru could be persuaded to do so. Imprisoned and forced to witness the torture and murder of his aides, the Ninth Guru maintained the right of all people to religious freedom. Aurangzeb beheaded him before a crowd of thousands. His son later wrote, "He has given his head, but not his determination."[9]

The martyred Ninth Guru was succeeded by his young son, who became the tenth master, Guru Gobind Singh (1666–1708). It was he who turned the intimidated Sikhs into saint-soldiers. In 1699 he reportedly told an assembly of Sikhs that the times were so dangerous that he had developed a new plan to give the community strength and unity. Total surrender to the master would be necessary, he said, asking for volunteers who would offer their heads for the cause of protecting religious ideals. One version of what happened next comes from

Abu-ul-Durani, who was reportedly a Hindu Brahmin who had converted to Islam and became a spy for the Mughal Emperor Aurangzeb. He wrote to the emperor that the Guru severed the heads of each volunteer with his sword in front of the congregation. The Guru then stitched the heads back onto different bodies, mixing their castes and transforming their identities, and covered the lifeless bodies with a cloth. He spent an hour and a half stirring water with a double-edged sword in an iron bowl and reciting hymns, and his wife added something to the water. The Guru then lifted the cloth off each body, poured holy water into the mouth, hair, and body, and demanded, "Say: 'The Khalsa is God's, and the victory is God's!'" whereupon each one arose and did so. The Guru called them his Five Beloved Ones (*Panj Piaras*).

Sikhs believe the willingness of the five men to sacrifice themselves for the Guru's mission was proven, and the **amrit** (nectar-like holy water) prepared by Guru Gobind Singh turned his followers into heroes, with sugar added by his wife symbolizing the ideal that they would also be compassionate. The Five Beloved Ones became models for Sikhs. It is noteworthy that they came from the lowest classes and different geographic areas.

After initiating the first five, the Guru (whose name up to that time was Gobind Rai) established a unique Guru–Sikh relationship by asking that they initiate him—thus underscoring the principle of equality among all Sikhs. The initiated men were given the surname *Singh* ("lion"); the women were all given the name *Kaur* ("princess") and treated as equals. Guru Gobind Rai took the name of Guru Gobind Singh. He called the initiates **Khalsa** (Pure Ones), a community pledged to a special code of personal discipline. According to Sikh belief about what happened in 1699, they were sworn to wear five distinctive symbols of their dedication: unshorn hair, a comb to keep it tidy, drawstring underbreeches for modesty, a small sword in a sheath symbolizing dignity and the willingness to stand up for justice and protection of the weak, and an iron bracelet worn as a personal reminder that one is a servant of God, and perhaps also offering some protection to the wrist in hand-to-hand combat.

These "**Five Ks**" (so called because all the words begin with a "k" in Punjabi) have been interpreted as proud hallmarks of Sikh identity dating from the birth of the Khalsa in 1699. They distinguished Sikhs from Muslims and Hindus, supporting the assertion that Sikhism constituted a third path with its own right to spiritual sovereignty. All these innovations are thought to have turned the meek into warriors capable of shaking off Mughal oppression and protecting freedom of religion; the distinctive dress made it impossible for the Khalsa to hide from their duty by blending with the general populace. In Sikh history, their bravery was proven again and again.

However, to interpret the Five Ks only as symbols of power and separate identity is to overlook the spiritual and egalitarian aspects of Sikhism. By mandating the same symbolic dress for people of all castes, both women and men, Sikhs gave both genders and all castes equal importance, contrary to Indian cultural traditions. There may also be significant spiritual symbols embedded in the Five Ks. The sword, for instance, is often used in the Guru Granth Sahib as a metaphor for divine wisdom that cuts through ignorance and egocentrism. The devotee who wields it—and even the sword itself—is commonly referred to in female terms. For example, "By taking up the sword of knowledge, she fights against her mind and merges with her self."[10] Uncut hair is important to observant Sikhs because through it they feel a close inner relationship to Guru Gobind Singh, who called it his "divine stamp."

It is thought that Guru Gobind Singh also commanded his Khalsa to follow a particular disciplinary code, including eschewing hair-cutting, adultery, tobacco, and the meat of animals slowly bled to death in Muslim fashion. Scholars debate the historicity of various versions of the code of conduct now in use, some of which contain hundreds of rules.

Guru Gobind Singh ended the line of bodily succession to Guruship. As he was passing on in 1708, he transferred his authority to the Adi Granth rather than to a human successor. Thenceforth, it was called the Guru Granth Sahib—the living presence of the Guru embodied in the sacred scripture, to be consulted by the congregation for spiritual guidance and decision-making.

As the Mughal Empire began to disintegrate and Afghans invaded India, the Sikhs fought for their identity and sovereignty, as well as to protect Hindu and Muslim women from the attackers, and to protect freedom of religion in the country. At the end of the eighteenth century and beginning of the nineteenth century under Maharaja Ranjit Singh, they formed the Sikh Empire, a non-sectarian government noted for its tolerance toward Muslims, despite the history of oppression by the Muslim rulers. Maharaja Ranjit Singh is said to have been unusually kind to his subjects and to have humbly accepted chastisement by the Sikh religious authorities for his rather immoral private life. The Sikh Empire attempted to create a pluralistic society, with social equality and full freedom of religion. It also blocked the Khyber Pass against invaders. The empire lasted only half a century, for the British subdued it in 1849.

Resistance to oppression became a hallmark of Sikhism, for the times were grim for India's people. Despite heavy losses, Guru Gobind Singh's outnumbered Sikhs began the protection of the country from foreign rule, a process that continued into the twentieth century. During the Indian struggle against British rule, despite their military abilities Sikhs set heroic examples of non-violent resistance to oppression. One story tells how British police began arresting, then beating and killing, Sikhs who went to Guru ka Bagh, a garden and shrine, to collect firewood for the community free kitchen. Every day a new wave of one hundred Sikhs came voluntarily to suffer fierce beatings and perhaps even be killed, without a murmur except for the Name of God on their lips, to resist injustice.

At one point, Sikh political prisoners arrested at Guru ka Bagh were being shifted by train. The Sikh community in Hasanavdal asked the stationmaster there to stop the train so they could offer food to the prisoners. He refused, saying it was a special train and would not stop at Hasanavdal. Determined to care for the prisoners, three leading Sikhs told the *sangat* (congregation) to bring food and then lie down on the tracks to force the train to stop. It ran over them, crushing their bodies, and then stopped. As the *sangat* tried to help the dying martyrs, one of them ordered, "Don't care for us. Feed the prisoners." Thus the *langar* (community meal) was served to the prisoners on the train, and the Sikhs who had laid their bodies on the track died.

Neither age, nor caste, nor gender has relevance in Sikh spirituality. In contrast to the restricted position of women in Indian society, the Gurus accorded full respect and freedom of participation to women.

> God is like sugar scattered in the sand. An elephant cannot pick it up. Says Kabir,
> the Guru has given me this sublime secret:
>   "Become thou an ant and partake of it."
>
> Kabir, Guru Granth Sahib p. 1377

Although the Sikh Gurus gave their followers no mandate to convert others, their message was spread in a non-sectarian way by the **Udasis**, renunciates who do not withdraw from the world but rather practice strict discipline and meditation while trying to serve humanity. Their missionary work began under Baba Siri Chand, the ascetic elder son of Guru Nanak. He had a close relationship with the Sikh Gurus and was respected by people of all castes and creeds because of his spiritual power, wisdom, and principles. During the reign of the Mughal emperor Shah Jahan, a census showed that he had the largest following of any holy person in India. Nevertheless, he directed all attention and praise to his father, and never claimed to be a Guru. Udasi communities and educational institutions are still maintained in the subcontinent, and old Udasi inscriptions have been discovered in Baku, Azerbaijan.

Central beliefs

Sikhism's major focus is loving devotion to one God, whom Sikhs recognize as the same One who is worshiped by different names around the world. God is formless, beyond time and space, the only truth, the only reality. This concept was initially set forth in Guru Nanak's *Mul Mantra* (basic sacred chant), which prefaces the Guru Granth Sahib, and *Jap Ji*, the first morning prayer:

> There is One God
> Whose Name is Truth,
> The Creator,
> Without fear, without hate,
> Eternal Being,
> Beyond birth and death,
> Self-existent,
> Realized by the Guru's grace.[11]

Following Guru Nanak's lead, Sikhs often refer to God as *Sat* ("truth") or as *Ik Onkar*, the One Supreme Being. God is pure being, without form.

Guru Gobind Singh, a great custodian of scholars who kept many poets in his court, offered a litany of praises of this boundless, formless One. His inspired composition, *Jaap Sahib*, includes 199 verses such as these:

> Immortal
> Omnipotent
> Beyond Time
> And Space
> Invisible
> Beyond name, caste, or creed
> Beyond form or figure

The ruthless destroyer
Of all pride and evil
The Salvation of all beings . . .
The Eternal Light
The Sweetest Breeze
The Wondrous Figure
The Most Splendid.[12]

The light of God is thought to shine fully through the Guru, the perfect master. In Sikh belief, the light of God is also present in the Guru Granth Sahib, the Holy Word of God, and in all of creation, in which **Nam**, the Holy Name of God, dwells. God is not separate from this world. God pervades the cosmos and thus can be found within everything. As the Ninth Guru wrote:

Why do you go to the forest to find God? He lives in all and yet remains distinctly detached. He dwells in you as well, as fragrance resides in a flower or the reflection in a mirror. God abides in everything. See him, therefore, in your heart.[13]

Sikhism does not claim to have the only path to God, nor does it try to convert others to its way. It has beliefs in common with Hinduism (such as *karma* and reincarnation) and also with Islam (such as monotheism). It is said that the respected Muslim mystic Mian Mir was invited to lay the cornerstone of the Golden Temple in Amritsar. It was constructed with four doors, inviting people from all traditions to come in to worship. When Guru Gobind Singh created an army to resist tyranny, he admonished Sikhs not to feel enmity toward Islam or Hinduism. The enemy, he emphasized, was oppression and corruption.

Sikh soldier-saints are pledged to protect the freedom of all religions. Sikhism is, however, opposed to empty ritualism, and Guru Nanak and his successors challenged hypocritical religious practices. "It is very difficult to be called a Muslim," said Guru Nanak. "A Muslim's heart is as soft as wax, very compassionate, and he washes away the inner dirt of egotism."[14] By contrast, said Guru Nanak, "The Qazis [Muslim legal authorities] who sit in the courts to minister justice, rosary in hand and the name of *Khuda* (God) on their lips, commit injustice if their palm is not greased. And if someone challenges them, lo, they quote the scriptures!"[15]

According to the Sikh ideal, the purpose of life is to realize God within the world, through the everyday practices of work, worship, and charity, of sacrificing love. All people are to be treated equally, for God's light dwells in all and ego is a major hindrance to God-realization. Since Guru Nanak, Sikhism has refused to acknowledge the Indian caste system. In social services, such as hospitals, free kitchens, and leprosariums, Sikhs serve everyone, regardless of caste or creed. A group known as Seva Panthis places great emphasis on this tradition, refusing to accept offerings to support their services to the needy.

In contrast to the low status of women in Indian society, the Gurus accorded considerable respect to women. Guru Nanak asked: "Why denounce her, who even gives birth to kings?"[16] Many women are respectfully remembered in Sikh history. Among them are Guru Nanak's sister Bibi Nanaki, who first recognized his great spiritual power and became his first devotee. When a group of Guru Gobind Singh's soldiers deserted him when his citadel at Anandpur was being besieged, their women threatened to dress in the men's clothes and return to

An Interview with Inderpreet Kaur

Inderpreet Kaur is a thirteen-year-old student in New Delhi, studying in an English-language, Christian-based school, as is the ideal of many middle- and upper-class families in India. She nonetheless maintains her family's Sikh traditions and tries to live by the essence of the teachings of the Sikh Gurus. She explains:

"We respect the Almighty. We just love Him infinitely. We don't seem to do external practices or rituals. But we should have a connection with the Divine Power, God. Our Gurus say if we love God with a pure heart, if we pray to Him with all our concentration, and meditate on Him, if we praise God and thank Him, God will surely help us.

"If I remember God with a pure heart, there is just God and me. God is always there to help me. If we thank God, praise Him, and we love Him dearly, I think we can even cross a mountain. It is written in our Holy Book, the Guru Granth Sahib, that there are no boundaries. The house of God is without walls. It is open for all. God asks for love and not anything else.

"There are many religious paths, but they are all leading to the one goal. I personally go to a [Hindu] temple, my school has a church, and I offer prayers to Lord Jesus. I may not know the rituals or the practices, how to offer prayers to Lord Jesus, but I love God with a pure heart, I really do love Jesus, and I think God helps us if we love Him. He also wants us not to create distinctions between the people. He just wants us to be good, to do good things in life, so that our sins can be washed away.

"The problems we face, the bad things that happen to us, are the result of our bad *karmas*, reborn. I think

the main goal in our life should be to respect every human being, to do good, and live by the principles of the religion which we follow, because every religion says one thing: The main thing is to love God with a pure heart.

"In Sikhism, we offer prayers every morning and evening, and we do *prakash* in the morning—we open our holy book, the Guru Granth Sahib. After reading from the holy scripture, we take *hukam*, that is, the teaching of the day, from the holy book. Our Gurus told that we should imbibe the teaching that is written in the book. They tell us what to do, how to lead a life, and we should follow those teachings. We see that every time we should always keep remembering God, we should take His Name, and we should always thank Him for whatever He has given us. Whatever He shall do, that will be given for our benefit. The problems which come in our life are for our own good, because we learn from them, and God will surely help us.

"In the evening after our day's work, again we read our holy scripture, and then in the night-time, we close the book and we offer prayers to the Lord. And then again in the morning, we open it.

"*Seva* means service. All beings are the creation of God, so we should help each other, but without expecting anything, and we should offer service to God. We should do good things in life and avoid crying for everything here. That is according to our Gurus' teachings. We wear an iron bracelet, *kara*, on our wrist. Whenever we are doing a wrong thing, as soon as we see it, it reminds us that, yes, we are dedicated to God and God is watching us. We can't hide anything from God."[17]

fight for the Guru. One woman—Mai Bhago—did so and helped to lead forty of the deserters back to battle on the Guru's side against Aurangzeb's army. The men all died on the battlefield, asking the Guru to forgive them, but Mai Bhago survived and remained in the Guru's personal security guard, dressed as a man, with his permission. When *amrit* was first prepared for Khalsa initiation, it was Guru Gobind Singh's wife who added sugar crystals to make the initiates sweet-tempered as well as brave. Women were active as missionaries carrying Guru Gobind Singh's program. During the Mogul persecutions of the eighteenth century, Sikh women were noted for their courage and steadfast faith.

A preference for sons nonetheless persisted, in part because of the heavy dowry burden traditionally expected of females in India. To counter this, Guru Gobind Singh reportedly forbade female infanticide, and in 2001, the chief Sikh authorities issued an order that anyone practicing female foeticide would be excommunicated from the faith.

In developing the military capabilities of his followers in order to protect religious freedom, Guru Gobind Singh set forth strict standards for battle. He established five stringent conditions for "righteous war": (1) Military means are a last resort to be used only if all other methods have failed; (2) Battle should be undertaken without any enmity or feeling of revenge; (3) No territory should be taken or captured property retained; (4) Troops should be committed to the cause, not mercenaries fighting for pay, and soldiers should be strictly disciplined, for-swearing smoking, drinking, and abuse of opponents' women; and (5) Minimal force should be used and hostilities should end when the objective is attained.

Like Hinduism, Sikhism conceives a series of lives, with *karma* (the effects of past actions on one's present life) governing transmigration of the soul into new bodies, be they human or animal. The ultimate goal of life is mystical union with the Divine, reflected in one's way of living.

I was separated from God for many births, dry as a withered plant,
But by the grace of the Guru, I have become green.
                                    Guru Arjun, Guru Granth Sahib, p. 102

Sacred practices

To be a true Sikh is to live a disciplined life of surrender and devotion to God, with hours of daily prayer, continual inner repetition of the Name of God (Nam), and detachment from negative, worldly mind-states. Nam carries intense spiritual power, capable of making a person fearless, steady, inwardly calm and strong in the face of adversity, willing to serve without reward, and effortlessly extending love in all directions. Why is it so powerful? It comes from the Guru as a trans-mission of spiritual blessing that automatically transforms people and links them with God. Some feel Nam is the essence of creation. The mystics and Gurus whose writings are included in the Guru Granth Sahib refer to many Names of God, such as *Sohang* (What You are, I am), *Narain* (the One present in water), *Allah*, and *Ram*. Some Sikhs recite *"Wahe Guru"* (God wondrous beyond words), some say *"Ik Onkar Sat nam Siri Wahe Guru"* (God is One, the Truth Itself, Most

Respectful, Wondrous beyond words), some recite the Mul Mantra, a key verse by Guru Nanak summarizing his philosophy, used at the beginning of the Guru Granth Sahib and in many other places in it.

In the Sikh path, at the same time that one's mind and heart are joined with God, one is to be working hard in the world, earning an honest living, and helping those in need. Of this path, the Third Sikh Guru observed:

The way of devotees is unique; they walk a difficult path.
They leave behind attachments, greed, ego, and desires, and do not speak much.
The path they walk is sharper than the edge of a sword and thinner than a hair.
Those who shed their false self by the grace of the Guru are filled with the fragrance
  of God.[18]

The standards set by Guru Gobind Singh for the Khalsa are so high that few people can really meet them. In addition to outer disciplines, such as abstaining from drugs, alcohol, and tobacco, the person who is Khalsa, said the Guru, will always recite the Name of God:

The Name of God is light, the Light which never extinguishes, day or night. Khalsa
recognizes none but the One. I live in Khalsa; it is my body, my treasure store.[19]

The one who is Khalsa renounces anger and does not criticize anybody. He fights on the front line against injustice and vanquishes the five evils (lust, anger, greed, attachment, and ego) in himself. He burns his *karmas* and thus becomes egoless. Not only does he not take another person's spouse, he doesn't even look at the things that belong to others. Perpetually reciting Nam is his joy, and he falls in love with the words of the Gurus. He faces difficulties squarely, always attacks evil, and always helps the poor. He joins other people with the Nam, but he is not bound within the forts of narrow-mindedness.[20]

The Sikh Gurus formed institutions to help create a new social order with no caste distinctions. One is **langar**, the community meal, which is offered to all who come, regardless of caste. This typically takes place at a **gurdwara**, the building where the Guru Granth Sahib is enshrined and public worship takes place. The congregation is called the **sangat**, in which all are equal; there is no priestly or servant class. During community worship as well as *langar*, all strata of people sit together, though men and women may sit separately, as is the Indian custom. People of all ethnic origins, ideologies, and castes, including untouchables, may bathe in the tank of water at Sikh holy places. Baptism into the Khalsa is thought to do away with one's former caste and make a lowly person a chief. At least one-tenth of one's income is to be contributed toward the welfare of the community. In addition, the Sikh Gurus glorified the lowliest forms of manual labor, such as sweeping the floor and cleaning shoes, especially when these are done as voluntary service to God.

The morning and evening prayers take about two hours a day, starting in the very early morning, when the first prayer is the *Jap Ji. Jap* means "recitation," and refers especially to using the Name of God (Nam) as the best way to approach the divine. Much of the *Jap Ji* is devoted to the Nam.

The devotees are forever in bliss, for by hearing the Nam their suffering and
  sins are destroyed.
Hearkening to the Nam bestows Truth, divine wisdom, contentment.

By hearing the Nam, the blind find the path of Truth and
  realize the Unfathomable.²¹

> *"The Lord is stitched into my heart and never goes out of it even for a moment."*
> *Guru Arjun Dev, Guru Granth Sahib, p. 708*

The second morning prayer is Guru Gobind Singh's universal *Jaap Sahib*. It names no prophet, nor creates any religion. It is sheer homage to God. The Guru addresses God as having no form, no country, and no religion but yet as the seed of seeds, song of songs, sun of suns, the life force pervading everywhere, ever merciful, ever giving, indestructible. Complex in its poetry and profound in its content, *Jaap Sahib* asserts that God is the cause of conflict as well as of peace, of destruction as well as of creation; God pervades in darkness as well as in light. In verse after verse, devotees learn there is nothing outside God's presence, nothing outside of God's control.

In addition to these and other daily prayers, passages from the Guru Granth Sahib are chanted or sung, often with musical accompaniment—the tradition of **kirtan**. The Guru Granth Sahib is placed on a platform, with a devotee waving a whisk over the sacred book to denote the royalty of the scripture. Worshipers bow to it, bring offerings, and then sit reverently on the floor before it. Every morning and evening, the spirit of God reveals its guidance to the people as an officiant opens the scripture at random, intuitively guided, and reads a passage that is to be a special spiritual focus for the day.

Some *gurdwaras*, including the Golden Temple in Amritsar, previously allowed only men to read publicly from the Guru Granth Sahib, to preach, to officiate at ceremonies, or to sing sacred songs. However, nothing in the Sikh scriptures or the Code of Conduct bars women from such privileges. Indeed, Guru Gobind Singh initiated women into the Khalsa and allowed them to fight on the battlefield. In 1996, the central setting policies for Sikh *gurdwaras* ruled that they should be allowed to perform sacred services.

In addition to group chanting, singing, and listening to collective guidance from the Guru Granth Sahib, devout Sikhs are encouraged to begin the day with private meditations on the name of God. As one advances in this practice and abides in egoless love for God, one is said to receive guidance from the inner Guru, the living word of God within each person.

Sikhism today

Sikhism has spread around the world, largely by emigration from India, but its center remains the Punjab, which is under Indian rule and was dramatically shrunk by the partition of India in 1947, for two-thirds of the Punjab was in the western area thenceforth called Pakistan. The two million Sikhs living there were forced to migrate to the eastern side of the border under conditions of extreme hardship. Through emigration, there are large Sikh communities in Britain, Canada, the United States, Malaysia, and Singapore.

In India, Sikhs and Hindus lived side by side until 1978 to 1992, when violent clashes occurred over anti-Sikh policies of the Indian government. Sikh separatists wanted to establish an independent Sikh state, called Khalistan, with a commitment to strong religious observances and protection for Sikhs from oppression and exploitation by Hindus. In 1984, Prime Minister Indira Gandhi attacked the Golden Temple, Sikhism's holiest shrine, for Sikh separatists were thought to be using it as a shelter for their weapons. This seemed an outrageous desecration of the holy place, and counter-violence increased. The Prime Minister was killed later in 1984 by her Sikh bodyguards. In retribution, mob killings of thousands of Sikhs followed.

Many Sikhs "disappeared" in the Punjab, allegedly at the hands of both separatists and police terrorists. Sikhs in India are going on with their lives now that violence has ended, but tensions are kept alive by Sikhs living outside India who persist in demanding the formation of Khalistan and promoting a militant, rigid version of the religion.

Historical tensions have arisen within Sikhism as it has been institutionalized. Leadership of *gurdwaras* is democratic, by elected committees, but this has not stopped fractiousness within the organizations. In 1998, factions of a Canadian *gurdwara* had a bloody fight over using chairs and tables in the *langar* rather than the tradition of sitting in rows on the ground.

From time to time, self-styled Sikh "saints" or "gurus" have claimed to have special powers and set themselves up as spiritual guides, antagonizing mainstream Sikhs, who believe the Tenth Sikh Guru turned over the role of guru to the Guru Granth Sahib, and that there will be no more worldly successors to the position. Some of the new gurus have split off from—or been ostracized by—the mainstream tradition and formed religious movements, such as Radhasoami (see chapter 11). In 2007, a newspaper published a photograph of a person who had gathered hundreds of thousands of followers. Dressed to look like Guru Gobind Singh, he was claiming spiritual authority and giving his followers *amrit* in his own way. A widespread conflict ensued between outraged mainstream Sikhs, who considered his actions blasphemous, and his followers.

Another issue is authority over the Sikh community. The Sixth Guru started a tradition of sitting on a high platform or *takht* ("throne") in Amritsar opposite the Golden Temple and issuing *hukamnamahs* (edicts). This place, the Akal Takht ("Eternal Throne"), remains the highest seat of both worldly and spiritual authority for Sikhs. In time, four more *takhts* associated with the life of Guru Gobind Singh were recognized, but the *jathedar* (leader) of the Akal Takht is still the most eminent. This system of control over the affairs of the Sikh Panth is challenged by some Sikhs as contrary to the original spirit of Sikhism. They argue that Sikhism rejects clergy and rigid authorianism in favor of the direct relationship between the devotee, the Guru, and God.

There are also tensions between Sikhs who favor a more spiritual and universal understanding of their religion and those who interpret it more rigidly and exclusively. When Sikhs were asserting their distinct identity, lest they be subsumed under Hinduism, the ecumenical nature of Sikhism was downplayed. There were no forcible attempts to convert anyone to Sikhism, but Sikhs became proud of their heroic history and tended to turn inward.

In the diaspora, many Sikhs have attempted to resist assimilation to the surrounding cultures and raise their children according to their Indian traditions.

His Holiness Baba Virsa Singh

For decades, His Holiness Baba Virsa Singh (c. 1934–2007) developed farms and communities in India in which people try to live by the teachings of the Sikh Gurus. Not only Sikhs but also Hindus, Muslims, and Christians, literate and illiterate, live and work side by side as brothers and sisters. Baba Virsa Singh himself was illiterate, the son of a village farmer. From childhood he had an intense yearning for communion with God:

> From childhood, I kept questioning God, "In order to love Jesus, must one become a Christian or just love?" He told me, "It is not necessary to become a Christian. It is necessary to love him."
>
> I asked, "To believe in Moses, does one have to observe any special discipline, or just love?" The divine command came: "Only love." I asked, "Does one have to become a Muslim in order to please Muhammad, or only love?" He said, "One must love." "To believe in Buddha, must one become a monk or a Buddhist?" He replied, "No. To believe in Buddha is to love." God said, "I created human beings. Afterward, human beings created sectarian religions. But I created only human beings."[22]

Intense spirituality is the base of the communities Baba Virsa Singh established, which are known collectively as Gobind Sadan ("The House of God"). Volunteers work hard to raise record crops on previously barren land. The harvests are shared communally and also provide the basis for Gobind Sadan's continual free kitchens (langar) for people of all classes, free medical services, and celebrations of the holy days of all religions. Devotions are carried on around the clock, with everyone from gardeners and pot washers to governors and professors helping to clean the holy areas and maintain perpetual reading of the Sikh scriptures. Everyone is empowered to do useful work, including children, elderly men and women, mentally disturbed people, and people with physical handicaps. Thus there is a living example of the power of Guru Nanak's straightforward, non-sectarian spiritual program: Work hard to earn your own honest living, share with others, and wake early to meditate upon and remember God in your everyday life.

Another social effect of the work of Baba Virsa Singh was an easing of the tensions between people of different religions. Even the most rigid proponents of their own religions came to him and were gently convinced to open their eyes toward the validity of other faiths.

Another area in which Baba Virsa Singh influenced public life in India and other countries was his effect on government officials. He urged them to attend to the practical needs of the people and to uphold order and justice in society.

Baba Virsa Singh also gave people spiritual hope for a new world order. To editors of a Russian magazine, he explained,

> Truth is always tested. Who tests it? Evil—evil attacks the truth. But truth never stops shining, and evil keeps falling back. Truth's journey is very powerful, with a very strong base. It never wavers. It is definitely a long journey, full of travails, but evil can never suppress the truth.[23]

Wherever communities of Sikhs have collected, they have tried to build a *gurdwara* for their worship services. One of the chief personal issues over assimilation is hair-cutting. Some Sikh men feel they cannot fit into the modern world wearing a turban, but their families may pressurize them not to cut their hair. Wearing the sword on a sling openly is also perceived as a problem in some non-Sikh environments, where would would be viewed with alarm, so some Khalsa initiates wear miniature symbols of the sword, comb, and *khanda* on a necklace, while wearing their drawstring underwear and keeping their hair bound under a turban or veil. After terrorist attacks in the United States and London, many Sikhs who had kept their traditional dress and long hair with beards and turbans were victims of hate crimes, since they were confused with Muslims. The Sikh community found it necessary to explain Sikhism publicly, and stressed its universality, democratic nature, and religious tolerance.

A strain of exclusivism continues among scholars and internet bloggers who deny the historic spiritual closeness of Sikhism to Hindu and Muslim traditions. Some scholars have insisted that the *Dasam Granth*, the purported writings of Guru Gobind Singh, was not entirely written by him because it contains positive references to Hindu deities and is sexually explicit in places. Major conflicts have arisen over calendar dates for Sikh holidays, with some factions rejecting the traditional—and somewhat inaccurate—Hindu way of accommodating differences between solar and lunar calendars. Such debates get mixed up with politics, with the elected *gurdwara* committee leadership issuing controversial rulings that are presented as authoritative and binding on all Sikhs.

Without going so far as to deny the uniqueness or continuing tradition of Sikhism, many contemporary Sikh and non-Sikh scholars are appreciating the message of the Sikh Gurus as supporting the underlying unity of people of all religions. In the words of Guru Gobind Singh:

> *Same are the temple and the mosque*
> *And same are the forms of worship therein.*
> *All human beings are one though apparently many,*
> *Realize, therefore, the essential unity of mankind.*[24]

Review questions

1. Describe the central beliefs of the Sikhs. Discuss God, *karma*, reincarnation, monotheism, freedom of religions, ritualism, sincerity, purpose of life, infanticide, five conditions for righteous war, various names of God, self-discipline, *langar, gurdwara, sangat*, baptism, and labor.
2. Describe the life and thoughts of Guru Nanak. Discuss Punjab, river, *amrit*, relations to Islam and Hinduism, three central teachings, kitchen, caste, class, and gender.
3. What roles did the following play in Sikh history? Sikh Empire, non-violent resistance, a train, Bibi Nanaki, Mai Bhago, and Udasis.

Discussion questions

1 How do Sikh Gurus differ from rabbis, priests, ministers, caliphs, or imams?
2. What does Sikh history illustrate about reforming religions?
3. What do you think of the problem seen by some Sikhs that a majority are Sikh by birth only and lack the commitment of conversion by choice?

CHAPTER 11

RELIGION IN A NEW ERA

"That yielding of the human mind to the divine"

The history of religions is one of continual change. Each religion changes over time, new religions appear, and some older traditions disappear. Times of rapid social change are particularly likely to spawn new religious movements, for people seek the security of the spiritual amidst worldly chaos. In the period since World War II, thousands of new religious groups have sprung up around the world. In sub-Saharan Africa, there are now over 7,000 different religions; every Nigerian town of several thousand people has up to fifty or sixty different kinds of religion.[1] In Japan, an estimated thirty percent of the population belongs to one of hundreds of new religious movements. Imported versions of Eastern traditions, such as Hinduism and Buddhism, have made many new converts in areas such as North America, Europe, and Russia, where they are seen as "new religions." Internet websites offer global opportunities for new religious movements to explain themselves and attract new followers.

New religious movements are often referred to as "cults" or "sects." These words have specific, neutral meanings: a **cult** represents a distinct break from other traditions, while a **sect** is a splinter group or a subgroup associated with a larger tradition. Both words have been used imprecisely and pejoratively to distinguish new religions from older ones. The word cult has often been used to signify a group temporarily gathered around a charismatic leader whose influence may be dangerous to his or her followers.

The label "new religious movement" seems more neutral and is widely used, particularly in academic circles, to avoid such negative connotations. However, the word "new" is itself imprecise, for many of these groups have a rather lengthy history and have survived long after the death of the original founder.

This chapter surveys representative examples of the religious movements that developed in the nineteenth to twenty-first centuries. All have some link with previous traditions but are sufficiently different to be studied independently. The pages that follow provide a sampling of these manifestations of the current burgeoning of spiritual vitality. The headings do not delineate separate categories, but rather common aspects of the new religious movements.

Apocalyptic and millennial expectations

As the twenty-first century began, according to Christian dating, speculations abounded that some major change was about to occur in the world. Some people expected better times ahead; some prophesied forthcoming planetary disaster. The disastrous weather patterns in 1997 and 1998 linked with the worst El Niño in history, unstable political and economic conditions around the world, the sudden collapse of the Asian "tiger" economies, and epidemic exposures of government scandals gave many people the impression that we were experiencing a global crisis of supernatural dimensions. After 2000 came and went without any world-shaking events, the 2001 terrorist attacks on the United States reawakened fears of worldwide calamity.

The expectation of major world changes appears in many established religions, including Hinduism, Zoroastrianism, Judaism, Christianity, Islam, and some indigenous religions. Hindus, for instance, anticipate that the current depraved age of Kali Yuga will be followed by the return of Sat Yuga (when *dharma* will again prevail). This leads periodically to the formation of movements which preach that the time of great changes is imminent. In Christianity, the last book in the Bible, Revelation, predicts an **apocalypse**, or dramatic end of the present world. Revelation foretells a titanic war at Armageddon between the forces of Satan and the forces of God, with great destruction, followed by the **millennium**, a thousand-year period of special holiness in which Christ rules the earth.

Catastrophic millennialism

People in some catastrophic millennial movements have led relatively normal lives despite their expectations of disaster. These include Jehovah's Witnesses. Others have taken a path leading to violence against themselves or others.

Jehovah's Witnesses   Jehovah's Witnesses foresee a new world in which people of all races (including many raised from the dead) will join hands in peace. They believe this will happen only after most of humanity is destroyed for not obeying the Bible. In their understanding, God will not let anyone, including "false Christians," ruin the earth. Those who are of the true religion will be saved from destruction, reunited with their dead loved ones in a paradise on earth (except for 144,000 who will live with God in heaven). In this paradise there will be no pain, no food shortages, no sickness, no death.

The founder of Jehovah's Witnesses, Charles Taze Russell (1852–1916), supported a prediction that 1873 or 1874 would be the date of this apocalypse. When that period passed uneventfully, the dates were changed to 1878, then 1914, 1925, and 1975. As they came and went without the world ending, Russell and his successors developed the idea that Christ had arrived, but was invisibly present. Only the faithful "Jehovah's Witnesses" would recognize his presence. Their mission is to warn the rest of the populace about what is in store. They thus go from door to door, encouraging people to follow their program of studying the Bible as an announcement of the millennium.

Violence in apocalyptic movements   There have been a number of tragic instances of catastrophic millennialism in recent times. In 1993, in Waco, Texas, the Branch Davidians, expecting Armageddon, had armed themselves to defend their devotional community. They were besieged by federal officials on weapons charges, and about eighty of them died when a blaze broke out as FBI agents moved into the compound to end the fifty-one-day siege. In 1994 and 1995, in Switzerland, France, and Quebec, seventy-four members of the Order of the Solar Temple, a group that claimed to be descendants of the medieval Knights Templar and to be receiving communications from super-human "Masters of the Temple," committed suicide, or were killed by the others. They apparently believed the apocalypse was near and that ritual death would transport them to another planet.

As we will see, religion-related violence is not limited to new religious movements; religious extremists who claim to be followers of major established religions are resorting to violence in many parts of the globe. Are the followers of new religious movements different? Research indicates that recruits to new religious movements tend to come from the mainstream of society. As sociology professor Lorne Dawson summarizes the research, people usually enter new religious movements by learning about them from their friends and relatives. They are often attracted by the joy, vibrancy, and enthusiastic outlook of other members, and tend to be middle- or upper-middle-class and well educated. Primarily young adults who do not have family commitments, they may be seeking answers to their questions about the meaning of life.

How, then, do such apparently reasonable people turn violent? One explanation that applies to some groups is that when, in sincere expectation of world changes, they have isolated themselves to prepare for the end, they distance themselves from other points of view. In isolation and group solidarity, seemingly irrational beliefs—such as the apocalyptic scenario of the biblical book of Revelation—seem to make perfect sense.

Religious movements may also turn violent in response to hostility from the surrounding culture. This is called "deviance amplification." New religious movements specialists Massimo Introvigne and Jean-François Mayer have observed that when some groups perceive threats from the outside, they encourage their members to feel they are not of this world. When under attack from the outside and also perhaps shaken by defections from within, they may conclude that suicide is their only good option. People enter the group of their own free will, but when the trend toward suicide or violence becomes apparent they may find it difficult to leave if the leader is extremely charismatic or even coercive.

Progressive millennial movements

In contrast to the violence that sometimes occurs in catastrophic millennial movements, progressive millennial movements tend to adopt a no less zealous but nonetheless peaceful approach, focusing on ushering in the new age. Here we will examine two examples: Rastafari and the Unification Movement.

Rastafari   In Jamaica, in 1895, Alexander Bedward of the Baptist Free Church prophesied a holocaust in which all white people would be killed, leaving the Blacks, "the true people," to celebrate the new world. A more generalized hopeful vision was spread by Marcus Garvey (1887–1940), who saw a fundamental change in society that would be led by Blacks, and linked this to the return of Blacks to Africa. A prophecy attributed to Garvey—"Look to Africa when a black king shall be crowned, for the day of deliverance is near"[2]—was mistakenly thought to have been realized when Ras (Prince) Tafari of Ethiopia was crowned as Haile Selassie, Emperor of Ethiopia.

Rastafarians intend to revive the "Way of the Ancients," their concept of the lost civilization of pre-colonial Africa, and to free people of African extraction from subservience. "Babylon," the oppressor, is the United States, Britain (the former colonial power in Jamaica), the state of Jamaica, and the Christian Church. In protest against Babylon, Rastafarians wear their hair in long uncombed curls, called "dreadlocks," symbolizing the natural non-industrial life. Some give use of marijuana (*ganja*) religious significance as a sacrament. A distinctive music, reggae, has evolved as an expression of Black pride, social protest, and Rastafarian millenarian ideals, with the legendary Bob Marley as its musical prophet. The Rastafari movement has spread beyond Jamaica to Blacks and a few whites elsewhere in the Caribbean, North America, Europe, Southern Africa, Australia, and New Zealand.

Unification Movement   Sun Myung Moon, the founder of the Unification Movement, has proclaimed himself and his second wife, Hak Ja Han, to be jointly the Messiah. Born in North Korea in 1935, by his account Jesus appeared to him in a vision in 1935 and asked him to complete the task of establishing God's kingdom on earth. To this end, Moon developed the "Unification Principle," according to which God created the universe in order to manifest true love. The family is considered the primary institution for the growth of love, and people are to live for the sake of others in all situations. However, according to Moon's theology, humans do not live according to God's design; selfishness prevails in human relationships and in relationships between ethnic groups and nations.

In the 1970s, the Unification Church staged a series of rallies in the United States and saw a rapid growth in membership. Middle-class youths put aside their previous lives, and devoted themselves to the religious path in what they saw as a rejection of the materialistic and hedonistic American lifestyle. However, parents accused the church of brainwashing their children. It was viewed with suspicion by the established Christian churches and vilified by the political left because of its anti-communist activities. Dodging controversy and mockery, the Unification Movement, which has become extremely financially successful, began large-scale activities reportedly designed to transform the world, creating international inter-religious dialogues among scholars of religion and political leaders, and service projects in many countries.

A unique aspect of the Movement's work is massive wedding ceremonies in which thousands of couples matched by the movement or already-wed couples wanting to dedicate themselves to "live for the sake of others" and "create an ideal family which contributes to world peace" are simultaneously "blessed" by Reverend and Mrs. Moon. With Reverend Moon announcing himself as the "Second Adam," Unificationists view these mass weddings as a movement to create one human family, with couples of all races and nationalities "engrafted" onto "God's lineage of true love."

An Interview with Ursula McLackland

Ursula is German and was matched by the Unification Movement to David McLackland from England; they have three children and live in Bahrain, where Ursula is a Regional Director for the Unification Movement. She explains why Unification appeals to her:

"I was raised in a Protestant church, but I was not interested in religion. When I was fifteen I followed my elder sister and left the church.

"Maybe the most motivating experience was when I was in a project trying to help drug addicts overcome their internal spiritual addiction to drugs. I confronted them with the question 'What is the purpose of life?' They said, 'I don't care if I die in two years or twenty years, so why?' So then I felt if I want to help drug addicts, I must give them the purpose of life. A friend had by that time introduced me to a yoga group. I felt the love among the people, the sacred singing, the meditation was what really drew and completely changed my life. Through the moral principles and starting a disciplined lifestyle, many questions in my life were answered, and I felt my mind got cleared up.

"When I met the Unification Movement, that is the point which really attracted me, because they had a very clear logical explanation about the relationship between man and woman, and they were teaching about the ideal of the family. I could see in their own members that even though they were married, now as a family they were sacrificing for society and for the world.

"David and I were matched and then engaged for one and a half years. We got to know each other through writing letters. When I met him, I felt tremendous love from God for my husband. I felt this love is not me for him; it is God's love coming through us.

"[In contrast to criticisms that the 'Moonies' are being exploited as cheap labor by the higher-ups in the movement] I see that the higher people are in the hierarchy, the more loving, the more sacrificial they are. I couldn't live like Reverend Kwak (Reverend Moon's direct assistant) or Reverend Moon. They sleep just a few hours a day, and all day they are active and busy. They are always loving, they are always there for you, they are always supporting you.

"Maybe what is most commonly accused is that our members start with sales to support our projects. But some of my most beautiful and wonderful experiences are doing these sales. This money is not for me, it is to help others. I have such beautiful experiences where I can just feel actually it is God who is selling it. It is not me. I think that is for all of our members who have these experiences: We have the most beautiful and wonderful experiences with God doing this.

"We feel that through this type of experience, for example going door to door, you meet all kinds of people in all levels of society. That is really Reverend Moon's internal motivation: To give members broad experience and to train them to get to know all kinds of people and relate to them and love them and understand them.

"When I met the movement, I felt, 'Wow—here are people who are more sincere than I am, people who are more sacrificial, who are more sincere to live for others.' I felt I want to become like them. I think that is really the motive of our members—we really want to live for others."

Supernatural powers and revelations

Numerous new religious movements operate in the realm of the supernatural, beyond the senses and therefore mysterious. Those interested in penetrating these mysteries may do so to attain personal power, or to use their presumed contacts with invisible realities to bring healing to those who are suffering and insights for those who want to understand what they cannot see.

The Mahikari movement was founded in Japan in 1959 by Sukui Nushi Sama, who believes he is the successor to the Buddha and Christ as God's representative on earth, and has become popular in the Caribbean. It does not claim to be a religion in itself, but rather that it brings all religions together, and involves practices centering on spiritual "light." Mahikarians are taught to heal by radiating light out of their hands, to send light to disturbed ancestral spirits to help them find peace, and to spread the divine civilization through the world by transmitting light. They are taught that the spiritual realm is the only reality; science and medicine are superstitions.

Communication with spirits of the dead has surfaced within a Christian context in the United States as Spiritualism, defined by the National Spiritualist Association of Churches as "the science, philosophy, and religion of continuous life." Its services include a sermon and hymns, and periods of spiritual healing in which trained "healing vehicles" are believed to serve as channels for God's healing power, which is transmitted through their hands. Equally important are messages transmitted by a medium to members of the congregation from deceased relatives "on the other side."

Offshoots of older religions

Since newer offshoots of older religions are often sufficiently different from the parent religion to be considered new religious movements—whether they regard themselves as such or not—we will examine two contemporary examples below: the Mormon Church and Radhasoami.

Mormon Church

The chief feature of the Mormon Church, more formally known as the Church of Jesus Christ of Latter-Day Saints, that distinguishes it from the many variations of mainstream Christianity is that Mormons believe not only in the Bible but also in another scripture, *The Book of Mormon*. Mormons believe that in 1822, under angelic guidance, Joseph Smith found the book in New York State, engraved on golden plates. *The Book of Mormon* purports to be the account of several of the lost tribes of Israel, who crossed the ocean to become the ancestors of the American Indians, and the appearance of Jesus to them in the Americas after his death and resurrection. Mormon is one of the faithful who is believed to have survived tribal conflict and managed to write down the teachings about Jesus in the Americas for posterity.

After Joseph Smith's death, several groups of Latter-Day Saints developed, the largest of which was led by Brigham Young (1801–1877) to Salt Lake City, Utah to build "Zion in the Wilderness" and restore what Mormons consider true

Christianity, as opposed to the **apostasy** (abandonment of principles) which they feel characterizes the Christian churches.

The Mormon Church has thirteen million followers worldwide and is one of the fastest-growing of all religions. Its members control great wealth and exercise considerable political influence in the United States. Its success is perhaps due partly to its 65,000 volunteer missionaries, and partly to its emphasis on clean living and strong family values in contrast to the prevailing Western culture; Mormons typically eschew alcohol, tobacco, coffee, and tea, and eat meat only sparingly. Sexual conduct outside marriage is discouraged, and only virgins can be missionaries. All men are ordained to the priesthood, and authority resides in fathers as the heads of households.

Mormon theology is still evolving, due to its principle of continuing revelation, by which all believers may receive revelations directly from God. Theological beliefs are also subject to change, the most controversial of which—from the point of view of other Christians—may be the nature of God. For some time, Mormons believed the "Heavenly Father" was originally a man but had risen to exaltation, and that humans can likewise become like gods. This belief still exists, but the current prophet, President Gordon Hinckley, has not stressed the controversial first part of this doctrine, and has restated the second half: "We believe in the progression of the human soul. We believe in the eternity and the infinity of the human soul, and its great possibilities."[3]

Radhasoami

Radhasoami is an outgrowth of Sikhism in India. Its leaders often have Sikh backgrounds, but while orthodox Sikhs believe in a succession of masters that stopped with the Tenth Guru and was transferred to the holy scripture, Radhasoamis believe in a continuing succession of living masters. The first of its gurus was Shiv Dayal Singh. In 1861, he offered to serve as a spiritual savior, carrying devotees into "Radhasoami," the ineffable Godhead. Some 10,000 took initiation under him. After his death, the movement eventually split into over thirty branches, each with its own living master, although there is theoretically only one of these at a time on the earth.

Initiates are taught a secret yoga practice of concentrating on the third eye with attention to the inner sound and inner light in order to commune with the all-pervading power of God, the "Word" or Nam—an experience that must be both initiated and guided by a perfected being. The Perfect Masters feel their lineage that includes Buddha, Jesus, Muhammad, and the Sikh Gurus.

The Radhasoami movement claims an estimated 1.7 million initiates, who are required to be vegetarians, to meditate every day, to forgo alcohol and, if possible, tobacco, and to be employed.

Combinations of older religions

Mixtures of more than one religion have historically arisen in many places. When this produces what seems to be a new religion of sorts as a combination of normally differing beliefs, it is referred to as **syncretism**.

Caodaism was formed in 1926 in Vietnam by several people who understood God was instructing them that religious leaders such as Moses, Yi king (in China), Buddha, Laozi, Confucius, and Jesus had all been God-inspired to start religions in their home regions. However, through lack of communication, the religions went their separate ways, and this kept people from living together harmoniously. Caodaists practice a religion made from parts of many world religions, including Judaism, Christianity, Islam, Buddhism, Confucianism, and Daoism, plus the indigenous Vietnamese religion Geniism. They see such a mixture as the basis for the Third Era of Religious Amnesty.

New religious movements in the Caribbean and Latin America evolved from mixtures of African religions carried by slaves and earlier Catholic traditions. They are characterized by an interest in contacting and cooperating with spirits. Santeria ("way of the saints," or Lukumi, as its practitioners prefer) blends some of the deities and beliefs of slaves from Dahomey, baKonga, and Yoruban cultures with images of Catholic saints. Since the slaves were prevented from openly practicing their ancestral faiths, they continued to do so in symbolic ways, such as hanging a white cloth from a doorway, and by worship of the African *orisa* in the form of Catholic saints.

Santeria specialists have techniques for "magical" intervention in people's lives. The *santeros* say they are able to clear away negative spiritual influences, for example, help them to get jobs, attract mates, and get ahead financially. They see the world as a mesh of interconnections among all beings, linked by the energy known as *ashe*. Human efforts are required to keep the *ashe* flowing properly through creation and to nourish the *orisa*.

Santeria has an estimated 100 million practitioners in Latin America and the United States, and there are pilgrimages to Nigeria for people seeking to explore the roots of their religion. It is strengthening its ties to Africa as it gains acceptance and feels less need to mask its practices as Catholic variants.

Syncretism has also developed in Africa. For example, a number of "new" religions in West Africa combine elements of indigenous and Christian traditions. The new religions take seriously problems with the spirit world, such as retaliations from spirits who have not been treated respectfully, and mix Christian prayers and incense with fetishes, talismans, divining, chanting, and drumming. These movements are most popular in urban areas, where they offer a refuge from unpleasant aspects of city life, and revive the traditional African community spirit as a stable support network within a changing society.

Nature spirituality

If religion is defined in the broadest sense as that which ties us back to the sacred, one of the strongest trends today is the religion of nature.

Revival of old models

Some who seek to practice a nature-oriented spirituality look to the past for models. This is sometimes called **Neo-Paganism**, referring to pre-Christian spiritual ways that are thought to have been practiced in Europe. Some call their way Witchcraft, despite the negative connotations of this label.

Some Neo-Pagans try to reproduce some of the sacred ways of earlier European peoples, such as the Celts in the British Isles or the Scandinavians. Reconstructing these is difficult, for they were largely oral rather than written traditions. The way known as **Wicca** can be partly traced to the writings of Gerald Gardner in England in the 1940s. He claimed to have been initiated into a secret coven of witches who allowed him to write about some of their practices as well as their historical persecutions by Christians.

Another version of the attempt to return to old models is **Goddess spirituality**. Archaeological evidence from many cultures was reinterpreted during the twentieth century as suggesting that worship of a female high goddess was originally widespread.

The Great Goddess had many names and identities, such as the Great Mother Nu Kwa of China, the Greek earth goddess Gaia, Coatlique the Mother of Aztec deities, Great Spider Woman of the Pueblo peoples of North America, and Mawu, omnipotent creator of the Dahomey. An address to Ishtar, an important Mesopotamian goddess, dating from some time between the eighteenth and seventh centuries BCE, suggests some of the powers ascribed to her:

> Unto Her who renders decision, Goddess of all things. Unto the Lady of Heaven and Earth who receives supplication; Unto Her who hears petition, who entertains prayer; Unto the compassionate Goddess who loves righteousness; Ishtar the Queen, who suppresses all that is confused. To the Queen of Heaven, the Goddess of the Universe, the One who walked in terrible Chaos and brought life by the Law of Love; And out of Chaos brought us harmony.[4]

To revive appreciation of the Goddess, including the goddess within themselves, as well as women's spirituality, contemporary women have pieced together and invented rituals for both individual and group use.

Yet other people seeking to return to old models are members of new religions known collectively as **ethnic religions**. These have emerged since the fall of communism as revivals of pre-Christian ethnic traditions in countries such as Russia and Eastern Europe. People are returning to the traditional agrarian rites for the earth's fertility and human links with the cosmic rhythms and energies.

Neo-Pagans often develop new forms of group ritual. Usually they are held outside, with trees and rocks and waters, the sun, moon, and stars as the altars of the sacred. Speakers may invoke the pantheistic Spirit within all life or the invisible spirits of the place, or prayers may be offered for healing the earth, the creatures, or the people. Certain spots have been known as places of high energy, and are often used for ceremonies. At Neo-Pagan festivals participants shed their usual identities and perhaps their clothes, create temporary "kinship groups," and enjoy ritual fires, storytelling, dancing, drumming, and workshops on subjects like astrology and herbal healing.

Deep ecology

Deep ecology is the experience of oneness with the natural world. By contrast, most Western religions have cast humans as controllers of the natural world. Australian deep ecologist John Seed refers to this as **anthropocentrism**— "human chauvinism, the idea that humans are the crown of creation, the source of all value, the measure of all things."[5]

> *What is man without the beasts? If all the beasts were gone, men would die from a great loneliness of spirit. For whatever happens to the beasts soon happens to the man. . . . The earth does not belong to man; man belongs to the earth. This we know. All things are connected like the blood which unites one family.*
>
> Attributed to Chief Seattle [6]

Biogeochemist James Lovelock (b. 1919) has proposed that the biosphere ("the entire range of living matter on Earth") plus the earth's atmosphere, oceans, and soil can be viewed as "a single living entity, capable of manipulating the Earth's atmosphere to suit its overall needs . . ."[7] He named this complex entity Gaia, after the Greek name for the Earth Goddess.

A corollary to the Gaia hypothesis is the concept that humans are becoming the global brain of the planet, and are thus becoming conscious of the dangers our activities pose to other parts of "our body"—the rainforests (the liver and/or lungs), the oceans (the circulatory system), and so on. In *The Global Brain*, Peter Russell warns that we have little time to become fully conscious of our potential destructiveness and take action to forestall disaster:

> As a species we are facing our final examination; . . . it is in fact an intelligence test—a test of our true intelligence as a species. In essence we are being asked to let go of our self-centred thinking and egocentric behaviour. We are being asked to become psychologically mature, to free ourselves from the clutches of this limited identity, and express our creativity in ways which benefit us all.[8]

Universalist religions

Efforts are being made to harmonize the world's religions. To cite examples, the Theosophical Society encourages the study of all religions and maintains interfaith libraries. Many Protestant ministers are trained at interfaith seminaries in the United States. Temples are being built to honor all religions. In addition, several groups have religious unity as their major focus.

Theosophical Society

Madame Helena Blavatsky (1831–1891) founded the Theosophical Society, one of the pioneering universalist religious movements, in nineteenth-century Russia with the motto, "There is no religion higher than truth." It was an attempt, she said, "to reconcile all religions, sects and nations under a common system of ethics, based on eternal verities."[9] The Society introduced ancient Eastern ideas to Western seekers, especially Hindu beliefs such as *karma*, reincarnation, and subtle energies. Madame Blavatsky was particularly interested in the secret esoteric teachings of each religion, which collectively she called the "Wisdom Religion" or the "secret doctrine." The Theosophical Society now has members in seventy countries.

Baha'i

The Baha'i faith, a major new religion that attempts to unite all humanity in the belief that there is only one God, the foundation of all religions, was foreshadowed in Persia in 1844 when a young man called the Bab ("Gate") announced that a new messenger of God to all the peoples of the world would soon appear. Because he proclaimed this message in a Muslim state, he was arrested and executed in 1850. One of his imprisoned followers was Baha'u'llah (1817–1892), a member of an aristocratic Persian family. He was stripped of his worldly goods, tortured, banished to Baghdad, and imprisoned in Palestine by the Turks. From prison, he revealed himself as the messenger proclaimed by the Bab. He wrote letters to the rulers of all nations, asserting that humanity was becoming unified and a single global civilization was emerging.

Despite vigorous initial persecution, this new faith has spread to over five million followers in 233 countries and territories around the world. They have no priesthood but they do have their own sacred scriptures, revealed to Baha'u'llah. Although Baha'is see him as the fulfillment of the prophecies of all religions, he did not declare himself to be the ultimate messenger. Rather, he prophesied that another would follow in a thousand years.

The heart of Baha'u'llah's message appears in the *Kitab-i-Iqan* ("The Book of Certitude"). God, Baha'u'llah says, is unknowable. Mere humans cannot understand God's infinite nature. However, God has become known through divine messengers, the founders of the great world religions. All are manifestations of God, pure channels for helping humanity to understand God's will. Humanity has been maturing, and each time a divine messenger appeared, the message was given at levels appropriate to humanity's degree of maturity. Baha'u'llah proclaimed his own message as the most advanced and the one appropriate for this time. It contains the same truths as the earlier revelations, but with some new features, which humanity is now ready to grasp, such as the oneness of all peoples, prophets, and religions, and a program for universal governance for the sake of world peace and social justice. Contemporary Baha'is are active in trying to develop a just order in the world.

Open to all, Baha'i Houses of Worship have nine doors and a central dome symbolizing the diversity and oneness of humanity. Services include readings from the scriptures of all religions, meditations, and prayers by the Bab, Baha'u'llah, and 'Abdu'l-Baha, his oldest son.

If the religions are true it is because each time it is God who has spoken, and if they are different it is because God has spoken in different "languages" in conformity with the diversity of the receptacles. Finally, if they are absolute and exclusive, it is because in each of them God has said "I."

Frithjof Schuon[10]

Baha'is' attempts to unite the earth in faith extend into the political sphere, where they actively support the United Nations' efforts to unify the planet.

New Age spirituality

A great variety of the spiritual movements that developed in the West in the 1970s and 1980s drew on many characteristics of older movements. In addition, they are often characterized by a quest for self-improvement but in highly individualistic, anti-institutional formats. Collectively, these ways, rather than being called "religions," are often therefore called "New Age spiritual movements." A hallmark of New Age spirituality is the feeling that there is some mechanism by which the consciousnesses of all members of our species are interlinked, and if enough of us change our way of thinking, the rest of us will spontaneously change as well.

As well as Western esotericism, Spiritualism, Theosophy, astrology, and introduction of the Eastern religions to the West, the roots of New Age Spiritual movements include discoveries about the power of the mind, as propagated by Phineas Parkhurst Quimby (1802–1866) and then developed into a full-fledged religious movement by Mary Baker Eddy (1821–1910) as Christian Science. In her *Science and Health with Key to the Scriptures*, Eddy proposed that negative inner states such as hatred, fear, selfishness, and envy obscure one's relationship with God's love. When they are surrendered, healing occurs naturally as one's true spiritual being emerges.

Another related trend utilizing the power of the mind is New Thought, which spread widely due to the efforts of Emma Curtis Hopkins (1849–1925). A website of one of its offshoots, the Unity School of Christianity, which dates back to 1886, includes an "Affirmation Machine" in which a person can choose a topic and instantly receive a brief message supporting positive spiritual thinking, such as "I am a beacon of light for others" or "I let my loving light encompass the world."

New Age spirituality is often mystical, favoring direct communion with the unseen. The Findhorn community is a striking example. One of its leaders, Dorothy Maclean, studied with Sufi masters, learning how to receive "inner guidance," before joining with Eileen and Peter Caddy in developing Findhorn, a transformation of desolate dunes on the coast of Scotland into a lush farming community. Dorothy developed a cooperative relationship with the energies she called the plant *devas*, after the Hindu term for the invisible "shining ones," asking for their "advice" on matters such as what nutrients the plants needed. The Findhorn community has its own Eco-village, and hosts workshops on topics designed to elevate human consciousness.

The main thrust of the 1970s and 1980s New Age movement was the belief that a new era was arising in which poverty, war, racism, and despair would give way to a new feeling of global human community, with peace, harmony, and happiness prevailing. Since this was not to be accomplished through any religious or political organization, the idea developed that groups of people could act as receivers for positive cosmic energies so that their effects would create a "planetary consciousness" that would spread to the rest of the world. Many New Age groups thus gathered to receive the cosmic energies and try to create enough critical mass to change the world.

The longed-for era of peace and harmony did not emerge, and talk of a "New Age" gradually faded away. However, the many professionals who were making a living as workshop leaders, holistic health practitioners, publishers of New Age literature, and the like were still on the scene. Collectively they shifted to emphasizing transformation in individual consciousness, perhaps coupled with the longer-term goal of global transformation.

While part of the New Age movement lost its millennial nature and focused instead on personal growth and the search for mystical communion through techniques such as meditation, a different millennial thrust developed in some circles: the idea that gradually "higher consciousness" will spread among enough humans for others to be drawn into the same enlightened world view and thus the whole world will "ascend."

Sociologists note that many people who participate in nature rituals and New Age movements are nomads who, in countries allowing freedom of religious choice, may wander through a growing supermarket of spiritual offerings, taking a bit here and there according to their needs of the moment. Sandra Duarte de Souza describes "spiritual nomadism" in contemporary Brazil, where most people remain nominally Christian but many are also attracted to nature-oriented New Age groups. As opposed to a "radical change of life, marking the biography of the converted forever and demanding his faithfulness, . . . the idea of 'religious transit' admits the 'walk through' several religions, does not demand intestinal changes in the way of life of the 'transilient,' and exempts or attenuates the commitment."[11]

Opposition to new religious movements

Throughout history, new religious movements have met with opposition from previously organized religions, which perceive them as threats to their own strength or brand them as heresies. In Russia, various foreign-based new religious movements are fighting for freedom of worship against a 1997 law passed at the behest of the Russian Orthodox Church and restricting the activities of groups that were newly introduced to Russia.

With or without prompting by established religions, nations may attempt to suppress new religious movements. China has taken strong measures to stamp out Falun Gong, one of many movements based on Daoist Qigong energy practices. Falun Gong's teacher, Li Hongzhi, lives in New York City, from where he has spread Falun Gong to thirty countries. He claims to have supernormal abilities and to help others to cultivate them, but warns that the simple exercises are of no value and may be destructive unless practiced in combination with "Zhen-Shan-Ren," the Daoist, Confucian, and Buddhist virtues of truthfulness, benevolence, and forbearance. Falun Gong members assert that Falun Gong is not a religion, but a set of exercises for self-cultivation which may be practiced by people of any religion. However, in 1999, the Chinese government declared Falun Gong an "evil cult," leading to 1,500 deaths by suicide or failure to seek medical care due to faith in the teachings.

In addition to negative reactions from governments and previously organized religions, new religious movements usually meet with opposition from the families of those who join. There is also concern that they may cause psychological damage, especially to vulnerable young people. In the United States, the "anti-cult" movement employed special agents who captured and "deprogrammed" followers of new religions, at the request of their parents. However, the claim that members of new religious movements had been "brainwashed" has been largely discredited.

In addition to the discrediting of the brainwashing theory, the coercive deprogramming techniques of the anti-cult movement have been deemed illegal in themselves. Nevertheless, what are now called "counter-cult" activities continue in the hands of other organizations, such as the American Family Foundation. The effort to eliminate or control new religious movements is also active in Europe, where governments are struggling with issues of religious freedom versus public safety.

Religious pluralism

No single religion dominates the world. Although authorities from many faiths have historically asserted that theirs is the best and only way, new religions and new versions of older religions continue to spring up and then divide, subdivide, and provoke reform movements. With migration, missionary activities, and refugee movements, religions have shifted from their country of origin. In Russia there are not only Russian Orthodox Christians but also Muslims, Catholics, Protestants, Jews, Buddhists, Hindus, shamanists, and members of new religions. Buddhism arose in India but is most pervasive in East Asia and popular in France, England, and the United States. Professor Diana Eck, Chairman of the Pluralism Project at Harvard University, describes what she terms the new "geo-religious reality":

> Our religious traditions are not boxes of goods passed intact from generation to generation, but rather rivers of faith—alive, dynamic, ever-changing, diverging, converging, drying up here, and watering new lands there.
> We are all neighbors somewhere, minorities somewhere, majorities somewhere. This is our new geo-religious reality. There are mosques in the Bible Belt in Houston, just as there are Christian churches in Muslim Pakistan. There are Cambodian Buddhists in Boston, Hindus in Moscow, Sikhs in London.[12]

Hardening of religious boundaries

As religions proliferate and interpenetrate geographically, a common response has been to deny the validity of other religions. In many countries there is tension between the religion most closely linked with national history and identity and other religions that are practiced or have been introduced into the country. People from established religions seek to find a balance between freedom of religion for all and the threat they perceive to their traditional values, customs, and national identity from religious minorities.

Registration for state funding is a means to control or at least track the introduction of religions into countries where they did not originate. Another is banning new or minority religions. In 1997, Russia passed a law prohibiting religions that had not officially existed in Russia longer than fifteen years from distributing religious materials or newspapers or running schools.

In France, in 2004, a law was passed forbidding wearing of religious symbols including Muslim veils, Jewish yarmulkes, and large Christian crosses in French public schools and colleges. The government has also tried to restrict the activities of new religious movements.

In some previously communist countries, old animosities between people of different ethnic groups resurfaced with great violence once totalitarian regimes toppled, as in former Yugoslavia where horrifying atrocities arose among largely Orthodox Christian Serbs, Roman Catholic Croats, and Muslims. Boundaries between religions have also hardened because of the clash between fundamentalism and "**modernism,**" the values of which include individualism, a preference for change rather than continuity, efficiency rather than traditional skills and aesthetics, and pragmatism and profiteering rather than eternal truths and values. Some fundamentalists perceive modernism as threatening the very existence of traditional religious values.

Some fundamentalists have tried to withdraw socially from the secular culture even while surrounded by it. Others have actively tried to change the culture. As described by the Project on Religion and Human Rights:

> Fundamentalists' basic goal is to fight back—culturally, ideologically, and socially—against the assumptions and patterns of life that are taken for granted in contemporary secular society and culture, refusing to celebrate them or to embrace them fully. They keep their distance and refuse to endorse the legitimacy of any culture that opposes what they perceive as fundamental truths. Secular culture, in their eyes, is base, barbarous, crude, and essentially profane. It produces a society that respects no sacred order and ignores the possibility of redemption.[13]

Although fundamentalism may be based on religious motives, it often turns to political means to accomplish its objectives. At the same time, political leaders have used the religious loyalty and absolutism of some fundamentalists to mobilize political loyalties. Buddhism, long associated with non-violence, became involved in the violent repression of the Hindu minority in Sri Lanka. Christians and Muslims are clashing in Indonesia, Nigeria, India and elsewhere. Violence among different branches of the same religion also rages, as in Northern Ireland where Catholic churches have been burned by Protestants. The Internet reveals a troubling number of hate groups promoting intolerance, bigotry, hatred, and violence against specific others in the name of religion.

Terrorism and counter-terrorism

The attacks by terrorists on United States targets in 2001 brought instant polarization along religious and ethnic lines. After September 11, Osama bin Laden proclaimed:

> These events have divided the world into two camps, the camp of the faithful and the camp of infidels. . . . Every Muslim must rise to defend his religion. . . . God is the greatest and glory be to Islam.[14]

Once groups have taken such oppositional standpoints, violence seems inevitable. People will sacrifice their lives as suicide bombers, kill innocent people in terrorist attacks, or conduct assassinations, for the sake of what they consider to be a holy cause. Pilots dropping bombs on Iraq and soldiers treating prisoners brutally may similarly be motivated by the conviction they are doing the right thing and attacking evil by "countering terrorism."

Some observers say the real problem is not conflict among religions but rather a "clash of ignorance."[15] Rigid exclusivist positions do not represent the heart of religious teachings; violence finds no support in any religion. Thus there has been a strong outcry against fundamentalist violence by the mainstream religions from which militants have drawn their faith.

Religion and politics

In many countries, religious groups have become associated with political parties or political interest groups—such as the linkage of Hindu religious fundamentalists with exclusivist nationalist political movements in India, and the linkage between neo-conservative politicians in the United States and evangelical Christian beliefs. Such politicians frequently legitimate their agendas by giving them a religious color or claiming they are defending religion. When religious groups are mobilized for political purposes, people oriented toward power rather than toward spirituality tend to be propelled into leadership roles, while still justifying their actions in religious terms. The political agenda can even become a global one, as in the case of Al Qaeda.

As the Bush administration responded to September 11 by attacking Afghanistan—and later, Iraq—President Bush also proclaimed a global politico-religious agenda: to attack any nation suspected of harboring terrorists and thus presumably bring peace, with God's blessings resting securely upon America. Many international observers feel this triumphalist policy has increased rather than decreased terrorism and violent deaths, and many religious leaders have questioned its ethics, as well as its political usefulness.

While separation of religion and state is one of the defining principles of modern democracy and also of some totalitarian states, certain religious beliefs and symbols are so deeply engrained in people's minds as part of their culture that they may still influence policies and worldviews. In Israel, for instance, even totally secular Jews beset by violence on their borders and terrorism within may subconsciously harbor the ancient Jewish dream of a world at peace—and thus rule out any consideration of ending the Zionist political experiment.

For other religious cultures such as Islam and Sikhism, the combination of religion and polity is perceived as a positive goal—the possibility of the mundane world reordered according to spiritual ideals. Even Buddhism has become engaged in politics, and to some Buddhists' thinking, a pro-active approach to political change is desirable.

Interfaith movement

While boundaries between religions are hardening in many areas, there has been a rapid acceleration of **interfaith dialogue**—the willingness of people of all religions to meet, explore their differences, and appreciate and find enrichment in each other's ways to the divine. This has been historically difficult, for many religions have made claims to being the best or only way.

Religions differ in their external practices and culturally-influenced behaviors. There are doctrinal differences on basic issues, such as the cause of and remedy for evil and suffering in the world, or the question of whether the divine is singular, plural, or nontheistic. And some religions make apparent claims to superiority which are difficult to reconcile with other religions' claims. For example, Christians read in John 14:6 that Jesus said, "I am the way, the truth, and the life; no one comes to the Father but by me." But some Christian scholars now feel that it is inappropriate to take this out of the context of Jesus's disciples asking how to find their way to him after they died, and interpret it to mean that the ways of Hindus, Buddhists, and other faiths are invalid. Many people of broad vision have noted that many of the same principles reappear in all traditions. All religions teach the importance of setting one's own selfish interests aside, loving others, harkening to the divine, and exercising control over the mind. What is called the "Golden Rule," expressed by Confucius as "Do not do unto others what you do not want others to do unto you" is found in every religion.

The absolute authority of scriptures is being questioned by scholars who are interpreting them in their historical and cultural context and thus casting some doubt upon their exclusive claims to truth. Some liberal scholars are also proposing that there is an underlying experiential unity among religions.

Responses to other faiths

People of different religions may relate to each other in different ways. Diana Eck, Professor of Comparative Religion and Indian Studies of Harvard Divinity School and Chair of the World Council of Churches committee on interfaith dialogue, observes there are three responses to contact between religions. One is exclusivism: "Ours is the only true way." Eck and others have noted that this has some value, for personal commitment to one's faith is a foundation of religious life and the first essential step in interfaith dialogue.

Eck sees the second response as **inclusivism**. This may take the form of trying to create a single world religion, such as Baha'i. Or it may appear as the belief that our religion is spacious enough to encompass all the others, that it supersedes all previous religions, as Islam said it was the culmination of all monotheistic traditions. In this approach, the inclusivists do not see other ways as a threat.

The third way Eck discerns is **pluralism**: to hold one's own faith and at the same time ask people of other faiths about their path, about how they want to be understood. Uniformity and agreement are not the goals—the goal is to collaborate, to combine our differing strengths for the common good.

Interfaith initiatives

Initially, ecumenical conferences involved pairs of related religions that were trying to agree to disagree, such as Judaism and Christianity. Now many interfaith organizations and meetings draw people from all religions in a spirit of mutual appreciation. In 1986, Pope John Paul II invited one hundred and sixty representatives of all religions to Assisi in honor of St. Francis, to pray together for world peace. "If the world is going to continue, and men and women are to survive in it, it cannot do without prayer. This is the permanent lesson of Assisi," he declared.[16]

In 1988, the Assisi idea was extended when some two hundred governmental leaders, scientists, artists, business leaders, and media specialists from around the globe, as well as spiritual leaders, in Oxford, England, in 1988 at the Global Forum of Spiritual and Parliamentary Leaders on Human Survival. There was shared concern about the environment, but it was spiritual camaraderie rather than shared fear that brought the participants together. Dr. Wangari Maathai, leader of the Green Belt movement in Kenya, observed:

> *All religions meditate on the Source. And yet, strangely, religion is one of our greatest divides. If the Source be the same, as indeed it must be, all of us and all religions meditate on the same Source.*[17]

In 1990, an assembly of spiritual leaders of all faiths with scientists and parliamentarians took place in Moscow. The final speaker was Mikhail Gorbachev, who called for a merging of scientific and spiritual values in the effort to save the planet.

Throughout 1993, special interfaith meetings were held around the world to celebrate the one hundredth anniversary of the Parliament of the World's Religions, held in Chicago. The provisional conference document signed by many of the leaders, "The Declaration Toward a Global Ethic," included agreement on the Golden Rule:

> *There is a principle which is found and has persisted in many religious and ethical traditions of humankind for thousands of years: What you do not wish done to yourself, do not do to others. Or in positive terms: What you wish done to yourself, do to others! This should be the irrevocable, unconditional norm for all areas of life, for families and communities, for races, nations, and religions.*[18]

The global gathering model has been replicated in various locations. Many people have had the vision that the United Nations could be home to representatives or leaders from all faiths, jointly advising the organization on international policy from a religious perspective.

"Spirituality is not merely tolerance. . . . It is the absolute recognition of the other's faith in God as one's own."

Sri Chinmoy

In addition to global projects, there are many local interfaith initiatives. In some places, these are applied to situations, such as the fighting between Protestants and Catholics in Northern Ireland. In Israel, the Interfaith Encounter Association brings Muslims, Christians, and Jews together to share cultural and spiritual experiences from each other's traditions. In India, where communal violence between people of varying religions is daily news, the Sikh-based interfaith work of Gobind Sadan brings together volunteers of all religions in practical farm work on behalf of the poor, and in celebrations of the holy days of all religions. Baba Virsa Singh, the spiritual inspiration of Gobind Sadan, continually quotes from the words of all the prophets and says:

All the Prophets have come from the same Light; they all give the same basic messages. None have come to change the older revealed scriptures; they have come to remind people of the earlier Prophets' messages which the people have forgotten. We have made separate religions as walled forts, each claiming one of the Prophets as its own. But the Light of God cannot be confined within any manmade structures. It radiates throughout all of Creation. How can we possess it?[19]

Where people have seen their relatives tortured and killed by fanatics of another faith, reconciliation is difficult but necessary if the cycle of violence and counter-violent reactions is to be halted. However, embedded within religions themselves is the basis for harmony, for all teach messages of love and self-control rather than murderous passions.

Religion and social issues

Within every religion, there are contemporary attempts to bring religious perspectives to bear on the critical issues facing humanity. Today we are facing new issues that were not directly addressed by older teachings, such as the ethics of genetic engineering. And some issues have reached critical proportions in our times, such as terrorism, injustice, the gap between rich and poor, racism and violence, poverty, and the deterioration of the natural environment. The Catholic liberation theologian Gustavo Gutierrez asserts:

In the last analysis, poverty means an unjust and early death. Now everything is subordinated to market economies, without taking into consideration the social consequences for the weakest. People say, for example, that in business there are no friends. Solidarity is out of fashion. We need to build a culture of love, through respect of the human being, of the whole of creation. We must practice a justice inspired by love. Justice is the basis of true peace. We must, sisters and brothers, avoid being sorry for or comforting the poor. We must wish to be friends of the poor in the world.[20]

The HIV/AIDS pandemic, which some feel is the greatest social crisis in the world, may continue to grow in the future, challenging religious groups and people to develop appropriate responses. Though late in starting, the response of religions is now growing rapidly, with dialogues, debates, and actions being undertaken from local to international levels by religious institutions. In Uganda, one of the worst-hit countries in Africa, the disease was identified in 1982. By 1992, the government recognized the country's future development could be seriously imperiled by the disease, so it organized the Uganda AIDS Commission. Catholic, Protestant, and Muslim leaders have been active members and chairs of the commission and have helped it to be candid about the problem and sensitive to the people's religious beliefs and practices.

Poverty is another issue that should be of great concern to religions and religious people. While every religion has some version of the "Golden Rule," there is an increasing gap between rich and poor, and poor people are homeless and dying from malnutrition and starvation in countries where wealthy people are benefiting from their cheap labor and politicians are benefiting from their votes.

In India, home to the world's largest tribal populations, and the world's largest democracy, over eighty percent of tribal peoples remain below the poverty line, sick, malnourished, ill-educated, lacking basic services, and hungry. Some faith-based NGOs such as the Swadhyaya Movement, based on the principles of ancient Hindu scriptures, and Gobind Sadan (Chapter 10) are trying to help people on a local scale, but there is as yet no concerted, sincere, large-scale effort by religiously conscientious people to change this bleak picture. To varying extents, the same widening gap between rich and poor is evident in other countries. Until individualism gives way to genuine concern for the community, this pattern may persist and worsen in years to come.

Religion and materialism

All religions teach that one should not hurt others, should not lie, should not steal, should not usurp others' rights, should not be greedy, but rather should be unselfish, considerate, and helpful to others, and humble before the Unseen. These universal spiritual principles were swamped by the expansion of capitalism in the twentieth century, as the profit motive triumphed as the most important value in economies around the world. Today, many people live by material greed alone, with no further meaning to their lives.

Many individuals and corporations have stepped back to consider how to reconcile spiritual motives with earning a living. Books on voluntary simplicity have proliferated on the bestseller lists. Typically, they encourage the relatively wealthy to cut back on their breakneck work pace for the sake of their own spiritual peace, and to cut back on unnecessary individual expenditures for the sake of sharing with others. Many people are also taking a second look at the effect of economic systems. Liberal capitalism, for example, is being reinterpreted not as a means of allowing industrious people to climb out of poverty, but as a potentially amoral system. In free market capitalism, as Pope Paul VI commented: "The right to the means of production is absolute. It has no limits. It has no social obligation."[21]

A new social consciousness that reflects religious values is beginning to enter some workplaces. Professor Syed Anwar Kabir, a faithful Muslim on the faculty of the Management Development Institute in New Delhi, India, teaches his managerial students to do mind-stilling meditation daily in order to listen to their own conscience and make ethical choices from a base of inner tranquility.

However, in the twenty-first century, power-mongering, self-interest, and corruption are at the forefront of economic and political activities; honesty, altruism, service, harmony, justice, and the public good are not the primary motivating forces in most government actions.

The world stage is ready for a true moral and spiritual revolution, in which people of every faith truly begin to practice in their own lives what their prophets have taught. The words of the late French sage Teilhard de Chardin are often quoted in these apocalyptic days:

> Some day, after mastering the winds, the waves, the tides, and gravity, we shall harness for God the energies of love. And then, for the second time in the history of the world, man will have discovered fire.

Jimmy Carter

When Jimmy Carter left the White House in 1981, he founded the Habitat for Humanity, which helps to build houses for the poor, and the Carter Center, which works to help governments solve conflict through peace talks rather than violence. The Center also promotes development, health, and human rights in many countries. Jimmy Carter explains the philosophy underlying these efforts:

War is the greatest violation of basic human rights that one people can inflict upon another. . . . War touches not only soldiers in battle and leaders in government but ordinary citizens—men, women, and children—as well. . . .

It is one thing to say that we each have the right not to be killed. It is another to say that we each have the right to live comfortably, . . . It is even more powerful to say that we each have the right to worship as we choose, to say what we choose, and to be governed by leaders we choose. And perhaps the most powerful statement of all is to say that we each hold these rights equally—that no one person is more entitled to any of these rights than the next, regardless of his or her sex, race, or station in life.[22]

Jimmy Carter is deeply religious, a committed Christian. He asserts:

Faith is the gift of God, and it is more precious than gold; . . . Without a central core of beliefs or standards by which to live, we may never experience the challenge and excitement of seeking a greater life.[23]

In the midst of difficulties, Jimmy Carter is comforted by a personal sense of the presence of God. He reflects:

We have an innate desire to relate to the all-knowing, the all-powerful, and the ever-present—to some entity that transcends ourselves. I am grateful and happy when I feel the presence of God within me, as a tangible influence on my thoughts and on the ultimate standards of my life.[24]

Jimmy Carter is one of the leaders engaged in a deep struggle to restore fundamental American values in government. He explains:

In recent years, I have become increasingly concerned by a host of radical government policies that now threaten many basic principles espoused by all previous administrations, Democratic and Republican. These include the rudimentary American commitment to peace, economic and social justice, civil liberties, our environment and human rights. . . . Instead of our tradition of espousing peace as a national priority unless our security is directly threatened, we have proclaimed a policy of "preemptive war," . . .

As the world's only superpower, America should be seen as the unswerving champion of peace, freedom and human rights. . . . It is time for the deep and disturbing political divisions within our country to be substantially healed, with Americans united in a common commitment to revive and nourish the historical political and moral values that we have espoused during the last 230 years.[25]

Review questions

1. What are the common themes and the differences among Neo-Paganism, Deep Ecology, and New Age Spirituality?
2. Describe the arguments between those opposed to tolerating new religions and those who favor religious toleration for them. Which is stronger now?
3. Explain five major themes in the interfaith movement.

Discussion questions

1. Why do you think that some new fundamentalist movements have turned to violence?
2. Do you think that religions should become involved with politics? Why?
3. Can you envision qualities and beliefs that would constitute a positive new religion?

NOTES

CHAPTER 1
RELIGIOUS RESPONSES

1 Karl Marx, from "Contribution to the Critique of Hegel's Philosophy of Right," 1884, *Karl Marx, Early Writings*, translated and edited by T. B. Bottomore, London: C. A. Watts and Co., 1963, pp. 43–44; *Capital*, vol. 1, 1867, translated by Samuel Moore and Edward Aveling, F. Engels, ed., London: Lawrence & Wishart, 1961, p. 79; "The Communism of the Paper 'Rheinischer Beobachter'," *On Religion*, London: Lawrence & Wishart, undated, pp. 83–84.

2 Karl Marx, "Religion as the Opium of the People," in Karl Marx and Friedrich Engels, *On Religions*, Moscow: Foreign Language Publishing House, 1955, p. 42.

3 Tenzin Gyatso, "The Monk in the Lab," *New York Times*, April 26, 2003, p. A29.

4 Mahatma Gandhi, quoted in Eknath Easwaran, *Gandhi the Man*, Petaluma, California: Nilgiri Press, 1978, p. 121.

5 *The Bhagavad-Gita*, portions of Chapter 2, translated by Eknath Easwaran, quoted in *Easwaran*, op. cit., pp. 121–122.

6 Buddha, *The Dhammapada*, translated by P. Lal, 162/92 Lake Gardens, Calcutta, 700045 India. (Originally published by Farrar, Straus & Giroux, 1967, p. 97.) Reprinted by permission of P. Lal.

7 *Brihadaranyaka Upanishad*, Fourth Adhyaya, Fourth Brahmana, 20, 13, translated by F. Max Müller, *Sacred Books of the East*, vol. 15, Oxford: Oxford University Press, 1884, pp. 178–179.

8 Jiddu Krishnamurti, *The Awakening of Intelligence*, New York: Harper & Row, 1973, p. 90.

9 Radhakrishnan, *The Hindu View of Life*, New Delhi: HarperCollins Publishers India, 1927, 1993, pp 17–18.

10 Martin Luther, as quoted in Gordon Rupp, "Luther and the Reformation," in Joel Hurstfield, ed., *The Reformation Crisis*, New York: Harper & Row, 1966, p. 23.

11 William James, *The Varieties of Religious Experience*, New York: New American Library, 1958, p. 298.

12 AE (George William Russell), *The Candle of Vision*, Wheaton, Illinois: The Theosophical Publishing House, 1974, pp. 8–9.

13 From *The Kabir Book* by Robert Bly, copyright 1971, 1977 by Robert Bly, copyright 1977 by Seventies Press. Reprinted by permission of Beacon Press.

14 Abu Yazid, as quoted in R. C. Zaehner, *Hindu and Muslim Mysticism*, London: University of London, The Athalone Press, 1960, p. 105.

15 Rudolf Otto, *The Idea of the Holy*, translated by John W. Harvey, New York: Oxford University Press, 1958, p. 1.

16 Sallie McFague, *Models of God: Theology for an Ecological, Nuclear Age*, Philadelphia: Fortress Press, 1987, p. 133.

17 Maimonides, "Guide for the Perplexed," 1, 59, as quoted in Louis Jacobs, *Jewish Ethics, Philosophy, and Mysticism*, New York: Behrman House, 1969, p. 80.

18 Guru Gobind Singh, *Jaap Sahib*, English translation by Surendra Nath, New Delhi: Gobind Sadan, 1992, verses 7, 29–31.

19 Antony Fernando, "Outlining the Characteristics of the Ideal Individual," paper for the Inter-Religious Federation for World Peace conference, Seoul, Korea, August 20–27, 1995, p. 9.

20 Pir Vilayat Inayat Khan, "The Significance of Religion to Human Issues in the Light of the Universal Norms of Mystical Experience," *The World Religions Speak on the Relevance of Religion in the Modern World*, Finley P. Ounne, Jr., ed., The Hague: Junk, 1970, p. 145.

21 Rev. Valson Thampu, "Religious Fundamentalisms in India Today," *Indian Currents*, November 2, 1995, p.3

22 Ilya Prigogine, abstract for "The Quest for Certainty," Conference on a New Space for Culture and Society, New Ideas in Science and Art, November 19–23, 1996.

23 Albert Einstein, *The World As I See It*, New York: Wisdom Library, 1979; *Ideas and Opinions*, translated by Sonja Bargmann, New York: Crown Publishers, 1954.

24 Stephen Hawking, *A Brief History of Time: From the Big Bang to Black Holes*, London: Bantam Press, 1988.

25 His Highness the Aga Khan, address to the School of International and Public Affairs, Columbia University, May 15, 2006.

CHAPTER 2
INDIGENOUS SACRED WAYS

1 Vine Deloria, Jr., *God is Red*, New York: Grosset & Dunlap, 1973, p. 267.

2 Lorraine Mafi Williams, personal communication, September 16, 1988.

3 Gerhardus Cornelius Oosthuizen, "The Place of Traditional Religion in Contemporary South Africa," in Jacob K. Olupona, *African Traditional Religions in Contemporary Society*, New York: Paragon House, 1991, p. 36.

4   Quoted by Bob Masla, "The Healing Art of the Huichol Indians," *Many Hands: Resources for Personal and Social Transformation*, Fall 1988, p. 30.

5   George Tinker, *Missionary Conquest: The Gospel and Native American Genocide*, Minneapolis: Fortress Press, 1993, p. 122.

6   John (Fire) Lame Deer and Richard Erdoes, *Lame Deer: Seeker of Visions*, New York: Pocket Books, 1972, p. 100.

7   Knud Rasmussen, *Across Arctic America*, New York: G. P. Putnam's Sons, 1927, p. 386.

8   Interview with Rev. William Kingsley Opoku, August 1992.

9   Josiah U. Young III, "Out of Africa: African Traditional Religion and African Theology," in *World Religions and Human Liberation*, Dan Cohn-Sherbok, ed., Maryknoll, New York: Orbis Books, 1992, p. 93.

10 Bill Neidjie, *Speaking for the Earth: Nature's Law and the Aboriginal Way*, Washington: Center for Respect of Life and Environment, 1991, pp. 40–41. Reprinted from *Kakadu Man* by Big Bill Neidjie, Stephen Davis, and Allan Fox, Northryde, New South Wales, Australia: Angus and Robertson.

11 Jaime de Angulo, "Indians in Overalls," *Hudson Review*, II, 1950, p. 372.

12 Kahu Kawai'i, interviewed by Mark Bochrach in *The Source*, as quoted in *Hinduism Today*, December 1988, p. 18.

13 Quoted in Matthew Fox, "Native teachings: Spirituality with power," *Creation*, January/February 1987, vol. 2, no. 6.

14 John (Fire) Lame Deer and Richard Erdoes, op. cit., p. 116.

15 Tlakaelel, talk at Interface, Watertown, Massachusetts, April 15, 1988.

16 As quoted in Georges Niangoran-Bouah, "The Talking Drum: A Traditional African Instrument of Liturgy and of Meditation with the Sacred," in Jacob K. Olupona, ed., *African Traditional Religions in Contemporary Society*, New York: Paragon House, 1991, pp. 86–87.

17 Leonard Crow Dog and Richard Erdoes, *The Eye of the Heart*, unpublished manuscript, quoted by Joan Halifax, *Shamanic Voices: A Survey of Visionary Narratives*, New York: E. P. Dutton, 1979, p. 77.

18 Quoted in John Neihardt, *Black Elk Speaks 1932*, Lincoln, Nebraska: University of Nebraska Press, 1961, pp. 208–209.

19 John (Fire) Lame Deer with Richard Erdoes, op. cit., pp. 145–146.

20 Tsering, in Ian Baker, "Shaman's Quest," *Hinduism Today*, November 1997, p. 23.

21 From an interview conducted for this book by Tatiana Kuznetsova.

22 Ruth M. Underhill, *Papago Woman*, New York: Holt, Rinehart and Winston, 1979, p. 9.

23 Leonard Crow Dog and Richard Erdoes, in Joan Halifax, *Shamanic Voices*, op. cit., p. 77.

24 Interview with Wande Abimbola, August 6, 1992.

25 Tlakaelel, op. cit.

26 In Lee Romney and James F. Smith, "Crowds hail Zapatistas' Arrival in Mexico City," *Los Angeles Times*, March 13, 2001.

27 Jameson Kurasha, "Plato and the Tortoise: A Case for the death of ideas in favour of peace and life?", paper presented at Assembly of the World's Religions, Seoul, Korea, August 1992, pp. 4–5.

28 Rigoberta Menchú, quoted in Art Davidson, *Endangered Peoples*, San Francisco: Sierra Club Books, 1994, p. ix.

29 Winona LaDuke, *Last Standing Woman*, Stillwater, Minnesota: Voyageur Press, 1997, p. 17.

30 Winona LaDuke, as quoted by Jamie Marks, "A campaignless campaign," *Becker County Record*, September 8, 1996, p. 1A.

31 Winona LaDuke, *Last Standing Woman*, op. cit., p. 299.

CHAPTER 3

HINDUISM

1   Sukta-yajur-veda XXVI, 3, as explained by Sai Baba in *Vision of the Divine* by Eruch B. Fanibunda, Bombay: E. B. Fanibunda, 1976.

2   *The Upanishads*, translated by Swami Prabhavananda and Frederick Manchester, The Vedanta Society of Southern California, New York: Mentor Books, 1957.

3   *Chandogya Upanishad*, ibid., p. 46.

4   *Brihadaranyaka Upanishad*, ibid.

5   Swami Sivananda, *Dhyana Yoga*, fourth edition, Shivanandanagar, India: The Divine Life Society, 1981, p. 67.

6   Ramana Maharshi, *The Spiritual Teaching of Ramana Maharshi*, Boston: Shambhala, 1972, pp. 4, 6.

7   Swami Vivekananda, *Karma-Yoga and Bhakti-Yoga*, New York: Ramakrishna-Vivekananda Center, 1982, p. 32.

8   Chapter II:49 (p. 36), chapter V:8, p. 12. All quotes from the *Bhagavad-Gita* are from *Bhagavad-Gita as It Is*, translated by A. C. Bhaktivedanta Swami Prabhupada, New York: Copyright 1972, The Bhaktivedanta Book Trust. Reproduced withpermission of The Bhaktivedanta Book Trust International.

9   Bhakta Nam Dev, as included in Sri Guru Granth Sahib, p. 693, adapted from the translation by Manmohan Singh, Amritsar, India: Shiromani Gurdwara Parbandhak Committee, 1989.

10 Bhakta Ravi Das, as included in Sri Guru Granth Sahib, p. 694, op. cit.

11 Ramakrishna, quoted in Carl Jung's introduction to *The Spiritual Teaching of Ramana Maharshi*, op. cit., p. viii.

12 Leela Arjunwadkar, "Ecological Awareness in Indian Tradition (Specially as Reflected in

Sanskrit Literature)," paper presented at Assembly of the World's Religions, Seoul, Korea, August 24–31, 1992, p. 4.

13 *The Thousand Names of the Divine Mother: Sri Lalita Sahasranama*, with commentary by T. V. Narayana Menon, English translation by Dr. M. N. Namboodiri, Amritapuri, Kerala, India: Mata Amritanandamayi Math, 1996, verses 1–2, 8, 158–161, 220–224, pp. 5–6, 11, 82–3, 106–107.

14 Swami Sivasiva Palani, personal communication, October 26, 1989.

15 T. M. P. Mahadevan, *Outlines of Hinduism*, second edition, Bombay: Chetana Ltd., 1960, p. 24.

16 A condensation by Heinrich Zimmer of the *Vishnu Purana*, Book IV, Chapter 24, translated by H. H. Wilson, London, 1840, in *Zimmer's Myths and Symbols in Indian Art and Civilization*, New York: Pantheon Books, 1946, p. 15.

17 Uttara Kandam, *Ramayana*, third edition, as told by Swami Chidbhavananda, Tiriuuparaitturai, India: Tapovanam Printing School, 1978, pp. 198–199.

18 *Bhagavad-Gita as It Is*, op. cit., III:30, p. 57.

19 Ibid., III:30, p. 57.

20 Ibid., IV:3, p. 64.

21 Ibid., IV:7–8, pp. 68–69.

22 Ibid., VII:7–8, 12, pp. 126, 128.

23 Ibid., IX:26, p. 157.

24 The Code of Manu, IV.43, as quoted in Roderick Hindery, *Comparative Ethics in Hindu and Buddhist Traditions*, second edition, Delhi: Motilal Banarsidass Publishers, 1996, p. 85.

25 Somjit Dasgupta, interviewed February 26, 2006.

26 *Thus Spake Sri Ramakrishna*, fifth edition, Madras: Sri Ramakrishna Math, 1980, p. 54.

27 Swami Prajnananda, introduction to *Light on the Path*, Swami Muktananda, South Fallsburg, New York: SYDA Foundation, 1981, p. x.

28 William F. Fisher, "Sacred Rivers, Sacred Dams: Competing Visions of Social Justice and Sustainable Development along the Narmada," in Christopher Key Chapple, and Mary Evelyn Tucker, eds., *Hinduism and Ecology*, Boston: Harvard University Press, 2000, p. 413.

29 Ibid., p.410.

30 Aditi Sengupta De, "The 'holy' mess," c/o editor@ip.eth.net, July 31, 2000.

31 Robert N. Minor, "Sarvepalli Radhakrishnan and 'Hinduism': Defined and Defended," in Robert D. Baird, ed., *Religion in Modern India*, New Delhi: Manohar Publications, 1981, p. 306.

32 Condensed Gospel of Sri Ramakrishna, Mylapore, Madras: Sri Ramakrishna Math, 1911, p. 252.

33 Ramakrishna, as quoted in Swami Vivekananda, *Ramakrishna and His Message*, Howra, India: Swami Abhayananda, Sri Ramakrishna Math, 1971, p. 25.

34 Shahid Faridi, "RSS is teaching distorted history in its schools," *Asian Age*, August 28, 2000, p. 3.

35 Abbreviation of Indian Supreme Court definition of Hinduism, as itemized in "The DNA of Dharma," *Hinduism Today*, December 1996, p. 33.

36 All quotations are from an interview with Dr. Karan Singh, November 17, 1998.

37 Karan Singh, *Essays on Hinduism*, second edition, New Delhi: Ratna Sagar, 1990, p. 43.

CHAPTER 4
BUDDHISM

1   Muhaparinibbana Sutta, Digha Nikaya, 2.99f, 155–156, quoted in *Sources of Indian Tradition*, William Theodore de Bary, ed., New York: Columbia University Press, 1958, pp. 110–111.

2   "A message from Buddhists to the Parliament of the World's Religions," Chicago, September 1993, as quoted in *World Faiths Encounter* no. 7, February 1994, p. 53.

3   Majjhima-Nikaya, "The Lesser Matunkya-putta Sermon," Sutta 63, translated by P. Lal in the introduction to *The Dhammapada*, op. cit., p. 19.

4   Walpola Sri Rahula, *What the Buddha Taught*, revised edition, New York: Grove Press, 1974, p. 17.

5   Ajahn Sumedho, "Now is the Knowing," undated booklet, pp. 21–22.

6   Sigalovada Sutta, Dighanikaya III, pp. 180–193, quoted in H. Saddhatissa, *The Buddha's Way*, New York: George Braziller, 1971, p. 101.

7   *The Dhammapada*, translated by P. Lal, op. cit., p. 152.

8   Ibid., p. 49.

9   Achaan Chah in *A Still Forest Pool*, Jack Kornfield and Paul Breiter, eds., Wheaton, Illinois: Theosophical Publishing House, 1985.

10 *The Mahavagga* 1.

11 *Suttanipatta* 1093–4.

12 *Majjhima-Nikaya* 1:161–4.

13 *The Dhammapada*, translated by P. Lal, op. cit., pp. 71–72.

14 Samyutta Nikaya, quoted in the introduction to *The Dhammapada*, translated by P. Lal, op. cit., p. 17.

15 Joko Beck, as quoted in Lenore Friedman, *Meetings with Remarkable Women*, Boston: Shambhala, 1987, p. 119.

16 *Mahaparinibbana Sutta* ii.142.

17 His Holiness the Fourteenth Dalai Lama, speaking on February 15, 1992, in New Delhi, India, Ninth Dharma Celebration of Tushita Meditation Centre.

18   As quoted in Lenore Friedman, *Meetings with Remarkable Women*, op. cit., p. 75.

19   Platform Scripture of the Sixth Patriarch, Hui-neng, quoted in *World of the Buddha*, Lucien Stryk, ed., New York: Doubleday Anchor Books, 1969, p. 340.

20   From "Hsin hsin ming" by Sengtsan, third Zen patriarch, translated by Richard B. Clarke.

21   Roshi Philip Kapleau, *The Three Pillars of Zen*, New York: Anchor Books, 1980, p. 70.

22   Bunan, quoted in *World of the Buddha*, Stryk, op. cit., p. 343.

23   Genshin, "The Essentials of Salvation," quoted in William de Bary, ed., *The Buddhist Tradition in India, China, and Japan*, New York: Modern Library, 1969, p. 326.

24   The Most Venerable Nichidatsu Fujii, quoted in a booklet commemorating the dedication for the Peace Pagoda in Leverett, Massachusetts, October 5, 1985.

25   The Most Venerable Nichidatsu Fujii, ibid.

26   "Rissho Kosei-kai, Practical Buddhism and Interreligious Cooperation," brochure from Rissho Kosei-kai, Tokyo.

27   Lama Drom Tonpa, as quoted in "Gems of Wisdom from the Seventh Dalai Lama," *Snow Lion Newsletter*, vol. 14, no. 4, Fall 1999, p. 14.

28   Stories and Songs from the Oral Tradition of Jetsun Milarepa, translated by Lama Kunga Rimpoche and Brian Cutillo in *Drinking the Mountain Stream*, New York: Lotsawa, 1978, pp. 56–57.

29   His Holiness the fourteenth Dalai Lama, *My Land and my People*, New York: McGraw-Hill, 1962; Indian edition, New Delhi: Srishti Publishers, 1997, p. 50.

30   His Holiness the fourteenth Dalai Lama, evening address after receiving the Nobel Peace Prize, 1989, in Sidney Piburn, ed., *The Dalai Lama: A Policy of Kindness*, second edition, Ithaca, New York: Snow Lion Publications, 1993, p. 114.

31   Thich Nhat Hanh, *Being Peace*, Indian edition, Delhi: Full Circle, 1997, pp. 53–54.

32   Walpola Rahula, "The Social Teachings of the Buddha," in *The Path of Compassion*, Fred Eppsteiner, ed., Berkeley, California: Parallax Press, 1988, pp. 103–104.

33   Metta Sutta, as translated by Maha Ghosananda, in "Invocation: A Cambodian Prayer," *The Path of Compassion*, op. cit., p. xix.

34   Sulak Sivaraksa, "Buddhism in a World of Change," in *The Path of Compassion*, op. cit., p. 16.

CHAPTER 5
DAOISM AND CONFUCIANISM

1   *The I Ching*, translated by Richard Wilhelm (German)/Cary F. Baynes (English), Princeton, New Jersey: Princeton University Press, 1967, pp. 620–621.

2   Excerpt from verse 1 in *Tao-te Ching*, translated by Stephen Mitchell. Translation copyright 1988 by Stephen Mitchell. Reprinted by permission of Harper & Row, Publishers, Inc.

3   *Tao-te Ching*, translated by Lin Yutang, New York: Modern Library, 1948, verse 1, p. 41.

4   Lao-tzu, *Tao-te Ching*, translated by D. C. Lau, London: Penguin Books, 1963, verse 25, p. 82.

5   Lao-tzu, op. cit., p. 82.

6   Chuang-tzu, *Basic Writings*, translated by Burton Watson, op. cit., p. 40.

7   *The Way to Life: At the Heart of the Tao-te Ching*, non-literal translation by Benjamin Hoff, New York/Tokyo: Weatherhill, 1981, p. 52, chapter 78.

8   *The Way to Life*, translated by Benjamin Hoff, op. cit., p. 33, chapter 35.

9   *Dao de jing*, trans. Ellen M. Chen, New York: Paragon House, 1989, Chapter 12.

10   Ibid., Chapter 67.

11   Ibid., Chapter 77.

12   Liu Zhongyu, trans. Lu Pengzhi, "Daoist Folk Customs: Burning Incense and Worshiping Spirits," http://www. eng.taoism.org.hk/religious-activities&rituals/daoist-folk-customs, accessed 3/22/2007.

13   *The Secret of the Golden Flower*, translated by Richard Wilhelm/Cary Baynes, New York: Harcourt Brace Jovanovich, 1962, p. 21.

14   Chuang-tzu, op. cit., p. 59.

15   Excerpted from Huai-Chin Han, translated by Wen Kuan Chu, *Tao and Longevity: Mind–Body Transformation*, York Beach, Maine: Samuel Weiser, 1984, pp. 4–5.

16   Sun Bu-er, in *Immortal Sisters: Secrets of Taoist Women*, translated by Thomas Cleary, Boston: Shambhala Publications, 1989, p. 50.

17   Quoted in *T'ai-chi, Cheng Man-ch'ing and Robert W. Smith*, Rutland, Vermont: Charles E. Tuttle, 1967, p. 106.

18   Yu Yingshi, "A Difference in Starting Points," *Heaven Earth*, ibid., p. 1.

19   The Analects, VII: 1, in *Sources of Chinese Tradition*, vol. 1, William Theodore de Bary, Wing-tsit Chan, and Burton Watson, eds., New York: Columbia University Press, 2000, p. 23.

20   Ibid. XIII: 6, p. 32, and Analects II: 1, as translated by Ch'u Chai and Winberg Chai in *Confucianism*, Woodbury, New York: Barron's Educational Series, 1973, p. 52.

21   Confucius, *The Analects*, translated by D. C. Lau, London: Penguin Books, 1979, VIII:19, p. 94.

22   *The Texts of Confucianism, Sacred Books of the East*, Max Müller, ed., Oxford: Oxford University Press, 1891, vol. 27, pp. 450–451.

23   The Analects, XI:11, in Ch'u Chai and Winberg Chai, *The Sacred Books of Confucius and Other Confucian Classics*, New Hyde Park,

New York: University Books, 1965, p. 46.

24 Ibid., X:25.

25 Ibid., X:103.

26 Mencius, in De Bary, op. cit., p. 91.

27 Ibid., p. 89.

28 From the Hsun Tzu, Chapter 17, in de Bary, op. cit., p. 101.

29 Zhang Zai's Western Inscription, in William Theodore de Bary et al., *Sources of Chinese Tradition*, op. cit.

30 *Quotations from Chairman Mao tse-Tung*, second edition, Peking: Foreign Language Press, 1967, pp. 172–173.

31 *China Daily*, January 30, 1989, p. 1.

32 Korean Overseas Information Service, Religions in Korea, Seoul, 1986, pp. 55–57.

33 Mary Evelyn Tucker, in Tu Weiming and Mary Evelyn Tucker, *Confucian Spirituality*, New York: Crossroad Publishing Company, 2003, p. 1.

CHAPTER 6
SHINTO

1 Yukitaka Yamamoto, *Way of the Kami*, Stockton, California: Tsubaki America Publications, 1987, p. 75.

2 Adapted from the *Nihon Shoki (Chronicles of Japan)*, I:3, in Stuart D. B. Picken, *Shinto: Japan's Spiritual Roots*, Tokyo: Kodansha International, 1980, p. 10.

3 Sakamiki Shunzo, "Shinto: Japanese Ethnocentrism," in Charles A. Moore, ed., *The Japanese Mind*, Hawaii: University of Hawaii Press, p. 25.

4 Kishimoto Hideo, "Some Japanese Cultural Traits and Religions," in Charles A. Moore, ed., *The Japanese Mind*, op. cit., pp. 113–114.

5 Ise-Teijo, Gunshin-Mondo, Onchisosho, vol. x., quoted in *Genchi Kato*, p. 185.

6 Unidentified quotation, Stuart D. B. Picken, ed., *A Handbook of Shinto*, Stockton, California: The Tsubaki Grand Shrine of America, 1987, p. 14.

7 Ibid.

8 Hitoshi Iwasaki, "Wisdom from the night sky," *Tsubaki Newsletter*, June 1, 1988, p. 2.

9 Motoori Norinaga (1730–1801), Naobi no Mitma, quoted in *Tsubaki Newsletter*, November 1, 1988, p. 3.

10 Tenri kyoso den ("Life of the Founder of the Tenrikyo Sect") compiled by the Tenrikyo doshi-kai, Tenri, 1913, quoted in Ichiro Hori, Folk *Religion in Japan*, Chicago: University of Chicago Press, 1968, p. 237.

11 Miki Nakayama, *Ofudesaki: The Tip of the Divine Writing Brush*, Tenri City, Japan: The Headquarters of the Tenrikyo Church, 1971, verses 1–3.

12 Ofudesaki, as quoted in *Aizen Newsletter of the Universal Love and Brotherhood Association*, no. 17, September–October 1997, p. 2.

ZOROASTRIANISM

1 *The Hymns of Zarathushtra*, translated by Jacques Duchesne-Guillemin/Mrs. M. Henning, London: John Murray Publishers, 1952, p. 7.

2 Yasna 33: 14, *Songs of Zarathushtra*, The Gathas translated by Dastur Framroze Ardeshir Bode and Piloo Nanavutty, London: George Allen and Unwin, 1952, p. 66.

3 Yasna 34: 5,4, ibid., p. 67.

4 T. R. Sethna, *Book of Instructions on Zoroastrian Religion*, Karachi, Pakistan: Informal Religious Meetings Trust Fund, 1980, p. 87.

CHAPTER 7
JUDAISM

1 Genesis 1:1. *Tanakh—The Holy Scriptures: The New JPS Translation According to the Traditional Hebrew Text*, Philadelphia: The Jewish Publication Society, 1985. This translation is used throughout this chapter.

2 Genesis 1:28.

3 Genesis 6:17.

4 Genesis 22:12.

5 Personal communication, March 24, 1989.

6 Deuteronomy 7:7.

7 Exodus 3:5.

8 Exodus 3:10.

9 Exodus 3:12, 14–15.

10 Exodus 34:13.

11 I Kings 9:3.

12 Daniel 7:13–14.

13 From the Talmud and Midrash, quoted in *The Judaic Tradition*, Nahum N. Glatzer, ed., Boston: Beacon Press, 1969, p. 197.

14 *Kaddish Shalem*, English translation by Rabbi Sidney Greenberg in *Likrat Shahhat: Worship, Study, and Song for Sabbath and Festival Services and for the Home*, Bridgeport, Connecticut: Media Judaica/The Prayer Book Press, 1981, p. 251.

15 Maimonides, *The Guide of the Perplexed*.

16 Quoted in S. A. Horodezky, *Leaders of Hasidism*, London: Ha-Sefer Agency for Literature, 1928, p. 11.

17 Elie Wiesel, *Night*, New York: Bantam Books, 1960, 1982, p. 64.

18 Aviezer Ravitzky, *Messianism, Zionism, and Jewish Religious Radicalism*, Chicago: The University of Chicago Press, 1993, p. 1.

19 Maimonides' "First Principles of Faith," as quoted in Louis Jacobs, *Principles of Jewish Faith*, Northvale, New Jersey: Jason Aronson, 1988, p. 33.

20 Ibn Gabirol, Keter Malkhut, quoted in Abraham J. Heschel, "One God," in *Between God and Man: An Interpretation of Judaism, from the Writings of Abraham J. Heschel*, Fritz A. Rothschild, ed., New York: Free Press, 1959, p. 106.

21 Abraham Joshua Heschel, *Man is not Alone*, New York: Farrar, Straus & Giroux, 1951, 1976, p. 112.
22 Abraham J. Heschel, "One God," op. cit., p. 104.
23 Martin Buber, in *The Way of Response: Martin Buber – Selections from His Writings*, Nahum N. Glatzer, ed., New York: Schocken Books, 1968, p. 53.
24 Isaiah 65:25, JPS Tanakh.
25 Ismar Schorsch, "Learning to Live with Less: A Jewish Perspective," in Steven C. Rockefeller and John E. Elder, *Spirit and Nature: Why the Environment is a Religious Issue*, Boston: Beacon Press, 1992, p. 35.
26 Job 1:20–21.
27 The Jewish Prayer Book, as quoted by Jocelyn Hellig, "A South African Jewish Perspective," in Martin Forward, ed., *Ultimate Visions*, Oxford: Oneworld Publications, 1995, p. 136.
28 Leviticus 11:45.
29 Talmud Berakhoth 11a, in *Ha-Suddur Ha-Shalem*, translated by Philip Birnbaum, New York: Hebrew Publishing Company, 1977, p. 14.
30 Sanhedrin 22a, quoted in *The Second Jewish Catalog*, Sharon Strassfeld and Michael Strassfeld, eds., Philadelphia: The Jewish Publication Society, 1976.
31 Rabbi Yochanan ben Nuri, Rosh Hashanah prayer quoted by Arthur Waskow, *Seasons of Our Joy*, New York: Bantam Books, 1982, p. 11.
32 Isaiah 55:6–7.
33 Michael Lerner, *Jewish Renewal: A Path to Healing and Transformation*, New York: HarperCollins, 1994, p. 365.
34 Prayer quoted by Arthur Waskow, op. cit., p. 175.
35 Rabbi Maria Feldman, "Why Advocacy is Central to Reform Judaism," Religious Action Center of Reform Judaism, http://rac.org/_kd_items/actions.cfm, accessed 14 April 2007.
36 Rabbi David Saperstein, Press Conference at the Dirksen Senate Office Building, http://www.interfaithalliance.org/site/pp.asp?c=8dKOOW<CE&b=120706, accessed 4/14/2007.
37 Rabbi David Saperstein, "Religious Under-pinnings of Social Justice," remarks on being given the Chernin Award by the Jewish Council for Public Affairs, 2003.
38 Mordecai M. Kaplan, "The Way I Have Come," in *Mordecai M. Kaplan: An Evaluation*, I. Eisenstein and E. Kohn, eds., New York: Jewish Reconstructionist Foundation, 1952, p. 293.
39 Rita M. Gross, "Steps toward Feminine Imagery of Deity in Jewish Theology," in Susannah Heschel, *On Being a Jewish Feminist: A Reader*, New York: Schocken Books, 1983, 1995, p. 237.
40 Jewish Orthodox Feminist Alliance, http://www.jofa.org/ about.php/who, accessed 4/18/2007.
41 Judith Plaskow, *Standing Again at Sinai*, San Francisco: HarperCollins, 1991, p. 120.
42 "Declaration of the ELCA to the Jewish Community," as quoted in Joel Beversluis, *A Sourcebook for Earth's Community of Religions*, revised edition, Grand Rapids, Michigan: CoNexus Press-Sourcebook Project, 1995, p. 170.
43 Rabbi Dovid Karpov, interviewed October 24, 1994.

CHAPTER 8
CHRISTIANITY

1 Publishing Department of Moscow Patriarchate, The Russian Orthodox Church, Moscow, 1980, p. 239 in English translation by Doris Bradbury, Moscow: Progress Publishers, 1982.
2 *The Gospel According to Thomas*, Coptic text established and translated by Guilloaumont et al., Leiden: E. J. Brill; New York: Harper & Row, 1959, verse 77.
3 Luke 2:47, 49. Most biblical quotations in this chapter are from the *Revised Standard Version of the Bible*, copyright 1946, 1952, 1971 by The Division of Christian Education of the National Council of the Churches of Christ in the USA. Used by permission.
4 Mark 1:10–11.
5 Matthew 6:25–27.
6 Matthew 7:7.
7 Luke 9:17.
8 John 6:48.
9 William, quoted in *The Gospel in Art by the Peasants of Solentiname*, Philip and Sally Scharper, eds., Maryknoll, New York: Orbis Books, 1984, p. 42.
10 Matthew 5:21–22.
11 Matthew 5:44–45.
12 Mark 10:27.
13 Matthew 22:39.
14 Matthew 5:3.
15 Mark 1:15.
16 Luke 4:43.
17 Matthew 6:10.
18 Matthew 24:29–31.
19 Matthew 15:10, *The New English Bible*.
20 Matthew 23:27–28, *The New English Bible*.
21 Mark 8:29–30.
22 John 11:27.
23 Matthew 17:2–5.
24 John 7:16, 8:12, 23, 58.
25 Matthew 26:28.
26 Mark 11:10.
27 Mark 14:36.
28 Joachim Jeremias, *New Testament Theology: The Proclamation of Jesus*, translated by John Bowden, New York: Charles Scribner's Sons, 1971, p. 40.
29 Mark 14:41.

30 Matthew 26:64.

31 Matthew 27:11.

32 John 18:35–38.

33 Matthew 27:46.

34 Matthew 28:18–20.

35 Elisabeth Schüssler Fiorenza, *In Memory of Her*, New York: Crossroad, 1983, 1994, p. xliv.

36 Acts 2:36.

37 Acts 26:18.

38 Philippians 3:8–10.

39 Acts 17:28.

40 The Gospel According to Thomas, op. cit., 82.

41 Confessions of St. Augustine, translated by Edward Bouverie Pusey, Chicago: Encyclopedia Britannica, vol. 18 of *Great Books of the Western World*, 1952, p. 64.

42 Rowan Williams, *Resurrection*, New York: The Pilgrim Press, 1984, p. 46 with quotations from John 14:19.

43 Archimandrite Chrysostomos, *The Ancient Fathers of the Desert*, Brookline, Massachusetts: Hellenic College Press, 1980, p. 78.

44 Ibid., p. 80.

45 Mikhail S. Gorbachev, quoted in Michael

Dobbs, "Soviets, Vatican to Establish Ties," *The Hartford Courant*, December 2, 1989, p. 1.

46 Father Feodor, interviewed October 29, 1994.

47 Fotini Pipili, in Iina Kyriakidou, "Greek women poised to take on all-male monastic community," *Asian Age*, October 14, 1997, p. 7.

48 St. Gregory Palamas, "Homily on the Presentation of the Holy Virgin in the Temple," in Sophocles, 22 Homilies of St. Gr. Palamas, Athens, 1861, pp. 175–177, quoted in Vladimir Lossky, *The Mystical Theology of the Eastern Church*, New York: St. Vladimir's Seminary Press, 1976, p. 224.

49 Jim Forest, *Pilgrim to the Russian Church*, New York: Crossroad Publishing Company, 1988, p. 50.

50 From *A Hopkins Reader*, John Pick, ed., New York: Oxford University Press, 1953, quoted in D. M. Dooling, ed., *A Way of Working*, New York: Anchor Press/ Doubleday, 1979, p. 6.

51 St. Francis, Testament, April 1226, p. 3, quoted in Jean Leclerc, Francois Vandenbroucke, and Louis Bouyer, eds., *The Spirituality of the Middle Ages*, vol. 2 of *A History of Christian Spirituality*, New York: Seabury Press, 1982, p. 289.

52 *The Cloud of Unknowing and The Book of Privy Counseling*, Garden City, New York: Image Books, 1973 edition, p. 56.

53 Martin Luther, "A Treatise on Christian Liberty," quoted in John Oillenberger and Claude Welch, *Protestant Christianity*, New York: Charles Scribner's Sons, 1954, p. 36.

54 Ulrich Zwingli, "On True and False Religion," quoted in Harry Emerson Fosdick, ed., *Great Voices of the Reformation*, New York: Random House, 1952, p. 169.

55 John Calvin, "Instruction in Faith," quoted in Fosdick, op. cit., p. 216.

56 John Wesley, as quoted in F. L. Cross and E. A. Livingstone, eds., *The Oxford Dictionary of the Christian Church*, Oxford: Oxford University Press, 1983, p. 1467.

57 St. Teresa of Avila, *The Interior Castle*, translated by E. Allison Peers from the critical edition of P. Silverior de Santa Teresa, Garden City, New York: Image Books, 1961, p. 214.

58 John Wesley, as quoted in John Dillenberger and Claude Welch, *Protestant Christianity*, New York: Charles Scribner's Sons, 1954, p. 134.

59 Sarah Grimke, "Letters on the Equality of the Sexes and the Condition of Women" (1836–1837), in *Feminism: The Essential Historical Writings*, M. Schneir, ed., New York: Vintage, 1972, p. 38.

60 *The Documents of Vatican II*, Walter M. Abbott, ed., New York: Guild Press, 1966, p. 665.

61 Ibid., pp. 661–662.

62 John 14:2–10, *The New English Bible*.

63 Paul Knitter, in John Hick and Paul F. Knitter, eds., T*he Myth of Christian Uniqueness: Toward a Pluralistic Theology of Religions*, Maryknoll, New York: Orbis Books, 1987, pp. 192–193.

64 Matthew 20:28.

65 John 3:16–17, *The New English Bible*.

66 Archbishop Desmond Tutu, "The Face of God," *Life*, December 1990, pp. 49–50.

67 Thomas Keating, *The Mystery of Christ: The Liturgy as Spiritual Experience*, Amity, New York: Amity House, 1987, p. 5.

68 (Thomas a Kempis), *The Imitation of Christ*, p. 139.

69 F. Ioann Kronshtadtsky, as quoted in F. Veniamin Fedchenkov, *Heaven on Earth*, Moscow: Palmnik, 1994, p. 70.

70 "Brief Order for Confession and Forgiveness," Lutheran Book of Worship, prepared by the churches participating in the Inter-Lutheran Commission on Worship, Minneapolis, Minnesota: Augsburg Publishing House, 1978, p. 56.

71 World Council of Churches, Baptism, Eucharist and Ministry, Faith and Order Paper No. 111, Geneva, 1982, p. 2.

72 John 1:9.

73 Thomas Merton, *Contemplative Prayer*, Garden City, New York: Image Books, 1969, p. 67.

74 *The Way of a Pilgrim and The Pilgrim Continues His Way*, translated by Helen Bacovcin, New York/London: Doubleday, 1978, 1992, p. 160.

75 Luke 1:38.

76   Quoted in Jim Forest, *Pilgrim to the Russian Church*, New York: Crossroad Publishing Company, 1988, p. 63.

77   *New York Times*, as reprinted in "The Gospel of Life," *Indian Currents*, April 8, 1995, p. 1.

78   Associated Press, Vatican City: "Only Catholicism 'proper': Vatican," *The Globe and Mail*, September 6, 2000, A14; Philip Pullella (Reuters), "Vatican says no religion equals Roman Catholicism," *Asian Age*, September 6, 2000, p. 5.

79   Quoted in Don A. Schanche and Russell Chandler, *Los Angeles Times*, "Tensions confront pope in U.S.," *The Hartford Courant*, September 11, 1987, p. 1.

80   Harvey Cox, *Fire from Heaven: The Rise of Pentecostal Spirituality and the Reshaping of Religion in the Twenty-first Century*, Reading, Massachusetts: Addison-Wesley, 1995.

81   I Corinthians 12:6–11.

82   Roman I. Bilas, interviewed October 25, 1994.

83   Members of African Independent Churches Report on their Pilot Study of the History and Theology of their Churches, "Speaking for Ourselves," Braamfontein, South Africa: Institute for Contextural Theology, 1985, pp. 23–24.

84   Martin Luther King, Jr., "An Experiment in Love," in *A Testament of Hope: The Essential Writings of Martin Luther King*, Jr., James Melvin Washington, ed., San Francisco: Harper & Row, 1986, p. 16.

85   Desmond Tutu, quoted in Charles Vila-Vicencio, "Tough and Compassionate: Desmond Mpilo Tutu," in Leonard Hulley, Louise Kretzschmar, and Luke Lungile Pato, eds., *Archbishop Tutu: Prophetic Witness in South Africa*, Cape Town: Human and Rousseau, 1996, pp. 41–42.

86   Ibid., p. 37.

87   Ibid., p. 38.

88   Francis Cull, "Desmond Tutu: Man of Prayer," in Hulley et al., op. cit., pp. 31–32.

89   Acts 4:32–35.

90   Gustavo Gutierrez, quoted in Phillip Berryman, *Liberation Theology*, New York: Pantheon Books, 1987, p. 33.

91   Bakole Wa Ilunga, *Paths of Liberation: A Third World Spirituality*, Maryknoll, New York: Orbis Books, 1984, p. 92.

92   James H. Cone, "Looking Back, Going Forward," in Dwight N. Hopkins, ed., *Black Faith and Public Talk*, Maryknoll, New York: Orbis Books, 1999, p. 257.

93   1 Corinthians 11:7–12.

94   Fiorenza, op. cit., p. xx.

95   Ivone Gebara and Maria Clara Bingemer, *Mary, Mother of God, Mother of the Poor*, Maryknoll, New York: Orbis Books, 1989, as excerpted in Ursula King, ed., *Feminist Theology from the Third World*, Maryknoll, New York, Orbis Books, 1994, pp. 277, 280–281.

96   Sallie McFague, *Models of God: Theology for an Ecological, Nuclear Age*, Philadelphia: Fortress Press, 1987, pp. 101, 106.

97   Thomas Berry, remarks at "Seeking the True Meaning of Peace" conference in San Jose, Costa Rica, June 27, 1989.

98   In Laurie Goodstein, "Evangelical Leaders Join Global Warming Initiative," *The New York Times*, February 8, 2006.

99   Father Denis G. Pereira, "A New Model for India's Pastoral Clergy," *Vidyajyoti Journal*, vol. 67, no. 1, January 2003, p. 67.

100 "Decade to Overcome Violence," World Council of Church website, www.wcc-coe.org, October 1, 2001.

CHAPTER 9
ISLAM

1   *The Holy Qur'an*, XCVI:1–5, English translation by Abdullah Yusuf Ali, Durban, R.S.A.: Islamic Propagation Center International, 1946. This translation is used throughout this chapter, by permission. Note that despite the layout of this translation, the Qur'an is not a work of poetry.

2   Abu Abdallah Muhammad Bukhari, Kitab jami as-sahih, translated by M. M. Khan as Sahih al-Bukhari, Lahore: Ashraf, 1978–80, quoted in Annemarie Schimmel, *And Muhammad is His Messenger*, Chapel Hill, North Carolina: University of North Carolina Press, 1985, p. 11.

3   *Sura* 8:18.

4   Maulana M. Ubaidul Akbar, *The Orations of Muhammad*, Lahore: M. Ashraf, 1954, p. 78.

5   *Sura* 41:6.

6   *Sura* 28:56.

7   Hadith quoted by Annemarie Schimmel, *And Muhammad is His Messenger*, Chapel Hill, North Carolina: University of North Carolina Press, 1985, pp. 48 and 55.

8   *The Holy Qur'an*, III:104.

9   Quoted by Mahmoud Ayoub, *The Qur'an and its Interpreters*, Albany: State University of New York Press, 1984, vol. 1, p. 14.

10 *Sura* 42:15.

11 Islamic Society of North America, "Islam at a Glance," Plainfield, Indiana: Islamic Teaching Center.

12 Abu Hashim Madani, quoted in Samuel L. Lewis, *In the Garden*, New York: Harmony Books/Lama Foundation, 1975, p. 136.

13 Frithjof Schuon, *Understanding Islam*, translated by D. M. Matheson, London: George Allen & Unwin, 1963, p. 59.

14 *Sura* 2:136.

15 Farid Esack, personal communication, March 29, 1998.

16 Farid Esack, *Qur'an, Liberation and Pluralism: An Islamic Perspective of Interreligious Solidarity against Oppression*, Oxford: Oneworld Publications, 1997, p. 4.

17 Ibid., p. 223.

18 Ibid., p. 222.

19 Farid Esack, personal communication, March 29, 1998.

20 *Sura* 32:16–17.

21 *Sura* 3:63.

22 *Sura* 41:37.

23 Quoted by Abdur-Rahman Ibrahim Doi, *"Sunnism," Islamic Spirituality: Foundations*, Seyyed Hossein Nasr, ed., New York: Crossroad, 1987, p. 158.

24 *Sura* 17:13–14.

25 *Sura* 70:16–18.

26 *Sura* 2:256.

27 Hadith quoted by Syed Ali Ashraf, "The Inner Meaning of the Islamic Rites: Prayer, Pilgrimage, Fasting, Jihad," in *Islamic Spirituality: Foundations*, op. cit., p. 114.

28 *Sura* 6:162.

29 Hammudah Abdalati, *Islam in Focus*, Indianapolis, Indiana: American Trust Publications, 1975, p. 88.

30 Syed Mousmen Hussain, interviewed October 18, 2006.

31 Quoted by Muhammad Rida al-Muzaffar, *The Faith of Shi'a Islam*, London: The Muhammadi Trust, 1982, p. 35.

32 Hadith #535 cited in Badi'uz-Zaman Furuzanfar, Ahadith-i Mathnawi, Tehran, 1334 sh./1955, in Persian, quoted in Annemarie Schimmel, *Mystical Dimensions of Islam*, Chapel Hill: University of North Carolina Press, 1975, p. 118.

33 Jalal al-Din Rumi, opening lines of the *Mathnawi*, as translated by Edmund Helminski, *The Ruins of the Heart: Selected Lyric Poetry of Jelaluddin Rumi, Putney*, Vermont: Threshold Books, 1981, p. 20.

34 Jalal al-Din Rumi, *Mathnawi-i ma'nawi*, ed. and translated by Reynold A. Nicholson, London, 1925–40, vol. 4, line 2102.

35 Hadith of the Prophet, #352 in *Zaman Furuzanfar*, Ahadith-i Mathnawi, op. cit.

36 Quoted in Javad Nurbakhsh, *Sufism: Meaning, Knowledge, and Unity*, New York: Khaniqahi-Nimatullahi Publications, 1981, pp. 19, 21.

37 Jalal al-Din Rumi, *Mathnawi, VI, 3220–3246*, as translated by Coleman Barks in *Rumi: We Are Three*, Athens, Georgia: Maypop Books, 1987, pp. 54–55.

38 Uzbek Khan, 1313 charter granted to Metropolitan Peter, as quoted in *Al Risala*, June 1994, p. 12.

39 Dalil-ul-Arifin, p. 37, as quoted in W. D. Begg, *The Holy Biography of Hazrat Khwaja Muinuddin Chishti*, Botswana, Africa: G. N. Khan, 1979, p. 41.

40 Indonesian President Suharto, quoted in *Hinduism Today*, July 1989, p. 20.

41 Jalal al-Din Rumi, Mathnawi, IV, in *Rumi: We Are Three*, op. cit., Barks, p. 52.

42 Seyyed Hossein Nasr, "The Pertinence of Islam to the Modern World," *The World Religions Speak on the Relevance of Religion in the Modern World*, Finley P. Dunne Jr., ed., The Hague: Junk, 1970, p. 133.

43 Ardeshir Cowasjee, "As Pak mocks education," Dawn, in *Asian Age*, January 8, 2004, p. 16.

44 Hadith of the Prophet, as quoted in *Fakhr al-Din Al-Razi, Tafsir al-Fakhr al-Razi*, 21 vols., Mecca: al-Kaktabah al-Tijariyyah, 1990, vol. 7, p. 232.

45 *Sura* 22:39–40.

46 *Sura* 2:217, 192.

47 Nical Al-Mughrabi, "Israelis kill five more in Gaza," *Asian Age*, April 22, 2004, p. 8.

48 *Asian Age*, April 22, 2004, p. 8.

49 Tony Blair, then Prime Minister, quoted in Alan Cowell, "Britain Proposes Allowing Schools to Forbid Full-Face Muslim Veils," *New York Times*, March 21, 2007, p. 21.

50 Mahmoon-al-Rasheed, "Islam, Nonviolence, and Social Transformation," Glenn D. Paige, Chaiwat Satha-Anand, and Sarah Gilliatt, eds., Honolulu: University of Hawaii, Center for Global Nonviolence Planning Project, 1993, p. 70.

51 M. R. Bawa Muhaiyaddeen, "Islam's Hidden Beauty: The Sufi Teachings of M. R. Bawa Muhaiyaddeen," tape from New Dimensions Foundation, SanFrancisco, 1989, side 1.

CHAPTER 10
SIKHISM

1 *Songs of Kabir*, translated by Rabindranath Tagore, New York: Samuel Weiser, 1977, p. 45.

2 Puratan, quoted in Khushwant Singh, *Hymns of Guru Nanak*, New Delhi: Orient Longmans Ltd., 1969, p. 10.

3 Guru Nanak, Guru Granth Sahib, p. 150 (as translated by Dr. Gopal Singh, New Delhi: World Book Centre, 1997).

4 Guru Nanak, as quoted in W. Owen Cole and Piara Singh Sambhi, *The Sikhs: Their Religious Beliefs and Practices*, London: Routledge & Kegan Paul, 1978, p. 39.

5 Sri Rag, p. 59, quoted in Trilochan Singh, Jodh Singh, Kapur Singh, Bawa Harkishen Singh, and Kushwant Singh, trans., *The Sacred Writings of the Sikhs*, reproduced by kind permission of Unwin Hyman Ltd., 1973, p. 72.

6 Bhagat Ravi Das, Rag Sorath, Guru Granth Sahib, p. 657.

7 Guru Granth Sahib, p. 724.

8 Guru Har Rai, as quoted in Dr. Gopal Singh, *A History of the Sikh People*, New Delhi: World Sikh University Press, 1979, p. 257.

9 Guru Gobind Singh, *Bachittar Natak*, autobiography.

10 Guru Granth Sahib, p. 1022.

11 Mul Mantra, quoted in *Hymns of Guru Nanak*, op. cit., p. 25.

12 *Jaap Sahib*, verses 84, 159, English translation by Harjett Singh Gill, New Delhi:
Gobind Sadan Institute for Advanced
Studies in Comparative Religion.
13 *Adi Granth* 684, quoted in Cole and Sambhi,
op. cit., p. 74.
14 Guru Nanak, Guru Granth Sahib, p. 141.
15 Ibid.
16 Guru Nanak, Guru Granth Sahib, p. 473.
17 Inderpreet Kaur, interviewed March 20,
2007.
18 *Anand Sahib*, verse 14.
19 Excerpt from Guru Gobind Singh,
Rahitnamas, as translated by Gurden Singh.
20 Excerpted from *Rahitnamas*, op. cit.
21 *Jap Ji* verses 9–10.
22 Baba Virsa Singh, quoted by Juliet Hollister
in *News from Gobind Sadan*, August 1997,
p. 1.
23 Baba Virsa Singh, in *News from Gobind Sadan*,
April 1997, p. 3.
24 Guru Gobind Singh, *Dasam Granth*.

CHAPTER 11
RELIGION IN A NEW ERA

1 Friday M. Mbon, "The Social Impact of
Nigeria's New Religious Movements," in
James A. Beckford, ed., *New Religious
Movements and Rapid Social Change*, Paris and
London: Unesco/Sage Publications, 1986,
p. 177.
2 Quoted in Ernest Cashmore, *Rastaman*,
London: Unwin Paperbacks, 1983, p. 22.
3 Gordon B. Hinkley, PBS interview broadcast
on July 18, 1997.
4 Quoted in Merlin Stone, *When God was a
Woman*, San Diego, California: Harcourt
Brace Jovanovich, 1976, p. x.
5 John Seed, "Anthropocentrism," *Awakening
in the Nuclear Age*, Issue #14 (Summer/Fall
1986), p. 11.
6 Chief Seattle, "Chief Seattle's Message,"
quoted in *Thinking Like a Mountain: Toward a
Council of All Beings*, John Seed, Joanna
Macy, Pat Fleming, and Arne Naess, eds.,
Santa Cruz, California: New Society
Publishers, 1988, p. 71.
7 J. E. Lovelock, *Gaia: A new look at life on
Earth*, Oxford: Oxford University Press,
pp. 9, 11.
8 Peter Russell, "Endangered Earth:
Psychological roots of the environmental
crisis," *Link Up*, Issue #38 (Spring 1989),
pp. 7–8.
9 H. P. Blavatsky, *The Key to Theosophy*, Los
Angeles: The United Lodge of Theosophists,
1920, p. 3.
10 Frithjof Schuon, *Understanding Islam*,
London: George Allen & Unwin Ltd., translated from French, 1963, p. 41.
11 Sandra Duarte de Souza, "Religious Transit
and Ecological Spirituality in Brazil," paper

presented at "The Spiritual Supermarket:
Religious Pluralism in the 21st Century,"
April 19–22, 2001, London School of
Economics, sponsored by the Center for
Studies on New Religions, Italy, p. 4.
12 Diana Eck, "A New Geo-Religious Reality,"
paper presented at the World Conference on
Religion and Peace Sixth World Assembly,
Riva del Garda, Italy, November 1994, p. 1.
13 Charles Strozier et al., "Religious Militancy
or 'Fundamentalism,'" *Religion and Human
Rights*, New York: The Project on Religion
and Human Rights, 1994, p. 19.
14 Osama bin Laden, videotaped address,
October 7, 2001, reprinted in Bruce Lincoln,
*Holy Terrors: Thinking about Religion after
September 11*, Chicago: University of Chicago
Press, 2003, p. 103.
15 His Highness the Aga Khan, Address to the
School of International and Public Affairs,
Columbia University, May 15, 2006.
16 Pope John Paul II, quoted in Richard N.
Ostling, "A Summit for Peace in Assisi,"
Time, November 10, 1986, p. 78.
17 Wangari Maathai, speaking at the Oxford
Global Survival Conference, quoted in *The
Temple of Understanding Newsletter*, Fall 1988,
p. 2.
18 "Towards a Global Ethic," Assembly of
Religious and Spiritual Leaders, at the
Parliament of World Religions, Chicago,
1993.
19 Baba Virsa Singh, in Mary Pat Fisher, ed.,
*Loving God: The Practical Teachings of Baba
Virsa Singh*, New Delhi: Gobind Sadan
Institute for Advanced Studies in
Comparative Religion, pp. 7–8.
20 Gustavo Gutierrez, address to the World
Conference on Religion and Peace, Riva del
Garda, Italy, November 1994.
21 Pope Paul VI, *Populorum Progressio Encyclical*,
1967.
22 Jimmy Carter, *Talking Peace*, New York:
Penguin Books, 1995, pp. xi–xii, 21.
23 Jimmy Carter, *Living Faith*, New York:
Random House, 1998, pp. 5, 13.
24 Ibid., p. 32.
25 Jimmy Carter, "This Isn't the Real America,"
Los Angeles Times, November 14, 2005.

GLOSSARY

In the glossary, most words are accompanied by a guide to pronunciation. This guide gives an accepted pronunciation as simply as possible. Syllables are separated by a space and those that are stressed are underlined. Letters are pronounced in the usual manner for English unless they are clarified in the following list.

a *as in*	flat		u	but
aa	father		ă, ě, ŏ, ŭ,	about (unaccented vowels
aw	saw			represented by "ə" in some
ay	pay			phonetic alphabets)
ai	there		er, ur, ir fern, fur, fir	
ee	see			
e	let		ch	church
i	pity		j	jet
ī	high		ng	sing
o	not		sh	shine
ŏŏ	book		wh	where
oo	food		y	yes
oy	boy		kh	guttural aspiration (ch in Welsh and
ō	no			German)
ow	now			

absolutist Someone who holds rigid, literal, exclusive belief in the doctrines of their religion.

Adi Granth (Guru Granth Sahib) Sacred scriptures of the Sikhs.

Advaita Vedanta (ad vī ee ta ve dan ta) Non-dualistic Hindu philosophy, in which the goal is the realization that the self is Brahman.

Advent The month of spiritual preparation leading up to Christmas.

African Instituted Churches Christian churches primarily founded or shaped in Africa.

Agni (aag nee) The god of fire in Hinduism.

agnosticism (ag nos ti siz ěm) The belief that if there is anything beyond this life, it is impossible for humans to know it.

Allah (aa lă) The one God, in Islam.

Ameshta Spenta In Zoroastrianism, six divine powers (The Good Mind, Righteousness, Absolute Power, Devotion, Perfection, and Immortality), personified and worshiped as deities with

shining eyes and beautiful forms after Zarathustra's death.

Amida (ă mee dă) (Sanskrit: Amitabha) The Buddha of infinite light, the personification of compassion whom the Pure Land Buddhists revere as the intermediary between humanity and Supreme Reality; esoterically, the Higher Self.

amrit (am ret) The water, sweetened with sugar, used in Sikh baptismal ceremonies.

anatman (Pali: **anatta**) The principle that there is no eternal self.

angel In the Zoroastrian, Jewish, Christian, and Islamic traditions, an invisible servant of God.

Anglicanism The Church of England, founded by Henry VIII when he split from Rome and formalized by Elizabeth I in 1559.

anitya (Pali: **anicca**) Impermanence.

Annunciation (ă nun see ay shun) In Christianity, the appearance of an angel to the Virgin Mary to tell her that she

would bear Jesus, conceived by the Holy
Spirit.

anthropocentrism (<u>an</u> thro po <u>sen</u> triz
ĕm) The assumption that the whole
universe revolves around the human
species.

anti-semitism Prejudice against Jews.

apocalypse (ă <u>paw</u> kă lips) In Judaism and
Christianity, the dramatic end of the
present age.

apostasy Accusation of abandonment of
religious principles.

apostle Missionary follower of Christ who
spread his word.

arhant (<u>aar</u> hănt) (Pali: *arhat* or *arahat*) A
"Worthy One" who has followed the
Buddha's Eightfold Path to liberation,
broken the fetters that bind us to the
suffering of the Wheel of Birth and
Death, and arrived at nirvana; the
Theravadan ideal.

Ark of the Covenant In Judaism, the
shrine containing God's commandments
to Moses.

Aryan Invasion Theory Speculation
originally advanced by Western scholars
that the Vedas were written by people
invading India rather than by people
already there.

Aryans (<u>ayr</u> ee ăns) The Indo-European
pastoral invaders of many European and
Middle Eastern agricultural cultures
during the second millennium BCE.

asana (<u>aa</u> să nă) A yogic posture.

Ascension The ascent of Jesus to heaven
forty days after his Resurrection.

Ashkenazim An ethnic grouping of the
Jews that migrated first to Italy, then
spread throughout central and eastern
Europe and thence on to the Americas.

ashram (<u>ash</u> ram) In Indian tradition, a
usually ascetic spiritual community of
those who have gathered around a guru.

Assumption Feast celebrating the bodily
ascent of Mary to heaven.

atheism (<u>ay</u> thee is em) Belief that there is
no deity.

atman (<u>aat</u> man) In Hinduism, the soul.

avatar In Hinduism, the earthly
incarnation of a deity.

Avesta Holy text of Zoroastrian teaching
and liturgy, only fragments of which
have survived.

awakening Awareness of invisible Reality.

Axial Age Period dating approximately
sixth century BCE during which a large
number of great religious leaders and
thinkers appeared in many parts of the
ancient world, including the authors of
the Upanishads, the Buddha, Mahavir,
Confucius, Laozi, Socrates, and
Zarathushtra.

baptism A Christian sacrament by which
God cleanses all sin and makes one a
sharer in the divine life, and a member
of Christ's body, the Church.

Baptists Protestant denomination in which
baptism takes place in adulthood.

barakah (bă <u>raa</u> ka) In Islamic mysticism,
the spiritual wisdom and blessing
transmitted from master to pupil.

Bar Mitzvah (baar <u>mitz</u> vă) The coming-
of-age ceremony for a Jewish boy.

Bat Mitzvah (bat <u>mitz</u> vă) The coming-of-
age ceremony for a Jewish girl in some
modern congregations.

Beatitudes (bee <u>at</u> ĕ toods) Short
statements by Jesus about those who
are most blessed.

Bhagavad-Gita (<u>ba</u> gă văd <u>gee</u> tă) A
portion of the Hindu epic *Mahabharata* in
which Lord Krishna specifies ways of
spiritual progress.

bhakta (<u>bak</u> taa) Devotee of a deity, in
Hinduism.

bhakti (<u>bak</u> tee) In Hinduism, intense
devotion to a personal aspect of the deity.

bhakti yoga In Hinduism, the path of
devotion.

bhikshu (bi kshoo) (Pali: *bhikkhu*;
feminine: *bhikshuni* or *bhikkhuni*). A
Buddhist monk or nun who renounces
worldliness for the sake of following the
path of liberation and whose simple
physical needs are met by lay supporters.

bodhisattva (<u>bŏo</u> dee <u>sat</u> vă) In Mahayana
Buddhism, one who has attained
enlightenment but renounces nirvana for
the sake of helping all sentient beings in
their journey to liberation from suffering.

Brahman (braa măn) The impersonal Ultimate Principle in Hinduism.

Brahmanas (braa mă năs) The portion of the Hindu Vedas concerning rituals.

brahmin (braa min) (brahman) A priest or member of the priestly caste in Hinduism.

Buddha-nature A fully awakened consciousness.

caliph (kay lif) In Sunni Islam, the successor to the Prophet.

Calvinism Protestant denomination founded by John Calvin in the sixteenth century and believing in predestination.

canon Authoritative collection of writings, works, etc., applying to a particular religion or author.

caste (kast) Social class distinction on the basis of heredity or occupation.

catholic Universal, all-inclusive. Christian churches referring to themselves as Catholic claim to be the representatives of the ancient undivided Christian church.

chakra (chuk ră) An energy center in the subtle body, recognized in *kundalini yoga*.

charisma (kă riz mă) A rare personal magnetism, often ascribed to a founder of a religion.

Christmas Feast on December 25 celebrating the birth of Jesus Christ.

Christology The attempt to define the nature of Jesus and his relationship to God.

Common Era Years after the traditional date used for the birth of Jesus, previously referred to in exclusively Christian terms as AD and now abbreviated to CE as opposed to BCE ("before Common Era").

communion *see* Eucharist.

comparative religion Scholarly discipline attempting to understand and compare religious patterns from around the world.

confirmation A Christian sacrament by which awareness of the Holy Spirit is enhanced.

Congregationalism Protestant denomination based on Calvinism, emphasizing the independence of each local congregation.

Conservative Judaism Branch that seeks to maintain traditional laws and practices while employing modern methods of scholarship.

cosmogony (kos mog ŏn ee) A model of the evolution of the universe.

Creationism Belief that all life forms were intentionally created by a Divine Being.

creed A formal statement of the beliefs of a particular religion.

Crucifixion In Roman times, the execution of a criminal by fixing him to a cross; with reference to Jesus, his death on the cross, symbolic of his self-sacrifice for the good of all humanity.

cult Any religion that focuses on worship of a particular person or deity.

Dao (dow) (also Tao) The way or path, in Far Eastern traditions. The term is also used as a name for the Nameless.

darsan (daar shan) Visual contact with the divine through encounters with Hindu images or gurus.

Darwinism Belief that life evolved by biological processes such as natural selection.

davening (daa věn ing) In Hasidic Judaism, prayer.

deity yoga (dee i tee yō gă) In Tibetan Buddhism, the practice of meditative concentration on a specific deity.

denomination (di nom ě nay shun) One of the Protestant branches of Christianity.

dervish (der vish) A Sufi ascetic, in the Muslim tradition.

deva (day vă) In Hinduism, a deity.

Dhammapada (dam ă pă dă) A collection of short sayings attributed to Buddha.

dharma (daar mă) (Pali: *dhamma*) In Hinduism, moral order, righteousness, religion. In Buddhism, the doctrine or law, as revealed by the Buddha; also the correct conduct for each person according to his or her level of awareness.

dhimmi (dě hem ee) A person of a non-Muslim religion whose right to practice that religion is protected within an Islamic society.

diaspora (dī <u>ass</u> po ra) Collectively, the practitioners of a faith living beyond their traditional homeland. When spelled with a capital "D", the dispersal of the Jews after the Babylonian exile.

dogma (<u>dog</u> mă) A system of beliefs declared to be true by a religion.

Dreaming (Dream Time) The timeless time of Creation, according to Australian Aboriginal belief.

dualistic Believing in the separation of reality into two categories, particularly the concept that spirit and matter are in separate realms.

dukkha (dŏŏ kă) According to the Buddha, a central fact of human life, variously translated as discomfort, suffering, frustration, or lack of harmony with the environment.

Durga (<u>dŏŏr</u> ga) The Great Goddess as destroyer of evil, and sometimes as *sakti* of Siva.

Easter Movable feast in spring celebrating the Resurrection of Jesus Christ.

ecumenism (ek <u>yoo</u> mĕ niz ĕm) Rapprochement between branches of Christianity or among all faiths.

enlightenment Wisdom that is thought to come from direct experience of Ultimate Reality.

epic A long historic narrative.

Epiphany (ee <u>pi</u> făni) "Manifestation"; in Christianity the recognition of Jesus's spiritual kingship by the three Magi.

Essenes (<u>es</u> eenz) Monastic Jews who were living communally, apart from the world, about the time of Jesus.

ethnic religions New religions which emerged since the fall of communism as revivals of pre-Christian ethnic traditions in Eastern Europe and Russia.

Eucharist (<u>yoo</u> kă rist) The Christian sacrament by which believers are renewed in the mystical body of Christ by partaking of bread and wine, understood as his body and blood.

evangelicalism Diverse Christian movement calling for a return to biblical

faith, personal conversion experience, and spreading of the gospel.

evangelism (i <u>van</u> jĕ liz ĕm) Ardent preaching of the Christian gospel.

exclusivism The idea that one's own religion is the only valid way.

excommunication Exclusion from participation in the Christian sacraments (applied particularly to Roman Catholicism), which is a bar to gaining access to heaven.

exegesis (ex a <u>gee</u> sis) Critical examination of a religious text.

Falun Gong/Falun Dafa A form of Qigong mixing Buddhism with Daoist energy practices, and emphasizing ethics—the development of truthfulness, benevolence, and forbearance.

Fatiha (fat <u>haa</u>) The first *sura* of the Qur'an.

fatwa In Islam, a legal opinion issued by an authority according to a particular school of law.

feng shui (fĕng <u>shwee</u>) The Taoist practice of determining the most harmonious position for a building according to the natural flows of energy.

Five Ks In Sikhism, the symbols worn by Khalsa members.

fundamentalism (fun dă <u>men</u> tăl iz ĕm) Insistence on what people perceive as the historical form of their religion, in contrast to more contemporary influences. This ideal sometimes takes extreme, rigidly exclusive, or violent forms.

Gamara In Judaism, commentaries on the Talmud, additional to the Mishnah.

Gathas In Zoroastrianism, metric verses or hymns which were the words of the prophet Zarathushtra.

Gayatrimantra (gī a<u>tree</u> man tră) The daily Vedic prayer of upper-caste Hindus.

Gentile (<u>jen</u> tīl) Any person who is not of Jewish faith or origin.

ghetto An urban area occupied by those rejected by a society, such as quarters for Jews in some European cities.

gnosis (nō sis) Intuitive knowledge of spiritual realities.

Gnosticism (<u>nos</u> ti siz ĕm) Mystical perception of spiritual knowledge.

Goddess spirituality Worship of a high goddess in ancient times, now revived in many places.

gospel In Christianity, the "good news" that God has raised Jesus from the dead and in so doing has begun the transformation of the world.

gurdwara (gŏŏr <u>dwa</u> rǎ) A Sikh temple.

guru (<u>gŏŏ</u> roo) In Hinduism, an enlightened spiritual teacher.

Guru Granth Sahib (goo roo granth <u>sa</u> heeb) The sacred scripture compiled by the Sikh Gurus.

Hadith (<u>haad</u> ith) In Islam, a traditional report about a reputed saying or action of the Prophet Muhammad.

haggadah (hǎ <u>gaa</u> dǎ) The non-legal part of the Talmud and Midrash.

hajj (haaj) The holy pilgrimage to Mecca, for Muslims.

halakhah (haa laa <u>khaa</u>) Jewish legal decision and the parts of the Talmud dealing with laws.

Haredi (**Ultra-Orthodox**) Favoring detachment from non-Jewish culture, to focus on the Torah.

Hasidism (<u>has</u> īd iz ĕm) Ecstatic Jewish piety, dating from eighteenth-century Poland.

hatha yoga (<u>ha</u> thǎ <u>yo</u>gǎ) Body postures, diet, and breathing exercises to help build a suitable physical vehicle for spiritual development.

havan In Hinduism, a sacred fireplace around which ritual fire ceremonies are conducted.

heretic (<u>hair</u> i tik) A member of an established religion whose views are unacceptable to the orthodoxy.

hermeneutics The field of theological study that attempts to interpret scripture.

heyoka (hay <u>yō</u> kǎ) "Contrary" wisdom or a person who embodies it, in some Native American spiritual traditions.

hijab (<u>hay</u> jab) The veiling of women for the sake of modesty in Islam.

hijrah (<u>hij</u> rǎ) Muhammad's migration from Mecca to Medina.

Holocaust (<u>haw</u> lō cawst) The genocidal killing of six million Jews by the Nazis during World War II.

Holy crusades Military expeditions undertaken by the Christians of Europe in the 11th–13th centuries to recover the Holy Land from the Muslims; any war carried on under Papal sanction.

Holy Trinity The Christian doctrine that in the One God are three divine persons: the Father, the Son, and the Holy Spirit.

icon (<u>ī</u> kon) A sacred image, a term used especially for the paintings of Jesus, Mary, and the saints of the Eastern Orthodox Christian Church.

iconoclast One who attacks cherished beliefs or destroys sacred images.

ijtihad (ij ti <u>haad</u>) In Islam, reasoned interpretation of sacred law by a qualified scholar.

Imam (i <u>maam</u>) In Shi'ism, the title for the person carrying the initiatic tradition of the Prophetic Light.

imam (i <u>maam</u>) A leader of Muslim prayer.

immanent Present in Creation.

incarnation Physical embodiment of the divine.

inclusivism The idea that all religions can be accommodated within one religion.

indigenous (in <u>dij</u> ĕ nĕs) Native to an area.

Indra (<u>in</u> drǎ) The old Vedic thunder god in the Hindu tradition.

indulgence In Roman Catholic Christianity, granting of a remission of sins.

infidel (<u>in</u> fid ĕl) The Muslim and Christian term for "nonbeliever," which each tradition often applies to the other.

Inquisition (in kwi <u>zi</u> shun) The use of force and terror to eliminate heresies and nonbelievers in the Christian Church starting in the thirteenth century.

intelligent design The concept that scientific discoveries and recognition of complex life processes prove the existence of a single being, an Intelligent Designer.

interfaith dialogue Appreciative communication between people of different religions.

Islam In its original meaning, complete, trusting surrender to God.

Islamist A person seeking to establish Islamic states in which the rule of God is supreme.

Jaap Sahib (jaap saa hib) Hymn of God's praises by Guru Gobind Singh.

Janam-sakhis Traditional Sikh biographies, especially stories of the life of Guru Nanak.

Jap Ji (jap jee) The first morning prayer of Sikhs, written by Guru Nanak.

Jehovah's Witnesses Movement holding that many modern Christian doctrines are false, and advocating what is regarded as early Christianity.

jihad (ji had) The Muslim's struggle against the inner forces that prevent God-realization and the outer barriers to establishment of the divine order.

jinn (jin) In Islam, an invisible being of fire.

jnana yoga (ya na yō gă) The use of intellectual effort as a yogic technique.

Jujiao (jee tzŭ yow) The Chinese term for the teachings based on Confucius.

justified In Christianity, having been absolved of sin in the eyes of God.

Kabbalah (kă baa lă) The Jewish mystical tradition.

Kali (kaa lee) Destroying and transforming Mother of the World, in Hinduism.

Kali Yuga (kaa lee yoo gă) In Hindu world cycles, an age of chaos and selfishness, including the one in which we are now living.

kami (kaa mee) The Shinto word for that invisible sacred quality that evokes wonder and awe in us, and also for the invisible spirits throughout nature that are born of this essence.

kannagara (kă nă gă ră) Harmony with the way of the *kami* in Shinto.

karma (kaar mā) (Pali: **kamma**) In Hinduism and Buddhism, our actions and their effects on this life and lives to come.

karma yoga (kaar mă yō gă) The path of unselfish service in Hinduism.

kensho (ken shō) Sudden enlightenment, in Zen Buddhism.

Khalsa (kal să) The body of the pure, as inspired by the Sikh Guru Gobind Singh.

kirtan (keer tan) Devotional singing of hymns from the Guru Granth Sahib in Sikhism.

koan (kō aan) In Zen Buddhism, a paradoxical puzzle to be solved without ordinary thinking.

kosher (kō sher) Ritually acceptable, applied to foods in Jewish Orthodoxy.

kshatriya (ksha tree ă) A member of the warrior or ruling caste in traditional Hinduism and Buddhism.

kufr (koo fer) In Islam, the sin of atheism, of ingratitude to God.

kundalini (koon dă lee nee) In Hindu yogic thought, the life-force that can be awakened from the base of the spine and raised to illuminate the spiritual center at the top of the head.

Lakshmi In Hinduism, the consort of Vishnu.

lama (laa mă) A Tibetan Buddhist monk, particularly one of the highest in the hierarchy.

langar (lan găr) In Sikh tradition, a free communal meal without caste distinctions.

Lent The forty days of spiritual preparation leading up to Easter.

li (lee) Ceremonies, rituals, and rules of proper conduct, in the Confucian tradition.

liberal Flexible in approach to religious tradition; inclined to see tradition as metaphorical rather than literal truth.

Liberal Judaism See Reform Judaism.

liberation theology Christianity expressed as solidarity with the poor.

lifeway An entire approach to living in which sacred and secular are not separate.

lingam (ling ăm) A cylindrical stone or other similarly shaped natural or sculpted form, representing for Saivite Hindus the unmanifest aspect of Siva.

literati The philosophical form of Daoism, followed by intellectuals and artists.

liturgy (<u>lit</u> ĕr jee) In Christianity and Judaism, the rites of public worship.

Lubavich Hasidim Highly structured Orthodox Jewish movement using modern technology for propagation but traditional lifestyles.

Lutheranism Modern denomination of the breakaway Protestant church founded by Martin Luther in 1517.

madrasa (mă <u>draa</u> să) In Islam, either a primary or secondary religious school, or an institution of higher learning in Islamic subjects, including the Qur'an, hadith, jurisprudence, and law.

Mahabharata (mă haa <u>baa</u> ră tă) A long Hindu epic that includes the *Bhagavad-Gita*.

Mahayana (maa hă <u>ya</u> nă) The "greater vehicle" in Buddhism, the more liberal and mystical Northern School, which stressed the virtue of altruistic compassion rather than intellectual efforts at individual salvation.

mandala (man <u>daa</u> lă) A symmetrical image, with shapes emerging from a center, used as a meditational focus.

mantra (<u>man</u> tră) A sound or phrase chanted to evoke the sound vibration of one aspect of creation or to praise a deity.

mass The Roman Catholic term for the Christian eucharist.

materialism The tendency to consider material possessions and comforts more important than spiritual matters, or the philosophical position that nothing exists except matter and that there are no supernatural dimensions to life.

maya (<u>mī</u> yă) In Indian thought, the attractive but illusory physical world.

medicine Spiritual power, in some indigenous traditions.

medicine person An indigenous healer.

Messiah The "anointed," the expected king and deliverer of the Jews; a term later applied by Christians to Jesus.

metaphysics Philosophy based on theories of subtle realities that transcend the physical world.

Midrash (<u>mid</u> rash) The literature of delving into the Jewish Torah.

mikva (<u>mik</u> vă) A deep bath for ritual cleansing in Judaism.

millennium One thousand years, a term used in Christianity and certain newer religions for a hoped-for period of a thousand years of holiness and happiness, with Christ ruling the earth, as prophesied in the Book of Revelation.

minyan (<u>min</u> yăn) The quorum of ten adult males required for Jewish communal worship.

Mishnah In Judaism, the systematic summation of the legal teachings of the oral tradition of the Torah.

misogi (mee <u>so̅</u> gee) The Shinto waterfall purification ritual.

mitzvah (<u>mitz</u> vă) (plural: *mitzvot*) In Judaism, a divine commandment or sacred deed in fulfillment of a commandment.

Modern Orthodoxy Branch of Orthodox Judaism, dedicated to the significance of Israel and Jewish law, which values secular knowledge and integration with non-Jews.

modernism Twentieth-century values including individualism, preference for change rather than continuity, quantity rather than quality, efficiency, pragmatism, and profiteering, all seen by some as threatening the existence of traditional religious values.

moksha (<u>mo̅ k</u> shă) In Hinduism, liberation of the soul from illusion and suffering.

monistic (<u>mon</u> iz tik) Believing in the concept of life as a unified whole, without a separate "spiritual" realm.

monotheistic (mon o̅ <u>thee</u> iz tik) Believing in a single God.

muezzin (moo <u>ez</u> in) In Islam, one who calls the people to prayer from a high place.

mujahid (<u>moo</u> jă hid) In Islam, a selfless fighter in the path of Allah.

murshid (<u>moor</u> shid) A spiritual teacher, in esoteric Islam.

mystic One who values inner spiritual experience in preference to external authorities and scriptures.

mysticism The intuitive perception of spiritual truths beyond the limits of reason.

myth A symbolic story expressing ideas about reality or spiritual history.

naga (naa gǎ) A snake, worshiped in Hinduism.

Nam (naam) The Holy Name of God reverberating throughout all of Creation, as repeated by Sikhs.

Neo-Confucianism Confucianism stressing the importance of meditation and dedication to becoming a "noble person" established during the Chinese Han and Sung dynasties.

Neo-Paganism Nature-oriented spirituality referring to pre-Christian sacred ways.

Nicene Creed Basic profession of faith for many Christian denominations in East and West, including all Orthodox churches, framed in a council held in Constantinople in 381 CE, and proposed as a basis for unifying all Christians.

nirvana (ner va na) (Pali: *nibbana*) In Buddhism, the ultimate egoless state of bliss.

nontheistic Perceiving spiritual reality without a personal deity or deities.

oharai Shinto purification ceremony.

OM (o⁻m) In Hinduism, the primordial sound.

original sin The Christian belief that all human beings are bound together in prideful egocentricity. In the Bible, this is described mythically as an act of disobedience on the part of Adam and Eve.

orisa The Yoruba term for a deity, often used in speaking of West African religions in general.

orthodox Adhering to the established tradition of a religion.

Orthodox Judaism Observing the traditional rabbinical *halakhah*; the strictest form of Judaism.

Pali (paa lee) The Indian dialect first used for writing down the teachings of the Buddha, which were initially held in memory, and still used today in the **Pali Canon** of scriptures recognized by the Theravadins.

Pahlavi Texts written or translated in Middle Persian from about the ninth century CE with detailed instructions about the rituals and customs of the Zoroastrians in Iran.

Panth In Sikhism, the religious community.

parable (par ǎ bŭl) An allegorical story.

Paraclete (par ǎ kleet) The entity that Jesus said would come after his death to help the people.

Parsis Persian Zoroastrians who avoided conversion to Islam by migrating to western India.

Parvati (paar vǎ tee) Siva's spouse, sweet daughter of the Himalayas.

passion narratives Descriptions in the gospels of Christ's suffering, betrayal, trial, and death.

patriarchal Group, society, or religion led by men in a fatherly role.

penance An act of self-punishment to atone for wrongdoings.

Pentateuch (pen tǎ took) The five books of Moses at the beginning of the Hebrew Bible.

Pentecost (pen tě kost) The occasion when the Holy Spirit descended upon the disciples of Jesus after his death.

Pentecostalism Charismatic Protestant denomination experiencing the manifestation of divinely inspired powers by signs such as "speaking in tongues."

Pharisees (fair ě seez) In Roman-ruled Judaea, liberals who tried to practice Torah in their lives.

phenomenology An approach to the study of religions that involves appreciative investigation of religious phenomena to comprehend their meaning for their practitioners.

pluralism An appreciation of the diversity of religions.

pogrom An attack against Jews.

polytheistic (pol ě thee iz ěm) Believing in many deities.

pope The Bishop of Rome and head of the Roman Catholic Church.

Prakriti (praak ri tee) In Samkhya Hindu philosophy, the cosmic substance.

prana (praa nă) In Indian thought, the invisible life-force.

prasad (pră saad) In Indian traditions, blessed food.

presbyter A governor of the Christian Reformed Church that sprung from Calvinism.

Presbyterianism Protestant denomination based on Calvinism, governed by presbyters or officials of the church.

profane Worldly, secular, as opposed to sacred.

puja (poo jă) Hindu ritual worship.

Puranas (pŏŏ raa năs) Hindu scriptures written to popularize the abstract truths of the Vedas through stories about historical and legendary figures.

Pure Land A Buddhist sect in China and Japan that centers on faith in Amida Buddha, who promised to welcome believers to the paradise of the Pure Land, a metaphor for enlightenment.

Purgatory (pur gă tor ee) In some branches of Christianity, an intermediate after-death state in which souls are purified from sin.

Purusha (poo roo shă) The Cosmic Spirit, soul of the universe in Hinduism; in Samkhya philosophy, the eternal Self.

qi (*ki*) (also *ch'i*) (chee) The vital energy in the universe and in our bodies, according to Far Eastern esoteric traditions.

Qigong (also **ch'i-kung**) (chee kung) A Daoist system of harnessing inner energies for spiritual realization.

Quakers Protestant denomination with no liturgy, but the expectation that God will speak through members of the congregation.

rabbi (rab ī) Historically, a Jewish teacher; at present, the ordained spiritual leader of a Jewish congregation.

raja yoga Mental concentration yoga (ancient technique for spiritual realization).

Ramayana (raa maa yă nă) The Hindu epic about Prince Rama, defender of good.

rapture Nineteenth-century belief amongst some Christians, using Paul's letter to the Thessalonians (I Thess. 4:17) to say that Christians would be caught up in clouds to meet Jesus when he returned to earth.

realization Personal awareness of the existence of Unseen Reality.

Reconstructionism Movement holding that Judaism is an evolving religious civilization.

redaction Editing, organizing.

Reform or **Liberal Judaism** Movement that began in the nineteenth century as a way of modernizing the religion and making it more accessible and open-ended.

reincarnation The transmigration of the soul into a new body after death of the old body.

relic In some forms of Christianity, part of the body or clothing of a saint.

religion A particular response to dimensions of life considered sacred, as shaped by institutionalized traditions.

Religious Zionism Holds as central the resettlement of the Jews in Israel.

ren (also *jen*) (yen) Humanity, benevolence—the central Confucian virtue.

Resurrection The rising of Jesus in his earthly body on the first Easter Day, three days after his Crucifixion and death.

Rig Veda (rig vay dă) Possibly the world's oldest scripture, the foundation of Hinduism.

rishi (rish ee) A Hindu sage.

ritual A repeated, patterned religious act.

Sabbath (sab ăth) The day of the week set aside for rest and worship in Judaism and Christianity.

sacrament Outward and visible signs of inward and spiritual grace in Christianity. Almost all churches recognize baptism and the eucharist as sacraments; some churches recognize five others as well.

sacred The realm of the extraordinary, beyond everyday perceptions, the supernatural, holy.

sacred thread In Hinduism, a cord worn over one shoulder by men who have been initiated into adult upper-caste society.

Sadducees (<u>saj</u> ŭ seez) In Roman-ruled Judaea, wealthy and priestly Jews.

sadhana (<u>saad</u> hǎ nǎ) In Hinduism, especially yoga, a spiritual practice.

sadhu (<u>sad</u> oo) An ascetic holy man, in Hinduism.

Saivite (<u>sīv</u> īt) A Hindu worshiper of the divine as Siva.

Sakta (<u>sak</u> ta) A Hindu worshiper of the female aspect of deity.

sakti (<u>sak</u> tee) The creative, active female aspect of Deity in Hinduism.

samadhi (sa <u>maa</u> dee) In yogic practice, the blissful state of superconscious union with the Absolute.

Samkhya (<u>saam</u> khyǎ) One of the major Hindu philosophical systems, in which human suffering is characterized as stemming from the confusion of Prakriti with Purusha.

samsara (sǎm <u>saa</u> rǎ) The continual round of birth, death, and rebirth in Hinduism and Buddhism.

Sanatana Dharma (sǎ <u>na</u> tǎ nǎ <u>daar</u> mǎ) The "eternal religion" of Hinduism.

sangat A Sikh congregation, in which all are ideally considered equal.

Sangha (<u>sung</u> ǎ) In Theravada Buddhism, the monastic community; in Mahayana, the spiritual community of followers of the *dharma*.

sannyasin (sun <u>yaa</u> sin) In Hinduism and Buddhism, a renunciate spiritual seeker.

Sanskrit (<u>san</u> skrit) The literary language of classic Hindu scriptures.

sant A Sikh holy person.

Santeria The combination of African and Christian practices which developed in Cuba.

satori (sǎ <u>taw</u> ree) Enlightenment, realization of ultimate truth, in Zen Buddhism.

scientific materialism School of thought which developed during the nineteenth and twentieth centuries claiming that the supernatural is imaginary; only the material world exists, and from this point of view religions have been invented by humans.

sect A sub-group within a larger tradition.

secularism Government policy of not favoring any one religion.

Seder Ceremonial Jewish meal in remembrance of the Passover.

see An area under the authority of a Christian bishop or archbishop.

Semite (sem ite) A Jew, Arab, or other, of eastern Mediterranean origin.

Sephardim An ethnic grouping of the Jews that migrated first to Spain and then to North Africa, the Americas, and back to West Asia.

Seventh Day Adventists Protestant denomination or sectarian movement believing in infallibility of the Bible, honoring Saturday as the Sabbath, and anticipating the "end times."

Shahadah (shǎ <u>haa</u> dǎ) The central Muslim expression of faith: "There is no god but God," and Muhammad is the messenger of God.

shaktipat (<u>shaak</u> tǎ pǎt) In the Siddha tradition of Hinduism, the powerful, elevating glance or touch of the guru.

shaman (<u>shaa</u> mǎn) A "medicine person," a man or woman who has undergone spiritual ordeals and can communicate with the spirit world to help the people in indigenous traditions.

Shangdi (also **Shang Ti**) In ancient China, a deity (or perhaps deities) with overarching powers.

Shari'ah (shǎ <u>ree</u> ǎ) The divine law, in Islam.

shaykh (shaik) A spiritual master, in the esoteric Muslim tradition.

Shekhinah (she <u>kī</u> nǎ) God's presence in the world, in Judaism.

Shi'a (adj. Shi'ite) (<u>shee</u> īt) The minority branch of Islam, which feels that Muhammad's legitimate successors were 'Ali and a series of Imams; a follower of this branch.

shirk (shirk) The sin of believing in any divinity except the one God, in Islam.

shudra (<u>shoo</u> drǎ) A member of the manual laborer caste in traditional Hinduism.

Sikh (seek) "Student," especially one who practices the teachings of the ten Sikh Gurus.

Siva/Shiva (<u>shee</u> vă) In Hinduism, the Supreme as lord of yogis, absolute consciousness, creator, preserver, and destroyer of the world; or the destroying aspect of the Supreme.

soma (<u>sō</u> ma) An intoxicating drink used by early Hindu worshipers.

spirituality Any personal response to dimensions of life that are considered sacred.

stupa (<u>stoo</u> pă) A rounded monument containing Buddhist relics or commemorative materials.

Sufism (<u>soo</u> fis ĕm) The mystical path in Islam.

Sunnah (<u>soo</u> nă) The behavior of the Prophet Muhammad, used as a model in Islamic law.

Sunni (<u>soo</u> nee) A follower of the majority branch of Islam, which feels that successors to Muhammad are to be chosen by the Muslim community.

sunyata (<u>soon</u> yă tă) Voidness, the transcendental ultimate reality in Buddhism.

sura (<u>sōō</u> ră) A chapter of the Qur'an.

sutra (<u>sōō</u> tră) (Pali: *suta*) Literally, a thread on which are strung jewels—the discourses of the teacher; in yoga, *sutras* are terse sayings.

symbol Visible representation of an invisible reality or concept.

synagogue (<u>sin</u> ă gog) A meeting place for Jewish study and worship.

syncretism (<u>sing</u> kri tis ĕm) A form of religion in which otherwise differing traditions are blended.

synod In Christianity, a council of church officials called to reach agreement on doctrines and administration.

synoptic (sin <u>op</u> tik) Referring to three similar books of the Christian Bible: Matthew, Mark, and Luke.

Taiji quan (also **T'ai-chi chu'an**) (tī chee hwaan) An ancient Chinese system of physical exercises, which uses slow movements to help one become part of the universal flow of energy.

talit (<u>ta</u> lit) A shawl traditionally worn by Jewish men during prayers.

Talmud (<u>tal</u> mŏod) Jewish law and lore, as finally compiled in the sixth century CE.

Tanakh (ta <u>nakh</u>) The Jewish scriptures.

Tantras (<u>tan</u> trăs) The ancient Indian texts based on esoteric worship of the divine as feminine.

Tantrayana (tăn tră <u>ya</u> nă) *see* Vajrayana.

tariqa (ta <u>ree</u> ka) In Islam, an esoteric Sufi order.

t'fillin (tĕ <u>fil</u> in) A small leather box with verses about God's covenant with the Jewish people, bound to the forehead and arm.

thangka (tang ka) In Tibetan Buddhism, an elaborate image of a spiritual figure used as a focus for meditation.

theistic (thee <u>is</u> tik) Believing in a God or gods.

Theravada (<u>ter</u> ă vă dă) The remaining orthodox school of Buddhism, which adheres closely to the earliest scriptures and emphasizes individual efforts to liberate the mind from suffering.

Tipitaka (ti <u>pi</u> ta ka) (Sanskrit: *Tripitaka*) the foundational "Three Baskets" of Buddha's teachings.

Torah (<u>tō</u> raa) The Pentateuch; also, the whole body of Jewish teaching and law.

transcendent Existing outside the material universe.

Transfiguration The phenomenon that took place when Christ, praying on the mountain, was irradiated with light and God spoke from the heavens.

transubstantiation (<u>tran</u> sŭb stan shee ay shun) In some branches of Christianity, the idea that wine and bread are mystically transformed into the blood and body of Christ during the eucharist sacrament.

Triple Gem ("Three Refuges") The three jewels of Buddhism: Buddha, *dharma*, *sangha*.

tsumi (tzoo mee) Impurity or misfortune, a quality that Shinto purification practices are designed to remove.

tzaddik (<u>tzaa</u> dik) An enlightened Jewish mystic.

Udasi (oo <u>daa</u> see) An ascetic Sikh order.

ulama (oo lă <u>maa</u>) The influential leaders in traditional Muslim society, including spiritual leaders, *imams*, teachers, state scribes, market inspectors, and judges.

ummah (o<u>maa</u>) The Muslim community.

Unitarianism Protestant denomination holding that God is One rather than Three persons.

universalism Acceptance that truth may be found in all religions.

untouchable The lowest caste in Brahmanic Hindu society.

Upanishads (oo <u>pan</u> i shăds) The philosophical part of the Vedas in Hinduism, intended only for serious seekers.

Ushas (<u>oo</u> shăs) Hindu goddess of dawn.

Vaishnavite (<u>vīsh</u> nă vīt) (or Vaishnava) A Hindu devotee of Vishnu, particularly in his incarnation as Krishna.

vaishya (<u>vīsh</u> yă) A member of the merchant and farmer caste in traditional Hinduism.

Vajrayana (văj ră <u>yaa</u> nă) (or Tantrayana) The ultimate vehicle used in Mahayana, mainly Tibetan, Buddhism, consisting of esoteric tantric practices and concentration on deities.

Vedas Ancient scriptures revered by Hindus.

vipassana (vi <u>pas</u> ă nă) In Buddhism, meditation based on watching one's own thoughts, emotions, and actions.

Vishnu (<u>vish</u> noo) In Hinduism, the preserving aspect of the Supreme or the Supreme Itself, incarnating again and again to save the world.

vision quest In indigenous traditions, a solitary ordeal undertaken to seek spiritual guidance about one's mission in life.

Vodou (<u>voo</u> doo) Latin American and Caribbean ways of working with the spirit world, a blend of West African and Catholic Christian teachings.

Wahhabism Islamic philosophy founded by Muhammad ibn 'abd al-Wahhab in the eighteenth century, discarding all practices not specifically approved by the Qur'an and Sunnah.

Wicca Neo-Pagan sect of secret coven of witches traced to the writings of Gerald Gardner in England in the 1940s.

wu wei (woo way) In Daoism, "not doing," in the sense of taking no action contrary to the natural flow.

yang In Chinese philosophy, the bright, assertive, "male" energy in the universe.

yantra (<u>yan</u> tră) In Hinduism, a linear cosmic symbol used as an aid to spiritual concentration.

yi (yee) Righteous conduct (as opposed to conduct motivated by desire for personal profit), a Confucian virtue stressed by Mencius.

yin (yin) In Chinese philosophy, the dark, receptive, "female" energy in the universe.

Yoga (<u>yō</u> gă) A systematic approach to spiritual realization, one of the major Hindu philosophical systems.

yoga (<u>yō</u> gă) Ancient techniques for spiritual realization, found in several Eastern religions.

yoni (<u>yō</u> nee) Abstract Hindu representation of the female vulva, cosmic matrix of life.

yuga (<u>yoo</u> gă) One of four recurring world cycles in Hinduism.

zakat (zak at) Spiritual tithing in Islam.

zazen (zaa <u>zen</u>) Zen Buddhist sitting meditation.

Zealots Jewish resistance fighters who fought the Romans and were defeated in the siege of Jerusalem.

Zen (zen) (Chinese: Ch'an) A Chinese and Japanese Buddhist school emphasizing that all things have Buddha-nature, which can only be grasped when one escapes from the intellectual mind.

Zion The original site of the Jerusalem Temples, now often used to refer to Jerusalem itself as the heavenly city, the goal of Judaism.

BIBLIOGRAPHY

CHAPTER 1 RELIGIOUS RESPONSES

Campbell, Joseph with Bill Moyers, *The Power of Myth*, New York: Doubleday, 1988. More brilliant comparisons of the world's mythologies, with deep insights into their common psychological and spiritual truths.

Capra, Fritjof, *The Tao of Physics*, third edition, Boston: Shambhala, 1991. A fascinating comparison of the insights of Eastern religions and contemporary physics.

Dawkins, Richard, *The God Delusion*, Boston: Houghton Mifflin; London: Transworld (Bantam Press), 2006. Controversial arguments against belief in a personal God by a leading atheistic evolutionary biologist.

Eliade, Mircea, *Patterns in Comparative Religion*, trans. Rosemary Sheed, Lincoln, Nebraska: University of Nebraska Press, 1958, 1996. A classic study in beliefs, rituals, symbols, and myths from around the world.

Fisher, Mary Pat, *Women in Religion*, New York: Pearson Longman, 2007. Many women's stories and analysis of how each major religion has included or excluded them.

King, Ursula, *Women and Spirituality: Voices of Protest and Promise*, second edition, University Park, Pennsylvania: Pennsylvania State University Press, 1993. Excellent cross-cultural survey of feminist theology and spiritual activism.

Marty, Martin E. and R. Scott Appleby, *The Fundamentalism Project*, 5 volumes, Chicago: University of Chicago Press, 1991–2000. Scholarly analyses of fundamentalist phenomena in all religions and around the globe.

McCutcheon, Russell T., *Manufacturing Religion: The Discourse on Sui Generis Religion and the Politics of Nostalgia*, New York and Oxford: Oxford University Press, 1997. Critique of the comparative study of religions as isolated phenomena without social and historical contexts.

Otto, Rudolf, *The Idea of the Holy*, second edition, London: Oxford University Press, 1950. An important exploration of "nonrational" experiences of the divine.

Paden, William E., *Interpreting the Sacred: Ways of Viewing Religion*, Boston: Beacon Press, 1992. A gentle, readable introduction to the complexities of theoretical perspectives on religion.

CHAPTER 2 INDIGENOUS SACRED WAYS

Beck, Peggy V. and Anna L. Walters, *The Sacred: Ways of Knowledge, Sources of Life*, Tsaile (Navajo Nation), Arizona: Navajo Community College Press, 1977. A fine and genuine survey of indigenous sacred ways, particularly those of North America.

Bell, Diane, *Daughters of the Dreaming*, 2nd ed., Minneapolis: University of Minnesota Press, 1993. A pioneering study of Australian aboriginal women, by an anthropologist who lived among them.

Berger, Julian, *The Gaia Atlas of First Peoples: A Future for the Indigenous World*, New York: Anchor Books, 1990. An illustrated survey of contemporary survival issues facing the original inhabitants of many lands, with particular reference to threats to their environment from invading cultures.

Ewen, Alexander, *Voice of Indigenous Peoples*, Santa Fe, New Mexico: Clear Light Publishers, 1994. Speeches and writings from indigenous speakers at the 1992 United Nations Human Rights Day, analyzing the political conditions facing indigenous peoples.

Gill, Sam D., *Native American Religions*, Belmont, California: Wadsworth, 1982. A sensitive academic survey of indigenous sacred ways in the United States.

Grim, John, ed., *Indigenous Traditions and Ecology: The Interbeing of Cosmology and*

Community, Cambridge: Harvard University Press, 2001. One of the excellent volumes of the series "Religions of the World and Ecology," this volume traces environmental themes across many different indigenous cultures.

Halifax, Joan, *Shamanic Voices: A Survey of Visionary Narratives*, New York: E. P. Dutton, 1979, and Harmondsworth, London: Penguin, 1980. First-hand accounts of shamanistic visionary experiences.

Harvey, Graham, *Indigenous Religions: A Companion*, London and New York: 2000. Scholarly articles about specific cultures, attempting to transcend the tendency to understand indigenous religions in terms of concepts taken from other religions.

Magesa, Laurenti, *African Religion: The Moral Traditions of Abundant Life*, Maryknoll, New York: Orbis Books, 1997. An African Catholic theologian describes African traditional beliefs and practices as teachings about how to live meaningfully and harmoniously.

Weaver, Jace, ed., *Native American Religious Identity: Unforgotten Gods*, Maryknoll, New York: Orbis Books, 1998. A varied collection of essays examining facets of contemporary religious identities among Native Americans.

Chapter 3   HINDUISM

Agnivesh, Swami, *Religion, Spirituality and Social Action: New Agenda for Humanity*, New Delhi: Hope India Publications, 2003. An outspoken social activist critiques contemporary problems in India and recommends dharmic solutions.

The Bhagavad-Gita, available in numerous translations. Central teachings about how to realize the immortal soul.

Chapple, Christopher Key and Mary Evelyn Tucker, eds., *Hinduism and Ecology*, Cambridge, Massachusetts: Harvard University Press, 2000. Perceptive contemporary essays about the relationship between various Hindu paths and environmental protection.

Eck, Diana, *Darsan: Seeing the Divine Image in India*, second edition, Chambersburg, Pennsylvania: Anima Books, 1985. A lively explanation of deity images and how the people of India respond to them.

Lopez, Donald S., Jr., ed., *Religions of India in Practice*, Princeton, New Jersey: Princeton University Press, 1995. An interesting anthology of popular texts with contemporary rather than stereotypical understandings, primarily from Hinduism but also including Buddhist, Jain, and Sikh material.

Prabhavananda, Swami, *Spiritual Heritage of India*, Madras: Sri Ramakrishna Math, undated. Classic explanation of Indian spirituality and philosophy since the Vedic age by a disciple of Ramakrishna.

Ramaswamy, Vijaya, *Walking Naked: Women, Society, Spirituality in South India*, Shimla, India: Indian Institute of Advanced Study, 1997. Groundbreaking study of movements in which women were able to transcend social restrictions and give free expression to their spirituality.

Sharma, Veena, *Kailash Mansarovar: A Sacred Journey*, New Delhi: Rol: Books, 2004. Fascinating and informative first-person account of Hinduism's most difficult and sacred pilgrimage.

Singh, Karan, *Essays on Hinduism*, New Delhi: Ratna Sagar, 1987 and 1990. An excellent and concise introduction to the many facets of Hinduism, interpreted in modern terms.

Sontheimer, Gunther-Dietz, and Hermann Kulke, *Hinduism Reconsidered*, New Delhi: Manohar, 1997. Provocative articles by Indian and Western scholars on controversal new ways of interpreting many facets of Sanatana Dharma.

Thapar, Romila, Jonathan Mark Kenoyer, Madhav M. Deshpande, Shereen Ratnagar, *India: Historical Beginnings and the Concept of the Aryan*, Delhi: National Book Trust, 2006. Essays surveying current archaeological, linguistic, and social research into the Aryan Invasion Theory.

CHAPTER 4   BUDDHISM

Batchelor, Martine and Kerry Brown, eds., *Buddhism and Ecology*, World Wide Fund for Nature, 1992. Buddhist teachings, stories, and activities from various countries, illustrating the sympathetic relationship between Buddhism and nature.

Carter, John Ross and Mahinda Palihawadana (trans.), *The Dhammapada: The Sayings of the Buddha*, Oxford: Oxford University Press, 2000. A basic book of sayings attributed to the Buddha that covers the essentials of Dharma in memorable, pithy verses.

Conze, Edward, I. B. Horner, David Snellgrove, and Arthur Waley, ed. and trans., *Buddhist Texts through the Ages*, Oxford, England: Oneworld Publications, 1995. A fine collection of Buddhist scriptures translated from the Pali, Sanskrit, Chinese, Tibetan, and Japanese.

Eppsteiner, Fred, ed., *The Path of Compassion: Writings on Socially Engaged Buddhism*, Berkeley, California: Parallax Press, 1988. A highly readable and relevant collection of essays by leading contemporary Buddhist teachers about the ways in which Buddhism can be applied to social problems.

Gross, Rita M., *Buddhism after Patriarchy*, Albany, New York: State University of New York Press, 1993. A feminist reconstruction of Buddhist history, revealing its core of gender equality but later overlays of sexism, plus analysis of key Buddhist concepts from a feminist point of view.

Habito, Ruben, *Experiencing Buddhism: Ways of Wisdom and Compassion*, Maryknoll, New York: Orbis Books, 2005. Clear and sensitive exploration of various ways that Buddhists are attempting to practice the Buddha's teachings, especially in the contemporary world.

Lopez, Donald S., Jr., ed., *Buddhism in Practice*, Princeton: Princeton University Press, 1995. Annotated translation of original sources dealing with Buddhist practice around the world, organized around the Triple Jewels of Buddha, Dharma, and Sangha.

Mitchell, Donald W., *Buddhism: Introducing the Buddhist Experience*, New York and Oxford: Oxford University Press, 2002. Detailed descriptions of general and culture-specific manifestations of Buddhism.

Queen, Christopher S. and Sallie B. King, eds., *Engaged Buddhism: Buddhist Liberation Movements in Asia*, Albany: State University of New York Press, 1996. A thorough survey of contemporary Buddhist activism in Asian countries.

Tsomo, Karma Lekshe, ed., *Out of the Shadows: Socially Engaged Buddhist Women*, Delhi: Sri Satguru Publications, 2006. Realistic in-depth expressions of Buddhist women's experiences in many cultures, and their efforts to uphold the Dharma therein.

CHAPTER 5   DAOISM AND CONFUCIANISM

de Bary, William Theodore, *East Civilizations: A Dialogue in Five Stages*, Cambridge: Harvard University Press, 1988. A masterful overview of 3,000 years of East Asian civilization, including the classical legacy, the Buddhist age, the Neo-Confucian stage, and East Asia's modern transformation.

Kindop, Jason and Carol Lee Hamrin, eds., *God and Caesar in China: Policy Implications of Church-State Tensions*, Washington, D.C.: The Brookings Institution, 2004. A survey of China's struggles to control religions throughout history, with particular reference to current Party efforts to compromise with the burgeoning public interest in religion.

Kohn, Livia, *The Taoist Experience*, Albany, New York: State University of New York Press, 1993. Interesting translations of ancient and more recent texts covering the various aspects of Daoism.

Kohn, Livia, *Daoism and Chinese Culture*, Cambridge, Massachusetts: Three Pines Press, 2001. Concise survey of different forms of Daoism in chronological order, considering comparative aspects and providing additional bibliography.

Lopez, Donald S., ed., *Religions of China in Practice*, Princeton, New Jersey: Princeton

University Press, 1996. Excellent articles illustrating the overlap between Confucianism, Daoism, and Buddhism in traditional and contemporary practice, with translations of original texts.

Sommer, Deborah, ed., *Chinese Religions: An Anthology of Sources*, New York/Oxford: Oxford University Press, 1995. Interesting primary source material from Daoist, Confucian, Buddhist, and communist writings about religious topics.

Tao-te Ching, attributed to Laozi, available in numerous translations, including the English translation by D. C. Lau, London: Penguin Books, 1963.

Tucker, Mary Evelyn and John Berthrong, *Confucianism and Ecology: the Interrelation of Heaven, Earth, and Humans*, Cambridge, Massachusetts; Harvard University Press, 1998. Interesting articles from a major series of conferences probing the relationships between particular religious teachings and the environment.

Weiming, Tu and Mary Evelyn Tucker, *Confucian Spirituality*, New York: Crossroad Publishing Company, 2003. Eastern and Western scholars analyze Confucianism as a spiritual path.

Yao, Xingzhong, *Introduction to Confucianism*, Cambridge: Cambridge University Press, 2000. A noted specialist blends traditional and contemporary scholarship to explore the many facets of Confucianism and their relevance today.

Chapter 6   SHINTO

Bocking, Brian, *A Popular Dictionary of Shinto*, Richmond, Surrey: Curzon Press, 1996. Thorough discussions of ancient and contemporary facets of Shinto, including shrines, festivals, *kami*, new religious movements, historical events, and key figures.

Breen, John and Mark Teeuwen, eds., *Shinto in History: Ways of the Kami*, Honolulu: University of Hawaii Press, 2000. Scholarly essays distinguishing between unnamed shrine cults and establishment Shinto in historical context.

Hardacre, Helen, *Shinto and the State, 1868–1988*, 1991, Princeton, NJ: Princeton University Press. Detailed analysis of state involvement with Shinto from the Meiji Restoration onward, plus Hardacre's theory that the idea of Shinto has also been used to benefit popular religious movements, individual political ambitions, and local government administrations.

Hori, Ichiro, *Folk Religion in Japan*, Chicago and London: University of Chicago Press, 1968. A lively study of Japanese folk traditions, such as shamanism and mountain worship, which contributed to Shinto.

Kitagawa, Joseph M., *On Understanding Japanese Religion*, Princeton, New Jersey and Guildford, Surrey: Princeton University Press, 1987. A scholarly history including Shinto and "new religions," making distinctions between shrine Shinto, folk Shinto, and sect Shinto.

Nelson, John K., *A Year in the Life of a Shinto Shrine*, University of Washington Press, 1995. Both an in-depth description of the ritual cycle at a major Shinto shrine and an accessible introduction to Shinto.

Picken, Stuart D. B., *Essentials of Shinto: An Analytical Guide to Principal Teachings*. Westport, Connecticut and London: Greenwood Press, 1994. A clear introduction by a minister of the Church of Scotland who is also a *misogi* practitioner.

Chapter 7   JUDAISM

Baskin, Judith R., ed., *Jewish Women in Historical Perspective*, Detroit: Wayne State University Press, second edition, 1998. Fifteen pioneering essays by modern scholars explore Jewish women and their activities in a variety of times and places.

Berger, Alan L., ed., *Judaism in the Modern World*, New York: New York University Press, 1994. Articles by leading contemporary Jewish scholars on facets of the changing identities and paradoxes of modern Jewry.

Encyclopedia Judaica, New York: Macmillan Press, 2006. The authoritative, multi-volume reference on all aspects of Judaism, as seen from a broad spectrum of points of view.

Greenburg, Blu, *On Women and Judaism: A View from Tradition*, Philadelphia: The Jewish Publication Society of America, 1998. An intimate personal attempt to reconcile Jewish feminism and the practice of Orthodox Judaism.

Henry, Sondra and Emily Taitz, *Written out of History: Our Jewish Foremothers*, New York: Biblio Press, 1990. The stories of significant Jewish women rediscovered and placed within their historical context.

Heschel, Abraham J., *Between God and Man: An Interpretation of Judaism*, ed., Fritz A. Rothschild, New York: The Free Press, 1959. An intimate exploration of the relevance of traditional Judaism for today's world, by a great twentieth-century theologian.

Holtz, Barry, *Back to the Sources*, New York: Schocken Books, 1984. Excellent introduction to classical Jewish religious texts. Each chapter takes the reader through a step-by-step approach on how to read representative selections of the Bible, Talmud, Midrash, the Zohar, liturgical texts, and others.

Lerner, Michael, *Jewish Renewal: A Path to Healing and Transformation*, New York: Harper-Collins, 1994. Profound and moving analyses of why Jews left Judaism and the revitalization that is drawing them back to faith.

Mendes-Flohr, Paul and Jehuda Reinharz, *The Jew in the Modern World: A Documentary History*, second edition, New York/Oxford: Oxford University Press, 1995. A wealth of historical documents from the seventeenth to the twentieth centuries tracing the many facets of Judaism as it encountered modernity.

Plaskow, Judith, *Standing Again at Sinai: Judaism from a Feminist Perspective*, San Francisco: Harper San Francisco, 1991. Studies of all aspects of Jewish feminism, including the reconstruction of women's history, women in Israel, gender-equal God-language, sexuality in feminist religious context, and women's role in the repair of the world.

Tanakh: The Holy Scriptures, The New JPS Translation according to the Traditional Hebrew Text, Philadelphia: The Jewish Publication Society, 1988. The preferred translation of the Hebrew scriptures, in graceful and spiritually sensitive modern English.

Umansky Ellen M. and Dianne Ashton, *Four Centuries of Jewish Women's Spirituality: A Sourcebook*, Boston: Beacon Press, 1992. First-hand accounts of the spiritual lives of a great variety of Jewish women.

CHAPTER 8   CHRISTIANITY

Achtmeier, Paul, J., general editor, *The HarperCollins Bible Dictionary*, 1966, New York: HarperCollins, 1996. Extensive contemporary scholarship on the Bible, with its historical contexts and modern interpretations.

Anderson, Allen, *An Introduction to Pentecostalism: Global Charismatic Christianity*, Cambridge: Cambridge University Press, 2004. A global picture of the fastest-growing movement in Christianity, in its many different cultural and historical variations.

Borg, Marcus J., *The Heart of Christianity*, San Francisco: HarperSanFrancisco, 2003. A major voice in Progressive Christianity discusses the relevance of Christianity to modern life.

Crossan, John Dominic, *Jesus: A Revolutionary Biography*, San Francisco: HarperSanFrancisco, 1994. A now-classic reconstruction of the life of Jesus through historical and textual analysis.

Crossan, John Dominic and Jonathan L. Reed, *In Search of Paul*, San Francisco: HarperSanFrancisco, 2004. Exploration of Paul's teachings in historical and social context.

Hopkins, Dwight N., ed., *Black Faith and Public Talk*, Maryknoll, New York: Orbis Books, 1999. Taking off from James H. Cone's influential *Black Theology and Black Power*, these essays probe how people of color relate Christian understanding to economic, social, and religious situations and ideals in today's world.

Irvin, Dale T. and Scott W. Sunquist, *History of the World Christian Movement, vol. 1: Earliest Christianity to 1453*. Maryknoll, New York: Orbis Books, 2001. An inclusive view of early Christian history extending to inputs from and influences on the cultures and people of Asia, Africa, and West Asia. Volume 2 (forthcoming) brings this survey up to the present.

King, Ursula, ed., *Feminist Theology from the Third World: A Reader*, Maryknoll, New York: Orbis Books, 1994. Excellent compendium of the voices of marginalized peoples, which give a special poignance and depth of meaning to efforts to give women a voice in shaping and interpreting Christianity.

Pope-Levison, Priscilla and John R. Levison, *Jesus in Global Contexts*, Louisville, Kentucky: Westminster/John Knox Press, 1992. Examinations of the question "Who is Jesus?" from poor cultures and feminist perspectives.

Robinson, James M., ed., *The Nag Hammadi Library*, San Francisco: Harper & Row, 1977. A fascinating collection of early scriptures that are not included in the Christian canon.

Ruether, Rosemary Radford, *Women and Redemption: A Theological History*, Minneapolis: Fortress Press, 1998. A major feminist theologian traces global and historical threads of women's place in Christian thinking.

Schüssler Fiorenza, Elisabeth, *In Memory of Her: A Feminist Theological Reconstruction of Christian Origins*, New York: Crossroad, 1983, 1994. Extensive scholarship about the role of women in early Christianity.

Ware, Timothy, *The Orthodox Church*, Middlesex, England and Baltimore, Maryland: Penguin Books, 1984, 1993. An overview of the history, beliefs, and practices of the Eastern Church.

Wilson, Ian, *Jesus: The Evidence*, Washington, D.C.: Regnery Publishing, 2000. Illustrated survey of historical and archaeological evidence of the life of Jesus.

CHAPTER 9   ISLAM

Ahmed, Akbar, S., *Islam Under Siege*, Cambridge: Polity Press, 2003. Careful explanation of Islamic ideals and concerns in the context of contemporary violence in the name of Islam.

Delong-Bas, Natana J., *Wahhabi Islam: From Revival and Reform to Global Jihad*, Oxford: Oxford University Press, 2004. Careful examination of the writings of Ibn 'abd al-Wahhab, with the thesis that they do not fit the stereotypical notion of Wahhabism as a major source of extremist movements.

The Holy Qur'an. Although the Qur'an is considered untranslatable, numerous translations from the Arabic have been attempted. Many Muslims' favorite English translation is by Abdullah Yusuf Ali (Durban, South Africa: Islamic Propagation Center International, 1946).

Lawrence, Bruce, *The Qur'an: A Biography*, New York: Atlantic Monthly Press, 2007. Insightful exploration of the life of the Qur'an, as it has been transmitted, recorded, translated, and understood during its 1400-year history.

McCloud, Aminah Beverly, *African American Islam*, New York and London: Routledge, 1995. An accessible inside view of contemporary African American Muslim communities and issues they face in a contrasting cultural context.

Nasr, Seyyed Hossein, *Ideals and Realities of Islam*, second edition, London: Unwin Hyman Ltd., 1985. Thoughtful presentation of both esoteric and exoteric features of Islam.

Nasr, Seyyed Hossein, ed., *Islamic Spirituality I: Foundations*, New York: Crossroad Publishing Company, 1987 and London: SCM Press, 1989. Excellent chapters on key features of Muslim spirituality, from fasting to angels, with sections on Sunnism, Shi'ism, and Sufism.

Ruthven, Malise, *Islam in the World*, 3rd edition, Oxford: Oxford University Press, 2006.

Explanations of mixtures of Islam with politics and culture throughout history, especially modern history.

Safi, Omid, ed., *Progressive Muslims: On Justice. Gender, and Pluralism*, Oxford: Oneworld Publications, 2003. Scholars and activists explore progressive ways of interpreting Islam in the context of modern issues.

Sajoo, Amyn B., ed., *Civil Society in the Muslim World: Contemporary Perspectives*, London: I. B. Tauris, 2004. Essays exploring the intimate relationships between secular, sacred, and state realms in Muslim society, both existing and ideal.

Wadud, Amina, *Qur'an and Woman*, New York/Oxford: Oxford University Press, 1999. Probing hermeneutic analysis of the Qur'an, revealing its principles of social justice, including gender equality.

Webb, Gisela, *Windows of Faith: Muslim Women Scholar-Activists in North America*, Syracuse, New York: Syracuse University Press, 2000. Articles revealing the depth of feminist scholarship within Islam, particularly with reference to the ideal of social justice as seen from the point of view of women of faith.

Zaman, Muhammad Qasim, *The Ulama in Contemporary Islam*, Princeton, New Jersey: Princeton University Press, 2002. Study of the evolution and contemporary importance of the *ulama* in several countries where these religious scholars have re-emerged as a significant factor in religiopolitical activism.

Chapter 10 SIKHISM

Cole, W. Owen, and Piara Singh Sambhi, *The Sikhs: Their Religious Beliefs and Practices*, second edition, Sussex, England: Academic Press, 1995. A clearly written survey of the Sikh tradition.

Duggal, K. S., *Secular Perceptions in Sikh Faith*, New Delhi: National Book Trust, revised edition, 1999. Clear and touching presentation of aspects of Sikh history and belief promoting universalist thought.

Macauliffe, Max Arthur, *The Sikh Religion: Its Gurus, Sacred Writings, and Authors*, Oxford: Oxford University Press, reprinted in Delhi: S. Chand and Company, 1963. The most respected general account of Sikhism in English, even though its author was not Sikh.

McLeod, W. H., *Exploring Sikhism: Aspects of Sikh Identity, Culture, and Thought*. Oxford: Oxford University Press, 2000. An influential non-Sikh scholar brings historical method and skepticism to bear on traditional Sikh beliefs.

Nesbitt, Eleanor, *Sikhism: A Very Short Introduction*. Oxford: Oxford University Press, 2005. Accessible explanations of Sikh practices and beliefs in contemporary context.

Singh, Dharam, *Sikhism: Norm and Form*, New Delhi: Vision and Venture, 1997. Discussion of Sikhism as a vision of a new social order: a classless and casteless brotherhood of enlightened humans.

Singh, Guru Gobind, *Jaap Sahib*, English translation by Surendra Nath, New Delhi: Gobind Sadan Publications, 1997. Powerful praises of the formless, ultimately unknowable God, without reference to any particular religion.

Singh, Harbans, ed., *The Encyclopedia of Sikhism*, Patiala: Punjabi University, 1992–1999. Four volumes on all aspects of Sikhism, prepared by leading scholars.

Singh, Manmohan, trans., *Sri Guru Granth Sahib*, eight vols., Amritsar: Shromani Gurdwara Parbandhak Committee, 1962. A good English translation of the Sikh sacred scripture.

Singh, Trilochan, Jodh Singh, Kapur Singh, Bawa Harkishen Singh, and Khushwant Singh, trans., *The Sacred Writings of the Sikhs*, New York: Samuel Weiser, 1973. Selections from the Adi Granth and hymns by Guru Gobind Singh in English translation.

CHAPTER 11   RELIGION IN A NEW ERA

Barney, Gerald O. and others, *Threshold 2000: Critical Issues and Spiritual Values for a Global Age*, Ada, Michigan: CoNexus Press, 2000. Projections of environmental and social crises in the twenty-first century, with multi-faith spiritual perspectives that may offer solutions.

Fisher, Mary Pat and Lee W. Bailey, *An Anthology of Living Religions*, second edition. Upper Saddle River, New Jersey: Prentice Hall, 2008. Readings from the various religions, following the outline of this book, to deepen understanding of the material herein.

Forward, Martin, *Ultimate Visions: Reflections on the Religions we Choose*, Oxford: Oneworld Publications, 1995. Interesting personal essays by scholars and leaders of many religions, reflecting upon why they like their religion and how it can contribute to a future of harmony among all religions.

Knitter, Paul F., *The Myth of Religious Superiority*, Maryknoll, New York: Orbis Books, 2004. Exclusivism, inclusivism, and pluralism as perceived from Hindu, Sikh, Buddhist, and Western perspectives.

Marshall, Katherine and Lucy Keough, *Mind, Heart and Soul in the Fight Against Poverty*, Washington: The World Bank, 2004. Encouraging report from the world's largest development bank as it attempts to work with religions to alleviate poverty, unemployment, debt, and HIV/AIDS.

Melton, J. Gordon, and Christopher Partridge, *New Religions: A Guide*, Oxford: Oxford University Press, 2004. Over 200 groups and new religious movements are described according to their roots in older traditions or New Age alternatives.

Plaskow, Judith, and Carol Christ, eds., *Weaving the Visions: New Patterns in Feminist Spirituality*, San Francisco: HarperCollins, 1989. Inclusive, goddess, feminist, and womanist perspectives from several religions.

Internet resources

CHAPTER 1   RELIGIOUS RESPONSES

Religion and Science: Stanford Encyclopedia of Philosophy
   http://plato.stanford.edu/entries/religion-science

Wabash Center Guide to Internet Resources
   http://www.wabashcenter.wabash.edu/resources/guide_headings.aspx

CHAPTER 2   INDIGENOUS SACRED WAYS

Australian Indigenous Spirituality and Sacred Sites
   http://www.trinity.wa.edu.au/plduffyrc/indig/sites.htm

Center for World Indigenous Studies http://www.cwis.org/wwwvl/indig-vl.html

Isizoh, Chidi Denis, ed., "African Traditional Religion." http://afrikaworld.net/afrel/

Native Americans http://www.nativeweb.org/

CHAPTER 3   HINDUISM

BBC Religion and Ethics: Hinduism http://www.bbc.co.uk/religion/religions/hinduism

Hinduism Website http://www.hinduwebsite.com/hinduindex.asp

Internet Sacred Text Archives: Hinduism http://www.sacred-texts.com/hin/index.htm

CHAPTER 4   BUDDHISM

Buddhanet http://www.buddhanet.net

Buddhist Studies WWW Virtual Library
   http://www.ciolek.com/WWWVL-Buddhism.html

Internet Sacred Text Archive: Buddhism http://www.sacred-texts.com/bud/index.htm

CHAPTER 5   DAOISM AND CONFUCIANISM

Asian Studies WWW Virtual Library
   http://coombs.anu.edu.au/WWWVL-AsianStudies.html

Chinese Religions http://www.asia.msu.edu/eastasia/China/religion.html

Daoist Texts http://www.sacred-texts.com/tao/index.htm

CHAPTER 6   SHINTO

Shinto and Japanese Religions Texts http://www.sacred-texts.com/shi/index.htm

Encyclopedia of Shinto http://eos.kokugakuin.ac.jp/modules/xwords/

CHAPTER 7   JUDAISM

Jewishnet http://www.jewishnet.net

Internet Sacred Text Archive http://www.sacred-texts.com/jud/index.htm

CHAPTER 8   CHRISTIANITY

Hartford Institute for Religion Research http://www.hirr.hartsem.edu

Internet Sacred Text Archive http://www.sacred-texts.com/chr/index.htm

Orthodox Christian Information Center http://www.orthodoxinfo.com/general

CHAPTER 9   ISLAM

Internet Sacred Text Archive http://www.sacred-texts.com/isl/index.htm

Islam.com http://www.islam.com

Resource for Islamic studies http://www.uga.edu/islam/

CHAPTER 10   SIKHISM

All About Sikhs http://www.allaboutsikhs.com

Internet Sacred Texts Archive: Sikhism http://www.sacred-texts.com/skh/index.htm

Sikhism Home Page http://www.sikhs.org/topics.htm

CHAPTER 11   RELIGION IN A NEW ERA

Gobind Sadan http://www.gobindsadan.org

Hartford Institute: New Religious Movements
   http://hirr.hartsem.edu/denom/new_religious_movements.html

Religious Tolerance http://www.religioustolerance.org/

The Pluralism Project at Harvard University http://www.pluralism.org

INDEX